ACCOUNTING

A SYSTEMS APPROACH
SECOND EDITION

HENRY J. KALUZA
PROFESSOR
Business and Computer
Studies Department
Faculty of Education
University of Western Ontario
London, Ontario

MURRAY B. HOWARD
Sarnia St. Clair Secondary School
Sarnia, Ontario

McGRAW-HILL RYERSON LIMITED

Toronto Montreal New York Auckland Bogotá Cairo Guatemala Hamburg
Lisbon London Madrid Mexico New Delhi Panama Paris San Juan São Paulo
Singapore Sydney Tokyo

ACCOUNTING
A SYSTEMS APPROACH
Second Edition

ISBN 0-07-548954-6

8 9 10 THB 4 3 2 1 0 9 8

Printed and bound in Canada

Canadian Cataloguing in Publication Data

Kaluza, Henry J., date
Accounting: a systems approach

Includes index.
ISBN 0-07-548954-6

1. Accounting. I. Howard, Murray B. II. Title.

HF5635.K34 1984 657 C84-098700-5

CONTENTS

PREFACE

This second edition of *Accounting: A Systems Approach* is designed for a full-year or two-year beginning accounting course, primarily at the high school level. It is intended for use by (1) students planning to take either general or advanced levels of instruction at the high school level, (2) those desiring to register in professional accounting courses at the university and college levels, and (3) those desiring an introduction to accounting for personal use.

THE PLAN OF THE BOOK

This edition is divided into four parts. Part 1 (the first six chapters) is concerned with concepts common to all accounting systems. The example of a real estate business is used to present the basic financial statements and their preparation through the steps of a simplied accounting cycle.

Part 2 (the next four chapters) introduces the learner to applications for accounts receivable, accounts payable, petty cash and banking, and a salaried payroll. A small dental practice is used to explain these common accounting applications.

Part 3 (the next six chapters) presents an accounting cycle for a merchandising firm.

Part 4 (the last two chapters) provides an introduction to the two main methods of processing accounting applications: the one-write system and the computer.

With the exception of the last two chapters, every chapter is divided into two or more Topics to facilitate lesson planning. Each Topic is followed by a series of problems presented in order of difficulty from the simple to the complex.

The contents (and the supporting materials, which will be discussed later) are so arranged that the book can be used for either a one- or a two-year program, and the material can be adapted for regular or more intensive study, according to the ability of the student.

USING THE BOOK

A One-Year Program

Parts 1, 2, and 4 offer an introduction to accounting principles and common accounting applications that would be useful, for example, to persons who hold clerical positions with service firms. These parts also provide an excellent background for a follow-up course emphasizing accounting applications on a one-write system and menu-driven applications on a computer.

Parts 1 and 2, and Chapters 11 to 14 of Part 3, offer a course combining a reasonable coverage of basic accounting principles with an introduction to merchandise accounting. For students who plan to register in an advanced accounting principles course at the high school level, or who are considering further study in post-high school accounting courses, it is recommended that all of Parts 1, 2, and 3 be covered.

A Two-Year Program

It may be that some schools will wish to use the text as part of a two-year clerical or general business program. In that case, Parts 1 and 2, or Parts 1, 2, and 4, are recommended for the first year. In the second year, Part 3 and 4, or Part 3, can be combined with one semester of accounting applications featuring the use of the one-write system and/or the computer. In general, instructors will find that the text can be combined with supporting material to extend an introductory course over two years.

In all of the previous cases, the first year of instruction could be at either the grade 10 or the grade 11 level, or their equivalents in an ungraded school system.

THE ILLUSTRATIVE METHOD VERSUS THE DEDUCTIVE METHOD

Traditionally, accounting courses have been based on the illustrative method. Using paper and pen, students learned how to do journal entries, income statements, and balance sheets as illustrated by examples in the text. In time, they mastered the knowledge and *induced* the underlying concepts and principles behind the accounting numbers. In the illustrative method, students can explain the accounting process and accounting principles by means of examples.

However, the wide use of computers in accounting practice has modified not only the bookkeeping aspects of accounting, but also how people solve accounting problems using a computer. Consider the following brief example.

In the illustrative method, if, for example, we show students how to calculate an increase in sales by ten percent of the previous month for the next eleven months, they do not have to be shown a step-by-step solution to do each subsequent month's calculation. Once an illustration has been given, students merely follow it.

But try communicating that same problem to a computer by means of the illustrative method. It can't be done. For a computer, you have to give exact instructions; otherwise, it will not know whether to increase sales of one month or two months or three months, etc. In short, it is very strong in *deductive* logic, but very weak when it comes to inductive logic.

For this reason, accounting educators have in the past left the deductive method to data processing and related courses. However, with the increasing use of microcomputers in small business and for personal use, we believe accounting educators can no longer ignore the deductive method of instruction. If they fail to train in the use of the micro to solve accounting problems, students will be missing out on one of the most important trends in business.

We do not suggest eliminating the illustrative method altogether. In our opinion, some degree of "pencil pushing" is absolutely necessary. In this period of transition, we believe that it is still the best way to begin an accounting course whose goal is an understanding of the accounting process and principles. On the other hand, with the availability of microcomputers and software for small business and personal use, we support the current trend to introduce the electronic spreadsheet in conjunction with the illustrative method in all accounting courses. Consequently, we offer in our supporting materials the *VisiCalc/FlashCalc Problem Supplement.**

NEW FEATURES OF THIS EDITION

Key Check Figures

Marginal notes called *Key Check Figures* have been placed beside the majority of problems in the text, so that students no longer have to ask their instructors or look to a separate list for the key figures to help them solve assigned problems.

The Six-Column Worksheet

In response to teacher requests, the six-column worksheet has been added to the steps of the simplified accounting cycle of Part 1.

The Application of GAAPs

We believe that beginning accounting courses at any level of instruction should present an introductory treatment of *generally accepted accounting principles* (GAAPs). Consequently, we offer an introduction to the principles of objectivity, revenue, expense, matching, and cost only as each can be applied to traditional high school topics. For example, the principle of objectivity is introduced in relation to the study of source documents. Similarly, specific financial reporting principles as supported by the *CICA Handbook* have been introduced only as they can be related to the presentation of financial statements for non-corporate service and merchandising firms.

---

*VisiCalc is a trademark of Software Arts, Inc. FlashCalc is a trademark of VisiCorp, Inc.

Accounting Careers

In accordance with requests from curriculum planners and guidance counsellors, Topic 3 of Chapter 6 presents an overview of possible careers in accounting. Students will learn about the requirements of becoming a professional accountant in Canada and be able to identify specialty careers in public, private, and governmental accounting. In addition, some chapters in Part 2 focus attention on clerical opportunities in the accounting applications for accounts receivable, accounts payable, and payroll.

Accounting Applications

Traditional accounting courses have emphasized the General Ledger application through the study of one or more accounting cycles. Although accounting cycles are presented in Parts 1 and 3, we believe equal attention should be given to the accounts receivable application, the accounts payable application, and the payroll application. These common applications are dealt with in Part 2 so that they can be related to the one-write system and computer menu-drive applications in Part 4.

The Combination Journal

In response to teacher requests, the Combination Journal is covered in Topic 4 of Chapter 12, the chapter introducing the accounting cycle for merchandising firms.

Credit Card Transactions

The wide use of "plastic money" necessitates an analysis of credit card transactions. Accordingly, these transactions are examined in Topic 2 of Chapter 13, the chapter on the accounting for special items.

The Electronic Spreadsheet

An introduction to the electronic spreadsheet in accounting is found in Chapter 18. In addition, we offer *Solving Accounting Problems Using VisiCalc* as explained under "Supporting Materials" in this preface.

FEATURES CARRIED FORWARD FROM THE FIRST EDITION

The Equation Approach

The accounting equation is used to present the introductory accounting cycle. Consequently, a solid foundation of accounting concepts and principles can be laid without the use of accounts, journals, and accounting jargon. With this foundation, students learn the *why* before the *how*.

Spiral Development

The Topics are arranged to proceed "from the simple to the complex and from the known to the unknown." Thus, Part 1 gives a simplified version of the accounting cycle by presenting an accounting system for a service firm that uses one journal and one ledger, and is without adjustments. Students can then proceed to the more complex Topics of Part 2, where special journals and subsidiary ledgers are explained; and to Part 3, where special journals, Combination Journals, subsidiary ledgers, and adjustments are analyzed for a merchandising firm.

Introduction to GAAPs

Students are introduced to those GAAPs that can be learned at the high school level. The emphasis has been placed on an understanding of accounting principles in relation to the study of source documents and the preparation of financial statements.

Current Terminology

In keeping with the updating of accounting terms generally accepted by the accounting profession, extreme care has been taken to adopt current, precise language throughout the text.

A Systems Approach

An accounting *system* may be defined as the method a business uses not only to process its data through the accounting cycle, but also to protect its cash and other assets from waste, fraud, and theft. This definition and approach characterizes Parts 1, 2, and 3.

Systems Flowcharts

Flowcharts are used throughout Parts 1, 2, and 3 to trace the flow of data in a continuous sequence from its origin to its ultimate use within an accounting system. They make use of standard symbols and thereby familiarize the students with a way of representing systems they will encounter in the business world.

Case Studies

A case study is found at the end of each chapter. More case studies are given in the *Teacher's Resource Book and Key.* Each of these studies challenges the student to analyze and interpret financial data and make an appropriate business decision. The case studies are ideal for promoting student-led discussions.

Wide Page Margins

On the text pages there is an extra-wide margin, to allow for printed notes and illustrations. The notes highlight key terms, definitions, and accounting principles for the students; the illustrations elaborate upon key concepts, reinforce graphically the content without interrupting the students' reading of text copy, and highlight portions of larger illustrations. The Key Check Figures, too, have been placed in the margin.

Conversion to SI

In spite of slow acceptance and, in some cases, stiff resistance to "metric," we have written the material to conform to the International System of Units (SI) in accordance with the *Metric Style Guide* published by the Council of Ministers of Education.

Also, by and large, the traditional comma in dollar amounts has been eliminated to conform to the following recommendation of the *Guide*: ". . . The use of the comma to separate sets of three digits to the left of the decimal point is now to be discontinued; a space is left where we used to put a comma." In addition, since dollar amounts in accounting commonly appear in columns with other numbers, the space is consistently used in numbers with only four digits, though this is not required by the *Guide*.

However, one exception occurs in illustrations which present actual applications of dollar amounts in current business usage. At the time of writing, dollar amounts in some computer printouts of accounting data show either the use of the traditional comma or a lack of spacing regardless of the number of digits. For practical reasons, no attempt has been made to change the simulated printout of such dollar amounts.

Although numeric dating — that is, expressing the date by means of numbers only (for example, *1985 01 14*) — is not part of SI, the *Metric Style Guide* also recommends its use. Thus, several instances of numeric dating may be found in the text where such applications do not clash with current accounting practice. However, in journals, in ledgers, and in financial statement headings, we follow the traditional practice of writing the month in words, followed by the day and the year in numbers, in order to conform to current accounting usage.

When identifying years, we use formats that avoid needless dating of this book. For example, *19—* refers to the current year, and *19-2* means two years after any given year. This is followed throughout the text.

SUPPORTING MATERIALS

A full assortment of supporting materials is available to accompany this text. These include:

Teacher's Resource Book and Key

This is published in two parts: book 1, which covers Chapters 1 to 10, and book 2, which covers Chapters 11 to 18.

Each chapter in book 1 is divided into seven sections, labelled A to G:

A. Instructional Objectives. This section contains a copy of the instructional objectives for a particular chapter that appears in the student's *Working Papers and Study Guides* booklet.

B. Solutions. This section contains keys to all topic problems and to the case study in the chapter. All solutions are camera-ready, allowing the teacher to prepare transparencies for use in taking up solutions in class.

C. Chapter Questions. This section contains questions and related solutions for a particular chapter. Each question is followed immediately by the answer. All questions and answers are camera-ready.

D. Supplementary Problems. This section contains extra problems for the chapter. These are camera-ready and may be used for testing/exam purposes. Camera-ready working papers and solutions are also included in this section.

E. Supplementary Case Studies. This section contains two extra cases for the chapter. These camera-ready cases may be used for testing/exam purposes. Suggested solutions to these supplementary case studies also appear in this section.

F. Progress Tests and Keys. This section contains the camera-ready progress tests to be administered after the completion of each chapter. A comprehensive progress test also appears in Chapters 6 and 10 to examine the work covered in Parts 1 and 2 respectively. Solutions to all questions making up the test also appear in this section.

G. Transparency Teaching Masters. This section contains teaching masters of the most commonly used forms and for each topic area covered in Chapters 1 to 10. Some of these masters include sets for the preparation of useful overlays.

Each chapter in book 2 is divided into six sections labelled A to F. These contain the material as described in similar sections for Chapters 1 to 10 (book 1). (Section G, "Transparency Teaching Masters," has not been included in book 2.)

Working Papers and Study Guides

Three sets of working papers and study guides, one for Part 1, one for Part 2, and one for Parts 3 and 4, are published separately from the text. The working papers allow the students to work on all Topic problems without the time-consuming task of ruling forms. The study guides consist of a list of instructional objectives, word study lists, chapter questions, and a test of the student's final reading of the chapter.

Accounting Projects and Simulations

Eight projects are also published separately from the text. In general, these are longer than Topic problems and give the students an opportunity to integrate the material they have learned in preceding chapters. Some of the projects offer simulated source documents from which students must analyze the transactions before recording their dollar results into accounting records. Other projects offer applications for the internal control of cash and merchandise inventory, an application featuring short-cuts in posting to subsidiary ledgers and a simulation designed to teach students more about GAAPs. Working papers are included for all projects which require accounting forms.

Solving Accounting Problems Using VisiCalc

The wide use of microcomputers and extensive availability of software packages to support the use of the electronic spreadsheet is a decided trend in the instruction of all accounting courses. Published separately from the text, we offer a selection of key text problems on the VisiCalc electronic spreadsheet.

One does not have to be a computer programmer to use the electronic spreadsheet on the microcomputer. Easy-to-follow instructions and step-by-step solutions are offered with the early problems to assist the student in running the software.

Like the columnar journal pad, the electronic spreadsheet allows the user to learn the computer's deductive method in recording and analyzing data and solving problems. The greatest advantage of using an electronic spreadsheet is in response to the many "what if" analytical questions. These accompany all problems in the supplement.

VisiCalc is the most successful "first generation" spreadsheet and is adaptable on microcomputers with at least 32K and the chip to run the software. FlashCalc is the "second generation" VisiCalc, which has greater flexibility for the user. It is available on the majority of microcomputers with at least 64K and the chip to run this updated spreadsheet. Both VisiCalc and FlashCalc are available from the majority of microcomputer dealers at a reasonable price.

ACKNOWLEDGEMENTS

Many people and organizations have contributed to the improvements in this edition.

In general, we are grateful to those of the many high school teachers who used the first edition who made useful suggestions for selecting topics, problems, and case studies. Similarly, we thank the students of past methodology classes at the Faculty of Education, University of Western Ontario, for taking time to evaluate the old edition and make suggestions for the second edition.

In particular, we are grateful to Fred Milsom, Business Education Director, Sarnia St. Clair Secondary School, who agreed to review the manuscript and offer suggestions.

We wish to acknowledge the support of the Canadian Institute of Chartered Accountants, who permitted us to display the cover of the *CICA Handbook* and allowed us to make reference to several specific financial reporting principles contained in the *Handbook*.

We wish to acknowledge the cooperation of the following firms for providing some of the illustrations we have used: Apple Canada Inc.; Bell Canada; Ford Motor Company of Canada, Limited; Grand and Toy Ltd.; IBM Canada Ltd.; Lyons Logic Limited; Mardan Business Systems Limited; Moore Business Forms Ltd.; Monroe Systems for Business — A Division of Litton Canada Inc.; Ron Nelson Photography Limited; Olivetti Canada Ltd.; the Royal Bank of Canada; and VisiCorp of San Jose, California.

And, finally, our wives also deserve a great deal of appreciation for their patience, assistance, and understanding.

Murray B. Howard
Sarnia, Ontario

Henry J. Kaluza
London, Ontario

TO THE STUDENT

Accounting, you will learn, is very much a part of every business. In fact, many persons believe that accounting is *the language of business*. Here are just some of the ways to study this language:

- Learn a complete definition of accounting and then discuss its many applications.
- Get an overview of the many different careers in accounting, such as auditor, tax specialist, or cost accountant.
- Study a number of clerical positions that are related to different areas of accounting, in the classified sections of your local newspapers.
- Study the organization of the accounting function in different types of business enterprises and at different levels of government work.
- Examine the course structure of Canada's three accounting bodies, and the professional designations they confer:

  C.A. (*Chartered Accountant,* offered by the Institute of Chartered Accountants)

  C.G.A. (*Certified General Accountant,* offered by the Certified General Accountants Association)

  R.I.A. (*Registered Industrial Accountant,* offered by the Society of Management Accountants)
- Invite someone actually engaged in accounting practice to give a talk about the field and possible career opportunities.
- Arrange to have shown a film about accounting and career opportunities, by contacting one of the accounting bodies above, or through a main library centre.

These are all valid study activities, but in our opinion they cannot take the place of a study of *introductory concepts* — accounting terms, principles, and any procedure within the accounting process. That is why this book begins with a look at what is required for a person to begin a business. In this way we can see how the problems of accounting arise, and how the concepts of accounting deal with these problems.

PART 1

BASIC CONCEPTS OF ACCOUNTING

CHAPTER 1

ESTABLISHING A BUSINESS

Profit-making business: produces goods; sells goods; or sells services.

Accounting is very much a part of every Canadian profit-making business. In Canada there are many different kinds of such businesses. Some (for example, farms, steel mills, paper mills, and automobile manufacturers) produce *goods;* others, known as wholesalers, buy the goods in large quantities from the producer and sell to the retailer, who, in turn, sells them to consumers. Not all businesses, however, are organized to produce or sell goods. Many (for example, beauty salons, dentists, lawyers, and dry cleaners) offer *services.* But all businesses, whether they produce or sell goods, or offer services, may be classified according to three forms of ownership: by one person: *sole (single) proprietorship;* by two or more persons: *partnership;* by (usually) three or more persons, who operate under a government charter: *business corporation.*

Forms of business ownership: sole proprietorship; partnership; corporations.

In this chapter, you will be introduced to the accounting concepts related to the creation of any Canadian business enterprise.

- Topic 1 deals with setting up and applying the accounting equation.
- Topic 2 deals with the preparation of a balance sheet.

TOPIC 1 ESTABLISHING THE ACCOUNTING EQUATION

Let's begin with an important question.

- *What does a person need to start a business?*

Your answers will probably include some of the following: money, that is, cash in the bank; a building; some equipment and furniture; a product or goods to sell; a delivery truck.

Of course, you and your classmates might have different answers. But let's consider an answer that can apply to all types of business enterprises. First, we will ask the same question in a slightly different way: What one word best describes all the items a person needs to start a business?

The word is *resources.*

Economic resources: items needed to establish a business.

To provide economic resources for businesses, natural resources such as land, water, forests, oil, nickel, copper, and so on are converted into such things as furniture and machinery. Economic resources can be considered scarce in that they require effort to produce and sell.

Cash

Building

Truck

Office Equipment

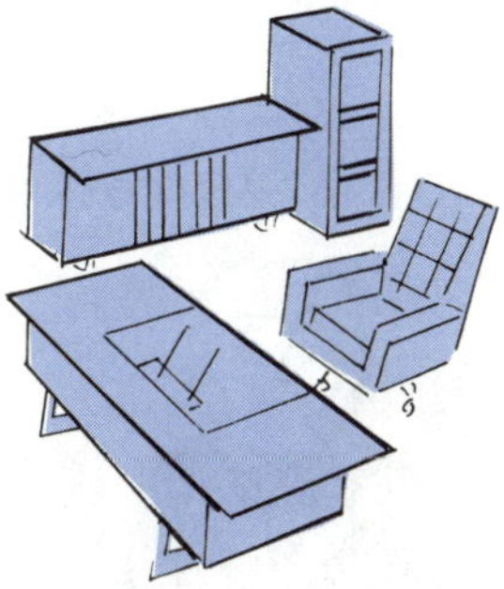

Furniture

Economic resources: scarce items which require effort to produce and for which a price must be paid.

Did your list of items needed include *people*? It is true that people are required to begin any successful business. But from an accounting standpoint, people are considered to be *human resources* or *labour*. Later in this text you will learn that business takes care of human resources by rewarding them through a payroll accounting system. People should therefore be excluded from the list of economic resources needed to begin any business. Now consider a second important question.

- *How does a business acquire the economic resources needed to begin operations?*

The answer is:

- partly through borrowing
- partly through the investment of the owner

Let's look at each aspect of the answer in greater detail.

When the owner or owners of the business obtains a loan from the bank or other lending institution, the money is used to obtain economic resources such as equipment, furniture, delivery trucks, etc. In this case, the bank is a creditor because it has

Creditor: a person or firm to whom money or goods are due; one to whom a debt is owed.

Credit: recognition granted a person who is allowed time to pay back money or goods owing.

Debt: something owed to another person or firm.

Debtor: a person or firm who owes money or goods to someone else.

Small claims court: an inexpensive, informal place for deciding small claims, usually of $1 000 or less.

granted credit (a loan to be repaid later) to the business. Of course, in borrowing from the bank the business acquires a debt and is a debtor.

The borrowing can also take other forms. For example, the business may buy a delivery truck from an auto dealer who allows the business a certain time, such as 30, 60, or 90 days, to pay for it. In this case the car dealer too is a creditor, having granted credit in the form of time to pay for the purchase.

Until the debts owed by the business are paid off, creditors have *claims* against its economic resources. For example, when money is borrowed from a bank, the bank has a legal claim against the economic resources of the borrower until that debt has been paid. Similarly, if a truck dealer gives a business 60 days to pay for a truck, the dealer has a claim on the borrower's economic resources.

Canada's legal system allows creditors to sue debtors for small overdue amounts in an appropriate court. For example, a banker who lent $500 to a business may place a claim before the small claims court of the province in which the business loan was made.

Not many new businesses, however, can get all the economic resources they need through borrowing. Usually, the owner or owners must invest some of their own money in the enterprise. In addition, they may invest other economic resources, such as furniture for the office. Therefore, another important source of economic resources is *owner investment,* and, since the owners have made this investment to establish the business, they too will have a claim against these resources.

Owner investment:

results in claim of owner against economic resources.

Let's pause to review the main concepts presented so far.

- To establish a business, economic resources are required.
- Some of these resources are obtained through borrowing; therefore, creditors will have claims against the economic resources until the debts are paid.
- Some of these resources are obtained through the investment of the owner or owners of the business; therefore, they too will have a claim against the economic resources of the business.

In the language of accounting, the shorthand way of stating what is needed to begin a business and how these things are acquired is by using an equation. Examine carefully the three equations that follow. Also, study the analysis of each equation given immediately below. *Note:* In this text, *analysis* simply means a way of learning the topic to be studied that involves breaking it into understandable parts.

Equation: a shorthand way of presenting mathematical or logical relationships.

Equation 1

ECONOMIC RESOURCES	=	CLAIMS AGAINST ECONOMIC RESOURCES
$100 000	=	*$100 000*

Analysis: This first equation simply says that the total economic resources of any business enterprise must be equal to the total claims against those resources. In Equation 1, the claims against economic resources totalling $100 000 are equal to $100 000. Notice that the economic resources have been placed on the left side of the equation and the claims against those resources on the right side.

Equation 2

ECONOMIC RESOURCES	=	CLAIMS OF CREDITORS	+	CLAIM OF OWNER
$100 000	=	*$30 000*	+	*$70 000*

Analysis: This second equation states the relationship between economic resources and how they were acquired. Note that the claims against the total economic resources are made up of:

- the claims of creditors (resulting from borrowing by the business)
- the claim of the owner of the business (resulting from investment)

The equal sign between the left and right sides of the equation means that the two sides must balance. In Equation 2, the dollar amounts for economic resources total $100 000. The sum of the total dollar amount claimed by all creditors ($30 000) and the dollar amount claimed by the owner ($70 000) must agree with this total.

The Accounting Equation

Assets: the economic resources of a business.

Liabilities: the claims of creditors against the assets of a business.

Owner's equity: the claim of the owner against the assets of a business.

In the language of accounting, economic resources are known as assets; the claims of creditors are known as liabilities; and the claim of the owner is called owner's equity. (The claim of more than one owner would be known as *owners'* equity.) In this way, we arrive at Equation 3 below, known as the *accounting equation.*

Equation 3

A	=	**L**	+	**OE**
ASSETS	=	**LIABILITIES**	+	**OWNER'S EQUITY**
$100 000	=	*$30 000*	+	*$70 000*

Analysis: Several important facts about the accounting equation should be remembered, as they will be used throughout your first course in accounting.

- The accounting equation contains three elements (or, in the language of mathematics, variables): assets, liabilities, and owner's equity.
- The symbols for the elements are *A*, *L*, and *OE*.
- Assets are shown on the left side of the accounting equation and liabilities and owner's equity on the right side.
- Assets are the economic resources required to establish any business. They represent what a business *owns.*
- Liabilities are the claims of the creditors against the assets. They represent the *debts* of the business.
- Owner's equity is the claim of the owner (or owners) against the assets. In accounting, *equity* refers to the claim or right of someone to the assets of a business. In this case, the

claim or right belongs to the owner. (Thus, one could speak of liabilities as *creditors' equity,* but the term is not used.)

- On the right side of the accounting equation, liabilities come *before* owner's equity. This order is very important, for in Canadian courts the claims of creditors are considered before those of an owner or owners. For example, if the business were to be declared bankrupt (incapable of paying its debts), in any sale of the assets the creditors' claims would have to be satisfied before the owner's.
- Since the accounting equation has only three elements, knowledge of the value of two of them enables one to figure out the value of the third. For example, if:

A (assets) = \$24 000
L (liabilities) = \$4 000

we can solve for OE (owner's equity) as follows:

$$
\begin{array}{llclcl}
\multicolumn{6}{l}{A = \$24\,000,\ L = \$4\,000,\ OE = ?} \\
A & = & L & + & OE \\
OE & = & A & - & L \\
OE & = & \$24\,000 & - & \$4\,000 \\
OE & = & \$20\,000 & &
\end{array}
$$

Similarly we can solve for A or L:

$$
\begin{array}{llclcl}
\multicolumn{6}{l}{A = ?,\ L = \$4\,000,\ OE = \$20\,000} \\
A & = & L & + & OE \\
A & = & \$4\,000 & + & \$20\,000 \\
A & = & \$24\,000 & &
\end{array}
$$

$$
\begin{array}{llclcl}
\multicolumn{6}{l}{A = \$24\,000,\ L = ?,\ OE = \$20\,000} \\
A & = & L & + & OE \\
L & = & A & - & OE \\
L & = & \$24\,000 & - & \$20\,000 \\
L & = & \$4\,000 & &
\end{array}
$$

Applying the Accounting Equation

Let's now apply the accounting equation to a specific business.

J. Emery Real Estate is a small business established as a single proprietorship owned by Jane Emery. Emery's operations consist entirely in buying and selling homes, office buildings, and other types of real estate for clients. They do not involve producing or selling goods. Emery is therefore a service firm.

J. Emery Real Estate began operations with the following assets and liabilities: Cash, $60 000; Automobile, $15 000; Furniture, $3 000; Office Equipment, $2 000; Bank Loan Payable, $20 000; Accounts Payable, $10 000. The firm's accounting equation can be obtained by classifying these items under the three elements of the equation as follows:

Assets				=	*Liabilities*		+ *Owner's Equity*
Cash	*Auto-mobile*	*Furniture*	*Office Equipment*		*Bank Loan Payable*	*Accounts Payable*	*J. Emery*
$60 000 +	*$15 000 +*	*$3 000 +*	*$2 000*	=	*$20 000 +*	*$10 000 +*	*$50 000*
$80 000				=	*$30 000*		+ *$50 000*

Analysis: From a study of Emery's accounting equation, you will see that the amount of owner's equity has been calculated, since it was the one unknown element in the equation.

Let's examine each element in a little more detail.

Assets Assets, in general, are economic resources owned by a business enterprise. Obviously, a business will have many different kinds of assets. Each of these kinds encompasses a number of different items. (In accounting practice, related assets are grouped into broad categories rather than dealt with separately.) For example, cash in accounting refers not only to money in the form of coins and paper money, but also to cheques and money orders received by the business and the amount that the business has deposited in its bank account.

Cash: currency, cheques, and money orders received, and bank deposits.

Under *Cash,* J. Emery Real Estate has a large amount, $60 000. The enterprise will need this amount not only to buy more economic resources as needed, but also to pay off debts as they fall due and, in particular, to meet operating expenses. For example, J. Emery Real Estate does not own a building, but rents office space. Thus it will regularly have to pay the landlord for rent. Rent and other expenses will be studied later in this book. What you should remember now is that cash is an important asset for every business.

The last three headings in the accounting equation — *Automobile, Furniture,* and *Office Equipment* — require only a brief explanation. The first is self-explanatory. Jane Emery needs a car to conduct her business. We assume that she uses it only for business purposes. Furniture refers to such items as desks, chairs, and tables. Office equipment covers calculators, typewriters, word processors, cash registers, copying machines, and the like.

Furniture: desk, chairs, tables, etc.

Office equipment: word processors, calculators, copiers, cash registers, etc.

Liabilities Most business enterprises have debts to pay. Two very common debts are illustrated in the equation for J. Emery Real Estate — *Bank Loan Payable* and *Accounts Payable*. First, bank loan payable,[1] or simply *Bank Loan,* is the accounting term for a loan from a bank. In the illustration, J. Emery Real Estate has borrowed $20 000 from a bank. This amount has been deposited in the name of the business as part of the total cash reported in the assets section.

Bank loan payable: the claim of a bank against the assets of a borrowing business.

In accounting, the term accounts payable is used to identify amounts due to creditors other than the bank for the purchase of goods or services on credit. J. Emery Real Estate must have acquired some assets on credit from an auto dealer, a furniture dealer, and/or an office equipment supplier. In the example, let's assume that these separate amounts are owing: to Bell Furniture Co., $3 000; to Ryan Equipment Co., $2 000; and to Westown Motors Ltd., $5 000. Notice that the sum of these debts is $10 000, the amount reported for accounts payable in the accounting equation.

Accounts payable: amounts owing to creditors (other than banks) for the purchase of goods or services on credit.

One other possible liability is worth mentioning here. In acquiring land and a building, some businesses find it necessary to borrow on a long-term basis — for example, for 20 or 30 years. Such a debt is usually supported by a document called a mortgage. A *mortgage* is a contract (written agreement) which states that if the debt is not paid as agreed the lender may sell the property to obtain the unpaid amount of the debt. This debt is called mortgage payable.

Mortgage payable: a long-term debt wherein the collateral consists of the properties bought.

Owner's Equity Owner's equity represents the claim of the owner against the assets of the business — the financial interest of the proprietor in the enterprise. In the case of J. Emery Real Estate, Jane Emery has an equity or claim against the assets in the amount of $50 000. This claim, like the claims of creditors, is not against any particular asset but against the assets in general.

You will recall from the equation that owner's equity is equal to total assets minus total liabilities:

$$\begin{aligned} OE &= A - L \\ &= \$80\,000 - \$30\,000 \\ &= \$50\,000 \end{aligned}$$

Thus, we could say that owner's equity is a *residual claim* — the amount Jane is entitled to after the claims of the creditors have been fully satisfied.

1. In accounting language, liabilities are usually identified by the word *payable*.

TOPIC 1 PROBLEMS

1-1 Solve for the unknown in each of the following equations:

	Assets	=	Liabilities	+	Owner's Equity
EXAMPLE:	$10 000	=	$1 200	+	(Answer: $8 800)
a	500	=	100	+	?
b	4 000	=	?	+	$2 500
c	740	=	300	+	?
d	?	=	800	+	1 000
e	9 000	=	?	+	6 200
f	4 800	=	2 100	+	?
g	18 000	=	6 900	+	?
h	?	=	4 500	+	6 900
i	1 435	=	?	+	700
j	3 890	=	0	+	?

1-2 On September 15 of this year Donna Lyon opened a law practice. Her business's assets and liabilities on that date were as follows: Accounts Payable, $200; Cash, $800; Bank Loan Payable, $1 200; Office Equipment, $2 200; Law Books, $2 400. Determine the owner's equity; then construct an accounting equation that *itemizes* (gives all the things that make up) the three elements as shown in the Emery equation on Page 8.

Key Check Figure
OE = $4 000

Note: Keep your answers for use in Problem 1-4.

1-3 Steven Oneschuk, owner of the Manitoba Car Rental Company, started his car rental business today with these economic resources and debts: Cash, $8 900; Land, $15 000; Buildings, $48 000; Automobiles, $40 000; Furniture, $1 200; Office Equipment, $4 800; Bank Loan Payable, $10 000; Accounts Payable, $3 700; and Mortgage Payable, $24 000.

a List the assets (beginning with cash) in one column and the liabilities in another; then calculate the owner's equity.

b Construct the accounting equation for the Manitoba Car Rental Company, *itemizing* the three elements.

Key Check Figure
OE = $80 200

Note: Keep your answers for use in Problem 1-4.

TOPIC 2 THE BALANCE SHEET

Balance sheet: a financial statement reporting assets, liabilities, and owner's equity as at a certain date.

One important purpose of accounting is to prepare formal reports detailing the assets and the claims against them for the benefit of creditors, the owner or owners, and/or other interested parties. Such a formal report or financial statement is known as a balance sheet.

Analyzing a Balance Sheet

From a study of the accounting equation, you have learned that a firm's liabilities represent the claims of creditors against its assets, and that owner's equity is the claim of the owner against those assets. (Assets = Liabilities + Owner's Equity.) The basic structure of a balance sheet is based upon this. Examine the two illustrations that follow. Then study the analysis.

Assets						*=*	*Liabilities*				*+ Owner's Equity*
Cash		*Automobile*		*Furniture*		*Office Equipment*	*Bank Loan Payable*		*Accounts Payable*		*J. Emery, Capital*
$60 000	*+*	*$15 000*	*+*	*$3 000*	*+*	*$2 000*	*= $20 000*	*+*	*$10 000*	*+*	*$50 000*
$80 000						*=*	*$30 000*			*+*	*$50 000*

J. Emery Real Estate
Balance Sheet
as at September 30, 19—

Heading

ASSETS		**LIABILITIES**		
Cash	*$60 000.00*	*Bank Loan Payable*		*$20 000.00*
Automobile	*15 000.00*	*Accounts Payable:*		
Furniture	*3 000.00*	*Bell Furniture Co.*	*$3 000.00*	
Office Equipment	*2 000.00*	*Ryan Equipment Co.*	*2 000.00*	
		Westown Motors Ltd.	*5 000.00*	*10 000.00*
		Total Liabilities		*$30 000.00*
		OWNER'S EQUITY		
		J. Emery, Capital		*50 000.00*
Total Assets	*$80 000.00*	*Total Liabilities and Owner's Equity*		*$80 000.00*

Body

Analysis: The balance sheet has two sections, the heading and the body.

- The heading of a balance sheet has three lines and each answers a question: Line 1: *who* (the name of the business); Line 2: *what* (the type of document that follows); Line 3: *when* (the date the information is valid for).
- The body of the balance sheet has two sides: assets are listed in detail on the left side, and the claims of creditors and the owner on the right side.

- Notice that assets are *itemized,* as in the accounting equation.
- Notice that liabilities are also itemized, and that accounts payable are broken down by the individual creditors.
- Look at the owner's equity section of the balance sheet. The heading *Owner's Equity* shows only the total claim of the owner against the assets; it does not explain the financial interest of the owner. Now notice the heading *J. Emery, Capital.* The word capital indicates what part of the owner's claim against assets is due to her investment. The amount shown is, of course, *equal* to the amount she invested.

Capital: the owner's claim against the assets through personal investment.

- There are similarities between the accounting equation and the balance sheet. First, since the accounting equation is now in the balance sheet, it may be called the balance sheet equation. Second, the balance sheet, like the accounting equation, balances (total assets are equal to total liabilities plus owner's equity).

Balance sheet equation: the accounting equation within the balance sheet.

Preparing a Balance Sheet

Balance sheets are prepared at least once a year. When they are used more frequently, such as once a month, and where facilities are available, balance sheets are prepared by means of a word processor or a computer.

Don't worry about being asked to prepare a computer program for a balance sheet. The study of how balance sheets and other accounting reports are actually prepared — by typewriter, word processor, printing press, or computer — is part of the study of business data processing. At this stage it is important only to acquire a basic knowledge of the concepts related to the preparation of any balance sheet. This is best done through learning to prepare it by hand. Only when you have learned the accounting theory should you begin to relate your knowledge to the actual way in which financial information is processed.

Business data processing: the study of how business (accounting) information is physically handled and processed.

To help you to learn how to prepare a handwritten balance sheet, an illustration is given on page 13. Follow closely the illustration and the following guidelines.

Let's first discuss the various sections.

Heading For a balanced appearance, centre the three lines of the heading over the body. Remember the order of these lines:

- *who*
- *what*
- *when*

Asset Section On the first writing line, centre the title *Assets* between the left side of the form and the first money column.

Look carefully at the order of listing the assets: cash, automobile, furniture, office equipment. This is the order of converting each asset into cash — the liquidity order. Most accountants

Liquidity order: the order resulting when assets are listed according to the sequence of converting them into cash.

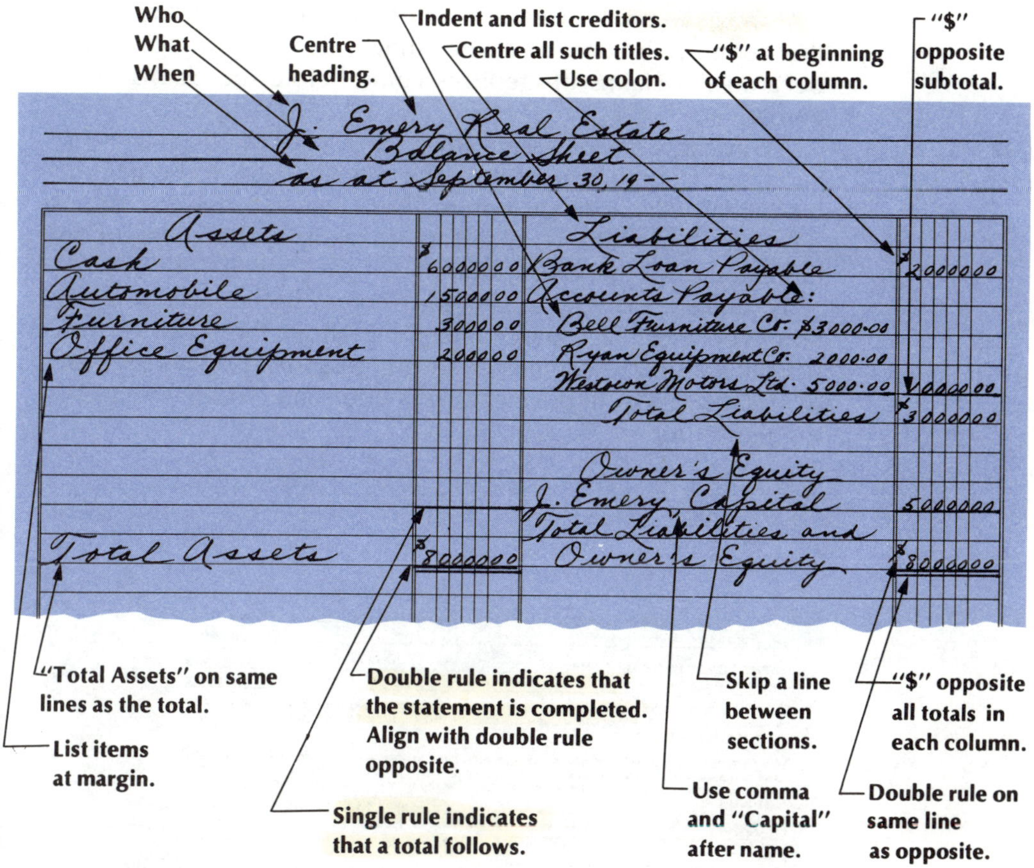

prefer this order. Begin with cash; follow with all assets which are converted into cash; and, finally, list all assets which are not converted into cash.

Observe how the assets are entered. Beginning with cash, each asset is listed along the left margin. Each word begins with a capital letter. The dollar amount of the asset is recorded in the money column on the same line.

Notice the dollar sign opposite the first asset in the money column. As a general rule for placement of dollar signs, show a dollar sign opposite the first amount in a column, whether the column is vertically ruled or not, and opposite each subtotal and total in a column. With a ruled money column do not use decimal points; a column is provided for the cents amounts.

Placement of dollar signs (general rules): (1) opposite first amount in any column; (2) opposite any subtotal or total in a column.

Finally, for even dollar amounts, remember to enter zeros in the cents columns. Do not leave a cents column blank (or use a dash) on a ruled balance sheet form. A balance sheet is a formal report and requires neatness, completeness, and legibility. More on this later.

Liability Section Centre the title *Liabilities* on the first line of the form. Liabilities must be shown *before* owner's equity because the claims of creditors come before the claims of the owner.

Order of listing liabilities: in the order of retiring debts.

As in the case of assets, there is a certain order of listing liabilities. Liabilities are debts; those which have to be paid immediately will be listed before those that fall due in, say, 30 days. A short note is necessary to explain the order of the liabilities of J. Emery Real Estate.

Demand loan: repayable when the creditor demands payment.

To understand why a bank loan comes before accounts payable, you must first know something about the types of loans usually granted to businesses. A business loan is generally a demand loan. To learn the meaning of "demand," study the following illustration.

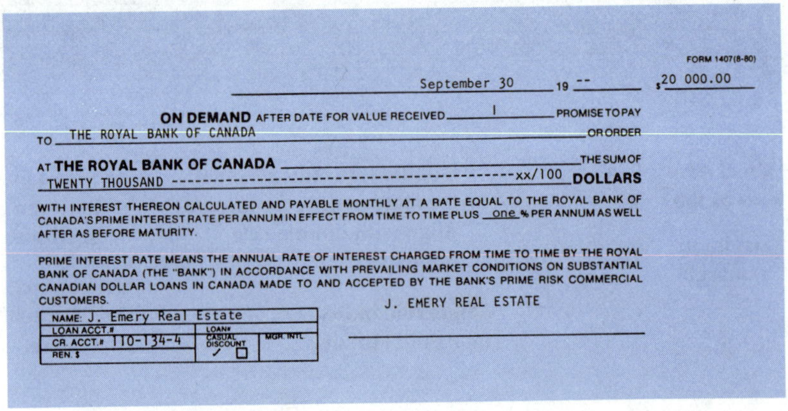
FORM 1407(8-80)

September 30 19 -- $20 000.00

ON DEMAND AFTER DATE FOR VALUE RECEIVED I PROMISE TO PAY

TO THE ROYAL BANK OF CANADA OR ORDER

AT THE ROYAL BANK OF CANADA THE SUM OF

TWENTY THOUSAND --xx/100 DOLLARS

WITH INTEREST THEREON CALCULATED AND PAYABLE MONTHLY AT A RATE EQUAL TO THE ROYAL BANK OF CANADA'S PRIME INTEREST RATE PER ANNUM IN EFFECT FROM TIME TO TIME PLUS one % PER ANNUM AS WELL AFTER AS BEFORE MATURITY.

PRIME INTEREST RATE MEANS THE ANNUAL RATE OF INTEREST CHARGED FROM TIME TO TIME BY THE ROYAL BANK OF CANADA (THE "BANK") IN ACCORDANCE WITH PREVAILING MARKET CONDITIONS ON SUBSTANTIAL CANADIAN DOLLAR LOANS IN CANADA MADE TO AND ACCEPTED BY THE BANK'S PRIME RISK COMMERCIAL CUSTOMERS.

J. EMERY REAL ESTATE

NAME: J. Emery Real Estate
LOAN ACCT.#
CR. ACCT.# 110-134-4
REN. $
LOAN# CASUAL DISCOUNT ✓ ☐
MGR. INTL.

Notice that this "I.O.U." is payable to the banker "on demand." This means that the business must repay the bank, with interest, whenever the bank asks for payment. By rights, the bank can grant the loan today and demand payment tomorrow. Ordinarily, it will allow the business to decide when it can pay the debt, as long as it is within a short time, but the point here is that there is no guaranteed time stated. Since the loan can be expected to be demanded at any time, this liability is usually listed first.

Accounts payable, on the other hand, are shown after the bank loan, since creditors usually give the business a longer time (30, 60, or 90 days) to repay. In our illustration individual creditors are reported under *Accounts Payable*. This is the method you should use until later in this book when you learn the method used in practice.

Those liabilities that must be paid within a year of the date of the balance sheet are placed ahead of those that must be paid over a longer period of time.

A mortgage payable (not shown in the illustration) is a long-term debt (for 20 years or more) and, therefore, it is placed at the end of the liability list.

One final point should be noted for the liability section of the balance sheet. Where two or more liabilities are reported, show the total liabilities on a separate line as shown in the margin illustration. Note the use of the dollar sign opposite the first dollar amount in a money column and opposite *Total Liabilities*. For only one liability, however, repeating the total is not necessary.

Several Accounts Payable

Liabilities		
Bank Loan Payable		$ 2 000 00
Accounts Payable:		
X Company Ltd.	$1 000 00	
Y Company Ltd.	2 000 00	3 000 00
Mortgage Payable		20 000 00
Total Liabilities		$25 000 00

One Liability Only

Liabilities	
Accounts Payable:	
M. Couse Company	$ 1 000 00
Owner's Equity	
J. Kershaw, Capital	39 000 00
Total	$40 000 00

Owner's Equity Section Leave one line after the liability section and centre the title *Owner's Equity*. As you will recall, this title refers to the claim of the owner against the total assets of the firm. To describe this claim, write on the next line the name of the owner, a comma, and the word *Capital*. *Capital* means investment, so the owner's claim against assets has been reported through his or her investment.

The foregoing concerns *sole proprietorships*. It is worth mentioning here how equity is reported for the two other common forms of business ownership. First of all, note that:

- In a *partnership*, the claims of partners against the total assets are usually known as *partners' equity*.
- In a *business corporation*, the owners are called shareholders, and their claims against the assets of the corporation are known as *shareholders' equity*.

Compare the three illustrations in the margin. Notice that, just as the name of a single proprietor is reported, so the names of all the partners are reported. In the case of shareholders, however, there may be hundreds or even thousands; it is impractical to list the name and equity of each. Instead, the term *share capital* (or *capital stock*) is used, and the total investment by persons holding shares (stock) is given.

Single Proprietorship

Owner's Equity	
Don Bain, Capital	13 000 00

Partnership

Partners' Equity	
Don Bain, Capital	6 500 00
Phil Page, Capital	6 000 00

Corporation

Shareholders' Equity	
Share Capital	250 000 00

Totalling and Ruling After the assets, liabilities, and owner's equity are entered, draw a line across each money column (as shown on page 13). Then add up the columns. Enter both totals (which should be equal) on the first available line immediately below the ruled line. Do not forget to show a dollar sign in front of each total.

Finally, draw a *double* line across each money column to indicate they are completed. *Note:* a single line indicates addition or subtraction; a double line indicates that the report has now been completed.

Let us now note a few general things about the form of the document.

No Abbreviations As we have stated, the balance sheet is a *formal* report and so should be easily readable. Short forms should not be used unless the word or name you are given is *already* an abbreviation. For example, if the firm's name is Fry Co., use the short form given (that is, Co.). On the other hand, if

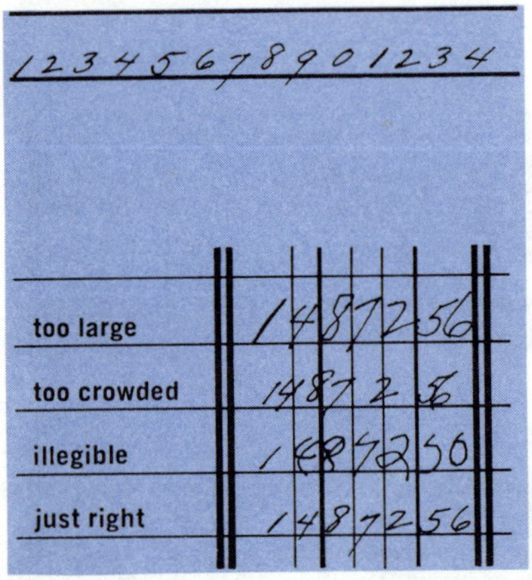

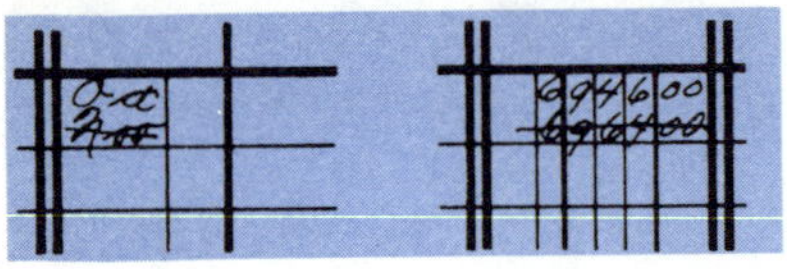

the name is Fry Company, write out the full name as given. If a name is too long for one line, you must use two lines.

This idea also applies to the date in the heading of a balance sheet. Do not abbreviate the month or the year, and do not use numerical dating.

Importance of Legibility Make sure your work is legible. One of the most costly problems in business is careless or unreadable writing, especially in the writing of numbers. It is a fact that numbers are still handwritten more often than they are typewritten or typeset. Ask yourself: *Could someone else read my numbers?*

Here are a few hints to improve your writing of numbers.

- Do not hurry. Take the time to form every number perfectly.
- Write the numerals slightly slanted to the right.
- The size of each number should be less than one-half the line space. This leaves enough space above the numbers to make a manual correction.

See the illustrations in the margin.

TOPIC 2 PROBLEMS

1-4 Refer back to the accounting equations solved for Problems 1-2 and 1-3.

a From the accounting equation solved for Problem 1-2, prepare the opening balance sheet for Donna Lyon, Barrister. Assume that the accounts payable is owing to Legal Publishing, Inc.

b From the accounting equation solved for Problem 1-3, prepare the opening balance sheet for the Manitoba Car Rental Company. Use the current date. Assume that the accounts payable are made up of: Bell Furniture Co., $2 000; Central Equipment Co., $1 700.

Key Check Figure
Capital = $4 000

1-5 The information below reflects Ruth Forrester's Photo Service as of December 31. First, classify the financial data by doing an accounting equation. Once you have determined the kind and amount of each asset and liability, use the accounting equation to calculate the amount of owner's equity. When the accounting equation is complete and in balance, prepare the opening balance sheet of the business.

(i) The business has $17 000 on deposit in its bank account.

(ii) Office equipment has been acquired at a cost of $3 400.

(iii) The business has contracted the following debts, to be paid within 60 days: to Hay Stationery Ltd., $5 400; to Star Equipment Co., $3 700; to Lennox Heating Co., $3 200.

(iv) The business owns land costing $20 000 and a building costing $50 000.

(v) The business has a 20-year mortgage payable, in the amount of $40 000.

(vi) Furniture has been acquired at a cost of $5 000.

Key Check Figure
OE = $43 100

1-6 James Martin established today the Atlantic Insurance Agency, with the following assets and liabilities: Cash, $14 800; Land, $20 000; Building, $55 000; Office Equipment, $6 450; Furniture, $4 550; Bank Loan Payable (on demand), $12 000; Mortgage Payable, $38 000; Accounts Payable (Roberts Supply Co.), $4 800.

Prepare a formal statement reporting the financial position of the business.

Key Check Figure
James Martin, Capital = $46 000

Case Study 1

Five high school students in accounting were watching an NHL hockey game featuring the Edmonton Oilers. After Wayne Gretzky had scored his fifth goal of the game, one student exclaimed: "I'll bet Gretzky is the most valuable asset the Oilers have on *their* balance sheet!"

Another student, however, quickly replied: "Sure, Gretzky is valuable, but I don't think he would appear on the Oilers' balance sheet as an asset."

Two other students agreed with the second speaker, while the remaining one sided strongly with the first speaker. What is your opinion? Explain your answer.

CHAPTER 2

ANALYZING CHANGES IN THE ACCOUNTING EQUATION

In Chapter 1, you learned that the accounting equation is made up of three parts or elements: assets, liabilities, and owner's equity.

In Chapter 2, you will learn how each of these three elements changes as a result of accounting or business transactions.

Business transaction: a financial event that affects one or more assets and/or liabilities, and owner's equity.

A business transaction is a financial event that affects one or more of the three parts of the accounting equation. When analyzing any financial event, keep in mind that the word *financial* simply means the event is expressed in terms of dollars or money. In this chapter, to help you analyze changes in the accounting equation:

- Topic 1 deals with business transactions that affect only the balance sheet.
- Topic 2 introduces two new sets of transactions that result in an expanded equation.
- Topic 3 shows you how to summarize the results of the expanded equation into two accounting reports.

TOPIC 1 ANALYZING BALANCE SHEET TRANSACTIONS

To illustrate how business transactions affect the three elements of the equation, we shall look at several business transactions of J. Emery Real Estate. As we have seen, the balance sheet for this business showed the following equation as at September 30.

Assets								=	Liabilities			+	Owner's Equity
Cash		Automobile		Furniture		Office Equipment			Bank Loan Payable		Accounts Payable		J. Emery, Capital
$60 000	+	$15 000	+	$3 000	+	$2 000		=	$20 000	+	$10 000	+	$50 000
$80 000								=	$30 000			+	$50 000

Now study the series of transactions below.

Transaction 1 On October 1, J. Emery Real Estate buys more furniture for $1 000 from Enns Furniture Ltd., and pays by cheque.

Assets					Liabilities			Owner's Equity	
Cash	Automobile	Furniture	Office Equipment	=	Bank Loan Payable	Accounts Payable	+	J. Emery, Capital	
$60 000 +	$15 000 +	$3 000 +	$2 000	=	$20 000 +	$10 000	+	$50 000	**Original balance**
−1 000		+1 000							**Transaction 1**
$59 000 +	$15 000 +	$4 000 +	$2 000	=	$20 000 +	$10 000	+	$50 000	**New balance**
$80 000				=	$30 000		+	$50 000	

Analysis: Since the furniture was purchased for cash, only assets are affected by this transaction. The business has obtained a new asset — Furniture — by decreasing another *asset* — Cash. Since one asset amount is increased while a second is decreased by the same dollar amount, the total assets do not change. And since this transaction did not change any variable on the right side of the accounting equation, the equation is still *in balance*. The total dollar amount on the left side is still equal to the total dollar amount on the right side.

Transaction 2 On October 3, J. Emery Real Estate buys more office equipment for $1 200 from the Ryan Equipment Co., on 60 days' credit (the creditor allows 60 days for payment of the debt).

Assets					Liabilities			Owner's Equity	
Cash	Automobile	Furniture	Office Equipment	=	Bank Loan Payable	Accounts Payable	+	J. Emery, Capital	
$59 000 +	$15 000 +	$4 000 +	$2 000	=	$20 000 +	$10 000	+	$50 000	**Previous balance**
			+1 200			+1 200			**Transaction 2**
$59 000 +	$15 000 +	$4 000 +	$3 200	=	$20 000 +	$11 200	+	$50 000	**New balance**
$81 200				=	$31 200		+	$50 000	

Analysis: Two elements of the accounting equation are affected by this transaction. On the left side, the *asset* Office Equipment increases by $1 200 because the business now owns more equipment. On the right side of the equation, the *liability* Accounts Payable increases by $1 200 because the business now owes more money to its creditors; in other words, the claims of the creditors against the total assets of the business have increased by $1 200.

Notice that the owner's equity of $50 000 is not affected by this transaction.

Look closely at the final result of this transaction on the equation. With the increase to Office Equipment, the total assets now amount to $80 000 + $1 200 or $81 200. The right side also totals $81 200 now because the total liabilities have been increased from $30 000 to $31 200. Since the left side has been increased by the same amount as the right side, the accounting equation is again in balance, but this time with new total amounts.

Transaction 3 On October 4, J. Emery Real Estate returns one piece of office equipment costing $200 to Ryan Equipment Co. because the equipment arrived in damaged condition. The creditor accepts the return.

	Assets								=	Liabilities			+	Owner's Equity
	Cash		*Automobile*		*Furniture*		*Office Equipment*			*Bank Loan Payable*		*Accounts Payable*		*J. Emery, Capital*
Previous balance	*$59 000*	+	*$15 000*	+	*$4 000*	+	*$3 200*		=	*$20 000*	+	*$11 200*	+	*$50 000*
Transaction 3							*−200*					*−200*		
New balance	*$59 000*	+	*$15 000*	+	*$4 000*	+	*$3 000*		=	*$20 000*	+	*$11 000*	+	*$50 000*
					$81 000				=		*$31 000*		+	*$50 000*

Analysis: Note that, when a business returns an asset purchased on credit but not yet paid for, the asset Cash does not change in any way. The two parts of the equation affected are assets and liabilities; both decrease. On the left, the *asset* Office Equipment decreases by $200 because the business now owns less equipment. On the right, the *liability* Accounts Payable decreases by $200 because the business now owes less money to its creditors. The final result is that the equation is still in balance, because the assets on the left and the liabilities on the right have been decreased by the same dollar amount.

Transaction 4 On October 5, J. Emery Real Estate writes a cheque for $5 000 to Westown Motors Ltd. in payment for the car Jane Emery purchased in September to establish the business. At the end of September, as a result of the purchase, Westown Motors Ltd. held a claim of $5 000 against the total assets of J. Emery Real Estate; the cheque therefore eliminates this claim.

Analysis: Two elements of the accounting equation are affected by this transaction — assets and liabilities. The *asset* Cash decreases by $5 000 because the business now has less money. The *liability* Accounts Payable decreases by $5 000 because a creditor no longer has a claim against the total assets

Assets				=	Liabilities		+ Owner's Equity	
Cash	Automobile	Furniture	Office Equipment		Bank Loan Payable	Accounts Payable	J. Emery, Capital	
$59 000 +	$15 000 +	$4 000 +	$3 000	=	$20 000 +	$11 000 +	$50 000	**Previous balance**
−5 000						−5 000		**Transaction 4**
$54 000 +	$15 000 +	$4 000 +	$3 000	=	$20 000 +	$ 6 000 +	$50 000	**New balance**
$76 000				=	$26 000		+ $50 000	

of the business. Since the left and right sides of the equation have decreased by the same amount, the equation remains in balance.

Transaction 5 On October 15, J. Emery Real Estate writes a cheque for $4 000 to the Royal Bank of Canada in partial payment of the bank loan.

Assets				=	Liabilities		+ Owner's Equity	
Cash	Automobile	Furniture	Office Equipment		Bank Loan Payable	Accounts Payable	J. Emery, Capital	
$54 000 +	$15 000 +	$4 000 +	$3 000	=	$20 000 +	$ 6 000 +	$50 000	**Previous balance**
−4 000					−4 000			**Transaction 5**
$50 000 +	$15 000 +	$4 000 +	$3 000	=	$16 000 +	$ 6 000 +	$50 000	**New balance**
$72 000				=	$22 000		+ $50 000	

Analysis: The analysis of this transaction is much the same as that of Transaction 4: the *asset* Cash and the *liability* Bank Loan Payable each decrease by $4 000. Since both sides of the equation decrease by the same amount, the equation balances.

Transaction 6 The previous five transactions have affected only the first two elements of the equation. This transaction will affect the third element, the owner's equity.

On October 16, Jane Emery decides to increase her investment in the business by taking $3 000 from her personal savings account and depositing it into the firm's chequing account.

Analysis: When an owner increases his or her investment in the business, two elements increase — assets and owner's equity. On the left, the *asset* Cash increases by $3 000 because the business now has more money. On the right, the *owner's equity* element, J. Emery, Capital, increases by $3 000 because Jane Emery has now increased her investment in the business. In

	Assets				=	Liabilities		+ Owner's Equity
	Cash	Automobile	Furniture	Office Equipment		Bank Loan Payable	Accounts Payable	J. Emery, Capital
Previous balance	$50 000 +	$15 000 +	$4 000 +	$3 000	=	$16 000 +	$ 6 000 +	$50 000
Transaction 6	+3 000							+3 000
New balance	$53 000 +	$15 000 +	$4 000 +	$3 000	=	$16 000 +	$ 6 000 +	$53 000
	$75 000				=	$22 000		+ $53 000

other words, she has increased her claim against the total assets. Since assets and owner's equity increase by the same amount, while liabilities remain the same, the equation must still balance.

Transaction 7 On October 30, Jane Emery withdraws $2 000 from her firm's bank account and deposits it into her personal chequing account.

As sole proprietor of the business, the owner is of course entitled to withdraw assets for personal use — in fact, regular cash withdrawals may be required in order to maintain a living. Assets such as office furniture could also be withdrawn for personal use.

	Assets				=	Liabilities		+	Owner's Equity
	Cash	Automobile	Furniture	Office Equipment		Bank Loan Payable	Accounts Payable	J. Emery, Capital	J. Emery, Drawing
Previous balance	$53 000 +	$15 000 +	$4 000 +	$3 000	=	$16 000 +	$ 6 000 +	$53 000	
Transaction 7	−2 000								− $2 000
New balance	$51 000 +	$15 000 +	$4 000 +	$3 000	=	$16 000 +	$ 6 000 +	$53 000 −	$2 000
	$73 000				=	$22 000		+	$51 000

Analysis: When the owner withdraws cash or other assets from the business for personal use, two elements are affected — assets and owner's equity. Both decrease. In this case, the *asset* Cash decreases by $2 000 because the business now has less cash.

Of course, the right side of the equation must also be lowered by $2 000. Since liabilities are not affected by this transaction, it must be owner's equity that is decreased. As you can see from the illustration, the decrease is made by subtracting $2 000 under a new subheading, *J. Emery, Drawing.*

You might ask: Why not show the decrease to owner's equity under *J. Emery, Capital?* The answer is that in accounting, capital means investment. Since the original investment has not decreased, we need to recognize a new item which can decrease owner's equity, referred to as drawing.

Drawing: a sub-element showing a decrease to owner's equity resulting from the owner's withdrawal of assets for personal use. See also "Drawings" later.

Notice that the addition of the new balances in the equation equalizes the two sides. Total assets of $73 000 are now equal to total liabilities of $22 000 plus the new owner's equity of $51 000.

Preparing a Summary Table

A useful table summarizing all of the above transactions can be prepared. See the illustration on page 24. A study of this table will help you do the problems that follow. Notice at the bottom of the table the reference to the *equality check*. This is a check to see that the two sides of the accounting equation are in balance once the final totals of the table are found.

TOPIC 1 PROBLEMS

2-1 On November 1, the balance sheet for Case Service Company showed these beginning balances:

A						=	L			+	OE
Cash		*Auto*		*Equip-ment*			*Bank Loan Payable*		*Accounts Payable*		*Carl Case, Capital*
$6 000	+	*$10 000*	+	*$4 000*		=	*$2 000*	+	*$6 000*	+	*$12 000*

a Enter the beginning balances of the various items into the accounting equation for Case Service Company on a summary table similar to the one illustrated on page 24. In this case there are three assets, two liabilities, and one owner's equity item.

b Show what happens to the accounting equation as a result of each of Carl Case's November transactions below.

c After you have analyzed the final transaction, add up all the columns in the table.

d Do an equality check below the summary table.

Transactions

(i) Bought equipment for $2 500 on 60 days' credit from Victoria Equipment Ltd.

(ii) Returned one piece of equipment costing $500 bought earlier on credit from Victoria Equipment Ltd.

(iii) Paid $4 000 cash to Vancouver Auto Ltd. in partial payment of a debt.

(iv) Invested another $5 000 cash in the business.

(v) Obtained another loan of $3 000 cash from the bank, which was immediately deposited into the firm's chequing account.

Key Check Figure
$26 000 = $9 000 +$17 000

SUMMARY TABLE

	ASSETS					= LIABILITIES			+ OWNER'S EQUITY		
Trans-actions	Cash	Auto-mobile	Furni-ture	Office Equip.	Total or Change in Assets	Bk. Loan Payable	Accts. Pay.	Total Lias.	J. Emery, Capital	J. Emery, Drawing	Total or Change in OE
(Orig. bal.)	$60 000	+$15 000	+$3 000	+$2 000	$80 000	$20 000	+$10 000	$30 000	$50 000		$50 000
1	−1 000		+1 000		∅						
2				+1 200	+1 200		+1 200	+1 200			
3				−200	−200		−200	−200			
4	−5 000				−5 000		−5 000	−5 000			
5	−4 000				−4 000	−4 000		−4 000			
6	+3 000				+3 000				+3 000		+3 000
7	−2 000				−2 000					−$2 000	−2 000
Totals	$51 000	+$15 000	+$4 000	+$3 000	$73 000	$16 000	+$6 000	$22 000	$53 000	−$2 000	$51 000

Equality Check: A = L + OE
$73 000 = $22 000 + $51 000
$73 000 = $73 000

2-2 The following transactions were performed by Kevin Heer during the month of October for the Kevin Heer Musical Band.

(i) Invested $5 000 cash for the formation of the band by depositing the amount into a chequing account under the name Kevin Heer Musical Band.

(ii) Bought musical instruments costing $1 200 on credit, payment to be made to Laxton Musical Store in 60 days.

(iii) Bought more musical instruments for $1 000 cash.

(iv) Returned one musical instrument purchased earlier for $200 cash; the supplier then issued a $200 cheque which was immediately deposited into the firm's chequing account.

(v) Bought various musical supplies for $1 700 cash.

(vi) Invested an additional $1 000 cash.

(vii) Issued a cheque for $200 to Laxton Musical Store in part payment of debt.

(viii) Withdrew $500 cash for personal use.

(ix) Borrowed $5 000 cash from a local banker, which was deposited into the firm's chequing account.

a Enter the following headings into a summary table similar to the one illustrated on page 24: Transactions; Cash; Musical Instruments; Musical Supplies; Total Assets; Bank Loan Payable; Accounts Payable; Total Liabilities; Kevin Heer, Capital; Kevin Heer, Drawing; Total Owner's Equity.

b Record the effects of the nine transactions in the correct columns of the table.

c After recording the results of the final transaction, add the columns in the table.

d Do an equality check below the table.

Key Check Figure
$11 500 = $6 000 +$5 500

2-3 Challenge Problem During the month of November, the following transactions concerning Radio Station CHJK took place.

Nov. 1 A licence was granted to Mrs. Edna Greenwood for the organization and operation of Radio Station CHJK. Mrs. Greenwood invested $40 000 cash.

3 Land was purchased for $13 000 from Dewling Development Company. A cash down payment of $3 000 was made, and credit of 90 days was extended.

4 A demand loan of $10 000 was obtained from the Royal Bank of Canada.

5 A transmitter was purchased for $25 000 from Radio Specialty, Ltd. A cash down payment of $15 000 was made. The balance was to be paid in monthly installments of $500 beginning November 18.

6 An office and broadcasting facility was erected at a cost of $18 000, paid in cash.

8 A turntable was purchased for $450 cash from Ferris Music Centre.

11 A tape recorder was purchased for $1 250 cash from Ferris Music Centre.

14 A record library was purchased for $3 750 from Ferris Music Centre. A

cash payment of $1 750 was made, with the balance to be paid within 30 days.

Nov. 16 Part of the record library, which had cost $250, was sold to the Civic Recreation Centre for the same price. The Civic Recreation Centre made payment by cheque.

18 $500 cash was paid to Radio Specialty, Ltd., as the first installment due that day.

30 Some new records were purchased from Ferris Music Centre for $1 125, to be paid within 30 days.

a Analyze and record the impact of each transaction on the accounting equation for this business enterprise by using a summary table with the following column headings: Transaction Date; Cash; Land; Buildings; Transmitter; Broadcasting Equipment; Record Library; Total Assets; Bank Loan Payable; Accounts Payable; Total Liabilities; Edna Greenwood, Capital.

b After recording the changes brought about by the final transaction, total all items in the table. Then prove the equality of the accounting equation by doing an equality check.

Key Check Figure Capital = $40 000

c Prepare the opening balance sheet for Radio Station CHJK.

TOPIC 2 ANALYZING AN EXPANDED EQUATION

Revenue and expense transactions: financial events that determine the profit (or loss) of a business.

The primary purpose of a business is to increase the owner's equity by earning a *profit* over a definite period of time. In the language of accounting, the financial events directly related to the calculation of a business profit (or loss) are known as revenue and expense transactions. Revenue transactions and expense transactions affect the accounting equation by expanding the right side of it. Let's begin the study of this expanded equation by analyzing the revenue aspect of accounting transactions.

Revenue Transactions

Let's analyze two further transactions that will affect Jane Emery's real estate business. Assume that these transactions simply follow the last transaction (Transaction 7 of October 30).

Commissions: the fees a business charges for buying or selling goods (for example, real estate) for clients.

Transaction 8 As of October 31, J. Emery Real Estate has received $6 800 cash for buying and selling homes, land, and other forms of real estate. In the language of real estate businesses, J. Emery Real Estate has earned and collected commissions totalling $6 800 for buying and selling real estate for clients.

Beginning Analysis: Identify what you already know. If the business has received $6 800 cash, then the *asset* Cash in the equation must be increased by $6 800. Next, the total of the left side of the equation must be changed, since the assets have now increased from $73 000 to $79 800. The accounting equation that follows illustrates these changes.

Assets						=	Liabilities			+	Owner's Equity		
Cash	+	Automobile	+	Furniture	+	Office Equipment	=	Bank Loan Payable	+	Accounts Payable	+	J. Emery, Capital	−	J. Emery, Drawing
$51 000	+	$15 000	+	$4 000	+	$3 000	=	$16 000	+	$6 000	+	$53 000	−	$2 000
+6 800								+ ?		+ ?		+ ?		+ ?
$57 800	+	$15 000	+	$4 000	+	$3 000	=							

$79 800

$6 800 must be shown as an increase on the right side of the equation. But where?

Tr. 8

Further Analysis: You now know that when the left side of the accounting equation is increased, the right side must be increased by the same amount. But are liabilities affected as a result of this transaction? Obviously not, because liabilities are the debts of a business. Then it must be the owner's equity that is increased. Now, you have learned that *J. Emery, Capital* means the claim of the owner through her investment; since she has not made any additional investment, it would be incorrect to show owner's equity as increased by an additional capital amount. You have also learned that *J. Emery, Drawing* is the heading under which we show a decrease to owner's equity resulting from an owner's withdrawal of assets for personal use. What, then, causes the owner's equity to go up in the accounting equation?

The answer is a new accounting concept to learn. Study the following illustration. See how the accounting equation has expanded on the right side to provide for revenue through commissions being earned and collected during October.

Assets							=	Liabilities			+	Owner's Equity				
Cash	+	Automobile	+	Furniture	+	Office Equipment	=	Bank Loan Payable	+	Accounts Payable	+	J. Emery, Capital	−	J. Emery, Drawing	+	Revenue
$51 000	+	$15 000	+	$4 000	+	$3 000	=	$16 000	+	$6 000	+	$53 000	−	$2 000		
+6 800															+	$6 800
$57 800	+	$15 000	+	$4 000	+	$3 000	=	$16 000	+	$6 000	+	$53 000	−	$2 000	+	$6 800

$79 800 = $22 000 + $57 800

Tr. 8

Final Analysis: When a business sells services for cash (as when earning and collecting commissions for real estate services), it acquires more cash. The illustration shows additional cash of $6 800, thus increasing the left side of the equation (the total assets) by this amount. Since the right side of the equation must also increase by the same amount, and since liabilities are not affected by this transaction, it must be the owner's equity that is increased. But capital (investment) and drawing (withdrawal of assets) are not affected, so a new subheading of owner's equity must be created: *Revenue.* Thus the right side of the equation is expanded and the expanded equation is in balance.

Transaction 9 As of October 31, J. Emery Real Estate earned commissions on credit by providing real estate services as follows: $2 000 for selling a building for Pat Rogers; $1 200 for selling a residence for R. Scobie; and $4 000 for buying properties for Shannon Development Co. All clients (customers) were given 30 days in which to pay the commissions earned.

	Assets			=	*Liabilities*		+	*Owner's Equity*		
	Cash	*Accounts Receivable*	*Auto*		*Bk. Loan Pay.*	*Accts. Pay.*		*J. Emery, Capital*	*J. Emery, Drawing*	*Revenue*
	$57 800 +		*+ $15 000 +*	=	*$16 000 +*	*$6 000*	+	*$53 000 −*	*$2 000 +*	*$6 800*
Tr. 9		*+$7 200*								*+7 200*
	$57 800 +	*$7 200*	*+ $15 000 +*	=	*$16 000 +*	*$6 000*	+	*$53 000 −*	*$2 000*	*+ $14 000*
		$87 000		=	*$22 000*		+		*$65 000*	

Accounts receivable: an asset representing amounts due from customers.

Analysis: As a result of earning commissions on credit, a new asset called accounts receivable comes into the business. On the left side, the accounting equation shows assets increasing by a total of $7 200 because the business now has claims on the property of three customers until their debts are paid. Notice that the heading *Accounts Receivable* is placed immediately after *Cash* in the equation. This is because the business expects to collect the customers' debts within 30 days.

Revenue:

an inflow of assets resulting from the sale of goods or services.

On the right side of the equation, owner's equity increases by $7 200 because of the additional source of revenue. This increase is shown as a second plus amount (an addition) under *Revenue.* The total revenue for October is now $14 000 ($6 800 in immediate cash collections of commissions plus $7 200 in commissions coming from accounts receivable). Since the two sides of the equation have been increased by the same amount, the equation is in balance.

Analysis of Transactions 8 and 9 gives you an excellent definition of revenue: an inflow of cash and accounts receivable to a business resulting from the sale of goods or services.

Remember, however, that the inflow of cash does not automatically mean revenue has been earned by the business. For example: (1) An inflow of cash resulting from a customer's paying a debt means simply an exchange of one asset (accounts receivable) for another (cash). (2) When a business gets cash by borrowing from a bank, this inflow of cash is offset by an increase in liabilities — usually in the form of a demand note payable to the bank. (3) Cash can come into a business through additional investment by the owner, in which case assets and owner's equity (under *Capital*) increase.

Remember that revenue for a given period is equal to the inflow of assets (cash and accounts receivable) in that period from the selling of goods or services. This inflow must be offset by an increase to owner's equity in the accounting equation.

When Is Revenue Recognized? You may be wondering at what point revenue from sales is recognized. For example, should it be recognized at the time the sale is made, or when the cash is received from the customer?

To answer this question and many other similar ones, the accounting profession has developed guidelines called generally accepted accounting principles (GAAPs for short). These guide accountants in preparing balance sheets and other useful financial statements. In this book you will be introduced to *basic* accounting principles only. One of these is the one for recognizing revenue, which may be stated here as follows:

Generally accepted accounting principles (GAAPs): broad guidelines used by accountants to answer accounting questions and to assist them in preparing financial statements.

Revenue must be recognized as at the time of the sale of goods, or as at the time of the rendering of services.

GAAP for Revenue Recognition

In Transactions 8 and 9, the sales of services were completed when assets such as cash or a promise to pay cash (accounts receivable) were transferred from the buyer to the seller in exchange for the services being completed.

If a sale of goods had been made, revenue would have been recognized when the seller received cash or the claim to cash (accounts receivable) in exchange for those goods.

Here's an easy way to remember the basic accounting principle for recognizing revenue:

- In cash sales transactions, sales revenue is recognized at the time when the good or service is received by the buyer and cash is received by the seller.
- In credit sales, sales revenue is recognized at the time the good or service is received by the buyer and the customer has agreed to pay within a certain time period (an account receivable).

Expense Transactions

All businesses have expenses for one reason only — to bring revenue into the business. For example, when money is spent on employee salaries, advertising, and the use of the telephone to attract customers, revenue may be obtained through the resulting sales.

In accounting terms, expenses are the dollar amounts *used up* to carry on business. Here are some examples:

- Salaries and wages are dollars *used up* by the business to pay employees.
- Monthly rent will be an expense because the cost of renting office space will be *used up* to bring customers to the place of business and to house the employees.
- A telephone bill received by a business will be an amount *used up* by the business to support activities which bring in revenue.
- A bill for advertising the goods or services of the business will be accounted for as dollars *used up* to help bring in revenue.

Expenses: costs incurred by a business in earning revenue.

Since the amounts paid for salaries, office space, telephone service, advertising, and other expenses are used up in the process of earning revenue, accountants define expenses as: the cost of goods and services used up by business to earn revenue.

The above definition of expenses emphasizes two ideas:

- that the cost (dollars) of operating the business must be *used up*
- that those dollars must be used to earn revenue

In other words, a business has expenses for one reason only — to create revenue or to support activities that create revenue.

Transaction 10 To obtain the $14 000 revenue from commissions earned during October, J. Emery Real Estate paid cash totalling $5 235 as of October 31 for the following expenses: Rent, $600; Salaries, $4 500; Utilities, $95; and Telephone, $40.

Beginning Analysis: Since the business paid $5 235 cash for four expenses, the left side of the equation decreases because the *asset* Cash has decreased. Therefore some element on the right side must decrease by a similar amount. Which element must it be, and what accounting concept causes this to happen in the following illustration?

	Assets			=	Liabilities		+	Owner's Equity		
	Cash	Accts. Rec.	Auto		Bk. Loan Pay.	Accts. Pay.		J. Emery, Capital	J. Emery, Drawing	Revenue
	$57 800 +	$7 200	+ $15 000 +	=	$16 000 +	$6 000	+	$53 000 −	$2 000	+ $14 000
Tr. 10	−5 235				− ?	− ?		− ?	− ?	− ?
	$52 565 +	$7 200	+ $15 000 +							
	$81 765									

Further Analysis: The element on the right side that must go down by $5 235 could not be liabilities because all of the expenses were paid in cash. If your answer was owner's equity, you are correct, but is J. Emery, Capital affected, or J. Emery, Drawing, or Revenue? Absolutely no in every case! Remember, J. Emery, Capital causes an increase to Owner's Equity through an owner's investment. J. Emery, Drawing causes a decrease to Owner's Equity only through the withdrawal of assets for the owner's personal use. And Revenue causes an increase to Owner's Equity through the inflow of cash and accounts receivable from sales.

What, then, causes Owner's Equity in the equation to decrease? The answer is the concept introduced earlier: *expenses.* The complete accounting equation below includes this new heading.

Assets			*= Liabilities*		*+ Owner's Equity*			
Cash	*Accts. Rec.*	*Auto*	*Bk. Loan Pay.*	*Accts. Pay.*	*J. Emery, Capital*	*J. Emery, Drawing*	*Revenue*	*Expenses*
$57 800 +	*$7 200 +*	*$15 000 +*	*= $16 000 +*	*$6 000 +*	*$53 000 −*	*$2 000 +*	*$14 000*	
−5 235								*−$5 235*
$52 565 +	*$7 200 +*	*$15 000 +*	*= $16 000 +*	*$6 000 +*	*$53 000 −*	*$2 000 +*	*$14 000 −*	*$5 235*
$81 765			*= $22 000*	*+*	*$59 765*			

Tr. 10

Final Analysis: When a business pays cash for its expenses the left side of the equation is decreased because the *asset* Cash decreases by the amount of the paid expenses. The right side of the equation must also be decreased by that amount. Because liabilities are not affected by the cash transaction, it is *Expenses* under *Owner's Equity* that causes the third element in the equation to decrease. Note that expenses are *not* going down — the minus sign is used for expenses simply to show that this item causes a decrease to owner's equity in the accounting equation. Without it, the accounting equation could not balance. Check the illustration once again to prove this point to yourself.

Transaction 11 On October 31, J. Emery Real Estate receives a bill for $600 from *The City Record,* a local newspaper, for running three large advertisements in October. The bill allows J. Emery Real Estate a period of 30 days in which to pay.

Analysis: The left side of the accounting equation is not affected because no asset is involved. J. Emery Real Estate is given 30 days to pay for the advertising and the *liability* Accounts Payable must be increased to record the new claim of creditors against the total assets of the business. At the same time, the expense *incurred* must be shown as a second minus sign under *Owner's Equity* because expenses cause a decrease to owner's equity.

Tr. 11

Assets			=	Liabilities		+	Owner's Equity			
Cash	Accts. Rec.	Auto		Bk. Loan Pay.	Accts. Pay.		J. Emery, Capital	J. Emery, Drawing	Revenue	Expenses
\$52 565 +	\$7 200 +	\$15 000 +	=	\$16 000 +	\$6 000	+	\$53 000 −	\$2 000 +	\$14 000 −	\$5 235
					+ 600					− 600
\$52 565 +	\$7 200 +	\$15 000 +	=	\$16 000 +	\$6 600	+	\$53 000 −	\$2 000 +	\$14 000 −	\$5 835
\$81 765			=	\$22 600		+	\$59 165			

Notice that the increase in liabilities (+\$600) is now offset by the decrease in owner's equity (−\$600). The accounting equation is in balance.

Notice, too, that the total expenses for October, \$5 835, are shown as a minus amount under *Owner's Equity*. Again, this minus sign does not mean that expenses have gone down by \$5 835. It simply means that owner's equity in the accounting equation has been decreased by this amount. If this were not true, the accounting equation could not possibly balance after any expense transaction.

The analysis of Transaction 11 introduces a second GAAP — the principle for recognizing expenses. Just as, earlier, revenue was recognized as at the point of sale, the principle for recognizing expenses says:

GAAP for Expense Recognition

Expenses must be recognized and recorded when they are incurred while making revenue.

It does not matter whether or not the business has paid the expenses; they must always be recognized as soon as they can be related to the earning of revenue within the same time period.

For example, if an advertising expense was incurred to bring revenue for October sales, it would be wrong to recognize the expense in November or in December when the bill was finally paid. Remember these two helpful questions as an aid to recognizing an accounting expense:

- Was the cost used up to earn revenue or to assist in revenue-making activities of the same time period?
- Does the item reduce the owner's equity in the accounting equation as well as reducing an asset or increasing a liability? If your answer to both questions is yes, then, under GAAPs, you will probably have to recognize a cost of operating the business.

One final point. You now know revenue transactions result in an inflow of cash and accounts receivable resulting from the sales of goods or services. Well, expenses may be viewed as the using up of economic resources or the *outflow* of assets in the process of earning revenue. As Transactions 10 and 11 showed, this outflow may occur directly, as a result of incurring expenses and paying cash for them; or indirectly, as when the outflow is delayed by recognizing the expense incurred as a result of the increase to the liability Accounts Payable. (You will recall that accounts payable are usually payable on 30 or 60 days' credit; therefore, the outflow of cash is delayed.)

What remains now is to relate the inflow (revenue) to the outflow (expenses) to determine whether the business has made a profit or loss.

Matching Revenues and Expenses

After accounting for revenue and expense transactions for a definite period of time, say one month, you must subtract the total revenue earned and the total expenses incurred to calculate the profit or loss for that period. This introduces what in the language of accounting is called the *matching principle*. To understand matching, study the five examples shown in the margin.

Example 1 There is a *mismatch* between revenues and expenses. Why? Revenues and expenses were not calculated for the same time period. A fair report of profit cannot be made. A valid matchup means *revenues and expenses must be related to the same time period.*

Example 2 Obviously, a serious mismatch of revenues and expenses has taken place. It is unfair to report a loss of $10 000 here, because revenues were reported for only six months while expenses for twelve months were deducted from revenues.

Example 3 This example does show a fair matchup. Why? Because revenues for one month are matched with expenses for the same month. Since revenues were greater than expenses *for that same time period,* a profit can be reported. Notice the use of the term *net profit. Net* simply means that all revenues and all expenses have been matched.

Example 4 This example also shows a fair matchup. Since total revenues for 19-5 exceeded total expenses for 19-5, a net profit for that year can be reported.

Example 5 Though this example shows a fair matchup, the net result is very different: it shows a net loss for the year. This is because total expenses are greater than total revenues for that time period.

Now the basic accounting principle for matching can be presented.

Example 1

Revenues (for Oct., Nov., Dec.)	$15 000
Expenses (for Oct., Nov.)	9 000
PROFIT	$ 6 000

Example 2

Revenues (for 6 months)	$50 000
Expenses (for 12 months)	60 000
LOSS	$10 000

Example 3

Revenues (for Sept. 19-5)	$10 000
Expenses (for Sept. 19-5)	4 000
NET PROFIT	$ 6 000

Example 4

Revenues (for year 19-5)	$150 000
Expenses (for year 19-5)	115 000
NET PROFIT	$ 35 000

Example 5

Revenues (for year 19-6)	$140 000
Expenses (for year 19-6)	160 000
NET LOSS	$ 20 000

GAAP for Matching

In reporting the net profit or loss of a business for a financial period, revenues must be matched with those expenses incurred in producing the profit or loss.

That is, revenues of one time period (called the *financial* or *accounting period)* must be matched with the related expenses incurred in the same period. Note that the length of the financial period can vary from one month to six months or even a year.

The Need for a Modern Term for Profit

Net income: the excess of revenue over expenses.

Net loss: the excess of expenses over revenues.

Many years ago, the term *profit* was used to report the favourable results of matching revenues with related expenses. However, this term can mean different things to different people. To avoid confusion, modern accounting practice speaks of *income* and loss rather than profit and loss. From now on, the student should use the modern terms net income and net loss. Remember: the word *net* means that all revenues and all expenses have been reported and matched, for the same accounting period.

Applying the Matching Principle to the Equation

To apply the matching principle, you must rearrange the expanded section (revenue and expenses) of the accounting equation by:

- placing the total expenses under the total revenue
- calculating the difference between the amounts

Examine the following rearranged and expanded equation for J. Emery Real Estate and study the analysis.

Assets				=	Liabilities		+	Owner's Equity				
Cash	Accts. Rec.	Auto			Bk. Loan Pay.	Accts. Pay.		J. Emery, Capital	J. Emery, Drawing		+$14 000 −5 835	Revenue Expenses
$52 565 +	$7 200 +	$15 000 +		=	$16 000 +	$6 600	+	$53 000 −	$2 000	+	$8 165	Net Income
		$81 765		=	$22 600		+			$59 165		

Analysis: Assuming the matching principle was used in this equation, the excess of revenue over related expenses is the *net income* — a plus amount under *Owner's Equity*. In other words, Owner's Equity is increased by the net income for the financial period. Of course, if total expenses had exceeded the total revenue, the final result would have been a *net loss* — a minus result. This result would naturally mean that the owner's equity for the period would be decreased by the amount of the loss. Study the two illustrations that follow.

In summary, revenue is the positive or plus part in calculating net income. Expenses are the negative or minus part in calculating net income. The difference between the two will determine

Owner's Equity		
		Net Income
		+ $14 000 Revenue
Capital	Drawing	−5 835 Expenses
$53 000 −	$2 000	+ $ 8 165 Increase

Owner's Equity		
		Net Loss
		+ $14 000 Revenue
Capital	Drawing	−16 000 Expenses
$53 000 −	$2 000	− $ 2 000 Decrease

whether the owner's equity is increased or decreased as a result of the business operations for a certain period of time.

TOPIC 2 PROBLEMS

2-4 Chan's Insurance Agency identified the following equation as a result of operations for the month of September, current year.

A				=	L	+	OE				
Cash	Accts. Rec.		Equip.		Bk. Loan Pay.		H. Chan, Capital		Revenue		Expenses
$2 510 +	$1 090	+	$6 400	=	$1 000	+	$5 000	+	$8 000	−	$4 000
$10 000				=	$1 000	+	$9 000				

a Rearrange the equation to show the matching of revenues and expenses for September.
b Did this matching produce a net income or a net loss for the period? Explain.

Key Check Figure
Total OE = $9 000

2-5 During the month of May, Davey Tree Service:
(i) Sold services for cash for $800.
(ii) Sold services on credit for $2 200.
(iii) Bought equipment for $600 in cash.
(iv) Received $100 from the sale of services.
(v) Paid $300 to a creditor to pay off an account payable.
(vi) Paid $80 for advertising expense.
(vii) Bought equipment for $75 on credit.
(viii) Paid $20 for utilities.
(ix) Received $200 from a customer on accounts receivable.
(x) Paid two employees each $600 for their monthly wages.
(xi) Received $300 from customers on accounts receivable.

a As of April 30, the business had the assets, liabilities, and owner's equity shown in the accounting equation that follows. Indicate what happens to the accounting equation as a result of each transaction. The first transaction is done as an example.

	Assets					=	Liabilities	+	Owner's Equity			
	Cash	+	Accts. Rec.	+	Equipt.	=	Accts. Pay.	+	D. Davey, Capital		Revenue	Expenses
April 30 bal.	$4 000	+	$ 400	+	$2 600	=	$ 800	+	$6 200			
Trans. a	+800										+$800	
New Balance	$4 800	+	$ 400	+	$2 600	=	$ 800	+	$6 200	+	$800	

Key Check Figure
Total OE = $8 000

b Rearrange the final equation to illustrate the matching of revenues and expenses for May. Did this matching produce a net income or a net loss for the financial period? Explain.

2-6 Joanne Guest opened a dental practice in Regina under the name J. Guest, D.D.S. She employed the services of one dental hygienist, one dental assistant, and one front-office person. The following transactions were recorded during the month of December.

(i) Joanne invested $10 000 of her personal savings kept in a bank account in the name of J. Guest, D.D.S.

(ii) She purchased dental equipment costing $20 000 on 60 days' credit from Western Dental Supply.

(iii) She returned dental equipment originally purchased on credit for $1 000 from Western Dental Supply.

(iv) She purchased more dental equipment by issuing a cheque for $9 000 to Saskatoon Dental Supply.

(v) She invested an additional $15 000 cash in the practice.

(vi) The practice earned $6 400 cash from fees charged for work done during the month.

(vii) As of December 31, J. Guest, D.D.S., earned the following fees on 30 days' credit by providing dental services to the patients mentioned: $100, K. Adams; $250, J. Harwood; $500, E. Lat; $75, D. Lee; and $800, E. Powell.

(viii) Joanne received a cheque for $75 from D. Lee, which cleared the debt.

(ix) To earn revenue during December, J. Guest, D.D.S., issued cheques totalling $8 138 as of December 31 to cover the following expenses: Rent, $1 400; Salaries, $5 200; Utilities, $80; Telephone, $38; Supplies, $1 420. *Note:* All of the supplies were used up during the month.

(x) A cheque for $1 000 was issued to Western Dental Supply in part payment of the debt owing to this creditor.

(xi) A bill for $100 was received on December 31 from City Cleaners. The bill was for the cleaning of dental uniforms for December. City Cleaners gave 30 days from the date of the bill to pay the amount owing.

(xii) Joanne withdrew $700 cash for personal use.

a Set up an accounting equation with the following elements: Cash; Accts.

Rec.; Equipment; Accts. Pay.; J. Guest, Capital; J. Guest, Drawing; Revenue; Expenses. Analyze and record what happens to the accounting equation as a result of each transaction. Use the procedure in Problem 2-5.

b Rearrange the final equation to illustrate the matching of revenue with related expenses. Did the dental practice produce a net income or a net loss for December? Explain the final effect on Owner's Equity.

Key Check Figure
Total OE = $24 187

TOPIC 3 INCOME STATEMENT AND RELATED BALANCE SHEET

From the previous section (Topic 2) you learned how revenue and expense transactions expand the accounting equation under *Owner's Equity* so that the net income or net loss may be calculated for a certain period of time. The results of this expanded equation may be summarized in two kinds of accounting reports:

- the income statement, which summarizes the revenue and related expenses to report the net income or net loss for the accounting period
- a new, related balance sheet to report the position of assets, liabilities, and owner's equity as at the end of the accounting period

Analyzing an Income Statement

The basic form of an income statement is based upon the expanded part of the accounting equation. Look closely at the illustration on page 38, and study the analysis of the points given below.

- An income statement has two sections, heading and body.
- The heading has three lines: line 1 shows the name of the business; line 2, the name of the financial statement; line 3, the specific accounting period for which revenues and related expenses have been matched to determine a net income or net loss.
- The first section of the body summarizes the reported revenue for the accounting period.
- The next section reports the related expenses for the same accounting period. Notice that total expenses are shown in order to match this amount against the reported revenue.
- The net result of operating the business — the net income or net loss for the accounting period — is shown.

Preparing an Income Statement

In Chapter 1 you learned that a balance sheet is prepared at least once a year for interested parties such as creditors, and that the people who manage a business may prepare them as often as

Assets				=	Liabilities			+	Owner's Equity				
Cash		Accts. Rec.			Bk. Loan Pay.		Accts. Pay.		J. Emery, Capital		J. Emery, Drawing		+$14 000 Revenue −5 835 Expenses
$52 565	+	$7 200	+ . . .	=	$16 000	+	$6 600	+	$53 000	−	$2 000	+	$8 165 Net Income
$81 765				=	$22 600			+	$59 165				

J. Emery Real Estate
Income Statement
For the Month Ended October 31, 19—

Revenue:		
Commissions Earned		$14 000.00
Expenses:		
Salaries Expense	$4 500.00	
Rent Expense	600.00	
Utilities Expense	95.00	
Telephone Expense	40.00	
Advertising Expense	600.00	
Total Expenses		5 835.00
Net Income		$ 8 165.00

once a month. You were also told that this financial statement is usually printed — by typewriter, printing press, computer, or word processor. These facts apply as well to the preparation of an income statement. However, as with the balance sheet, you can learn the important guidelines for preparing an income statement by doing some by hand. Refer to the following illustration as you study the guidelines.

J. Emery Real Estate
Income Statement
For the Month Ended October 31, 19--

Revenue:		
Commissions Earned		$14 000 00
Expenses:		
Salaries Expense	$4 500 00	
Rent Expense	600 00	
Utilities Expense	95 00	
Telephone Expense	40 00	
Advertising Expense	600 00	
Total Expenses		5 835 00
Net Income		$8 165 00

Heading Notice that the heading of an income statement answers the questions *who, what,* and *when.*

The *when* is very important. It explains the accounting period covered by the statement. In the income statement illustrated for J. Emery Real Estate, the accounting period is one particular month. Note that the one-month period *has ended* — the transactions matching revenue and related expenses have taken place. Thus, it would be incorrect to use the expression "ending" in the date line.

Once the accounting period has been established, it must be stated on the date line of the statement. For example, if the accounting period covers three months — say January, February, and March — the date line would read "For the Quarter Ended March 31, 19—" or "For the Three Months Ended March 31, 19—." If the accounting period covers a calendar year, the date line would read "For the Year Ended December 31, 19—."

Revenue Section On the first line at the margin, enter the title *Revenue* followed by a colon. Underneath, indent and list the sources of revenue, beginning each word with a capital letter. When there is only one source, as in the example for J. Emery Real Estate, show the amount directly in the second money column. If there are several sources, as in the example in the margin, the individual amounts would be listed in the first money column and the total amount in the second money column.

Revenue:		
Admissions Revenue	$8 000 00	
Concessions Revenue	4 500 00	
Parking Fees Earned	2 500 00	
Total Revenue		$15 000 00

Sales: the main source of revenue for firms that sell goods.

Retailing, wholesaling, or manufacturing firms earn revenue mainly by selling goods, so they describe their source as sales revenue or simply Sales. But the source of revenue depends on the nature of a business's operations. Service firms report their main source of revenue by describing the nature of their business operations. Firms that charge a commission for their services may report their revenue as *Commissions Earned.*

Fees Earned: the main source of revenue for professions such as doctors, lawyers, etc.

Many service firms are in the professions — law, medicine, dentistry, accountancy, etc. These charge a fee for their services. Therefore, the income statement of these firms usually describes their main source of revenue as Fees Earned.

Expense Section On the line below the last entry in the revenue section, enter the title *Expenses* followed by a colon. Indent and list the expenses beneath this title. Begin every word with a capital letter. If there is only one expense, list the amount in the second money column (that is, the main money column for reporting the matchup of revenue with related expenses). If there is more than one expense, as there usually is, the amount for each expense is listed in the first money column, and the total of the expenses is extended in the second money column. By showing the total expenses in the same column as the total revenue, you have indicated the concept of matching all revenues against all expenses for the same accounting period.

Net Income or Net Loss Section The last section of the income statement is the one for income or net loss — the final result of operating a business for an accounting period. First draw a single line across the money column under the amount of the total expenses. Next, subtract the total expenses from the total revenue and record the difference in the second money column on the next line. (In the example illustrated for J. Emery Real Estate, the result is a net income; if the total expenses were greater than the total revenue for the accounting period, you would show the final result under *Net Loss.*) Finally, draw a double line across the second money column to show that the matchup of revenue and related expenses, and thus the statement, is completed.

Reporting a Net Loss

Total Revenue	*$18 000*	*00*
Total Expenses	*20 000*	*00*
Net Loss	*$ 2 000*	*00*

Dollar Signs Since an income statement is a *formal* financial report, dollar signs should appear opposite the first amount in each money column and the final result in the second money column. Refer to the income statements illustrated so far in this chapter for the correct placement of dollar signs.

Income statement: a financial report of the results of matching revenues with related expenses for a definite accounting period.

At this point, you should have no difficulty in defining the term income statement. One good definition is: a financial report of revenues, expenses, and the net income or net loss for a definite accounting period. Another is: a financial report of the matchup of revenues and expenses for a stated accounting period. Remember that any definition must include the idea of a definite accounting period that *has ended.*

Preparing a Related Balance Sheet

In the income statement for J. Emery Real Estate, the net income reported ($8 165) agrees with the amount shown in the accounting equation. It is important to remember, however, that this income is the amount remaining after revenues and related expenses have been matched for an accounting period. If revenue means an inflow of assets (cash and/or accounts receivable) through sales, and if expenses mean an outflow of assets (cash) or an increase in liabilities (incurring an expense through a liability), then certain balance sheet items must have been changed during the accounting period. To report the new balances in assets, liabilities, and owner's equity as at the end of the accounting period, a new balance sheet must be prepared immediately after the income statement.

Analysis: Look at the illustration on page 42 and study the following points.

- The heading of the new balance sheet reports a different date from that of the opening balance sheet. Here, the sheet reports the assets and the claims against those assets as at October 31. In other words, the new balances for assets, liabilities, and owner's equity are reported as at October 31.
- Only one new point has to be learned on the assets side of the balance sheet. Accounts Receivable (an asset) is reported immediately after Cash, because the business expects to collect amounts due from customers within 30 days. The customers' names and the amounts of their debts are listed in a separate column. The total is then placed in the main column.
- The liabilities report amounts owing to creditors as at October 31. These amounts will differ from those reported in the opening balance sheet of September 30 because changes were made during October. The firm now owes the bank only $16 000, not $20 000. Under *Accounts Payable,* the firm no longer owes any money to Westown Motors Ltd.; therefore, no debt is reported. However, because of Transaction 11, a new creditor, *The City Record,* is listed. Also, a new balance is reported for Ryan Equipment Co., because $3 000 is the amount owing as at October 31. No change is reported for Bell Furniture Co., because no transaction involving this creditor took place in October.
- From the owner's standpoint, the most important changes are reported in the owner's equity section of the new balance sheet. To understand the changes, remember the meaning of owner's equity: *the claim of the owner against the total assets of the business.* In the opening balance sheet, the owner had only one claim: $50 000 through an investment (capital). One month later, however, the owner's equity section reports two claims: the investment of $53 000 ($50 000 plus an additional

Assets					=	Liabilities		+	Owner's Equity		
Cash	Accts. Rec.	Auto	Furn.	Office Equip.		Bk. Loan Pay.	Accts. Pay.		J. Emery, Capital	Net Income	J. Emery, Drawing
$52 565 +	$7 200 +	$15 000 +	$4 000 +	$3 000	=	$16 000 +	$6 600	+	$53 000 +	$8 165 –	$2 000
$81 765					=	$22 600		+	$59 165		

J. Emery Real Estate
Balance Sheet
as at October 31, 19—

ASSETS

Cash		$52 565.00
Accounts Receivable:		
Pat Rogers	$2 000.00	
R. Scobie	1 200.00	
Shannon Development Co.	4 000.00	7 200.00
Automobile		15 000.00
Furniture		4 000.00
Office Equipment		3 000.00
Total Assets		$81 765.00

LIABILITIES

Bank Loan Payable		$16 000.00
Accounts Payable:		
Bell Furniture Co.	$3 000.00	
The City Record	600.00	
Ryan Equipment Co.	3 000.00	6 600.00
Total Liabilities		$22 600.00

OWNER'S EQUITY

J. Emery, Capital	$53 000.00	
Add: Net Income	8 165.00	
	61 165.00	
Deduct: Drawing	2 000.00	
Total Owner's Equity		59 165.00
Total Liabilities and Owner's Equity		$81 765.00

investment) and the net income of $8 165 earned through business operations.

- Note the net income being added to the capital part of the owner's equity to report those two claims against the total assets of the business. The final equation has now been rearranged to show this.

Owner's Equity				
J. Emery, Capital		Net Income		J. Emery, Drawing
$53 000	+	$8 165	−	$2 000
		$59 165		

- The last part of the owner's equity section shows under *Drawing* the deduction for withdrawals. (As you will recall, the owner has the right to withdraw assets for personal use.) Here, the owner's withdrawal of $2 000 assets decreases Owner's Equity to $59 165. Notice that the total of Owner's Equity agrees with the result you get when you solve the accounting equation for *OE*. You should always make this calculation when you do problems on the balance sheet. See the illustration in the margin.

A = $81 765, *L* = $22 600, *OE* = ?

A	=	L	+	OE
OE	=	A	−	L
OE	=	$81 765	−	$22 600
OE	=	$59 165		

- Observe that the deduction for Drawing comes *after* net income is added to capital. This order is also shown in the rearranged accounting equation. To understand why, remember that a person who invests money hopes to make profits (nowadays called net income). A sole owner does not expect to be paid a salary for working in his or her business. The owner's main goal is to increase his or her equity, which results from the business's earning net incomes. Of course, before those net incomes can be accounted for, the owner will have to withdraw cash in order to live. In accounting, these drawings are considered to be payments out of profits not yet accounted for — payments made in advance out of net income. That is why it is very important to report withdrawals only *after* Net Income has been added to Capital in the owner's equity section.

Drawings: payments made in advance out of profits (net income). See also "Drawing" earlier.

Since the owner's withdrawals represent payments made in advance out of net income, owner's withdrawals are *not* business expenses. No transaction involving the withdrawal of assets for the owner's personal use should ever be reported in the income statement. Remember the accounting definition of expenses: costs of goods and services used up by the business *to earn revenue*. When an owner withdraws assets for *personal* use, the asset is used up but no revenue is earned from that withdrawal.

For the above reasons, always report Drawings in the balance sheet after Net Income is added to Capital.

- The illustration of the components of owner's equity above showed Net Income being added to Capital. Suppose, however, there was a net loss during the accounting period. This would be reported on the balance sheet as a *deduction* from Capital. Again, show any drawings after reporting the net loss. See the illustration in the margin.

Total Liabilities		$22 600
OWNER'S EQUITY		
J. Emery, Capital	$53 000	
Less: Net Loss	3 000	
	50 000	
Less: Drawing	2 000	
Total Owner's Equity		48 000
Total L + OE		$70 600

TOPIC 3 PROBLEMS

2-7 Vivian Rabethge operates the Circle Theatre, which derives revenue from admissions and parking fees, and from operating concessions. Between January 1 and December 31 of this year, the Circle Theatre reported revenues and expenses as shown below. Prepare an income statement for the accounting period.

Key Check Figure Net Income = $29 865

Admissions Revenue......	$116 320	Concessions Revenue............	$33 500
Salaries Expense	88 635	Building Rental Expense	12 000
Insurance Expense..........	300	Film Rental Expense...............	30 220
Parking Fees Earned........	12 300	Projection Rental Expense......	600
Advertising Expense.......	240	Utilities Expense	130
Telephone Expense........	96	Miscellaneous Expense..........	34

2-8 Refer to the solutions for Problem 2-6, Topic 2 of this chapter.

a Prepare an income statement for J. Guest, D.D.S., for the accounting period given in Problem 2-6.

Key Check Figure Net Loss = $113

b Prepare a related balance sheet reporting the assets and claims against assets as at the end of the accounting period.

2-9 Challenge Problem R. Philip organized Philip's Moving and Storage Co. on August 1 this year. The firm earns revenue by performing long-distance moves of household furniture, appliances, and other household items, and by leasing storage space. The business recorded the following business transactions during August.

Aug. 1 Investment of $250 000 cash by Philip, deposited into a bank account in the name of Philip's Moving and Storage Co.

3 Purchase of land and a building for a total cost of $120 000, of which one-third was applicable to the land, and two-thirds to the building. A cheque was issued for the full amount.

5 Purchase of four trucks from Hamilton Motors at a cost of $50 000 each. A cash down payment of $75 000 was made, the balance to be paid in 60 days.

6 Purchase of office equipment for $6 800 cash.

6 Moving of furniture for Mr. A. Stockwell from Hamilton to Halifax for $4 000. Collected $1 000 in cash, the balance to be paid within 30 days.

11 Moving of household items for various clients for $10 800. Collected cash for the entire amount.

12 Issuing of a cheque for $40 in payment of a telephone bill received today.

14 Receipt of cash totalling $3 500 from clients who stored household goods during the past two weeks.

15 Payment of $10 000 in salaries for first half of the month.

15 Issuing of a cheque for $50 000 to Hamilton Motors in part payment of the debt.

Aug. 19 Moving of furniture for various clients for $18 500. Collected $15 400 in cash; the balance to be paid by R. Wilkinson within 30 days.
22 Payment of utilities bill, $70 in cash.
24 Moving of furniture for various clients for a total of $4 680. Cash collected in full.
29 Issuing of bills for storage fees earned to date to the following customers: R. Browne, $200; G. Martin, $300; and E. Powell, $350. All customers were given 30 days to pay.
30 Receipt of a cheque for $3 000 from A. Stockwell in full payment of this customer's amount owing to the business.
31 Loan of $20 000 cash from the Royal Bank of Canada on a demand note. The cash was deposited into the firm's chequing account.
31 Payment of $10 000 in salaries for the second half of the month.
31 Receipt of bill for $300 for repair work on trucks during August by Hamilton Motors. Terms given were 30 days.
31 Receipt of a gasoline bill totalling $8 900 for the month of August from Esso Oil Company. The bill allowed payment to be made within 15 days of the date printed on it.
31 Receipt of a bill from Central Advertisers Ltd. for advertising the firm's services during August. The bill totalled $2 400 and allowed 30 days' credit.
31 Issuing of a cheque for $1 200 to City Insurance Co. in payment of the August premium for insurance of the trucks, the building, and their contents.
31 Withdrawal of $2 000 cash by R. Philip, for personal use.
31 Payment of $125 cash to Office Specialty Co. for the cost of office supplies used up during August.

a Set up a summary table on two pages as follows. On a left-hand page, make columns for (1) Transaction Date, (2) Cash, (3) Accts. Rec., (4) Land, (5) Building, (6) Trucks, (7) Office Equipment, (8) Total Assets. On a right-hand page, make columns for (9) Bank Loan Payable, (10) Accts. Pay., (11) Total Liabilities, (12) R. Philip, Capital, (13) Revenues, (14) Expenses, (15) R. Philip, Drawing, (16) Total Owner's Equity.

b Analyze each business transaction by recording the effects on the elements of the accounting equation in the appropriate columns of the table.

c After recording the final transaction, total the table. Then do an equality check on the main elements of the accounting equation.

d Prepare an income statement for the first month's operations. *Hint:* there are two sources of revenue and eight expenses to report in the statement.

e Prepare a balance sheet reporting details of individual assets, liabilities, and the owner's equity as at August 31.

Key Check Figure
Net Income = $9 295

Case Study 2

A student in a beginning accounting class turned in, for marking, the financial statements illustrated here.

Income Statement
Debbie Couse, M.D.
as at May 31, 19--

Income:		
Professional Fees Earned		$ 11 060 00
Expenses:		
Salaries Expense	$ 7 500 00	
Rent Expense	800 00	
Utilities Expense	150 00	
Telephone Expense	50 00	
Insurance Expense	120 00	
D. Couse, Drawing	1 000 00	
Medical Supplies on Hand	3 000 00	
Total Expenses		12 620 00
Net Loss		$ 1 560 00

Balance Sheet
Debbie Couse, M.D.
For the Month Ending May 31, 19--

Assets		Liabilites	
Cash	$ 6 500 00	Bank Loan Payable	$ 4 000 00
Accounts Recievable:		Accounts Payable:	
P. Abban $600.00		A + B Co. Ltd.	3 000 00
C. Blake 500.00		Total Liabiltes	$ 7 000 00
S. Cary 300.00	1 400 00		
Medical Supplies Used	650 00	Owners Equity	
Medical Instruments	12 000 00	D. Couse, Capital $19 610.00	
Office Equipment	4 500 00	Less: Net Loss 1560.00	
		Total Owners Equity	18 050 00
		Total Liabiltes and	
Total Assets	$ 25 050 00	Owners Equity	$ 25 050 00

a List and explain your criticisms of the income statement. *Hint:* There are eight things wrong with it.

b List and explain your criticisms of the balance sheet. *Hint:* There are nine things wrong with it.

c Prepare a corrected income statement in good form.

d Prepare a corrected balance sheet in good form.

CHAPTER 3

USING ACCOUNTS

In Chapters 1 and 2 you were shown how to analyze business transactions affecting the key elements of the accounting equation. For example, you will recall that when a customer paid cash to repay a debt to the business, the asset Cash was increased and the asset Accounts Receivable was decreased — both on the left side of the equation. On the other hand, when the business paid cash to eliminate the claim of a creditor, the asset Cash was decreased on the left side and the liability Accounts Payable was decreased on the right side.

Now suppose that during a normal business day the asset Cash was involved in 300 transactions. To find out the balance of Cash at the end of the day: (1) Would you record the increases and decreases to Cash directly on one equation as in the illustration? (2) Would you prepare 300 separate accounting equations? (3) Or would you prepare a new balance sheet after each change in Cash?

A					=	L	+	OE
Cash	+	Accounts Receivable	+	Office Equipment	=	Accounts Payable	+	Owner's Capital
~~$8 000~~		~~$500~~		~~$3 500~~		~~$2 000~~		~~$10 000~~
~~$8 500~~		Ø		$4 500		~~$1 200~~		$14 000
~~$7 500~~						$ 500		
~~$6 700~~								
~~$6 000~~								
$10 000								

Recording changes directly on the accounting equation is inefficient.

Obviously, these are inefficient ways to record the daily changes to an asset like Cash. (Choice 3 would involve 300 separate balance sheets!) A new device is needed to record changes to the items within the accounting equation — the account.

Account: a device for recording the effects of transactions under one title.

- Topic 1 will examine the nature of the account and how a set of accounts are established for any business.
- Topic 2 will show you how to record changes to asset and liability accounts.
- Topic 3 will show you how to record changes to owner's equity accounts.

TOPIC 1 ESTABLISHING ACCOUNTS

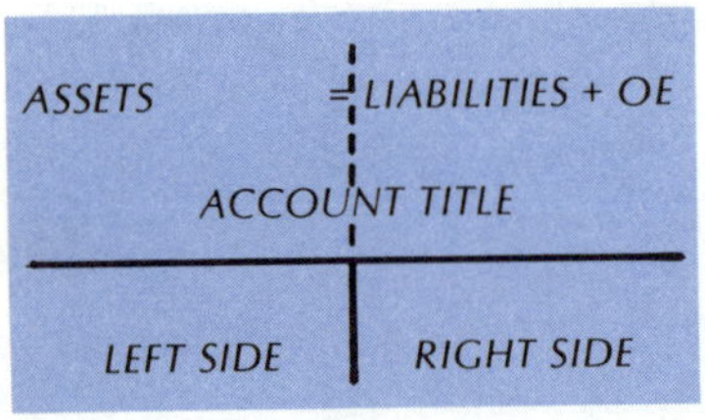

Several different forms of accounts are in actual use; only a very simple one is presented here — other forms will be introduced in later chapters. This simple account resembles the accounting equation. Just as the equation has two sides, so this device has two sides also, as shown in the first margin illustration here.

The various account forms illustrated, which are in the shape of a large T, may be called *T-accounts.* The space above the horizontal line is used to identify the item in the accounting equation for which the account is being made. A separate account can be identified for each asset and liability, and for each part of owner's equity.

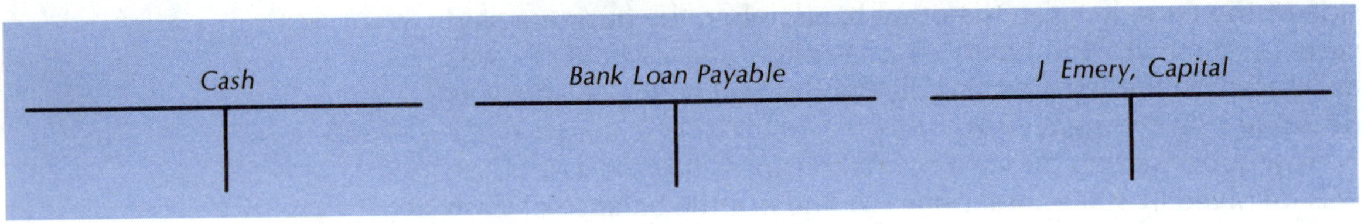

Debits and Credits

Debit: the left side of an account.

Credit: the right side of an account.

In the language of accounting, the left side of every account is known as the debit (DR.) side and the right side is known as the credit (CR.) side. When you see a reference to the debit side of an account, you should always think only of the left side of that account; when you see a reference to the credit side, think only of the right side of that account. Do not attach any further meaning to debit and credit. *The term* debit *refers to the left side, and the term* credit *to the right side, of an account.*

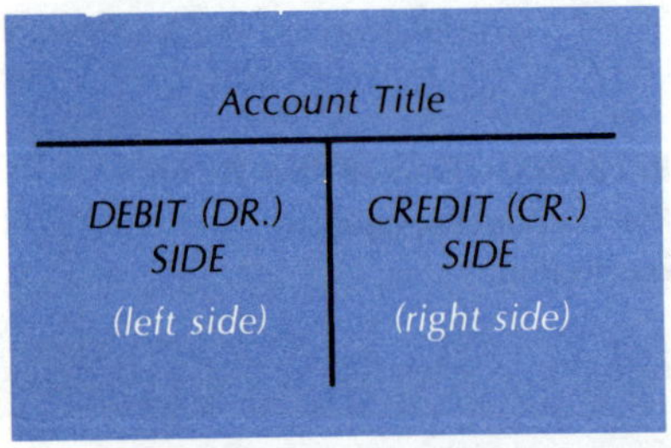

Starting Position for All Accounts

Look at the first accounting equation for J. Emery Real Estate, illustrated below. Do you see any relationship between the position of each element in the accounting equation and the position of the beginning dollar amount in each T-account?

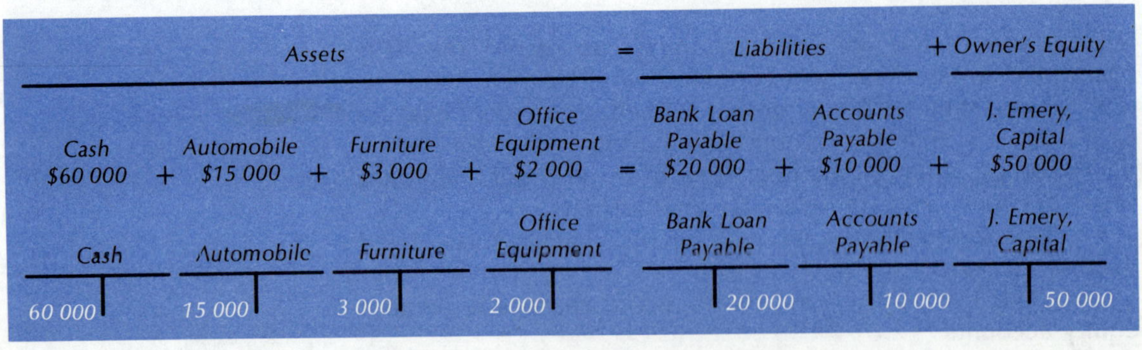

The illustration shows all the first entries on the same side of the account as the side of the beginning accounting equation the account appears on. These entries are called *opening balances.* Because assets are located on the left side of the accounting equation, all asset accounts will show their beginning balances on the left side — that is, on the debit side.

Positions of Opening Balances

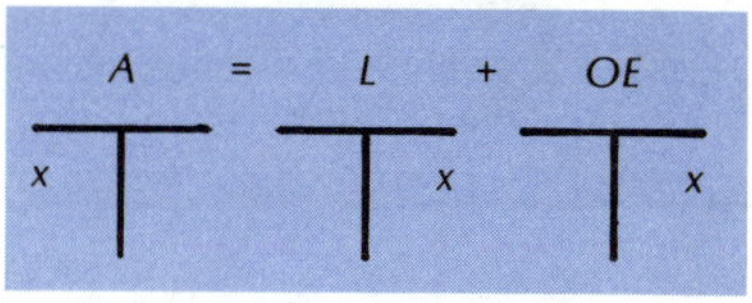

Where would you locate the opening balance amounts for the liabilities and the owner's equity element Capital? On the credit side, of course, because liabilities and owner's equity were placed on the right (credit) side of the accounting equation. You should now have little difficulty in understanding this important rule:

Rule for Opening Accounts

Accounts are set up by placing their beginning amounts, called opening balances, on the side of the account on which the accounts appear in the first accounting equation.

Opening Accounts for a Business

To illustrate how accounts are actually established for a business, consider the example of J. Emery Real Estate in Chapter 1. Jane Emery began her business on September 30 by buying and investing assets. Against these assets, two claims were made: (1) the claim of creditors, called liabilities, and (2) the claim of the owner, called owner's equity. Thus, an accounting equation was formed for Jane Emery's new business.

After the beginning accounting equation was formed, a beginning balance sheet was prepared so that the elements of the equation could be summarized in a more detailed financial report. Since this opening balance sheet contains the details of the beginning accounting equation as well, it is possible to use the information of the balance sheet to open a set of accounts for the business. Study how the opening balance sheet relates to the T-accounts in the illustration on page 50.

From the illustration, you can easily see the similarities. There are, however, important differences.

- Each asset account has the date of the opening balance sheet on the debit (left) side of the account. The opening balance for each asset account must be placed on the left (debit) side.
- For all liabilities and the owner's equity, the date of the opening balance sheet is identified on the side where *L* and *OE* appear in the accounting equation. The opening balance for each account on the right side of the balance sheet must be placed on the credit (right) side.
- A separate account is opened for each creditor so that the amount owed to each can be quickly calculated. The abbreviation *Accts. Pay.* is placed before the creditor's name to identify it

J. Emery Real Estate
Balance Sheet
as at September 30, 19—

ASSETS		LIABILITIES		
Cash	$60 000.00	Bank Loan Payable		$20 000.00
Automobile	15 000.00	Accounts Payable:		
Furniture	3 000.00	Bell Furniture Co.	$3 000.00	
Office Equipment	2 000.00	Ryan Equipment Co.	2 000.00	
		Westown Motors Ltd.	5 000.00	10 000.00
		Total Liabilities		$30 000.00
		OWNER'S EQUITY		
		J. Emery, Capital		50 000.00
Total Assets	$80 000.00	Total Liabilities and Owner's Equity		$80 000.00

Cash

19—
Sept. 30 60 000 |

Automobile

19—
Sept. 30 15 000 |

Furniture

19—
Sept. 30 3 000 |

Office Equipment

19—
Sept. 30 2 000 |

Bank Loan Payable

| 19—
| Sept. 30 20 000

Accts. Pay./Bell Furniture Co.

| 19—
| Sept. 30 3 000

Accts. Pay./Ryan Equipment Co.

| 19—
| Sept. 30 2 000

Accts. Pay./Westown Motors Ltd.

| 19—
| Sept. 30 5 000

J. Emery, Capital

| 19—
| Sept. 30 50 000

ASSETS $80 000 = LIABILITIES $30 000 + OWNER'S EQUITY $50 000

as an account payable. (When the business has customer accounts, the short form *Accts. Rec.* is placed before the customer's name to identify it as an account receivable.)

- Dollar signs are not required when recording dollar amounts in T-accounts, because T-accounts are not formal financial reports like the income statement and the balance sheet.
- There is no *account* called "Owner's Equity." Since this term means *all* the claims of the owner against the total assets of the business, a T-account must be opened for each claim of the owner. The first is through his or her investment, and an investment account called *Capital* is opened to show this.

The Ledger

When accounts have been opened for all assets and liabilities, and the owner's equity, the entire group of accounts forms the ledger. Strictly speaking, a ledger is a file containing all the accounts of a particular type or nature; in actual practice, there are many different types and forms of ledgers. Some of these will be examined in future chapters. At this point, think of "the ledger" as simply the group of T-accounts.

Ledger: a file or group of accounts.

Note that the ledger for J. Emery Real Estate contains all of the accounts for the beginning accounting equation. Since these accounts were established with opening balances that related to their placement within the equation, the effect is that the accounting equation has been transferred from the opening balance sheet to the ledger in total form.

To prove this point, check the T-account ledger illustrated on page 50. The debit or left-side balances represent the assets in the equation, while the total credit or right-side balances represent the total liabilities plus owner's equity. The equation in the ledger will always show that the total debits are equal to the total credits, as shown below.

J. Emery Real Estate
Summary of Ledger Account Balances
as at September 30, 19—

TOTAL DEBIT (LEFT) BALANCES			TOTAL CREDIT (RIGHT) BALANCES	
Cash	*$60 000.00*		*Bank Loan Payable*	*$20 000.00*
Automobile	*15 000.00*		*Accts. Pay./Bell Furniture Co.*	*3 000.00*
Furniture	*3 000.00*		*Accts. Pay./Ryan Equipment Co.*	*2 000.00*
Office Equipment	*2 000.00*		*Accts. Pay./Westown Motors Ltd.*	*5 000.00*
			J. Emery, Capital	*50 000.00*
Total Debits	*$80 000.00*		*Total Credits*	*$80 000.00*
Total Assets	*$80 000.00*	=	*Total Liabilities + Owner's Equity*	*$80 000.00*

TOPIC 1 PROBLEMS

3-1 Refer to the opening balance sheet solved for Problem 1-4b (Manitoba Car Rental Company).

a Open a T-account ledger including every asset and liability, and the owner's equity. For each account enter the opening balance and the date.

b Prepare a summary of ledger account balances similar to that illustrated on page 51. What do the totals prove?

3-2 Refer to the opening balance sheet solved for Problem 2-3 (Radio Station CHJK).

a Open a T-account ledger including every asset and liability, and the owner's equity. For each account enter the opening balance and the date.

b Prepare a summary of ledger account balances similar to that illustrated on page 51. What do the totals prove?

Key Check Figure Total Credits = $72 625

3-3 Paul Young purchased a car wash, paying the original owner $38 700 cash. Taking over the assets and liabilities of the old firm, he prepared the opening balance sheet under his own name as shown below.

Paul's Auto Wash
Balance Sheet
August 1, 19—

ASSETS			LIABILITIES	
Cash		$ 4 600	Bank Loan	$36 000
Accounts Receivable:			Accounts Payable:	
Frank Higgins	$100		Bates Equipment Co.	4 000
John Mills	200	300	Total Liabilities	$40 000
Supplies		2 800		
Land		25 000	**OWNER'S EQUITY**	
Building		20 000	Paul Young, Capital	38 700
Equipment		26 000		
Total		$78 700	Total	$78 700

a Open a T-account ledger including every asset and liability, and the owner's equity.

b Prepare a summary of ledger account balances similar to that illustrated on page 51. What do the totals prove?

Key Check Figure Total Debits = $78 700

3-4 The following financial events took place by July 14 to establish the Oakridge Animal Clinic, owned by Dr. W.M. Branan.

(i) Dr. Branan invested $25 000 cash, placing it into the bank account of Oakridge Animal Clinic.

(ii) He purchased equipment costing $18 000 from City Equipment Ltd. on 60 days' credit.

(iii) He purchased more equipment costing $2 000, issuing a cheque to Lambeth Equipment Co.

(iv) He returned equipment originally purchased on credit for $750 from City Equipment Co.

(v) He borrowed $10 000 cash from his banker, signing a demand note. The money was deposited into the firm's chequing account.

(vi) For $14 000 he purchased a station wagon for the business from Eastown Motors. The terms of the purchase were: 10% in cash; the balance on 30 days' credit. A cheque was issued for the correct amount.

a Analyze and record the effects of each transaction on the accounting equation for the Oakridge Animal Clinic by using a summary table with the following columns: Transaction No.; Cash; Equipment; Station Wagon; Total Assets; Bank Loan Payable; Accts. Pay./City Equipment Ltd.; Accts. Pay./Eastown Motors; Total Liabilities; W.M. Branan, Capital.

b Total all items in the Table. Then, do an Equality Check.

c Prepare the opening balance sheet for the Oakridge Animal Clinic as at July 14, current year.

d Open a T-account ledger for each asset, liability, and owner's equity element listed on the opening balance sheet.

e Prepare a summary of ledger account balances similar to that illustrated on page 51. What do the totals prove?

Key Check Figure
Total Credits
= $64 850

TOPIC 2 T-ACCOUNT RECORD OF ASSET AND LIABILITY CHANGES

In this section, you will learn how to use debits and credits to record changes in asset and liability accounts. (The rules for using debits and credits to record changes in the owner's equity section of the equation will be studied in Topic 3.)

It is very important to learn not only how the increases and decreases are recorded in asset and liability accounts, but also *why* each is recorded on a particular side of an account. Here is the rule for recording increases to any account:

Rule for Increasing All Accounts

An increase in an account is recorded on the side on which the account is placed in the accounting equation.

Let's apply this rule to the recording of increases in *asset* accounts.

Rule for Recording Increases in Asset Accounts

An increase in an asset account is recorded on the debit side, because assets appear on the left side of the beginning accounting equation.

This rule explains why increases in asset accounts are recorded on one side of the account only. Since asset accounts are located on the left side of the equation, an increase to any asset account must be recorded on the same side, that is, on the debit side. For example, suppose a transaction causes an increase of $5 000 to the cash account. To record this increase, you would simply show the $5 000 on the left or debit side of the cash account as shown in the margin.

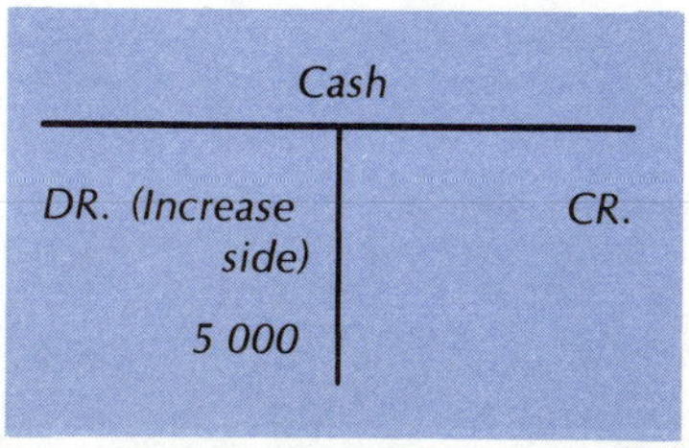

Accountants sometimes use short expressions such as "Debit Cash for $5 000." All this means is to record the $5 000 on the left side of the cash account. And instead of saying "recording Cash with an amount on the left side," accountants simply say "debiting Cash." Thus, the *noun* "debit" means the left side of an account, and the *verb* "debit" means to *record* an amount on the left side of the account.

Debiting: recording an amount on the left side

Let's now apply the rule for recording increases to *liability* accounts.

Rule for Recording Increases in Liability Accounts

An increase in a liability account is recorded on the credit side, because liabilities appear on the right side of the beginning accounting equation.

The above rule is easy to understand because it is logical. Since liabilities are located on the right side of the accounting equation, all liabilities must be increased on that side, that is, on the credit side. For example, to record an increase of $100 to Accounts Payable, you would credit this account as shown in the left-hand illustration below.

Crediting: recording an amount on the right side

In recording the credit, one is of course crediting the account.

If accounts are increased on the side on which they appear in the accounting equation, the following rule makes sense.

Rule for Decreasing All Accounts

A decrease in an account is recorded on the side opposite to that on which the account is placed in the accounting equation.

Let's apply this to the recording of decreases in *asset* accounts.

Rule for Recording Decreases in Asset Accounts

A decrease in an asset account is recorded on the side opposite to that on which the element *A* is placed in the beginning accounting equation — in other words, the credit side.

The above explains why decreases are only recorded on *one* side of asset accounts. Decreases must be recorded on the credit side because that is the side opposite to the one on which the account appears in the accounting equation. For example, to decrease the Cash account by $400, you would credit it as shown in the right-hand illustration below.

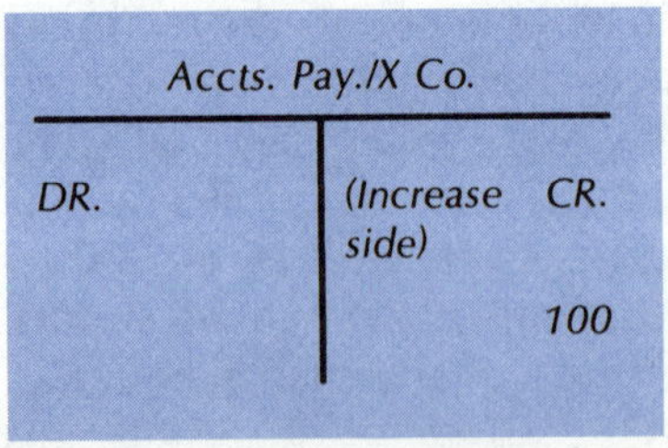

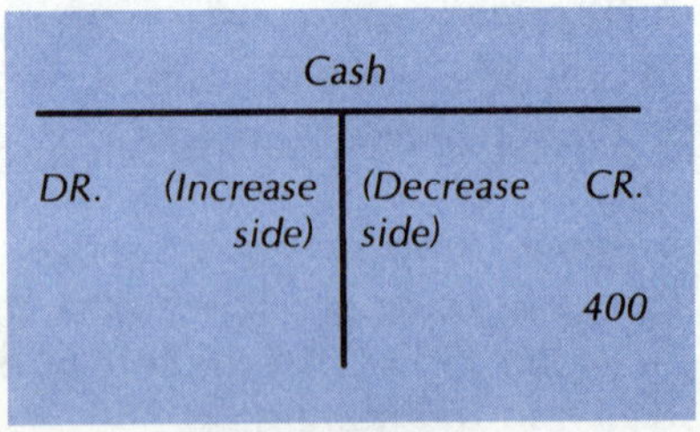

The rule for recording decreases can now be applied to all *liability* accounts as follows.

Rule for Recording Decreases to Liability Accounts

A decrease in a liability account is recorded on the side opposite to that on which the element *L* is placed in the beginning accounting equation — in other words, the debit side.

For example, to record a decrease of $25 to Accts. Pay./X Co., debit the account as shown in the margin. Why? The rule says that all decreases must be recorded on the side opposite to the one on which the account is found in the accounting equation. Since liabilities are found on the right side, the opposite is the left — debit — side.

Accts. Pay./X Co.

DR. (Decrease side)	(Increase side) CR.
25	

Here's a good question. On what side would you show the balance in any account after recording increases and decreases? The following rule makes accounting sense.

Rule for Showing a Normal Balance in an Account

The balance of an account will normally appear on the side on which the account appears in the accounting equation.

This final rule is an important one. It explains how you would place the difference between the total debits and the total credits recorded in any account. Suppose the Cash and the Accounts Payable accounts contained entries as illustrated below.

Cash

DR.	CR.
5 000	400
2 000	1 600

$5 000 debit balance

Accts. Pay./X Co.

DR.	CR.
25	400

$375 credit balance

Account balance: the difference between the total debits and the total credits.

The Cash account shows a record of two debits and two credits. The difference between the sums on both sides is $5 000 and is called the account balance. Since the Cash account, an asset, appears on the left side of the equation, it normally has a *debit* balance ("DR. balance" for short). In other words, total debits are usually greater than total credits in accounts on the left side of the equation.

In the case of a liability account, total credits are normally greater than total debits. A liability account, therefore, is expected to have a *credit* balance ("CR. balance"). This follows from the general rule because all liabilities are found on the right or credit side of the equation.

Accts. Pay./Y Co.	
DR.	CR.
500	500
Ø	

Suppose the debit side and the credit side of an account are equal. How would you identify the balance? Of course, there would be a zero balance. One way to show an account with such a balance is to write a large zero with a slash as illustrated in the margin.

Here's a useful summary of the basic rules for recording increases and decreases to asset and liability accounts:

A		=	L + OE	
Asset Accounts			Liability Accounts	
DR. (Left)	(Right) CR.		DR. (Left)	(Right) CR.
Record increases here.	Record decreases here.		Record decreases here.	Record increases here.

- *All* accounts are *increased* on the *same* side as that on which the account is found in the beginning accounting equation.
- *All* accounts are *decreased* on the *opposite* side from that on which the account is found in the beginning accounting equation.
- *Asset* accounts (which appear on the left side of the accounting equation) are *increased on the debit side* and *decreased on the credit side.*
- *Liability* accounts (which appear on the right side of the accounting equation) are *increased on the credit side* and *decreased on the debit side.*
- The balance of *any* account will normally be placed on the *same* side as that on which the account is found in the accounting equation.
- The balance of an *asset* account will normally be on the *debit* side.
- The balance of any *liability* account will normally be on the *credit* side.

Illustrating Asset and Liability Changes in T-Accounts

In the October transactions for J. Emery Real Estate, the opening balances were recorded from the beginning balance sheet of September 30.

October 1 J. Emery Real Estate buys more furniture for $1 000 from Enns Furniture Ltd., and pays by cheque.

ANALYSIS CHART

WHAT HAPPENS	ACCOUNTING RULE	ACCOUNTING ENTRY
The asset Furniture increases by $1 000.	*To increase an asset, debit the account.* Reason: *Assets increase on the side on which they appear in the accounting equation — the debit side.*	*Debit: Furniture $1 000*
The asset Cash decreases by $1 000.	*To decrease an asset, credit the account.* Reason: *Assets decrease on the side opposite to that on which they appear in the accounting equation — the credit side.*	*Credit: Cash $1 000*

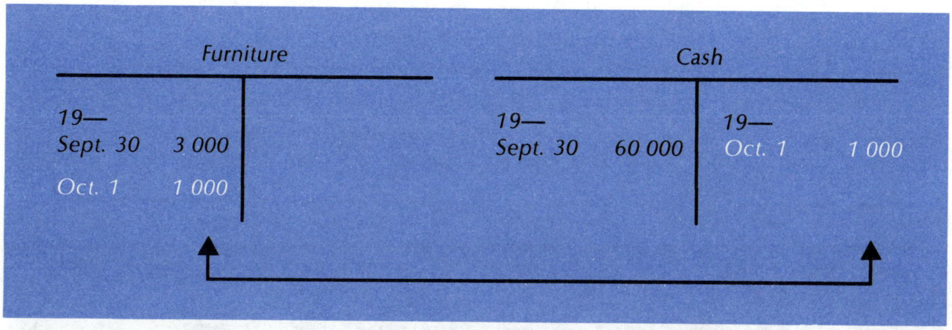

Analysis: In recording this first transaction, notice that only two asset accounts are affected. (1) Since the Furniture account must be increased, the amount must be recorded on the debit side. This follows the rule that increases in an account always occur on the side on which the account appears in the accounting equation. (2) Since the business has given a cheque in payment, the asset Cash must be decreased. In accordance with the rule for decreasing an account, the amount of the cheque must be recorded on the credit side of the Cash account.

Here is another important point. The transaction results in an increase to one asset account and a decrease to another, by the same dollar amount. In fact, this is the same transaction you studied in Topic 1 of Chapter 2. But in this chapter, the analysis has to be done in terms of debits and credits. Thus, you say that one asset account has been debited and another credited for the same amount. In other words, the debit half of the entry is the same as the credit half. This idea is brought out in the two T-accounts above by the arrows. When you analyze a recorded transaction, always check that the idea of *equal debits and credits* has been followed.

October 3 J. Emery Real Estate buys more office equipment for $1 200 from the Ryan Equipment Co. on 60 days' credit.

ANALYSIS CHART

WHAT HAPPENS	ACCOUNTING RULE	ACCOUNTING ENTRY
The asset Office Equipment increases by $1 200.	*To increase an asset, debit the account. Reason: Assets increase on the side on which they appear in the accounting equation — the debit side.*	*Debit: Office Equipment $1 200*
The liability Accts. Pay./Ryan Equipment Co. increases by $1 200.	*To increase a liability, credit the account. Reason: Liabilities increase on the side on which they appear in the accounting equation — the credit side.*	*Credit: Accts. Pay./ Ryan Equipment Co. $1 200*

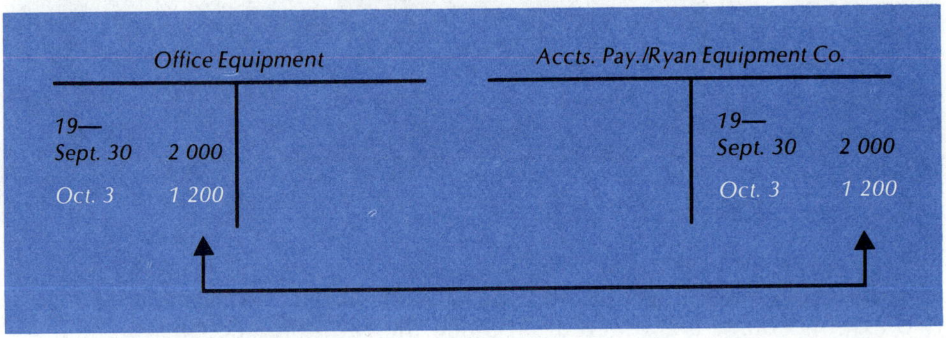

Analysis: Two different classes of accounts are affected by this second transaction: both the asset Office Equipment and the liability Accts. Pay./Ryan Equipment Co. are increased. The Office Equipment account is debited for $1 200 and the Accts. Pay./Ryan Equipment Co. account is credited for the same amount. Again the debit dollar amount is equal to the credit dollar amount.

October 4 J. Emery Real Estate returns one piece of office equipment costing $200 to Ryan Equipment Co. because it arrived damaged. The creditor has accepted the return.

Analysis: The two accounts affected by this transaction decrease by the same amount. Since a piece of office equipment has been returned, the asset Office Equipment must be decreased by the amount of the return. And since J. Emery Real Estate no longer owes the $200 to Ryan Equipment, the liability

ANALYSIS CHART

WHAT HAPPENS	ACCOUNTING RULE	ACCOUNTING ENTRY
The liability Accts. Pay./Ryan Equipment Co. decreases by $200.	*To decrease a liability, debit the account. Reason: Liabilities decrease on the side opposite to that on which they appear in the accounting equation.*	*Debit: Accts. Pay./ Ryan Equipment Co. $200*
The asset Office Equipment decreases by $200.	*To decrease an asset, credit the account. Reason: Assets decrease on the side opposite to that on which they appear in the accounting equation.*	*Credit: Office Equipment $200*

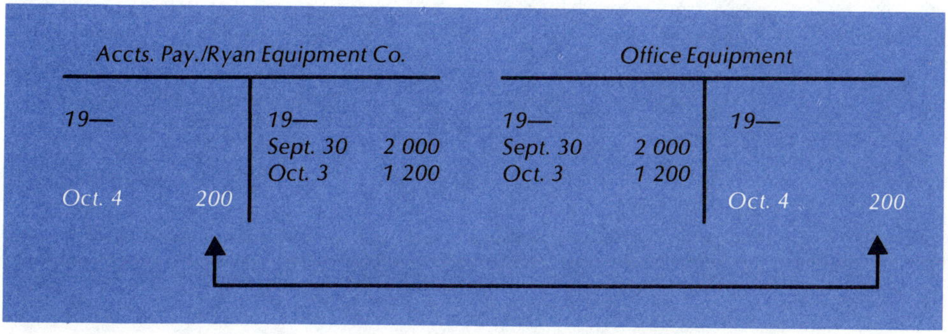

Accts. Pay./Ryan Equipment Co. decreases by $200, as the analysis chart shows. The rule says that, to record a decrease to any liability account, the amount must be recorded on the side opposite to that on which the element *L* appears in the accounting equation. Office Equipment is credited because all assets decrease only on the side opposite to that on which the element *A* appears in the accounting equation.

Note that for the third time in a row, a business transaction has resulted in an accounting entry that debits one account and credits another the same dollar amount. In fact, you can take it as a rule that *equal debits and credits* must be recorded for every business transaction. This is the double-entry system.

Double-entry system: the system of recording transactions now in general use in modern accounting practice: for every transaction, the debit entry must equal the credit entry.

October 5 J. Emery Real Estate makes out a cheque for $5 000 to Westown Motors Ltd.

Analysis: Notice the use of the double-entry system in the record of this transaction. The total of the debit entry is equal to the total of the credit entry — $5 000. Notice also the large zero with the slash, centred at the bottom after recording the debit to Accts. Pay./Westown Motors Ltd. It is customary to show this

ANALYSIS CHART

WHAT HAPPENS	ACCOUNTING RULE	ACCOUNTING ENTRY
The liability Accts. Pay./ Westown Motors Ltd. decreases by $5 000.	*To decrease a liability, debit the account.* Reason: *Liabilities decrease on the side opposite to that on which they appear in the accounting equation.*	*Debit: Accts. Pay./ Westown Motors Ltd. $5 000*
The asset Cash decreases by $5 000.	*To decrease an asset, credit the account.* Reason: *Assets decrease on the side opposite to that on which they appear in the accounting equation.*	*Credit: Cash $5 000*

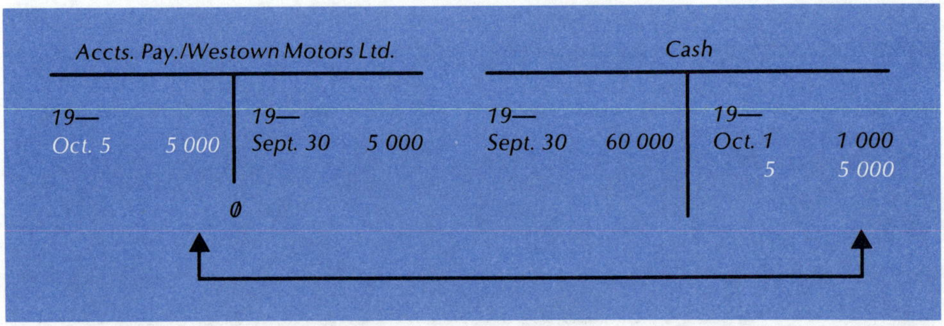

large "no balance" sign in the account when the recording of an entry results in a zero balance.

October 15 J. Emery Real Estate makes out a cheque for $4 000 to the Royal Bank of Canada in part payment of the bank loan.

Analysis: You should now be able to interpret on your own the double-entry system of recording transactions in T-accounts.

Here are three guidelines that will help you analyze business transactions in the problems that follow:

- Every transaction affects *at least* two accounts.
- If *only* two accounts are affected, the debit entry in the one account must be equal to the credit entry in the other.
- If *more than* two accounts are affected, the total debits must be equal to the total credits.

Once you have determined the accounts involved in the transaction, you can apply the basic rule for increasing and decreasing accounts.

One final point. Notice that in all transactions analyzed and recorded so far, the debit side of the entry came before the credit

ANALYSIS CHART

WHAT HAPPENS	ACCOUNTING RULE	ACCOUNTING ENTRY
The liability Bank Loan Payable decreases by $4 000.	*To decrease a liability, debit the account. Reason: Liabilities decrease on the side opposite to that on which they appear in the accounting equation.*	*Debit: Bank Loan Payable $4 000*
The asset Cash decreases by $4 000.	*To decrease an asset, credit the account. Reason: Assets decrease on the side opposite to that on which they appear in the accounting equation.*	*Credit: Cash $4 000*

Bank Loan Payable

Debit		Credit	
19—		19—	
Oct. 15	4 000	Sept. 30	20 000

Cash

Debit		Credit	
19—		19—	
Sept. 30	60 000	Oct. 1	1 000
		5	5 000
		15	4 000

side. It is good procedure always to think of the debit entry as coming before the credit entry.

In doing the problems that follow, consult the illustrations given earlier.

TOPIC 2 PROBLEMS

3-5 Study the following T-accounts.

Cash

Debit	Credit
5 000	700
200	1 800
300	500
	600
	100

Accts. Rec./J. Forrester

Debit	Credit
200	200

Supplies

Debit	Credit
700	200

Equipment

Debit	Credit
1 200	
1 800	

Accts. Pay./Chayka Corp.

Debit	Credit
500	1 200
600	

Dale Green, Capital

Debit	Credit
100	5 000
	300

a Determine the balance for each and indicate whether it is a debit or a credit by entering DR. or CR. in the appropriate space.

Key Check Figure
OE = $5 200

b Below the T-account ledger, prove that the accounting equation is in balance within the ledger by completing the totals for $A = L + OE$.

3-6 On a form similar to the one below, show what happens to the fundamental elements — assets or liabilities — in each transaction, and name the accounts that are involved.

EXAMPLE: Purchased land for cash in the amount of $7 000.

Debit Entry		*Credit Entry*	
What Happens	*Account Debited*	*What Happens*	*Account Credited*
Assets increase	Land	Assets decrease	Cash

(i) Bought tools for $750 in cash.
(ii) Returned tools purchased for $10 in cash.
(iii) Bought building costing $18 000 on a 20-year mortgage payable.
(iv) Received $100 from a customer in part payment of an amount owing.
(v) Paid $45 to a creditor in part payment of the debt owing to the creditor.
(vi) Borrowed $2 000 from the bank on a demand note.
(vii) Bought office equipment for $12 000 on credit.
(viii) Returned one piece of office equipment costing $250. The equipment was bought earlier on credit.

3-7 Set up two T-accounts for each transaction given below. Treat the transactions as separate cases. Give a title to each account, and record the amount on the correct side of each account. Show the left account as the debit entry in each case, as in the following example.

EXAMPLE:
Paid $100 in cash to E. Cox on account.

Accts. Pay./E. Cox		*Cash*	
100			*100*

a Received $75 from P.A. Belliveau on account.
b Bought equipment for $500 in cash.
c Returned one piece of equipment purchased for $100 in cash.
d Received $300 from Francis Dalton "on account" — that is, on credit.
e Bought furniture for $5 000 on credit from Landry Furniture Co.
f Paid $225 to D. LeBlanc, a creditor.
g Obtained $10 000 cash from a bank loan on a demand note.
h Bought equipment costing $1 000 on 30 days' credit from Jay Co.

3-8 Challenge Problem Mary Ann Gillett established a sole-proprietorship accounting office under her name, M.A. Gillett, C.A. The following transactions took place in May.

May 1 Mary Ann deposited $10 000 in personal funds into a bank account in the name of the new business.
2 She bought two standard electric typewriters for the office at a total cost of $2 400 from IBM Co. The terms were 30 days' credit.
3 She bought one desktop electronic calculator from Monroe Co. for $600. Issued a cheque in payment.
4 She decided that only one of the two typewriters was needed for the office. Instead of returning one, she agreed to sell it at cost to a friend. The friend, R. Stevens, agreed to pay M. A. Gillett, C.A. $1 200 within 30 days. *Hint:* This transaction does not involve a sale of services. It simply eliminates the cost of one piece of office equipment.
5 She purchased one IBM word processor for $4 000. The terms were one-half cash, the balance owing to IBM Co. on 30 days' credit.
8 She bought three more calculators for the office from Monroe Co. at a total cost of $1 800. The terms allowed for 30 days' credit.
9 She returned one of the calculators bought on credit on May 8 from Monroe Co., because it was the wrong model. It had cost $600.
10 She borrowed $12 000 cash from the bank by signing a demand note. This amount was deposited immediately into the firm's bank account.
11 She bought a car from Westown Motors for business use. The cost was $14 000. The terms were 20% in cash and the rest on 30 days' credit.
15 She purchased desks, chairs, and tables from Office Specialty Ltd. The total cost was $6 500. The terms given were 30 days' credit.
17 One of the desks purchased on May 15 proved to be defective. Mary Ann returned it to Office Specialty Ltd. for a full credit of $500 — the price shown on the bill made out to M.A. Gillett, C.A.
30 She issued a cheque to IBM Co. for $2 400 in full payment for the typewriters bought on May 2.
30 She issued a cheque to Monroe Co. for $1 200 in full settlement of the balance owing to this creditor.
31 R. Stevens paid $600 cash in part payment of the debt owing to M.A. Gillett, C.A.
31 Mary Ann purchased accounting and tax books to be used as a professional library in the business. She issued a cheque for $4 000 to C.C.H. Canada Ltd. for the total cost of the books.

a Set up a T-account ledger for M.A. Gillett, C.A. with the following accounts: Cash; Accts. Rec./R. Stevens; Office Equipment; Furniture; Automobile; Accounting Library; Bank Loan Payable; Accts. Pay./IBM Co.; Accts. Pay./Monroe Co.; Accts. Pay./Office Specialty Ltd.; Accts. Pay./Westown Motors; M.A. Gillett, Capital.

b Record each of the transactions by date in the T-account ledger. Use only the accounts set up for the business.

c After you record the final transaction, calculate the balance for each account. Draw a single line across the entire account and show the balance below this line on the correct side as shown below.

	Cash	
	4 000	200
	100	800
	1 900	1 000
Balance	4 000	

d Prepare a Summary of Account Balances as at May 31. It should prove that the accounting equation in total balances within the T-account ledger.

Key Check Figure Cash Balance = $9 600

e The banker has asked the owner for a copy of the firm's latest balance sheet. This document is required to enable the banker to support the existing demand loan. Prepare the balance sheet in good form. Report the assets and claims against assets as at May 31.

TOPIC 3 T-ACCOUNT RECORD OF OWNER'S EQUITY CHANGES

In Chapter 2, you learned that Owner's Equity in the accounting equation may be changed as a result of four types of business transactions:

- additional investment by the owner of the business
- revenue transactions
- expense transactions
- a withdrawal of assets for the owner's personal use

An account called "Owner's Equity" as such does not exist in accounting. You must remember this before you use debits and credits to record changes to owner's equity. Owner's equity is the claim of the owner against the total assets as shown in the accounting equation and as reported by the balance sheet at the end of the financial period. Look at the *complete accounting equation:*

$$A = L + \overbrace{C + R - E - D}^{\textbf{OE}\ \textit{(owner's equity)}}$$

It shows four separate sections under *OE*:

- *capital:* the owner's investment
- *revenue:* the inflow of cash and accounts receivable resulting from sales
- *expenses:* the operating costs incurred in bringing revenue into the business
- *drawing:* withdrawals of assets for the owner's personal use

The complete accounting equation also shows these important facts about Owner's Equity:

- Capital transactions cause an increase to *OE* in the accounting equation, so there is a plus sign in front of *C*.
- Revenue transactions cause an increase to *OE* in the accounting equation, so there is a plus sign in front of *R*.
- Expense transactions cause a decrease to *OE* in the accounting equation, so there is a minus sign in front of the *E*.
- Drawing transactions cause a decrease to *OE* in the accounting equation, so there is a minus sign in front of *D* in the equation.

It follows, therefore, that four separate accounts are needed to record those transactions that cause increases and decreases to Owner's Equity — capital, revenue, expenses, and drawing.

Debit and Credit Rules to Record Changes to Owner's Equity

The rules in Chapter 2 for increasing and decreasing asset and liability accounts can also be used for recording changes to the owner's equity. But there is one more point to learn here. Since Owner's Equity is not an account, you must use a separate account for each transaction which causes an increase, and a separate account for each which causes a decrease, to *OE* in the accounting equation. Study the two rules that follow.

Rule for Recording an Increase to Owner's Equity

An increase to *OE* is recorded in the account that caused the increase, and on the side on which *OE* is placed in the accounting equation — the credit side.

This rule says that you must first identify what item causes the increase to Owner's Equity. For example, an additional investment of cash by the owner causes an increase to Assets on the left side of the equation. A similar increase results on the right side to Owner's Equity. Since the increase to Owner's Equity was caused by an additional investment, the owner's Capital account is used to record this increase. Because *OE* appears on the credit (right) side of the accounting equation, the increase will be recorded on the credit side of the account which caused this increase. In this case, the credit side of the Capital account will be used.

Rule for Recording a Decrease to Owner's Equity

A decrease to *OE* is recorded in the account that caused the decrease, and on the side opposite to that on which *OE* is placed in the accounting equation — the debit side.

This rule follows the rule given for all accounts. To decrease any element of the accounting equation (*A*, *L*, or *OE*), you have to use the opposite side. In the case of *OE*, the debit (left) side must be used.

Recording Capital Transactions

Perhaps the most fundamental business transaction is the initial investment of the owner in his or her business. For example, where the owner invests cash to establish the business, the Cash account is opened with a debit balance. Likewise, the owner's Capital account is opened with a credit balance. If an additional investment is made later on, an accounting entry must be made to record the increase to Owner's Equity and an increase to Cash or another asset.

October 16 Jane Emery decides to increase her investment in the business by taking $3 000 from her personal savings account and depositing the cash into the firm's chequing account.

Analysis: From the double entry shown below, you can see the asset Cash being debited for an increase of $3 000. You already know that all increases to Assets, which are done on the left side, must be balanced by similar increases on the right side of some other account or accounts. Since the owner has invested additional cash, the right side of the equation must be increased by recording an increase to some part of Owner's Equity. Under

ANALYSIS CHART

WHAT HAPPENS	ACCOUNTING RULE	ACCOUNTING ENTRY
The asset Cash increases by $3 000.	*To increase an asset, debit the account. Reason: Assets increase on the side on which they appear in the accounting equation.*	*Debit: Cash $3 000*
Owner's Equity in the accounting equation increases by $3 000.	*To increase Owner's Equity, credit the account which caused the increase. Reason: Owner's Equity can increase only on the side on which it appears in the accounting equation — the credit side.*	*Credit: J. Emery, Capital $3 000*

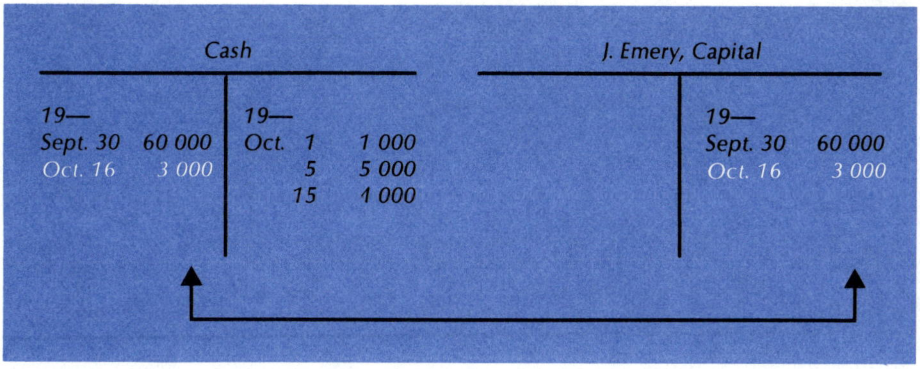

Owner's Equity, investment is recorded under Capital. Therefore, the increase must be recorded in the Capital account, on the credit side.

Recording Owner's Withdrawals of Assets

In Chapter 2, you learned that when an owner withdraws cash from the business for personal use, a sub-element called Drawing is used to record the transaction.

October 30 Jane Emery withdraws $2 000 from her firm's bank account and deposits it in her personal chequing account.

Analysis: From the double entry shown, you can see Owner's Equity being decreased by $2 000. The rule on decreasing elements of the equation says that a record of the decrease to *OE* is made by choosing the account that caused the decrease. Here,

ANALYSIS CHART

WHAT HAPPENS	ACCOUNTING RULE	ACCOUNTING ENTRY
Owner's Equity in the accounting equation decreases by $2 000.	*To decrease Owner's Equity, debit the account which caused the decrease. Reason: Owner's Equity can decrease only on the side opposite to that on which it appears in the accounting equation — the debit side.*	*Debit: J. Emery, Drawing $2 000*
The asset Cash decreases by $2 000.	*To decrease an asset, credit the account. Reason: Assets decrease on the side opposite to that on which they appear in the accounting equation — the credit side.*	*Credit: Cash $2 000*

J. Emery, Drawing			
19—			
Oct. 30	2 000		

Cash			
19—		19—	
Sept. 30	60 000	Oct. 1	1 000
Oct. 16	3 000	5	5 000
		15	4 000
		30	2 000

the owner's Drawing account is used to record the decrease to *OE*. This decrease must be recorded on the side opposite to that on which the element is located in the equation — the debit side.

The credit entry is easy to follow because you have now analyzed many entries to decrease the Cash account.

Do not confuse the owner's withdrawals of cash for personal use with expense transactions. For example, it would be a serious accounting error to consider a monthly cash withdrawal by the owner of a business as his or her salary. True, an owner uses all or part of his or her time to carry on the business. But the owner invests money and time in the business for one reason only: to make as much income as possible. The owner's incentive is the healthy increase in his or her equity in the firm that will result if the business earns a large net income. All of the owner's "salaries" must be accounted for as a debit to his or her Drawing account.

Watch out for other kinds of transactions dealing with personal withdrawals by the owner. For example, an owner of a business may issue a cheque to pay a *home* telephone bill. In this case, again, the owner's Drawing account must be used to show a decrease to Owner's Equity. Of course, a credit to Cash would be made to record the decrease to the Asset account. It would be a serious error to debit an expense account — for example, Telephone Expense — since this account only records *business* expenses.

Recording Revenue Transactions

As you will recall, revenue is the inflow of cash and accounts receivable that result from the sale of goods and services. It causes an increase in Owner's Equity within the accounting equation. To record this increase within a ledger system, a revenue account must be credited.

October 31 J. Emery Real Estate has received $6 800 cash for buying and selling homes, land, and other forms of real estate for a variety of clients.

ANALYSIS CHART

WHAT HAPPENS	ACCOUNTING RULE	ACCOUNTING ENTRY
The asset Cash increases by $6 800.	*To increase an asset, debit the account.* Reason: *Assets increase on the side on which they appear in the accounting equation.*	*Debit:* *Cash $6 800*
Owner's Equity in the accounting equation increases by $6 800.	*To increase Owner's Equity, credit the account which caused the increase.* Reason: *Owner's Equity can increase only on the side on which it appears in the accounting equation — the credit side.*	*Credit:* *Commissions Earned* *$6 800*

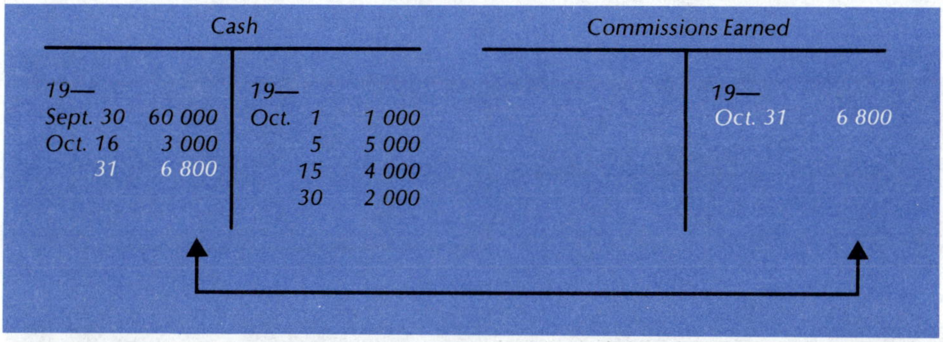

Analysis: As explained in Chapter 2, the name of the revenue account depends on the nature of the business operations. Since a real estate broker earns revenue by charging a commission, the revenue account would usually be called *Commissions Earned,* as here. Dentists, lawyers, doctors, accountants, and other professionals charge a fee for their services, so it is common to see a revenue account called *Professional Fees Earned* or simply *Fees Earned.* Retail stores sell goods, and the revenue account is usually called *Sales Revenue,* or simply *Sales.*

October 31 J. Emery Real Estate earned commissions on credit by providing real estate services as follows: $2 000 for selling a building for Pat Rogers; $1 200 for selling a residence for

ANALYSIS CHART

WHAT HAPPENS	ACCOUNTING RULE	ACCOUNTING ENTRY
Three assets increase as follows: Accts. Rec./Pat Rogers by $2 000; Accts. Rec./R. Scobie by $1 200; Accts. Rec./Shannon Development Co. by $4 000.	*To increase assets, debit the separate accounts involved.*	*Debit: Accts. Rec./Pat Rogers $2 000 Accts. Rec./R. Scobie $1 200 Accts. Rec./Shannon Development Co. $4 000*
There is a second inflow of revenue causing an increase of $7 200 to OE in the accounting equation.	*To increase OE, credit the account which caused the increase. (Here, it is revenue that caused it.)*	*Credit: Commissions Earned $7 200*

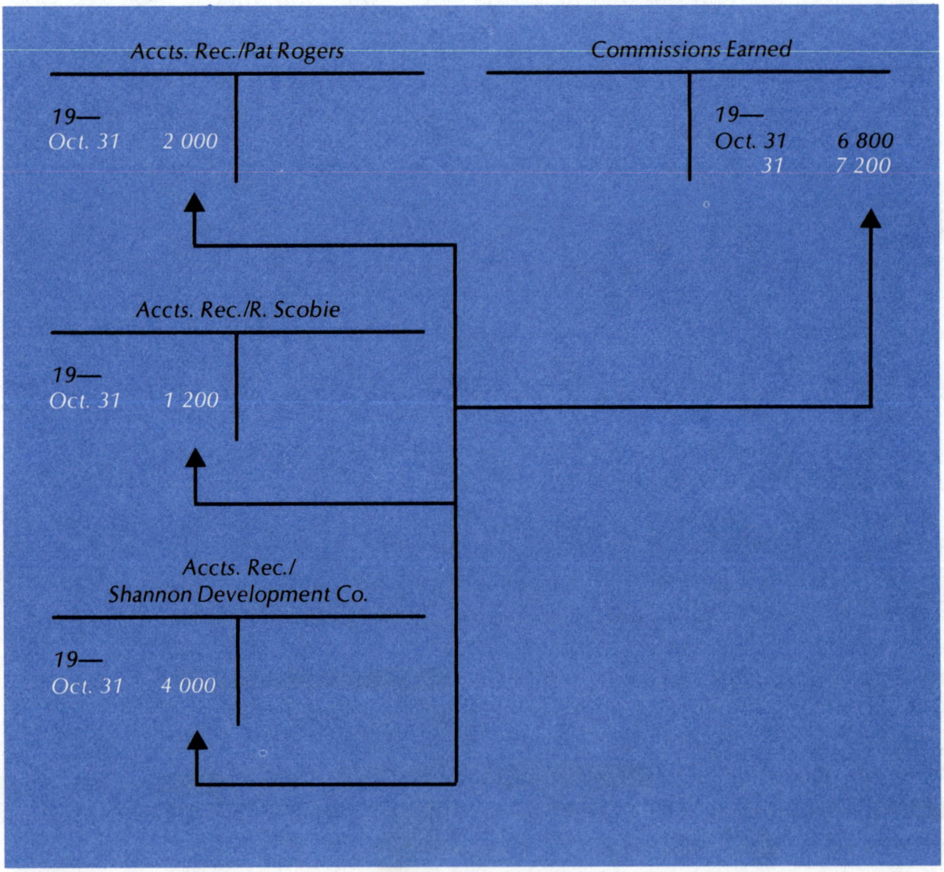

R. Scobie; $4 000 for buying properties for Shannon Development Co. All clients were given 30 days in which to pay.

Analysis: The credit to the revenue account Commissions Earned should be easy to follow. Observe carefully the three debits to three customer accounts. Obviously, the total of the three debits must be equal to the one credit to the revenue account.

Recording Expense Transactions

Chapter 2 explained the nature of a business expense and how it results in a decrease to Owner's Equity in the accounting equation. This is an important point because it explains why the *debit* side of an expense account must be used to record any expense transaction. Also, expenses may be incurred because of an immediate cash payment or because of owing a sum through a liability. Study the analysis of how the next two expense transactions are recorded.

October 31 J. Emery Real Estate pays cash totalling $5 235 for the following expenses: Rent, $600; Salaries, $4 500; Utilities, $95; Telephone, $40.

Analysis: Notice that a separate expense account describing the cost used up is shown. A separate expense account gives better information to the owner, who must make sure that those costs do not get too high. Notice also that the total of the debits equals the one credit.

ANALYSIS CHART

WHAT HAPPENS	ACCOUNTING RULE	ACCOUNTING ENTRY
Four expenses are incurred. These cause OE in the accounting equation to decrease by their sum.	*To decrease Owner's Equity, record the amount in the account that caused the decrease, on the side opposite to that on which OE is placed in the accounting equation.*	*Debit:* *Rent Expense $600* *Salaries Expense $4 500* *Utilities Expense $95* *Telephone Expense $40*
The asset Cash decreases by the sum of the expenses, $5 235.	*To decrease an asset, credit the account.*	*Credit:* *Cash $5 235*

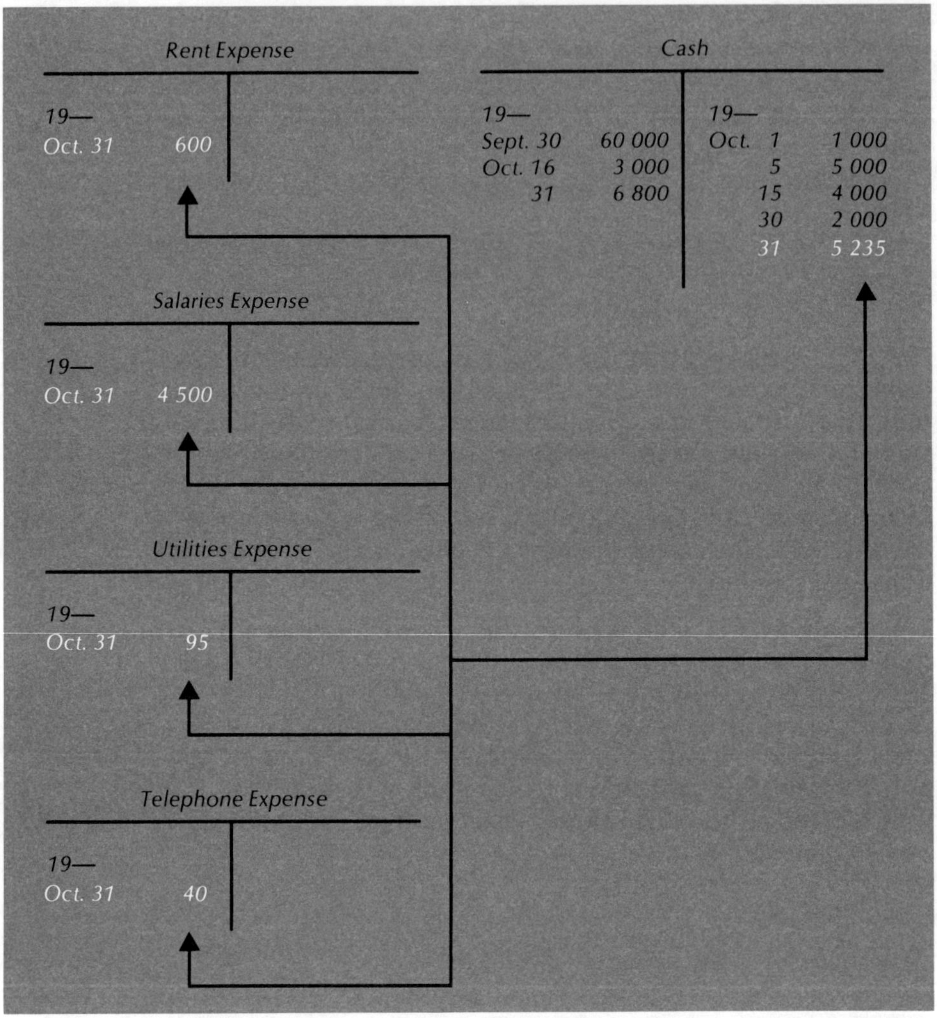

October 31 J. Emery Real Estate receives a bill for $600 from *The City Record,* a local newspaper, for three large advertisements during October. The bill allows the firm a period of 30 days in which to pay.

ANALYSIS CHART

WHAT HAPPENS	ACCOUNTING RULE	ACCOUNTING ENTRY
An expense for advertising is incurred. This expense decreases Owner's Equity by $600 in the accounting equation.	*To decrease Owner's Equity, debit the account which caused the decrease.* Reason: *Owner's Equity can decrease only on the side opposite to that on which OE appears in the accounting equation — the debit side.*	*Debit: Advertising Expense $600*

The liability Accts. Pay./ The City Record increases by $600 in the accounting equation.	*To increase a liability, credit the account.* Reason: *Liabilities appear on the right side of the equation. Thus, the increase side is the credit side.*	*Credit: Accts. Pay./The City Record $600*

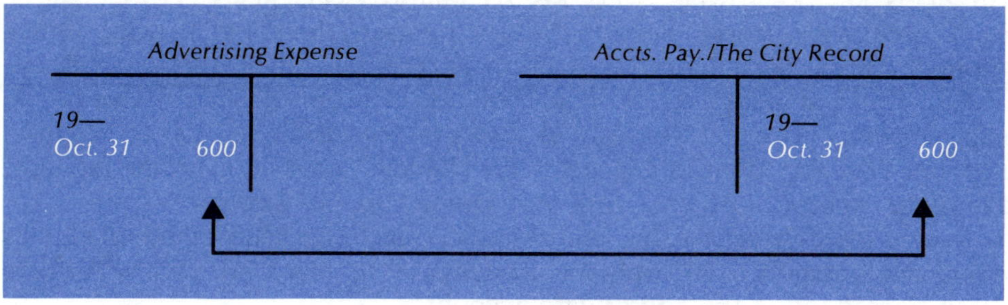

TOPIC 3 PROBLEMS

3-9 Set up a *separate* T-account for *each* of the following transactions. Give an appropriate title to each account, and record the amount on the correct side of the account. Always show the debit entry on the left side in the T-account.

EXAMPLE: Frank Towes started an auto repair shop with $30 000 in cash.

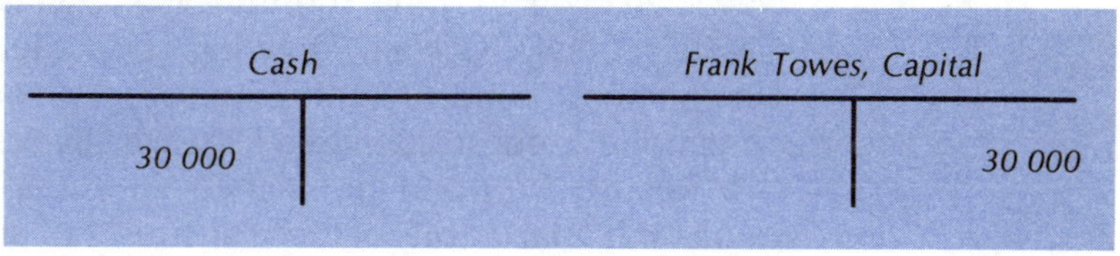

a Frank Towes bought tools for $2 400 on credit from Market Tools Ltd.
b He earned repair service revenue by charging $310 for repairing Mark Howe's car. He gave him 30 days' credit.
c He bought equipment for $6 000 in cash.
d He returned equipment costing $200 originally purchased for cash.
e He borrowed $1 000 from the Bank of British Columbia on a demand note.
f He received $100 from Mark Howe on account.
g He paid $600 for monthly rent.
h He collected $800 cash for servicing customers' cars during week.
i He paid $400 to Market Tools Ltd. on account.
j He paid $30 to settle a telephone bill.
k He withdrew $1 000 from the business for his personal use.
l He received a bill for $800 from *The Daily Record* for advertising, with credit terms of 30 days.

3-10 Refer to Problem 2-5 of Chapter 2, page 35. Set up a *separate* T-account for *each* of the 11 transactions shown for Davey Tree Service. Use an account called *Tree Service Revenue* for all transactions involving the sale of services. Always show the debit entry on the left side.

3-11 Refer to Problem 2-9 of Chapter 2, page 44.

a Set up the following T-account ledger for Philip's Moving and Storage Co.: Cash; Accts. Rec./R. Browne; Accts. Rec./G. Martin; Accts. Rec./E. Powell; Accts. Rec./A. Stockwell; Accts. Rec./R. Wilkinson; Land; Building; Trucks; Office Equipment; Bank Loan Payable; Accts. Pay./Central Advertisers Ltd.; Accts. Pay./Esso Oil Company; Accts. Pay./Hamilton Motors; R. Philip, Capital; R. Philip, Drawing; Moving Fees Earned; Storage Fees Earned; Salaries Expense; Telephone Expense; Utilities Expense; Truck Repairs Expense; Gasoline Expense; Advertising Expense; Insurance Expense; Office Supplies Expense.

b Record the transactions for August in the T-accounts established for Philip's Moving and Storage Co. Use only the accounts set up in **a** above. Show the date of each transaction in the appropriate accounts.

Key Check Figure Cash Balance = $33 145

c Calculate and show the balance on the correct side of the account at the close of business on August 31.

3-12 Challenge Problem On November 1, Gerald O'Neil began his Spot-Free Cleaners with the following assets and liabilities: Cash, $30 000; Government of Canada Bonds, $20 000; Equipment, $25 000; Store Fixtures, $2 000; Bank Loan Payable (on demand), $10 000; Accts. Pay./King Furniture Co., $5 000.

a Open the following T-account ledger for Spot-Free Cleaners: Cash; Government of Canada Bonds; Accts. Rec./Eastview Garage; Accts. Rec./S. Harvey; Equipment; Store Fixtures; Truck; Bank Loan Payable; Accts. Pay./The Daily News; Accts. Pay./King Furniture Co.; Accts. Pay./Swan's Auto; Gerald O'Neil, Capital; Gerald O'Neil, Drawing; Dry Cleaning Revenue; Interest Earned on Government Bonds; Rent Expense; Advertising Expense; Salaries Expense; Telephone Expense; Utilities Expense; Bank Interest Expense.

b Record the opening balances in the appropriate accounts. Check the total debits and total credits of these accounts to prove that the equation is in balance as at November 1. (HINT: One element must be calculated.)

c Record the following transactions for November in the T-accounts established for Spot-Free Cleaners. Identify each transaction by date.

Nov. 2 Gerald O'Neil made an additional investment of $5 000 in the business.
3 He bought a new truck from Swan's Auto for $15 000 on 60 days' credit.
4 He provided drycleaning services for $175 in cash.
5 He paid $700 cash for rent.
7 He rendered drycleaning services to S. Harvey for $125 on 30 days' credit.
9 He paid $26 cash for the business telephone bill.
11 He rendered drycleaning services for $100 in cash.
12 He rendered drycleaning services for $225 in cash.
14 He paid $300 to King Furniture on account.

15 He received $50 from S. Harvey on account.
17 He provided drycleaning services to Eastview Garage for $680 on 30 days' credit.
19 He paid $120 cash for utilities.
20 He ordered newspaper advertising at a cost of $90, payment to be made within 30 days to *The Daily News.*
21 He issued a cheque to Bell Canada for $12 in payment of his home telephone bill.
23 He rendered drycleaning services for $600 in cash.
28 He paid a monthly salary of $1 000 *each* to two employees. He also paid himself $2 000 as salary for the month.
30 He issued a cheque for $7 500 to Swan's Auto on account.
30 He received $200 from Eastview Garage on account.
30 He rendered drycleaning services for $850 in cash.
30 He received a cheque for $250 for one month's interest earned on Government of Canada bonds. He deposited the cheque into the firm's bank account.
30 He received a note from the bank informing him that $125 had been deducted from the bank account of Spot-Free Cleaners for one month's interest on the demand loan.

d Calculate the balance of each account at the close of business on November 30. Show each balance on the correct side of the account.

e Prepare a Summary of Ledger Account Balances as at November 30 to prove that the accounting equation is in balance within the ledger.

f From the Summary, prepare an income statement for the month of November.

g From the Summary and the result reported in the income statement, prepare a balance sheet in good form as at November 30.

Key Check Figure
Net Loss = $56
Cash Balance = $24 667

Case Study 3

Four beginning accounting students, after a final lesson on debits and credits, were overheard as follows:

Student 1: "I'm really confused. Expenses mean decreases in the owner's equity. Decreases in liabilities and owner's equity are recorded on the debit side of the account. Yet to record an increase in an expense, you debit the account. How come?"

Student 2: "You have to learn your debit and credit rules. Here are mine. Debit anything that's bad for the business. Credit anything that's good. Since any expense cuts profits down, that's bad for the business and you debit an expense account. When you sell something, that's good for the business. So you will credit a revenue account."

Student 3: "I don't have any problem with the rules for debits and credits. I simply debit anything which comes into the business, and credit what goes out."

Student 4: "I have a very easy way to do debits and credits. It works every time. Every transaction will have one easy part to it. So I do that part first. The other part must be the opposite because debits always equal credits. For example, for a cash sale, Cash has to be debited — everyone knows that. So Sales revenue must be credited. As long as debits equal credits, you can't go wrong."

a Give your reactions to *each* student's approach.

b What approach would *you* recommend, if you were teaching someone when to debit and when to credit?

(Use lined notepaper to answer a and b above.)

CHAPTER 4

IDENTIFYING THE BOOKKEEPING BASE OF ACCOUNTING

At this point you are ready to learn how to perform accounting in a more organized way so that you can prepare financial statements easily and accurately at the end of each accounting period. In the language of accounting, this organized way of doing accounting is made up of a series of steps known as the accounting cycle.

In this chapter, you will be shown the first four steps of the accounting cycle.

Accounting cycle: the complete sequence of accounting activities repeated in every accounting period.

- Topic 1 explains how transaction information originates on business papers called source documents.
- Topic 2 examines the recording of information contained in source documents in an accounting record known as the journal.
- Topic 3 shows how these recorded transactions are transferred from the journal to the ledger.
- Topic 4 covers the preparation of a series of accounting proofs before any financial statements are prepared.

TOPIC 1 ORIGINATING TRANSACTION DATA

Accountants cannot make a record of any financial event unless there is proof that the business transaction actually did take place. This is because they must follow the guidelines called GAAPs.

Two of these basic guidelines, which have already been given to you in Chapter 2, are the revenue recognition principle and the matching principle. The first helps accountants to recognize and record revenue transactions in accounts. The second guides the accountant to report revenues earned with expenses incurred in the same time period in a formal report called the income statement.

The GAAP used by accountants to prove that a business transaction did occur is known as the *objectivity principle.* It may be simply stated as follows:

GAAP for Objectivity

All accounting transactions must be supported by business papers called source documents.

Source documents: business forms (papers) that give evidence of business transactions on a certain date.

To understand the meaning of "objectivity," think of the word *object.* An object is something you can see. When you can see it, you know it's for real. The objectivity principle, then, allows the accountant to record actual business transactions on the basis of "objects" called source documents.

Four common source documents are described below.

The First Balance Sheet

When a business is established, the assets, the liabilities, and the owner's equity are presented on the *first balance sheet.* This becomes the source document as at the date when the owner began his or her business. Of course, this date is the one reported in the heading of the balance sheet. Then, a T-account is opened for each asset and liability, and for the owner's capital as at the opening balance sheet date.

Handwritten Sales Slip

The Invoice

When a business buys an asset either for cash or on credit, the seller completes a bill of sale often called the sales invoice or simply the *invoice.*

The name of the document varies according to the type and need of each business: the bill of sale may be called an invoice, a sales slip, a sales ticket, or a cash register tape. Regardless of its name, the buyer will receive a copy, which becomes the source document for the transaction.

For example, when J. Emery Real Estate buys additional office equipment costing $1 200 from the Ryan Equipment Co. on 60 days' credit, the buyer expects to receive a business form known as the invoice. See the next illustration.

Purchase invoice: a copy of an invoice, received by the buyer, to give evidence of the purchase made.

The invoice is called the purchase invoice by the buyer, because he or she receives a copy for buying the asset. The copy of the invoice kept by the seller becomes the source document for the sale — that is, proves in the seller's books that a sale occurred. The seller's name for it is the *sales invoice.* A good way to remember the difference between the terms "sales invoice" and

Invoice: a source document that gives evidence of a sale.

RYAN EQUIPMENT CO.
379 KING STREET
KITCHENER, ONTARIO N2G 1G6

INVOICE
No. 04879

SOLD TO: J. Emery Real Estate
Any Street
Any Town, Canada

INVOICE DATE: 19-- 10 03
TERMS: Net, 60 days
SHIPPED VIA: Truck

SHIP TO: Same

QUANTITY	DESCRIPTION	UNIT PRICE	AMOUNT
2	Electronic Printing Calculators, Model 15X, Serial Numbers 487876 and 787877	$200.00	$ 400.00
1	Electric Typewriter, Model AC5, Serial Number 878994	800.00	800.00
		Total Amount Payable	$ 1 200.00

"purchase invoice" is to follow the arrows in the diagram below. *Remember:* the two are the same document, the invoice, looked at from two points of view.

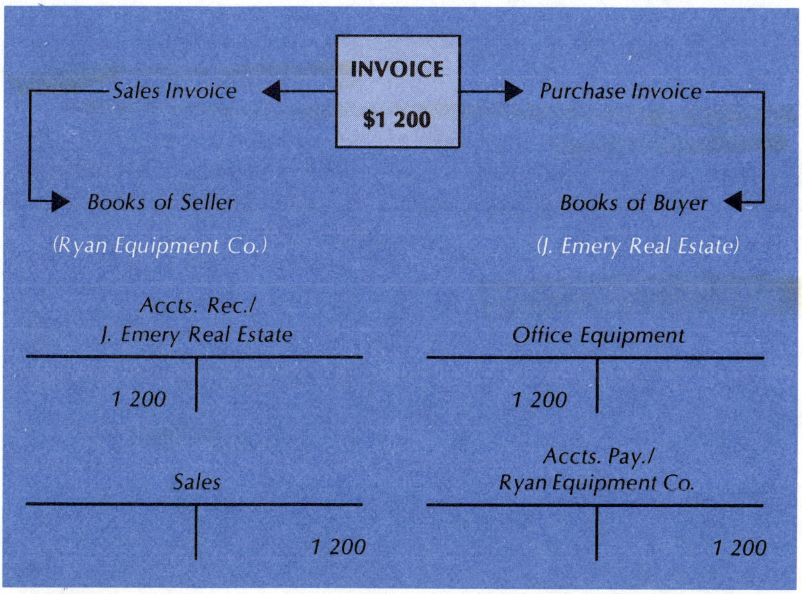

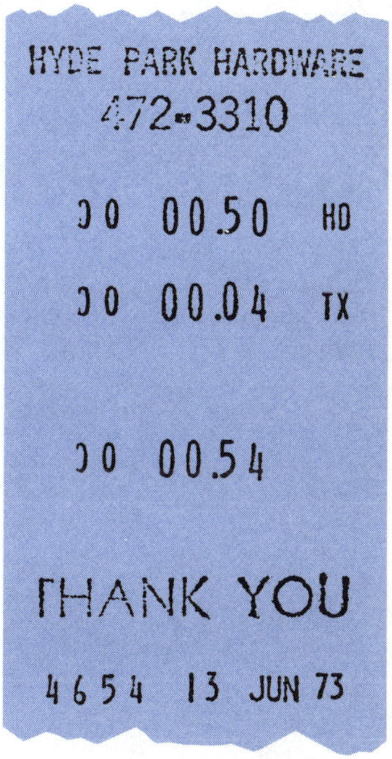

Cash Register Tape

BELL CANADA 787900
P.O. Box 9000
DON MILLS, ONT.
M3C 2X7

To: J. EMERY REAL ESTATE
ANY STREET
ANY TOWN, CANADA

Date of bill: October 10, 19--

Your telephone no.: 479-8622

TOTAL AMOUNT DUE: $40.00

The invoice can also be used to originate a sale of services. The common telephone bill is a good example of this. For the user of telephone services, the telephone bill is the source document proving the telephone expense transaction. For the telephone company — the seller of these services — a copy of the source document becomes the sales invoice allowing accounting to record the revenue earned for the period.

The Cheque Record

Many businesses use a *cheque record* to give evidence of each cash payment. It may take many forms. One is the cheque stub. Study the stub and the attached cheque shown below. The cheque is in payment of the telephone bill for October.

DATE Oct. 11, 19-- No. 3
ORDER OF Bell Canada
For: Telephone Expense
$40.00

DEPOSITS		JOURNAL		
		BALANCE	$54 000	00
		ADD DEPOSIT(S)	—	
		BALANCE	54 000	00
		DEDUCT CHEQUE	40	00
TOTAL		BALANCE	$53 960	00

THE ROYAL BANK OF CANADA
MAIN BRANCH
ROYAL BANK PLAZA
TORONTO, ONT.

No. 3 October 11, 19--

PAY TO THE ORDER OF Bell Canada $40.00
Forty ——— 00/100 DOLLARS

J. EMERY REAL ESTATE
Jane Emery

⑆00002⑉003⑆110⑉134⑉4⑉

BELL CANADA 787900
P.O. Box 9000
DON MILLS, ONT.
M3C 2X7

To: J. EMERY REAL ESTATE
ANY STREET
ANY TOWN, CANADA

Date of bill: October 10, 19--

Your telephone no.: 479-8622

PAID
Cheque No. 3
Oct. 11, 19--

TOTAL AMOUNT DUE: $40.00

Cheque stub: kept by buyer as a record of the cash payment

Completed cheque: sent to the seller of services (Bell Canada)

Bill: marked "Paid" with cheque number and date.

In this example, J. Emery Real Estate has two documents proving that a cash payment occurred. The cheque stub is the main source document, and the bill marked *Paid* becomes a supporting source document. With objective evidence like this, the accountant can record the result of the transaction by debiting the Telephone Expense account, and crediting the Cash account, for the amount shown on the cheque record.

The Remittance Slip

Remittance slip: a source document proving the receipt of a customer's cheque.

When a customer pays a debt by cheque, many businesses prepare a business form called the remittance slip. The slip becomes the source document for the record of the dollar amount received. The document may also be called the receipt. Receipts often come in a book of forms. For J. Emery Real Estate, assume the form is a remittance slip as shown below.

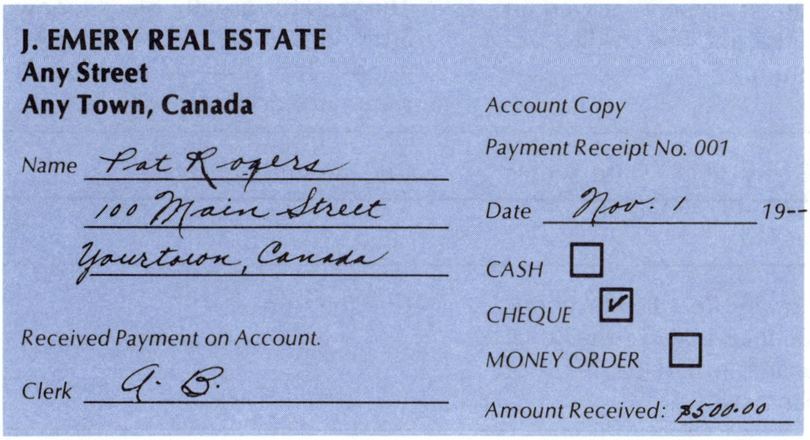
J. EMERY REAL ESTATE
Any Street
Any Town, Canada

Account Copy

Payment Receipt No. 001

Name Pat Rogers
100 Main Street
Yourtown, Canada

Date Nov. 1 19--

CASH ☐

CHEQUE ☑

MONEY ORDER ☐

Received Payment on Account.

Clerk G. B.

Amount Received: $500.00

The remittance slip would be prepared *before* the customer's cheque is deposited into J. Emery Real Estate's bank account. This is important, because accounting requires evidence that a cheque has been received. Once prepared, the remittance slip becomes the source document for analyzing and recording a debit to Cash and a credit to Accts. Rec./Pat Rogers for the amount of the cheque ($500 in this case).

The chart below summarizes the source documents identified for the transactions of J. Emery Real Estate during October.

Transaction	*Source Document*
Oct. 1 J. Emery Real Estate buys additional furniture for $1 000 from Enns Furniture Ltd., and pays by cheque.	1. Cheque stub 2. Invoice from Enns Furniture Ltd. (marked *Paid* with cheque number and date)
Oct. 3 J. Emery Real Estate buys additional office equipment costing $1 200 from the Ryan Equipment Co. on 60 days' credit.	Invoice from Office Equipment Co. (which becomes the purchase invoice)

Oct. 4 J. Emery Real Estate returns one piece of office equipment costing $200 to Ryan Equipment Co. because the equipment arrived in damaged condition. The creditor accepts the return.	1. Copy of letter (a note to the creditor) stating the details of the return of the equipment 2. The creditor usually mails a note after receiving the returned goods. The note is attached to the source document above.
Oct. 5 J. Emery Real Estate writes out a cheque for $5 000 to Westown Motors Ltd.	Cheque stub
Oct. 15 J. Emery Real Estate writes out a cheque for $4 000 to the Royal Bank of Canada in part payment of the bank loan payable.	Cheque stub
Oct. 16 Jane Emery decides to increase her investment in the business by taking $3 000 from her personal savings account and depositing the cash into the firm's chequing account.	1. Note called a *memorandum* (or *memo*), which is usually prepared to identify the additional investment 2. Copy of the deposit slip, which shows the amount invested in the firm's bank account
Oct. 30 Jane Emery withdraws $2 000 from her firm's bank account and deposits it into her personal chequing account.	Cheque stub
Oct. 31 J. Emery Real Estate has received $6 800 cash for buying and selling homes, land, and other forms of real estate for a variety of clients.	1. Copies of the individual sales invoices (sales slips) totalling $6 800 for commissions earned 2. Copy of a deposit slip showing the total cash received, $6 800, deposited into the firm's bank account
Oct. 31 J. Emery Real Estate earned commissions on credit by providing real estate services as follows: $2 000 for selling a building for Pat Rogers; $1 200 for selling a residence for R. Scobie; $4 000 for buying properties for Shannon Development Co. All clients were given 30 days to pay the commissions.	Copies of the invoices (totalling $7 200) made out to these customers

Oct. 31 J. Emery Real Estate pays cash totalling $5 235 for the following expenses: Rent, $600; Salaries, $4 500; Utilities, $95; Telephone, $40.	1. Individual cheque stubs for rent, $600; salaries, $4 500; utilities, $95; telephone, $40. 2. The following supporting documents, which would be marked *Paid* with the cheque number and date: the landlord's bill (sometimes the landlord gives only a receipt after payment is made); the utilities bill; the telephone bill
Oct. 31 J. Emery Real Estate receives a bill for $600 from *The City Record,* a local newspaper, for running three large advertisements during October. The bill allows the firm 30 days to pay for the advertising.	Advertising bill (invoice) from *The City Record*

TOPIC 1 PROBLEMS

4-1 Study the invoice below. Then answer the questions.

J. EMERY REAL ESTATE
MEMBER BROKER
Any Street
Any Town, Canada
Telephone: 471-8622

INVOICE NO. 00007

INVOICE DATE: October 31, 19--

TERMS: Net 30 days

Services Rendered
To: Pat Rogers
68 Central Avenue
Yourtown, Canada

For the following services rendered:	*Amount*
Oct. 30/-- Sold building located at 40 Main Street West, under your name, for $40 000. Commission: 5% of the amount equal to the sales price	$2 000.00
Please Pay This Amount	$2 000.00

When Remitting: Please indicate Invoice No. on reverse of your cheque.
Interest: will be charged at 2% per month on overdue accounts (after 30 days from Invoice Date).

a Who is the seller?
b Who is the buyer?
c Who prepared the source document?
d How do you know whether the invoice gives evidence to a credit sale?
e What was sold to the buyer?
f Why is an invoice number an important feature of every invoice?
g How was the amount owing calculated?
h By what date must the buyer pay the amount owing?
i What will be charged if the buyer does not pay within the terms given by the invoice?
j In one sentence, describe the transaction from the viewpoint of the seller indicated on the source document.
k Show the double entry in T-accounts that would be made in the seller's books.
l In one sentence, describe the transaction from the viewpoint of the buyer indicated on the source document.
m Show the double entry in T-accounts that would be made in the buyer's books. *Hint:* An expense account must be debited.

4-2 Study the source document below. Then answer the questions.

THE CITY RECORD
5000 Main Street East
Yourtown, Canada N6H 4H9

INVOICE NO.
74034

SOLD TO: J. Emery Real Estate
Any Street
Any Town, Canada

DATE: October 31, 19--

TERMS: Net 30 days

Half-page advertisement in evening editions of October 13, 24, and 25.	$600.00

a Who prepared this source document?
b What would it be called by the party who prepared it?
c Why has it been prepared?
d What would it be called by the party who receives it?
e When must the buyer named on the document make his or her payment?
f In one sentence, describe the transaction from the viewpoint of the seller named on the document.

g Show the double entry in T-account form that would be made in the seller's books.

h In one sentence, describe the transaction from the viewpoint of the buyer named on the document.

i Show the double entry in T-account form that would be made in the buyer's books.

4-3 Refer to Problem 3-8. For each of the business transactions outlined for M.A. Gillett, C.A., name a source document. Also, suggest any supporting document where it may be needed. Use a form similar to the one below.

Date	*Transactions*	*Source Documents*

4-4 Refer to Problem 3-12. For each of the business transactions outlined for Spot-Free Cleaners, name a source document. Also, suggest any supporting document where it may be needed. Use a form similar to the one used for Problem 4-3.

TOPIC 2 JOURNALIZING TRANSACTION DATA

In earlier chapters, you learned how to record the debits and credits for each business transaction directly into a T-account ledger. But although business transactions *could* be recorded directly into accounts, there are several disadvantages to showing debits and credits only in the ledger.

- First, the debit side of the entry would appear in one or more accounts, and the credit entry would appear in one or more different accounts, but which ones? You would have to search the entire ledger just to analyze one complete business transaction.
- Second, the account does not by itself show a record of all the business transactions for a particular date. Again, you would have to search through many accounts to discover how many business transactions occurred on a given day.
- Finally, if an error were made in the debit or the credit entry, the error would be difficult to locate quickly because the double entry has been separated into two or more accounts.

Journal: a daily record of business transactions in debit and credit form; a book of original entry.

To overcome these disadvantages, many accounting systems make an accounting record known as the journal before the debits and credits are entered into the ledger accounts. The journal is like a diary: it shows, for each day, the debits and credits analyzed from the source documents. The debits and credits can later be transferred to individual ledger accounts. Under this system, the debit and credit entries appear for the first time, in date order, in the journal. The journal is also known as the *book of original entry*.

General Journal: a two-column journal.

Journalizing: the process of analyzing transactions into debits and credits, and recording the results in a journal.

Before we examine how transactions are recorded in a journal, the following points should be considered.

- There are many different kinds of journals. One is the two-column form called the General Journal. This is a simple way of journalizing — analyzing a transaction and recording the debits and credits in the journal.
- Journalizing does not require any knowledge of how to debit and credit accounts.
- You will learn how to record journal entries manually. Journalizing may also be done by computer, but the manual method will be shown in this book because it is easier to learn. In fact, the practice of recording transactions manually in some journals persists even in some large businesses that use computers.
- For most business transactions to be recorded in the journal, one or more source documents will have provided the accounting data. Journalizing, therefore, follows the creation of source documents and is the second step in the accounting cycle.

Journalizing: An Illustration

Suppose that, on November 3, a business bought two desks costing $300 each from Wood Company on 30 days' credit. In journalizing this transaction, follow these steps:

Step 1 Analyze (break up) the effects of the transaction in the usual way, but this time try to think of the debit entry *before* the credit entry. (To review the rules for debiting and crediting accounts, go back to Chapter 3.) It may help you to think of the T-account analysis as follows:

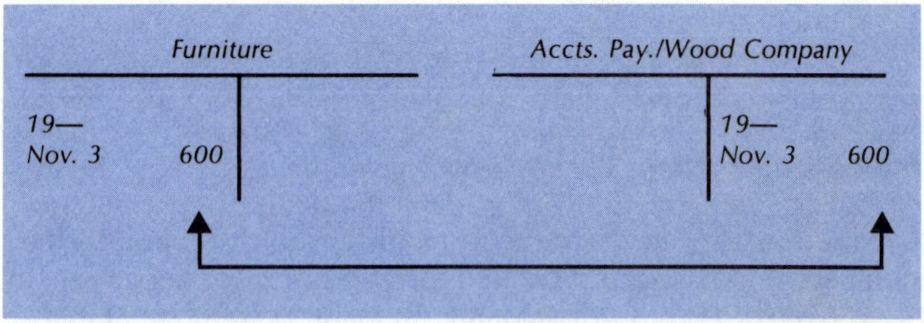

Step 2 Turn to the General Journal sheet as illustrated on page 87.

All journal sheets are numbered consecutively. In this illustration, *Page 10* appears on the top line of the journal, because earlier transactions were recorded on previous pages.

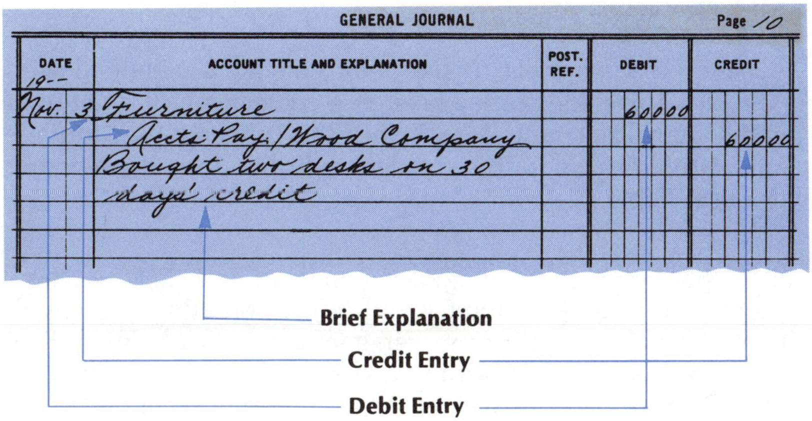

no $ sign

Next record the date of the transaction in the *Date* column. When you begin a page of the journal, indicate the year just above the left part of the date column, below the heading. Since space is limited, abbreviate the month and enter it into the left side of the date column. Then write the day of the month of the transaction on the right side.

For the next transaction, only the day of the month is recorded. The month and year are repeated only at the top of a new page, or when either the month or the year changes. See the illustrations in the margin.

The year and month are written at the top of every new journal page.

Only the day of the month is recorded for the next transaction on the same journal page.

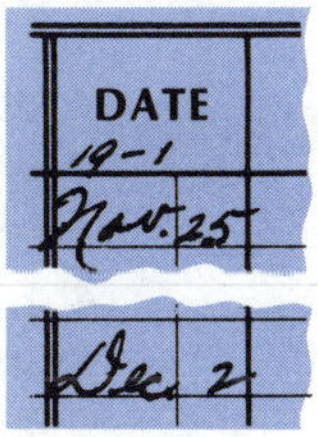

When the month changes on the same journal page, the new month is written.

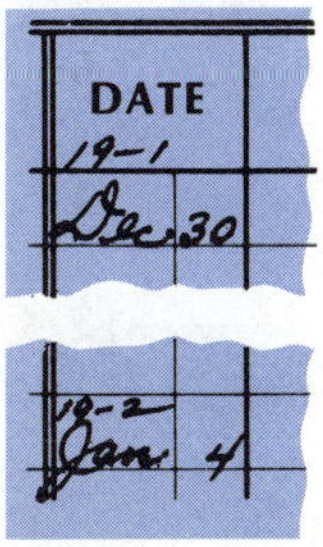

When the year changes on the same journal page, the new year and month are written.

Step 3 Record the debit entry, beginning to the right of the date. Write the title of the account to be debited. Then carefully enter the debit amount in the debit column (the left-hand money column). Notice that the dollar sign has been omitted from the money column because it is only in the income statement, the balance sheet, and other *formal* financial reports that dollar signs may be used. The journal is not a formal financial statement.

Step 4 See the illustration on page 90 to follow better this step and step 5. On the line below the debit entry, indent about 1.5 cm from the date column and write the title of the account to be credited. Then, on this same line, enter the amount credited in the credit column (the right-hand money column). The reason for indenting is simply to make it easier to distinguish the credit entry from the debit entry. It may remind you to indent if you remember that credit means "to the right."

Step 5 Finally, on the line below the credit entry, begin at the date column and record an explanation of the transaction. (In the example, the account title for the debit entry does not explain what type of furniture was acquired; however, a short but clear explanation could be shown.) In addition, many accountants like to see an identification of the source documents involved.

The Posting Reference Column

A narrow column next to the debit column is identified with *Post. Ref.* This is the Posting Reference column, which is not used in the journalizing procedure. Rather, this column is used in *posting* (transferring) data to the ledger, which will be explained in the next Topic.

Journal Entries: An Illustration

To show how a set of journal entries is recorded in a two-column General Journal, the earlier transactions for J. Emery Real Estate will be repeated with two changes. First, individual sales and expenses are listed as they would normally occur during the month. Second, appropriate source documents are identified for every transaction.

Date		*Transactions*	*Source Documents*
19-1			
Sept.	30	Jane Emery began the firm J. Emery Real Estate with the following assets and liabilities: Cash, $60 000; Automobile, $15 000; Furniture, $3 000; Office Equipment, $2 000; Bank Loan Payable, $20 000; Accts. Pay./Bell Furniture Co., $3 000; Accts. Pay./Office Equipment Co., $2 000; Accts. Pay./Westown Motors Ltd., $5 000. The opening balance sheet was prepared.	Opening balance sheet as at Sept. 30.
Oct.	1	J. Emery Real Estate buys more furniture for $1 000 from Enns Furniture Ltd., and issues Cheque No. 1 in payment.	Cheque record; purchase invoice marked *Paid*
	3	J. Emery Real Estate buys additional office equipment — two calculators and one typewriter — costing $1 200 from the Ryan Equipment Co. on 60 days' credit.	Purchase invoice
	4	J. Emery Real Estate returns one calculator costing $200 to Ryan Equipment Co. because the equipment arrived in damaged condition. The creditor has accepted the return.	Copy of letter, note, or return slip
	5	J. Emery Real Estate makes out Cheque No. 2 for $5 000 to Westown Motors Ltd.	Cheque record
	11	Cheque No. 3 is issued in payment of a business telephone bill for $40.	Cheque record
	12	Cheque No. 4 is issued in payment of the monthly rent, $600.	Cheque record; landlord's bill marked *Paid*

Oct.	15	Cheque No. 5 is issued to the Royal Bank of Canada in part payment of the $4 000 bank loan payable.	Cheque record
	16	Jane Emery decides to increase her investment by taking $3 000 from her personal savings account and depositing the cash into the firm's chequing account.	Memo; copy of bank deposit slip
	18	Cheque No. 6 is issued to Public Utilities Commission, in payment of $95 utilities bill.	Cheque record; utilities bill marked *Paid*
	20	$3 400 cash is received for commissions earned buying and selling real estate. (The invoice slips are numbered 00001, 00002, 00003, and 00004.)	Individual sales invoices; copy of bank deposit slip.
	30	Cheque No. 7 in the amount of $2 000 is issued to Jane Emery for personal use.	Cheque record
	31	$3 400 cash is received for commissions earned from real estate transactions. (Invoice slips 00005 and 00006.)	Individual sales invoices; copy of bank deposit slip
	31	Cheque No. 8 in the amount of $2 250 is issued to clerk Wendy Thomas for monthly salary; also Cheque No. 9 in the amount of $2 250 to clerk Jim Trafford for monthly salary.	Individual cheque records
	31	The following sales invoices are issued: No. 00007 to Pat Rogers for $2 000 in commissions earned selling a building for the client; No. 00008 to R. Scobie for $1 200 in commissions earned selling a residence for the client; No. 00009 to Shannon Development Co. for $4 000 in commissions earned buying properties for the client. Terms for all customers: net 30 days.	Copies of the invoices
	31	A bill for $600 is received from *The City Record* for advertisements during the month. Terms: net 30 days.	Purchase invoice

The following points relate to the entries recorded in the General Journal for J. Emery Real Estate:

- The journal pages are numbered consecutively.
- The first column is for the date of the transaction. Since this date is usually supported by a source document, the date in the journal is also the date of the transaction document. If there were no source document, the date in the journal would become the date of the transaction.
- A line is skipped after each entry. In a two-column journal, this spacing causes each entry to stand out clearly so that the

GENERAL JOURNAL — Page 1

DATE 19-1		ACCOUNT TITLE AND EXPLANATION	POST. REF.	DEBIT	CREDIT
Sept.	30	Cash	101	6000000	
		Automobile	110	1500000	
		Furniture	112	300000	
		Office Equipment	114	200000	
		Bank Loan Payable	201		2000000
		Accts. Pay./Bell Furniture Co.	202		300000
		Accts. Pay./Ryan Equipment Co.	204		200000
		Accts. Pay./Westown Motors Ltd.	205		500000
		J. Emery, Capital	301		5000000
		To record the opening			
		balance sheet into accounts.			
Oct.	1	Furniture	112	100000	
		Cash	101		100000
		Cheque No. 1 to Enns Furniture			
		Ltd. for additional furniture.			
	3	Office Equipment	114	120000	
		Accts. Pay./Ryan Equipment Co.	204		120000
		2 calculators and 1 typewriter			
		on 60 days' credit.			
	4	Accts. Pay./Ryan Equipment Co.	204	20000	
		Office Equipment	114		20000
		Returned 1 calculator received			
		in damaged condition.			
	5	Accts. Pay./Westown Motors Ltd.	205	500000	
		Cash	101		500000
		Cheque No. 2 on account.			
	11	Telephone Expense	502	4000	
		Cash	101		4000
		Cheque No. 3 to Bell Canada			

Opening entry: the entry that results in the opening of a set of books for a business.

Compound entry: an entry that involves more than two accounts.

separate transactions can easily be seen.

• The first entry is known as the opening entry because it identifies the accounts that open a set of accounting records for a business. The source document for the opening entry is the beginning balance sheet of the new business.

• An entry which includes more than one debit and more than one credit (such as the opening entry in the illustration) is called a compound entry. In every compound journal entry, the debits are listed before any credits, and the total of all debits

GENERAL JOURNAL Page 2

DATE 19-1		ACCOUNT TITLE AND EXPLANATION	POST. REF.	DEBIT	CREDIT
Oct.	12	Rent Expense	501	600 00	
		Cash	101		600 00
		Cheque No. 4 for monthly rent.			
	15	Bank Loan Payable	201	4 000 00	
		Cash	101		4 000 00
		Cheque No. 5 to The Royal			
		Bank of Canada in part			
		payment of demand loan.			
	16	Cash	101	3 000 00	
		J. Emery, Capital	301		3 000 00
		Additional investment.			
	18	Utilities Expense	503	95 00	
		Cash	101		95 00
		Cheque No. 6 to Public			
		Utilities Commission.			
	20	Cash	101	3 400 00	
		Commissions Earned	401		3 400 00
		Invoices 00001, 00002, 00003,			
		and 00004.			
	30	J. Emery, Drawing	302	2 000 00	
		Cash	101		2 000 00
		Issued Cheque No. 7 to			
		owner for personal use.			
	31	Cash	101	3 400 00	
		Commissions Earned	401		3 400 00
		Invoices 00005 and 00006.			

must be equal to the total of all the credits. This total is not shown in a two-column journal but should be checked mentally before the next journal entry is done.

- Only *complete* journal entries are shown on a journal page. In other words, a transaction is not recorded unless there are enough lines to journalize all of it, including the brief explanation. This is for the reader's convenience: it is better to leave a few blank lines at the bottom of a page than to use two pages to record an entry.

GENERAL JOURNAL — Page 3

DATE		ACCOUNT TITLE AND EXPLANATION	POST. REF.	DEBIT	CREDIT
19-1					
Oct.	31	Salaries Expense	504	4 500 00	
		Cash	101		4 500 00
		Cheque No. 8 for $2,250 to Wendy Thomas; Cheque No. 9 for $2,250 to Jim Trafford.			
	31	Accts. Rec./Pat Rogers	103	2 000 00	
		Accts. Rec./R. Scobie	104	1 200 00	
		Accts. Rec./Shannon Development Co.	105	4 000 00	
		Commissions Earned	401		~~6 200 00~~ 7 200 00 W.T.
		Sales Invoices issued as follows: No. 00007 to Pat Rogers; No. 00008 to R. Scobie; No. 00009 to Shannon Development Co. Terms on all invoices: 30 days.			
	31	Advertising Expense	505	600 00	
		Accts. Pay./The City Record	203		600 00
		Advertising bill, terms given: net 30 days			

• Page 3 of the General Journal shows how a correction in a recorded amount is made. The clerk simply rules out the mistake with a single neat line and neatly inserts the correct amount in full above, with his or her initials. Thus, the reader can see the error, the correction, and who made the correction. An error is never erased.

Advantages of the Journal

From a study of the journal entries just illustrated, the following advantages to the use of a journal can be seen:

• The journal lists all the financial events by date. Thus, if you needed information about a transaction months or even years ago, all you would need is the date of the transaction to find it in the journal.

• Since the journal provides a record of all transactions in date order, you can compare the volume of transactions from day to day.

• Because the equality of debits and credits can be checked at a glance, errors can be discovered before the transactions are transferred to the ledger.

• The journal not only shows all numerical information about a transaction in one place, but also explains the transaction.

- The journal is a factual proof of financial events in case such proof should be required in a court of law. For example, if any source document should be lost or destroyed, a valuable proof of business transactions is available in the form of the journal record.

TOPIC 2 PROBLEMS

4-5 On a sheet of two-column General Journal paper, record the entries for the following transactions. Explain each entry. Use a second sheet of journal paper if necessary.

May 1 John Moore started his business, J. Moore Repair Service, with the following assets and liabilities: Cash, $1 075; Tools, $500; Accts. Pay./David Green, $150.
2 Cheque No. 01 was issued for tools costing $125.
3 Repair services were rendered for $445 to Elmer Good on 30 days' credit. Sales Invoice No. 1 was issued.
4 Repair services were rendered for $340 in cash on Sales Invoice No. 2. The cash was deposited into the firm's bank account.
5 Cheque No. 02 for $35 was issued to the Public Utilities Commission in payment of a utility bill received today.
7 Cheque No. 03 for $500 was issued to pay the monthly rent.
10 $1 000 was borrowed from the bank, to be repaid on a demand note.
11 An invoice was received for office equipment (a calculator) bought for $250 on credit from David Green.
12 $245 was received from Elmer Good on account. The customer's cheque was deposited into the bank account.
13 The $250 calculator was returned to David Green because it was the wrong model. A covering letter explaining the return was included.
14 An invoice was received for a new $350 printing calculator purchased on credit from David Green.
17 A memo was issued stating that John Moore had invested $757 additional cash in the business. The cash was deposited into the firm's bank account.
18 Sales Invoices No. 3, 4, and 5 were issued for repair services performed for a total of $1 400 cash. The total cash received was deposited into the firm's bank account.
19 Cheque No. 04 for $500 was issued to David Green in full payment of the account.
20 Cheque No. 05 for $45 was issued to Bell Canada in payment of the monthly telephone bill.

4-6 Refer to Problem 3-12. Use two-column General Journal paper to record the opening investment of Gerald O'Neil in his firm Spot-Free Cleaners. Then journalize the rest of the business transactions given for November. Explain each journal entry.

Key Check Figure
The owner's Drawing account is debited twice.

4-7 The Baird Real Estate Company, owned by Nora Baird, was involved in the following transactions in September and October. Journalize these transactions into a two-column General Journal. Explain each journal entry.

Sept. 1 Nora Baird went into business with an investment of $50 000 cash.
3 Land was bought for a future office site for $9 000 cash. Cheque No. 1 was issued.
5 A building was bought for $24 000; the cost included moving it to its new site on the recently acquired land. Cheque No. 2 for $10 000 was issued to Kay Properties Limited, the balance being payable within 90 days.
10 An unused part of the land was sold to Mary's Beauty Shop at cost, $4 000. Mary Clements, owner of the beauty shop, agreed to pay for the lot within three months.
14 Office equipment costing $1 800 was bought on credit from General Equipment Co.: two filing cabinets, a printing calculator, and an electric typewriter.
15 A filing cabinet costing $150 was returned to General Equipment Co.
20 A cheque for $500 was received from Mary's Beauty Shop in part payment of its account.
30 Cheque No. 3 for $1 000 was issued to General Equipment Co. on account.

Oct. 1 Cheque No. 4 for $120 was issued to pay for newspaper advertising.
6 $750 cash was earned on Sales Invoice No. 1 and collected as commission for selling a residence on behalf of a client. The cash was deposited into the firm's bank account.
16 Newspaper advertising was ordered from *The Daily News.* The bill totalled $90, giving 30 days' credit.
20 A commission was earned on Sales Invoice No. 2 by selling a home to Lynda Paulley. The commission of $1 130 was to be received in 60 days.
30 $900 cash was paid in salaries for October. Cheque No. 5 was issued.
30 A telephone bill totalling $48 was received from Manitoba Telephone Co., which gave 15 days' credit.
31 Nora Baird withdrew $600 cash on Cheque No. 6 for personal use.

Key Check Figure
Land is credited for $4 000 on September 10.

4-8 Journalize the transactions below. Select the account titles from the following list: Cash; Accts. Rec./A. Couse; Accts. Rec./B. Doan; Accts. Rec./C. Fairs; Accts. Rec./D. Good; Accts. Rec./E. Hey; Accts. Rec./J. Pool; Land; Building; Automobiles; Office Equipment; Bank Loan Payable; Accts. Pay./Ace Motors; Accts. Pay./The Daily News; Accts. Pay./Esso Oil Co.; Accts. Pay./Public Utilities Commission; Mortgage Payable; John Ross, Capital; John Ross, Drawing; Rental Revenue; Advertising Expense; Utilities Expense; Repairs Expense; Telephone Expense; Salaries Expense; Gasoline Expense. Provide a brief explanation for each entry. It may be necessary at times to begin a new journal page.

Oct. 1 Mr. John Ross deposited $200 000 cash into Ross Car Rental System's bank account.
2 Land was purchased on the company's behalf for $15 000; a building

on the land was also purchased, for $35 000. A cash payment of $20 000 was made on Cheque 001, and a 20-year mortgage note was signed for the balance.

Oct. 3 Twenty new automobiles were purchased at $5 200 each from Ace Motors. A cash down payment of $50 000 was made on Cheque 002, the balance to be paid in 60 days.

4 An automobile was sold to J. Pool, one of the company's employees, at cost. Pool paid $1 000 in cash and agreed to pay the balance within 30 days.

5 An automobile proved to be defective and was returned to Ace Motors. The amount due the car company was reduced by $5 200.

9 $2 000 cash was borrowed from the bank on a demand note.

10 A cash register and office desks were purchased for $2 800, payment being made on Cheque 003.

25 Ace Motors was paid $10 800 cash with Cheque 004.

26 An advertising bill totalling $250 was received, payable to *The Daily News* within 30 days.

27 The hydro bill from the Public Utilities Commission amounted to $75, to be paid before November 10.

28 Repair bills for servicing automobiles totalled $2 400, and were paid by issuing Cheque 005.

29 Gasoline charges totalled $4 000, payable in 30 days to Esso Oil Co.

30 Salaries amounting to $6 800 were paid to employees; Cheques 006, 007, and 008 were issued.

31 An accounting of $4 000 cash was obtained by renting cars to cash customers for the month. Invoices numbered 01, 02, 03, 04, and 05 were issued.

31 Revenue totalling $6 000 was earned in October through car rentals on a credit of 30 days to the following customers: Invoice 06, A. Couse, $1 000; Invoice 07, B. Doan, $1 400; Invoice 08, C. Fairs, $600; Invoice 09, D. Good, $1 500; Invoice 10, E. Hey, $1 500.

31 Mr. Ross withdrew $1 200 cash for personal use on Cheque 009.

31 Cheque 010 for $56 was issued to Bell Canada to pay the monthly telephone bill.

Key Check Figure Mortgage Payable is credited for $30 000 on October 2.

TOPIC 3 POSTING TRANSACTION DATA

A chronological record of business transactions in a journal has many uses; however, accounts that classify accounting information under one title are also needed, so that a set of financial statements can be prepared at the end of any accounting period. Also, during the accounting period, the owner-manager will want information such as:

- how much cash is available in the bank account
- how much is owing from customers on account
- how much is owing to the bank

- how much is owing to creditors on accounts payable
- how much revenue has been earned
- how many expenses have been incurred

While the journal will have a record of all transactions, it would be inefficient to search the journal for all entries affecting one account. Therefore, once the debits and credits have been recorded in the journal, accounting information must be transferred from the journal to the individual accounts in the ledger. The process is called posting.

Posting: transferring debits and credits from the journal to the ledger.

The Modern Ledger

You learned in Topic 2 that business transactions are analyzed and recorded in debit and credit form for the *first* time in the journal; hence, the journal was called the "book of original entry." Since these debits and credits are then transferred to the ledger, you could say the ledger is the "book of secondary entry"; but no further transfer of debits and credits is required and therefore the ledger is better called the *book of final entry.*

Ledger (1): the book of secondary or final entry.

In the past, the ledger in which accounts were kept was an actual bound book. This was the basis for the original definition of the ledger as the "book of accounts." Today, we still use the word *book* even though accounts may not be stored or filed in a book. Some small businesses still use a bound ledger, but the system of filing or storing the ledger accounts varies according to the method of data processing used by the business.

In the manual processing of ledger information, some businesses use loose-leaf forms printed on paper or cards. The accounts can then be kept in a loose-leaf binder, a filing cabinet, or ledger trays. A loose-leaf ledger offers great flexibility: the accounts can be rearranged if necessary, and the sheets or cards can be easily removed so that manual entries can be made.

Of course, the most modern method of processing a ledger is

Grand and Toy Ltd.

Loose-Leaf Binder

Grand and Toy Ltd.

Ledger Tray

Grand and Toy Ltd.

Open Tub File

by computer. The computer stores the account information on magnetic tape or disks. A modern ledger, then, is a group of accounts filed according to the method of data processing used by the business.

Ledger (2): a group or file of accounts; the book of final entry.

The Need for a Formal Ledger Account

When the idea of the *account* was introduced in Chapter 3, the "T-account" form was used to communicate the meaning of debits and credits, how to properly record increases and decreases in accounts, and how to calculate and show account balances.

In modern practice, the simple T-account does not exist. You will not see it used with any manual method or computer method of processing the ledger. Instead, forms are designed according to the type of information required from the account and the method of processing data used in the firm's accounting system. For example, an account form posted by hand will be quite different from one posted by computer. One type of account form that is in widespread use is the three-column form as shown below (three *money* columns).

Magnetic Disks: can store the entire ledger.

Analysis: The three money columns are:

- the *debit* column, which receives the debits recorded first in the debit column of the journal
- the *credit* column, which receives the credits recorded first in the credit column of the journal
- the *balance* column, which is used to record the balance remaining in the account immediately after the debit or credit has been posted from the journal to the ledger

Since the current balance can be shown after each posting, the

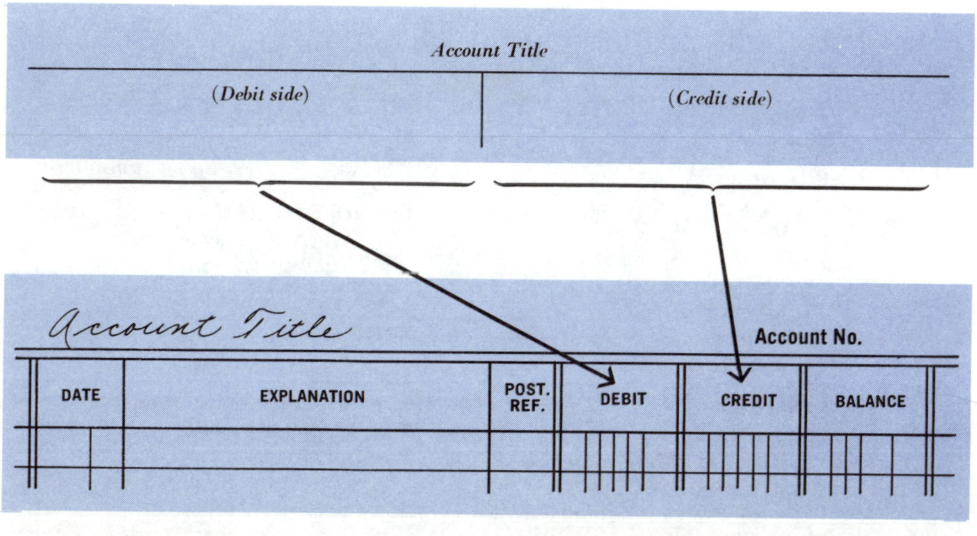

T-Account

Balance Ledger Form

Balance ledger form: a three-column account with a "running balance" column.

three-column form is more commonly called the balance ledger form.

The other columns in the balance ledger form are:

- *Date.* This column shows the date of the business transaction as recorded in the journal.
- *Explanation.* This shows a brief explanation when one is required. Often, the source document is identified or an unusual entry is explained. A brief description is not necessary for every entry in the ledger account, however, because the source of posting is usually given in the next column.
- *Post. Ref. (Posting Reference).* This column shows the name of the journal and the page from which the information has been transferred.

When the name of the account is shown, it appears at the left, above the date column. However, today, accounts are usually identified by a number code at the top right-hand side of the balance ledger form. These accounts are filed in the General Ledger.

General Ledger: the ledger filing those accounts which supply information for the preparation of financial statements.

Chart of Accounts

The number code given to each account identifies the account and indicates the order in which this account is listed in the General Ledger. Such a number plan is important because it enables financial statements to be prepared later from the numerical sequence of accounts in the General Ledger. The complete list of account titles and the number codes assigned to them is called the chart of accounts.

Chart of accounts; a numbering plan, listing all account titles in the order in which they appear in the accounting equation, and the numbers assigned to them.

Many number plans are in use today. The three-digit plan is common. A three-digit plan for J. Emery Real Estate is shown below.

Notice that the first digit of the code identifies the major class

J. Emery Real Estate
Chart of Accounts

ASSETS
101 Cash
103 Accts. Rec./Pat Rogers
104 Accts. Rec./R. Scobie
105 Accts. Rec./Shannon Development Co.
110 Automobile
112 Furniture
114 Office Equipment

LIABILITIES
201 Bank Loan Payable
202 Accts. Pay./Bell Furniture Co.
203 Accts. Pay./The City Record
204 Accts. Pay./Ryan Equipment Co.
205 Accts. Pay./Westown Motors Ltd.

OWNER'S EQUITY
301 J. Emery, Capital
302 J. Emery, Drawing

REVENUE
401 Commissions Earned

EXPENSES
501 Rent Expense
502 Telephone Expense
503 Utilities Expense
504 Salaries Expense
505 Advertising Expense

of accounts, while the second and third digits provide a further breakdown. For example, account numbers beginning with 1 indicate asset accounts; those beginning with 2 indicate liability accounts; and so on. The next two digits indicate the position of the account within its group. Most charts of accounts leave gaps in the sequence of numbers so that new accounts can be added later on. Notice also that an account is not usually assigned the first whole number. For example, Number 100 is omitted here so that it may be used for the heading *Assets* when a balance sheet is later prepared on a computer listing.

This numbering system makes it easy to locate an account quickly because it identifies it as an asset, liability, owner's equity, revenue, or expense account. Remember that accounts related to the balance sheet are given lower code numbers while accounts related to the income statement are given higher ones.

Chart of Accounts

Asset accounts:	*101 through 199*
Liability accounts:	*201 through 299*
Owner's Equity accounts:	*301 through 399*
Revenue accounts:	*401 through 499*
Expense accounts:	*501 through 599*

The Mechanics of Posting

The mechanics of posting data to the ledger will vary from business to business. It will naturally depend on the method of processing used: manual or computer. The manual method has been chosen for this chapter to simplify matters.

To see the mechanics of posting by hand, examine the illustrations that follow for J. Emery Real Estate's opening entry. The top diagram shows how the first account named in the opening entry is posted to the Cash account in the General Ledger.

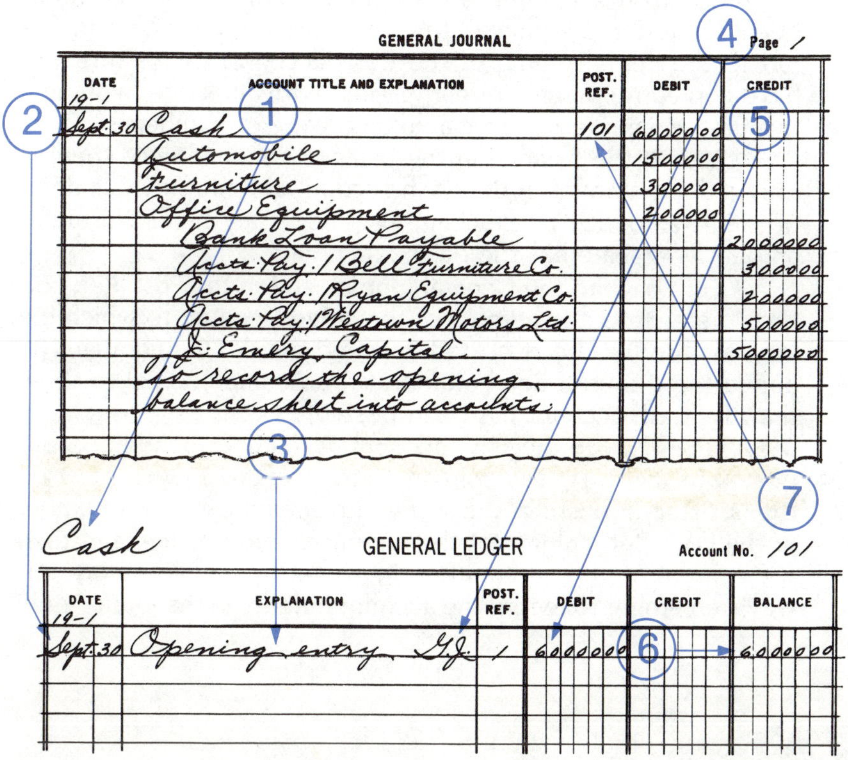

Posting may be done manually.

Posting may be done by computer.

Courtesy of IBM Corporation

Analysis: In posting the first line of the opening entry, these steps are followed:

Step 1: Locate the ledger account.

- For the first account recorded in the General Journal, locate the ledger account. Obviously, the Cash account would be easily found in the General Ledger.

Step 2: Record the date.

- Record the date in the date column. It should be exactly the same as the date recorded on each source document and journal record.
- Record the year, month, and day for the first entry only. Do not put down the month or the year for the rest of the entries unless a change is involved or the account must be continued on another page.

Step 3: Show an explanation, if needed.

- Enter an explanation of the entry, if one is needed to make the entry clear. In the Cash account shown, the words "Opening entry" are written as the explanation to distinguish the opening balance from the changes recorded during the month. In practice, however, the explanation column in the General Ledger is seldom used. The posting reference to the journal page from which the information was transferred allows a clerk or accountant to quickly locate a complete explanation of the transaction.

Step 4: Fill out the Post. Ref. column of the account.

- Just before the Post. Ref. column of the account, enter the letters *G.J.* (for *General Journal*). Then, enter the number of the journal page from which the entry is being posted. In the example, the source of posting reference is G.J. 1, referring to page 1 of the General Journal.

Step 5: Record the amount in the correct money column.

- Record the amount in the correct column. Since Cash has been debited in the journal, this debit amount must be transferred to the debit column of the Cash account. (Make sure you have copied the figure correctly. Most errors in ledger work in a manual system are due to careless copying of numbers.)

Step 6: Record the correct balance in the balance column.

- Record the balance in the balance column. Since there is only a debit amount in the Cash account and no previous debit or credit amounts, no calculation is necessary here. The debit amount is repeated as the balance amount.

Step 7: Complete the Post. Ref. column in the General Journal.

- Turn back to the General Journal, and in the Post. Ref. column there, enter the number of the ledger account to which the journal entry has been posted. In the example, the number 101 appears in the Post. Ref. column of the General Journal to show that the Cash account has been posted.

Important: Recording the accounting number of the account posted in the Post. Ref. column of the General Journal must be the last step in posting. Why? If you placed the account number in the Post. Ref. column of the journal before posting, and then were interrupted, you could easily forget to post the entry. Always remember to record the account number in the journal only after having posted and recorded the balance in the Balance column of the ledger account.

When you have finished posting the first account, locate the next one to be posted. If it involves a debit, repeat the foregoing procedure. If it involves a credit, apply the same procedure but with one change: record the amount in the credit column.

General Ledger Accounts after Posting

The illustrations that follow on the next few pages show how the accounts should look after the opening entries, and a selection of the other transactions, of J. Emery Real Estate have been posted from the General Journal to the General Ledger. (See pages 102-104.) Remember: account numbers are entered in the Post. Ref. column in the General Journal only *after* each entry is posted.

GENERAL JOURNAL Page 1

DATE		ACCOUNT TITLE AND EXPLANATION	POST. REF.	DEBIT	CREDIT
19-1					
Sept.	30	Cash	101	60 000 00	
		Automobile	110	15 000 00	
		Furniture	112	3 000 00	
		Office Equipment	114	2 000 00	
		Bank Loan Payable	201		20 000 00
		Accts. Pay./Bell Furniture Co.	202		3 000 00
		Accts. Pay./Ryan Equipment Co.	204		2 000 00
		Accts. Pay./Westown Motors Ltd.	205		5 000 00
		J. Emery, Capital	301		50 000 00
		To record the opening			
		balance sheet into accounts.			
Oct.	1	Furniture		1 000 00	
		Cash			1 000 00
		Cheque No. 1 to Enns Furniture			
		Ltd. for additional furniture.			
	31	Advertising Expense	505	600 00	
		Accts. Pay./The City Record	203		600 00
		Advertising bill; terms			
		given: net 30 days			

General Ledger

Cash → Account No. 101

DATE 19-1		EXPLANATION	POST. REF.	DEBIT	CREDIT	BALANCE
Sept.	30	Opening entry	G.J. 1	6000000		6000000
Oct.	1		G.J. 1		100000	5900000
	5		G.J. 1		500000	5400000
	11		G.J. 1		4000	5396000
	12		G.J. 2		60000	5336000
	15		G.J. 2		400000	4936000
	16		G.J. 2	300000		5236000
	18		G.J. 2		9500	5226500
	20		G.J. 2	340000		5566500
	30		G.J. 2		200000	5366500
	31		G.J. 2	340000		5706500
	31		G.J. 3		450000	5256500

Accts. Rec. / Pat Rogers Account No. 103

DATE 19-1		EXPLANATION	POST. REF.	DEBIT	CREDIT	BALANCE
Oct.	31	Invoice 00007	G.J. 3	200000		200000

Accts. Rec. / R. Scobie Account No. 104

DATE 19-1		EXPLANATION	POST. REF.	DEBIT	CREDIT	BALANCE
Oct.	31	Invoice 00008	G.J. 3	120000		120000

Bank Loan Payable Account No. 201

DATE 19-1		EXPLANATION	POST. REF.	DEBIT	CREDIT	BALANCE
Sept.	30	Opening entry	G.J. 1		2000000	2000000
Oct.	15		G.J. 2	400000		1600000

Accts. Pay. / Ryan Equipment Co. — Account No. 204

DATE 19-1		EXPLANATION	POST. REF.	DEBIT	CREDIT	BALANCE
Sept.	30	Opening entry	G.J. 1		200000	200000
Oct.	3		G.J. 1		120000	320000
	4		G.J. 1	20000		300000

Accts. Pay. / Westown Motors Ltd. — Account No. 205

DATE 19-1		EXPLANATION	POST. REF.	DEBIT	CREDIT	BALANCE
Sept.	30	Opening entry	G.J. 1		500000	500000
Oct.	5		G.J. 1	500000		0

J. Emery, Capital — Account No. 301

DATE 19-1		EXPLANATION	POST. REF.	DEBIT	CREDIT	BALANCE
Sept.	30	Opening entry	G.J. 1		5000000	5000000
Oct.	16		G.J. 2		300000	5300000

J. Emery, Drawing — Account No. 302

DATE 19-1		EXPLANATION	POST. REF.	DEBIT	CREDIT	BALANCE
Oct.	30		G.J. 2	200000		200000

Commissions Earned — Account No. 401

DATE 19-1		EXPLANATION	POST. REF.	DEBIT	CREDIT	BALANCE
Oct.	20		G.J. 2		340000	340000
	31		G.J. 2		340000	680000
	31		G.J. 3		720000	1400000

Rent Expense — Account No. 501

Date 19-1		Explanation	Post. Ref.	Debit	Credit	Balance
Oct.	12	G.J.	2	600 00		600 00

Important: Although the accounts illustrated on the previous pages show several accounts on one page, in actual practice each account would be shown on a separate sheet or card, as illustrated below.

GENERAL LEDGER

Account Name *J. Emery, Capital* — Account No. *301*

Date 19-1		Explanation	Post. Ref.	Debit	Credit	Balance
Sept.	30	Opening Entry G.J.	1		50 000 00	50 000 00
Oct.	16	G.J.	2		3000 00	53 000 00

Calculating a New Balance

From the foregoing it would seem that it is simple to calculate the current balance of an account in a balance ledger form. Let us check this by calculating the new balances in three accounts.

In the Cash account shown on page 102, Account No. 101, the opening entry on September 30 shows a debit balance of $60 000. This balance does not need to be identified as a debit balance because (as you learned from the accounting equation) assets normally have debit balances.

The second posting, on October 1, shows a credit of $1 000 from issuing a cheque to buy additional furniture. Since this cheque decreases the amount of cash, the account is credited, and the new balance is calculated at $59 000. This balance is understood to be a debit, because all assets are found on the debit (left) side of the accounting equation.

On October 5, J. Emery Real Estate issued Cheque No. 2 in payment of the account payable to Westown Motors Ltd. Since this payment decreases the amount of cash, the account is credited, and the balance is now calculated at $54 000 ($59 000 − $5 000).

Similar decreases to the Cash account appear on October 11, 12, and 15. For each of these postings, the Cash account is *credited*. The balance after posting the decrease on October 15 will be $49 360 ($53 360 − $4 000).

On October 16, however, the Cash account shows a *debit* posting of $3 000. This results in an increase to the Cash account. The new balance will now be $52 360 ($49 360 + $3 000). Further debits will be added to the previous balance and further credits will be subtracted, so that the current balance is always shown in the account.

Look at Account No. 205 on p. 103, the Accts. Pay./Westown Motors Ltd. liability account. The first entry (Sept. 30) shows the opening entry with a credit balance. This balance need not be identified as a credit balance because liabilities normally have credit balances in the accounting equation, as do the owner's equity elements Capital and Revenue.

The second entry (October 5) shows a debit of $5 000 resulting from a cheque being issued to this creditor. Since this is a liability account and the debit must show a decrease, the new balance is calculated by subtracting the debit from the current (credit) balance. This calculation gives a "zero balance" or "no balance," because the previous $5 000 credit balance is wiped out by the equal debit entry. The "no balance" sign is written in the balance column.

Now look at Account No. 401, Commissions Earned. This is a revenue account and will normally have a credit balance, because revenue causes an increase to *OE* in the accounting equation. Of course, each new credit entry will be added to the balance because commissions earned result in increases to owner's equity. For the Commissions Earned account, and for all revenue accounts, every balance is understood as a CR. balance.

The Accounting Cycle So Far

You have now been introduced to the first three steps in the accounting cycle:

- *Step 1:* originating the transaction data
- *Step 2:* journalizing the transaction data
- *Step 3:* posting the transaction data

TOPIC 3 PROBLEMS

4-9 Refer to Problem 4-5 in Topic 2. Assume that the following general ledger accounts have been identified from the chart of accounts for John Moore's business: Cash, 101; Accts. Rec./Elmer Good, 103; Tools, 110; Equipment, 112; Bank Loan Payable, 201; Accts. Pay./David Green, 202; John Moore, Capital, 301; Repair Service Revenue, 401; Utilities Expense, 501; Rent Expense, 502; Telephone Expense, 503.

Key Check Figure Cash Account Balance = $3 612

Post the journal entries made in Problem 4-5 of this chapter to the General Ledger. *Note:* Save the journal and the ledger for use in the final topic of this chapter.

4-10 Refer to Problem 4-6 in Topic 2. Assume that the following general ledger accounts have been identified from the chart of accounts for Gerald O'Neil's Spot-Free Cleaners: Cash, 101; Government of Canada Bonds, 102; Accts. Rec./Eastview Garage, 103; Accts. Rec./S. Harvey, 104; Equipment, 110; Store Fixtures, 112; Truck, 114; Bank Loan Payable, 201; Accts. Pay./The Daily News, 202; Accts. Pay./King Furniture Co., 203; Accts. Pay./Swan's Auto, 204; Gerald O'Neil, Capital, 301; Gerald O'Neil, Drawing, 302; Dry Cleaning Revenue, 401; Interest Earned on Government Bonds, 402; Rent Expense, 501; Telephone Expense, 502; Utilities Expense, 503; Advertising Expense, 504; Salaries Expense, 505; Bank Interest Expense, 510.

Key Check Figure Cash Account Balance = $24 667

Post the journal entries made in Problem 4-6 to the General Ledger. *Note:* Save the journal and the ledger for use in the final topic of this chapter.

4-11 Refer to the General Journal you made up for the Baird Real Estate Company in Problem 4-7.

a Go through all the entries made in the journal for Problem 4-7 and set up a chart of accounts for Nora Baird's business. Follow the plan in the chart illustrated on page 99.

b Using your chart, set up a General Ledger for the Baird Real Estate Company.

c Post the journal entries made in Problem 4-7 to the General Ledger. *Note:* Save the journal and the ledger for use in the final topic of this chapter.

Key Check Figure Cash Account Balance = $29 630

4-12 Refer to the General Journal you made up for the Ross Car Rental System in Problem 4-8.

a Go through all entries made in the journal and set up a chart of accounts for John Ross's business. Follow the plan in the chart illustrated on page 99.

b Using your chart, set up a General Ledger for the Ross Car Rental System.

c Post the journal entries made in Problem 4-8 to the General Ledger. *Note:* Save the journal and the ledger for use in the final topic of this chapter.

Key Check Figure Cash Account Balance = $112 944

TOPIC 4 PREPARING ACCOUNTING PROOFS

Topics 1, 2, and 3 of this chapter introduced the first three steps of the accounting cycle as follows:

- *Step 1:* originating transaction data
- *Step 2:* journalizing — analyzing transactions and recording the debits and credits from those transactions in a book of original entry
- *Step 3:* posting — transferring debits and credits from the journal to the ledger

After the third step, financial statements can be prepared from the accounts filed in the General Ledger. Before such statements are prepared, however, accountants recommend the practice of taking a number of accounting *proofs* — procedures to ensure (1) that the data recorded in the journal and the ledger are accurate and (2) that all transactions have been accounted for.

Courtesy of Olivetti Canada Ltd.

Preparing the Journal Proof

The double entry in the journal is a sound checking system in itself. For each transaction recorded in the General Journal, equal amounts are recorded in the debit column and the credit column. This important rule of "debit equals credit" makes it possible to prove the journal in two ways:

- by routinely totalling each column on a journal page *before* any posting is done
- by totalling the money columns *before* the next page in the journal is used

A journal proof is prepared either manually or through a computer program. The computer method is presented in Chapter 18; a short description of the preparation of a journal proof by hand is given below.

In the manual method, an adding machine or electronic

Courtesy of Monroe, the Calculator Company

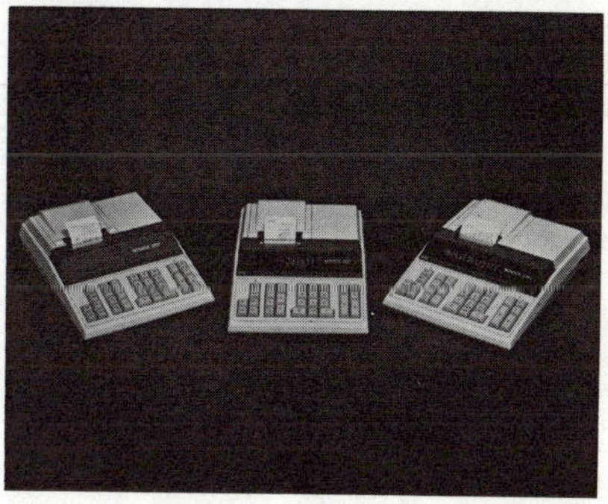

calculator with a tape printer is often used to perform the addition. A printing machine is preferred because it permits checking the information inputted at any time. In the illustration below, the tape shows the addition of the debit and credit columns on page 1 of the General Journal for J. Emery Real Estate.

Journal Proof.

GENERAL JOURNAL Page 1

DATE		ACCOUNT TITLE AND EXPLANATION	POST. REF.	DEBIT	CREDIT
19-1					
Sept.	30	Cash		6000000	
		Automobile		1500000	
		Furniture		300000	
		Office Equipment		200000	
		Bank Loan Payable			2000000
		Accts. Pay./Bell Furniture Co.			300000
		Accts. Pay./Ryan Equipment Co.			200000
		Accts. Pay./Westown Motors Ltd.			500000
		J. Emery, Capital			5000000
		To record the opening			
		balance sheet into accounts.			
Oct.	1	Furniture		100000	
		Cash			100000
		Cheque No. 1 to Enns Furniture			
		Ltd. for additional furniture.			
	3	Office Equipment		120000	
		Accts. Pay./Ryan Equipment Co.			120000
		2 calculators and 1 typewriter			
		on 60 days' credit.			
	4	Accts. Pay./Ryan Equipment Co.		20000	
		Office Equipment			20000
		Returned 1 calculator received			
		in damaged condition.			
	5	Accts. Pay./Westown Motors Ltd.		500000	
		Cash			500000
		Cheque No. 2 on account.			
	11	Telephone Expense		4000	
		Cash			4000
		Cheque No. 3 to Bell Canada			

Journal Proof
Page 1
Oct. 11, 19-1

```
      0.00 T

 60 000.00 + ✓
 15 000.00 + ✓
  3 000.00 + ✓
  2 000.00 + ✓
  1 000.00 + ✓
  1 200.00 + ✓
    200.00 + ✓
  5 000.00 + ✓
     40.00 + ✓
 87 440.00 T

 20 000.00 + ✓
  3 000.00 + ✓
  2 000.00 + ✓
  5 000.00 + ✓
 50 000.00 + ✓
  1 000.00 + ✓
  1 200.00 + ✓
    200.00 + ✓
  5 000.00 + ✓
     40.00 + ✓
 87 440.00 T
```

If the totals of the debit and the credit columns agree, this is reasonable mathematical proof that the figures in the journal are accurate. This proof is commonly known as the journal proof. Posting can now be done to the ledger, and page 2 of the journal can be set up without fear that an error may exist on the previous page.

Journal proof: what an accountant has when the total of the debit column is equal to the total of the credit column on a journal page.

As you can see from the illustration, when these machine tapes are saved and kept with the accounting records, a reference notation is made at the top. Sometimes, the tapes are attached to the documents being proved.

Important warning: It is considered good accounting practice to double-check the figures against the source document *before* recording the next transaction.

Proving Individual Account Balances

Instead of rechecking each horizontal calculation throughout the account, you can easily check the final balance on rough working paper or with the aid of an adding machine.

If you use the "rough paper" approach, first add the debits in the debit column. Show a total on the working paper. Do the same with the credits in the credit column. Then subtract the total credits from the total debits. Your answer should be the same as the final balance in the account. For example, the final balance of the Cash account in J. Emery Real Estate's General Ledger is a debit of $52 565 because the total credits subtracted from the total debits proves this final balance to be correct. See illustration below.

Cash   Account No. 101

DATE 19-1		EXPLANATION	POST. REF.	DEBIT	CREDIT	BALANCE	
Sept.	30	Opening entry	G.J. 1	60000 00		60000 00	
Oct.	1		G.J. 1		1000 00	59000 00	
	5		G.J. 1		5000 00	54000 00	
	11		G.J. 1		40 00	53960 00	
	12		G.J. 2		600 00	53360 00	
	15		G.J. 2		4000 00	49360 00	
	16		G.J. 2	3000 00		52360 00	
	18		G.J. 2		95 00	52265 00	
	20		G.J. 2	3400 00		55665 00	
	30		G.J. 2		2000 00	53665 00	
	31		G.J. 2	3400 00		57065 00	
	31		G.J. 3		4500 00	52565 00	DR.

Total debits	$69 800	
Total credits	-17 235	
Cash balance	$52 565	DR.

Once you have checked and proved the final balance in the account, it is useful to indicate it as a DR. or a CR. balance. Of course, the final balance in a Cash account will be a DR. balance, as illustrated.

Acct. No. 101
Oct. 31, 19-1

```
      0.00 T

60 000.00 +
 3 000.00 +
 3 400.00 +
 3 400.00 +
 1 000.00 -
 5 000.00 -
     40.00 -
    600.00 -
 4 000.00 -
     95.00 -
 2 000.00 -
 4 500.00 -
52 565.00 T
```

Here are the steps for checking the same Cash account if you use an adding machine or calculator tape.

- Clear the machine of any previous figures. Then enter each *debit* figure with the *plus* (+) bar.
- Next, enter each *credit* figure with the *minus* (—) bar.
- Take a total.

If the figures have been entered correctly, the total should verify the final balance in the account. In the case of this Cash account, the margin illustration gives the final result in the line "52 565.00 T."

Here are the steps for checking an account which must have a final CR. balance. In J. Emery Real Estate's General Ledger, Account No. 204 is a liability account. The final balance is checked on an adding machine or calculator tape as illustrated below.

- Clear the machine of any previous figures. Then enter each *debit* figure with the *plus* (+) bar.
- Next, enter each *credit* figure with the *minus* (—) bar.

After the last credit figure is entered, take a total. For a liability account, the final total should be interpreted as a CR. balance. Depending on the machine used, you will find the balance either printed in red with a star or the letters CR. beside it, or printed in black with a minus sign.

It is useful to show the final balance as being a DR. or CR. balance in the account, but this should be done only after you have proved its accuracy. In the case of Account No. 204, the final balance on the proof will be shown as $3 000 CR.

Accts. Pay./Ryan Equipment Co. — Account No. 204

DATE		EXPLANATION	POST. REF.	DEBIT	CREDIT	BALANCE
19-1						
Sept.	30	Opening entry	G.J. 1		2 000 00	2 000 00
Oct.	3		G.J. 1		1 200 00	3 200 00
	4		G.J. 1	200 00		3 000 00 cr.

Acct. No. 204
Oct. 31 19-1

```
    0.00 T

  200.00 +
2 000.00 -
1 200.00 -
3 000.00 T
```

You should now have little difficulty in determining whether an account has a final debit or credit balance. Chapter 3 gave you three rules for increasing and decreasing accounts. The third is well worth repeating.

The balance of an account will normally appear on the side on which it is shown in the accounting equation.

Applying this to the classes of accounts introduced in the chart of accounts, you can now show this summary:

Class of Account	*Type of Final Balance Normally Shown*
Asset	DR., because assets are found on the left side of the accounting equation
Liability	CR., because liabilities are found on the right side of the accounting equation
Owner's Equity elements:	
Capital	CR., because the owner's investment increases *OE* in the accounting equation
Drawing	DR., because owner's drawings decrease *OE* in the accounting equation
Revenue	CR., because revenue accounts increase *OE* in the accounting equation
Expense	DR., because expense accounts decrease *OE* in the accounting equation

Proving the Ledger

If the debits and credits are posted correctly to the accounts, the ledger must balance, not only within the ledger accounts but overall.

Actually, you have already learned how to "prove the ledger." In Chapter 3, after completing the T-account ledger, you were asked to do a summary to prove that the accounting equation in total is in balance within the T-account ledger. This summary showed that the total of the debit balances agreed with the total of the credit balances of accounts within the ledger. Such a summary is known as a *trial balance.*

Examine the illustration on the next page.

Formal Trial Balance: a list or summary of the balances of accounts in a ledger as at a certain date.

J. Emery Real Estate
Trial Balance
October 31, 19-1

ACCOUNT TITLE	ACCT. NO.	DEBIT	CREDIT
Cash	101	52 565 00	
Accts. Rec./Pat Rogers	103	2 000 00	
Accts. Rec./R. Scobie	104	1 200 00	
Accts. Rec./Shannon Development Co.	105	4 000 00	
Automobile	110	15 000 00	
Furniture	112	4 000 00	
Office Equipment	114	3 000 00	
Bank Loan Payable	201		16 000 00
Accts. Pay./Bell Furniture Co.	202		3 000 00
Accts. Pay./The City Press	203		600 00
Accts. Pay./Ryan Equipment Co.	204		3 000 00
J. Emery, Capital	301		53 000 00
J. Emery, Drawing	302	2 000 00	
Commissions Earned	401		14 000 00
Rent Expense	501	600 00	
Telephone Expense	502	40 00	
Utilities Expense	503	95 00	
Salaries Expense	504	4 500 00	
Advertising Expense	505	600 00	
		89 600 00	89 600 00

Preparing the Formal Trial Balance

Study these points as you refer to the illustration:

- Check the accuracy of the final balance reported in each account in the ledger, and show whether it is a debit or a credit balance by placing the letters DR. or CR. after it.
- To begin the trial balance, centre a three-line heading as shown. The heading answers three questions: *who* (the name of the business); *what* (the name of the accounting proof); and *when* (the date as of which the summary is prepared).
- Deal with the accounts in the order in which they are filed in the General Ledger. List only accounts that have a (non-zero) balance; accounts without a balance do not need to be listed in the trial balance. Write the account title and the account number in their respective columns, and the account balance in the appropriate money column.
- After all the account balances have been entered, draw a single line across both money columns and total the columns. If

you have journalized and posted correctly, the total debit balances will equal the total credit balances. If this happens, the trial balance is then completed by drawing a double line across both money columns and the account number column.

You may wonder what the adjective *trial* means. In simple terms, you are putting the General Ledger "on trial" for accuracy. If $A = L + OE$, then this equation as it appears in the ledger must balance.

You may also be wondering: If all expense account balances and owner's drawing account balances are shown on the right side of the accounting equation, why are they listed with debit balances? The answer is that since all accounts have only two sides, debit and credit (the balance column is their result), any account causing a decrease to *OE* must be shown on the side opposite to that on which *OE* is found in the accounting equation. So when you list a debit balance for any expense account or for the owner's drawing account, you are recognizing that these accounts *decrease* owner's equity.

On the other hand, the owner's capital account and all revenue account balances *increase* owner's equity. Since all increases to *OE* are shown on the side on which *OE* is found in the equation, these account balances are always listed in the credit column of the trial balance.

Trial Balance
Zero Proof

Preparing an Informal Trial Balance

When a formal trial balance is not required, an adding-listing machine may be used. To save time, the accounts with a balance can be entered directly onto the machine tape from the ledger. Here are the main procedures for a quick trial balance.

- Check the accuracy of the balance in each account and indicate whether it is a debit or a credit. (Place a large "DR." or "CR." to the right of the final balance.)
- Clear the machine with the "Total" key.
- Listing all accounts in account-number order, enter all debit balances on the machine with the plus (+) key and all credit balances with the minus (−) key.
- When the last balance has been listed, depress the "Total" key to print the result.

If the result is a zero, you have a zero proof and the ledger is in balance — total debits equal total credits.

Trial Balance
Zero Proof
Oct. 31, 19–1

0.00 T
52 565.00 +
2 000.00 +
1 200.00 +
4 000.00 +
15 000.00 +
4 000.00 +
3 000.00 +
16 000.00 −
3 000.00 −
600.00 −
3 000.00 −
53 000.00 −
2 000.00 +
14 000.00 −
600.00 +
40.00 +
95.00 +
4 500.00 +
600.00 +
0.00 T

Informal Trial Balance

Zero proof: what an accountant has when deducting all of the credit balances from all of the debit balances gives a zero result.

A	=	*L*	+	*C*	+	*R*	−	*E*	−	*D*
$81 765	=	*$22 600*	+	*$53 000*	+	*$14 000*	−	*$5 835*	−	*$2 000*
$81 765	=	*$81 765*								

If the result is not zero an error has been made in the ledger and the tape can be used to find it. (Of course, it may happen that an error has been made in producing the zero proof.)

Uses of the Trial Balance

A trial balance is useful because:

- It proves the equality of the total debits and credits in the General Ledger.
- It provides a listing of all the account balances, giving a brief picture of every account that has a balance in the ledger.
- It may be used as a basis for the preparation of financial statements.

The Accounting Cycle So Far

Although each of the accounting proofs presented in this topic is important, the taking of the trial balance is considered the key checkpoint before any financial statements are prepared.

Here are the steps in the accounting cycle we have covered so far:

- *Step 1:* originating the transaction data (originating transactions on source documents)
- *Step 2:* journalizing (analyzing and recording transactions from source documents to a book of original entry)
- *Step 3:* posting (transferring debit and credit information from the journal to the ledger)
- *Step 4:* preparing a trial balance

Bookkeeping Defined

Bookkeeping: the process of journalizing business transactions, posting transactions to ledger accounts, and proving the ledger to be in balance.

With the completion of the trial balance stage of the accounting cycle, you can now learn the meaning of the term bookkeeping.

In simple terms, bookkeeping is journalizing, posting, and preparing the trial balance. It thus consists of steps 2, 3, and 4 of the accounting cycle.

BOOKKEEPER

We have an immediate opening for an experienced bookeeper.

This person will be capable of:

—Maintaining a complete set of books up to and including the general ledger trial balance;
—Controlling and balancing subsidiary ledgers;
—Reconciling bank accounts;
—Maintaining payroll records, being knowledgable of current government regulations relevant thereto.

Applications must be in writing and should include a work resume for the past 5 years and salary history, together with whatever personal information the applicant may wish to provide.

All applications will be kept in strict confidence.

THE CONTROLLER,

LONDON FURNITURE CO. LTD.,

655 DUNDAS STREET

Formerly, nearly everyone who worked with financial records was called a bookkeeper. (Records were actually kept in book form for many years.) As financial record-keeping grew in importance and stature, the term *accountant* came into popular usage.

Today, the title "accountant" is usually reserved for those who have the responsibility of establishing and maintaining an entire accounting system, interpreting the results of recorded data to management, and assisting in management decisions. The title "bookkeeper" is used for those who work under an accountant, usually recording transactions, posting to the ledger, and providing mathematical checks of documents, journals, account balances, and the ledger.

LONDON HOUSING AUTHORITY

requires an

Accountant

SALARY RANGE $10,400 TO $12,200

In the capacity of accountant you will be responsible for the implementation and operation of a recognized accounting system, the receipt and deposit of cash disbursements, balancing of accounts and preparation of accounting statements.

You will co-ordinate and prepare budget submissions, be responsible for training and efficiency of accounting staff and provide financial advice to management.

QUALIFICATIONS—The candidate selected will preferably be a member of a recognized accounting association with several years of progressive experience. Preference will be given to a graduate from a university of recognized standing.

Submit detailed resume outlining educational and business background to:

THE OPERATIONS MANAGER

LONDON HOUSING AUTHORITY

291 King St.

LONDON, Ont.

CONSTRUCTION COMPANY—WEST TORONTO

REQUIRES

ACCOUNTS PAYABLE CLERK

For Accounts Payable up to and including trial balance on McBee system, and varied duties. Typing a necessity. Please submit the following: personal resume, education, experience, references, previous employment and salary.

BOX 1802, THE GLOBE

ACCOUNTS RECEIVABLE CLERK

REQUIRED

The maintenance of A/R subsidiary ledger with approx. 100 active accounts. Call for interview.

In large organizations, especially where computers are now used to process accounting data, the term "bookkeeper" is gradually disappearing and "accounting clerk" is taking its place. In small businesses the person in charge of financial records is still usually called a bookkeeper, even though he or she may be performing the duties of an accounting clerk.

In general, the following distinction can be made. The accountant holds a professional position, and the bookkeeper or accounting clerk performs clerical duties under the supervision of an accountant.

TOPIC 4 PROBLEMS

4-13 Refer to the journal you made up for Problem 4-5 and the ledger for Problem 4-9 (J. Moore Repair Service).

a Make up a journal proof for each page of the General Journal used to solve Problem 4-5. Use separate working paper or use a tape if you have access to an adding machine or a calculator.

b Check the accuracy of the final balance for each account in the General Ledger in Problem 4-9. Then print DR. or CR. in the General Ledger after each final balance.

c Prepare a formal trial balance of the General Ledger done for Problem 4-9. Use May 20 as the date.

Key Check Figure Trial Balance Total = $5 367

d If you have access to an adding machine or tape calculator, prepare a zero proof or quick trial balance of the General Ledger you prepared in Problem 4-9.

4-14 Refer to the General Journal you made up for Problem 4-8 and the General Ledger for Problem 4-12 (Ross Car Rental System).

a Make up a journal proof for each page of the General Journal used to solve Problem 4-8. Use separate working paper or use a tape.

b Check the accuracy of the final balance for each account in the General Ledger in Problem 4-12. Then print DR. or CR. in the General Ledger after each balance.

c Prepare a formal trial balance of the General Ledger done for Problem 4-12.

Key Check Figure Trial Balance Total = $284 325

d If you have access to an adding machine or tape calculator, prepare a zero proof of the General Ledger you prepared in Problem 4-12.

4-15 The following accounts and their balances have been taken from the General Ledger of a dental business established under the name Ken Hardy, D.D.S. Assume that all the balances have been checked for accuracy as at December 31, the firm's year-end. Also assume that all account balances are *normal* — that they are credits if on the right side of the equation and debits if on the left.

Accts. Pay./Mardan Systems	$ 230	Accts. Rec./J. Burtch	$ 300
Cash	2 460	Accts. Pay./AB Dental Co.	265
Accts. Rec./S. Jones	300	Bank Loan Payable	5 600
Mortgage Payable	20 000	Land	10 500
Dental Equipment	5 700	Office Equipment	2 880
Ken Hardy, Capital	48 000	Ken Hardy, Drawing	25 410
Professional Fees Earned	93 440	Building Repairs Expense	470
Dental Supplies Expense	9 350	Electricity Expense	930
Salaries Expense	41 985	Telephone Expense	400
Mortgage Interest Expense	1 850	Bank Interest Expense	110
Building	64 000	Laundry Expense	890

a Assign appropriate number codes to the individual accounts, following the chart of accounts on page 99. (In other words, make up a chart.)

b Prepare a formal trial balance.

Key Check Figure Trial Balance Total = $167 535

c Write the balances of the accounts listed in your trial balance under the elements of the expanded accounting equation, $A = L + C + R - E - D$. Then prove that Ken Hardy's General Ledger balances.

4-16 The following accounts and codes are used for the Halifax Moving Company: 101 Cash; 102 Accts. Rec./A. Long; 103 Accts. Rec./Mary Wallace;

110 Land; 112 Building; 114 Trucks; 116 Office Equipment; 201 Bank Loan Payable; 202 Accts. Pay./Central Motors; 301 A. MacPherson, Capital; 302 A. MacPherson, Drawing; 401 Moving Fees Earned; 501 Salaries Expense; 502 Truck Repairs Expense; 503 Telephone Expense. During September, the following transactions occurred:

Sept. 1 A. MacPherson deposited $150 000 cash into a bank account in the name of the Halifax Moving Company.
2 Land was purchased for $27 000 and a building for $42 000 by issuing a cheque for the total.
3 Four trucks were purchased from Central Motors at a cost of $15 000 each. A cheque was issued for $25 000 as a down payment, the balance to be paid by November 12.
6 Furniture was moved from Toronto to Halifax for Mr. and Mrs. A. Long for $1 800. $400 in cash was collected, the balance to be paid within 30 days.
7 Office equipment was purchased for $5 000 cash.
9 Furniture was moved from Halifax to Regina for Mary Wallace for $3 100. $500 cash was collected, the balance to be paid within 30 days.
15 $3 700 in salaries was paid to drivers for the first half of the month.
23 Furniture was moved for various clients for a total of $6 500. Cash was collected in full.
30 $3 495 in salaries was paid to drivers for the second half of September. Appropriate cheques were issued.
30 A bill for $150 was received from Central Motors for repair work on trucks during September. The terms of credit given were 30 days.
30 $1 000 in cash was borrowed from the Royal Bank on a demand note.
30 A cheque for $45 was issued to pay the monthly telephone bill.
30 A. MacPherson withdrew $600 cash for personal use.

a Journalize the above transactions using only the account titles used by the company.

b Open a General Ledger for the accounts. Post the journal entries from the General Journal to the General Ledger.

c Check the accuracy of the final balance in each account in the General Ledger. Identify the final balance by placing DR. or CR. immediately after the final balance.

d Prepare a formal trial balance.

e If you have access to an adding machine or tape calculator, prepare a zero proof of the General Ledger.

f Write the balances of accounts listed in your formal trial balance under the elements of the expanded accounting equation: $A = L + C + R - E - D$. Then prove that the company's General Ledger balances.

Key Check Figure
Trial Balance Total = $197 550

Case Study 4

The manager for the Rockwood Village Playhouse is anxious to prepare a set of financial statements. However, before these statements are prepared, the manager asks a neighbour of yours to check the bookkeeping records.

Your neighbour finds the journal pages to be in order. But the general ledger accounts appear to be in bad shape. None of the accounts has a number and the owner's capital and drawing accounts are missing.

The best your neighbour can do to help is to supply the summary of account balances as at November 30. But your friend tells you that the owner withdrew cash totalling $200 for personal use on November 30 and that the withdrawal was not recorded in the journal.

Summary of Account Balances

Accts. Pay./G. Aziz	$ 2 685	Mortgage Payable	12 450
Accts. Rec./F. Goodman	1 412	Office Equipment	2 725
Admissions Revenue	3 850	Salaries Expense	2 875
Advertising Expense	1 150	Stage Equipment	6 000
Bank Loan Payable	2 000	City Taxes Payable	610
Building	35 050	Utilities Expense	175
Cash	2 200	Helen Zimmerman, Capital	(file missing)
Land	18 000	Helen Zimmerman, Drawing	(file missing)
Lighting Equipment	5 600		

a Calculate the balance of the two accounts whose balance is unknown.

b Prepare a formal trial balance for the Rockwood Village Playhouse at November 30.

CHAPTER 5

PREPARING FINANCIAL STATEMENTS

Chapter 4 introduced the accounting cycle, giving the first four steps: (1) originating transaction data through the creation of source documents; (2) journalizing source documents; (3) posting data to the ledger; (4) preparing a trial balance. These steps lead to one goal — to prepare a set of financial statements.

When a trial balance is correct and contains only a short list of General Ledger accounts, a set of financial statements can easily be prepared. However, many accountants first prepare a working paper called the *worksheet.*

This chapter covers the next two steps of the accounting cycle.

- Topic 1 deals with step 5, preparing the worksheet.
- Topic 2 deals with step 6, preparing financial statements from the worksheet.
- Topic 3 deals with what financial statements say and what they do not say, and contains a review of the basic accounting principles presented up to that point.

TOPIC 1 THE SIX-COLUMN WORKSHEET

A *worksheet* is a working paper used to summarize all the information needed to prepare an accurate set of financial statements. It is *not* regarded as part of the permanent accounting records of the business. It is only a temporary record. As such, it is usually prepared (neatly) in pencil, so that errors may be easily corrected.

The worksheet can contain six or more money columns. The six-column type will be explained in this chapter, because it is the easiest to learn. A six-column worksheet is shown on page 120.

Analysis: Notice the following about the worksheet for J. Emery Real Estate:

- In the *heading,* Line 1 shows the name of the firm, Line 2 the name of this working paper, and Line 3 the date completing the accounting period.

J. Emery Real Estate
Worksheet
For the Month Ended October 31, 19-1

ACCOUNT TITLE	ACCT. NO.	TRIAL BALANCE		INCOME STATEMENT		BALANCE SHEET	
		DEBIT	CREDIT	DEBIT	CREDIT	DEBIT	CREDIT
Cash	101	52 565 00					
Accts. Rec./Pat Rogers	103	2 000 00					
Accts. Rec./R. Scobie	104	1 200 00					
Accts. Rec./Shannon Dev. Co.	105	4 000 00					
Automobile	110	15 000 00					
Furniture	112	4 000 00					
Office Equipment	114	3 000 00					
Bank Loan Payable	201		16 000 00				
Accts. Pay./Bell Furn. Co.	202		3 000 00				
Accts. Pay./The City Press	203		600 00				
Accts. Pay./Ryan Equip. Co.	204		3 000 00				
J. Emery, Capital	301		53 000 00				
J. Emery, Drawing	302	2 000 00					
Commissions Earned	401		14 000 00				
Rent Expense	501	600 00					
Telephone Expense	502	40 00					
Utilities Expense	503	95 00					
Salaries Expense	504	4 500 00					
Advertising Expense	505	600 00					
		89 600 00	89 600 00				

Worksheet: an expanded trial balance, classifying and sorting account balances prior to the preparation of formal financial statements.

- The *body* consists of the following headings and columns: *Account Title*, for all General Ledger accounts having a balance as at the end of the accounting period; *Account Number*, for the related number of each account listed; *Trial Balance*, a pair of money columns for the trial balance information; *Income Statement*, a pair of money columns for entering later the amounts that make up the income statement; *Balance Sheet*, a pair of money columns for entering later the figures that make up the balance sheet.

Because it begins with a trial balance and then expands to other statement columns, the worksheet may be defined as an expanded trial balance.

The two columns at the right will be referred to as the "financial statement columns."

Steps in Completing the Six-Column Worksheet

To complete a six-column worksheet, the following procedure is used. (After reading the instructions for each step, look at the completed worksheet illustrated opposite.)

J. Emery Real Estate
Worksheet
For the Month Ended October 31, 19-1

ACCOUNT TITLE	ACCT. NO.	TRIAL BALANCE		INCOME STATEMENT		BALANCE SHEET	
		DEBIT	CREDIT	DEBIT	CREDIT	DEBIT	CREDIT
Cash	101	52 565 00				52 565 00	
Accts. Rec./Pat Rogers	103	2 000 00				2 000 00	
Accts. Rec./R. Scobie	104	1 200 00				1 200 00	
Accts. Rec./Shannon Dev. Co.	105	4 000 00				4 000 00	
Automobile	110	15 000 00				15 000 00	
Furniture	112	4 000 00				4 000 00	
Office Equipment	114	3 000 00				3 000 00	
Bank Loan Payable	201		16 000 00				16 000 00
Accts. Pay./Bell Furn. Co.	202		3 000 00				3 000 00
Accts. Pay./The City Press	203		600 00				600 00
Accts. Pay./Ryan Equip. Co.	204		3 000 00				3 000 00
J. Emery, Capital	301		53 000 00				53 000 00
J. Emery, Drawing	302	2 000 00				2 000 00	
Commissions Earned	401		14 000 00		14 000 00		
Rent Expense	501	600 00		600 00			
Telephone Expense	502	40 00		40 00			
Utilities Expense	503	95 00		95 00			
Salaries Expense	504	4 500 00		4 500 00			
Advertising Expense	505	600 00		600 00			
		89 600 00	89 600 00	5 835 00	14 000 00	83 765 00	75 600 00
					5 835 00		
Net Income					8 165 00	→	8 165 00
						83 765 00	83 765 00

Step 1: Complete the Heading Remember: the date line always reports the length of the accounting period. It is important to recognize the complete accounting period because the link between the financial statement columns on the worksheet will be the net income (or loss). As you now know, the net income (or loss) is the result of matching revenues with related expenses for a definite time period.

Step 2: Copy the Trial Balance onto the Worksheet Enter account titles, account numbers, and the debit and credit balances exactly as listed for the trial balance prepared as part of the fourth step of the accounting cycle. Include the totals, to prove that the General Ledger is in balance.

Step 3: Transfer and Separate the Balances This means that if an account has a debit balance in the trial balance section, it becomes a debit balance in the column related to the financial statement in which that account is properly reported. Begin with the first account title at the top.

An account with a credit balance becomes a credit balance in the column related to the financial statement in which that account is reported.

Always remember these two rules when moving balances from the trial balance column to the financial statement columns:

- Move a debit balance to the debit side of the related financial statement column.
- Move a credit balance to the credit side of the related financial statement column.

Check your understanding of these two rules by studying the completed worksheet for J. Emery Real Estate on page 121.

The first account balance, that of the Cash account, shows a debit balance of $52 565. This is moved to the *debit side* of the *balance sheet column* because Cash is an asset and all assets are reported on the balance sheet.

Since the next six accounts are all assets with debit balances, they are moved to the *debit side* of the *balance sheet column.*

Bank Loan Payable, listed on line 8, has a credit balance and so is moved to the *credit side* of the *balance sheet column.* The same procedure is followed for the three accounts payable.

The owner's Capital account is listed on line 12. Move the credit balance of this owner's equity account to the *credit side* of the *balance sheet column.*

Next is the owner's Drawing account. Since the balance is a debit in the trial balance, it is moved to the *debit side* of the *balance sheet column.* Why? Because Drawings are to be reported in the Balance Sheet as an eventual deduction from Owner's Equity. Remember, a debit in the trial balance column must be moved to the debit column of the related financial statement where the account is reported.

Commissions Earned is next. Since this is a revenue account with a credit balance, move the balance to the *credit side* of the *income statement column.*

Five expense accounts are listed next. Since each shows a debit balance, move each balance to the *debit side* of the *income statement column.*

Step 4: Add the Financial Statement Columns Rule a single line across all statement columns as shown. Then add the figures in the debit column under *Income Statement*, the credit column under *Income Statement*, the debit column under *Balance Sheet*, and the credit column under *Balance Sheet.* The totals are written below the single line. Refer once again to the completed worksheet on page 121.

Step 5: Complete the Income Statement Section Since the income statement section is shown in the form of debit and credit money columns, a procedure is followed which is slightly different from that used to prepare an income statement.

- On the line below the totals, place the *smaller amount* under the larger one. In the example, the amount $5 835 is placed under the $14 000 in the credit column.

- Draw a single line under this smaller amount to indicate a calculation.
- Subtract the two figures and enter the answer on the next line. Since the smaller figure normally represents total expenses, and since this figure is subtracted from the larger total revenue, the answer must be the net income for the month. Thus, in the example, the net income is $8 165, shown on line 22 of the worksheet. See the margin illustration.
- Finally, at the far left of the worksheet, in the *Account Title* column, enter the words *Net Income*.

Completing the Income Statement Section: Calculating a Net Income

	INCOME STATEMENT	
	DEBIT	CREDIT
20	*5 835*	*14 000*
21		*5 835*
22		*8 165*

Step 6: Complete the Balance Sheet Section This is the last step. See the illustration.

Completing the Balance Sheet Section: Reporting a Net Income

INCOME STATEMENT		BALANCE SHEET		
DEBIT	CREDIT	DEBIT	CREDIT	
5 835	*14 000*	*83 765*	*75 600*	20
	5 835			21
	8 165		*8 165*	22
		83 765	*83 765*	23

- Move the Net Income figure along the same line to the *credit side* of the balance sheet column. Why? Since the net income in the income statement shows a *credit balance*, it must increase owner's equity in the balance sheet only on the credit side. As you have learned, a credit balance must be moved to the credit column in the financial statement. In the illustration this is emphasized with an arrow, which the student may wish to use at this stage.
- Draw a single line across both the debit and the credit columns of the balance sheet section to indicate a calculation.
- Total the balance sheet columns. Of course, the sums must agree. In the example, the sums are both $83 765.
- Finally, draw a double line across both financial statement columns as shown.

The worksheet is now complete.

Calculating and Reporting a Net Loss

In J. Emery Real Estate's worksheet, the *matchup* between the total revenue and the total expenses in the income statement section resulted in a net *income*. Suppose, however, that the total expenses (the total of the debit column) were greater than the total revenue (the total of the credit column). Then matching revenue with related expenses would show a net loss.

Calculating and Reporting a Net Loss

INCOME STATEMENT		BALANCE SHEET		
DEBIT	CREDIT	DEBIT	CREDIT	
15 000	*14 000*	*74 600*	*75 600*	20
14 000				21
1 000 →		→ *1 000*		22
		75 600	*75 600*	23

The procedure for reporting a Net Loss on the worksheet is shown in the illustration. Note that the total of the debit column of the income statement is greater than the total of the credit column. This means that the total expenses are greater than the total revenue. The matchup is done by placing $14 000 under the $15 000 in the greater column. The net debit balance is moved to the debit column of the balance sheet column, because a net loss must decrease owner's equity in any balance sheet. Of course, the balance sheet columns will balance now that the Net Loss has been transferred to the debit side.

Finally, the words *Net Loss* are entered on the far left in the *Account Title* column, and a double line is drawn across the financial statement columns, to complete the worksheet.

TOPIC 1 PROBLEMS

5-1 A trial balance of the General Ledger for the Moncton Secretarial Service after the first month's business, which ended March 31, revealed the following balances: Cash (101), $2 758; Accts. Rec./A. Daoust (103), $540; Accts. Rec./C. Gagne (104), $380; Accts. Rec./F. Larmer (105), $1 410; Office Equipment (110),

$6 400; Delivery Equipment (112), $16 000; Bank Loan Payable (201), $1 500; Accts. Pay./Central Supply Ltd. (202), $790; Accts. Pay./Fox Auto Service (203), $210; T. Perrault, Capital (301), $24 000; T. Perrault, Drawing (302), $1 200; Fees Earned (401), $6 278; Rent Expense (501), $600; Salaries Expense (502), $1 900; Telephone Expense (503), $110; Utilities Expense (504), $220; Office Supplies Expense (505), $900; Advertising Expense (506), $150; Truck Expense (507), $210.

Prepare a six-column worksheet for the Moncton Secretarial Service for the month ended March 31.

Key Check Figure
Net Income = $2 188

5-2 After its first year of business, Allan's Auto Repair showed the following balances from the General Ledger as at June 30, 19-2: Cash (101), $6 260; Accts. Rec./D. Hawerchuk (103), $520; Accts. Rec./E. Staniowski (108), $1 000; Land (110), $12 000; Building (112), $28 000; Repair Equipment (114), $7 580; Office Equipment (116), $2 400; Truck (118), $18 000; Bank Loan Payable (201), $6 000; Accts. Pay./Winnipeg Auto (202), $400; Property Taxes Payable (205), $200; Mortgage Payable (220), $12 000; Tom Allan, Capital (301), $66 000; Tom Allan, Drawing (302), $7 200; Repair Service Revenue (401), $48 400; Wages Expense (501), $38 200; Repair Parts Expense (502), $5 520; Property Taxes Expense (503), $2 400; Utilities Expense (504), $540; Truck Expense (505), $1 900; Telephone Expense (506), $180; Interest Expense (520), $1 300.

Prepare a six-column worksheet for Allan's Auto Repair for the year ended June 30, 19-2.

Key Check Figure
Net Loss = $1 640

5-3 Challenge Problem After its first year of business, the Maritime Survey Co. showed the following year-end General Ledger account balances as at December 31: Cash (101), $9 250; Government of Canada Bonds (102), $10 000; Accts. Rec./Dartmouth Construction (103), $2 400; Accts. Rec./Halifax Properties (104), $1 600; Accts. Rec./Saint John Construction (105), $3 500; Land (110), $25 000; Buildings (112), $75 000; Survey Equipment (114), $30 000; Office Equipment (116), $5 000; Trucks (118), $36 000; Bank Loan Payable (201), $4 500; Accts. Pay./Fredericton Supply (202), $3 000; Accts. Pay./Newcastle Motors (203), $2 500; Salaries Payable (204), $1 200; Mortgage Payable (220), $48 000; Don Kelly, Capital (301), $50 930; Don Kelly, Drawing (302), $32 000; Fees Earned (401), $188 870; Interest Revenue (402), $1 000; Salaries Expense (501), $41 970; Survey Supplies Expense (502), $1 800; Office Supplies Expense (503), $2 400; Telephone Expense (504), $890; Utilities Expense (505), $1 950; Insurance Expense (506), $390; Maintenance Expense (507), $11 250; Gasoline Expense (508), $3 800; Truck Repairs Expense (509), $1 200; Property Taxes Expense (510), $1 200; Bank Interest Expense (520), $400; Mortgage Interest Expense (521), $3 000.

Prepare a six-column worksheet for the Maritime Survey Co. *Special instructions:* This worksheet will require the use of two forms. Draw a single line across all money columns after the second-last line (line 25) of the first worksheet form. On the last line (line 26), in the account title column, write *Totals Carried Forward.* Show the total in each money column.

On a second form, show in the heading the name of the firm, the title *Worksheet, Page 2,* and the date of the accounting period. Then on the line

Key Check Figure
Net Income = $119 620

below the heading *Account Title,* write *Totals Brought Forward.* Copy all the totals from the first page to this line in the proper money columns.

You can now complete the worksheet in the usual way.

TOPIC 2 PREPARING THE FINANCIAL STATEMENTS

This section deals with how to prepare the financial statements from a completed worksheet. Also, it presents some new guidelines for reporting the balance sheet.

Preparing the Income Statement

The first financial statement to be prepared is the income statement. The data for this are found in the columns headed *Income Statement* on the worksheet. The income statement for J. Emery Real Estate is shown below.

J. Emery Real Estate
Worksheet
For the Month Ended October 31, 19-1

Account Title	Income Statement Debit	Income Statement Credit
Commissions Earned		14 000
Rent Expense	600	
Telephone Expense	40	
Utilities Expense	95	
Salaries Expense	4 500	
Advertising Expense	600	
	5 835	14 000
		5 835
Net Income		8 165

J. Emery Real Estate
Income Statement
For the Month Ended October 31, 19-1

Revenue:		
Commissions Earned		$14 000 00
Expenses:		
Rent Expense	$ 600 00	
Telephone Expense	40 00	
Utilities Expense	95 00	
Salaries Expense	4 500 00	
Advertising Expense	600 00	
Total Expenses		5 835 0
Net Income		$ 8 165 0

Preparing the Related Balance Sheet

As you have learned, the related balance sheet is prepared *after* the income statement. Of course, the data for the balance sheet are found in the columns headed *Balance Sheet* on the worksheet.

In Chapter 2, the balance sheet was prepared with the assets on the left and the claims against those assets on the right, as in the accounting equation ($A = L + OE$). This form is also known as the account form type of balance sheet, because two sides are used. But the account form is only one way to report a balance sheet. Another method is shown in the illustration on page 128. It is called the report form. Examine it first, and then study the following points.

Account form: type of balance sheet with assets on the left side, and the claims against them on the right.

pag 42

Report form: type of balance sheet with assets, liabilities, and owner's equity arranged vertically.

- In the heading, Line 1 reports the name of the firm, Line 2 the name of the document, and Line 3 the *as at* date for reporting the balances of assets, liabilities, and the accounts which make up the owner's equity.
- The body reports the details of $A = L + OE$. Note that the three elements of the accounting equation are placed *vertically*.
- It is easier to prepare a balance sheet in the report form because you need not balance the totals of $A = L + OE$ on the same line.
- No matter which form is used, all balance sheets should report useful information about the assets, the liabilities, and the owner's equity. In earlier chapters, you learned a simple form of balance sheet. In the present illustration, notice that the assets and liabilities have been divided into groups or classes. Such a balance sheet is called a classified balance sheet. Since the elements of the accounting equation are also reported vertically here, it may be referred to as a *classified balance sheet prepared in report form*.

Classified balance sheet: one in which assets and liabilities are reported under meaningful groups or classes.

Assets may be put into as many as six classes, but only two are shown in the illustration: *Current Assets* and *Fixed Assets*. Liabilities may be put into as many as four classes, but only one class, *Current Liabilities*, is shown. (A second class will be presented later.) These three classes will now be explained.

6 Assets classes
4 Liabil. Classes.

Reporting Current Assets

Current assets: assets expected to be converted into cash within one year of the balance sheet date. (Introductory definition.)

The meaning of current assets reflects the idea of the liquidity order of reporting assets — that assets are reported in the order in which they will be converted into cash.

In the case of J. Emery Real Estate, Accounts Receivable are reported right after Cash because the business expects to collect from the customers within a short time — perhaps 30 days.

If the firm had Canada Savings Bonds, they would be reported ahead of Accounts Receivable, as shown in the margin. This is because these bonds can be converted into cash by "cashing them in" at the bank or through a broker.

Current Assets:	
Cash	*$ 6 400*
Canada Savings Bonds	*20 000*
Accounts Receivable	*1 200*

Notice that the definition of current assets ends with the words "introductory definition." This is because other current assets are included in this class which are *not* converted into cash. You will learn about these assets, as well as other aspects of current asset accounting, in Chapter 15.

Classified Balance Sheet in Report form

J. Emery Real Estate
Worksheet
For the Month Ended October 31, 19-1

Account Title	Balance Sheet Debit	Balance Sheet Credit
Cash	52 565	
Accts. Rec./Pat Rogers	2 000	
Accts. Rec./R. Scobie	1 200	
Accts. Rec./Shannon Dev. Co.	4 000	
Automobile	15 000	
Furniture	4 000	
Office Equipment	3 000	
Bank Loan Payable		16 000
Accts. Pay./Bell Furn. Co.		3 000
Accts. Pay./The City Press		600
Accts. Pay./Office Equip. Co.		3 000
J. Emery, Capital		53 000
J. Emery, Drawing	2 000	
	83 765	75 600
Net Income	→	8 165
	83 765	83 765

J. Emery Real Estate
Balance Sheet
as at October 31, 19-1

Assets			
Current Assets:			
Cash		$52 565 00	
Accounts Receivable:			
Pat Rogers	$2000.00		
R. Scobie	1200.00		
Shannon Development Co.	4000.00	7 200 00	
Total Current Assets			$59 765 00
Fixed Assets (at cost):			
Automobile		$15 000 00	
Furniture		4 000 00	
Office Equipment		3 000 00	
Total Fixed Assets			22 000 00
Total Assets			$81 765 00
Liabilities			
Current Liabilities:			
Bank Loan Payable (on demand)		$16 000 00	
Accounts Payable:			
Bell Furniture Co.	$3000.00		
The City Press	600.00		
Ryan Equipment Co.	3000.00	6 600 00	
Total Liabilities			$22 600 00
Owner's Equity			
J. Emery, Capital		$53 000 00	
Add: Net Income		8 165 00	
		61 165 00	
Less: Drawings		2 000 00	
Total Owner's Equity			59 165 00
Total Liabilities and Owner's Equity			$81 765 00

Finally, note that the total of Current Assets is reported. This always appears on a balance sheet.

Reporting Fixed Assets

Fixed assets: tangible, long-lived assets held for use within the firm to support revenue-making activities for several years beyond the balance sheet date.

Fixed assets are also known as *long-lived* assets, *operational* assets, *plant* assets, or *property, plant, and equipment.* Being more or less permanent in nature, they are *not* converted into cash. Instead, they are kept in the business to assist in revenue-making activities for several years beyond the balance sheet date. Fixed assets are always reported under a separate heading in the balance sheet.

Look at the fixed assets section in the handwritten balance sheet for J. Emery Real Estate. Notice the words *at cost* after *Fixed Assets.* They are put there because of a very important basic accounting principle called the *cost principle.* In its introductory form, it may be stated as follows:

Fixed Assets (at cost):

GAAP for Cost (Introductory Definition)

All assets purchased by a business must be recorded as follows: (1) All assets must be recorded at the price at which they were purchased. This price is known as the cost price or cost value. (2) The original cost values of assets must be retained throughout the accounting cycle.

Cost price (sometimes known as Historical cost price): the price originally agreed upon by buyer and seller.

When applied to fixed assets, the cost principle assures readers of financial statements that these assets are reported on the balance sheet on the basis of what it cost the business to obtain them. For example, if a parcel of land cost $20 000 ten years ago, the cost principle requires accountants to report it at its original cost, $20 000 — even if it can now be bought or sold for $50 000. However, to avoid any misunderstanding, the words *at cost* are used, either after the particular asset or after the class name *Fixed Assets.*

Though we have been talking about assets, the cost principle sets guidelines for recording every element and sub-element in the accounting equation. It also sets guidelines for transactions when a cash price is not involved. Since these areas of applying the cost principle can become very complex, they are best studied in more advanced courses at the post-secondary level. In this chapter and later ones, always show the words *at cost* after *Fixed Assets* on a balance sheet. Of course, you should be able to explain the two parts of the cost principle as given earlier.

In the illustration, notice that *Total Fixed Assets* is reported.

And finally, notice that, when the report form of balance sheet is used, a double line is drawn below the figure for total assets. This closes the assets section so that the figure can be kept separate from the figures for liabilities and the owner's equity.

Reporting Current Liabilities

Current liabilities: debts owing which will fall due within one year of the balance sheet date.

Liabilities, like assets, are reported on a balance sheet under groups or classes of accounts. A common class is current liabilities.

Current liabilities are simply those debts which the business expects to pay within a year of the balance sheet date. For J. Emery Real Estate, note that the bank loan is payable "on demand." This means that the bank can ask Emery to pay back the loan at any time. Therefore, it is reported as the first current liability on the balance sheet.

Amounts owing to creditors, too, would normally have to be paid within one year of the balance sheet date. Thus Emery's balance sheet also reports Accounts Payable as a current liability.

Although Emery shows only two current liabilities, it is useful to remember that *any debt which will be paid out of current funds (funds available under current assets) should be included in current liabilities.* Keep this in mind when you study other balance sheets in this book.

In Emery's balance sheet, the total of current liabilities is also the total liabilities. When only one class of liabilities is reported, the total is commonly shown as *Total Liabilities.* When more than one class of liabilities is reported, the total of each class should be shown.

The owner's equity section need not be explained here. You learned about this section in Chapter 2.

The Classified Balance Sheet in Account Form

When the balance sheet is to be included in a published annual report, most Canadian businesses prefer to use the account form, described earlier. The reason is its understandability, due to the use of two pages, the left listing the assets and the right listing the liabilities and owner's equity elements.

Study the illustrated balance sheet for Southview Cleaning Shop. Then study the following points.

- When the account form is used, there may not be enough space to group the accounts in preliminary columns. In this case, the accepted practice is to place the figures for each classified item in one column and enclose the total figure for that classification between two single ruled lines.
- Note how each current asset — Cash, Government of Canada Bonds, and the total of accounts receivable — is placed in the final money column. The total of current assets is then enclosed between two single lines.
- The same procedure is followed for the five fixed assets. Thus the separate totals enclosed between the single lines can easily be added to report *Total Assets* at the bottom on this side.

Account form

Southview Cleaning Shop
Balance Sheet
as at December 31, 19—

ASSETS

Current Assets		
Cash		$ 2 250.00
Government of Canada Bonds		10 000.00
Accounts Receivable:		
Alma Services	$2 000.00	
Vancouver Auto	2 800.00	4 800.00
Total Current Assets		17 050.00
Fixed Assets (at cost):		
Land (security for mortgage payable)		10 000.00
Building (security for mortgage payable)		50 000.00
Dry Cleaning Equipment		20 000.00
Delivery Equipment		12 000.00
Office Equipment		5 000.00
Total Fixed Assets		97 000.00
Total Assets		$114 050.00

LIABILITIES

Current Liabilities		
Bank Loan Payable (on demand)		$ 2 000.00
Accounts Payable:		
Bute Supply Co.	$1 500.00	
Kingsway Ltd.	3 500.00	5 000.00
Property Taxes Payable		200.00
Current portion of mortgage payable		1 000.00
Total Current Liabilities		8 200.00
Long-Term Liabilities		
10% Mortgage Payable, due 1999 (secured by land and building)	$20 000.00	
Less current portion	1 000.00	
Total Long-Term Liabilities		19 000.00
Total Liabilities		$ 27 200.00
OWNER'S EQUITY		
L.A. Fortier, Capital	$ 71 850.00	
Add: Net Income for Year	40 000.00	
	111 850.00	
Less: Withdrawals	25 000.00	
Total Owner's Equity		86 850.00
Total Liabilities and Owner's Equity		$114 050.00

- In the Liabilities section, on the right page, observe the two classes of debts: *Current Liabilities* and *Long-Term Liabilities*.
- As we have said, current liabilities consist of all the debts of the business payable within one year of the date of the balance sheet. Long-term liabilities, on the other hand, represent the debts of a business that are *not* due within a year. The illustration reports one common long-term debt, Mortgage Payable.
- A mortgage is a pledge of property to a creditor as security against a debt (the loan of money). Since a pledge of property is involved, accountants report as much information as possible about a mortgage. For example, if a fixed rate of interest is used, the interest rate payable on the mortgage should be reported. Also, the due date should be reported.
- The mortgage is "secured by land and building." This means that the lender of the money (the *mortgagee*) will have a

Long-term liabilities: debts which, in the ordinary course of business, will not be liquidated within one year of the balance sheet date.

claim on the firm's land and building if the borrower (the *mortgagor*) fails to make the payments.

- On the assets side of the balance sheet under *Fixed Assets,* notice how the fact that the land and building are pledged as securities against the mortgage is reported. After each asset the words "security for mortgage payable" appear in parentheses. Thus the reader of the balance sheet knows what liability is secured and what assets are pledged as securities.
- The current portion of the long-term debt is reported under *Current Liabilities.* This is an important procedure, because any portion of long-term debt obligations payable within a year out of current funds (out of current assets) should be included in current liabilities.
- When the current portion of a long-term debt is reported it is also subtracted from the long-term amount to report what amount remains to be paid beyond a year from the balance sheet date (in this case, in 1999).
- Finally, on the left page total assets must be reported on the same line as the total liabilities and owner's equity on the right page.

The Accounting Cycle So Far

We have now covered these steps in the accounting cycle:

- *Step 1:* originating the transaction data
- *Step 2:* journalizing
- *Step 3:* posting
- *Step 4:* preparing the trial balance
- *Step 5:* preparing the worksheet
- *Step 6:* preparing financial statements

TOPIC 2 PROBLEMS

Key Check Figure
Total OE = $24 988

5-4 Using the completed worksheet for Problem 5-1, prepare an income statement and a classified balance sheet in report form for the Moncton Secretarial Service.

Key Check Figure
Total OE = $57 160

5-5 Using the completed worksheet for Problem 5-2, prepare an income statement and a classified balance sheet in report form for Allan's Auto Repair. *Important:* Of the $12 000 balance reported for Mortgage Payable, $800 is due within one year of the balance sheet date. The mortgage is secured by the pledging of the land and building. Finally, the final amount payable on the mortgage is due in 10 years.

5-6 Using the worksheet completed for Problem 5-3, prepare an income statement and a classified balance sheet in report form for the Maritime Survey Co. *Important:* Assume that the mortgage payable carries a fixed rate of interest at 7 1/2%. Of the $48 000 balance reported on the mortgage payable, assume that $5 000 is payable within one year of the balance sheet date. The mortgage is secured by the pledging of the company's land and buildings. Assume that the mortgage payable is due 20 years from now.

Key Check Figure Total Assets = $197 750

5-7 Challenge Problem After the second year of business, Miller's TV Repair Service reported the following year-end trial balance.

Miller's TV Repair Service
Trial Balance
December 31, 19-2

Cash	101	$ 10 000	
Canada Savings Bonds	102	15 000	
Accts. Rec./F. Allen	103	1 000	
Accts. Rec./S. Foster	104	800	
Accts. Rec./A. Leung	105	210	
Repair Service Equipment	120	18 000	
Truck	122	15 000	
Office Equipment	124	2 400	
Bank Loan Payable (on demand)	201		$ 3 000
Accts. Pay./Aurora Ltd.	202		210
Accts. Pay./Markham Supply	203		1 100
Wages Payable	204		400
Business Licence Fee Payable	205		200
3-Year Note Payable	220		12 000
J. Miller, Capital	301		53 542
J. Miller, Drawing	302	24 000	
Repair Services Revenue	401	68 940	
Bond Interest Earned	402		1 800
Property Rent Expense	501	9 600	
Wages Expense	502	36 920	
Business Licence Fee Expense	503	200	
Advertising Expense	504	1 400	
Telephone Expense	505	360	
Utilities Expense	506	1 300	
Supplies Expense	507	870	
Truck Repairs Expense	508	1 200	
Gas and Oil Expense	509	1 120	
Interest Expense	520	1 812	
		$210 132	$72 252

Here is some additional information:

(i) The 3-Year Note Payable is a written promise to pay Canada Trust by not later than December 31, 19-5. According to the agreement, $4 000 is due to be paid within one year of the balance sheet date. Also, the note payable is secured by pledging of the firm's repair service equipment.

(ii) Due to an obvious error in reporting an account balance, the trial balance does not balance.

a Find the error. Show a correct trial balance on a six-column worksheet.

b Complete the six-column worksheet.

Key Check Figure Net Income = $15 958

c Prepare an income statement in good form.
d Prepare a classified balance sheet in report form.

TOPIC 3 INTERPRETING AN INCOME STATEMENT AND BALANCE SHEET

You have learned much about how to prepare two of the most important financial statements — the income statement and the balance sheet. No matter how you prepared these statements, by hand or through a computer, it is important to understand and interpret both statements. What does an income statement say, and what does a balance sheet say, to readers?

Let us first review the basic accounting principles and the guidelines given in earlier chapters, for they will help you.

Basic accounting principles: broad accounting guidelines followed by professional accountants in all countries.

Review of Basic Accounting Principles

When you hear the term basic accounting principles, think of those broad principles which are accepted in all countries in which accounting is carried on as a profession. Accountants in Canada, the U.S.A., the United Kingdom, Europe, Australia, New Zealand, etc. all follow the same *basic* principles.

So far, you have learned: the revenue recognition principle, the expense recognition principle, the matching principle, the objectivity principle, and the cost principle. (We have also called them *GAAPs*.)

- *Revenue recognition principle* (often shortened to *revenue principle):* This one assumes that you can define revenue, and, simply, it says that revenue must be recognized at the point in time when the sale of services (or goods) is made, and not when the cash is received from the customer.
- *Expense recognition principle* (often shortened to *expense principle):* This principle assumes you can define expense, and, simply, it says that an expense must be accounted for when it is *incurred,* and not when the cash payment is made.
- *Matching principle:* Revenues recognized during one accounting period must be paired up with expenses incurred during the same accounting period. All these matchings result in the net income or net loss for an accounting period. The accounting period may be any designated length of time up to one year.
- *Objectivity principle:* A transaction must have occurred before that transaction can be recorded in accounts. Second, there must be physical proof (evidence) that this financial event did occur. Such evidence is called a source document.
- *Cost principle:* First, all assets must be accounted for on the basis of how much was paid to get those assets. Second,

these same cost figures must be kept in the assets accounts even if the so-called market or current value has gone up.

These are only five of at least ten basic accounting principles. The others are more complex and are best studied in specialized courses at the post-secondary level.

Specific Accounting Principles

Every country also follows its own specific accounting principles which serve as guidelines for accountants practicing in that country. For example, in Canada, the three accounting bodies — Chartered Accountants (which grants the C.A. designation), Society of Management Accountants (R.I.A.), and Certified General Accountants (C.G.A.) — follow the *CICA Handbook* published by the Canadian Institute of Chartered Accountants, which contains a large number of these more specialized guidelines. Since they have to do with financial reporting requirements, these guidelines are often collectively called the *financial reporting principle.*

Specific accounting principles: more specific guidelines followed by accountants in a particular country.

CICA Handbook: published by the Canadian Institute of Chartered Accountants; contains specific accounting guidelines for use in Canada.

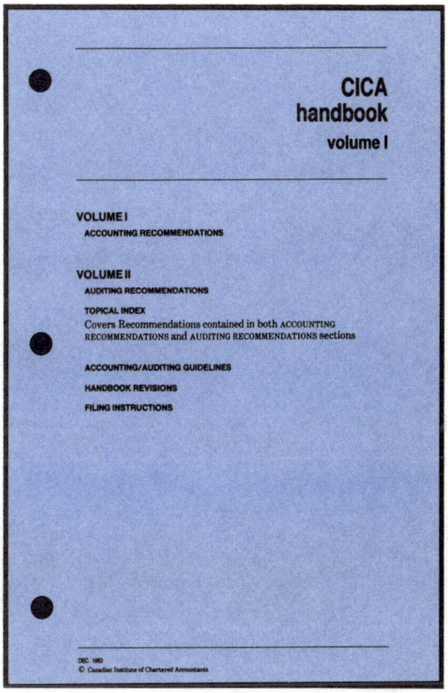

Here are the guidelines you have learned so far:

- Financial statements should be prepared in such form and use such words and classifications that readers can easily understand the information being reported.
- Assets reported on the balance sheet should be classified under at least two classes: current and fixed.
- The main items making up current assets should be reported separately; for example, cash, temporary investments, and accounts receivable.
- Fixed assets should be reported by major category; for example, land, buildings, and machinery.
- The cost value of fixed assets should be disclosed on every balance sheet.
- If assets of the business are promised as security against liabilities, the nature of such assets should be disclosed. In other words, readers of the balance sheet should know which assets have been pledged as security against which debts.
- Liabilities reported on the balance sheet should be classified under at least two classes: current and long-term.
- The Current Liability classification should report separately all debts payable within a year from the date of the balance sheet; for example, bank loans, accounts payable, other loans payable, taxes payable, and current payments on long-term debt.
- If any of the liabilities are secured, they should be stated separately and the fact that they are secured should be indicated.
- Any portion of a long-term debt obligation payable within a year out of current funds should be included in current liabilities.

- The income statement should report at least the following items: the main sources of revenue earned by the business for a specific accounting period, the major expenses incurred for the same accounting period, and the net income or net loss for the period.
- The financial statements of an unincorporated business (sole proprietorship) should clearly indicate the name of the business and, when necessary, the name of the owners.
- Any "salary" paid to the owner of a single proprietorship should be considered part of the payment of the net income to the owner of that unincorporated business. Such "salaries" should be accounted for in a separate, drawing account.

It should be kept in mind that other countries may follow different principles from the ones above.

What an Income Statement Says

Let us summarize what you have learned so far about the income statement.

- Every income statement follows the matching principle, by which the accountant matches revenues earned for an accounting period and the expenses incurred for the same period. Remember that, regardless of how complex the income statement appears to be, only two key elements are reported: revenue items matched with expense items.
- A glance at the heading of any income statement tells the reader the name of the business, the name of the statement, and the length of the accounting period for which revenues and expenses have been matched. It is important to understand that this accounting period has *ended.* The date line should contain the word "ended" (*not* "ending").
- The income statement reports the main and secondary source(s) of revenue earned by the business during the accounting period. For example, the main source of revenue for a dental practice is charging fees for services rendered. Thus, professional fees earned would be the main or primary source of revenue. The firm may also have invested money in Canada Savings Bonds. The interest earned from the bond investment would be the firm's secondary source of revenue. Other common sources of secondary revenue are the dividends earned from investing in stocks, and rental revenue earned from renting part of the firm's land or building.

Main or primary source of revenue: regular operations of the business that bring in revenue.

Secondary source of revenue: a source of revenue which is not part of the regular operations of the business; usually an investment.

- Various terms are used by businesses to describe their main source of revenue. The nature of the main business operation will give you a hint. Service firms sell services so the name of their main source of revenue depends on what their services are.

A real estate broker charges a commission for buying and selling properties so his or her main source of revenue would be given as *Commissions Earned.* Most of the professional practices charge fees for their services. Hence, such people as lawyers, doctors, dentists, and accountants would report their main source of revenue as *Fees Earned.* Retailers and wholesalers buy goods and sell them to their customers. These merchandising or trading firms would report their main source of revenue as *Sales Revenue* or simply *Sales.*

- It is important to know what revenue means. The revenue principle defines the main source of business revenue as an inflow of assets (cash and/or accounts receivable) from the sale of goods and services. This means that, for a service firm, revenue must be recognized when the services are rendered. For example, when a dentist performs dental services such as giving an X-ray or cleaning and examining the patient's teeth, the total *on the bill* must be recognized as revenue earned. You do not wait until the cash is received to recognize revenue.

- Every source of revenue reported should be traced back to a source document. Of course, this important idea comes from the objectivity principle. The reader of an income statement must have confidence that all revenues reported are accurate. To give this confidence to readers, special accountants called auditors are hired to ensure that all business transactions are supported by source documents.

Auditors: specialized accountants who conduct an examination of the accounting records and other supporting evidence of a business.

- The expense principle gives the meaning of expenses and guides accountants in deciding when to record expenses in accounting records.

- Business expenses, of course, are the costs of operating a business. For example, when a telephone is used in a dentist's practice, the cost of using the telephone helps bring in revenue. In accounting language, the cost is "used up" and so becomes *expired.* That expired cost is accounted for as a business expense and reported under *Telephone Expense.* All expired costs, therefore, are business expenses.

Expired costs: expenses to be matched against revenue in the income statement.

- The expense principle not only defines an expense but tells readers when those expenses are to be accounted for. Expenses are recorded when they are *incurred* and not when they are eventually paid. For example, a telephone bill received today shows the cost of business telephone use during a period of time. The expense should be recognized and recorded at that time. If a cheque is issued immediately, then the expense is recognized along with the cash payment; but if management decides to wait until next month to pay, the expense must be recorded as an account payable.

- All expense transactions must be recorded in accordance with the objectivity principle. The income statement is based on this principle, since all reported expenses can be traced to source documents.

• The result of matching revenues with related expenses — the net income or net loss — may be considered the most important piece of information reported by the income statement.

Earnings Statement: another name for the income statement.

Profit and Loss Statement: an old name for the income statement.

When the statement is called the "Income Statement," the net result would be reported as *Net Income*. Some firms, however, prefer to name their statement the Earnings Statement (or "Statement of Earnings"). In this case, the net result would be reported as *Net Earnings*.

Many years ago, firms called their statement the Profit and Loss Statement; the net result was called *Net Profit*.

The terms *net income, net earnings,* and *net profit* all have the same meaning. However, *net profit* is becoming rare in today's accounting practice.

• It is important to remember that net income is related to the matching principle. To put it simply, net income is made up of more revenues than the matched expenses. If revenue refers to an inflow of assets, and expenses refer to expired costs, net income must mean that the business has increased the dollar amount of assets during the accounting period. On the other hand, if a net loss is the result, this means that the total dollar amount of assets must have decreased during the accounting period.

What an Income Statement Does Not Say

In interpreting an income statement for a given accounting period, many persons try to read too much into the document. Here are a few of the things an income statement does *not* say:

An income statement is a HISTORICAL statement reporting the matching of revenues with related expenses for a period that HAS ENDED.

• An income statement does not predict the net income for any *future* accounting period. It is merely a matching of revenues and related expenses for a period which has ended — a historical report of revenues and expenses for a past accounting period. Since the future is filled with uncertainty, the reader of a historical income statement cannot rely on the reported results of any single year for an indication of future results. However, by comparing income statements of past accounting periods, for example 10-year periods or 5-year periods, one may be able to predict with greater confidence the future results of a business. Management may try to predict the future by preparing a budgeted income statement, which would be described as such.

Budgeted income statement: a statement estimating future revenues matched with future expenses in order to predict net income or net loss for some future accounting period.

• An income statement, even if it is well prepared, does not provide an exact measurement of net income for the period. At best, it shows an *appreciation* of net income for the accounting period. Here is why. Ideally, all expenses should be identified with certain revenues during a specified accounting period.

However, it is often impossible to get a precise matching. For example, it is difficult to assign the costs of such items as Advertising Expense. Consider the decision by management to incur an advertising cost of $1 000 in order to produce revenue for the month of December. If revenues from sales totalled $5 000 for December, the plain fact is that there is no way to guarantee that the benefits of using up the $1 000 of advertising cost did bring in this exact amount of revenue. Furthermore, it is probable that some of January's revenue was a result of the advertising expense of December. So, whenever it is difficult to measure the benefits of any cost used up to bring in revenue, one simply accounts for the entire cost as an expense in the time period when the expense was incurred.

An income statement reports only a fair approximation of net income for an accounting period.

- An income statement does not report the so-called "true profit" of any business. Rather, it reports the profit for the accounting period. To get the true profit, you would have to calculate the difference between the assets invested during the lifetime of the business and the amount finally received from remaining assets after winding up the business. You would also have to deduct any withdrawals of funds made by the owner during the lifetime of the business, because personal withdrawals are actually payments made out of profits in advance of accounting for them. Suppose, for example, that your total investment in a business over 20 years amounted to $100 000, and that during this period your withdrawals for personal use totalled $240 000. Suppose also that after 20 years you sold the business for $160 000 cash. Your true profit, therefore, would be $160 000 + $240 000 − $100 000, or $300 000 for the 20 years.

True profit: the difference between total funds invested over the life of the business and funds realized from sale of business.

Owners and other interested persons need, not this "true profit," but periodic information on the progress of the business. To get this information, accountants prepare income statements at least annually, and in a great many cases quarterly or more often.

- Some readers of net income statements, unfortunately, interpret net income as cash. Always keep in mind that net income is the *excess* of revenue over the *related* expenses for a specific accounting period. Cash has very little to do with the determination of net income. Some are misled into thinking that, since revenue is the inflow of cash and expense is the outflow, the difference must be a cash balance. True, revenue refers to an inflow of cash (or claims to cash) and expense to an outflow for some of the operating expenses. But cash is often reused as soon as it becomes available. For example, sales revenue is often used to buy other assets for the purpose of bringing in more revenue. Or the cash may be invested in bonds and stocks so that revenue from secondary sources may flow in. Another point to consider is that not all expenses result in an outflow of cash. For example, the business may have incurred an advertising expense for which

Net income does not mean cash.

30 or 60 days have been given before a cash payment is required. Later on in this book, you will also learn that for some expenses, such as depreciation, there is *no* cash outflow whatsoever.

In accounting, expenses must be treated as *expired costs*. And net income must always be regarded as the net increase to owner's equity as a result of having revenues greater than their related expenses for a given accounting period.

Summary An income statement reports mainly the following information:

- the sources of revenue earned for a given accounting period
- those expenses which are related to the revenue for the same accounting period
- the income result of matching the two — the net income or loss

What a Balance Sheet Says

Here is a summary of what you have learned so far about the balance sheet.

Accounting entity: the business as a unit distinct from its owner(s), for accounting purposes.

- A balance sheet gives the reader the name of the business in the first line of the heading. This name also identifies the accounting entity. This means that accounting separates the idea of the business from that of the owner or owners. For example, when J. Emery invested some of her own money in her real estate business, only the amount of that investment is included in the assets of J. Emery Real Estate. The accountant is not concerned with Emery's *personal* assets such as her home, car, or boat. Nor is accounting concerned with the owner's personal debts. It is concerned only with the accounting entity — J. Emery Real Estate.
- A balance sheet gives readers a detailed summary of the assets, and claims against those assets, as at a particular date. The details about the assets come from the balances of the asset accounts filed in the General Ledger. The details of the claims of creditors come from the balances of the liability accounts filed in the General Ledger. And the claims of the owner come from the balance of the owner's Capital account in the General Ledger, plus the net income (or less the net loss) reported by the income statement, less the balance of the owner's Drawing account in the General Ledger.
- A balance sheet provides the reader with information about the financial position of the firm with regard to its ability to pay current debts. If all debts payable out of current funds are reported correctly under current liabilities, the reader can turn to the list of current assets to see if there are enough funds. For example, by comparing the available current assets against the current debts of J. Emery Real Estate, you learn that the firm has

$52 565 of potential cash available to clear the total current debts of $22 600. This would suggest that the business is in a favourable financial position not only to meet its obligations to creditors, but also to pay for expenses in operating the business.

- A balance sheet gives the reader a view of the firm's ability to carry on its business operations. Such an interpretation may be made by analyzing the fixed assets section. For example, in the case of J. Emery Real Estate, the reader can see that the business has $22 000 of fixed assets to assist in revenue-making activities.
- Finally, a balance sheet reveals the strength of the owner's claim against the assets. In the case of J. Emery Real Estate, the claim appears to be a strong one. The balance sheet as at October 31, 19-1 shows total assets of $81 765. Of this total, creditors claim $22 600 or approximately 27%. J. Emery's claim of $59 165 is approximately 73%. You must remember, however, that this is a residual ("remaining") claim because the claims of creditors must always be satisfied before the owner's claim.
- In accordance with specific guidelines published in the *CICA Handbook,* a balance sheet tells the reader what debts are secured.
- In accounting, any liability that is reported as being secured has one or more assets pledged as the security. Again in accordance with the *CICA Handbook,* a balance sheet will report which assets have been pledged.

A balance sheet can say other things to readers, but further analysis cannot be done until you learn more about additional assets, liabilities, and owner's equity elements, and, especially, how they are applied to different types of businesses.

What a Balance Sheet Does Not Say

One of the most important problems facing many readers of a balance sheet is the possibility of misinterpreting it altogether. Here is a summary of some of the things that a balance sheet does *not* say.

- A balance sheet does not report the details of how profits were made by the business. These details are reported in the income statement.
- A balance sheet does not show the claims of creditors and the owner(s) against specific assets. For example, the total claim of creditors reported in J. Emery Real Estate, $22 600, is not against the cash of the business or against any other specific asset. Nor is the claim of J. Emery, the owner, against any specific asset. The claims are *against the assets in general* — the total assets only.
- The word *Capital* under the owner's equity must not be interpreted as cash. Although it is true that the owner has invested money, it is also true that the new business has used some of this

money to acquire additional assets. No balance sheet, therefore, reveals how money invested by the owner has been used by the business. Because balance sheets do not disclose actual transactions, it is important that the meaning of *capital* be restricted only to *investment.* A correct interpretation of *J. Emery, Capital,* therefore, is simply J. Emery's claim against total assets through her investment.

- This final limitation is very important to remember. A balance sheet does not report the so-called market value, current value, or worth of any business. Unfortunately, many readers believe that the total assets represent a bundle of future cash resources. While there is little difficulty in assigning a dollar value to *current* assets such as cash and accounts receivable, there are *fixed* assets to consider as well. Such assets are kept by the business to produce revenue and not to be converted into cash.

In Topic 2, you learned that accountants follow the basic guideline called the cost principle. This principle simply means that accountants are required to record assets on the basis of the dollars that have been used to buy these economic resources. Therefore, the dollar amounts listed on the balance sheet do not indicate the prices at which assets could be sold. In the language of business, the value of an asset simply means *the cost of that asset* and not its present value or worth.

Value: in accounting, the cost of assets.

You have also learned that to avoid any reader misunderstanding, accountants are directed in the *CICA Handbook* to disclose the cost basis of reporting assets. For this reason, all fixed assets are reported "at cost."

You can now learn a second way to define assets in general. If assets are reported at cost and are still usable to produce revenue, then at least part of these costs must not have been used up — in other words, there are unexpired costs. All assets, therefore, represent unexpired costs reported on the balance sheet to be used up in the future. As you have learned from analyzing the income statement, all costs used up become expired costs and are reported as expenses matched against revenue in the period in which they expired. In Part III of this book, you will learn how assets which start as unexpired become expired, and how these expired costs are transferred to expense accounts.

Unexpired costs: assets carried forward in the balance sheet to be expired in some future accounting period.

The illustration opposite should clarify the differences between expired and unexpired costs.

In conclusion, a balance sheet is a statement of a firm's financial position that gives three main pieces of information:

- It summarizes the position of assets, liabilities, and owner's equity as at a specific date.
- It allows the reader to analyze the financial position of the firm — its ability to meet its debts.

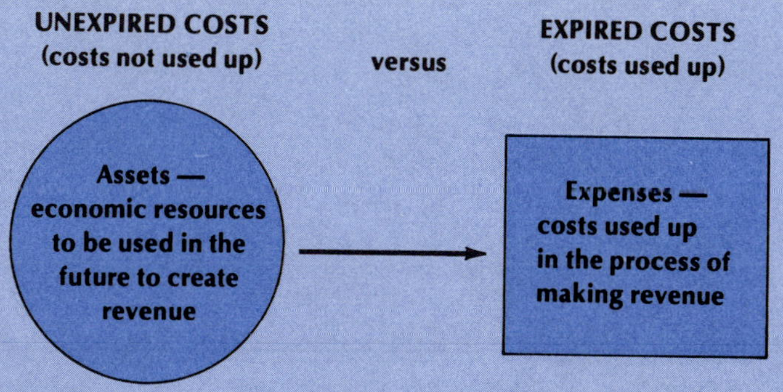

- *They are recorded at their original costs.*
- *They are called "unexpired" because their costs have not been used up.*
- *They are reported on the balance sheet at their unexpired cost.*

- *When the cost of any asset is used up, that cost "expires" — is no longer there.*
- *All expired costs are expenses and must be matched against revenue on the income statement.*

EXAMPLE: *When a business pays a salesperson a salary, it must:*

DR. Salaries Expense
CR. Cash

The Cash account is credited because the business has used it to create revenue (pay for salesperson's services). The expired portion is shown as a debit to an expense account.

- It allows the reader to analyze those economic resources to be used to bring in revenue for the firm.

A balance sheet, therefore, may properly be interpreted as a *statement of financial position.*

Balance sheet: a statement of financial position.

TOPIC 3 PROBLEMS

5-8 In each of the income statement headings offered below, find errors that make it difficult to interpret the statement correctly. Then rewrite any statement heading to conform to current accounting practices.

a

D. Muir Travel Service
Income Statement
As at December 31, 19—

b

Ashworth Auto Repair
Statement of Income & Expenses
For the Year Ended March 31, 19—

c

Beaulieu Music Conservatory
Operating Statement
For the Accounting Year April 1—April 30, 19—

d

Statement of Earnings
Barclay Investment Service
As at April 30, 19—

e

Guenther Air Services
Profit and Loss Statement
For the Month Ending May 31, 19—

f

Statement of Revenue and Expenses
Groleau Parking System
Six Months Ended June 30, 19—

5-9 On a form similar to the one below, enter the following types of businesses in column 1: bank; manufacturer of steel products; wholesale merchandiser; doctor; retail clothier; lawyer; newspaper company; dentist; accountant; mortgage and savings corporation; telephone company; airline company; movie theatre; real estate agency; insurance agency.

Then complete columns 2 and 3 for each type of business listed.

Type of Business (1)	*Main Business Operations (2)*	*Description of Revenues (3)*
EXAMPLE: Bank	Lending of money	Interest revenue

5-10 The balance sheet for the Greater Winnipeg Car Rental Company is illustrated below.

Greater Winnipeg Car Rental Company
Balance Sheet
as at September 30, 19—

ASSETS		**LIABILITIES**	
Cash	$ 6 000	Bank Loan	$ 4 000
Accounts Receivable	2 000	Accounts Payable	2 000
Land	8 000	Mortgage Payable (20-year)	14 000
Buildings	12 000	Total Liabilities	$20 000
Automobiles	20 000		
Furniture	8 000	**OWNER'S EQUITY**	
Office Equipment	4 000	D. Rybachuk, Capital	40 000
Total	$60 000	Total	$60 000

The bank loan is payable on demand. The current portion of Mortgage Payable is $1 500. The mortgage is secured by the land and buildings. The net income for the month of September is $2 000. The balance in the owner's drawing account as at September 30 showed a debit of $2 000.

a List and explain your criticisms of the above balance sheet.

b Using the above data, prepare a balance sheet in report form that meets the requirements of the basic accounting principles and the specific guidelines from the *CICA Handbook* studied so far.

c Answer the following questions on interpreting this balance sheet. **(i)** Who is the owner of the business? **(ii)** Does the owner represent the accounting entity? Explain why or why not. **(iii)** What is the claim of creditors against the economic resources of the business? **(iv)** Why are automobiles listed as part of the economic resources of this business? **(v)** Interpret the financial position of the firm as to its ability to meet its debts. **(vi)** Is the business in a strong financial position to carry out its operations? Explain your answer. **(vii)** Does the owner have a strong or weak claim against the assets of the business? Explain your answer. **(viii)** Does the balance sheet report how much profits were made by the business? Explain your answer. **(ix)** Explain the word *Capital* in *D. Rybachuk, Capital.* **(x)** Does the balance sheet report the true worth of the business? Explain your answer.

Key Check Figure
Total Current Liabilities = $7 500

5-11 Challenge Problem The balance sheet for Central Rent-A-Car is illustrated below.

Balance Sheet
Central Rent-A-Car
For the Year Ended December 31, 19-1

ASSETS		**LIABILITIES**	
Cash	$ 100	Accounts Payable	$ 9 000
Automobiles	25 500	Bank Loan Payable (on demand)	1 000
Furniture	5 000	3-year Note Payable, due December 31, 19-4	18 000
Office Equipment	6 000	J. Taylor, Capital	9 000
Accounts Receivable	400	Net Income for Year	18 000
J. Taylor, Drawing	18 000		
Total Assets	$55 000	Total Liabilities	$55 000

The 3-year note payable was made out to City Chev-Olds Ltd. This note was secured by pledging the entire amount reported for Automobiles. The current portion of the long-term note payable is $6 000.

a List and explain your criticisms of the above balance sheet.

b Using the above data, prepare a balance sheet in report form that meets the requirements of the basic accounting principles and the specific guidelines from the *CICA Handbook* studied so far.

c Answer the following questions on interpreting this balance sheet. **(i)** Does Central Rent-A-Car own premises from which it can conduct business operations? Explain why or why not. **(ii)** What is the claim of creditors against the assets of the business? **(iii)** Analyze the financial position of this firm as to its

Key Check Figure
Total Current Liabilities = $16 000

ability to meet its debts. **(iv)** Does the owner have a strong or weak claim against the assets of the business? Explain your answer. **(v)** Is the business in a strong financial position to create revenue through the service of renting cars? Explain your answer. **(vi)** Summarize the main weaknesses of this business as you have concluded from your analysis of the firm's balance sheet.

Case Study 5

Mr. Ron Florendine is in the cattle business in Alberta and owns 400 ha of land for grazing purposes. Originally this land cost Mr. Florendine $100/ha. For accounting purposes, the land was listed correctly in the assets section of the first and subsequent balance sheets with a dollar amount of $40 000. Recently, large oil reserves were discovered by an oil company in a piece of land next to the Florendine ranch. An official of the company offered Mr. Florendine $2 000/ha for all of his land. Although he refused this offer, Mr. Florendine called his accountant in and said, "I've recently been offered $2 000/ha for my land and yet you still show the land to be worth only $100/ha in the financial records. Why don't you report the true value of the land on the next balance sheet? I know I can get $800 000 for my 400 ha of land."

If you were the accountant, how would you answer that question? How would you justify your position to Mr. Florendine?

CHAPTER 6

CLOSING THE LEDGER AND COMPLETING THE ACCOUNTING CYCLE

This chapter will complete the study of the accounting cycle. The previous six steps were: (1) originating transaction data, (2) journalizing, (3) posting, (4) preparing the trial balance, (5) preparing the worksheet, (6) preparing financial statements.

- Topic 1 of this chapter deals with step 7, closing the General Ledger.
- Topic 2 deals with the last step, step 8, preparing the postclosing trial balance.
- Topic 3 completes Part 1 of this book by offering you information about accounting careers.

TOPIC 1 CLOSING THE LEDGER

The Need for Closing

The word *closing* in "closing the ledger" (or "closing the books") has a special meaning in accounting. To learn the correct meaning of *closing* in accounting it is helpful first to understand the need for closing the ledger. Study the illustrations on page 148 for J. Emery Real Estate.

The top illustration shows the accounting equation for J. Emery Real Estate for transactions that have ended on October 31, 19-1. Notice that the net income is added to the owner's capital before the drawings are deducted. Obviously, this is also reported in the owner's equity section of the partial balance sheet. In the two illustrations, note that the total owner's equity is the same, $59 165.

So far, this information presents nothing new to you. But now, check the figure for *J. Emery, Capital* as shown in the General Ledger and partial trial balance. *Does the balance in the Capital account agree with the new owner's equity figure of the accounting equation and balance sheet?*

The answer is no! The new owner's equity (the claim of the

Acc. Eq. after Balance Sheet

Assets		=	Liabilities	+	Owner's Equity					
Current Assets	Fixed Assets		Current Liabilities		J. Emery, Capital		+$14 000 / −5 825	Revenue / Expenses		J. Emery, Drawings
$59 765 +	$22 000	=	$22 600	+	$53 000	+	$ 8 165	Net Income	−	$2 000
$81 765		=	$22 600	+	$59 165					

Partial Balance Sheet
as at October 31, 19-1

OWNER'S EQUITY

J. Emery, Capital	$53 000	
Add: Net Income	8 165	
	61 165	
Less: Drawings	2 000	
Total Owner's Equity		$59 165

Conclusion: *The new Total Owner's Equity of $59 165, as reported in the accounting equation and balance sheet, does not agree with the figure reported in the trial balance and J. Emery's Capital account in the General Ledger ($53 000).*

Partial Trial Balance
October 31, 19-1

Cash	101	52 565	
J. Emery, Capital	301		53 000

GENERAL LEDGER

J. Emery, Capital — Account No. 301

Date	Explanation		PR	DR.	CR.	Bal.
Sept. 30	Opening entry	GJ	1		50 000	50 000
Oct. 16	Add. invest.	GJ	2		3 000	53 000

owner against total assets) is reported as $59 165, while the claim shown by the Capital account is only $53 000.

Now we can begin to see the need for closing the ledger. Simply, closing the ledger is a method of getting the net income figure into the owner's Capital account so that the balance of this account agrees with the total owner's equity of the balance sheet and the accounting equation. As you will learn shortly, the method of getting the net income into the Capital account is to transfer the net income through the ledger accounts. For now, keep in mind this first need of updating the Capital account so that the ledger balance can be in agreement with the balance sheet and the accounting equation.

One more need will help to explain the meaning of closing the ledger. As you know, the calculation of net income is the result of matching revenues for a certain accounting period with related expenses for that accounting period. And, as you now know, it is important for a year-end matching to occur so that the net income for the year can be reported to interested persons outside the firm. (One of those interested parties is the Department of National Revenue — Taxation. The Department requires all businesses to report their net income (or net loss) at least once a year.)

Now, if the revenue and expense accounts contain balances for a specific year, these figures cannot appear in the next accounting period. If they did, the next year's figures would contain not only the current year's amounts, but also last year's. That is why the balances of all revenue and all expense accounts at the end of the accounting year must be "closed" — brought down to zero. By closing all revenue and all expense accounts, these accounts are cleared to receive the figures of revenue and expense for the next accounting period.

Two aspects of closing can now be identified. First, there is the need for updating the Capital account balance so that it can agree with the total owner's equity in the balance sheet. This agreement can be brought about by transferring the net income through ledger accounts so that it can be added to the Capital account. Second, there is the need to prepare all revenue and expense accounts at the end of the accounting year so that they can receive only the figures of the next accounting period. To accomplish this, all revenue and expense accounts must be closed (brought down to zero). Keep these two meanings in mind when you go through the actual mechanics of closing the ledger.

The Mechanics of Closing

To understand the actual mechanics of closing, it is helpful to first visualize the ideas by means of a series of T-accounts. In the illustration below, the separate stages of the closing process are

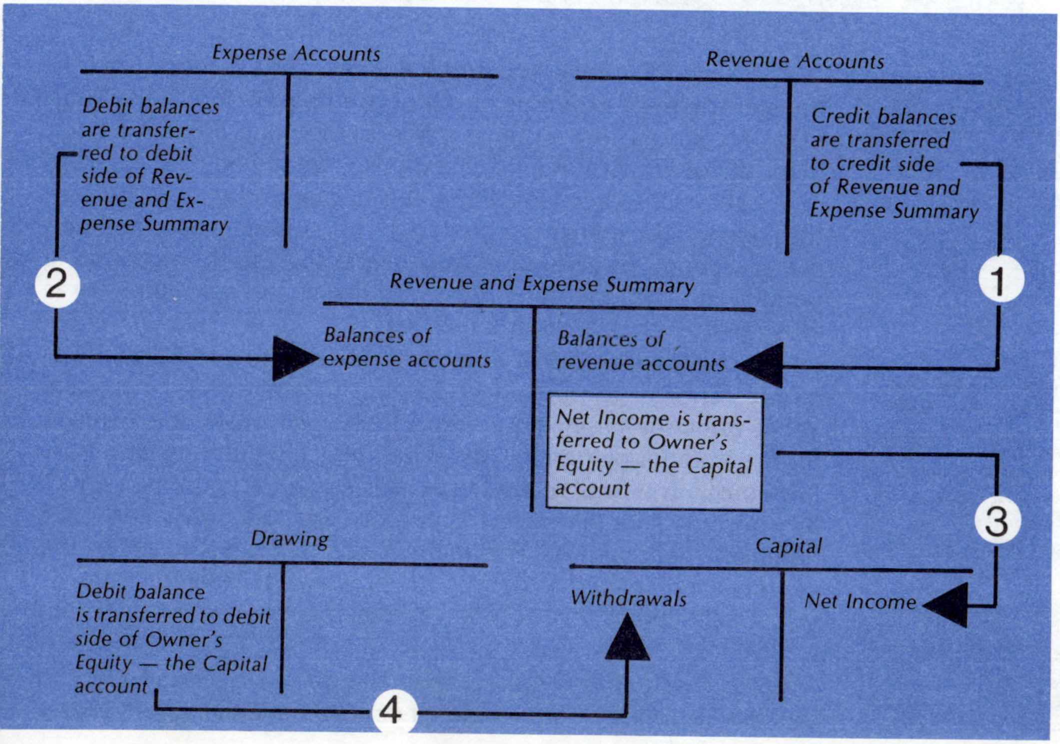

numbered in chronological order. You will also observe that one new account, *Revenue and Expense Summary,* appears in the set of accounts. Can you guess its nature and purpose? Follow the sequence closely; then study the number-keyed explanation that follows.

1. Transfer Revenue Account Balances The first step in closing the ledger is to transfer the revenue for the accounting period to a special summary account called Revenue and Expense Summary (often abbreviated R & E Summary where space is limited). To make this transfer, the Revenue account or accounts must be debited and the Summary account must be credited. Once this entry is posted, the Revenue account will be closed. Thus the balance of the account will be zero, and the Revenue and Expense Summary account will have a credit balance.

For J. Emery Real Estate, this entry may be shown in T-account form as follows:

Commissions Earned	401
Oct. 31 (to close) 14 000	*Oct. 31 bal. 14 000*

Revenue and Expense Summary	399
	Oct. 31 14 000

Revenue and Expense Summary	399
Oct. 31 5 835 (total expenses)	*Oct.31 14 000 (total revenue)*

2. Transfer Expense Account Balances The second step is to transfer the total expenses of the accounting period to the Summary account. This transfer is made by debiting the R & E Summary account with the *total expenses* and crediting each individual expense account. Once this compound entry is posted, the individual expense accounts will be closed, while the Summary account receives the total expenses for the accounting period. This compound entry may be shown in T-account form as illustrated at the top of the next page.

Revenue and Expense Summary	399
Oct. 31 5 835 (total expenses)	*Oct.31 14 000 (total revenue)*
	Oct. 31 balance 8 165
	This account has a credit balance. It must be the net income.

3. Transfer the R & E Summary Balance to the Capital Account Look at the Summary account illustrated in the margin. What does the credit figure represent? Obviously, the revenue for the accounting period. And what does the debit figure mean? Obviously, the total related expenses for the accounting period. By now, you should realize the purpose and function of the R & E Summary account. As the name suggests, it summarizes the revenue and related expenses in the General Ledger. Actually, you can think of this account as the income statement in the ledger.

If the credit side is greater than the debit side, what will the balance be called? Net income, of course, since there is an excess

Rent Expense 501

Oct. 31 bal.	600	Oct. 31 (to close)	600

Revenue and Expense Summary 399

Oct. 31	5 835		

Telephone Expense 502

Oct. 31 bal.	40	Oct. 31 (to close)	40

Utilities Expense 503

Oct. 31 bal.	95	Oct. 31 (to close)	95

Salaries Expense 504

Oct. 31 bal.	4 500	Oct. 31 (to close)	4 500

Advertising Expense 505

Oct. 31 bal.	600	Oct. 31 (to close)	600

of revenue over related expenses. This net income, or credit balance, can now be transferred (cleared) to the owner's capital account by debiting Summary account and crediting the Capital account. This entry may be shown in T-account form as follows:

Revenue and Expense Summary 399

Oct. 31	5 835	Oct. 31	14 000
Oct. 31 (to close)	8 165		

J. Emery, Capital 401

		Oct. 31	53 000
		Oct. 31	8 165

The R & E Summary account is now down to zero because the credit balance of $8 165 (the net income) has been transferred to the owner's Capital account. This transfer shows that the net income has been added to the owner's Capital.

If there were a debit balance in the Summary account, this debit balance would mean a net loss, since there would be an excess of expenses over related revenue. Of course, this net loss would be transferred to the owner's Capital account by debiting the Capital account (a decrease to owner's equity) and crediting the Summary account. Study the analysis of the following T-account:

X Capital			*301*
Net Loss	*4 000*	*Original Balance*	*8 900*

Revenue and Expense Summary			*399*
Expenses	*12 000*	*Revenue*	*8 000*
Bal 4000		*To close Net Loss*	*4 000*

From the closing entry above, the net loss of $4 000 (the debit balance in the Summary account) is transferred to the debit side of the owner's Capital account. Since the owner's Capital account is part of owner's equity in the accounting equation, debit has the effect of decreasing owner's equity in the equation. The same idea was shown on the worksheet: net loss was transferred from the debit column of the income statement section to the debit column of the balance sheet.

Chart of Accounts

OWNER'S EQUITY
301 J. Emery, Capital
302 J. Emery, Drawing
399 Revenue and Expense Summary

Note the account number given to this Summary account: Account No. 399. Since the whole idea of the Summary account is to transfer the net income (or net loss) to the owner's Capital account, you can say that the Summary account is related to Owner's Equity in the General Ledger. For this reason, many charts of accounts will show the Summary account under Owner's Equity.

4. Transfer Drawings to the Capital Account The final step in closing is to transfer the owner's drawings to the owner's Capital account. This is accomplished by debiting the Capital account and crediting the Drawing account. This last step is identical to the sequence used in the accounting equation and the

J. Emery, Drawing			*302*
Oct. 31 (balance)	*2 000*	*Oct. 31 (to close)*	*2 000*

J. Emery, Capital			*301*
Oct. 31	*2 000*	*Oct. 31*	*53 000*
		Oct. 31	*8 165*
		Balance	*59 165*

OWNER'S EQUITY		
J. Emery, Capital	*$53 000*	
Add: Net Income	*8 165*	
	61 165	
Less: Drawings	*2 000*	
Total Owner's Equity		*$59 165*

balance sheet. Once this entry is posted, the Drawing account is closed and the Capital account agrees with the new total of Owner's Equity as shown by the balance sheet and accounting equation.

Closing the Ledger: An Illustration

The General Ledger for J. Emery Real Estate will be used to illustrate the actual closing process. Although closing would normally occur at the end of a complete fiscal (accounting) year, we will close the ledger at the end of one month for J. Emery Real Estate for the sake of simplicity.

It is essential to remember one other point: journal entries must come before all ledger postings. Follow the illustrations on the next pages. Then study the short summary that follows.

GENERAL JOURNAL — Page 4

DATE 19-1		ACCOUNT TITLE AND EXPLANATION	POST. REF.	DEBIT	CREDIT
Oct.	31	Commissions Earned	401	14 000 00	
		Revenue and Expense Summary	399		14 000 00
		To close the revenue account.			
	31	Revenue and Expense Summary	399	5 835 00	
		Rent Expense	501		600 00
		Telephone Expense	502		40 00
		Utilities Expense	503		95 00
		Salaries Expense	504		4 500 00
		Advertising Expense	505		600 00
		To close the expense accounts.			
	31	Revenue and Expense Summary	399	8 165 00	
		J. Emery, Capital	301		8 165 00
		To transfer the net income.			
	31	J. Emery, Capital	301	2 000 00	
		J. Emery, Drawing	302		2 000 00
		To transfer the drawings.			

Important: *The presence of account numbers in the Post. Ref. column suggests that all accounts on this page have been posted to the General Ledger.*

GENERAL LEDGER
(after closing entries have been posted)

Cash — Account No. 101

DATE 19-1		EXPLANATION		POST. REF.	DEBIT	CREDIT	BALANCE	
Sept.	30	Opening entry	G.J.	1	6000000		6000000	
Oct.	1		G.J.	1		100000	5900000	
	5		G.J.	1		500000	5400000	
	11		G.J.	1		4000	5396000	
	12		G.J.	2		60000	5336000	
	15		G.J.	2		400000	4936000	
	16		G.J.	2	300000		5236000	
	18		G.J.	2		9500	5226500	
	20		G.J.	2	340000		5566500	
	30		G.J.	2		200000	5366500	
	31		G.J.	2	340000		5706500	
	31		G.J.	3		450000	5256500	Dr.

Accts. Rec./Pat Rogers — Account No. 103

DATE 19-1		EXPLANATION		POST. REF.	DEBIT	CREDIT	BALANCE	
Oct.	31	Invoice 00007	G.J.	3	200000		200000	Dr.

Accts. Rec./R. Scobie — Account No. 104

DATE 19-1		EXPLANATION		POST. REF.	DEBIT	CREDIT	BALANCE	
Oct.	31	Invoice 00008	G.J.	3	120000		120000	Dr.

Accts. Rec./Shannon Development Co. — Account No. 105

DATE 19-1		EXPLANATION		POST. REF.	DEBIT	CREDIT	BALANCE	
Oct.	31	Invoice 00009	G.J.	3	400000		400000	Dr.

Automobile — Account No. 110

DATE 19-1		EXPLANATION	POST. REF.	DEBIT	CREDIT	BALANCE	
Sept.	30	Opening entry G.J.	1	1500000		1500000	Dr.

Furniture — Account No. 112

DATE 19-1		EXPLANATION	POST. REF.	DEBIT	CREDIT	BALANCE	
Sept.	30	Opening entry G.J.	1	300000		300000	
Oct.	1	G.J.	1	100000		400000	Dr.

Office Equipment — Account No. 114

DATE 19-1		EXPLANATION	POST. REF.	DEBIT	CREDIT	BALANCE	
Sept.	30	Opening entry G.J.	1	200000		200000	
Oct.	3	G.J.	1	120000		320000	
	4	G.J.	1		20000	300000	Dr.

Bank Loan Payable — Account No. 201

DATE 19-1		EXPLANATION	POST. REF.	DEBIT	CREDIT	BALANCE	
Sept.	30	Opening entry G.J.	1		2000000	2000000	
Oct.	15	G.J.	2	400000		1600000	Cr.

Accts. Pay./Bell Furniture Co. — Account No. 202

DATE 19-1		EXPLANATION	POST. REF.	DEBIT	CREDIT	BALANCE	
Sept.	30	Opening entry G.J.	1		300000	300000	Cr.

Accts. Pay./The City Record — Account No. 203

DATE 19-1		EXPLANATION	POST. REF.	DEBIT	CREDIT	BALANCE	
Oct.	31	G.J.	3		60000	60000	Cr.

Accts. Pay./Ryan Equipment Co. Account No. 204

DATE 19-1		EXPLANATION	POST. REF.	DEBIT	CREDIT	BALANCE	
Sept.	30	Opening entry G.J.	1		200000	200000	
Oct.	3	G.J.	1		120000	320000	
	4	G.J.	1	20000		300000	Cr.

Accts. Pay./Westown Motors Ltd. Account No. 205

DATE 19-1		EXPLANATION	POST. REF.	DEBIT	CREDIT	BALANCE
Sept.	30	Opening entry G.J.	1		500000	500000
Oct.	5	G.J.	1	500000		0

J. Emery, Capital Account No. 301

DATE 19-1		EXPLANATION	POST. REF.	DEBIT	CREDIT	BALANCE	
Sept.	30	Opening entry G.J.	1		5000000	5000000	
Oct.	16	G.J.	2		300000	5300000	Cr.
	31	Net income G.J.	4		816500	6116500	
	31	Drawings G.J.	4	200000		5916500	Cr.

J. Emery, Drawing Account No. 302

DATE 19-1		EXPLANATION	POST. REF.	DEBIT	CREDIT	BALANCE	
Oct.	30	G.J.	2	200000		200000	Dr.
	31	To J. Emery, Capital G.J.	4		200000	0	

Revenue and Expense Summary Account No. 399

DATE 19-1		EXPLANATION	POST. REF.	DEBIT	CREDIT	BALANCE
Oct.	31	Total revenue G.J.	4		1400000	1400000
	31	Total expenses G.J.	4	583500		816500
	31	To close net income G.J.	4	816500		0

Commissions Earned

Account No. 401

DATE 19-1		EXPLANATION	POST. REF.	DEBIT	CREDIT	BALANCE	
Oct.	20		G.J.	2		340000	340000	
	31		G.J.	2		340000	680000	
	31		G.J.	3		720000	1400000	Cr.
	31	To R+E Summary	G.J.	4	1400000		-0-	

Rent Expense

Account No. 501

DATE 19-1		EXPLANATION	POST. REF.	DEBIT	CREDIT	BALANCE	
Oct.	12		G.J. 2	60000		60000	Dr.
	31	To R+E Summary	G.J. 4		60000	-0-	

Telephone Expense

Account No. 502

DATE 19-1		EXPLANATION	POST. REF.	DEBIT	CREDIT	BALANCE	
Oct.	11		G.J. 1	4000		4000	Dr.
	31	To R+E Summary	G.J. 4		4000	-0-	

Utilities Expense

Account No. 503

DATE 19-1		EXPLANATION	POST. REF.	DEBIT	CREDIT	BALANCE	
Oct.	18		G.J. 2	9500		9500	Dr.
	31	To R+E Summary	G.J. 4		9500	-0-	

Salaries Expense

Account No. 504

DATE 19-1		EXPLANATION	POST. REF.	DEBIT	CREDIT	BALANCE	
Oct.	31		G.J. 3	450000		450000	Dr.
	31	To R+E Summary	G.J. 4		450000	-0-	

Advertising Expense

Account No. 505

DATE 19-1		EXPLANATION	POST. REF.	DEBIT	CREDIT	BALANCE	
Oct.	31		G.J. 3	60000		60000	Dr.
	31	To R+E Summary	G.J. 4		60000	-0-	

Summary

Temporary accounts: revenue and expenses, R&E Summary, and drawing accounts.

Permanent accounts: asset, liability, and capital accounts.

Revenue and Expense Summary: a temporary account used to transfer (clear) the net income (net loss) to the owner's capital account.

Closing the ledger, or "closing the books," is done at the end of the accounting year for two purposes:

- to update the Capital account so that its balance can agree with the total owner's equity figure as calculated by the balance sheet and accounting equation
- to prepare the ledger so that the revenue and expense amounts for the next accounting period can be received without mixing them with the previous accounting period

To achieve these goals, all revenue and expense accounts are closed. Because these accounts are closed at the end of the accounting period, they are known as the temporary accounts of the General Ledger. On the other hand, the balance sheet accounts (except for the owner's Drawings) are not closed. Therefore, all balance sheet accounts (except for Drawings) are called permanent accounts.

The owner's Drawing account must be considered a temporary account because its balance is closed (transferred) to the owner's Capital account. This means that the only permanent owner's equity account in the General Ledger is the owner's Capital account.

Remember, too, that the Revenue and Expense Summary account is itself a temporary owner's equity account because it is used only at the end of the accounting period when the books are being closed. Nevertheless, it serves two very useful functions in the accounting cycle: (1) it simplifies the closing of the temporary revenue and expense accounts, and (2) it provides a convenient record of the net income (or net loss) for the accounting period in the ledger.

Closing the ledger is the seventh and next-to-last step of the accounting cycle. Can you name all seven in order?

TOPIC 1 PROBLEMS

6-1 After one year's operations, the trial balance for Bernik's TV Service revealed the information in the next illustration.

a From the trial balance, prepare a six-column worksheet.

b From the completed worksheet, prepare a set of financial statements in good order. Use the report form of the balance sheet.

c From the trial balance, set up a General Ledger for Bernik's TV Service. Include an account for Revenue and Expense Summary (No. 399). Show all account

Bernik's TV Service
Trial Balance
December 31, 19-1

Cash	101	$ 2 075	
Accts. Rec./R. Auld	102	250	
Accts. Rec./C. Baechler	103	125	
Accts. Rec./F. Benton	104	50	
Repair Equipment	110	8 415	
Office Equipment	111	785	
Bank Loan Payable (on demand)	201		$ 400
Accts. Pay./Bradford & Son	202		225
Accts. Pay./Brookfield Ltd.	203		275
John Bernik, Capital	301		11 025
John Bernik, Drawing	302	8 400	
Repairs Revenue	401		18 135
Wages Expense	501	6 960	
Rent Expense	502	900	
Advertising Expense	503	465	
Repair Supplies Expense	504	1 035	
Telephone Expense	505	120	
Utilities Expense	506	480	
		$30 060	$30 060

balances carried forward as of December 31. For example, the Cash account would be opened as follows:

Cash — Account No. 101

DATE	EXPLANATION	POST. REF.	DEBIT	CREDIT	BALANCE
19-1					
Dec. 31	Balance forward	✓			2 075 00 Dr.

d Journalize the required closing entries in the General Journal, beginning with journal page 12.

e Post the closing entries to the appropriate ledger accounts. *Note:* The new balance in John Bernik, Capital, after all postings are complete, should be $10 800. Does your balance agree?

Key Check Figure
Net Income =
$8 175

6-2 Peggy Chivers is the owner-manager of Supreme Carpet & Upholstery Cleaners. Her firm's year-end trial balance is as follows:

Supreme Carpet & Upholstery Cleaners
Trial Balance
March 31, 19-2

Cash	101	$ 4 700	
Canada Savings Bonds	102	10 000	
Accts. Rec./T. Adams Ltd.	103	1 000	
Accts. Rec./S. Roy	104	300	
Cleaning Equipment	110	6 000	
Office Equipment	112	2 000	
Truck	114	7 000	
Bank Loan Payable (on demand)	201		$ 1 200
Accts. Pay./Rex Supply Ltd.	202		3 000
Accts. Pay./Woods & Co.	203		800
Long-Term Note Payable	210		5 200
Peggy Chivers, Capital	301		15 000
Peggy Chivers, Drawing	302	9 600	
Fees Earned	401		45 000
Interest Revenue	402		900
Advertising Expense	501	9 600	
Wages Expense	502	18 000	
Cleaning Supplies Expense	503	1 400	
Truck Expense	504	1 100	
Telephone Expense	505	250	
Miscellaneous Expense	506	50	
Interest Expense	520	100	
		$71 100	$71 100

Here is some additional information:

(i) The long-term note payable is due in the year 19-5.

(ii) It is secured by the pledging of the amount reported for the cleaning equipment.

(iii) The current portion of the long-term note payable, due within the next accounting year, is $1 200.

a From the trial balance, prepare a six-column worksheet.

b From the completed worksheet and additional information given in the question, prepare a set of financial statements in good order. Use the report form of the balance sheet.

c From the trial balance, set up a General Ledger for Supreme Carpet & Upholstery Cleaners. Include an account for Revenue and Expense Summary (No. 399). Show all account balances carried forward as of March 31, 19-2.

d Journalize the required closing entries in the General Journal, beginning with journal page 23.

e Post the closing entries to the appropriate ledger accounts. *Note:* The new balance in Peggy Chivers, Capital, after all postings are complete, should be $20 800. Does your balance agree?

Key Check Figure
Net Income =
$15 400

6-3 The year-end trial balance for Paul's Armoured Car Service is illustrated below.

Paul's Armoured Car Service
Trial Balance
November 30, 19-2

Cash	101	$ 200	
Accts. Rec./C. Price Co.	102	5 000	
Accts. Rec./B. Walker & Sons	103	3 000	
Land	110	4 000	
Garage Buildings	112	16 000	
Armoured Cars	114	18 000	
Office Equipment	116	4 000	
Bank Loan Payable	201		$ 4 000
Accts. Pay./Daily News	202		1 500
Accts. Pay./Exeter Supply Co.	203		4 500
Accts. Pay./Farr Motors Ltd.	204		6 000
Mortgage Payable	220		30 000
Paul Williams, Capital	301		22 500
Paul Williams, Drawing	302	12 000	
Fees Earned	401		60 000
Wages Expense	501	54 000	
Advertising Expense	502	1 200	
Repairs Expense	503	1 800	
Gasoline and Oil Expense	504	3 100	
Insurance Expense	505	1 500	
Utilities Expense	506	1 800	
Telephone Expense	507	200	
Miscellaneous Expense	508	300	
Bank Interest Expense	520	400	
Mortgage Interest Expense	521	2 000	
		$128 500	$128 500

Here is some additional information:

(i) The bank loan is payable on demand.

(ii) The mortgage payable is due on November 30, 19-2.

(iii) It is secured by the pledging of the cost of both the land and the garage buildings.

(iv) The current portion of the mortgage payable, due within the next accounting year, is $3 000.

a From the trial balance, prepare a six-column worksheet.

b From the completed worksheet and additional information, prepare a set of financial statements in good form. Use the report form of balance sheet.

c From the trial balance, set up a General Ledger for Paul's Armoured Car Service. Include an account for Revenue and Expense Summary (No. 399). Show all account balances carried forward as of November 30, 19-2.

d Journalize the required closing entries in the General Journal, starting with journal page 15.

Key Check Figure
Net Loss = $6 300

e Post the closing entries to the appropriate ledger accounts. *Note:* The new balance in the owner's Capital account, after all postings are complete, should be $4 200. Does your balance agree?

TOPIC 2 COMPLETING THE ACCOUNTING CYCLE

After all closing entries have been posted, the General Ledger should reveal these facts:

- All revenue and expense accounts, the Revenue and Expense Summary account, and the owner's Drawing account should have zero balances.
- Only the accounts that supply data for the year-end balance sheet should contain balances.
- The balance in the owner's Capital account should agree with the total of Owner's Equity in the year-end balance sheet.

Postclosing trial balance: a trial balance taken after closing the ledger.

To prove these facts, an after-closing trial balance called the postclosing trial balance is prepared. This procedure represents the final step in any accounting cycle. The postclosing trial balance for J. Emery Real Estate is illustrated below:

J. Emery Real Estate
Postclosing Trial Balance
October 31, 19–1

ACCOUNT TITLE	ACCT. NO.	DEBIT	CREDIT
Cash	101	52 565.00	
Accts. Rec./Pat Rogers	103	2 000.00	
Accts. Rec./R. Scobie	104	1 200.00	
Accts. Rec./Shannon Development Co.	105	4 000.00	
Automobile	110	15 000.00	
Furniture	112	4 000.00	
Office Equipment	114	3 000.00	
Bank Loan Payable	201		16 000.00
Accts. Pay./Bell Furniture Co.	202		3 000.00
Accts. Pay./The City Press	203		600.00
Accts. Pay./Ryan Equipment Co.	204		3 000.00
J. Emery, Capital	301		59 165.00
		81 765.00	81 765.00

From the postclosing trial balance, you can see that the accounts listed are the balance sheet accounts. As stated in Topic 1, these balance sheet accounts are the *permanent accounts* because their balances are carried forward into the next accounting period. On the other hand, all revenue and expense accounts, the Revenue and Expense Summary account, and the owner's

Drawing account do not appear in the postclosing trial balance because their account balances are closed. For this reason, these accounts are only *temporary accounts* — their balances are reduced to zero at the end of each accounting cycle.

If the postclosing trial balance agrees in total, then the accounting equation, after closing the ledger, must also balance. This can easily be checked by doing the accounting equation from the postclosing trial balance as follows:

Final Acc. Eq. after post trial Bal

Assets					=	Liabilities		+	Owner's Equity
Cash	Accts. Rec.	Auto	Furn.	Office Equip.		Bk. Loan Pay.	Accts. Pay.		J. Emery, Capital
$52 565 +	$7 200 +	$15 000 +	$4 000 +	$3 000	=	$16 000 +	$6 600	+	$59 165
$81 765					=	$22 600		+	$59 165
$81 765					=	$81 765			

Summary of the Entire Accounting Cycle

The preparation of the postclosing trial balance completes the accounting cycle. The cycle begins with originating the data on

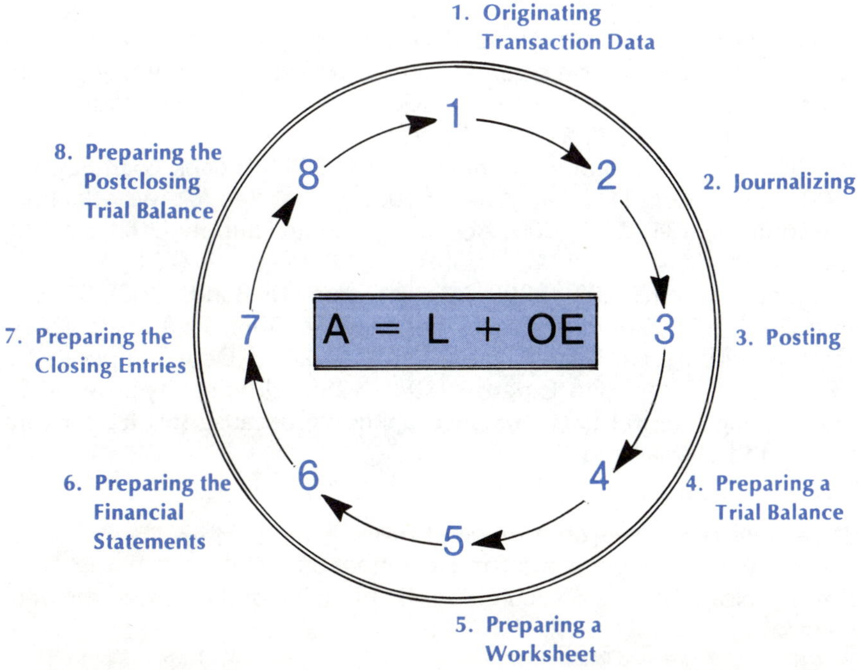

source documents and ends with the preparation of a postclosing trial balance. Then the cycle is repeated for the next accounting year. To review, the eight steps in the accounting cycle may be visualized as in the preceding illustration.

TOPIC 2 PROBLEMS

6-4 Refer to your solution for Problem 6-1.

a From the General Ledger, prepare a postclosing trial balance for Bernik's TV Service.

Key Check Figure Postclosing Trial Balance Total = $11 700

b Prepare a final accounting equation from the postclosing trial balance to prove that the equation balances. For Accounts Receivable and Accounts Payable, show totals only.

6-5 Refer to your solution for Problem 6-2.

a From the General Ledger, prepare a postclosing trial balance for Supreme Carpet & Upholstery Cleaners.

Key Check Figure Postclosing Trial Balance Total = $31 000

b Prepare a final accounting equation from the postclosing trial balance to prove that the equation balances. For Accounts Receivable and Accounts Payable, show totals only.

6-6 Refer to your solution for Problem 6-3.

a From the General Ledger, prepare a postclosing trial balance for Paul's Armoured Car Service.

Key Check Figure Postclosing Trial Balance Total = $50 200

b Prepare a final accounting equation from the postclosing trial balance to prove that the equation balances.

6-7 Challenge Problem Karen Wong, D.D.S. completed her first year of professional practice. Her dental firm's general ledger reported the following year-end account balances: Cash (101), $3 600; Government of Canada Bonds (102), $20 000; Interest Expense (520), $1 400; Accts. Rec./C. Best (103), $200; Licence Fee Expense (507), $400; Dental Equipment (110), $30 000; Bank Loan Payable (201), $4 000; Accts. Rec./D. Ellen (104), $100; Accts. Rec./G. Wood (105), $750; Office Equipment (112), $6 000; Accts. Pay./Central Supply (202), $2 500; Karen Wong, Drawing (302), $18 000; Professional Fees Earned (401), $66 530; Accts. Pay./Mardan Systems (203), $800; Interest Earned on Bonds (402), $2 000; Rent Expense (501), $7 200; Professional Dues Expense (506), $200; Salaries Expense (502), $34 000; 3-Year Note Payable (220), $10 000; Dental Supplies Expense (503), $5 600; Telephone Expense (504), $280; Utilities Expense (505), $1 100; Karen Wong, Capital (301), balance unknown because this ledger card could not be found at year-end.

Here is some additional information:

(i) The bank loan payable is on a demand basis.

(ii) The 3-Year Note Payable is due on December 31, 19-4.

(iii) The 3-Year Note Payable is secured by the pledging of the cost of the dental equipment.

(iv) The current portion of the 3-Year Note Payable is $3 000.
(v) The firm's year-end is December 31.

a Arrange the accounts in numerical order on a six-column worksheet. Enter all given account balances in their normal balance position, and assume they are correct. Find the amount for Karen Wong, Capital by "plugging in" the figure. Complete the six-column worksheet.

b From the completed worksheet and additional information, prepare a set of financial statements in good order. Use the report form of balance sheet.

c From the trial balance, set up a General Ledger for the dental practice. Include an account for Revenue and Expense Summary (No. 399). Show all account balances carried forward as of the year-end.

d Journalize the required closing entries in the General Journal, starting with page 20.

e Post the closing entries to the appropriate ledger accounts. *Hint:* The balance in the owner's Capital account after all postings are complete should be $43 350.

f Prepare a postclosing trial balance.

Key Check Figure
Net Income = $18 350

TOPIC 3 CAREERS AND THE PROCESS OF ACCOUNTING

To understand some of the possible careers in accounting, it is necessary first to know what makes up the entire accounting process within any firm. An accounting systems flowchart will show you the process. Study the flowchart on the next page.

Systems flowchart: a chart showing the flow of procedures, and the flow of data and documents, in an accounting system.

The Systems Flowchart

Think of the large rectangle as a business of any size or kind. Steps of the accounting process which take place within the firm are shown inside the rectangle; those which take place outside the firm are shown outside the rectangle.

Within any business organization, all accounting begins with the *origination of data.* In a systems flowchart, the *input symbol* has been used to show this data coming into the business.

Not all data or information, however, results in business transactions. Therefore, the flowchart *decision symbol* asks an impor-

Input Symbol

Indicates data put into the system

Decision Symbol

Indicates that a decision must be made

tant question: *Is an accounting entry required?* For example, a person may offer the owner a sum of money to buy the business. This information will not become a business transaction because the "transaction" is not complete unless the offer is accepted by the owner. Instead, it ends. The systems flowchart shows a "no" answer to the question by means of the arrow pointing to the *terminal point.* The *terminal symbol* ends any further consideration of this data.

Terminal Symbol

Indicates the ending in a flowchart

On the other hand, much of the data originating within the firm will form completed business transactions — for example, when a sale of goods or services is made to a customer. This is shown on a source document called an invoice. The invoice will be used to record the results of the transaction.

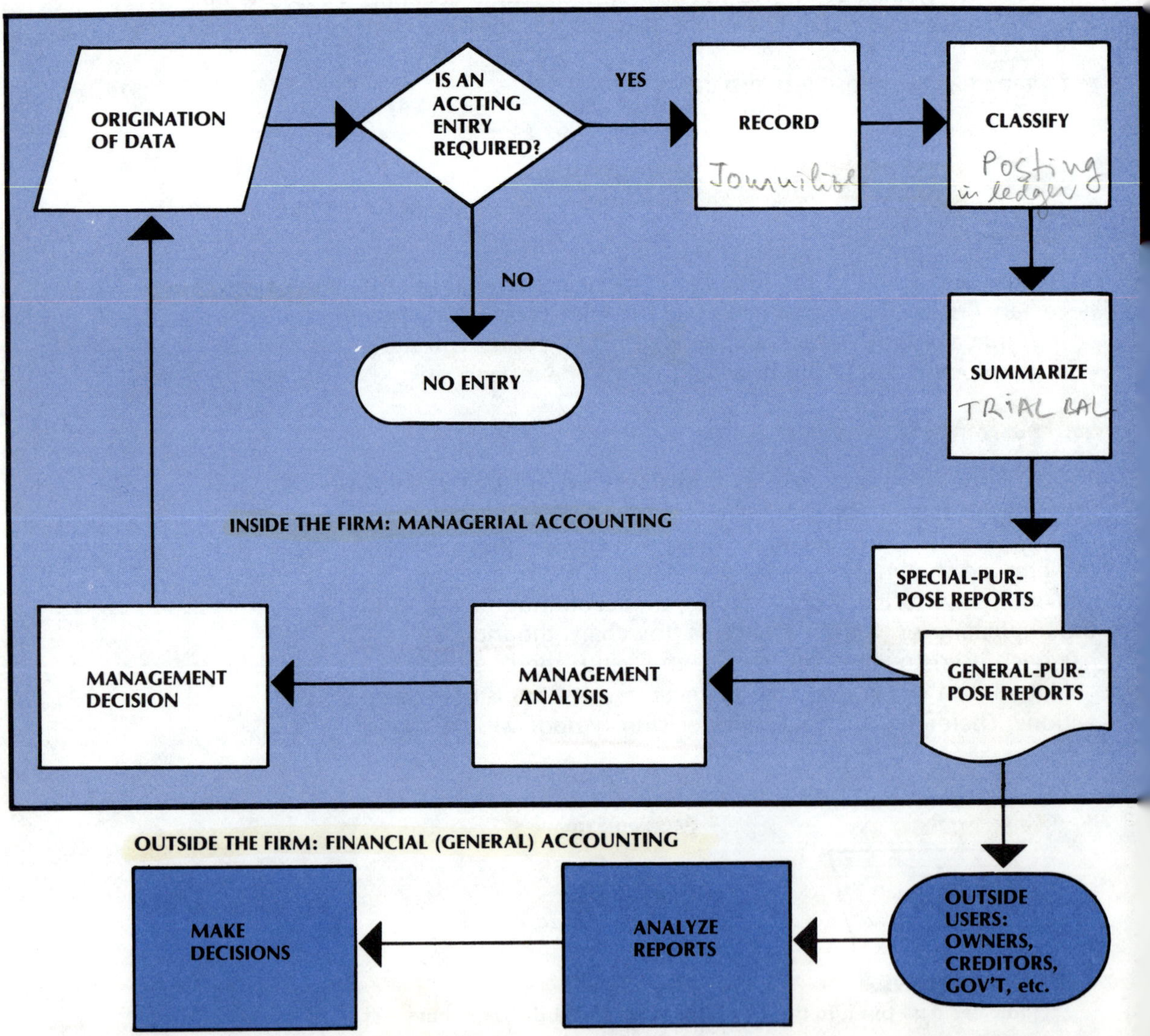

Process Symbol

Indicates that an activity of some kind must be performed

All completed business transactions will enter the accounting process. The systems flowchart now shows a "yes" answer with an arrow leading to the symbol labelled RECORD, which refers to the action of recording the results of that transaction.

The action of recording is shown in the chart by the *process symbol.* You already know that a record of any business transaction is made by analyzing the information shown by the source document and recording that information in a journal — that is, journalizing those business events.

Document (Report) Symbol

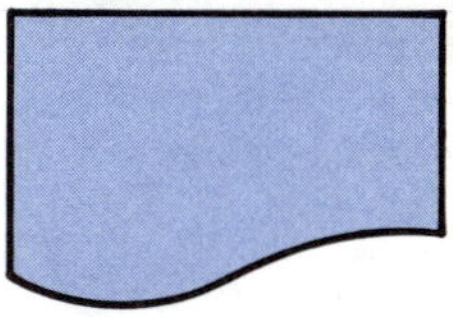

Indicates any source document: journals, ledgers, trial balances, financial statements, and other accounting statements and reports

The arrow now leads from RECORD to another process symbol labelled CLASSIFY. Classifying accounting information is simply the action of posting accounting data to appropriate accounts in a ledger file.

The next arrow leads to SUMMARIZE. Many different summaries are made before accounting reports are prepared — the trial balance is one example of a valuable summary of General Ledger accounts before financial statements are prepared.

The chart now shows the output of reports. The reports are indicated in the chart by the *document or report symbol.* Two distinct types of reports are produced by the accounting process, one aimed at persons within the firm, the other at persons outside the firm.

Special-purpose reports: detailed sales reports, expense reports, budgets, and other financial reports aimed at the managers (insiders) of a business.

Reports which stay *within* the firm are called special-purpose reports. These are produced for the use of managers. Among them will be reports covering periodic sales, expense reports, budgets, and monthly financial statements.

The chart shows that these special-purpose reports may serve as the basis for a management decision that sets off a new series of economic events. Such a decision may result in the recording of more business transactions, ending in another series of reports.

Managerial accounting: that part of the accounting process which prepares special-purpose reports to meet the needs of managers.

Because special-purpose reports are intended for managerial decision-making only, the systems flowchart shows this "flow" of the accounting process as one main branch of accounting. This branch is called managerial accounting or management accounting. As you will learn shortly, many careers are possible in this branch of accounting.

General-purpose reports: financial statements prepared in accordance with GAAPs and for outside users.

The other type of report shown in the flowchart is general-purpose reports for interested parties *outside* the firm. These outsiders include owners who do not manage their businesses, such as shareholders of corporations. Other interested outsiders could be potential investors, banks and other lending institutions, government agencies, and labour unions. *Note:* Since a symbol for "outsiders" does not exist, a symbol has been selected for our purposes. It is not basic to accounting systems flowcharting.

For outside groups, the reports must be general in nature, so that all outsiders can use them. Thus the traditional year-end financial statements — year-end income statements and balance sheets — make up these reports. With these, the would-be lender will want to analyze and interpret the firm's financial position to decide whether the firm is secure and offers a good return on investment.

For obvious reasons, general-purpose financial statements *must* be prepared according to pre-established guidelines — GAAPs. In Chapter 5 you learned that every country follows basic accounting principles, and also specific ones as published by that country's leading accounting authority (the *CICA Handbook* in Canada). Since general-purpose financial statements are prepared only for outside parties, in accordance with GAAP, this branch of accounting is referred to as financial accounting or general accounting.

Financial (general) accounting: that part of the accounting process which prepares general-purpose statements for outside users.

The following table summarizes the main features of, and differences between, financial accounting and managerial accounting. See also the illustrated want ads.

THE TWO BRANCHES OF ACCOUNTING COMPARED

Financial (General)	Managerial
1. *Deals with the preparation of useful general-purpose reports aimed at interested parties outside the firm.*	1. *Deals with the preparation of useful specific-purpose reports aimed at managers inside the firm.*
2. *The reports must be general in nature, in order to be of interest to many different outsiders such as business owners who do not manage (shareholders), potential investors, bankers and other creditors, labour unions, and Revenue Canada — Taxation.*	2. *The reports must be specific in nature, to be of interest to specific managers such as sales managers, production managers, and purchasing managers.*
3. *Common examples of general reports are the year-end financial statements such as the income statement and the balance sheet.*	3. *Common examples of specific reports are a variety of sales reports for different marketing managers, cost and expense reports for purchasing and production managers, specific budgets for specific managers, and monthly financial statements.*
4. *To be useful to outsiders, all general-purpose reports (year-end financial statements) must be prepared in accordance with GAAPs.*	4. *For specific-purpose reports to be useful, GAAPs do not have to be followed. For example, a budgeted income statement is only an estimated forecast of future net income which matches estimated revenues and estimated expenses for a future period.*

Your study of the systems flowchart should enable you to understand the following definition:

A modern definition of accounting.

Accounting may be described as the process of recording, classifying, and summarizing business transactions so that useful specific-purpose reports can be prepared for management decision-making, and useful general-purpose reports in accordance with GAAPs can be prepared for interested parties outside the firm.

QUALIFIED MANAGEMENT ACCOUNTANTS

We have several openings in our management accounting group for qualified accountants with a good educational background and extensive professional or industrial accounting experience. Our management accounting group are involved in a broad range of assignments in such areas as:

Budgetary Control Systems
Responsibility Accounting
Cost Systems
Profitability Analysis
Return on Investment Analysis
Interpretation of Financial Results
Distribution Cost Analyses
Work Simplification
General Administrative Procedures

If you have the experience and qualifications to make a meaningful contribution and would like to broaden your management abilities and perspectives, we would like to hear from you.

Replies, which will be treated in strict confidence, should state full personal details, including education, business experience, and present salary. Please apply to:

MANAGER FINANCIAL ACCOUNTING

Position: Direct and control the complete financial accounting functions of a progressive Canadian company in the forest industry. Major duties will also include systems development and taxation. Reporting to the Divisional Controller, this person will also assist in major planning projects.

Qualifications: C.A. designation. Preference will be given to candidates with data processing background and supervision experience in industry.

Salary commensurate with experience and ability. Apply in confidence to:

Accounting Careers

Large firms often hire clerks to work in a particular area of the firm's accounting. For example, an accounts receivable clerk will work in the accounts receivable department, a payroll clerk will work in the payroll department, and so on. Such an area of accounting is called an accounting application.

Accounting application: the several accounting activities related to one area of the firm's accounting. For example, all accounting related to customer accounts forms the accounts receivable application.

Smaller firms, however, do not divide their accounting duties into departments. Instead, they may hire only one clerk — the bookkeeper — to do the work of several.

Most large firms employ one or more professional accountants, who supervise the clerks. In small firms, the owner-manager may hire a professional accounting firm to set up the firm's accounting system and to look after the preparation of financial statements on a regular basis. Of course, the bookkeeper in this small firm would follow the accounting system designed by the professional accountant.

To become an accounting clerk or bookkeeper normally requires a high school education. One or more high school courses in accounting would help you get started in a clerical position. To become a *professional* accountant, however, you will need more.

Becoming a Professional Accountant

In Canada, three accounting bodies have been created by law to educate and train professional accountants:

- the Institute of Chartered Accountants, whose members are entitled to the designation *Chartered Accountant,* or *C.A.*
- the Society of Management Accountants, whose members are entitled to the designation *Registered Industrial Accountant,* or *R.I.A.* CMA Certified Management Acc.
- the Canadian Certified General Accountants' Association, whose members are entitled to the designation *Certified General Accountant,* or *C.G.A.*

In all three cases, the letters C.A., R.I.A., and C.G.A. do not indicate university degrees — universities do not award these letters. They are, rather, *professional designations.*

C.A.: the designation Chartered Accountant.

The Chartered Accountant (C.A.) To be able to write the letters C.A. after your name, you must complete the requirements stated by your provincial Institute of Chartered Accountants. For example, the Institute of Chartered Accountants of Ontario controls the program for education and training students to become C.A.s in Ontario. Briefly, here are the requirements to become a C.A. in Ontario. (Although there are minor differences in other provinces, the majority have the same requirements.)

- A university degree such as B.A. (Bachelor of Arts), B.Sc. (Bachelor of Science), B.Comm. (Bachelor of Commerce), or M.B.A. (Master of Business Administration) is necessary. However, you must take 45 credit hours of university courses, in courses recognized as acceptable. The courses may be divided into two classes: "pure" and "related."
- In "pure" accounting courses, a minimum grade of 60% is normally required. The recognized "pure" accounting courses are:

Financial Accounting: When you complete this text, you will have covered only a few of the topics in an introductory course of financial accounting. If you continue your education, there are many other topics which have to be covered in depth at the university level.

Management Accounting: This is sometimes called Cost and Management Accounting.

Auditing: This prepares a person to examine the records and financial reports of a variety of firms and business corporations.

Taxation: This covers the details of individual and corporate income tax.

- The recognized "related" accounting courses for which university passing grades are required are:

Computer Science: No professional accountant can practice without some exposure to the computer.

Quantitative Methods: This is a specialized course in business statistics.

Business Finance: This is sometimes called Financial Management.

Economics: This is an introduction to the two main fields of economics, called Microeconomics and Macroeconomics.

Business Law: This is sometimes called Commercial Law.

Introduction to Business: This is an introduction to how businesses are formed and managed.

- You must be hired by a C.A. firm to obtain *on-the-job* training. (In general, C.A. firms require a university degree with at least 28 credit hours of approved accounting and related courses before students are hired.)

● After completing the 45 semester-hour credits, C.A. students are required to successfully complete a course of study at the Institute's professional School of Accountancy. The Institute's Uniform Final Examination is written by all students across Canada. Once a student passes these exams, the designation C.A. is awarded and he or she can practice in any province.

New C.A.s may open their own public accounting office, or they may be employed in private or government positions. The majority of C.A.s specialize in fields like external auditing, taxation, and information systems. These careers and others are summarized at the end of this Topic.

The Registered Industrial Accountant (R.I.A.) Like the C.A., the R.I.A. is a professional. However, an R.I.A. prefers to specialize in the management side of accounting. This means that R.I.A. courses will emphasize cost and management accounting. The word *industrial* is used in the title because the majority of R.I.A.s do their work in large industrial firms such as Stelco, Dominion Foundries, and Algoma Steel.

R.I.A.: the designation Registered Industrial Accountant.

However, at the time of this writing, many provincial chapters of the R.I.A. have agreed to change the title to *C.M.A.* — Certified Management Accountant. If and when all provinces agree to make the change, the letters C.M.A. will replace R.I.A. so that members can emphasize their involvement in *management* accounting.

The governing body for R.I.A.s is the Society of Management Accountants of Canada. Each province is also organized into a branch or chapter. For example, the Society of Management Accountants of Ontario supervises the education and training of R.I.A.s for Ontario. Like C.A.s, the R.I.A.s must complete an educational program. The R.I.A. program is made up of the following courses:

Financial Accounting
- Introductory Accounting
- Intermediate Accounting I
- Intermediate Accounting II
- Taxation
- Advanced Financial Accounting

Management Accounting
- Cost and Management Accounting (an introductory course)
- Advanced Management Accounting
- Quantitative Methods I (a statistical math-oriented course)
- Quantitative Methods II (an advanced statistics course)
- Financial Management
- Internal Auditing (checking the records and control measures within the firm)

Management Studies
- Organizational Behaviour (the behaviour of people working

in groups; also includes topics such as leadership and authority, communication, and decision-making)
Commercial Law
Economics
Communication and Case Analysis (proper language usage, business letter writing, and report writing)
Data Processing
Information Systems
Management: Processes and Problems

The majority of R.I.A. students now take the required courses at post-secondary levels of education. Exemptions from R.I.A. courses are granted to students who have covered the equivalent course material in a recognized university or community college program. Generally, a student must achieve a pass mark of 60% before an exemption is given in an approved course.

Unlike the C.A. designation, the R.I.A. can be obtained without a university degree or college diploma. For example, a high school graduate who passes a special R.I.A. mathematics admission test may be approved for taking R.I.A. courses through part-time study while working. The Society has arranged with several community colleges and universities to offer all the required R.I.A. courses through evening classes. If a person cannot attend these classes, the Society offers correspondence courses. National examinations are held after each course. The pass mark on each exam is 60%.

You need not be working in an accounting position to enrol for R.I.A. studies, but a minimum of two years' work experience is required before receiving the R.I.A. designation. All work experience is evaluated and approved by the Society's admissions committee.

C.G.A.: the designation Certified General Accountant.

The Certified General Accountant (C.G.A.) The C.G.A., too, is a professional accountant who qualifies for a variety of career positions.

C.G.A.s are organized under a national body, the Canadian Certified General Accountants' Association. This association also has a chapter in each province. For example, the C.G.A. Association of Ontario governs the education and training of students in Ontario.

Like C.A.s and R.I.A.s, C.G.A.s need to pass an approved list of "pure" and "related" accounting courses. The courses must be as follows:

- three levels of financial accounting
- two levels of cost and management accounting
- two levels of taxation
- two levels of auditing
- a basic course in statistics
- a course in information and computer systems
- an introductory course in economics

- an introductory course in management
- a basic course in public finance and administration

Since each province lays down its own requirements for becoming a C.G.A., you should contact the main office of the province in which you live for additional information. Students may complete the requirements by taking correspondence courses offered by the provincial association, or obtain exemptions by taking approved university or community college courses.

Obtaining More Than One Designation The three Canadian accounting bodies have a working relationship enabling them to confer each other's designations. For example, an R.I.A. graduate with a university degree may become a C.A. in Ontario by completing 12 semester-hour subject requirements, the practical experience requirements, the School of Accountancy, and the Uniform Final Examination. Similarly, a C.A. can become an R.I.A. and/or a C.G.A. by completing the requirements stated by the provincial chapter of the accounting body whose designation is sought.

Summary of Accounting Careers

Accountants tend to specialize just as lawyers and doctors do. The large field of accounting is composed of three sectors:

- public accounting
- private accounting
- governmental accounting

Public Accounting A public accountant is one who offers professional services to the public for a fee. Many small businesses will hire a public accountant rather than employ an accountant themselves.

An accountant in public practice may work alone or in partnership, or may be a member of a large firm with many partners and offices throughout the country. Some of the larger firms have branches in several countries. The chief areas in which the public accountant will serve are:

General accounting: In this area, the public accountant may check the accounting records once a month, prepare monthly statements, and eventually the year-end statements.

External auditing: To perform an audit, the public accountant makes a careful review of the accounting system and the financial statements of the firm.

This independent service is especially important to corporations because the owners — the shareholders — rely on the audit to present the financial statements fairly and consistently.

Tax services: The public accountant is often called upon to prepare the annual tax returns of individuals, small firms, and large firms. Another important service is to offer the client tax

CHARTERED ACCOUNTANT

QUALIFIED C.A. with at least 3 years experience required by medium sized accounting firm with rapidly growing practice. Ideal candidate will be an independent self-starter and able to supervise staff. Respond in confidence to

CHARTERED ACCOUNTANTS

Progressive, expanding CA firm in North Toronto requires graduates with 1-2 years post qualification experience to handle an account group.

The successful candidates must be capable of supervising staff and dealing directly with clients in tax planning and consulting to medium sized businesses. Professional development program provided "in house" to assist in career growth.

Please reply in confidence to:

plans so that the client can pay as little income tax as possible within the framework of Canada's complex tax laws.

Management advisory services: The public accountant may advise the management of the firm on matters such as classifying job positions and the hiring of qualified people. In recent years, very large public accounting firms have organized special departments that give advisory services to management about company mergers and employee pension plans.

Systems design and installation: The public accountant may be hired to study a firm's system of processing accounting information and suggest changes in the overall accounting system.

In Canada, the majority of accountants in public practice are C.A.s.

CORPORATE ACCOUNTANT

A dynamic Canadian group of companies located in rural southwestern Ontario involved in the highway transportation industry.

THE OPPORTUNITY:
To utilize and expand your financial skills in a rapidly expanding environment.

THE CHALLENGE:
To take immediate control of the corporate financial area: To design and implement accounting systems.

THE CANDIDATE:
Should have a C.A., R.I.A. or C.G.A. designation with at least 2 years' industrial experience. Experience in highway transportation preferred.

Please send resumes in confidence to:

WARD & UPTIGROVE
BOX 127, LISTOWEL, ONTARIO N4W 3H2
OR CALL TED, 519-335-3575

Private Accounting Accountants hired as employees of a firm that is not a public accounting firm — such as Stelco — are said to be in private accounting.

There are far more private accountants than public accountants. The chief employers of professional accountants are modern business corporations that may have several hundred employees working in a number of special accounting departments. In these firms, accountants are hired to perform accounting functions ranging all the way from general (financial) accounting duties to such management functions as cost accounting, budgeting, internal auditing, and other special phases of management accounting.

Controller or comptroller: the chief accounting officer in a large business.

The chief accounting officer in a large business is generally called the controller or comptroller because he or she not only manages the accounting staff, but also is part of the management team responsible for *controlling* the financial operation of the business. One of the attractions of the accounting or finance department of a large corporation is the fact that the accounting division has often been the springboard for promotion to key jobs in sales, purchasing, production planning, manufacturing, and personnel. Indeed, it is quite common for vice presidents and presidents to hold accounting titles such as C.A., R.I.A., and C.G.A.

Newell Industries is a leading organization in the hard ware/houseware field. A large measure of our success is due to the quality of our employees. Due to a promotion, we now require a

CONTROLLER

for one of our companies located in Toronto.

Applicants must have their accounting designation and previous supervisory experience. Your resume will demonstrate a results oriented career to date.

The successful candidate will be responsible for the complete financial function including budgeting, reporting, internal control, credit, collections, financial analysis and office administration.

Newell Industries is an achievement oriented organization that offers excellent growth prospects. Resumes must indicate salary history to be considered. Interested candidates should send their resume to: W. Lamon

A MEMBER OF The newell group™ Newell Industries Canada Inc.
Suite 202, 387 Bloor Street East,
Toronto, Ontario M4W 1H7

Government Accounting Governments at all levels — federal, provincial, and municipal — hire accountants to perform specialized services. Of course, the federal government is the largest employer, for whom accountants may perform such services as preparing budgets, auditing the accounting records of departments, and examining the millions of income tax returns filed by individuals and corporations.

Provincial governments, too, hire accountants, but on a smaller scale. These accountants would perform services such as preparing budgets, auditing the accounting records of various provincial departments, and examining income tax returns and sales tax returns for that province.

ACCOUNTING

A sporting goods company in Toronto seeks an experienced accountant. Candidate must have several years practical experience in all areas of accounting and supervision and be enrolled in the RIA or CGA Course. Position should be of interest to a person earning $22K-$25K per annum.

Please forward resume in confidence to:

BOX 1761, THE GLOBE
444 Front St. W.
Toronto, Ont. M5V 2S9

SASKATCHEWAN
Public Service Commission

PROFESSIONAL ACCOUNTANTS

The Saskatchewan Public Service offers a challenging opportunity to professional accountants interested in senior financial management or auditing positions. We require the talents of innovative and dynamic professionals interested in the development, control and maintenance of major government financial systems. Positions currently available in Regina include:

Chief Financial Officers responsible for directing the design, implementation and maintenance of accounting and financial information systems for the varied and complex operations of a major government Department.

Financial Consultants responsible for the evaluation of government accounting and financial systems, identifying internal control deficiencies and recommending improvements, and participating in the development of accounting policies and procedures.

Senior Audit Supervisors responsible for directing subordinate audit teams in the audit of financial operations of Crown Corporations, boards, agencies and Commissions.

Successful candidates will be members of a recognized Canadian professional accounting body with experience in financial management or auditing.

For further information please call the Public Service Commission at 525-8355 (Area Code 306).

Forward application forms and or resumes to the Public Service Commission, 1820 Albert Street, Regina, S4P 2S8 quoting competition number 107010-7-281, as soon as possible,

Auditors

The MINISTRY OF REVENUE has immediate openings for graduates of the RI or CGA program and for students who have successfully completed the second year of the RIA or CGA program.

These responsibilities could entail field or desk audits of either inventory, financial or corporate records or audits of an investigative nature. Some will require considerable travel by car within the Toronto area or throughout the Province.

Starting salary will be commensurate with qualifications. There are opportunities for advancement.

Please submit a resume as soon as possible to: "Auditors", Recruitment Branch, Civil Service Commission, 151 Bloor Street West, Toronto

ONTARIO
PROVINCE OF OPPORTUNITY

Municipalities hire an accountant to act as the city or town treasurer and to perform services such as audits and the preparation of budgets.

Another important field of governmental accounting is made up of accountants who are hired to assist appointed and elected representatives in administering the many separate funds that have been set up for specific purposes. Because each fund is kept separate, and because there are income or loss concepts in the same sense as in private accounting (though governments are not designed to make profits), governmental accounting is often known as fund accounting.

Fund accounting: the accounting of government funds which are used for a variety of purposes.

TOPIC 3 PROBLEMS

6-8 Three key action words within the accounting process are shown in column 1 below.

Key Concepts from the Accounting Process (1)	*Matching Words from the Accounting Cycle (2)*
Recording	
Classifying	
Summarizing	

a Complete column 2 by giving the one word or words from the steps of the accounting cycle which match(es) the meaning of the word in column 1.

b Give *one* word which defines all the words in both columns. *Hint:* the correct word has been used in an earlier chapter.

6-9 Several significant happenings in the life of a business are listed below. For each of these events, explain whether or not it will enter into the accounting process.

a Vaughan Minor invested $50 000 cash under the firm name Vaughan Minor, Chartered Accountant, and deposited it into the bank account.

b The owner looked at three different office buildings in order to decide where to establish his public accounting practice.

c A cheque for $700 was made out to City Properties Ltd. for the payment of one month's office space in City Towers.

d Vaughan Minor interviewed three candidates for the position of office receptionist.

e The owner was permitted to try out three different microcomputer systems without charge.

f The owner signed a contract to purchase one of the tested microcomputer systems. Payment was to be made in 60 days.

g Lawrence Philp, C.A. opened a competing accounting practice in a modern office building across the street.

h Lawrence Philp, C.A. offered Vaughan Minor $20 000 cash to join him as an equal partner in a firm to be called Philp and Minor, Chartered Accountants.

6-10 Search newspapers and magazines for classified ads announcing positions in bookkeeping, management accounting, and financial (general) accounting. From the advertisements, list the following information: title of position, starting salary, education or knowledge required, experience asked for (if any), and type of work performed.

6-11 Suppose that a friend asks you what is needed to become a professional accountant in Canada. In about 750 words, describe how one qualifies to become a professional accountant in your province. *Hint:* you may have to call the office of your nearest accounting body to obtain specific information.

Case Study 6

Swan Dry Cleaners
Five-Year Financial Summary

	Year 19-5	Year 19-4	Year 19-3	Year 19-2	Year 19-1
Revenue	$20 000	$26 000	$30 000	$40 000	$50 000
Expenses	25 000	27 000	28 000	30 000	35 000
Net Income (Loss)	(5 000)	(1 000)	2 000	10 000	15 000
Current Assets	3 000	4 000	6 000	8 000	7 000
Current Liabilities	4 000	4 000	3 000	4 000	6 000
Fixed Assets	60 000	60 000	60 000	65 000	65 000
Long-Term Liabilities	40 000	38 000	35 000	34 000	32 000
J. P. Swan, Capital	19 000	22 000	28 000	35 000	34 000

J.P. Swan, owner of Swan Dry Cleaners, has been in business for the past five years. To expand, she applies to her bank for a long-term loan of $50 000. She provides the bank with the statement illustrated, showing financial highlights over the life of the business.

a If you were the bank manager, would you accept this form of statement rather than the traditional year-end set of financial statements? Explain why or why not.

b Would you grant Swan Dry Cleaners the loan? Give your reasons for your decision.

PART 2

SYSTEMS AND PROCEDURES FOR A DENTAL FIRM

In Part 1 a simple accounting cycle was presented so you could learn a few of the basic concepts of accounting systems. Also, Part 1 emphasized the use of the General Ledger to prepare useful financial statements at the end of each accounting period. This accounting of the General Ledger is known as the General Ledger application.

General Ledger application: updating the GL to prepare financial statements.

Although the General Ledger application is very important, it is not the only common use of accounting today. In Part 2 you will learn about common applications used to account for individual accounts receivable, individual accounts payable, and the details of the firm's regular payroll.

Such accounting is known as the *accounts receivable application,* the *accounts payable application,* and the *payroll application* respectively.

ACCOUNTING CLERK

We have an immediate opening for a hard working individual who attains a complete understanding of accounting principles and who must be experienced in payroll and account reconciliations.

We offer excellent company benefits, pleasant working environment and the opportunity to learn and benefit from an exciting business.

Apply in confidence to:

BOOKKEEPER

with experience to trial balance. Able to work independently and willing to participate in general office duties. Salary range $12,000-$15,000.

SECRETARY/BOOKKEEPER REQUIRED

- *The maintenance of A/R subsidiary ledger with approx. 100 active accounts.*
- *A bi-weekly payroll for approx. 50 persons on a one-write system.*
- *The job requires reconciling the banks each month and close-off of the journals, posting the general ledger, and a trial balance.*

BOOKKEEPER

Duties include general bookkeeping functions.

Must be experienced in accounts receivable, accounts payable and payroll.

Salary commensurate with experience. The company offers a wide range of benefits.

Please send resume and salary expectations to:

CHAPTER 7

THE ACCOUNTS RECEIVABLE APPLICATION

Assume that a small dental practice has been operating for the first year under the name John H. Johnson, D.D.S. To assist with his practice, Dr. Johnson has hired Kathy Lewis as the dental assistant/hygienist, and Lynn Fortier as the front-office person. Since the dental practice is small, the front-office person is required to perform several duties: receptionist, secretary, and accounting clerk for accounts receivable.

In the first year, the dental practice's accounting system recorded all entries in the general journal and posted all entries in one ledger — the general ledger. At the end of the first year, the chart of accounts for the general ledger contained the following information. *Note:* Not all accounts have been included in this chart. Several others will be added when individual applications

John H. Johnson, D.D.S.
Dental Surgeon
Chart of Accounts

CURRENT ASSETS
101 Cash
102 Bank Deposit Receipts
103 Accts. Rec./Ms. Mary Brown
104 Accts. Rec./B. Campbell
105 Accts. Rec./T. Douglas
106 Accts. Rec./Ms. B. Farr

FIXED ASSETS
110 Dental Euipment
112 Office Equipment

CURRENT LIABILITIES
201 Bank Loan Payable
202 Accts. Pay./Denco Supply
203 Accts. Pay./Mardan Business Systems Ltd.

LONG-TERM LIABILITIES
210 5-Year Note Payable

OWNER'S EQUITY
301 John H. Johnson, Capital
302 John H. Johnson, Drawing
399 Revenue and Expense Summary

REVENUE
401 Professional Fees Earned
402 Interest Revenue

EXPENSES
501 Rent Expense
502 Salaries Expense
503 Dental Supplies Expense
504 Office Supplies Expense
505 Telephone Expense
506 Utilities Expense
507 Lab Fees Expense
508 Professional Fees Expense
530 Interest Expense

are presented. Other, complex accounts which are common in business have been omitted here. They will be studied in Part 3.

In its simplest form, the accounts receivable application deals with all of the accounting related to customer accounts. (In a dental practice, of course, the customers are the patients.)

Accounts receivable application: all accounting dealing with customer accounts.

- Topic 1 of this chapter deals with originating and analyzing dental charges.
- Topic 2 deals with journalizing and posting these charges to the appropriate accounts.
- Topic 3 deals with the steps taken to control cash receipts.
- Topic 4 deals with the accounting of cash received on account or in full.
- Topic 5 deals with month-end procedures for accounts receivable.

TOPIC 1 ORIGINATING AND ANALYZING DENTAL CHARGES

A dental patient will make an appointment for dental services such as an examination, cleaning, filling, extraction, bridge work, and so on. The majority of small dental practices use a source document called the dental fee bill to account for the services carried out. Examine the sample dental fee bill illustrated.

Dental fee bill: a source document showing charges to and payments from dental patients.

Dental Fee Bill

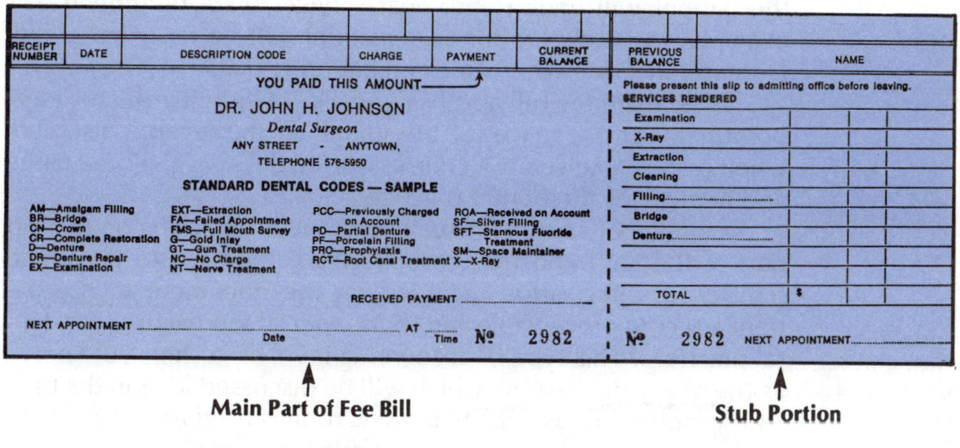

Analysis: Read these points carefully as you study the illustration:

- There are two parts to the bill: a right-hand section called the *stub* and a left-hand portion which is the main part or the fee bill itself.
- A perforated edge separates the stub portion from the

main part of the form. This perforation allows you to tear off the stub from the main fee bill when necessary.

- Each part of the document is pre-numbered with the same number. This number identifies the source document so every part can be accounted for.
- The stub portion is completed *before* the dental patient is treated. Thus the name of the patient is entered in the space above *Name*. Also, any previous balance owed by the patient is entered in the space above *Previous Balance*.
- In general, the stub portion travels from the receptionist/clerk's office to the examining room (the room where dental services are performed). After the treatment, the stub is completed by the dentist, dental assistant, or receptionist/clerk. In some practices, the dentist may prefer to record the services rendered on the stub portion and indicate also when the next appointment is to take place. *When a dental fee is to be charged to a patient's account, the stub is commonly used to originate the transaction.*
- The left-hand side (the fee bill) is completed by the receptionist/clerk only after services are performed as shown on the stub portion. Since a patient may pay part or all of the dental fee immediately, the fee bill also acts as a receipt (remittance slip) in cases where money is paid.
- Notice that the fee bill has the following columns at the top edge: *Receipt Number, Date, Description Code, Charge, Payment,* and *Current Balance.*
- The codes for common dental services are listed so that the patient will understand what services were performed. For example, the code *EX* (for *examination*) will be recorded above *Description Code* when an examination is made.
- The main fee bill also has a space for entering the next appointment, and a space for the initials of the receptionist/clerk when cash is received. Of course, the fee bill also gives the name and address of the dental practice.
- A layer of carbon is usually present as a backing on the top part of the stub and the fee bill. This carbon makes it easy to transfer all information recorded on the document to the patient's account receivable and to the special journal used for dental practices. This type of accounting involves a short-cut known as the one-write system, which will be discussed later in the text. At this point, just assume that the carbon is used to make a copy of the source document for accounting purposes.

One-write system: a manual accounting system in which two or more documents and accounting records are prepared at the same time.

Preparation of a Dental Fee Bill: An Illustration

Case 1 The Gray family, of Any Street and Any Town, Canada includes Mr. D. Gray, Mrs. Joan Gray, and two children, Ann and Don. When the Grays make an appointment to see the

STATEMENT

JOHN H. JOHNSON, D.D.S.
Dental Surgeon
ANY STREET - ANYTOWN, CANADA
TELEPHONE 576-5950

STANDARD DENTAL CODES — SAMPLE

MR.
MRS.
ANN
DON

Mr. D. Gray
Any Street
Any Town, Canada

NUMBER	DATE	DESCRIPTION (SEE CODE BELOW)	CHARGE	PAYMENT	CURRENT BALANCE

PLEASE PAY THE LAST FIGURE IN THIS COLUMN ▲

AM—Amalgam Filling
BR—Bridge
CN—Crown
CR—Complete Restoration
D—Denture
DR—Denture Repair
EX—Examination
EXT—Extraction
FA—Failed Appointment
FMS—Full Mouth Survey
G—Gold Inlay
GT—Gum Treatment
NC—No Charge
NT—Nerve Treatment
PCC—Previously Charged on Account
PD—Partial Denture
PF—Porcelain Filling
PRO—Prophylaxis
RCT—Root Canal Treatment
ROA—Received on Account
SF—Silver Filling
SFT—Stannous Fluoride Treatment
SM—Space Maintianer
X—X-Ray

THIS IS A COPY OF YOUR ACCOUNT AS IT APPEARS ON YOUR LEDGER CARD

dentist, a receptionist/clerk first prepares a "patient's ledger card" similar to the one illustrated.

Analysis: The following points should be related to the illustrations.

- In dental practice (and many other health-care practices), the patient's ledger card is actually the accounts receivable ledger account.
- The accounts receivable ledger card is labelled with the name of the head of the family, usually the person who pays the bills.
- The other members of the family are listed at the top right corner of the card.
- The accounts receivable card becomes the family financial profile. It identifies services performed for individual members of the family as well as the total amount owing by the family.

• As shown in the illustration, the family or patient's ledger card includes the traditional three money columns: (1) the left-hand column, to record the charge (the debit column); (2) the middle column, to record the payment (the credit column); (3) the far right column, to record the running or current balance (the balance column). The headings *Charge* and *Payment* are used to make this card easier to understand for the patient.

Suppose that Mrs. Gray is the first member of the Gray family to be treated at Dr. Johnson's office. Since she is a new patient, the first entry which must be made by the front-office person is a zero balance on the stub portion of the two-part source document. This stub may be completed as shown below.

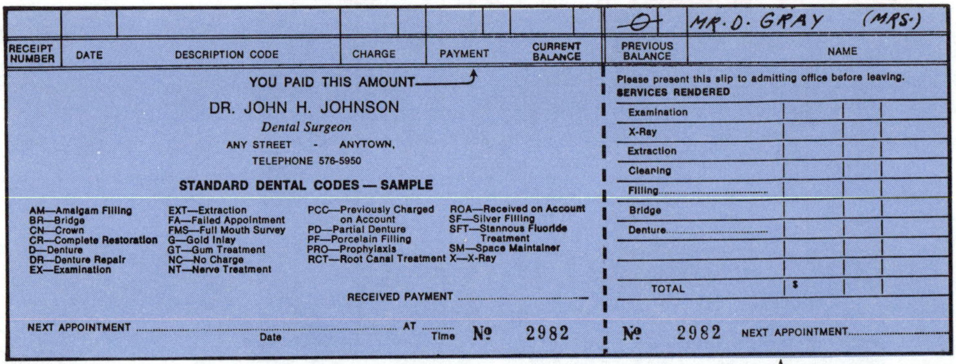

RECEIPT NUMBER	DATE	DESCRIPTION CODE	CHARGE	PAYMENT	CURRENT BALANCE

YOU PAID THIS AMOUNT

DR. JOHN H. JOHNSON

Dental Surgeon

ANY STREET - ANYTOWN,

TELEPHONE 576-5950

STANDARD DENTAL CODES — SAMPLE

AM—Amalgam Filling
BR—Bridge
CN—Crown
CR—Complete Restoration
D—Denture
DR—Denture Repair
EX—Examination
EXT—Extraction
FA—Failed Appointment
FMS—Full Mouth Survey
G—Gold Inlay
GT—Gum Treatment
NC—No Charge
NT—Nerve Treatment
PCC—Previously Charged on Account
PD—Partial Denture
PF—Porcelain Filling
PRO—Prophylaxis
RCT—Root Canal Treatment
ROA—Received on Account
SF—Silver Filling
SFT—Stannous Fluoride Treatment
SM—Space Maintainer
X—X-Ray

RECEIVED PAYMENT ....

NEXT APPOINTMENT .... Date AT .... Time № 2982

PREVIOUS BALANCE	NAME
Ø	MR. D. GRAY (MRS.)

Please present this slip to admitting office before leaving.
SERVICES RENDERED

Examination			
X-Ray			
Extraction			
Cleaning			
Filling..........			
Bridge			
Denture..........			
TOTAL	$		

№ 2982 NEXT APPOINTMENT..........

Completed Stub with Zero Balance

Analysis: Notice that the zero balance symbol Ø has been entered in the *Previous Balance* section of the stub. (We have seen that the zero with the slash is commonly used to indicate a zero balance.)

• Next *Mr. D. Gray,* the person who must pay the fee, is printed (or written neatly and legibly) on the stub in the section above *Name.*

• Next, *Mrs.* is printed to the right of *Mr. D. Gray*. This identifies the member of the family who will receive the treatment.

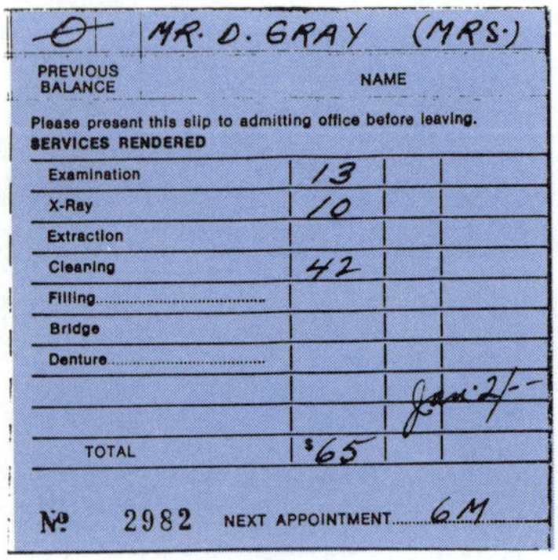

PREVIOUS BALANCE	NAME
Ø	MR. D. GRAY (MRS.)

Please present this slip to admitting office before leaving.
SERVICES RENDERED

Examination	13		
X-Ray	10		
Extraction			
Cleaning	42		
Filling..........			
Bridge			
Denture..........			
TOTAL	$65		

Jan 2/--

№ 2982 NEXT APPOINTMENT.......... 6M

Once the stub has been completed, it is detached from the main portion and is taken with the patient's dental chart to the examining room. Here, the dentist (or an assistant) completes the stub after dental services are performed. In this case, Mrs. Gray received the services illustrated on the stub in the margin.

Analysis: The stub shows a breakdown for the total fee of $65. Note that the next appointment is to be in "6M" — an abbreviation for six months in dental practice.

The stub is returned to the receptionist/clerk, who uses it to complete the left side of the document. Of course, the corresponding document number, in this case 2982, is used to complete the fee bill portion, as illustrated below. Study this illustration carefully. Then refer to the analysis.

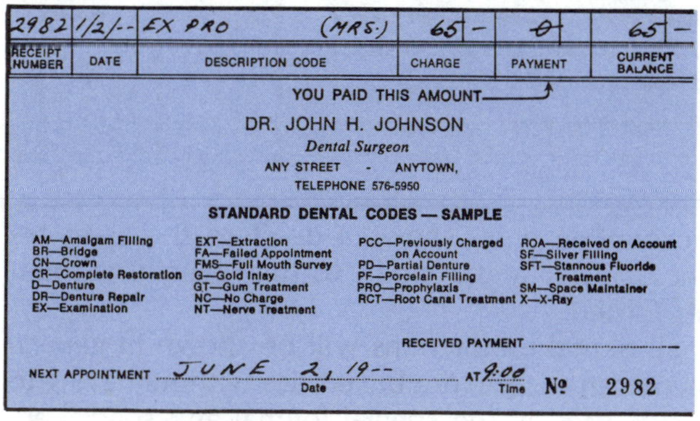

RECEIPT NUMBER	DATE	DESCRIPTION CODE	CHARGE	PAYMENT	CURRENT BALANCE
2982	1/2/--	EX PRO (MRS.)	65 –	∅	65 –

YOU PAID THIS AMOUNT

DR. JOHN H. JOHNSON
Dental Surgeon
ANY STREET - ANYTOWN,
TELEPHONE 576-5950

STANDARD DENTAL CODES — SAMPLE

AM—Amalgam Filling
BR—Bridge
CN—Crown
CR—Complete Restoration
D—Denture
DR—Denture Repair
EX—Examination
EXT—Extraction
FA—Failed Appointment
FMS—Full Mouth Survey
G—Gold Inlay
GT—Gum Treatment
NC—No Charge
NT—Nerve Treatment
PCC—Previously Charged on Account
PD—Partial Denture
PF—Porcelain Filling
PRO—Prophylaxis
RCT—Root Canal Treatment
ROA—Received on Account
SF—Silver Filling
SFT—Stannous Fluoride Treatment
SM—Space Maintainer
X—X-Ray

RECEIVED PAYMENT

NEXT APPOINTMENT JUNE 2, 19-- (Date) AT 9:00 (Time) № 2982

Original Fee Bill: *original copy given to patient, carbon copy kept for accounting purposes*

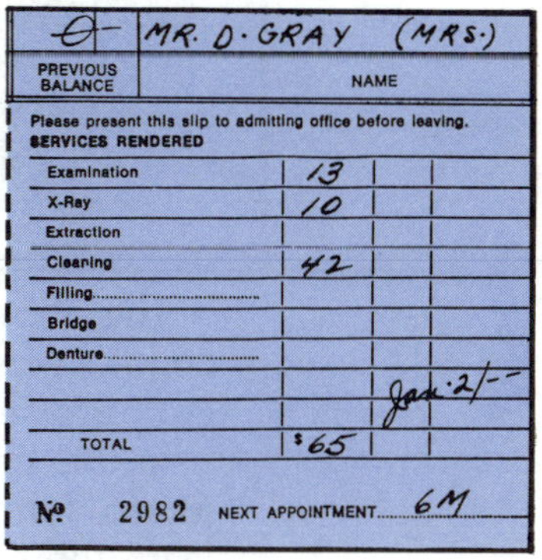

PREVIOUS BALANCE	NAME
∅ –	MR. D. GRAY (MRS.)

Please present this slip to admitting office before leaving.

SERVICES RENDERED

Examination	13		
X-Ray	10		
Extraction			
Cleaning	42		
Filling			
Bridge			
Denture			
			Jan. 2/--
TOTAL	$65		

№ 2982 NEXT APPOINTMENT 6M

Completed Stub: *original copy given to patient, carbon copy kept for accounting purposes*

Analysis: The following points should be noted as you refer to the completed fee bill illustrated.

- The receptionist/clerk uses the information on the stub to complete the patient's fee bill.
- The receipt number is recorded in the *Receipt Number* column. Since no cash was paid by the patient, the receipt number is the fee bill number. This pre-printed number is the same on both the main form and the stub portion.
- Next, the date of the transaction is recorded in the *Date* column. Because the column is narrow, some clerks prefer numerical dating: for example, 1/2/— for January 2, 19-.
- In the left side of the *Description Code* column is recorded the code. Here, EX covers the examination and X-ray, and PRO (short for *prophylaxis*) covers the cleaning.
- In the right side of the *Description Code* column is recorded *Mrs.* It is not necessary to complete the full name of the patient since the stub is available for this information.
- The total fee, $65, is recorded in the *Charge* column.
- Since no payment was made in this case, a Ø is shown in the *Payment* column.
- Since there was no previous balance (as shown on the stub portion), the *Current Balance* column shows $65.
- To complete the fee bill, the date and time of the next appointment are recorded in the appropriate spaces.

The originals of the fee bill and stub are given to the patient, and the carbon copy is kept for the accounting records. The accounting of this fee bill would be analyzed in general journal form as shown on the next page.

GENERAL JOURNAL Page 53

DATE	ACCOUNT TITLE AND EXPLANATION	POST. REF.	DEBIT	CREDIT
19-2				
Jan 2	Accts. Rec./D. Gray		65 00	
	Professional Fees Earned			65 00
	To record fee bill No. 2982;			
	Ex Pro rendered to Mrs. Gray.			

The above accounting entry shows a debit to the asset account *Accts. Rec./D. Gray* and a credit to the revenue account *Professional Fees Earned.*

In this topic, all dental transactions will be shown in general journal form so you can analyze double entries without having to learn the short cuts used in the special journal and special accounts receivable ledger.

Two More Dental Fee Bills: An Illustration and Analysis

Case 2 Ms. Mary Brown has appeared by appointment to have a tooth removed. Mary Brown's balance from an earlier appointment is $20. If the fee for the present appointment were $30, the completed stub and fee bill portions would appear as illustrated below, assuming that she made no payment in this case.

RECEIPT NUMBER	DATE	DESCRIPTION CODE	CHARGE	PAYMENT	CURRENT BALANCE	PREVIOUS BALANCE	NAME
2983	1/2/--	EXT	30 —	-0-	50 —	20 —	MS. MARY BROWN

YOU PAID THIS AMOUNT

DR. JOHN H. JOHNSON
Dental Surgeon
ANY STREET - ANYTOWN,
TELEPHONE 576-5950

STANDARD DENTAL CODES — SAMPLE

AM—Amalgam Filling
BR—Bridge
CN—Crown
CR—Complete Restoration
D—Denture
DR—Denture Repair
EX—Examination
EXT—Extraction
FA—Failed Appointment
FMS—Full Mouth Survey
G—Gold Inlay
GT—Gum Treatment
NC—No Charge
NT—Nerve Treatment
PCC—Previously Charged on Account
PD—Partial Denture
PF—Porcelain Filling
PRO—Prophylaxis
RCT—Root Canal Treatment
ROA—Received on Account
SF—Silver Filling
SFT—Stannous Fluoride Treatment
SM—Space Maintainer
X—X-Ray

RECEIVED PAYMENT ....

NEXT APPOINTMENT MARCH 5, 19-- (Date) AT 10:00 (Time) № 2983

Please present this slip to admitting office before leaving.
SERVICES RENDERED

Examination	
X-Ray	
Extraction	30
Cleaning	
Filling..........	
Bridge	
Denture..........	
	Jan. 2
TOTAL	$30

№ 2983 NEXT APPOINTMENT 3M

Analysis: The following points should be noted when studying the illustrations above.

- Ms. Mary Brown's previous account balance of $20 is copied onto the stub from the last balance shown on her ledger card.
- Since Mary Brown will pay the bill (there is no other family member), her name is not repeated on the fee bill portion but only on the stub part.
- Notice that the current balance is now $50 (the original $20 plus the new fee of $30).

The accounting of this second fee bill, in general journal form, would be analyzed as follows:

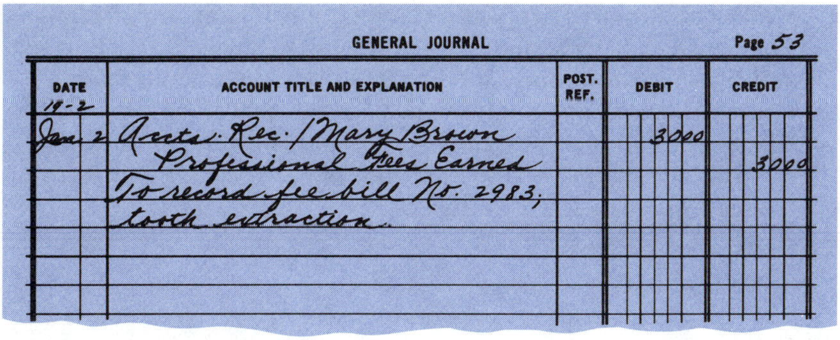

GENERAL JOURNAL Page 53

DATE		ACCOUNT TITLE AND EXPLANATION	POST. REF.	DEBIT	CREDIT
19-2					
Jan.	2	Accts. Rec./Mary Brown		30 00	
		Professional Fees Earned			30 00
		To record fee bill No. 2983;			
		tooth extraction.			

Once the above entry is posted to Ms. Mary Brown's account, the new balance would be the sum of the previous balance plus the new charge. This new balance may be analyzed in T-account form as shown in the margin.

Accts. Rec./Ms. Mary Brown	
Prev. balance 20	
Jan. 2 charge 30	
New balance 50	

Case 3 Mr. D. Gray and his daughter, Ann, receive dental services on the same day. Ann receives treatment first with an X-ray, examination, and cleaning for a total fee of $53. Mr. Gray then has two silver fillings inserted for a fee of $57. In some dental practices, the above transactions would be completed on the stub and fee bill as follows. *Note:* Some dental practices might prefer to issue separate fee bills, one for services to daughter Ann, the other to Mr. Gray. Both fees, however, would be charged to Mr. Gray.

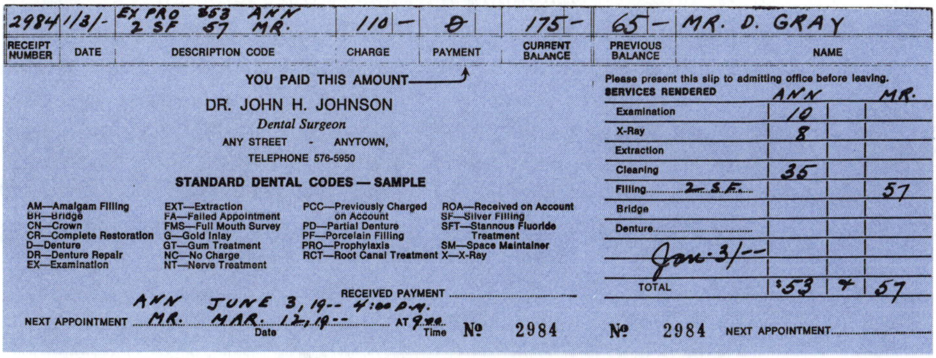

RECEIPT NUMBER	DATE	DESCRIPTION CODE	CHARGE	PAYMENT	CURRENT BALANCE	PREVIOUS BALANCE	NAME
2984	1/3/-	EX PRO $53 ANN 2 SF 57 MR.	110 —	0	175 —	65 —	MR. D. GRAY

YOU PAID THIS AMOUNT

DR. JOHN H. JOHNSON
Dental Surgeon
ANY STREET - ANYTOWN,
TELEPHONE 576-5950

STANDARD DENTAL CODES — SAMPLE

AM—Amalgam Filling
BH—Bridge
CN—Crown
CR—Complete Restoration
D—Denture
DR—Denture Repair
EX—Examination
EXT—Extraction
FA—Failed Appointment
FMS—Full Mouth Survey
G—Gold Inlay
GT—Gum Treatment
NC—No Charge
NT—Nerve Treatment
PCC—Previously Charged on Account
PD—Partial Denture
PF—Porcelain Filling
PRO—Prophylaxis
RCT—Root Canal Treatment
ROA—Received on Account
SF—Silver Filling
SFT—Stannous Fluoride Treatment
SM—Space Maintainer
X—X-Ray

RECEIVED PAYMENT ....

NEXT APPOINTMENT ANN JUNE 3, 19-- 4:00 P.M.; MR. MAR. 12, 19-- AT 9:00 (Date, Time) № 2984

Please present this slip to admitting office before leaving.

SERVICES RENDERED	ANN	MR.
Examination	10	
X-Ray	8	
Extraction		
Cleaning	35	
Filling 2 S.F.		57
Bridge		
Denture		
Jan. 3/--		
TOTAL	$53 +	57

№ 2984 NEXT APPOINTMENT ....

Analysis: The following points should be noted when studying the illustrations above:

- Since the Gray family's previous account balance (in Case 1) was $65, this balance is recorded on the stub portion.
- Notice that the clerk used two columns on the stub, to originate separate fees for Mr. Gray and his daughter, Ann. The

total charge is easily given by adding the separate charges (in this case, $110).

- The main fee bill is completed by subdividing the description code to show separate charges to Mr. Gray and Ann.
- The *Charge* column of the fee bill receives the total charge of $110, because the accounting is done on a family basis.
- Since no payment on account was made, the new current balance is $175 ($110 plus the previous balance of $65).

The accounting of this third fee bill, in general journal form, would be analyzed as follows:

GENERAL JOURNAL — Page 53

DATE 19-2		ACCOUNT TITLE AND EXPLANATION	POST. REF.	DEBIT	CREDIT
Jan	3	Accts. Rec./D. Gray		110 00	
		Professional Fees Earned			110 00
		To record fee bill No. 2984;			
		Ann, $53 ExPro; Mr., $57, 2 SF.			

Important Questions on GAAPs

You have learned how a dental charge originates on a two-part source document called a dental fee bill. It is also important to know how to apply the GAAPs related to this source document.

- *What basic GAAP is recognized with the creation of this source document?*

The objectivity principle.

- *What is the essential meaning of this principle?*

Think of the word *object.* An object can be seen. It's for real. In accounting, every transaction must be a real one. That is, you should be able to prove that the transaction actually took place. The objectivity principle says that there must be evidence to prove the existence of every accounting transaction. That proof or evidence is known as the source document.

- *What other basic GAAP is recognized with the creation of the source document called the dental fee bill?*

The revenue principle.

- *In simple terms, what two things does the revenue principle say when applied to the dental fee bill?*

The revenue principle has two meanings. First, it defines revenue as the inflow of assets (accounts receivable in this case) resulting from the sale of dental services. Second, it gives the guideline for recognizing revenue. In a service firm, revenue is recognized only after the services have been completed. This recognition is easy because a source document — here, the dental fee bill — is made out showing the details of the services rendered.

TOPIC 1 PROBLEMS

7-1 Dr. Penny Thornton has just graduated as a dental surgeon and is about to begin her practice with the following assets and liabilities: Cash, $10 000; Government of Canada Bonds, $50 000; Dental Equipment, $80 000; Office Equipment, $4 000; Furniture, $6 000; Bank Loan Payable (on demand), $5 000; Accts. Pay./Denco Equipment & Supply, $10 000; Accts. Pay./Mardan Business Systems Ltd., $3 000; 5-Year Note Payable, $38 000 ($7 600 to be paid off the principal each year, interest to be accounted for separately at the rate of 12% per annum). The dental equipment has been pledged as security for the 5-Year Note Payable.

a Prepare an opening balance sheet for Dr. Penny Thornton's dental practice as at December 1, 19-1. Prepare the balance sheet in report form.

b Record the opening entry in the general journal, page 1. Use appropriate general ledger account titles.

Key Check Figure
Total Assets = $150 000

7-2 The first patient of Dr. Penny Thornton's practice is Mrs. Cindy Vandenberk. Her husband, Howard Vandenberk, pays the family bills. The Vandenberks have two children, Roberta and Tom. Mrs. Vandenberk has received the following dental services: Examination, $10; X-ray, $8; Cleaning, $35. No payment was made on the day of the services, December 2. The next appointment is to be in 6 months.

a Prepare the new patient's ledger card. Make up a suitable address for the family.

b Prepare the stub of the dental fee bill. Show how it would be completed with the breakdown of services rendered and total as of December 2. The stub is numbered 0001.

c Prepare the fee bill portion of the bill. The next appointment is booked for June 2, 19-2, 9:00 a.m.

d In general journal form, analyze the accounting of the dental fee bill.

7-3 Illustrated below is a completed dental fee bill and stub for Dr. Penny Thornton's practice.

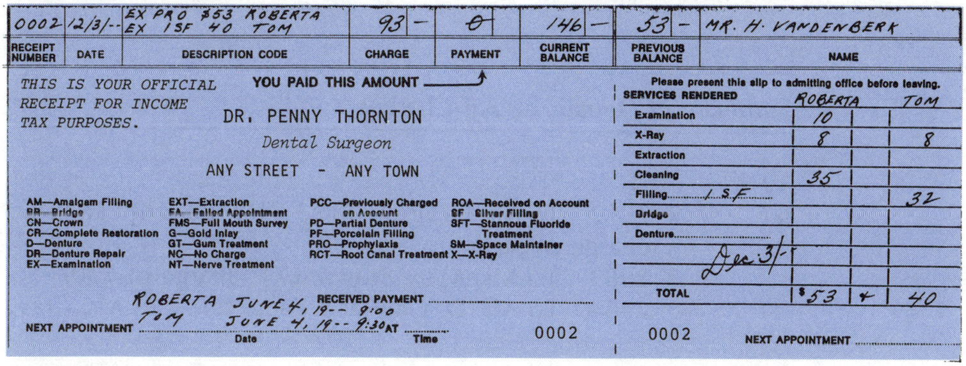

RECEIPT NUMBER	DATE	DESCRIPTION CODE	CHARGE	PAYMENT	CURRENT BALANCE	PREVIOUS BALANCE	NAME
0002	12/3/--	EX PRO $53 ROBERTA EX 1SF 40 TOM	93 —	0	146 —	53 —	MR. H. VANDENBERK

THIS IS YOUR OFFICIAL RECEIPT FOR INCOME TAX PURPOSES.

YOU PAID THIS AMOUNT

DR. PENNY THORNTON
Dental Surgeon
ANY STREET - ANY TOWN

AM—Amalgam Filling
BR—Bridge
CN—Crown
CR—Complete Restoration
D—Denture
DR—Denture Repair
EX—Examination
EXT—Extraction
FA—Failed Appointment
FMS—Full Mouth Survey
G—Gold Inlay
GT—Gum Treatment
NC—No Charge
NT—Nerve Treatment
PCC—Previously Charged on Account
PD—Partial Denture
PF—Porcelain Filling
PRO—Prophylaxis
RCT—Root Canal Treatment
ROA—Received on Account
SF—Silver Filling
SFT—Stannous Fluoride Treatment
SM—Space Maintainer
X—X-Ray

RECEIVED PAYMENT

NEXT APPOINTMENT ROBERTA JUNE 4, 19-- 9:00 / TOM JUNE 4, 19-- 9:30 AT
Date Time

0002

Please present this slip to admitting office before leaving.

SERVICES RENDERED	ROBERTA		TOM
Examination	10		
X-Ray	8		8
Extraction			
Cleaning	35		
Filling 1 S.F.			32
Bridge			
Denture			
Dec 3/-			
TOTAL	$53	+	40

0002 NEXT APPOINTMENT

a How many parts are there to this source document? Name them.

b What is common to these parts? Why is this item important?

c When is the top line of the stub portion completed?

d Where did the recording of the previous balance come from?

e How many important columns appear at the top edge of the left or fee bill portion?

f Name the three money columns from left to right on the dental fee bill. What are these called in accounting terms?

g How is the explanation of dental services recorded on the dental fee bill?

h What is the total fee charged on the bill? How is the amount calculated?

i What amount is currently owed by the patient? How is this amount calculated?

j Analyze the results of the source document by showing the accounting entry in general journal form.

k Name two basic GAAPs which can be related to this completed source document. Explain them.

TOPIC 2 JOURNALIZING AND POSTING DENTAL CHARGES

In this section, you will learn how and why to record all dental fees *charged* in a special journal. You will also learn to post those charges to individual-patient ledger accounts and to accounts in the general ledger.

The Need for a Fees Earned Journal

Suppose the summary of transactions below represents the dental fees charged to various patients of Dr. John H. Johnson's dental practice for the month of January, 19-2. Only those transactions affecting dental fees *charged* — the amount in the *Charge* column — are summarized here. Transactions affecting the *Payment* column of the fee bill will be analyzed in Topic 4. In all cases, assume that copies of the stub and the main fee bill portion were kept for the accounting records.

Summary of Dental Fee Bill Charges

19-2

Jan. 2 2982 To Mr. D. Gray. (Mrs.) (New patient.) EX PRO, charge of $65.

2 2983 To Ms. Mary Brown, EXT, charge of $30.

3 2984 To Mr. D. Gray and daughter Ann: Mr. Gray,

two SF, charge of $57; Ann, EX PRO, charge of $53. Total charge of $110.

Jan. 3 2985 To Mary, daughter of Mr. B. Campbell, for temporary filling. Total fee of $45.

5 2987 To David, son of Mr. R. Diloreto (new patient), for examination, X-ray, and cleaning. Total fee, $65.

8 2990 To Jane and Mary, daughters of Mr. J. Fountain (new patient). Jane's treatment: exam, X-ray, cleaning, and fluoride, $68. Mary's treatment: exam, X-ray, and cleaning, $60. Total charge of $128.

9 2991 To Mr. T. Jacques (new patient). Exam, X-ray, and cleaning; total fee of $65.

10 2994 To Ms. Clemence Lee (new patient). EXT, charge of $35.

11 2995 To David, son of Mr. W. Maksymiuk (new patient). Exam, X-ray, and root canal. Total fee of $160.

13 2997 To Mr. R. Diloreto, for examination, X-ray, and cleaning. Total fee of $65.

14 2998 To Mr. J. Fountain, for exam, X-ray, and cleaning. Total fee, $65.

17 2999 To Ms. Brenda Toy (new patient). Total charge of $800 for a bridge.

18 3000 To Mr. T. Jacques. Total fee of $400 for a crown.

20 3002 To Ms. Christine Zander (new patient). Exam, X-rays, root canal treatment, $480.

22 3003 To Mr. H. Chan (new patient). Exam, X-rays, cleaning, $65.

24 3005 To Ms. Clemence Lee, cleaning, $35.

25 3006 To Mr. D. Cook (new patient). Exam, X-rays, cleaning, $65.

26 3007 To Andrew, son of Mr. D. Cook. Exam, X-rays, cleaning, $65. Also to Brenda, daughter of Mr. Cook. Exam, X-rays, cleaning, $65. Total bill, $130.

29 3009 To Mr. S. Lesniak (new patient). Exam, X-ray, cleaning, $65.

30 3010 To Mr. H. Chan. Root canal treatment plus crown, $700.

31 3011 To Ms. Gwenda Tuck (new patient). Exam, X-ray, and partial denture, $400.

31 3012 To Mr. H. Chan. Lab fee of $92.

31 3014 To Ms. Anne Gomes (new patient). Total fee of $600 for bridge.

Now suppose that the above 23 transactions were recorded in the general journal as shown below.

GENERAL JOURNAL — Page 53

DATE	ACCOUNT TITLE AND EXPLANATION	POST. REF.	DEBIT	CREDIT
19-2				
Jan. 2	Accts. Rec./D. Gray		65 00	
	Professional Fees Earned			65 00
	To record fee bill No. 2982;			
	Ex Pro rendered to Mrs. Gray.			
2	Accts. Rec./Mary Brown		30 00	
	Professional Fees Earned			30 00
	To record fee bill No. 2983;			
	tooth extraction.			
Jan 31	Accts. Rec./Ms. A. Gomes		600 00	
	Professional Fees Earned			600 00
	To record fee bill No. 3014;			
	services rendered, bridge.			

Until now, you have analyzed each fee charged by debiting Accts. Rec./(Name of Patient) and crediting the revenue account Professional Fees Earned. If all 23 transactions were recorded in the general journal, this would mean that Accounts Receivable would be debited, and Professional Fees Earned credited, 23 times. Furthermore, if each entry required at least three or four lines (one for the debit entry, one for the credit entry, and one or two for the brief explanation), the entire 23 transactions would use up at least 69 or 92 writing lines. Moreover, a typical dental practice would probably have 15 to 20 transactions *per day*. Add to this other business transactions which may also be recorded in the general journal, and you would probably have to search through many pages of the journal to find the total fees earned for a given day or month. To overcome these difficulties, many firms use a special journal to record revenue earned called the Fees Earned Journal.

Fees Earned Journal: a special journal recording all fees earned in chronological order.

The Fees Earned Journal: An Illustration

The next illustration shows how the 23 transactions discussed above may be recorded in the special revenue journal called the fees earned journal. In actual practice, this journal is custom-designed to meet the needs of individual firms. For example, some firms may prefer to use only one money column to record dental fees earned. Such is the case when a firm uses a one-write system to record all charges (this system will be studied in Chapter 17). Other firms may prefer to use a fees earned journal with several money columns.

Study the one-column fees earned journal presented below.

FEES EARNED JOURNAL — Page 1

RECEIPT NUMBER	DATE		ACCOUNT DEBIT	DESCRIPTION CODE	POST. REF.	AMOUNT	
	19-2						
2982	Jan.	2	D. Gray	Ex Pro (Mrs.)		65	—
2983		2	Ms. Mary Brown	Ext.		30	—
2984		3	D. Gray	Ex Pro $53 (Ann) 2 SF 57 (Mr.)		110	—
2985		3	B. Campbell	A M (Mary)		45	—
2987		5	R. Diloreto	Ex Pro (David)		65	—
2990		8	J. Fountain	Ex Pro $68 (Jane) Ex Pro 60 (Mary)		128	—
2991		9	T. Jacques	Ex Pro		65	—
2994		10	Ms. C. Lee	Ext.		35	—
2995		11	W. Maksymiuk	Ex X RCT (David)		160	—
2997		13	R. Diloreto	Ex Pro		65	—
2998		14	J. Fountain	Ex Pro		65	—
2999		17	Ms. B. Toy	BR		800	—
3000		18	T. Jacques	CN		400	—
3002		20	Ms. C. Zander	EX X RCT		480	—
3003		22	H. Chan	EX PRO		65	—
3005		24	Ms. C. Lee	PRO		35	—
3006		25	D. Cook	EX PRO		65	—
3007		26	D. Cook	EX PRO (Brenda & Andrew)		130	—
3009		29	S. Lesniak	EX PRO		65	—
3010		30	H. Chan	RCT CN		700	—
3011		31	Ms. D. Tuck	EX X PD		400	—
3012		31	H. Chan	Lab fee		92	—
3014		31	Ms. A. Gomes	BR		600	—

Analysis: Note the following facts from the illustration:

- Since the fees earned journal records all revenue earned, this journal is in effect the revenue journal.
- As in all journals, page numbers are given on the top line.
- The main column headings are: (1) *Receipt Number,* to record the number on the fee bill, (2) *Date,* to record the transaction date appearing on the source document, (3) *Account Debit,* to record each account debited in each transaction, (4) *Description Code,* to record the description code of the dental services provided, (5) *Post. Ref. (Posting Reference),* to be used later to transfer each amount debited to appropriate accounts, and (6) *Amount,* to record the dollar result of each fees earned transaction.

After studying the headings, you may ask yourself: *Where is the column to record the credit to Professional Fees Earned?* This credit will be posted as part of the total only once at the end of the month. For each line entry, the credit is understood as having been recorded each time the debit entry is made.

You can now see one of the main advantages of any special journal: recording the complete entry on one line. However, think of each transaction in general journal form so you can record correctly the debit entry. For example, in the first transaction, the entry in general journal form shows four lines as shown below. That same entry, with all information, is recorded on one line in the special journal. Remember, however, that the credit to Professional Fees Earned is understood to be there and will be seen as part of the total amount at the end of the month.

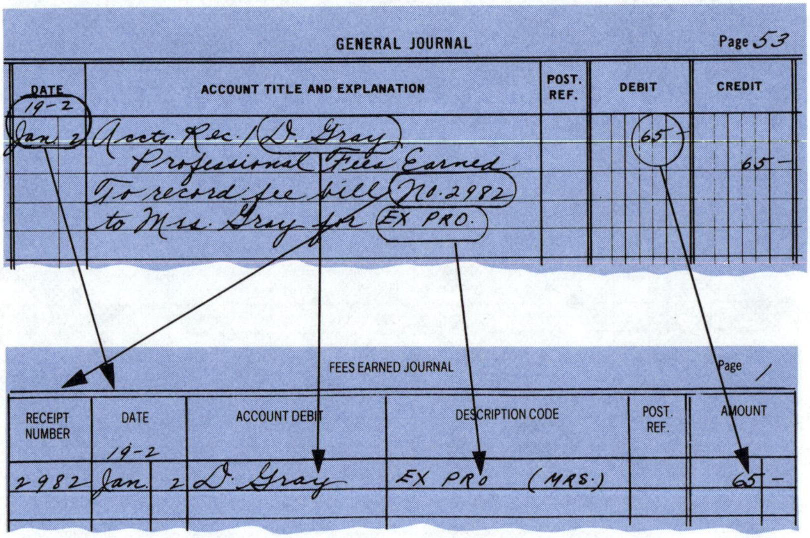

Here are three more points to keep in mind:

- All receipt numbers will be accounted for in the fees earned journal. For example, receipt number 2986 is missing. This would suggest that 2986 was used to record no fee charged but only the receipt of cash on account. As you will learn in Topic 4, payments of cash received will be recorded in another special journal.
- There are no "cents" amounts recorded for dental fees charged. This practice is common in dental and other practices. It cuts down on errors in adding long columns of figures.
- In journals and ledger accounts, when only dollars are used, it is permissible to show a dash instead of ciphers (zeros).

The dash should not be used when reporting dollars in financial statements. Such statements are treated as *formal* accounting reports. Journals and ledgers, on the other hand, are merely internal records.

The Need for an Accounts Receivable Ledger

In Part 1 of this book, all transactions involving accounts receivable were posted to a few individual customer accounts that were filed together with other asset accounts in the same general ledger. In practice, however, nearly all professional practices (health-care, law, accounting, etc.) have a large number of individual accounts receivable. So do nearly all other businesses which sell services (or goods) on credit. Consider the following problems of using only one ledger:

- It would become quite crowded.
- It would be heavy and awkward to work with.
- Only one person could post at any one time.
- The trial balance would take several pages.
- If the trial balance did not balance, it would be very difficult to find the error within a reasonable time.
- The current asset section of the balance sheet would be extremely long.

To overcome these problems, the majority of firms will file individual customer accounts in a separate ledger called the Accounts Receivable Ledger (or *customers' ledger,* or, in dental practice, *patients' ledger*).

Accounts Receivable Ledger: the file of all individual customer or patient accounts.

Organizing a Separate Accounts Receivable Ledger

When individual customer accounts are pulled from the original or main ledger, it is important to remember that a general account known as Accounts Receivable must be kept in the General Ledger. The process of pulling out the four individual patient accounts at the start of January, 19-2 to replace them with one account for Dr. Johnson's dental practice is shown next.

Accounts Receivable: a current asset account in the General Ledger.

Analysis: Study the illustration and note the following facts:

- There are two ledgers: the Accounts Receivable Ledger containing the individual patient (customer) accounts, and the main ledger, the General Ledger, which now contains the general account called Accounts Receivable.
- The Accounts Receivable account in the General Ledger will show the total amount owed by all the customers. For example, the last illustration showed four patient accounts receivable totalling $320. This total is seen clearly on the debit side of the Accounts Receivable account in the General Ledger.
- This Accounts Receivable account is said to "control" the individual customer accounts in total form. Therefore, this account may be called Accounts Receivable Control. In practice, the word *control* is usually dropped from the account name because it is understood.

Accounts Receivable Control: the General Ledger account which contains the total of all individual customer account balances. (In practice, the word control is not used, being understood.)

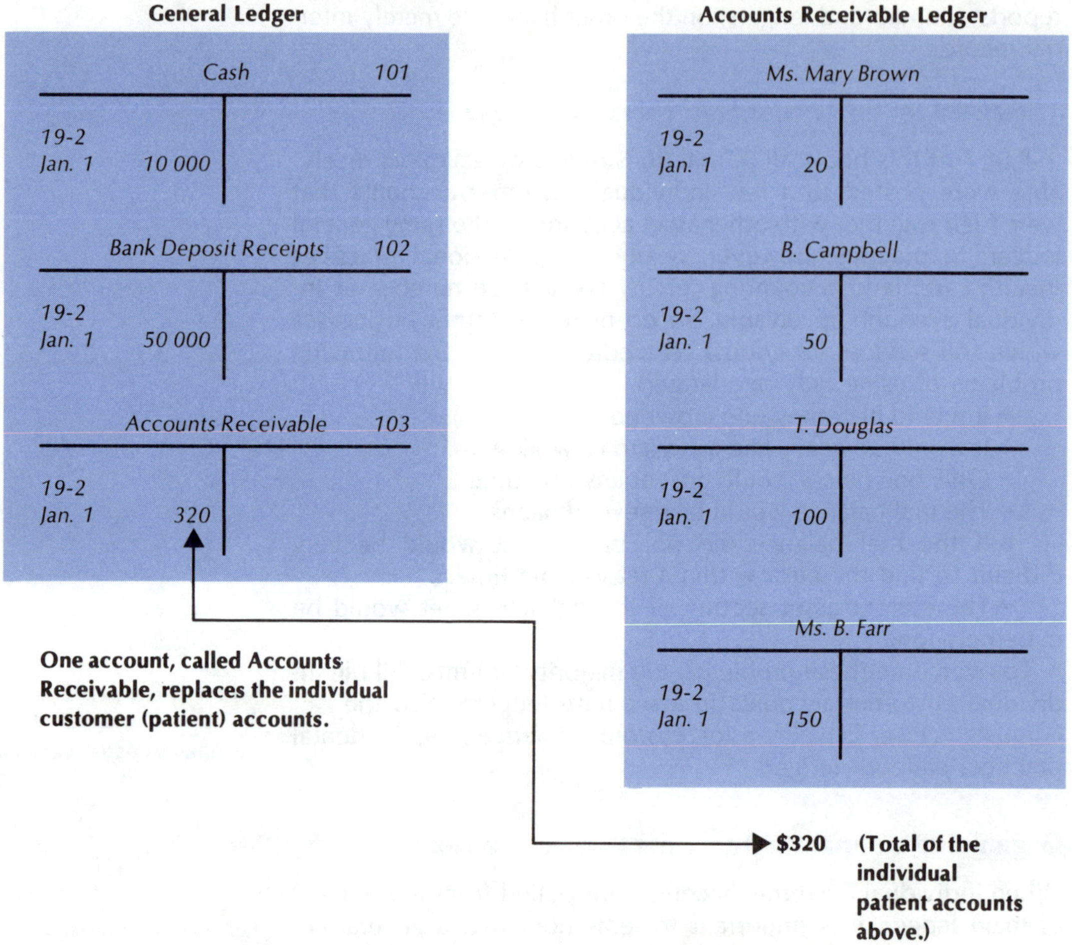

Subsidiary ledger: a secondary ledger which stores the details of all the accounts of only one type.

• The General Ledger is the *main ledger* — that is, it contains all of the information necessary to prepare financial statements. The Accounts Receivable Ledger is a secondary or a subsidiary ledger. The subsidiary ledger does not contain all of the accounts of the business; it contains only *one class* of account. In a large accounting system, there will always be one General Ledger and one or more subsidiary ledgers.

• Accounts stored in the subsidiary ledger are coded differently from the accounts filed in the General Ledger. In the T-account illustration above, the accounts in the Accounts Receivable Ledger are kept in alphabetical order. On the other hand, the accounts in the General Ledger are filed in numerical order as listed by a chart of accounts.

Posting Individual Customer Accounts

When a General Ledger and an Accounts Receivable Ledger form part of a total accounting system, the posting of *credit sales*

(sales on account) is done in two stages. In the case we are examining, the credit sales are dental fees charged to patient accounts. The first stage is the posting to the Accounts Receivable Ledger *on a daily basis;* the second is to the General Ledger *at the end of the month.*

The individual credit sales (dental fees charged) are posted to the customer (patient) accounts filed in the Accounts Receivable Ledger on the *same days* on which the sales of dental services occur. This is necessary because the owner-manager or even the customer may request information on the balance owing at any time.

In some practices, posting to the Accounts Receivable Ledger may be done from the revenue journal (in the case of a dental practice, the Fees Earned Journal). This system of posting will be used here to illustrate the case of Dr. Johnson's practice. Turn to page 198, where posting is shown from the Fees Earned Journal to Mr. D. Gray's account. Read the following points of analysis when you study the illustration on the next page.

- Note that all important information is transferred from the Fees Earned Journal to the patient's account.
- From left to right, the clerk transfers the number, date, and description.
- In the *Description* column, the source of posting is given. Here, the information is taken from the Fees Earned Journal, page 1, so *FEJ1* is printed next to the *Charge* column. This way, you can always refer to the source if any question arises about the individual transaction.
- Once the complete explanation and source of posting are recorded in the *Description* column, the clerk transfers the total fee to the *Charge* column — which is, of course, the left column.
- After posting the amount of the total fee to the *Charge* (debit) column, the current balance is entered.
- Finally, since the individual accounts in the Accounts Receivable Ledger are filed in alphabetical order, a check mark is placed in the *Post. Ref.* column of the Fees Earned Journal to show that the transfer of information from this special journal to the customer's account has taken place.

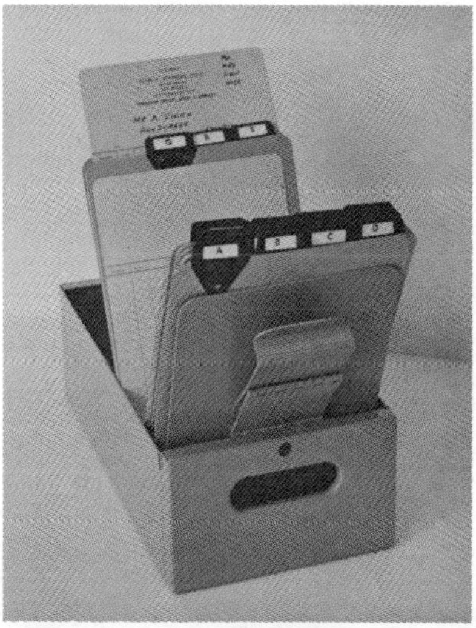

Postings to other individual patient accounts would be done in the same manner. A separate card would be used for each customer's account. When a card has been completed to the bottom line, a second card is used to follow the first one. After each customer's account is posted, the patient's accounts receivable card is filed in alphabetical order. (See the illustration of the filing tray in the margin.)

In some accounting systems, posting to the Accounts Receivable Ledger is done *directly* from the source document (the fee bill) to the individual customer's account. In others, posting is automatically done through the one-write system at the time the

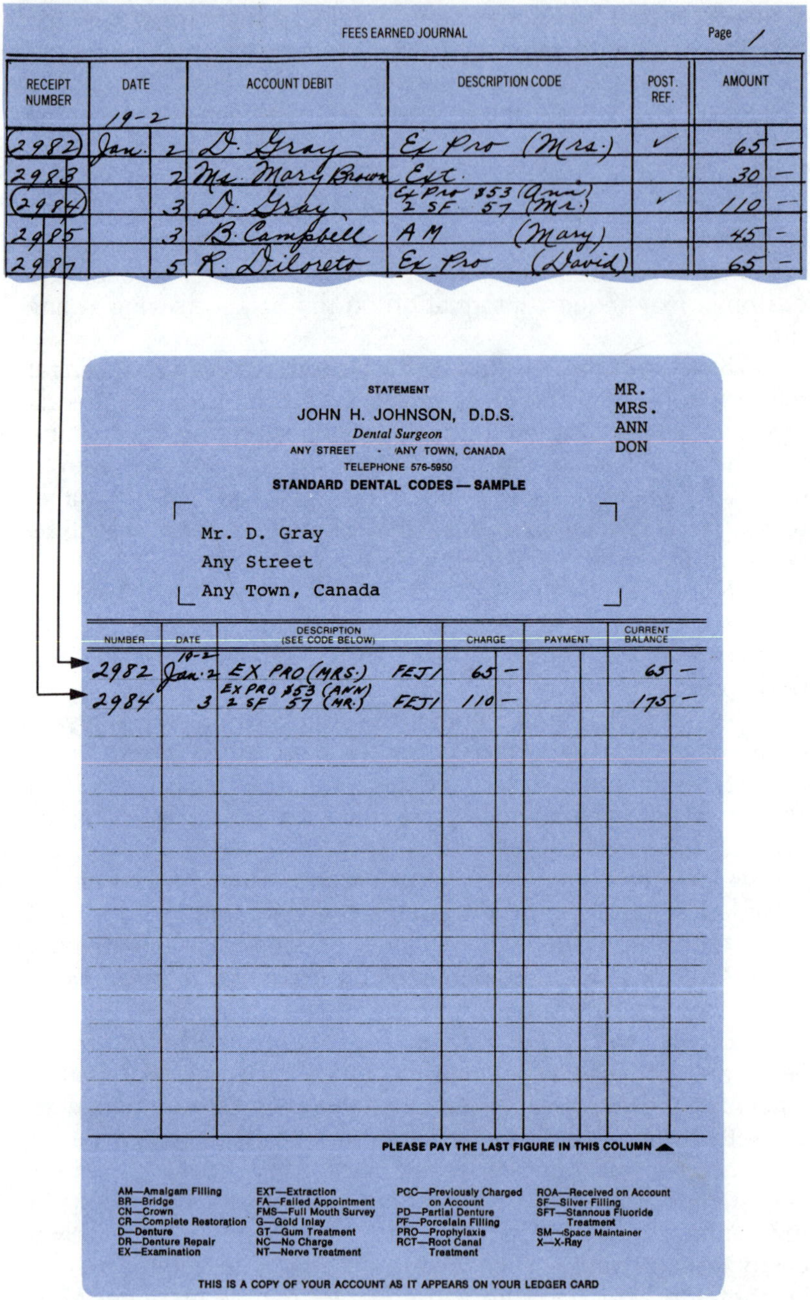

FEES EARNED JOURNAL Page 1

RECEIPT NUMBER	DATE	ACCOUNT DEBIT	DESCRIPTION CODE	POST. REF.	AMOUNT
	19-2				
2982	Jan. 2	D. Gray	Ex Pro (Mrs.)	✓	65 —
2983	2	Ms. Mary Brown	Ext.		30 —
2984	3	D. Gray	Ex Pro $53 (Ann) 2 SF 57 (Mr.)	✓	110 —
2985	3	B. Campbell	A M (Mary)		45 —
2987	5	R. Diloreto	Ex Pro (David)		65 —

STATEMENT

JOHN H. JOHNSON, D.D.S.
Dental Surgeon
ANY STREET · ANY TOWN, CANADA
TELEPHONE 576-5950

STANDARD DENTAL CODES — SAMPLE

MR.
MRS.
ANN
DON

Mr. D. Gray
Any Street
Any Town, Canada

NUMBER	DATE	DESCRIPTION (SEE CODE BELOW)		CHARGE	PAYMENT	CURRENT BALANCE
2982	19-2 Jan. 2	EX PRO (MRS.)	FEJ1	65 —		65 —
2984	3	EX PRO $53 (ANN) 2 SF 57 (MR.)	FEJ1	110 —		175 —

PLEASE PAY THE LAST FIGURE IN THIS COLUMN ▲

AM—Amalgam Filling
BR—Bridge
CN—Crown
CR—Complete Restoration
D—Denture
DR—Denture Repair
EX—Examination
EXT—Extraction
FA—Failed Appointment
FMS—Full Mouth Survey
G—Gold Inlay
GT—Gum Treatment
NC—No Charge
NT—Nerve Treatment
PCC—Previously Charged on Account
PD—Partial Denture
PF—Porcelain Filling
PRO—Prophylaxis
RCT—Root Canal Treatment
ROA—Received on Account
SF—Silver Filling
SFT—Stannous Fluoride Treatment
SM—Space Maintainer
X—X-Ray

THIS IS A COPY OF YOUR ACCOUNT AS IT APPEARS ON YOUR LEDGER CARD

fee bill is prepared. These short-cuts will be examined in Part IV of this book.

Posting to the General Ledger

At the end of the month, the Fees Earned Journal is totalled to determine the amount to be posted to the General Ledger. But before such a posting occurs, it is important to check the mathematical accuracy of this column. These preliminary steps are recommended at each month-end.

1 List the individual amounts on an adding machine tape. After obtaining the total, check off the figures on the tape against the individual amounts in the Fees Earned Journal.

FEES EARNED JOURNAL Page 1

RECEIPT NUMBER	DATE		ACCOUNT DEBIT	DESCRIPTION CODE	POST. REF.	AMOUNT
	19-2					
2982	Jan.	2	D. Gray	Ex Pro (Mrs.)		65 —
2983		2	Ms. Mary Brown	Ext.		30 —
2984		3	D. Gray	Ex Pro $53 (Anne) 2 SF 57 (Mr.)		110 —
2985		3	B. Campbell	A M (Mary)		45 —
2987		5	R. Diloreto	Ex Pro (David)		65 —
2990		8	J. Fountain	Ex Pro $68 (Jane) Ex Pro 60 (Mary)		128 —
2991		9	T. Jacques	Ex Pro		65 —
3011		31	Ms. G. Tuck	EX X PD		400 —
3012		31	H. Chan	Lat fee		92 —
3014		31	Ms. A. Gomes	BR		600 —

Fees Earned Journal, Page 1

0. *
65.00 +✓
30.00 +✓
110.00 +✓
45.00 +✓
65.00 +✓
128.00 +✓
65.00 +✓
35.00 +✓
160.00 +✓
65.00 +✓
65.00 +✓
800.00 +✓
400.00 +✓
480.00 +✓
65.00 +✓
35.00 +✓
65.00 +✓
130.00 +✓
65.00 +✓
700.00 +✓
400.00 +✓
92.00 +✓
600.00 +✓
4 665.00 *

2 If you do not have an adding machine, add the amounts in the *Amount* column yourself. Then record the total in small, pencilled figures directly under the last entry in the money column. This is known as a pencil footing or *pinhead total* and is used to double-check the addition of the money column before a figure is shown in ink.

Pencil footing: small, pencilled figures entered at the foot (bottom) of a money column.

3 After the total of the *Amount* column has been checked, draw a single line under the last figure to indicate that the column is to be totalled.

4 On the next writing line, enter the last day of the month in the *Date* column. Then, beginning on that same line, show the total in the form of a complete double entry:

- a debit to the Accounts Receivable controlling account
- a credit to the revenue account called Professional Fees Earned.

5 To show that the special journal has been completed for the month, draw a double horizontal line across the *Amount, Post. Ref., Date,* and *Receipt Number* columns.

The total of the *Amount* column is now ready to be transferred to the General Ledger. Observe that in the illustrations on page 200 the posting references are entered for both the Accounts Receivable account and the Professional Fees Earned account.

After the total has been posted to the General Ledger, the ledger must be in balance because the total to the debit side of

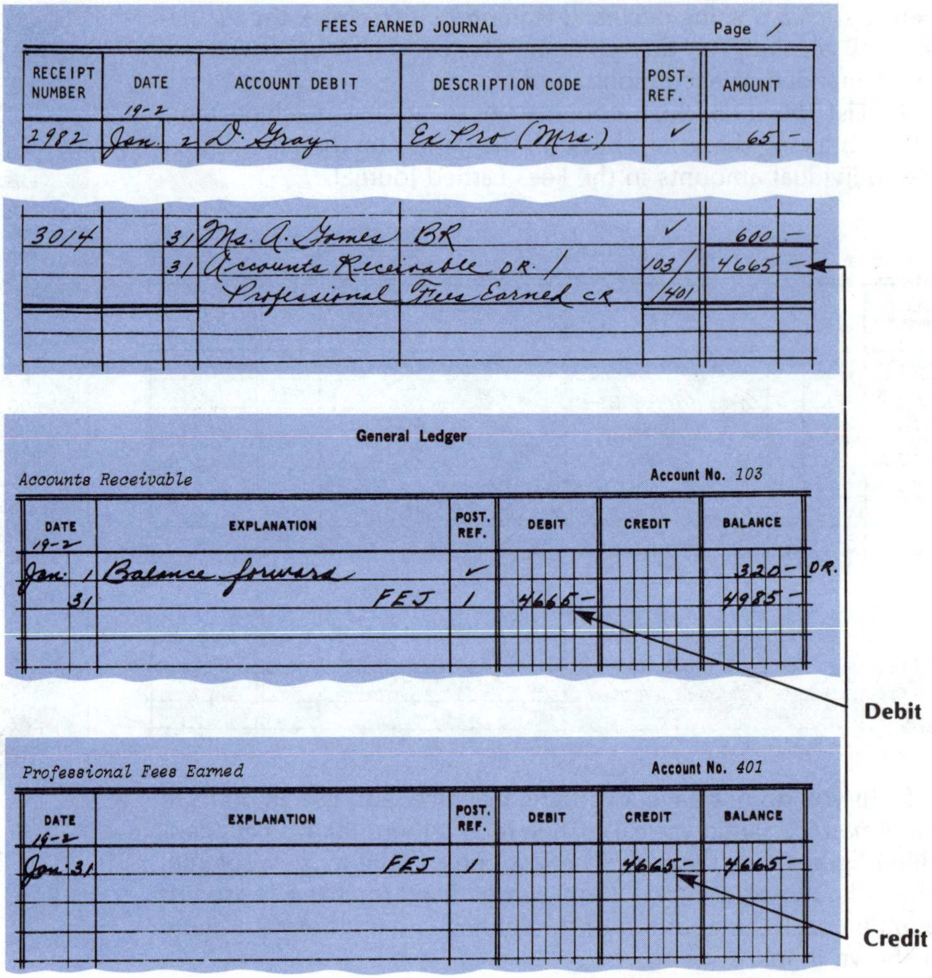

FEES EARNED JOURNAL — Page 1

RECEIPT NUMBER	DATE 19-2		ACCOUNT DEBIT	DESCRIPTION CODE	POST. REF.	AMOUNT
2982	Jan.	2	D. Gray	Ex Pro (Mrs.)	✓	65 —
3014		31	Ms. A. Gomes	BR	✓	600 —
		31	Accounts Receivable DR. / Professional Fees Earned CR		103 / 401	4665 —

General Ledger

Accounts Receivable — Account No. 103

DATE 19-2		EXPLANATION	POST. REF.	DEBIT	CREDIT	BALANCE
Jan.	1	Balance forward	✓			320 — DR.
	31	FEJ	1	4665 —		4985 —

Professional Fees Earned — Account No. 401

DATE 19-2		EXPLANATION	POST. REF.	DEBIT	CREDIT	BALANCE
Jan.	31	FEJ	1		4665 —	4665 —

Accounts Receivable equals the posted total to the credit side of the Professional Fees Earned.

Advantages of the Special Journal

Here are the main advantages to using a special journal to record the professional fees earned:

- Only one line is needed to record an entry in a special journal. Thus valuable time and space are saved.
- The dollar amount is written only once for each double entry because the credit to Professional Fees Earned is understood.
- Time is saved because only the total is posted to the General Ledger at the end of the month — to the debit of Accounts Receivable and to the credit of Professional Fees Earned.
- Division of responsibility among accounting clerks is possible. In a large firm, one clerk can be responsible for recording and posting accounts receivable.

Other Special Journals

Other special journals exist in the efficient organization of any accounting system for most businesses. Often, a special journal may be used to record only transactions that are similar and very repetitive in nature. For example, the inflow of cash is highly repetitive and, therefore, justifies the use of a special journal to record cash receipts. (The Cash Receipts Journal will be dealt with in Topic 4.)

A special journal such as the Fees Earned Journal does *not* eliminate the need for a General Journal. Think of the General Journal as the non-specialized journal. It is the record that contains all the entries that cannot be recorded in any special journal. For example, because an opening entry happens only once, the General Journal is used to record the opening balance sheet of a new firm. Remember, special journals are used to record transactions that are similar and repetitive.

TOPIC 2 PROBLEMS

7-4 Dr. L.M. Munro opened his dental practice during the final week of January, 19-1 with the following assets and liabilities: Cash, $5 000; Government of Canada Bonds, $30 000; Dental Equipment, $40 000; Office Equipment, $10 000; Bank Loan Payable, $5 000; Accts. Pay./Bell Equipment Ltd., $10 000; Accts. Pay./Riverside Systems Ltd., $2 000. The transactions below represent the dental fees charged to various patients for that final week.

Jan.	26	0001	To Ms. M. Micsinski, EX PRO. Total fee, $65.
	27	0002	To Susan, daughter of Mr. L. McGraw. EX 2BW PRO, $68.
	28	0003	To Mr. L. McGraw, CN. Total fee of $225.
	28	0004	To Mr. S. Katz. Lab fee of $120.
	29	0005	To Richard and Ronald, sons of Mr. S. Ketcheson. Richard, EX PRO, $65. Ronald, EX X 2SF, $48.
	30	0006	To Ms. J. Laing, EX BW PRO, $70.
	31	0007	To Mr. I. Ryder, EX PRO, $65.

a Record the opening entry for Dr. Munro's dental practice in the General Journal.

b Analyze each of the above dental charges in general journal form. Continue the General Journal used in **a** above. Show a complete explanation for each entry.

c Record the transactions analyzed in **b** on page 1 of a Fees Earned Journal.

Key Check Figure Accounts Receivable DR. = $726

7-5 The summary of transactions below represents the dental fees charged to various patients of Dr. Penny Thornton's dental practice for the month of December, 19-1.

Dec. 2 0001 To Mr. H. Vandenberk for dental services rendered to Mrs.Vandenberk. Total fee for EX PRO, $53.
3 0002 To Mr. H. Vandenberk for dental services rendered to the two children: Roberta, EX PRO, $53; Tom, EX 1SF, $40.
4 0003 To Mr. Geoff Dean, X SF, $32.
4 0004 To Mr. H. Vandenberk, EX PRO, $65.
5 0005 To Mrs. Liepner, wife of Mr. M. Liepner, X SF, $66.
8 0006 To Ms. E. Revell, $152, for EX X and ENDO (endodontics).
9 0007 To Mr. T. Taller, $65, for EX PRO.
10 0008 To Mr. T. Murphy, $34, for 2SF.
11 0009 To Ms. L. Kretchman, $65, for EX PRO.
14 0010 To Mr. B. Gibson, $100, for dental services performed on two children: Don, $35, for PRO; David, $65, for EX PRO.
15 0011 To Mrs. Vandenberk, wife of H. Vandenberk, $63, for 2SF.
16 0012 To Ms. M. Kingsbury, $400, for CN.
17 0013 To Ms. C. Pratt, $180, for BR.
18 0014 To Mr. R. Kendall, $65, for EX PRO.
21 0015 To Mr. M. Robineau, $235, for lab fee.
22 0016 To Mr. Jack Wilson, $65, for EX PRO.
23 0017 To Ms. M. McKim, $68, for EX BW PRO.
24 0018 To Ms. B. Johnson, $145, for lab fee.
27 0019 To Mr. D. Schearer, $189, for PFM (type of crown).
30 0020 To Mr. D. Milks, $32, for 1SF.
30 0021 To Mrs. J. Borron, wife of Mr. Wm. Borron, $65, for EX PRO.
31 0022 To Mr. Wm. Borron, $65, for EX PRO.
31 0023 To Ms. Mary Ryan, $72, EX 2BW PRO.
31 0024 To Ms. V. Hume, $119, EX 2BW 1PA PRO.

Key Check Figure Accounts Receivable DR. = $2 488

a Analyze each of the above transactions in general journal form. Include the source document number and description code in the explanation.

b Record the same transactions on page 1 of a Fees Earned Journal.

7-6 Refer to Problem 7-4 (Dr. L.M. Munro's dental practice) and the solution for that problem.

a Open separate patient accounts receivable cards for Mr. S. Katz, Mr. S. Ketcheson, Ms. J. Laing, Mr. L. McGraw, Ms. M. Micsinski, and Mr. I. Ryder. Invent appropriate mailing addresses.

b Post the transactions from the Fees Earned Journal (from Problem 7-4) to the individual patient accounts in the Accounts Receivable Ledger.

Key Check Figure Accounts Receivable Balance = $726

c Total the Fees Earned Journal. Record the appropriate double entry for this total; post the total to appropriate General Ledger accounts; and rule off the special journal for the month.

7-7 Refer to Problem 7-5 (Dr. Penny Thornton's dental practice) and the solution for that problem.

a List all the patients identified in the December transactions. Then arrange the names in alphabetical order.

b From that list, set up an Accounts Receivable Ledger in T-account form.

c Post the transactions from the Fees Earned Journal to the T-accounts set up for the Accounts Receivable Ledger.

d Set up a patient's ledger card for Mr. H. Vandenberk. Post the transactions from the Fees Earned Journal to this account.

e Total the Fees Earned Journal and show this total *journalized* for the month of December. Then rule off the journal for the month.

f Set up the two appropriate General Ledger accounts and post the total from the Fees Earned Journal to these accounts.

Key Check Figure Accounts Receivable Balance = $2 488

TOPIC 3 A SYSTEM FOR CONTROLLING CASH RECEIPTS

The owner(s) of a business rely on accounting to develop a system to ensure that:

- all cash receipts are recorded efficiently and accurately
- the cash is protected from fraud (dishonesty) and outright theft

To do this, accounting must take measures to control cash receipts. Since these measures are taken within the firm, they are called an internal control system in accounting.

Internal control system: activities organized within a firm for the purpose of (1) protecting its assets against waste, fraud, and theft and (2) ensuring the accuracy and reliability of the data in accounting reports.

The basic measures forming an internal control system for cash receipts are summarized below. (However, as a business grows and the number of employees increases, more steps become necessary to ensure a more efficient system to account for cash receipts and other transactions.)

(1) Create pre-numbered source documents.
(2) Prepare a daily cash proof.
(3) Open a chequing account at a bank.
(4) Deposit intact all cash received.
(5) Deposit daily all cash received.
(6) Obtain receipts for all cash deposited.
(7) Divide the responsibility.
(8) Use a special journal to record cash receipts.

The first seven will be covered in this Topic. The eighth will be covered in Topic 4.

Create Pre-Numbered Source Documents

As soon as any cash item is received, the business should immediately prepare a *pre-numbered*[1] source document that indicates:

---

1. This means that each document should have a stamped or printed number so that it can be controlled and accounted for, and that someone in the accounting department itself should be responsible for having the forms printed with consecutive and continuous numbers before they are used as source documents for cash receipts.

- how much cash was received
- the date on which the cash was received
- why the cash was received

and, in some cases,

- who made the payment

This document will be used to account for the cash received.

In practice, the source documents used to originate cash receipts will vary with the type of business. Here are a few common examples.

Cash Register Tapes Cash register tapes are used in various food and drug stores. One copy, stored within the cash register, would be used for the accounting of cash receipts; the original would be given to the customer.

Pre-Numbered Sales Slips Numbered sales slips are commonly used in many specialty shops such as clothing stores. Some managers use a sales book or pad. One copy of the document would be used to account for cash receipts.

Other managers insist on more control through the use of a forms register. Here, the accounting copy drops to the bottom compartment of the register, where it remains locked until accounting personnel remove all copies at the end of the day.

Cash Register

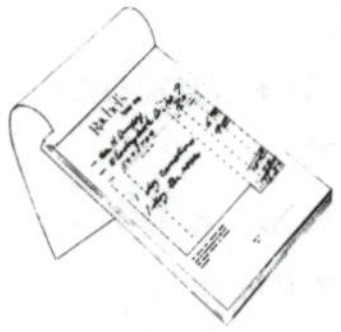

Sales Book or Sales Pad

Forms Register

Remittance Slips Some businesses prefer the source document known as a remittance slip when cheques and money orders are received by mail. See the first illustration opposite.

One copy of these slips (often called simply receipts) would be used to account for cash receipts.

Receipted Fee Bills In the case of Dr. Johnson's dental practice, suppose that on Jan. 8, fee bill no. 2986 was correctly receipted to Ms. Mary Brown, who sent in her cheque for $50. Study the second illustration opposite.

The bill shows the receipt of Ms. Mary Brown's cheque for $50. The *Description Code* column now shows *ROA* ("received on account"). The amount received is entered in the *Payment* column and, of course, there is no current balance because payment was made in full.

KELLY'S OFFICE SERVICES

Remittance Slip No. **RS-24**

Name June Cooper

Amount	Cheque Number	Cheque Date
$50.00	191	Feb. 21, 19-

Explanation

Received on account

Date Feb 25, 19 | Received By B.H.

BUXTON'S 2401 CAMBIE ST. VANCOUVER, B.C. ACCT. COPY—PAYMENT RECEIPT

069868

ACCOUNT NO. 13071 CLERK #104 25.92/100

NAME Dunster, S. J.

ADDRESS 89-904 Clarke Rd. Port Moody, B.C.

CASH ☐ CHEQUE ☒ MONEY ORDER ☐

DATE: -- 10 15
YEAR MONTH DAY

PAYMENT ON ACCOUNT ☒ DEPOSIT ON C.O.D. ☐ DEPOSIT ON LAY-A-WAY ☐ DEPOSIT ON SPECIAL ORDER ☐

The fee bill becomes an official receipt only when the clerk's initials appear opposite *Received Payment.* Of course, a copy of this document is kept to record the future debit to Cash and a credit to Accts. Rec./Ms. Mary Brown. The receipt number is also the number of the source document.

RECEIPT NUMBER	DATE	DESCRIPTION CODE	CHARGE	PAYMENT	CURRENT BALANCE	PREVIOUS BALANCE	NAME
2986	1/8/--	ROA	0	50 —	0	50 —	MS. MARY BROWN

YOU PAID THIS AMOUNT

DR. JOHN H. JOHNSON
Dental Surgeon
ANY STREET - ANYTOWN,
TELEPHONE 576-5950

STANDARD DENTAL CODES — SAMPLE

AM—Amalgam Filling, BR—Bridge, CN—Crown, CR—Complete Restoration, D—Denture, DR—Denture Repair, EX—Examination, EXT—Extraction, FA—Failed Appointment, FMS—Full Mouth Survey, G—Gold Inlay, GT—Gum Treatment, NC—No Charge, NT—Nerve Treatment, PCC—Previously Charged on Account, PD—Partial Denture, PF—Porcelain Filling, PRO—Prophylaxis, RCT—Root Canal Treatment, ROA—Received on Account, SF—Silver Filling, SFT—Stannous Fluoride Treatment, SM—Space Maintainer, X—X-Ray

RECEIVED PAYMENT L. F.

NEXT APPOINTMENT .... AT .... Date Time № 2986

Please present this slip to admitting office before leaving.
SERVICES RENDERED
Examination / X-Ray / Extraction / Cleaning / Filling / Bridge / Denture / TOTAL
ROA $50— Jan. 8/--

№ 2986 NEXT APPOINTMENT........

Look closely at this next illustration.

From Topic 2, you will recall that this transaction only accounted for the dental charge. If Ms. Anne Gomes also paid $100

RECEIPT NUMBER	DATE	DESCRIPTION CODE	CHARGE	PAYMENT	CURRENT BALANCE	PREVIOUS BALANCE	NAME
3014	1/31/--	BR	600 —	100 —	500 —	0	MS. ANNE GOMES

YOU PAID THIS AMOUNT

DR. JOHN H. JOHNSON
Dental Surgeon
ANY STREET - ANYTOWN,
TELEPHONE 576-5950

STANDARD DENTAL CODES — SAMPLE

AM—Amalgam Filling, BR—Bridge, CN—Crown, CR—Complete Restoration, D—Denture, DR—Denture Repair, EX—Examination, EXT—Extraction, FA—Failed Appointment, FMS—Full Mouth Survey, G—Gold Inlay, GT—Gum Treatment, NC—No Charge, NT—Nerve Treatment, PCC—Previously Charged on Account, PD—Partial Denture, PF—Porcelain Filling, PRO—Prophylaxis, RCT—Root Canal Treatment, ROA—Received on Account, SF—Silver Filling, SFT—Stannous Fluoride Treatment, SM—Space Maintainer, X—X-Ray

RECEIVED PAYMENT L. F.

NEXT APPOINTMENT .... AT .... Date Time № 3014

Please present this slip to admitting office before leaving.
SERVICES RENDERED
Examination / X-Ray / Extraction / Cleaning / Filling / Bridge 600 / Denture / TOTAL $600
Jan. 31/--

№ 3014 NEXT APPOINTMENT........

on account, however, the fee bill would be receipted and the patient's current balance would be shown as $500, as illustrated. When a patient is charged a fee and then pays all or part of it, it is important to analyze two separate accounting entries:

- Debit Accts. Rec./Ms. Anne Gomes 600 *and* credit Professional Fees Earned 600 to record the amount of the fees earned from the *Charge column.* This entry would be recorded in the Fees Earned Journal.

- Debit Cash 100 *and* credit Accts. Rec./Ms. Anne Gomes 100 to record the cash received from the *Payment* column of the receipted fee bill. (As discussed in Topic 4, this entry will be recorded in a special journal called the Cash Receipts Journal.)

Prepare a Daily Cash Proof

The amount of cash received should be verified *before* the total cash is deposited and *before* the cash received is recorded in the accounting records. This proof is needed to make sure that the asset Cash is protected from fraud (dishonesty) and outright theft.

Ideally, it is a supervisor, the owner of the business, or the owner's spouse, rather than the person who prepared the source document, who should verify that the day's cash intake agrees with the total amount of cash receipts recorded on the source documents. Of course, any cash shortage should be investigated immediately.

In practice, cash proofs will vary according to the type of source document used. Below, we'll examine the proof of cash register tapes, sales slips, and remittance slips only. From these examples, you should be able to learn how any cash proof works.

Proving Cash Register Tapes When a cash register system is used, the clerk is generally instructed to prepare a daily cash summary form from his or her actual count. To provide for maximum control, the clerk would prepare this daily cash summary without the knowledge of the totals on the cash register tape. Ideally, a supervisor, or any person other than the clerk who created the source documents, should verify that the amount of cash counted in the cash drawer at the end of the day is equal to:

- the total of the cash sales as recorded on the cash register tape *plus*

- the total of the cash received on account (if any) from customers

plus

- the amount of the change fund, that is, money placed in the drawer at the beginning of the day to allow the cashier to make change

Change fund: a small amount of currency used to make change.

less

- any money taken out of the drawer to refund a customer's return of merchandise

Where management allows cash refunds, the clerk must record on the cash register tape the amount taken out as a refund; otherwise, the daily cash summary will not balance. Look closely at the illustrations below.

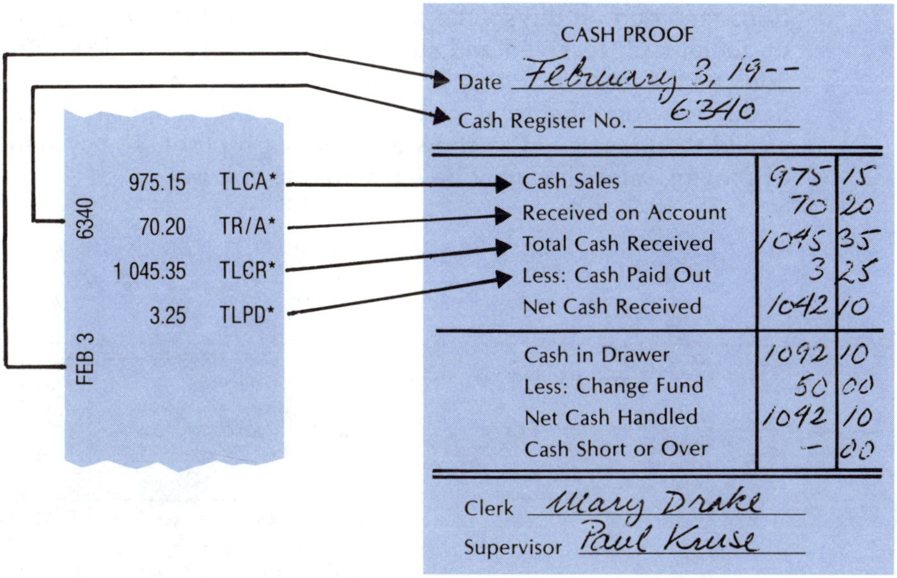

If the cash summary does not balance with the source document, the difference will be a cash shortage or cash overage on the cash summary form. Notice that both the cash register clerk and the supervisor must sign the summary form.

Once the cash proof has been made, the total cash receipts can be forwarded to the cashier's or treasurer's department, where the total cash can be prepared for bank deposit. Of course, a copy of the cash proof, together with the source documents, would be submitted to accounting, where a record would eventually be made of the total cash received for the day.

Proving Sales Slips As you will recall, pre-numbered sales slips are used to account for the receipt of cash when a cash register system is not used. When sales slips are used, the supervisor or someone other than the person creating the document takes the following steps to prove the cash at the end of the day.

(1) All copies of the sales slips are arranged in numerical order so that all the slips can be accounted for, including spoiled ones.

(2) The supervisor or another clerk lists each cash amount received on an adding machine tape to determine the total received on sales slips.

(3) If the sales slips have been used to record cash received on accounts receivable, a separate listing of these items appears on the adding machine tape. Obviously, the cash received from cash sales and cash received from customers in payment on their accounts must be separated for the future accounting record of these transactions.

(4) The supervisor or other clerk checks the total cash transactions recorded on the source documents against the total count of actual cash received and summarized by the sales clerk. (Of course, the amount of any change fund would have to be deducted from the total cash count.) A cash summary form would then be signed to show a proper cash proof. The system of proving sales slips may be illustrated as follows:

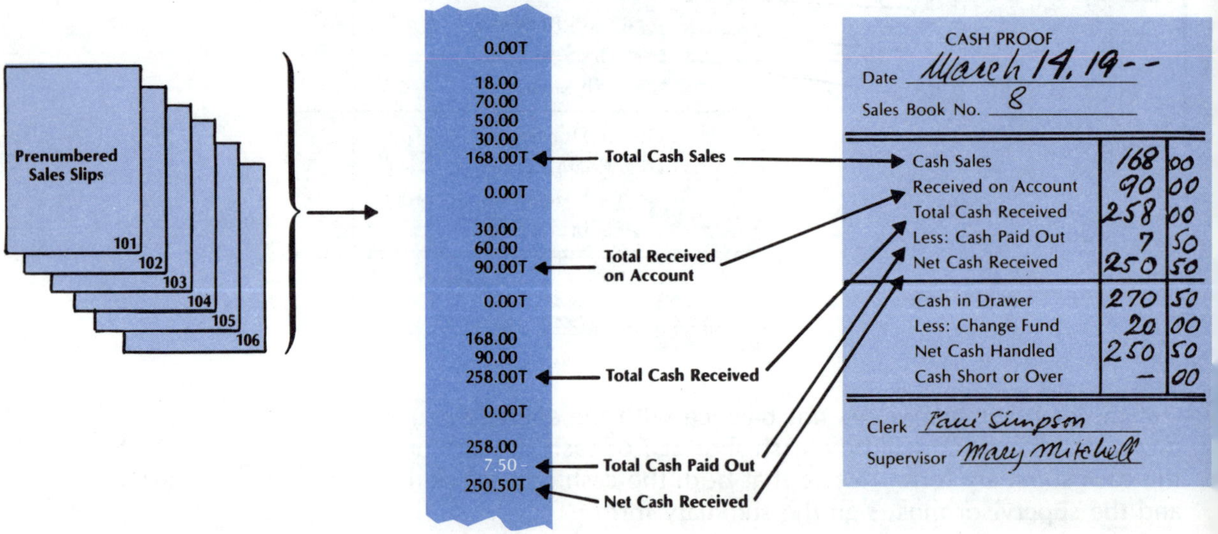

Once the cash receipts from cash transactions have been verified against the sales slips, the total cash can be forwarded to the cashier's or treasurer's office, where it can be prepared for bank deposit. In addition, one copy of each sales slip and the cash proof can also be forwarded to accounting, where the individual transactions shown on the source documents can be correctly recorded in the accounting records.

Proving Remittance Slips A remittance slip is created to account for each cash item received by mail. Since all copies are continuously and consecutively numbered, the proof of cash would be similar to the procedure for proving cash received on the numbered sales slips. In this case, no change fund is necessary and therefore would not be considered in the cash proof.

Once the cash receipts by mail have been verified, all cash and remittance copies must be forwarded to the cashier's or treasurer's office in preparation for bank depositing. And finally, one copy of each remittance slip, together with a copy of the cash proof, can be forwarded to the accounting office where a correct accounting entry can be made for each transaction.

Open a Bank Chequing Account

Most well-run businesses open a chequing account at a bank to ensure a measure of control over their most valuable asset. Such a chequing account is called a current account. A current account offers the following advantages:

Current account: a business bank account used to account for a firm's cash receipts and cash payments.

- The business hires the banker to act as the custodian (guardian) of the firm's most valuable asset (cash). Thus, the banker safeguards the depositor's cash until the depositor instructs the banker to pay some person or some business. In this way, the business does not have to keep large sums on its premises.
- The business will receive all cheques back once the issued cheques are paid. Thus, the *paid* cheques become valuable receipts — documents proving that payments were made.
- The banker provides the depositor with a monthly statement showing the accounting of the depositor's receipts and payments from the banker's point of view. The statement allows the depositor to check the information against his or her own records and make sure that any disagreement is accounted for. By having this separate accounting, the business gains one more check on the accuracy of its procedures.

Deposit Intact All Cash Received

This control measure places great emphasis on the word *intact.* Never should even one dollar of cash receipts be used to make any payment. "Intact" means that *all* cash received must be deposited into the firm's current account. Unless this measure is followed, the total cash received cannot later be checked against the total cash recorded in the accounting records. To prepare all cash receipts for bank deposit, many firms use these additional control measures:

- All cash received in the form of currency (money) should be sorted separately for deposit. Bank of Canada notes (paper money) would be separated into their respective denominations and wrapped together with an elastic band. Each separate denomination would appear on the bank deposit slip. For example, all one-dollar bills would be summarized and totalled, as would all twos, fives, and other denominations. (See the opposite page for two illustrations of completed deposit slips.) All *loose* coins should be placed in separate envelopes or coin wrappers according to denomination. Banks provide coin wrappers to roll 50 pennies (50 cents), 40 nickels ($2.00), 50 dimes ($5.00), 40 quarters ($10.00), and 20 half-dollars ($10.00).

Banks usually request that the name of the business be written or stamped on each wrapper. If there are not enough coins of any one denomination to complete a wrapper, they may be put in small coin envelopes supplied by the bank or in any envelope showing the total coins enclosed. Of course, the total value of the coins wrapped and placed in envelopes would be shown on the appropriate line of the bank deposit slip.

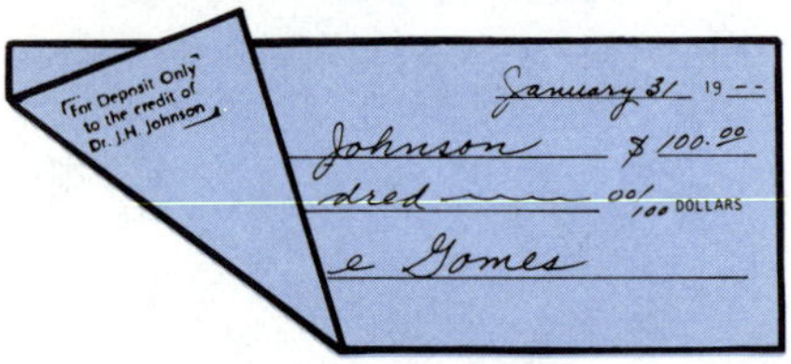

- All cash in the form of cheques, promissory notes, and bank money orders are first endorsed *For Deposit Only*. This means that every cheque and every money order received would be marked on the back with this *restrictive endorsement* before it can be deposited. Cheques and money orders so endorsed cannot be cashed or transferred to someone else. They can only be deposited into the firm's bank account. Since all forms of cash must generally be prepared for deposit, banks allow the depositing firm to use an approved rubber stamp to print the restrictive endorsement. See the example in the margin.

Drawer: the person signing a cheque or money order.

- Once each negotiable instrument has been stamped with the restrictive endorsement, the clerk preparing the deposit slip lists every cheque and money order in the *Cheque* section of the deposit slip. It is considered good practice to show on the deposit slip the name of the drawer of the cheque or money order and the amount of the cheque or money order. When the number of cheques and money orders is great, banks usually allow all negotiable instruments for deposit to be listed on an adding machine tape. The tape can be clipped to the deposit slip, while the total of the negotiable instruments can be written on the first line of the *Cheque* section, with the words *See list attached*.

Deposit Daily All Cash Received

All cash should be deposited daily. Any delay increases the danger of theft. For the convenience of many firms, banks provide night depository facilities. If an evening deposit cannot be made, the deposit is made the next morning.

Obtain a Receipt for All Cash Deposited

Always prepare the deposit slip in *duplicate*. To assist firms that make deposits, banks often supply deposit slips in books

CURRENT ACCOUNT DEPOSIT SLIP

ROYAL BANK

Oct. 24, 19--
DATE

DEPOSITOR'S INITIALS	TELLER'S INITIALS
P.M.	

CREDIT ACCOUNT OF

Sportsman Specialty Shop
843 Driftwood Rd.
Any Town, Canada

PLEASE LIST FOREIGN CHEQUES ON A SEPARATE DEPOSIT SLIP

VISA AND CHEQUES		DETAILS	CASH (INCL. COUPONS)
	VISA VOUCHER TOTAL	6 X 1	6 00
P. Bain	11 20	5 X 2	10 00
L. Cao	12 00	6 X 5	30 00
D. Ellis	25 00	3 X10	30 00
J. Moore	27 96	1 X20	20 00
		X	
		X	
		COIN	27 84
		CANADIAN CASH TOTAL	123 84
TOT	76 16	VISA & CHQS. FORWARDED	76 16
U.S. CASH		RATE	
U.S. CHQS		RATE	
NET DEPOSIT			200 00

⑆0000 2⑈003⑆ 51

CURRENT ACCOUNT DEPOSIT SLIP

ROYAL BANK

Oct. 25, 19--
DATE

DEPOSITOR'S INITIALS	TELLER'S INITIALS
P.M.	

CREDIT ACCOUNT OF

Sportsman Specialty Shop
843 Driftwood Rd.
Any Town, Canada

PLEASE LIST FOREIGN CHEQUES ON A SEPARATE DEPOSIT SLIP

VISA AND CHEQUES		DETAILS	CASH (INCL. COUPONS)
250 00	VISA VOUCHER TOTAL	18 X 1	18 00
359 10		12 X 2	24 00
(see cheque list attached)		5 X 5	25 00
		7 X10	70 00
		2 X20	40 00
		1 X	50 00
		X	
		COIN	38 67
		CANADIAN CASH TOTAL	265 67
TOT	609 10	VISA & CHQS. FORWARDED	609 10
U.S. CASH		RATE	
U.S. CHQS		RATE	
NET DEPOSIT			874 77

⑆0000 2⑈003⑆ 51

Cheque List
Deposit
Oct. 25, 19--

0.00 T
18.00
20.90
19.40
10.00
28.70
35.80
30.00
17.45
46.30
40.00
55.65
20.00
16.90
359.10 T

designed to make duplicate copies. If an individual slip is used, a carbon copy should always be made. When the cash is actually deposited, the bank clerk will stamp both the original and the copy. The original will be kept by the bank, while the stamped copy will be returned to the depositor. If the night depository has been used, the stamped duplicate copy will be mailed to the depositor. The duplicate stamped deposit slip then becomes an effective proof that all cash receipts have been deposited intact into the firm's bank account. The business keeps a permanent file of these receipted deposit slips so a proper audit (check) of the books can be made. An illustration of the duplicate deposit slip, receipted by the bank teller, is given on the next page.

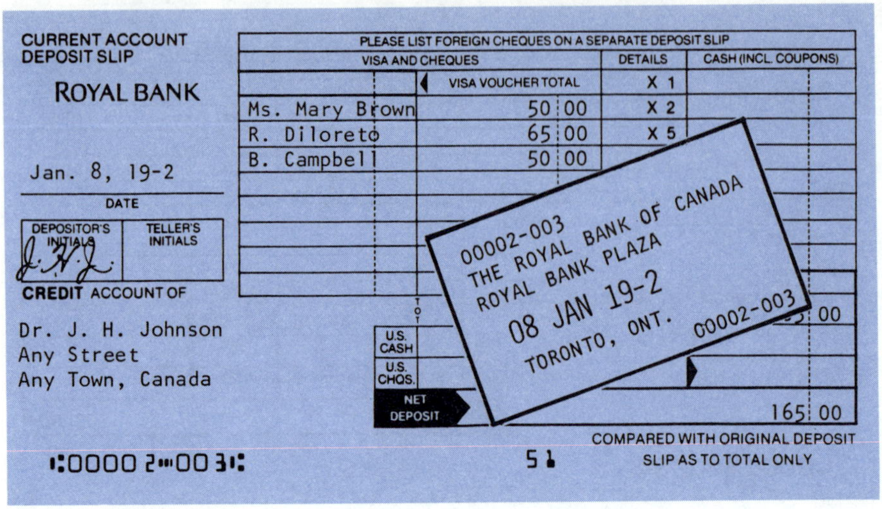
CURRENT ACCOUNT DEPOSIT SLIP
ROYAL BANK

Jan. 8, 19-2
DATE

DEPOSITOR'S INITIALS | TELLER'S INITIALS

CREDIT ACCOUNT OF
Dr. J. H. Johnson
Any Street
Any Town, Canada

PLEASE LIST FOREIGN CHEQUES ON A SEPARATE DEPOSIT SLIP

VISA AND CHEQUES		DETAILS	CASH (INCL. COUPONS)
	VISA VOUCHER TOTAL	X 1	
Ms. Mary Brown	50 00	X 2	
R. Diloreto	65 00	X 5	
B. Campbell	50 00		

U.S. CASH
U.S. CHQS.
NET DEPOSIT 165 00

COMPARED WITH ORIGINAL DEPOSIT SLIP AS TO TOTAL ONLY

⑆00002⑉003⑆ 51

Divide the Responsibility

In a small business, the owner-manager controls the entire operation; he or she participates directly in the daily activities of the firm and personally supervises the one or two clerks who may be hired as employees. As the business grows, however, the owner-manager may find it difficult to buy all the assets, goods, and services for the business, and to supervise the employees and sign all the cheques. At this point, he or she must rely on a strong system of measures to control valuable assets. One important step in any system of controlling assets is: *Divide the responsibility so that people who handle an asset do not also record transactions relating to the asset in the accounting records.*

When this measure is applied to controlling cash, we arrive at the following measures, some or all of which even the smallest of businesses would support:

- The person who prepares the source documents for cash receipts (this person handles the cash) should *not* prepare the daily cash proof. As stated earlier, a supervisor or the owner of the business should double-check to prove that the amount of cash received during the day agrees with the total of the cash receipts recorded on the source document.
- The person who handles the cash and source documents for cash received should *not* make the daily deposit. The owner or some other responsible person should do this. In a very large business, the actual deposit may be performed by personnel working in a separate cashier's or treasurer's office.
- In a large business, the person who handles the cash should *not* be the person who eventually makes the accounting entry to record the cash receipts. In a small business, the clerk who originated the source document for cash received records the cash receipts transaction, but the owner closely supervises

this activity. In large businesses, a separate accounting clerk is assigned the task of recording accounting transactions.

Use a Special Journal to Record Cash Receipts

Since transactions involving cash received every day are common and numerous, many firms will use a special journal known as the Cash Receipts Journal to ensure a better control of recording all cash receipts. This special journal will be discussed in the next Topic.

Cash Receipts Journal: a special journal in which only cash receipts are recorded.

Examine closely the systems flowchart below. Can you identify the basic measures for controlling cash receipts from this chart?

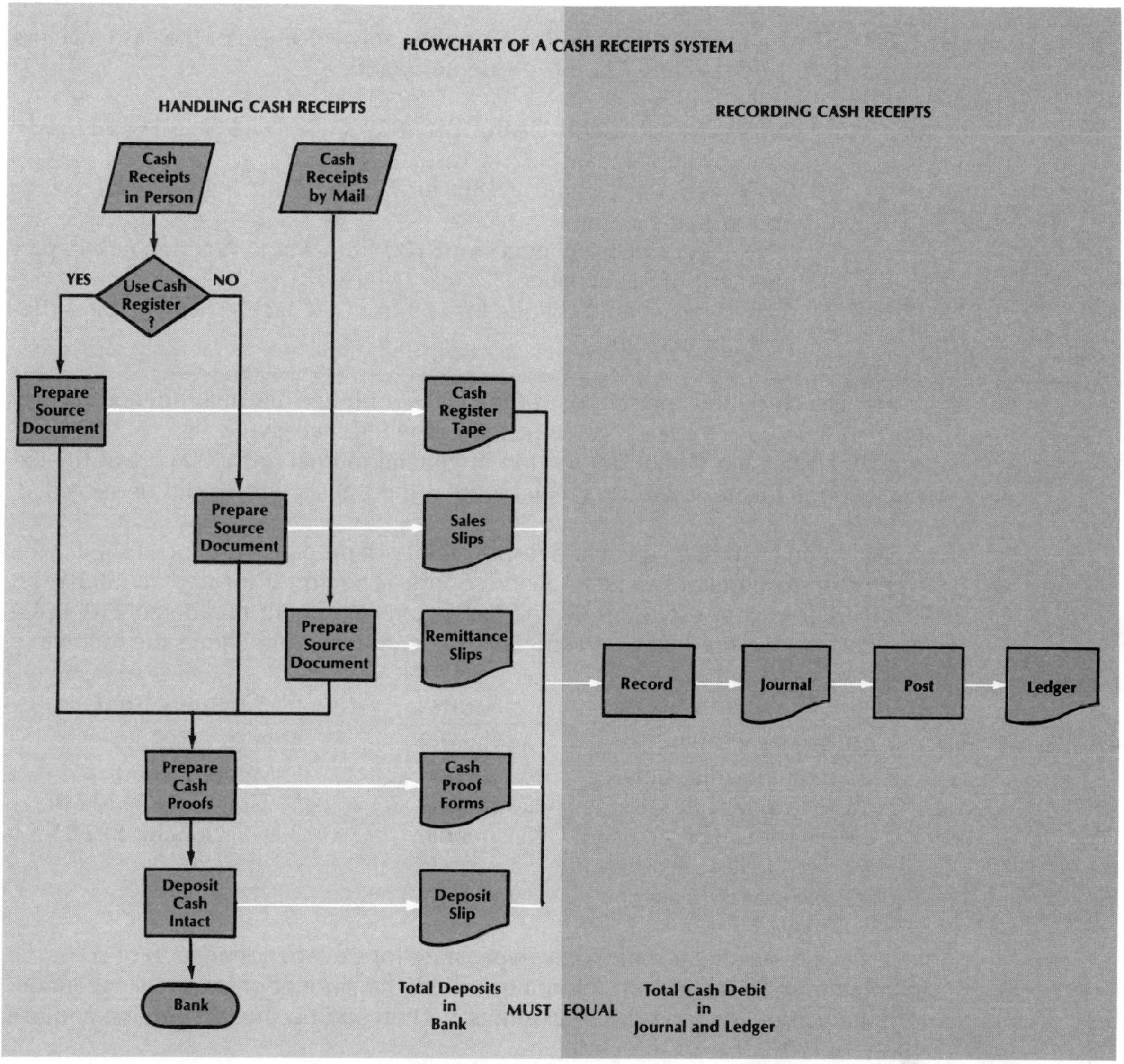

Observe that the chart illustrates the basic internal control measures for controlling cash receipts: create source documents, prepare cash proofs, deposit all cash receipts intact, and divide the responsibility. Notice how it highlights two operations that are involved in processing cash within any business: (1) handling the cash and (2) recording the cash. And notice also that the chart attempts to emphasize a clear division of responsibility between the custodial function (handling the cash) and the accounting function (recording the cash).

TOPIC 3 PROBLEMS

7-8 The four transactions below represent only a portion of the cash receipts transactions of Dr. Penny Thornton's dental practice.

Dec. 2 0003 To Mr. Geoff Dean, X SF, $32 (X-ray = $10, SF = $22). Mr. Dean promptly paid $32 in cash.

17 0013 To Ms. C. Pratt, $180, for BR. Ms. Pratt issued a cheque for $80 in part payment.

31 0025 Received a cheque for $100 from Mr. H. Vandenberk in part payment of his account.

31 0026 Received a cheque for $65 from Mr. Jack Wilson in full settlement of account.

a For each dental transaction, prepare the stub and the main dental fee bill portion. Use your initials to receipt the bill where necessary.

b Analyze each dental transaction in general journal form. As part of the explanation, indicate in which special journal the transaction would be recorded.

7-9 You have been given the responsibility of preparing a deposit slip for the day's cash receipts of Peacock Cycle & Sports. The firm is located at 1595 West 10th Street in your town or city and has a current account numbered 110-134-4 at a nearby chartered bank. A summary of the cash receipts shows the following:

Bank of Canada Notes	Coins	Cheques from
10 fifty-dollar bills	84 quarters	S. Roth, $125.80
26 twenty-dollar bills	82 dimes	L. Milne, $95.00
18 ten-dollar bills	223 nickels	D. Gemeroy, $132.50
36 five-dollar bills	184 pennies	B. MacDonald, $72.25
40 two-dollar bills		
93 one-dollar bills		

a On a form similar to the one given, state for each denomination of coins the number of rolls, the amount of money rolled, the amount of loose change (under *Amount Unrolled*), and the total amount. Then add up the last column and use the sum for part **b** of this problem.

	Coins	No. of Rolls	Amount Rolled	Amount Unrolled	Total
EXAMPLE:	84 quarters	2	$20.00	$1.00	$21.00

b Using today's date, prepare the deposit slip for Peacock Cycle & Sports. Assume the deposit form you are using is in duplicate.

Key Check Figure
Net Deposit = $2 020.74

7-10 Using today's date, prepare a deposit slip for The Janzen Shop, located at 5 Bolton Avenue in your town or city. The firm has a current account numbered 110-734-2 at a nearby chartered bank or trust company. A summary of the cash receipts shows the breakdown illustrated below. *Note:* If you have access to an adding machine, itemize the cheques on it and attach the adding machine tape to the deposit slip. If you do not, itemize the cheques on a separate sheet. Record the total of the cheques in the *Cheque* section of the slip and write the short note *See separate tape attached.*

Bank of Canada Notes	Coins
2 fifty-dollar bills	185 quarters
97 twenty-dollar bills	210 dimes
35 ten-dollar bills	321 nickels
138 five-dollar bills	380 pennies
270 two-dollar bills	
148 one-dollar bills	

Cheques from

D. Shearer, $78.50	D. Stevenson, $110.00	K. Gloster, $24.80
J.MacLean, $62.30	K. Hartsell, $89.00	M. Elliot, $129.75
E. Carleton, $37.90	S. Lindeblom, $23.10	G. McSweeney, $98.40
M. Farewell, $56.00	R.Lewis, $198.75	G. Leal, $225.80
D. Merizzi, $68.90	D. Walduck, $32.80	J. Harrington, $98.56

Key Check Figure
Net Deposit = $5 189.66

7-11 For each case below, identify one major problem of inadequate cash control. Then suggest an internal control measure that would solve the problem.

a The owner of a city parking lot charges a flat fee of $5.00. Two attendants have been hired. One collects cash and supervises parking during the day; the other does the same during the evening. To simplify his records system, the owner instructs each attendant to turn over all cash collected at the end of the shift with a simple summary showing the number of parked cars under his or her supervision.

b To account for the cash received for each day's movie showing, the manager of a movie theatre uses pre-numbered tickets and a different-coloured ticket roll for each different price of admission. At the end of each day's showing, the box office clerk is instructed to turn over the unused roll of tickets to an accounting clerk and the cash collected to the manager. The accounting clerk records a debit to Cash and a credit to Admissions Revenue in the accounting records for the total amount of sales as calculated from the unused ticket rolls. The manager prepares a deposit slip for the total cash and then places the total cash receipts in the bank's night depository facilities.

c The manager of a large clothing store has a current account with a nearby chartered bank but, for personal reasons, prefers to deposit cash receipts at the end of the week only. For safekeeping prior to the weekly bank deposit, he puts the cash into a vault in his office. His weekly cash receipts are in the range of $20 000 to $25 000.

d The dance committee of Central High School has collected $900 in advance ticket sales for a school dance that is to be held in three days. From the cash received to date, $200 has been turned over to the decorating committee with instructions to buy all necessary decorations. Another $300 in cash has been given to a student with instructions to purchase two loudspeakers. The remaining $400 has been deposited into a bank account under the name of Central High School, Student's Council.

e Mary Parker has been elected treasurer of her school's athletic committee. Her duties include the sale of tickets for each contest, proving the cash for all cash receipts prior to the bank deposit, completing a bank deposit slip, depositing the cash into the school's bank account, and recording the total cash receipts for each event held at the school.

TOPIC 4 JOURNALIZING AND POSTING CASH RECEIPTS

In Topic 3, you learned these important measures for controlling cash receipts:

- Create source documents to account for each cash receipt transaction.
- Prepare cash proofs to check the actual count of cash with the total recorded on the source document.
- Deposit daily and intact all cash receipts into the firm's bank current account.
- Obtain a receipted copy of the bank deposit slip.
- Divide the work so that the person who handles the cash is not also the person who records the dollar results of the cash transaction.

With a copy of the source document to originate the cash receipts transaction, you can now proceed to the second and third steps of the accounting cycle: to record the debits and credits of those cash receipts in a journal, and to post the transactions to appropriate accounts.

In this Topic, you will learn how to record cash receipt transactions in a special Cash Receipts Journal and to post those transactions from this journal to appropriate accounts in the Accounts Receivable Ledger and the General Ledger.

The Need for a Cash Receipts Journal

When transactions involving cash receipts are recorded in a two-column general journal, the Cash account is debited for the amount of cash received. What account is credited depends upon the source from which cash was received. Since a dental practice is being used to illustrate Part II of this book, assume that the cash is received from dental patients. Each patient's account is credited for the amount of cash received. This means that the patient's account balance will be reduced.

The Cash Receipts Journal: An Illustration

Assume that the summary of transactions below represents the cash received from various patients of Dr. John H. Johnson's dental practice for the month of January.

Summary of Fee Bill Receipts

Jan.	8	2986	Received a cheque for $50 from Ms. Mary Brown in full settlement of account.
	8	2988	Received a cheque for $65 from Mr. R. Diloreto in full settlement of account.
	8	2989	Received a cheque for $50 from Mr. B. Campbell in full settlement of account.
	10	2992	Received a cheque for $100 from Mr. T. Douglas in full settlement of account.
	10	2993	Received a cheque for $50 from Ms. B. Farr in part payment of her account.
	13	2996	Received a cheque for $100 from Ms. B. Farr in full settlement of her account.
	20	3001	Received a cheque for $193 from Mr. J. Fountain in full settlement of his account.
	24	3004	Received a cheque for $200 from Ms. Christine Zander in part payment of her account.
	29	3008	Received a cheque for $465 from Mr. T. Jacques in full settlement of his account.
	31	3013	Received a cheque for $160 from Mr. W. Maksymiuk in full settlement of his account.
	31	3014	Ms. Anne Gomes paid $100 by cheque in part payment of the $600 dental fee charged today for a bridge.
	31	3015	Received a cheque for $65 from Mr. D. Gray in part settlement of his account.
	31	3016	Received a cheque for $300 from Mr. H. Chan in part payment of his account.
	31	3017	Received a cheque for $195 from Mr. D. Cook in full settlement of his account.

A count shows a total of 14 transactions. Until now, you have analyzed each cash receipt by debiting Cash and crediting Accts. Rec./(Name of Patient) for each transaction. But if all 14 transactions were recorded in the General Journal, then Cash would be debited 14 times and Accounts Receivable would be credited 14 times. Since each entry requires at least three writing lines (one more for each explanation), the entire 14 transactions would take up at least 42 writing lines. If other business transactions were also recorded in the General Journal, you would probably have to search through many pages of the journal to find the total cash received for a given day or a given month.

A better method is to use a special journal to record all cash receipts. Carefully study the one-money column Cash Receipts Journal presented below.

CASH RECEIPTS JOURNAL **Page** *1*

Receipt No.	Date *19-2*		Account Credited	Description	Post. Ref.	Amount
2986	*Jan.*	*8*	*Ms. Mary Brown*	*Full settlement*		*50* —
2988		*8*	*R. Diloretto*	*Full settlement*		*65* —
2989		*8*	*B. Campbell*	*Full settlement*		*50* —
2992		*10*	*T. Douglas*	*Full settlement*		*100* —
2993		*10*	*Ms. B. Farr*	*ROA*		*50* —
2996		*13*	*Ms. B. Farr*	*Full settlement*		*100* —
3001		*20*	*J. Fountain*	*Full settlement*		*193* —
3004		*24*	*Ms. Christine Zander*	*ROA*		*200* —
3008		*29*	*T. Jacques*	*Full settlement*		*465* —
3013		*31*	*W. Maksymiuk*	*Full settlement*		*160* —
3014		*31*	*Ms. Anne Gomes*	*ROA*		*100* —
3015		*31*	*D. Gray*	*ROA*		*65* —
3016		*31*	*H. Chan*	*ROA*		*300* —
3017		*31*	*D. Cook*	*Full settlement*		*195* —

Analysis: Refer to the systems flowchart in Topic 3 of this chapter as you study the points below.

- The name of the special journal appears above the top line along with the journal page number.
- Journal pages are numbered consecutively, beginning with 1.
- The main column headings are: (1) *Receipt Number,* to record the number of the fee bill which is receipted, (2) *Date,* to record the transaction date appearing on the source document, (3) *Account Credit,* to record each account *credited* in each cash receipts transaction, (4) *Description,* to record a brief explanation of the transaction, (5) *Post. Ref. (Posting Reference),* to transfer later each account credited to appropriate accounts,

and (6) *Amount,* to record the dollar result of each cash receipts transaction and the total at the end of the month.

- For each line except the final total line, it is helpful to think of each transaction in general journal form so that the correct credit entry may be recorded. For example, in the case of the first transaction, the entry in general journal form would be analyzed as follows: Cash (debit) and Accts. Rec./Ms. Mary Brown (credit). Of course, Cash (debit) is understood and will be shown at the end of the month when the amount column is totalled.
- On any transaction date, accounting personnel should be able to check the accuracy of the total bank deposit made against the accounting record for that total. For example, the receipted copy of the bank deposit slip for January 8 must agree with the total cash debited on that date in the accounting records. If the two figures do not match, the cash received on that day has not been deposited intact. Accounting personnel can then bring this to the attention of management for immediate action.

CASH RECEIPTS JOURNAL **Page** *1*

Date 19—		**Account Credited**	**Amount**
Jan.	8	Ms. Mary Brown	50 —
	8	R. Diloreto	65 —
	8	B. Campbell	50 —

Total of $165

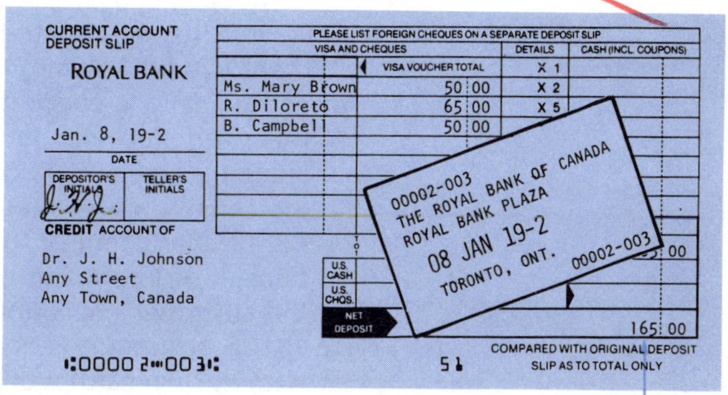

Posting the Cash Receipts Journal

As you know, posting means transferring information from the journal to appropriate accounts filed in a ledger. When a special journal like the Cash Receipts Journal is used together with the General Ledger and Accounts Receivable Ledger, it is helpful to think of the transfer procedure as being divided into two stages:

- *daily* postings to the credit side of individual customer (patient) accounts filed in the Accounts Receivable Ledger
- *month-end* transferring of the *total* of the *Amount* column to the debit side of the Cash account and the credit side of the Accounts Receivable (controlling) account in the General Ledger

Daily Posting to Customer Accounts Posting to individual customer (patient) accounts is no different from the procedure you learned in Topic 2 of this chapter. As a general rule, posting information to customer accounts is done daily. In the case of Dr. Johnson's dental practice, posting is shown from the Cash Receipts Journal to Mr. D. Gray's account in the illustration opposite.

Analysis: Study the following points in connection with the illustration:

- All important information is transferred from the Fees Earned Journal to the patient's account.
- From left to right, the clerk transfers the source document number, the date, and the description.
- In the *Description* column, two items are entered: (1) the description code *ROA* (received on account), (2) next to the *Charge* column, the source of posting. Here, the information is taken from Cash Receipts Journal, page 1, so show the symbol *CRJ1* next to the *Charge* column. In this way, you can always tell where to refer if any question arises as to the individual transaction.
- After recording the explanation and source of the posting in the *Description* column, the clerk transfers the amount of the cash receipt to the *Payment* (credit) column.
- After posting the amount of the cash receipt in the *Payment* (credit) column, enter the Current Balance.
- Finally, a check mark is shown in the *Post. Ref.* column of the Cash Receipts Journal opposite the account just posted. Since the individual accounts are filed in the Accounts Receivable Ledger in alphabetical order, a check mark is placed in the *Post. Ref.* column of the Cash Receipts Journal to show that the transfer of information has occurred from this special journal to the customer's account.

The postings to the other individual patient accounts (each with its own card) would be done in exactly the same manner as shown for Gray's account. After posting each customer's account, the patient's accounts receivable card is filed alphabetically in the tray.

Month-End Posting of the Column Total At the end of the month, the total of the *Amount* column must be posted to the debit side of the Cash account and the credit side of Accounts Receivable (Control) in the General Ledger. But before such a posting occurs, it is important to check the mathematical accuracy of this column. These preliminary steps are recommended at each month-end.

- If you have an adding machine, list the individual amounts on the tape. Be sure the symbol on the tape is printed clearly before beginning the addition. After finding the total, check off the figures on the tape against the individual amounts in the Cash Receipts Journal. (See the illustration.)
- If you do not have an adding machine, add up the *Amount* column and record the total in small pencil figures directly under

CASH RECEIPTS JOURNAL — **Page 1**

Receipt Number	Date 19—		Account Credited	Description	Post. Ref.	Amount
3015		31	D. Gray	ROA		65 —
3016		31	H. Chan	ROA		300 —
3017		31	D. Cook	Full settlement		195 —

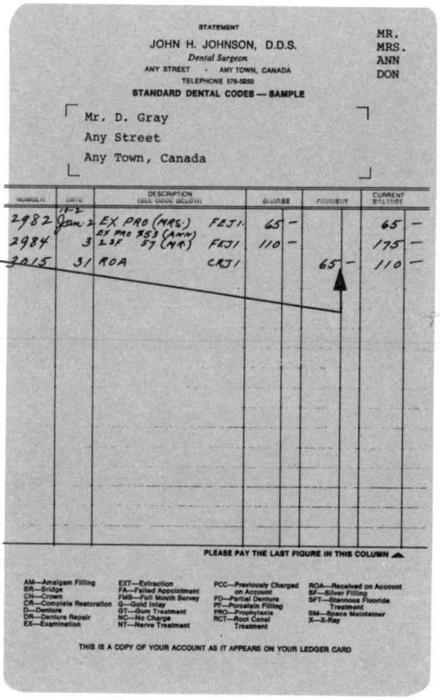
STATEMENT

JOHN H. JOHNSON, D.D.S.
Dental Surgeon
ANY STREET - ANY TOWN, CANADA
TELEPHONE 576-5950
STANDARD DENTAL CODES — SAMPLE

MR.
MRS.
ANN
DON

Mr. D. Gray
Any Street
Any Town, Canada

[illegible]	[illegible]	DESCRIPTION (SEE CODE BELOW)		[illegible]	[illegible]	CURRENT BALANCE
2982	19-2 Jan. 2	EX PRO (MRS.)	FEJ1	65 —		65 —
2984	3	EX PRO #53 (ANN) 2 SF 57 (MR.)	FEJ1	110 —		175 —
3015	31	ROA	CRJ1		65 —	110 —

PLEASE PAY THE LAST FIGURE IN THIS COLUMN

AM—Amalgam Filling
BR—Bridge
CN—Crown
CR—Complete Restoration
D—Denture
DR—Denture Repair
EX—Examination
EXT—Extraction
FA—Failed Appointment
FMS—Full Mouth Survey
G—Gold Inlay
GT—Gum Treatment
NC—No Charge
NT—Nerve Treatment
PCC—Previously Charged on Account
PD—Partial Denture
PF—Porcelain Filling
PRO—Prophylaxis
RCT—Root Canal Treatment
ROA—Received on Account
SF—Silver Filling
SFT—Stannous Fluoride Treatment
SM—Space Maintainer
X—X-Ray

THIS IS A COPY OF YOUR ACCOUNT AS IT APPEARS ON YOUR LEDGER CARD

the last entry in the money column. This small pencil footing is used to double-check the addition of the money column before an ink figure is shown.

- List the daily bank deposits of cash on an adding machine tape and total. The total of all deposit slips for the month must agree with the total cash recorded in the special journal, for management will insist on depositing all cash receipts intact.
- After the total of the *Amount* column has been checked, draw a single line under the last figure in that column to indicate that it is to be totalled.
- On the next writing line, enter the last day of the month in the *Date* column, and the words *Cash DR./Accounts Receivable*

CASH RECEIPTS JOURNAL — **Page 1**

Receipt Number	Date 19-2		Account Credited	Description	Post. Ref.	Amount
2986	Jan.	8	Ms. Mary Brown	Full settlement	√	50 —
2988		8	R. Diloreto	Full settlement	√	65 —
2989		8	B. Campbell	Full settlement	√	50 —
2992		10	T. Douglas	Full settlement	√	100 —
2993		10	Ms. B. Farr	ROA	√	50 —
2996		13	Ms. B. Farr	Full settlement	√	100 —
3001		20	J. Fountain	Full settlement	√	193 —
3004		24	Ms. Christine Zander	ROA	√	200 —
3008		29	T. Jacques	Full settlement	√	465 —
3013		31	W. Maksymiuk	Full settlement	√	160 —
3014		31	Ms. Anne Gomes	ROA	√	100 —
3015		31	D. Gray	ROA	√	65 —
3016		31	H. Chan	ROA	√	300 —
3017		31	D. Cook	Full settlement	√	195 —
		31	Cash DR./Accounts Receivable CR.			2 093 —

Cash Receipts Journal - Page 1
Jan. 31, 19-2

```
      0.00 T
     50.00 +✓
     65.00 +✓
     50.00 +✓
    100.00 +✓
     50.00 +✓
    100.00 +✓
    193.00 +✓
    200.00 +✓
    465.00 +✓
    160.00 +✓
    100.00 +✓
     65.00 +✓
    300.00 +✓
    195.00 +✓

  2 093.00 T
```

CR. stretching across the *Account Credited* and *Description* columns.

- To show that the special journal has been completed for the month, draw a double horizontal line across the *Amount, Post. Ref., Receipt No.,* and *Date* columns. The double line indicates that the next month's transactions begin below.

The total of the *Amount* column is now ready to be transferred to the General Ledger in the form of a double entry:

- A debit must be transferred to the Cash account.
- A credit must be transferred to Accounts Receivable (Control).

CASH RECEIPTS JOURNAL — **Page** *1*

Receipt No.	Date 19-2		Account Credited	Description	Post. Ref.	Amount
2986	Jan.	8	Ms. Mary Brown	Full settlement		50 —
3017		31	D. Cook	Full settlement		195 —
		31	Cash DR./Accounts Receivable CR.		101/103	2 093 —

GENERAL LEDGER

Cash — **Account No.** *101*

Date 19-2		Explanation		Post. Ref.	Debit	Credit	Balance	
Jan.	2	Balance forward		√			20 000 —	DR.
	31	Total Cash Receipts	CRJ	1	2 093 —		22 093 —	

Accounts Receivable — **Account No.** *103*

Date 19-2		Explanation		Post. Ref.	Debit	Credit	Balance	
Jan.	2	Balance forward		√			320 —	DR.
	31	Total charges	FEJ	1	4 665 —		4 985 —	
	31	Total payments	CRJ	1		2 093 —	2 892 —	

Recording the Opening Entry Many accountants prefer always to show the opening entry in the General Journal, because this entry is non-recurring. Furthermore, a permanent record of the opening balances can be made in one place where cash and other assets are invested. For example, the opening entry to record Dr. Johnson's investment of both cash and other assets may be shown in the General Journal as follows:

GENERAL JOURNAL **Page** *1*

Date		Account Title and Explanation	Post. Ref.	Debit		Credit	
19-1							
Jan.	*2*	*Cash*		*26 000*	*00*		
		Dental Equipment		*70 000*	*00*		
		Office Equipment		*4 000*	*00*		
		Accts. Pay./Denco Supply				*8 000*	*00*
		Accts. Pay./Mardan Business Systems Ltd.				*2 000*	*00*
		Notes Payable — 5-Year				*30 000*	*00*
		John H. Johnson, Capital				*60 000*	*00*
		To record the opening entry for John H. Johnson, D.D.S.					

The Cash debited in the General Journal will be posted immediately to the Cash account to open the books for that account. Since this opening entry occurs only once, it is common to record it in the General Journal. Of course, if the opening entry consisted of a cash investment only (Cash debited and Capital credited), the opening entry could be recorded in the Cash Receipts Journal. To be consistent, however, all opening entries should be recorded in the General Journal.

Advantages of the Cash Receipts Journal

Let's summarize the main advantages of using a special journal to record all cash receipts:

- Only one line is required to record an entry in the Cash Receipts Journal, instead of three or four. This saves time and space.
- The dollar amount is written only once for each double entry because *Cash debit* is understood.
- Valuable time is saved because only the total is posted to the General Ledger at the end of the month. The total is posted to the debit of Cash, and to the credit of the controlling account, Accounts Receivable.

- A division of responsibility among accounting clerks is made possible. In a large firm, one clerk can be assigned responsibility for recording and posting credits to accounts receivable.

TOPIC 4 PROBLEMS

7-12 The transactions below represent the cash receipts from various patients of Dr. L.M. Munro's dental practice for the final week of January, 19-1.

Jan. 26 0001 Ms. M. Micsinski today issued a cheque for $65 in full payment of the dental fee.
28 0003 Mr. L. McGraw issued a cheque for $100 in part payment of his account.
30 0006 Ms. J. Laing paid $70 cash to clear her account.
31 0007 Mr. I. Ryder issued a cheque for $65 in full payment of his dental fee.
31 0008 Received a cheque for $193 from Mr. L. McGraw in full settlement of his account.
31 0009 Received a cheque for $50 from Mr. S. Katz in part payment of his account.
31 0010 Received a cheque for $100 from Mr. S. Ketcheson in part payment of his account.

a Record the transactions above in a Cash Receipts Journal. Begin on "page 1."

b Refer to Problem 7-6 and its solution. Post the transactions from the Cash Receipts Journal to the separate patient accounts receivable cards used for Problem 7-6.

c Total the Cash Receipts Journal and show this total *journalized* for the month of January. Then rule off the journal for the month.

d Set up two General Ledger accounts and post the total from the Cash Receipts Journal to these accounts. *Note:* The Cash account has a debit balance forward of $5 000; the Accounts Receivable controlling account has a debit balance forward of $726.

Key Check Figure Cash DR. = $643

7-13 Brian Prong, C.A. owns and operates a tax service bureau in a medium-sized community. All clients are given 30 days in which to pay their bills. Brian uses pre-numbered fee bills which serve also as official receipts when cash is received on account.

a Open General Ledger accounts and enter account balances forwarded as of March 1, 19-2 as follows: Cash (101), $29 000; Accounts Receivable (103), $4 500; Office Equipment (110), $6 500; Automobile (112), $20 000; Bank Loan Payable (201), $1 200; B. Prong, Capital (301), $58 800.

b Set up a T-account Accounts Receivable Ledger for the following clients: Howden's Electric (balance, $350 DR.), Munro Boats (balance, $650 DR.), J. North (balance, $2 000 DR.), Orr Cleaners (balance, $1 000 DR.), Wm. A. Smith (balance, $500 DR.). *Note:* In setting up each T-account, show the balance on the proper side. This balance represents the balance carried forward from the previous accounting period.

Howden's Electric	
Balance 350	

c Record the following cash receipts transactions in a Cash Receipts Journal. Number the page "12."

Mar. 4 Receipt No. 6040. Issued to Howden's Electric for cheque received in full payment of account.
6 Receipt No. 6041. Received a cheque for $650 from Munro Boats in full settlement of account.
10 Receipt No. 6042. J. North appeared at the office to issue his cheque for $1 000 in part settlement of his account.
22 Receipt No. 6043. Received a cheque for $500 from Orr Cleaners on account.
28 Receipt No. 6044. Received a cheque for $500 from Wm. A. Smith in full settlement of account.

d Post the daily entries from the Cash Receipts Journal to the appropriate accounts.
e Check the addition (using an adding machine tape or the footing procedure), total, and then rule off the Cash Receipts Journal for the month.
f Post the month-end total from the Cash Receipts Journal to the General Ledger.

Key Check Figure
Cash DR. = $3 000

7-14 The transactions below represent the cash received from various patients of Dr. Penny Thornton's dental practice for the month of December, 19-1.

Dec. 4 0003 Received $32 in cash from Mr. Geoff Dean in full settlement for the dental services rendered today.
17 0013 Received a cheque for $80 from Ms. C. Pratt in part payment of the dental fee charged today.
31 0025 Received a cheque for $100 from Mr. H. Vandenberk in part payment of his account.
31 0026 Received a cheque for $65 from Mr. Jack Wilson in full settlement of account.
31 0027 Received a cheque for $66 from Mr. M. Liepner in full settlement of account.
31 0028 Received a cheque for $152 from Ms. E. Revell in full settlement of account.
31 0029 Received a cheque for $65 from Mr. T. Taller in full settlement of account.

Dec. 31 0030 Received a cheque for $34 from Mr. T. Murphy in full settlement of account.
31 0031 Received a cheque for $65 from Ms. L. Kretchman in full settlement of account.
31 0032 Mr. B. Gibson appeared at the office to pay $50 cash in part payment of his account.
31 0033 Received a cheque for $100 from Ms. M. Kingsbury in part payment of her account.
31 0034 Received a cheque for $65 from Mr. R. Kendall in full settlement of account.

a Record the transactions above in a Cash Receipts Journal, Page 1.

b Use the T-account Accounts Receivable Ledger solved for Problem 7-7 to post the transactions from the Cash Receipts Journal to the individual patient accounts.

c Use the patient's ledger card set up for Mr. H. Vandenberk in Problem 7-7 to show how this family card would receive the appropriate posting from the Cash Receipts Journal.

d Check the addition of the Cash Receipts Journal using an adding machine tape or the footing procedure. Total and record the appropriate double-entry for this total, then rule off the Cash Receipts Journal for the month.

e Post the month-end total from the Cash Receipts Journal to the General Ledger. *Note:* The Cash account shows a balance of $10 000. Check the solution to Problem 7-7 for the correct balance forward for Accounts Receivable DR.

Key Check Figure
Cash DR. = $874

TOPIC 5 MONTH-END PROCEDURES

So far in this chapter you have gone through the first three steps of the accounting cycle for transactions affecting customer (patient) accounts:

Step 1: Originating transaction data through the analysis of the charge on the dental fee bill, and of the payment on the receipted dental fee bill.

Step 2: Journalizing the dental charge in the Fees Earned Journal and journalizing the cash received in the Cash Receipts Journal.

Step 3: Posting transactions daily from the Fees Earned Journal and the Cash Receipts Journal to the patient accounts in the Accounts Receivable Ledger, and posting the monthly total from those special journals to appropriate accounts in the General Ledger.

This final Topic involves the fourth step of the accounting cycle: the preparation of monthly trial balances.

Preparing Monthly Trial Balances

When a General Ledger and one or more subsidiary (secondary) ledgers are used in the accounting system, it is important that a trial balance be taken at the end of each month for each ledger. Also, when many customer account balances appear in the Accounts Receivable Ledger, it is most important to prepare at month-end what is known as an *aged trial balance.*

Preparing the General Ledger Trial Balance

In the General Ledger Trial Balance, all accounts with balances in the General Ledger are listed in the order in which they appear in the ledger. The only difference from the trial balances studied earlier is that the controlling account for Accounts Receivable appears instead of the listing of the individual customer (patient) account balances. Similarly, the controlling account for Accounts Payable appear instead of the listing of the individual creditor accounts. In the case of Dr. Johnson's dental practice (assuming that the previously treated fees charged and cash receipts represent the only transactions for the first month of the new accounting period), the monthly General Ledger Trial Balance would appear as follows:

John H. Johnson, D.D.S.
Trial Balance
January 31, 19-2

Account Title	Post. Ref.	Debit		Credit	
Cash	101	22 093	00		
Bank Deposit Receipts	102	15 680	00		
Accounts Receivable	103	2 892	00		
Dental Equipment	110	70 000	00		
Office Equipment	112	4 000	00		
Accounts Payable	202			10 000	00
5-Year Note Payable	210			30 000	00
John H. Johnson, Capital	301			70 000	00
Professional Fees Earned	401			4 665	00
		114 665	00	114 665	00

Trial balance: a summary of General Ledger account balances.

The above illustration merely shows the heading Trial Balance. It is understood that the words *General Ledger* go along with this heading; a quick glance at the accounts listed will support this idea. So when you merely see the title *Trial Balance,* think of the report as the *General Ledger Trial Balance.*

Preparing the Accounts Receivable Trial Balance

Schedule of Accounts Receivable: a list of individual customer account balances.

Posting to the various customer accounts in the Accounts Receivable Ledger is done on a daily basis. To check on the accuracy of this posting for the whole month, the balances of all the accounts in the Accounts Receivable Ledger at the end of the month are listed on a form called the Schedule of Accounts Receivable, as shown below.

John H. Johnson
Schedule of Accounts Receivable
January 31, 19-2

B. Campbell	45	00
H. Chan	557	00
R. Diloreto	65	00
Ms. A. Gomes	500	00
D. Gray	110	00
Ms. C. Lee	70	00
S. Lesniak	65	00
Ms. B. Toy	800	00
Ms. G. Tuck	400	00
Ms. C. Zander	280	00
Total Accounts Receivable	2 892	00

Accounts Receivable **Account No.** *103*

Date 19-2		Explanation	Post. Ref.	Debit		Credit		Balance		
Jan.	2	Balance forward	√					320	—	DR.
	31	Total charges FEJ	1	4 665	—			4 985	—	
	31	Total payments CRJ	1			2 093	—	2 892	—	

The total of the Schedule of Accounts Receivable at the end of the month must agree with the balance of the Accounts Receivable controlling account in the GL (General Ledger). In effect, a type of *trial balance* has been made to prove that the subsidiary ledger agrees with the related controlling account in the GL. Notice also the title of the report. The term *Accounts Receivable Trial Balance* might have been used, but to avoid confusion with the trial balance of the GL, *Schedule of Accounts Receivable* will be used throughout this book.

If the total of the Schedule of Accounts Receivable agrees with the balance in the Accounts Receivable controlling account, their agreement is treated as an accounting proof that the posting done in the subsidiary ledger is accurate. If they are not identical and the GL Trial Balance has been proved, errors or omissions must have occurred in the subsidiary ledger. For example, a clerk may have posted a charge directly to a patient's account without including this charge in the Fees Earned Journal. Of course, the mistakes must be identified and corrected before any financial statements are prepared. In general, as a useful internal control measure, *it is essential that the Accounts Receivable account in the GL agree with the Accounts Receivable subsidiary ledger before any financial statements are prepared.*

Preparing the Aged Trial Balance

When a firm has many customer accounts with month-end balances as shown by the Schedule of Accounts Receivable, it is common to prepare an aged trial balance of those receivables.

Aged trial balance: a list of customer account balances according to their "age" (current, 31-60 days, 61-90 days, or over 90 days).

What is meant by *aging?* Aging is the procedure of listing each customer's month-end balance and indicating whether that balance is currently due or overdue. In giving credit terms, most firms usually award their reliable customers with 30 days from the date of the bill to pay their account in full. Any such balance in a customer's account is then regarded as current — not past due.

On the other hand, if a customer's account balance shows an amount not paid for, say, 40 days from the date of the bill, accountants say that this amount is past due or is *aged* beyond 30 days. To control these past-due or older account balances, accountants recommend the classification of aged amounts under at least the following headings: *31 – 60 days, 61 – 90 days,* and *over 90 days.*

Suppose a patient's account shows the information on page 230.

To age this account, one would say that the $61 shown on Jan. 14, 19-2 is past due between 31 – 60 days. Therefore, the $61 would be entered in the 31 – 60 days aged column. The remaining $442 (balance owing of $503 less the $61) is not past due because the date of the charge, Feb. 10, 19-2 is within the current 30-day credit period. This amount would be reported in the current column of the aged trial balance as illustrated.

Analysis: As you can see, amounts past due are clearly indicated. Now the owner/manager must collect the amounts. The longer the amounts remain past due, the less likely the firm will collect these amounts. Remember these important points:

- Overdue accounts receivable may never be collected. This means having to account for what are known as bad debts. Of

STATEMENT

MARY E. WEST, D.D.S.
Dental Surgeon
ANY STREET - ANY TOWN
TELEPHONE 888-7880

MR.
MRS.
JANE
780-4398

Mr. C. A. Black
Any Street
Any Town, Canada

NUMBER	DATE	DESCRIPTION (SEE CODE BELOW)		CHARGE	PAYMENT	CURRENT BALANCE
6040	19-2 Jan. 14	EX PRO (MRS.)	FEJ 70	61 —		61 —
6900	Feb. 10	BR	FEJ 85	592 —		653 —
6900	10	ROA	CRJ 18		150 —	503 —

PLEASE PAY THE LAST FIGURE IN THIS COLUMN ▲

AM—1, 2, 3 etc. Surfaces Amalgam Restoration
BR—Bridge
CN—Crown
CR—Composite Restoration
CX—Complete Series X-Rays
D—Dentures
DR—Denture Reline
ET—Endodontic Therapy
EX—Examination
EXT—Extraction
FA—Failed Appointment
FT—Fluoride Treatment
G—Gold Inlay
NC—No Charge
O—Orthodontic Treatment
OHI—Oral Hygiene Instruction
PD—Partial Denture
PRO—Prophylaxis
PT—Periodontal Treatment
ROA—Recevied on Account
SM—Space Maintainer
TF—Temporary Filling
X—X-Ray

THIS IS A COPY OF YOUR ACCOUNT AS IT APPEARS ON YOUR LEDGER CARD.

course, bad debts result in extra expenses which decrease the firm's net income and even may result in a net loss. (The accounting of bad debts is explained in Chapter 15.)

• Overdue accounts receivable mean that the owner has no money coming in within an expected time (within 30 days). This means a poor *cash flow*. If money is not coming in on time from receivables, the owner may have to borrow money to pay the firm's accounts payable. And borrowing money means extra accounting for an extra cost called interest expense, which can also lead to future net losses.

• Overdue accounts receivable also mean that the business cannot invest the amounts which should be flowing in. If the business thus loses the opportunity to invest, it is actually losing the chance to make more money through interest earned or dividends earned on investments. We call such losses *opportunity costs*.

Mary E. West, D.D.S.
Aged Trial Balance as of February 28, 19-2

Family Name	Phone No.	Total Owing	Current	Days Past Due			Current Month	
				31 – 60	61 – 90	Over 90	Debits	Credits
J. Acker	487-7890	42.00				42.00		
C.A. Black	780-4398	503.00	442.00	61.00			592.00	150.00
S. Byrd	459-6070	204.00			204.00			
J. Cruse	236-8902	59.00		52.00		7.00	52.00	100.00
E. Doney	679-4598	100.00				100.00		
E. Flynn	579-8945	19.00				19.00		
B. Goetz	887-4532	153.00	153.00				153.00	
E. Harris	334-2378	100.00	100.00				100.00	
J. Jacobs	456-0990	981.00	100.00	100.00	100.00	681.00	100.00	
L. Larsen	324-0345	109.00	2.00	107.00			302.00	300.00
M. Matz	567-9823	20.00			20.00			
H. Novak	456-4588	15.00				15.00		
W. Petty	234-6789	523.00	375.00	148.00			875.00	500.00
J. Robey	788-8000	306.00		274.00		32.00	274.00	400.00
T. Schmidt	471-8666	109.00	2.00	107.00			302.00	300.00

Controlling a firm's accounts receivable, therefore, is just as important as controlling the asset Cash. One way of controlling accounts receivable is to take time to (1) prepare an aged trial balance each month, (2) study the results, and (3) take steps to get the debtors to pay.

For Dr. Johnson's practice, an aged trial balance as of January 31, 19-2, from the data presented in this chapter, may be shown as follows:

John H. Johnson, D.D.S.
Aged Trial Balance as of January 31, 19-2

Family Name	Phone No.	Total Owing	Current	Days Past Due			Current Month	
				31 – 60	61 – 90	Over 90	Debits	Credits
B. Campbell	489-7772	45.00	45.00				45.00	50.00
H. Chan	457-8976	557.00	557.00				857.00	300.00
R. Diloreto	324-0090	65.00	65.00				130.00	65.00
Ms. A. Gomes	443-1177	500.00	500.00				600.00	100.00
D. Gray	678-0923	110.00	110.00				175.00	65.00
Ms. C. Lee	432-0987	70.00	70.00				70.00	
S. Lesniak	323-4356	65.00	65.00				65.00	
Ms. B. Toy	449-3345	800.00	800.00				800.00	
Ms. G. Tuck	679-9834	400.00	400.00				400.00	
Ms. C. Zander	299-0093	280.00	280.00				480.00	200.00

Preparing the Statement of Account

Statement of account: a statement mailed monthly to customers showing the balances they owe.

One step taken by many firms to control their accounts receivable is to prepare a statement of account. In some businesses, a statement of account is mailed to each customer (or patient) showing a month-end balance on the Schedule of Accounts Receivable. Since the preparation and mailing of many monthly statements is costly, dental practices (and other firms) often send statements only to those customers whose accounts are past due.

The type of statement of account prepared will vary with management's methods of keeping costs down. The simplest shows only the balance due at the end of the month. This type of statement is used by some professional people. For example, an accountant may prepare a statement of account as shown below.

Statement of Account

JOHN KERSHAW, C.A.
1500 Bloor Street E.
Toronto, Canada

471-8622

TO: T. J. Atkins
16 Yonge Street N.
Toronto, Ontario

June 30, 19--

For professional services, balance due $300.00

Many businesses, including professional practices, prefer to make a photocopy of the customer's (patient's) ledger card once this card is completely posted for the month. In the case of Dr. Johnson's dental practice, the copy of Mr. D. Gray's ledger card would appear as shown in the margin.

Where computers are used to process the accounts receivable application, it is common to prepare an aged monthly statement of account.

This shows which amounts are currently due and which ones are past due in ages of 31 – 60 days, 61 – 90 days, and over 90 days. The computerized application for accounts receivable will be covered in Chapter 18.

STATEMENT
JOHN H. JOHNSON, D.D.S.
Dental Surgeon
ANY STREET · ANY TOWN, CANADA
TELEPHONE 576-5950
STANDARD DENTAL CODES — SAMPLE

MR.
MRS.
ANN
DON

Mr. D. Gray
Any Street
Any Town, Canada

NUMBER	DATE	DESCRIPTION (SEE CODE BELOW)		CHARGE	PAYMENT	CURRENT BALANCE
2982	19-2 Jan. 2	EX PRO (MRS.)	FEJ1	65 —		65 —
2984	3	EX PRO #53 (ANN) 2 SF 57 (MR.)	FEJ1	110 —		175 —
3015	31	ROA	CRJ1		65 —	110 —

PLEASE PAY THE LAST FIGURE IN THIS COLUMN ▲

AM—Amalgam Filling
BR—Bridge
CN—Crown
CR—Complete Restoration
D—Denture
[illegible]
EX—Examination

EXT—Extraction
FA—Failed Appointment
FMS—Full Mouth Survey
G—Gold Inlay
GT—Gum Treatment
[illegible]
NT—Nerve Treatment

PCC—Previously Charged on Account
PD—Partial Denture
PF—Porcelain Filling
PRO—Prophylaxis
[illegible] Treatment

ROA—Received on Account
SF—Silver Filling
SFT—Stannous Fluoride Treatment
SM—Space Maintainer
[illegible]

THIS IS A COPY OF YOUR ACCOUNT AS IT APPEARS ON YOUR LEDGER CARD

TOPIC 5 PROBLEMS

7-15 Refer to Problem 7-14.

a Calculate and show balances in each patient's T-account in the Accounts Receivable Ledger solved in Problem 7-14b.

b Prepare a Schedule of Accounts Receivable as at December 31, 19-1.

c What check can you make to prove that the total obtained in your Schedule of Accounts Receivable is accurate?

Key Check Figure Total of Accounts Receivable = $1 614

Problems 7-16 and 17 are related.

7-16 Challenge Problem On March 1, Dr. Robert Wong, D.D.S. acquired a dental practice from a retired dentist. Dr. Wong's opening balance sheet revealed the following: Cash, $50 000; Accounts Receivable, $2 400; Dental Supplies on Hand, $5 000; Dental Equipment, $70 000; Office Equipment, $5 000; Furniture, $2 600; Bank Loan Payable, $35 000.

a In a General Journal, Page 1, make the opening entry to record the assets, liabilities, and owner's equity reported in the opening balance sheet of March 1.

b Open the following General Ledger accounts with account numbers as indicated in parentheses: Cash (101), Accounts Receivable (103), Dental Supplies on Hand (105), Dental Equipment (110), Office Equipment (112), Furniture (114), Bank Loan Payable (201), Robert Wong, Capital (301), Professional Fees Earned (401).

c Post the opening entry from the General Journal to the appropriate accounts in the General Ledger.

d Set up separate patient accounts receivable *cards* to make up the Accounts Receivable Ledger for the following patients (names in parentheses represent *the other family members)*: Mr. J.M. Boersema (Mrs.), Ms. H. Cheng, Mrs. Helen Dye, Mr. H. Fisher (Mrs., Terry), Ms. Janet Gamble (new patient), Mr. R. Green (Mrs., Linda, Jim), Mrs. Jane Kaplan, Mr. John Lee (new patient), Mr. R. Mandel (Mrs., Betty, Barbara), Ms. Pat Nash (new patient). For each patient, invent appropriate street and city or town addresses.

e For each *old* patient account acquired by the business, record the following balance forward as of March 1: Mr. J. M. Boersema, balance of $100; Ms. H. Cheng, balance of $200; Mrs. Helen Dye, balance of $250; Mr. H. Fisher, balance of $500; Mr. R. Green, balance of $175; Mrs. Jane Kaplan, balance of $450; Mr. R. Mandel, balance of $725.

Key Check Figure Boersema's Balance = $100

Note: Keep all forms for use in the next question.

7-17 Challenge Problem The transactions below represent the dental fees charged and the cash received from the various patients of Dr. Robert Wong's dental practice for the month of March, 19-1.

Mar. 2 1001 Mr. John Lee. EX PRO, total fee of $65. No payment received.
3 1002 Received cheque for $100 from Mr. J.M. Boersema in full settlement of account.
6 1003 Mr. R. Mandel. EX PRO, total fee of $65. No payment received.

Mar. 7 1004 Ms. Janet Gamble. Total fee of $70 for X-Ray, Examination, and Cleaning. Received $20 cash in part payment of account.
9 1005 Ms. Pat Nash. EX PRO, total fee of $65. Received $25 cash on account.
10 1006 Received cheque for $175 from Mr. R. Green in full settlement of account.
13 1007 Received cheque for $100 from Mrs. Helen Dye, in part payment of account.
14 1008 Total charge of $700 to Mrs. Boersema, wife of Mr. J.M. Boersema, for a bridge. No payment was received.
15 1009 Total charge of $450 to Mr. John Lee for a crown. Received a cheque for $100 in part payment of account.
16 1010 Received a cheque for $500 from Mr. H. Fisher in full settlement of account.
17 1011 Received a cheque for $150 from Mrs. Jane Kaplan in part payment of account.
20 1012 Received a cheque for $40 from Ms. Pat Nash in full settlement of account.
21 1013 Total fee charged to Mr. R. Green for dental services rendered to Linda, his daughter, $80 for a white filling.
22 1014 Received a cheque for $150 from Mrs. Helen Dye in full settlement of account.
23 1015 Ms. Pat Nash, total fee of $200 charged for gold inlay. No payment received.
24 1016 Received a cheque for $50 from Ms. Janet Gamble in full settlement of account.
27 1017 Received a cheque for $500 from Mr. R. Mandel in part settlement of account.
28 1018 Received a cheque for $200 from Ms. H. Cheng in full settlement of account.
29 1019 Ms. Janet Gamble. Total fee of $600 charged for root canal treatment. No payment received.
30 1020 Received a cheque for $100 from Mr. J.M. Boersema on account.
31 1021 To Terry, son of Mr. H. Fisher, total fee of $32 charged for tooth extraction. No payment received.
31 1022 Received from Mrs. Jane Kaplan a cheque for $50, on account.

a Analyze each of the dental transactions summarized above. Then record each *Charge* in a Fees Earned Journal, Page 1. Also record each *Payment* in a Cash Receipts Journal, Page 1.

b On a *daily basis,* post the information from the special journals to appropriate patient accounts receivable cards. (Use the Accounts Receivable Ledger established in Problem 7-16.)

c Total the Fees Earned Journal and the Cash Receipts Journal and show each total *journalized* for the month of March.

d Post the total from each special journal to appropriate accounts in the General Ledger. Use the General Ledger prepared for Problem 7-16.

e Prepare a trial balance of both the General Ledger and the Accounts Receivable Ledger.

Key Check Figure Trial Balance Total = $137 327

7-18 Challenge Problem The Accounts Receivable Ledger of Dr. P. Mazzone, Dental Surgeon shows the following data on December 31, 19-1:

R. Abel (phone number 478-9500); total owing, $70; no current-month debits or credits; the last transaction shows a charge of $70 on October 15, 19-1.

J. Angel (587-4000); current debits of $695; total credits of $400.

F. Barton (748-6920); no current-month debits or credits; balance owing of $85 dates back to Nov. 1, 19-1.

J. Bogart (417-9939); current-month debit of $52; current-month credit of $100; total owing of $59, made up of the $52 charge dating back to Nov. 12 and the $7 charge dating back to Oct. 1.

A. Carson (670-4000); current-month debit of $153; no current credits; no past-due amounts.

M. Chester (448-1740); current-month debits of $302; current-month credits of $300; a charge of $107 dates back to Nov. 14, 19-1.

H. Dennis (515-6800); total owing of $100, resulting from a current debit of $100.

C. Dunn (715-8958); no current debits or credits; a charge of $40 dates back to Oct. 10, 19-1.

D. Fair (238-7400); no current debits or credits; a charge of $150 dates back to Sept. 1, 19-1.

D. Ganz (678-4333); total owing of $523; current debits of $875; current credits of $500; a charge of $148 dates back to Nov. 8, 19-1.

R. Hansen (540-9009); total owing of $981; current debit of $100; no current credits; a charge of $100 dates back to Aug. 10, 19-1; a charge of $100 dates back to Oct. 15, 19-1; a charge of $681 dates back to Nov. 4, 19-1.

Prepare an aged trial balance for Dr. Mazzone's dental practice as of December 31, 19-1. Use a form similar to the first one shown on page 231.

Key Check Figure
R. Abel, $70, Aged 61 - 90 days

Case Study 7

A cashier in a large business is also permitted to post information to various accounts receivable. Charlie Brown, a customer, sends in $100 to be credited to his account. The funds are cashed by the cashier, but he keeps the $100 instead of crediting the customer's account.

Next there is a second $100 remittance from a customer named Charles Sanderson. To cover the discrepancy in Brown's account, the cashier posts the $100 credit to Brown instead of Sanderson. Still later, a third customer's remittance is posted to Sanderson's account. Once again, the credit to the proper account is not made but, in fact, delayed. The cashier feels quite safe in indulging in this *lapping* practice because the majority of customers do not pay very strict attention to their accounts.

a In the language of business, what has the cashier done?

b Suggest at least two measures that would discourage this practice.

CHAPTER 8

THE ACCOUNTS PAYABLE APPLICATION

The accounts payable application deals with two related transactions: (1) the purchase of assets or services on *credit*, and (2) the cash payment to creditors to eliminate the accounts payable.

Many firms transact all of their purchases of assets and services on a credit basis. This means that for every debit to the asset account or expense account (for the service rendered) there will be a credit to Accounts Payable. A cheque would follow to eliminate the current liability.

Other businesses acquire assets or services by issuing a cheque as soon as they receive the invoice (bill of sale). Their "accounts payable application" would naturally be limited to the accounting of cash payments only. A debit would be made to the asset and a credit to Cash for the cheque. This would still be regarded as an accounts payable transaction because the bill was paid.

Profit-seeking businesses design accounts payable systems and procedures in keeping with the needs and costs of the enterprise. For example, large firms usually have a separate accounts payable department. Within such a department, there would be specialized accountants and clerks, specialized journals and ledgers, specialized trial balances, and probably computers to process the firm's individual accounts payable and cash payments.

ACCOUNTS PAYABLE CLERK

Required by computer service and supply company. Previous experience in computerized accounts payable a must. Downtown location. Excellent salary and benefits. Send resume to:

IST - HEALTH COMP INC.
Attn. P. Hendrickson
123 Edward St., Ste. 1325
Toronto, Ontario. M5G 1E2

A small firm, though, would probably not have a separate department for accounts payable. Instead, a general clerk would be employed who would take advantage of short-cuts and the manual method to account for individual creditor transactions.

- Topic 1 of this chapter deals with originating and analyzing accounts payable transactions.
- Topic 2 deals with journalizing and posting such transactions.
- Topic 3 deals with accounting for cash payments.
- Topic 4 deals with month-end procedures related to accounts payable.

TOPIC 1 ORIGINATING AND ANALYZING THE TRANSACTIONS

All accounts payable applications begin with transactions related to accounts payable. Of course, each of these transactions starts with a source document called the invoice. Earlier, you learned that the vendor (seller) makes one copy, usually the original, for the buyer. This "customer's copy" becomes the source document for the purchase transaction.

Invoice: a bill of sale made out by the vendor (seller).

Look at the invoice received and approved by Dr. Johnson's dental practice on January 4.

IBM CANADA LTD
P.O. BOX 5100
TORONTO, ONTARIO
M4Y 2T5

INVOICE

INVOICE TO: DR JOHN H JOHNSON
ANY STREET
ANY TOWN, CANADA

INVOICE DATE: JANUARY 3, 19-2
INVOICE NO. **TA22809**
TERMS: NET 30 DAYS

QTY	DESCRIPTION	UNIT PRICE	AMOUNT
1	SELECTRIC III TYPEWRITER		
	RAVEN BLACK		
	SERIAL NO. 921082611	600.00	600.00
	PLUS ONTARIO SALES TAX 7.00%		42.00

CUSTOMER'S COPY **PLEASE PAY THIS AMOUNT** ► 642.00

Analysis: The invoice contains the following information: the name and address of the vendor, the name and address of the customer, the invoice number, the invoice date, the terms of the sale, details of what was sold, and the total amount payable.

Net amount of an invoice: the final amount — the amount owing on the invoice.

• The terms of the sale are stated as *net 30 days.* This means that the seller expects to receive payment from the buyer for the *amount owing* — the net amount — within 30 days of the invoice date. In Dr. Johnson's case, a cheque should be mailed no later than the due date, February 2. To be sure that the cheque is

Calculation of due date Feb. 2:

Days in Jan.	**31**
Minus date of invoice	**3**
Days remaining in Jan.	**28**
Plus days to due date (Feb. 2)	**2**
Net days	**30**

Purchase invoice: customer's copy of an invoice — the copy in the hands of the buyer.

John H. Johnson, D.D.S.
Dental Surgeon
Chart of Accounts

FIXED ASSETS
110 Dental Equipment
112 Office Equipment

received on time, many firms will date cheques for the due date but mail them ahead of time by one or two days.

• In the hands of the buyer, the invoice becomes the purchase invoice. Of course, this purchase invoice proves the cost of buying something. Here, the proof is for the cost of a new office typewriter.

An accounting entry must now be analyzed and recorded for this purchase invoice. This means breaking up the source document information into debits and credits. The chart of accounts for Dr. Johnson's dental practice, in the margin here, shows the account Office Equipment. Look at the accounting entry in General Journal form:

19-2			
Jan. 4	*DR. Office Equipment*	642	
	CR. Accts. Pay./IBM Canada Ltd.		642
	Purchase Invoice No. TA22809. Invoice date, Jan. 3, 19-2. Terms net 30 days. Due date, Feb. 2, 19-2.		

Analysis: The new typewriter is part of the office equipment, so the fixed asset Office Equipment would be selected from the firm's chart of accounts for the debit entry. Of course, the credit would be to a new current liability called Accts. Pay./IBM Canada Ltd.

• Modern accounting practice requires that the accounting entry be recorded *on the date of receiving and approving the invoice.* In Dr. Johnson's case, an accounting record of the asset purchased must be made on January 4.

• The purchase invoice shows $642 as the total amount payable for the typewriter: the cost, $600, plus the provincial sales tax, $42. Which amount should be used for the debit to the Asset account, $600 or $642? The answer is given by the *cost principle.* This GAAP is the accountant's guideline for recording and reporting the correct value of any fixed asset: the correct value is what the fixed asset purchased has *cost* the buyer. This value is reported on the firm's balance sheet by placing the words *at cost* after the title *Fixed Assets.* This tells the readers that the cost at the date of acquiring the asset was used and that no other so-called "market value" or "worth" is intended.

John H. Johnson, D.D.S.
Partial Balance Sheet
As at January 2, 19-1

FIXED ASSETS (at cost):

Dental Equipment	*$70 000*
Office Equipment	*4 000*

Though all of the above sounds straightforward, in real life the accounting of "cost" as required by the cost principle can be most complicated. Why? Because purchase invoices often have more than one cost figure, as shown by the illustrated IBM invoice. What's more, you could buy assets involving more than one "purchase invoice." For example, to bring equipment across the Canadian border, our government will bill the buyer for a special tax called a customs duty. Do you add this customs duty tax to the cost of the equipment itself? Suppose also that you had to install the machine to get it ready for its intended use. Would you include the cost of installation as well as the price of the machine?

To answer these and other questions, accounting has defined "cost" differently for different applications. Two common definitions can be presented here.

(1) Cost is all of the costs necessary to acquire the asset and to prepare it so that it can create revenue or assist in revenue-making activities. In the case of purchased equipment coming across the border and which has an installation charge, cost is the invoice cost of the equipment, plus the customs duty, plus the cost of installation.

(2) Cost is measured by the cash or cash equivalent price of obtaining the asset and getting it ready for its intended use. If the invoice reads *Amount Now Due,* cost is the cash necessary to pay the bill. If the invoice reads *Net 30 days,* cost is the cash equivalent price as established on the day the invoice was received and approved. *Cash equivalent price* is the net amount owing on the day the invoice was received and approved. *Net* means the final amount shown on the invoice. The net amount owing (cash equivalent price) can always be identified by this question: How much cash would it take to buy the asset (or service) if the business were to pay cash on the day the invoice is received and approved? The answer is usually shown on the invoice as *Net Amount Owing, Total Owing,* or simply *Amount Owing.*

Cost as defined in the cost principle: the cash equivalent price on the invoice as of the day of receiving and approving that invoice.

These two ideas can now be used to answer the question of what cost is, in the illustrated IBM invoice. The cost principle requires the *total cost* of $642 to be used in recording the correct amount in the accounting records. The total cost is the cost of the typewriter (cash bargained price) plus the provincial sales tax. This is reported on the IBM invoice with the words *Please Pay This Amount.* This is the net (final) amount payable because the invoice terms show *Net 30 Days.*

In any future accounting problem in this book which calls for analyzing purchase invoices, always remember that you record, as the cost of the asset being acquired, the net amount owing (cash equivalent price) on the invoice. *Note:* The required accounting of the provincial sales tax, from the seller's viewpoint, will be examined in Topic 1 of Chapter 13.

• The cost principle is not the only basic GAAP you can relate to the study of this invoice. The *objectivity principle* is also involved. This says that you cannot record any transaction without proof. In this case, the source document giving proof of the purchase of the fixed asset is the approved invoice.

Below is another invoice received and approved by Dr. Johnson on January 5.

DENCO SUPPLY
DON MILLS, ONTARIO
M3C 3G1

INVOICE NO. 92524

INVOICE DATE: Jan. 4, 19-2

SOLD TO: Dr. J. H. Johnson
Any Street
Any Town, Canada

TERMS: NET 10 DAYS AFTER STATEMENT DATE

2.00% service charge on overdue amount.

QUANTITY			ITEM NUMBER	ITEM DESCRIPTION	PRICE PER		AMOUNT
ORDERED	SHIPPED	B/O					
1	0	1	E4606	ELEVATORS STR W/J STR	21.25	EA	0.00
1	1	0	E4606	ELEVATORS STR W/J LEFT	21.25	EA	21.25
1	1	0	E4606	ELEVATORS STR W/J RIGHT	21.25	EA	21.25
2	2	0	SP99T	CAULK REPAIR KIT FOR CAULK VARI-MIX	23.00	EA	46.00

TOTAL ITEMS SHIPPED 4

SUBTOTAL	88.50
P.S.T. ONTARIO 7.00%	6.20
TOTAL AMOUNT ►	94.70

Analysis: Examine the illustration as you study the following points:

- The terms of the sale are stated as Net 10 Days after Statement Date. Clearly, the vendor expects to receive a remittance no later than January 14, 19-2.
- If the remittance is not received by the due date, a service charge of 2% will be calculated on overdue amounts. This means a charge of 2% per month or 24% per year.
- The first item ordered was not shipped. Under *Quantity,* the item is placed in the column *B/O* — "back order." Because the item was not shipped, no amount is shown.

An accounting must be made of this purchase invoice. All items received are dental supplies. Dr. Johnson's chart of accounts shows an account for Dental Supplies Expense. Look at the accounting entry in General Journal form:

19-2			
Jan. 5	*DR. Dental Supplies Expense ....*	*94.70*	
	CR. Accts. Pay./Denco Supply		*94.70*
	Purchase Invoice No. 92524. Invoice date, Jan. 4, 19-2. Terms net 10 days. Due date, Jan. 14, 19-2.		

Analysis:

- The credit side of the double entry is easy to follow. Since payment is not made for ten days, the current liability Accts. Pay./Denco Supply is credited.
- At this point you may ask: Why was the cost of these dental supplies not debited to an asset account such as Dental Supplies on Hand? After all, the supplies have just been received and have yet to be used. The answer is that, while some firms debit the asset account for a large quantity of supplies purchased, others debit the expense account in the belief that the cost of those supplies will be used up during the current accounting period. In Part 1 you learned that all costs used up in the process of earning revenue become expired costs, which are then recorded as expenses. Since Dr. Johnson's practice follows the policy of accounting for all supplies received as expired costs, the debit to Dental Supplies Expense is correct.

Expired costs: expenses to be matched against revenue.

What happens at the end of the accounting period if all the supplies have not been used up? Accounting will make adjusting entries at the end of the accounting period to record the actual cost of the supplies used (the expense) and the actual cost of supplies on hand (the asset). These adjusting entries will not be examined until Part 3, because they are part of every General Ledger application. For problems assigned in Part 2, you will be referred to the firm's chart of accounts for the selection of the appropriate debit in any "purchase" transaction.

- The date of recording the entry is January 5, the date of receiving and approving the invoice. Since an expense account was used for the debit, the expense was recognized on January 5 and not on the date of payment. This follows the GAAP for expense recognition. In Dr. Johnson's case, the supplies received will help create the revenue called Professional Fees Earned. Since Dr. Johnson follows the policy of using up all supply costs during the accounting period, these costs become expired and will be accounted for as expenses. This expense will be recognized on the day of receiving and approving the invoice and not when the actual cash payment is made.

In summary, three basic GAAPs can be identified in the analysis of this second invoice.

- The *objectivity principle* applies because the approved invoice gives evidence of the purchase of dental supplies.
- The *cost principle* is used to determine the dollar amount to be used in the accounting entry. In this case, cost is the cash equivalent price (the total amount) on the purchase invoice.
- Since management has decided to expire this cost, the *expense recognition principle* is used to record the expense transaction on the day of receiving and approving the invoice.

Assume Dr. Johnson receives a third "purchase" invoice on January 6 as illustrated next.

PUBLIC UTILITIES COMMISSION
BOX 3060 ANY TOWN, CANADA **01 095 08184 02**

Inquiries — 8:15 to 4:30 — Monday to Friday *Telephone: 679-5503*

DR. J.H. JOHNSON ANY STREET ANY TOWN, CANADA

READING DATE	JAN 03, 19-2		
ELECTRIC READING	0000		
WATER READING	0000		
ELECTRIC	0000 KWH	0.00	
WATER	0000 CU FT	0.00	
INSTALLATION CHARGES		65.00	
AMOUNT DUE IF PAID AFTER JAN. 18		65.00	E & O E
AMOUNT DUE IF PAID BY JAN. 18		61.75	

Analysis:

- Obviously, this third "purchase" invoice is a utility bill received on January 6 for electricity and water services rendered up to January 3, 19-2. Of course, the bill will be accounted for as a Utility Expense.
- Notice that the bill comes to $65. The notation *E & OE* after this amount stands for *errors and omissions excepted*. This is sometimes put on an invoice to inform the buyer that the seller has the right to make corrections if errors are found after the bill is made out and mailed.
- Notice also that the utility company will allow its customer to pay a lower amount, $61.75, if the customer pays the bill by January 18. This is a very common practice among utility companies.
- Like any other bill received, an accounting entry is required on the day the bill is received and approved. But which amount should you record as the debit to Utility Expense, $65.00 or $61.75?

The answer is shown in the double entry, analyzed in General Journal form:

19-2			
Jan. 6	*DR. Utilities Expense ....*	*61.75*	
	CR. Accts. Pay./Public Utilities Commission		*61.75*
	Utility Bill No. 01 095 08184 02. Date of bill, Jan. 3, 19-2. Due date, Jan. 18, 19-2.		

Analysis:

- The correct amount used in the double entry is $61.75. But how did you decide which to use? The answer is known to accountants who have mastered the theory of using the cost principle.

From the analysis of the first two invoices, you learned that the "cost" of any invoice is the total cost to be paid. You also learned to express this idea by saying cost is the net amount owing on the day of recording the invoice.

It's worth repeating an earlier point that accountants have an exact way of defining "cost" according to the cost principle. In their language, cost is the cash equivalent price as evidenced by the source document. The words *cash equivalent price* refer to the exact amount of cash needed if you were to pay cash on the date of receiving and approving the purchase invoice. The utility bill shows the first amount (the gross amount of $65 payable after January 18 and usually not later than 30 days from the date of the invoice.) However, the net amount payable is $61.75 if the bill were to be paid by January 18. Accounting theory prefers to use this figure, because it is the amount of cash required if the bill were to be paid on the date of recording and approving the bill.

Since the "cost" in this invoice is used up (the installation charges for electricity and water have been completed), the cost becomes expired, and, therefore, must be accounted for as an expense. The accounting of this expense will use the cash equivalent price — the amount of cash needed if the bill were to be paid on the date of recording the entry.

Here's a good question. What accounting would be needed if, for some reason, Dr. Johnson failed to pay the bill by the due date? For example, say a cheque for $65 was mailed on January 31. Look at the following accounting entry in General Journal form:

Jan. 31	*DR. Accts. Pay./Public Utilities Commission*	*61.75*	
	DR. Discount Lost Expense	*3.25*	
	CR. Cash		*65.00*
	Issued cheque for the gross amount of Utility Bill 01 095 08184 02 and to record the discount lost due to late payment.		

Analysis:

- In the above entry, the credit to Cash is the exact amount of the issued cheque.
- The first debit to Accts. Pay./Public Utilities Commission eliminates the current liability recorded on January 6.

Chart of Accounts

EXPENSES
510 Discount Lost Expense

● The second debit records the difference between the gross and net amounts of the bill — the discount of $3.25. Because the discount was lost, a special expense account called Discount Lost Expense is used. (See the margin illustration.) Like all expenses, this one would be reported in the income statement. Of course, a well-run business would take steps to avoid these lost discounts by organizing an efficient cash payments system. The control of cash payments will be discussed in Topic 3.

Now take a look at this final "purchase" invoice below. Assume that the bill was received in Dr. Johnson's office on January 18, 19-2.

Date of Bill	Your Telephone No.
19-2 01 16	576-5950
Bill No.	981390

TO: DR. J.H. JOHNSON
ANY STREET
ANY TOWN, CANADA

**See reverse for important information*
***Accounts are payable on receipt*

BELL

1 Previous Bill	
2 Payments	
3 Adjustments	
4 Balance	
5 *Late Payment Charge	
6 *Directory Advertising	
7 *Monthly Rate	14.80
Tax	1.04
8 Chargbl. Msgs.	64.94
Tax	4.55
9 Other Charges or Credits	
Tax	
** TOTAL NOW DUE	85.33

Analysis:

● The striking feature of this bill is the fact that the total amount of $85.33 is "now due." To emphasize this point, the bill also states that "accounts are payable on receipt."

● Since the bill must be paid "on receipt," a cheque will be issued on the same day the bill is received and approved. The accounting entry may be shown, in General Journal form, as follows:

19-2			
Jan. 18	*DR. Telephone Expense*	*85.33*	
	CR. Cash		*85.33*
	Issued cheque in payment of telephone bill No. 981390 due today.		

• In the above entry, notice that no accounts payable account is used. Why not? The simple explanation is that the bill had to be paid "on receipt." Most firms will follow this practice when no credit is shown on the invoice. Since the amount was due on receipt, accounting simply records the cash payment. As you will learn in Topic 3, all cheques issued are recorded in a special journal called the Cash Payments Journal. However, it is important to learn that all cash payments form part of the total accounts payable application in any accounting system.

Important Questions on GAAPs

You have learned how accounts payable transactions originate through various "purchase" invoices received. But it is also important to know how to relate basic GAAPs to each invoice received and approved by the buyer. The following questions and answers will serve as a useful review.

• *What GAAP is recognized with the receipt of any purchase invoice?*
The objectivity principle.

• *Suppose an invoice is received for the purchase of some office equipment on credit. What GAAP can be identified in addition to the objectivity principle?*
The cost principle.

• *What is the meaning of* cost *in the term* cost principle?
Cost is the net amount payable on the invoice as at the day of receiving and approving it. This means the total cost in cases where a sales tax or any other amount like a shipping charge is added to the price of the office equipment.

• *What other meaning can you give to the cost principle?*
Once the cost of the asset is recorded, this value remains on the books even if prices for that asset later go up.

• *How do accountants tell readers of financial statements that assets acquired were recorded and remain at their original cost?*
On all balance sheets, the words *at cost* are placed opposite the title *Fixed Assets*.

• *Suppose a utility bill for electrical and water services is received. It offers 30 days' credit for the gross amount and 15 days' credit for the net amount. What GAAP decides which "cost" to use in recording the entry?*
The cost principle. "Cost" is always the *cash equivalent price*

(net amount payable) on the invoice as of the day the invoice is received and approved.

- *What other GAAP is related to the analysis of this utility bill?*

The expense recognition principle.

- *What two things does the expense recognition principle say when applied to the utility bill?*

(1) It defines expense as a cost amount used up in the process of earning revenue (that is, expired cost). (2) It requires the accounting entry for the expense on the day the invoice is received and approved.

- *Suppose an invoice is received and approved for the purchase of dental supplies. What GAAPs may be used in analyzing the accounting of this purchase invoice?*

Three are possible. (1) If management decides to record the supplies as an asset, then the *cost principle* must be used to record the correct "cost value." This means the cash equivalent price on the invoice — the amount payable on the invoice on the day the invoice is received and approved. (2) If management believes that the cost of the supplies will be completely used up during the current accounting period, the *expense recognition principle* requires you to select an appropriate expense account for the debit entry. (3) The *objectivity principle* can be identified, because the purchase invoice gives evidence of the accounting transaction.

TOPIC 1 PROBLEMS

8-1 Assume that the invoice on page 247 has been received and approved by Dr. Penny Thornton's dental practice on December 5, 19-1.

a By what date must this bill be paid? Show how you arrived at your answer.

b On what date should an accounting entry be recorded for this invoice? Why?

c Show the analysis of this invoice in General Journal form.

d What type of account did you use for the debit entry? Why?

e What type of account did you use for the credit entry? Why?

Key Check Figure Correct Dollar Amount = $1 414.01

f What GAAP helped you to choose the correct dollar amount in your double entry? Explain the full meaning of this principle.

g What other GAAP can be related to the analysis of this purchase invoice? Briefly explain the meaning of this principle.

8-2 Dr. R.B. Cousins, Orthodontist, operates a dental firm in Regina, Saskatchewan. On June 14, 19-2, Dr. Cousins received and approved a utility bill from Saskatchewan Power Corp. It showed the following information: Invoice No. 14896701; Reading Date, June 10, 19-2; Amount Due If Paid after June 25, 19-2, $74.00; Amount Due If Paid by June 25, 19-2, $70.30.

EXPRESS DENTAL INC.
DOWNSVIEW, ONTARIO

SOLD TO: Dr. Penny Thornton
Any Street
Any Town, Canada

INVOICE NO. 748960
INVOICE DATE: Dec. 2, 19-1
TERMS: NET 30 DAYS

QUANTITY	DESCRIPTION	UNIT PRICE	AMOUNT
1	TRANSLUX VISIBLE LIGHT CURING UNIT	875.00	875.00
1	#2001 PULP TESTER	340.00	340.00
3	RIMLOCK CAULK TRAYS	10.50	31.50
2	RUBBER DAM CLAMP FORCEP	37.50	75.00
Note: A 2% late charge will be added to all accounts over 30 days.		**SUBTOTAL**	1 321.50
		ONTARIO SALES TAX 7.00%	92.51
		AMOUNT PAYABLE ►	1 414.01

Problem 8-1 (cont.)

Problem 8-2 (cont.)

a By what date must this bill be paid? Explain your answer.

b On what date should an accounting entry be recorded for this bill? Explain your answer.

c Show the analysis of this bill in General Journal form.

d What dollar amount did you use in the double entry for **c** above? What GAAP helped you decide on your amount? Explain the full meaning of this principle.

e What other GAAP can be related to the analysis of this utility bill? Briefly explain the meaning of this principle.

f Suppose this dental practice paid the bill by issuing a cheque on June 30, 19-2. Show the required accounting of this cheque.

Key Check Figure Discount Lost Expense = $3.70

8-3 On February 13 of the current year, MacPherson Plumbing & Heating of Fredericton, N.B. received and approved the monthly telephone bill from New Brunswick Telephone Co. The bill contained the following information: Date of Bill, February 10; Bill No. 1689480; Monthly Rate, $18.00; Tax (10%), $1.80; Chargeable Messages, $56.40; Tax (10%), $5.64; Total Now Due, $81.84.

a What *basic* GAAP is immediately involved in this bill? Briefly explain the meaning of this principle.

b By what date must this bill be paid? Explain your answer.

c Show the required double entry in General Journal form.

d What GAAP helped you to select the account title for the debit side of the entry? Explain the full meaning of this principle.

Key Check Figure Telephone Expense = $81.84

e What GAAP helped you to choose the correct dollar amount in your double entry? Explain the full meaning of this principle.

8-4 Challenge Problem Dr. E.M. Sawchuck, Dental Surgeon, operates a dental firm in Winnipeg, Manitoba. Assume that the invoice below has been approved by Dr. Sawchuck on July 5, 19-1. *Note:* Dr. Sawchuck's accounting policy is to treat the cost of all dental supplies received as expenses. At the end of the accounting period, an adjustment is made to record dental supplies on hand.

Telephone
(204) 875-9000

LARR DENTAL PRODUCTS
2020 Portage Ave.
Winnipeg, Manitoba
R3J 0K0

INVOICE NO. 168470
INVOICE DATE: July 2, 19-1
TERMS: Net 30 days

SOLD TO: DR. E. M. SAWCHUCK
2799 Roblin Blvd.
Winnipeg, Manitoba
R3J 0B8

QUANTITY	DESCRIPTION	UNIT PRICE	AMOUNT
1 only	POLY-F PLUS SUPPLY KIT	34.50	34.50
10 bottles	*GERMICIDAL CONCENTRATE (SULTAN)	12.00*	120.00*
1 PKG	IMPRESSION COMPOUND (KERR)	205.00	205.00
1 PKG	*FACIAL TISSUE (ROYALE)	39.95*	39.95*
1 only	*INSTRUMENT STERILIZATION TRAY (BARD PARKER)	133.60*	133.60*
1 set	*AIR TWIST DENTAL DRILLS	795.00*	795.00*
**All items starred are subject to provincial sales tax.*		**SUBTOTAL**	1 328.05
		MANITOBA SALES TAX 6.00%	65.31
A CHARGE OF 2% PER MONTH IS LEVIED ON OVERDUE AMOUNTS		**NET AMOUNT OWING**	► 1 393.36

a The items shown on the purchase invoice may be classified under the headings *Dental Supplies* and *Dental Equipment*. What items would you list under each of these classes?

b By what date must this invoice be paid? Show your calculation.

c Check the accuracy of the provincial sales tax reported on the invoice. Show your calculation.

d On what date would an accounting entry be made for this source document? Why?

e Show the required accounting entry in General Journal form. Include all necessary computations for key figures in the entry.

Key Check Figure Dental Equipment Debit = $984.32

f What GAAPs can you identify in the complete analysis of the source document? Briefly explain the meaning of each principle as related to the document.

8-5 Challenge Problem The legal firm Wilkinson, Philip & Groleau is located in Hamilton, Ontario. Earlier, the firm ordered some valuable reference books for its library. All the books have been received in good condition. Because of the large number of books, the publisher offers a trade discount of 20% off the list price of each. The McGraw-Hill Ryerson Ltd. invoice, approved on October 10, 19-1, gives the following information: Invoice Number, 293945; Invoice Date, October 9, 19-1; Terms, Net 10 days; Total List Price, $1 278.40; Total Trade Discount (20% off List), $255.68; Total Net Price, $1 022.72; Applicable Ontario Sales Tax (7.00%), $71.59; Subtotal, $1 094.31; Delivery Charges (Special Delivery), $35.00; Invoice Total, $1 129.31.

a By what date should this invoice be paid?

b On what date should an accounting entry be made of this invoice? Why?

c On what figure was the Ontario sales tax applied? Show your calculation.

d Show an accounting entry in General Journal form with appropriate account titles.

e What GAAPs did you follow in support of your accounting entry in **d** above? Briefly explain the meaning of these principles in relation to the invoice.

Key Check Figure Accts. Pay./ McGraw-Hill CR. = $1 129.31

TOPIC 2 JOURNALIZING AND POSTING THE TRANSACTIONS

Once a purchase invoice on credit is received and approved by accounting as a valid source document, accounting must journalize and post the results of that invoice in the accounting records.

Journalizing Accounts Payable Transactions

The method of recording debits and credits for accounts payable differs from one type of business to another. Some firms use a special Purchases Journal to record all purchase invoices on credit. Since this type of special journal is common among merchandising firms, the Purchases Journal will be discussed in Part III of the text.

Many firms, particularly those in the health science field, will not use a special journal for purchase invoices. For example, many dental firms prefer to store all invoices to be paid in an accounts payable file. When a bill comes due for payment, these firms often use a special Cash Payments Journal to record the cash disbursement side of the accounts payable application.

Other firms prefer to record the initial accounts payable transactions in the General Journal and keep a separate ledger for individual creditor accounts. The General Journal is often preferred when very few purchase invoices on credit are received during any month. Cheques for payment of those invoices can then be recorded in a special Cash Payments Journal because cash disbursements occur very frequently in every month.

The dental practice of Dr. Johnson uses (1) a General Journal for recording all credit purchases of assets and services, (2) a subsidiary ledger to keep track of individual creditor accounts, and (3) a special Cash Payments Journal to record all issued cheques. To illustrate the initial accounts payable transactions for Dr. Johnson's practice, assume the following entries were made in the General Journal for January:

GENERAL JOURNAL — **Page** 2

Date 19-2		**Account Title and Explanation**	**Post. Ref.**	**Debit**		**Credit**	
Jan.	4	Office Equipment		642	—		
		Accts. Pay./IBM Canada Ltd.				642	—
		Purchase Invoice TA22809. Invoice date, Jan. 3, 19-2. Terms net 30 days. Due date, Feb. 2, 19-2.					
Jan.	5	Dental Supplies Expense		94	70		
		Accts. Pay./Denco Supply				94	70
		Purchase Invoice 92524. Invoice date, Jan. 4, 19-2. Terms net 10 days. Due date, Jan. 14, 19-2.					
Jan.	6	Utilities Expense		61	75		
		Accts. Pay./Public Utilities Commission..				61	75
		Utility Bill No. 01 095 08184 02. Date of bill, Jan. 3,19-2. Due date, Jan. 18, 19-2.					

Accounts Payable Ledger: a subsidiary ledger storing individual creditor (vendor) accounts.

Accounts Payable: a controlling account in the General Ledger.

Posting Accounts Payable Transactions

Many businesses have a separate Accounts Payable Ledger to control amounts owed to vendors so all creditor accounts are removed from the General Ledger. When such a transfer occurs, a controlling account called Accounts Payable must replace all creditor accounts. Dr. Johnson's original chart of accounts showed two creditor accounts. The transfer of those accounts to a subsidiary ledger for accounts payable may be analyzed as follows:

General Ledger

Accounts Payable	202
	19-2 Jan. 2 Bal. 10 000*

*The balance in this controlling account must agree with the total of all individual creditor account balances in the subsidiary ledger.

Accounts Payable Ledger

Denco Supply	
	19-2 Jan. 2 Bal. 8 000

Mardan Business Systems Ltd.	
	19-2 Jan. 2 2 000

If formal ledger account forms were used, the above information would be shown as follows:

General Ledger

Accounts Payable — Account No. 202

DATE		EXPLANATION	POST. REF.	DEBIT	CREDIT	BALANCE	
19-2							
Jan.	2	Balance forward	✓			10 000 —	CR.

Accounts Payable Ledger

Name Denco Supply
Address Don Mills, Ontario M3C 3G1

DATE		EXPLANATION	POST. REF.	DEBIT	CREDIT	BALANCE	
19-2							
Jan.	2	Balance forward	✓			8 000 —	CR.

Name Mardan Business Systems Ltd.
Address 48 Preston Street, Kitchener, Ontario N2G 3W4

DATE		EXPLANATION	POST. REF.	DEBIT	CREDIT	BALANCE	
19-2							
Jan.	2	Balance forward	✓			2 000 —	CR.

Remember the following points about the creation of the Accounts Payable controlling account in the GL and the individual creditor accounts in the subsidiary ledger:

- The General Ledger account for Accounts Payable has a credit balance equal to the total of the account balances of the individual creditor accounts in the subsidiary ledger. This means that the GL account *controls by total* the individual balances of the related creditor accounts in the subsidiary ledger.
- The word *control* or *controlling* is rarely used in the name of the GL account — the word is understood.
- The form of each individual creditor account varies with the need for information. We have shown a three-column form with more information in the heading lines of the account.
- The accounts in the subsidiary ledger are listed in alphabetical order so there is no need to use account numbers.
- Notice how a balance is forwarded as at a particular date. The date of carrying forward the balance is shown. *Balance forward* is placed in the *Explanation* column. Because there is no posting, a check mark is placed in the *Post. Ref.* column. Finally, the balance forwarded is placed only in the *Balance* column.
- The Accounts Payable account in the GL will always supply the amount to report under *Current Liabilities* when a future balance sheet is prepared.
- The Accounts Payable Ledger will always be used to find out how much is owing to any individual creditor at any time.
- At the end of each month, the balance in the controlling account must agree with the total balances taken from the individual creditor accounts in the subsidiary ledger. Financial statements should never be prepared without first checking that the control account "controls" the balances in the related subsidiary ledger.

After the controlling account and the Accounts Payable Ledger are established, you can turn to the mechanics of posting accounts payable transactions. Look back to the General Journal illustrated on page 250. The transactions would be posted in this order:

(1) Post the information affecting individual creditor accounts on a daily basis. Then management can control the amounts owing to individual creditors on any given day. Refer to the posted General Journal illustrated next. Notice how a check mark is placed in the *Post. Ref.* column to indicate that posting has occurred to the individual creditor account in the subsidiary ledger.

(2) Post information affecting GL accounts at the end of the month. Posting every day to the GL is not necessary because financial statements are normally prepared at the end of the month. Notice in the posted General Journal that the GL account number is shown to indicate that posting has been completed to this GL account. The credit line, therefore, of an accounts pay-

able entry in the General Journal must be posted once to the individual creditor account in the subsidiary ledger and once to the controlling account in the GL.

Here's how the General Journal and the two ledgers would appear after all postings have been completed:

GENERAL JOURNAL — **Page** 2

Date 19-2		Account Title and Explanation	Post. Ref.	Debit		Credit	
Jan.	4	Office Equipment	112	642	—		
		*Accts. Pay./IBM Canada Ltd.	202/✓			642	—
		Purchase Invoice TA22809. Invoice date, Jan. 3, 19-2. Terms net 30 days. Due date, Feb. 2, 19-2.					
Jan.	5	Dental Supplies Expense	503	94	70		
		*Accts. Pay./Denco Supply	202/✓			94	70
		Purchase Invoice No. 92524. Invoice date, Jan. 4, 19-2. Terms net 10 days. Due date, Jan. 14, 19-2.					
Jan.	6	Utilities Expense	506	61	75		
		*Accts. Pay./Public Utilities Commission	202/✓			61	75
		Utility Bill No. 01 095 08184 02. Date of bill, Jan. 3,19-2. Due date, Jan. 18, 19-2.					

*Notice that this credit line is posted twice: once to Accounts Payable No. 202 in the GL; and once to the individual creditor account in the Accounts Payable Ledger. Posting references to the individual creditor accounts are shown by a check mark because these accounts are filed in alphabetical order.

General Ledger

Accounts Payable — **Account No.** 202

DATE 19-2		EXPLANATION	POST. REF.	DEBIT	CREDIT	BALANCE	
Jan.	2	Balance forward	✓			10000 —	CR.
	4	G.J.	2		642 —	10642 —	
	5	G.J.	2		94 70	10736 70	
	6	G.J.	2		61 75	10798 45	

Accounts Payable Ledger

Name *Denco Supply*
Address *Don Mills, Ontario M3C 3G1*

DATE		EXPLANATION	POST. REF.	DEBIT	CREDIT	BALANCE
19-2						
Jan.	2	Balance forward	✓			8000 — CR.
	5	Inv. 92524; due Jan. 14 G.J.	2		94 70	8094 70

Name *IBM Canada Ltd.*
Address *Toronto, Ontario M4Y 2T5*

DATE		EXPLANATION	POST. REF.	DEBIT	CREDIT	BALANCE
19-2						
Jan.	4	Inv. TA22809; due Feb. 2 GJ	2		642 —	642 —

Name *Mardan Business Systems Ltd.*
Address *48 Preston Street, Kitchener, Ontario N2G 3W4*

DATE		EXPLANATION	POST. REF.	DEBIT	CREDIT	BALANCE
19-2						
Jan.	2	Balance forward	✓			2000 — CR.

Name *Public Utilities Commission*
Address *Box 3060, Any Town, Canada*

DATE		EXPLANATION	POST. REF.	DEBIT	CREDIT	BALANCE
19-2						
Jan.	6	Bill 010950818402; due Jan. 18 GJ	2		61 75	61 75

The GL account shows posting for each date of entry in the General Journal. Posting dates are the dates of transactions and not the day on which the transfer occurs. The GL account also shows the posting reference — the GJ page from which the information was posted.

Explanation columns are usually completed for the subsidiary ledger accounts. This is true for any subsidiary ledger account. Why? The subsidiary ledger supplies complete information about any individual account. Here, management can look to any creditor account to find out when payments are required to eliminate a debt.

TOPIC 2 PROBLEMS

8-6 As outlined in problems for Chapter 7, Dr. Penny Thornton's dental practice began business on Dec. 1, 19-1 with the following General Ledger account balances: Cash (101), $10 000; Government of Canada Bonds (102), $50 000; Dental Equipment (110), $80 000; Office Equipment (112), $4 000; Furniture (114), $6 000; Bank Loan Payable (201), $5 000; Accts. Pay./Denco Equipment & Supply (202) (Don Mills, Ontario M3C 3G1), $10 000; Accts. Pay./Mardan Business Systems Ltd. (203) (48 Preston Street, Kitchener, Ontario N2G 3W4), $3 000; 5-Year Note Payable (220), $38 000; P. Thornton, Capital (301), $94 000.

During December, 19-1 Dr. Penny Thornton's practice received and approved several accounts payable invoices as summarized below. Dr. Thornton accepted the advice of her accountant to introduce the following accounting policies: (1) the cost of all dental and office supplies will be expired in the belief that all such supplies will be used up completely by the end of the accounting period; (2) all purchase invoices on credit will be recorded in the General Journal; (3) all purchase invoices will be recorded in accordance with GAAPs; and (4) a separate Accounts Payable Ledger will be used to control amounts owing to individual creditors.

A summary of purchase invoices received and approved is as follows:

Dec. 5 From Express Dental Inc., Downsview, Ont.; Invoice No. 748960; Invoice Date, Dec. 2, 19-1; Terms Net 30 Days; dental equipment, $1 321.50; Ontario Sales Tax, $92.51; Amount Payable, $1 414.01.

7 From Mardan Business Systems Ltd.; Invoice No. 67891; Invoice Date, Dec. 4, 19-1; Terms Net 30 Days; accounting supplies, $300; Ontario Sales Tax, $21; Net Amount Payable, $321.

12 From Public Utilities Commission, Box 3060, Any Town, Canada; Bill No. 16250; Reading Date, Dec. 10, 19-1; Total Amount Due, after Dec. 27 for installation of electricity and water, $50; Amount Due If Paid by Dec. 27, $47.50.

29 From Denco Equipment & Supply; Invoice 84762; Invoice Date, Dec. 27; Terms Net 10 Days; dental supply kits, $400; dental equipment, $600; Applicable Ontario Sales Tax, $70; Total Amount, $1 070.

a Set up a General Ledger showing the beginning balances of GL accounts as at December 1, 19-1. Include a controlling account for Accounts Payable (202).

b Transfer the beginning balances of the two accounts payable accounts to the subsidiary ledger.

c Analyze each purchase invoice. Then record each invoice in the General Journal, beginning on page 2.

d Post the accounts payable information from the General Journal to the individual creditor accounts in the subsidiary ledger.

e Post all entries affecting the GL from the General Journal to appropriate accounts in the GL.

Key Check Figure GL Balance for Accounts Payable, Dec. 29 = $15 852.51

8-7 MacPherson Plumbing & Heating of Fredericton, N.B. approved purchase invoices on credit as summarized below. The firm supported the following accounting policies: (1) all supplies are to be expired immediately; (2) all purchase invoices on credit are to be recorded in the General Journal; (3) all purchase invoices are to be recorded in accordance with GAAPs; and (4) a separate Accounts Payable Ledger is to be used to control amounts owing to individual vendors.

On February 1, current year, the Accounts Payable account in the GL (No. 202) showed a credit balance forward of $18 000. The related subsidiary ledger showed the following individual accounts: Maritime Truck Centre, 442 Canada Street, Fredericton, N.B., E3A 4A6, $10 000; Newcastle Manufacturing Co. Ltd., 102 Main Street, Newcastle, N.B., E1V 3E7, $6 000; Smith Business Equipment, 124 George St., Fredericton, N.B., E3A 4E2, $2 000.

A summary of approved purchase invoices on credit is as follows:

Feb. 8 Newcastle Manufacturing Co. Ltd.; Invoice No. 148012; Invoice Date, Feb. 5; Terms Net 30 Days; small tools costing $1 000; Provincial Sales Tax, 10%, Net Amount Payable, $1 100. (Charge Account No. 116, Small Tools.)

12 Smith Business Equipment; Invoice No. 35418; Invoice Date, Feb. 10; Terms Net 15 Days; total cost of office supplies, $80; Provincial Sales Tax, 10%, Net Amount Owing, $88.

18 Maritime Truck Centre; Invoice No. 8045; Invoice Date, Feb. 18; Terms Net EOM (end of current month); repairs and tune-up of truck, $150; Provincial Sales Tax, $15; Total Amount, $165. (Charge Truck Expense, Account No. 515.)

20 New Brunswick Electric Power Commission; Utility Bill No. 2A4747; Reading Date, Feb. 16; Amount Due If Paid by Feb. 28, $85.50; Amount Due If Paid after Feb. 28, $90.

25 St. John Wholesale Plumbing Supplies Ltd., 287 Duke St., St. John, N.B., E2L 1P4; plumbing supplies, $400; Special Delivery Charge, $50; Total Owing, $450; Invoice No. A41217; Invoice Date, Feb. 24; Terms Net 30 Days.

a Analyze each approved purchase invoice. Then record each in the General Journal, beginning on page 15.

b Set up an Accounts Payable Ledger with the following creditor accounts: Maritime Truck Centre; New Brunswick Electric Power Commission; Newcastle Manufacturing Co. Ltd.; Saint John Wholesale Plumbing Supplies Ltd.; Smith Business Equipment. Show beginning balances for appropriate accounts as at February 1, current year.

c Post all recorded entries from the General Journal to creditors in the Accounts Payable Ledger.

Key Check Figure Accounts Payable Balance, Feb. 25 = $19 888.50

d Open General Ledger accounts for all GL accounts involved in this problem. Show any required balances forward as of May 1, current year.

e Post information from the General Journal to the General Ledger.

8-8 Challenge Problem Dr. John Reddon, Dental Surgeon, began his dental practice in Red Deer, Alberta on September 1 with the following assets and liabilities: Cash $50 000; Land, $50 000; Building, $150 000; Dental Equipment, $20 000; Bank Loan Payable (on demand), $20 000; Accounts Payable, $15 000 (to Edmonton Dental Supply, 3911 — 126th St., Edmonton, Alberta, T6J 2A5); Mortgage Payable, $100 000.

a Record the opening entry in the General Journal.

b Set up a General Ledger with the following accounts: Cash (101); Dental Supplies on Hand (105); Office Supplies on Hand (106); Land (110); Land Improvements (111); Building (113); Dental Equipment (115); Office Equipment (117); Bank Loan Payable (201); Accounts Payable (202); Mortgage Payable (220); John Reddon, Capital (301); Utilities Expense (501); Lab Fees Expense (502).

c Post the opening entry to the General Ledger.

d Open an Accounts Payable Ledger with the following creditor accounts: Alberta Power Ltd., 4700 — 26th Ave. SW, Calgary, Alberta, T3E 0R3; Edmonton Dental Supply; HealthCo. (Canada) Ltd., 511 North Railway St., Medicine Hat, Alberta, T1A 2Z4; Mardan Business Systems Ltd., 3000 Elbow Dr. SW, Calgary, Alberta, T2S 2J3; Pratt Dental Laboratory, 5701 West Park Cres., Red Deer, Alberta, T4N 1E4; Western Construction Ltd., Box 5000, Lethbridge, Alberta, T1K 1L7.

e Post the opening entry affecting the individual creditor accounts from the General Journal to the subsidiary ledger.

f During September, Dr. Reddon received and approved the following purchase invoices on credit:

Sept. 4 From Mardan Business Systems Ltd.; Invoice A7489; Invoice date, Sept. 3; Terms Net 30 Days; cost of office supplies, $300; one file cabinet, $1 200; one reception desk, $1 000; one conference table, $800; four office chairs at $100 each, $400; Total Amount Payable, $3 700.

5 Returned one office chair (wrong colour) to Mardan Business Systems Ltd. on Invoice A7489. Permission granted to ship the chair back on a collect basis.

8 From HealthCo (Canada) Ltd.; Invoice No. 78989; Invoice date, Sept. 6; Terms Net 30 Days; dental supply kits, $500; dental equipment, $800; Total Amount Owing, $1 300.

9 From Alberta Power Ltd., Bill No. AB24890; Reading Date, Sept. 7; installation charges for electricity and water system, $65 if paid by Sept. 17, $70 if paid after Sept. 17.

20 From Edmonton Dental Supply; Invoice 162480; Invoice Date, Sept. 19; dental equipment, $1 500; special shipping charge of $150 for delivery of equipment; Terms Net 30 Days.

21 From Edmonton Dental Supply; Invoice 162485; Invoice Date, Sept. 20; charge for installing dental equipment on Invoice 162480; Total Charge, $125; Terms Net 30 Days.

30 From Pratt Dental Laboratory; Invoice No. 7580; Invoice Date, Sept. 30; lab fees to date, $700; Terms Net 15 Days.

30 From Western Construction Ltd.; Invoice WA64891; Invoice date, Sept. 30; for completion of needed parking lot, $4 500 (use fixed asset account No. 111, Land Improvements); Terms Net 30 Days.

Also, management has approved the following accounting policies regarding the accounting of the accounts payable application: (1) all dental supplies and office supplies are to be charged to asset accounts No. 105 and 106 respectively; (2) all expired costs of dental supplies and office supplies will be charged to expenses at the end of the accounting period as part of the required adjusting entries; (3) all purchase invoices on credit are to be recorded in the General Journal; (4) all purchase invoices are to be recorded in accordance with GAAPs; (5) a separate subsidiary ledger for vendor accounts is to be maintained.

Analyze each approved purchase invoice. Then record each in the General Journal immediately after the opening entry.

Key Check Figure Accounts Payable Balance, Sept. 30 = $26 940

g Post all recorded entries from the General Journal to creditors in the Accounts Payable Ledger.

h Post the required information from the General Journal to appropriate General Ledger accounts.

TOPIC 3 CASH PAYMENTS

In setting up an efficient system for cash payments, the owner of every business turns to accountants to introduce internal measures both for controlling the *handling* of cash payments and for controlling the *recording and posting* of cash payments.

This topic examines nine basic measures for controlling cash payments. These measures may be adapted or expanded to suit a firm's particular needs. These nine basic measures are:

- Check the bill or invoice.
- Use a tickler file system to make sure that bills are paid on time.
- Pay by cheque.
- Use pre-numbered cheques.
- Prepare a cheque record for every payment.
- Void and keep all spoiled cheques.
- Cancel all bills and invoices after they have been paid by cheque.
- Divide the responsibility.
- Use a special journal for cash payments.

Check the Bill (Invoice)

It is important to take steps to check the bill (invoice) before paying it. Two things should be checked:

(1) The assets or services identified on the bill should be checked to see that they were actually ordered and received.

(2) The amount of the bill should be checked to see that it has been computed accurately.

To make sure these two steps are carried out, large businesses often require all bills to be immediately forwarded to their purchasing department where they are checked against the original purchase orders and warehouse receiving reports. In smaller businesses a general office clerk or secretary may be given this responsibility.

Remember, *all* invoices (bills) must be checked and approved before a cash payment is made.

Use a Tickler File System

Tickler file: a reminder file arranged by date.

Many businesses use what is called a tickler file to remind accounts payable clerks that bills must be paid on a certain date. The tickler file "tickles" the clerk's memory — it is checked first thing every day. Whether it is a card file or folder file, its basic system is always the same: an arrangement by date order.

A *card* tickler file is illustrated in the margin for Dr. Johnson's dental practice.

Card-sized reminders are obviously filed in a card tickler file. For example, Dr. Johnson's practice has recorded purchase invoice number 92524 from Denco Supply with terms of net 10 days counting from the invoice date of January 4. To make sure the cheque gets to the vendor on time, a reminder card is made out on January 12, two days before the due date (January 14). The instructions on the card direct the accounts payable clerk to issue the cheque dated January 14 but to mail that cheque on January 12. Obviously, this tickler card would be filed behind the divider labelled "12."

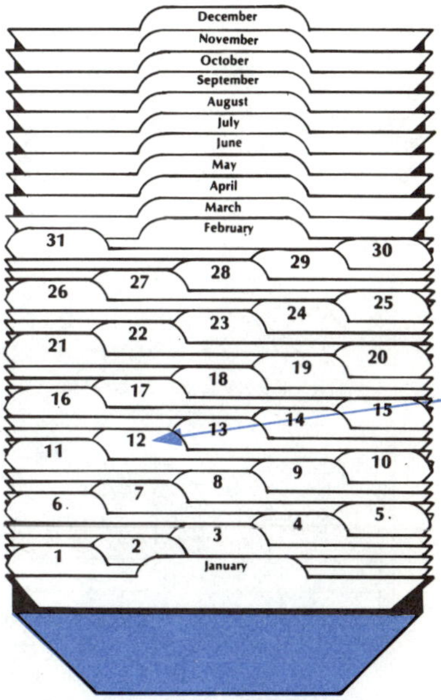

Card Tickler File

January 12, 19-2

Issue cheque dated Jan. 14 to Denco Supply in payment of Invoice No. 92524.

Pay by Serially Pre-Numbered Cheque

In Chapter 7 you learned that all cash receipts should be deposited "intact" into the bank. In other words, no payments should ever be made from those cash receipts. Instead, all cash payments should be made with pre-numbered cheques. (There is one exception. Since some payments are very small, management often creates a system to take care of those "petty" expenditures — the *petty cash* system. This system will be explained fully in Topic 1 of Chapter 9.)

Why is it a good control measure to pay by cheque?

- It eliminates the need for handling large amounts of money.
- It provides proof of each payment, because the bank returns each cancelled (paid) cheque to the drawer (the person signing the cheque).
- Paying by cheque through a current account at a bank automatically provides an independent accounting of each payment, because the banker gives the depositor a monthly bank statement on which each cheque transaction is listed.
- Serially pre-numbered cheques help keep track of the cheques issued.

Prepare a Cheque Record for Every Payment

A cheque record is an important accounting document, for it supplies the information upon which an accounting entry is made for each cash payment. Obviously, the objectivity principle is being followed when a cheque record is available to prove a cash payment transaction.

A perforated stub known as the *cheque stub* is often used to make a permanent record of each cheque issued and to make the future accounting entry to record the cash payment. The cheque stub may also be used by the person handling the cheques to record amounts deposited, thus providing a running balance of cash in the bank. A typical cheque and cheque stub are illustrated below.

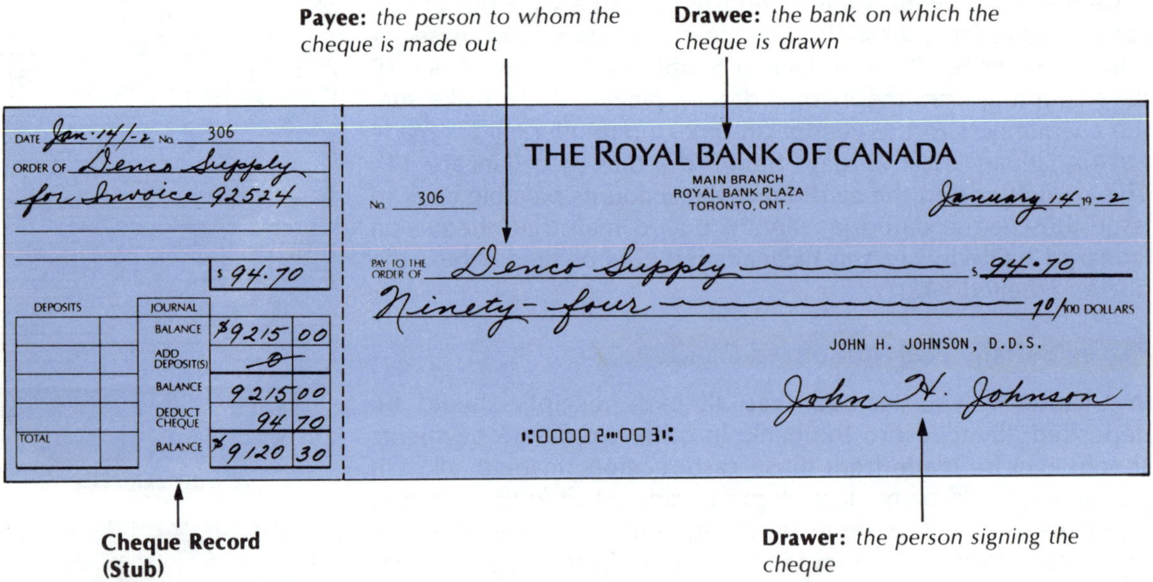

When a standard cheque book with a stub is used, the stub section must be completed first. Otherwise, it may be overlooked and no record of the cheque would exist once the cheque is signed and mailed. Completing the stub first not only decreases errors when writing the cheque proper, it allows you to check whether you have enough cash in the bank to cover the cheque.

Void and Keep All Spoiled Cheques

To void a cheque: to mark it so it cannot be cashed.

If a cheque is spoiled, it is important to void both the cheque record and the cheque itself as illustrated next.

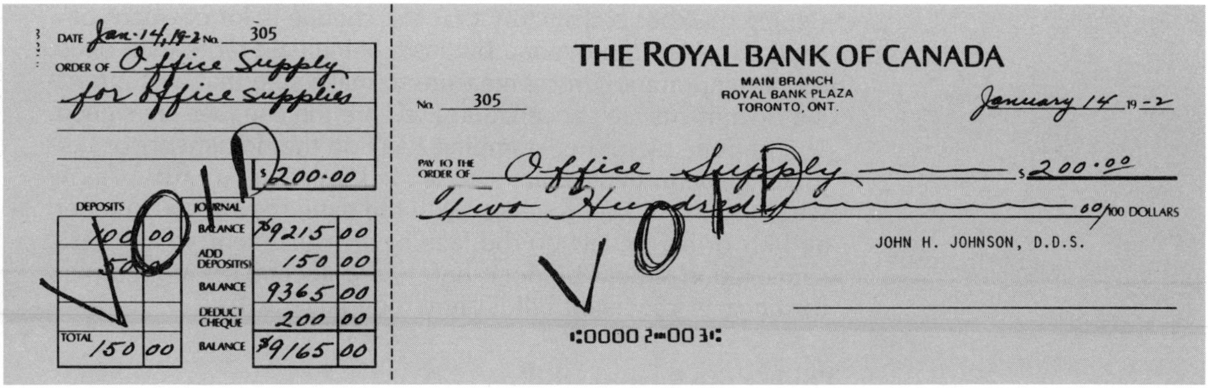
DATE Jan. 14, 19-2 No. 305
ORDER OF Office Supply
for Office supplies
$200.00

DEPOSITS		JOURNAL	
100	00	BALANCE	$9215 00
50	00	ADD DEPOSIT(S)	150 00
		BALANCE	9365 00
		DEDUCT CHEQUE	200 00
TOTAL 150	00	BALANCE	$9165 00

VOID

THE ROYAL BANK OF CANADA
MAIN BRANCH
ROYAL BANK PLAZA
TORONTO, ONT.
No. 305
January 14 19-2
PAY TO THE ORDER OF Office Supply $200.00
Two Hundred 00/100 DOLLARS
JOHN H. JOHNSON, D.D.S.
⑆00002⑉003⑆

VOID

Void means "without legal force" or "not binding"; a cheque with this word on the face has no legal force and cannot be cashed. When serially pre-numbered cheques are used, even spoiled cheques must be carefully voided and kept on file because every number must be accounted for.

Cancel All Bills Paid by Cheque

When a cheque has been presented to the appropriate person for signature, it should be accompanied by the invoice and other supporting documents (such as the warehouse receiving report and the purchase order, if they exist). This allows the person

DENCO SUPPLY
DON MILLS, ONTARIO
M3C 3G1

INVOICE NO. 92524

SOLD TO: Dr. J. H. Johnson
Any Street
Any Town, Canada

INVOICE DATE: Jan. 4, 19-2
TERMS: NET 10 DAYS AFTER STATEMENT DATE
2.00% service charge on overdue amount.

QUANTITY			ITEM NUMBER	ITEM DESCRIPTION	PRICE PER	AMOUNT
ORDERED	SHIPPED	B/O				
1	0	1	E4606	ELEVATORS STR W/J STR	21.25 EA	0.00
1	1	0	E4606	ELEVATORS STR W/J LEFT	21.25 EA	21.25
1	1	0	E4606	ELEVATORS STR W/J RIGHT	21.25 EA	21.25
2	2	0	SP99T	CAULK REPAIR KIT FOR CAULK VARI-MIX	23.00 EA	46.00
TOTAL ITEMS SHIPPED 4					**SUBTOTAL**	88.50
				P.S.T. ONTARIO 7.00%		6.20
Paid by Cheque 306, Jan. 14, 19-2					**TOTAL AMOUNT ►**	94.70

signing the cheque to verify that the cheque is for payment of a valid bill. And to prevent a bill from being paid more than once, it is an important control measure to make sure that all supporting documents are cancelled at the time the cheques are signed. This is done by rubber-stamping *PAID* on the documents or perforating them. In smaller firms, a clerk or secretary may simply write the word *paid*, together with the date, the cheque number, and his or her initials on the face of the document. In any case, cancellation should be done before the documents are returned for filing. A cancelled bill is shown on page 261.

Divide the Responsibility

In a small business with only one clerk, the owner-manager usually controls all cash payments by preparing and signing all cheques. Where there are two or more employees, their duties must be organized to ensure that no employee has responsibility for more than a part of the cash payments function. The responsibility for handling the cheques and recording the payments should be divided so that the work of one employee can be checked against that of another. Here are four ways this can be achieved:

- The purchasing department should definitely be separated from the accounting, receiving, and shipping departments.
- Divide the responsibility for verifying and for approving invoices. The purchasing clerk checks the bill; the head of purchasing approves the bill; the accounting clerk double-checks the bill before making the accounting entry.
- All documents associated with accounts payable should be controlled and go directly to accounting. This includes copies of purchase orders and receiving documents. Unauthorized persons should *never* have access to blank forms.
- Once the invoice has been approved, the accounting clerk prepares the cheque for signature; however, some other authorized person does the actual signing. Those authorized to sign cheques should not prepare the cheques or maintain accounting records for cash receipts and cash payments.

Use a Special Journal to Record Cash Payments

Cash Payments Journal (also known as Cash Disbursements Journal): a special journal in which all cheques are recorded.

A special journal should be used to record all cash payments transactions. This is known as the Cash Payments Journal or Cash Disbursements Journal. Before we examine this special journal, here's an important note on the mailing of signed cheques.

Mailing Signed Cheques

In small businesses, a cheque in payment of accounts payable is mailed together with a short note or letter of explanation. This becomes the *remittance advice* — a statement advising the payee of the item or items covered by the cheque. In large businesses, a special cheque form known as a voucher cheque is commonly used. The most common voucher cheque has a perforated rider attached. The rider is removed by the recipient before the cheque is presented for payment. See the illustration below.

Voucher cheque: a two-part cheque with a detachable statement form.

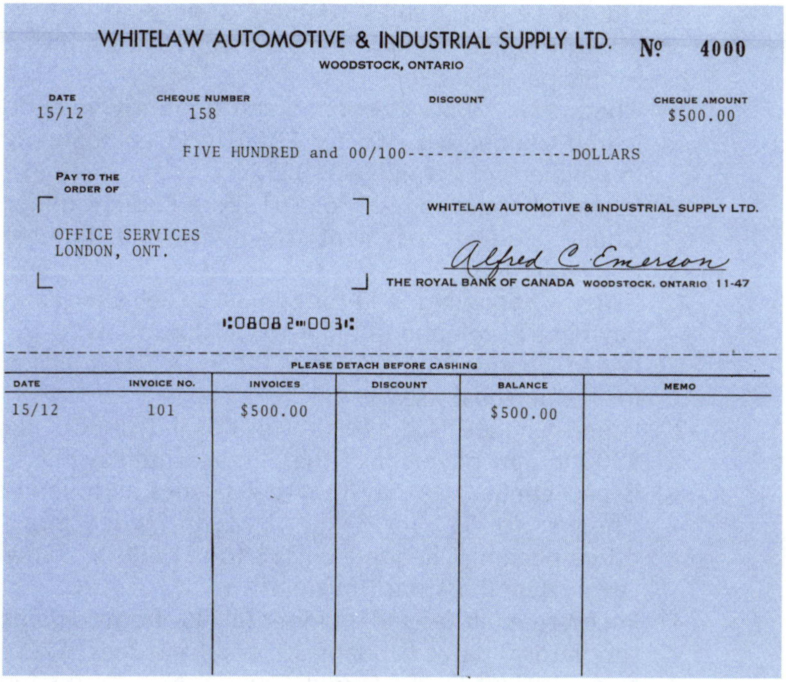

WHITELAW AUTOMOTIVE & INDUSTRIAL SUPPLY LTD. Nº 4000
WOODSTOCK, ONTARIO

DATE	CHEQUE NUMBER	DISCOUNT	CHEQUE AMOUNT
15/12	158		$500.00

FIVE HUNDRED and 00/100----------------DOLLARS

PAY TO THE ORDER OF

OFFICE SERVICES
LONDON, ONT.

WHITELAW AUTOMOTIVE & INDUSTRIAL SUPPLY LTD.

Alfred C. Emerson

THE ROYAL BANK OF CANADA WOODSTOCK, ONTARIO 11-47

⑆08082⑈003⑆

PLEASE DETACH BEFORE CASHING

DATE	INVOICE NO.	INVOICES	DISCOUNT	BALANCE	MEMO
15/12	101	$500.00		$500.00	

Journalizing Cash Payments Transactions

The most common reasons for issuing cheques are to pay for assets purchased, to pay operating expenses, to pay creditors, and to pay the owner when he or she makes regular withdrawals of cash for personal use.

To save time in journalizing and posting, many businesses use a Cash Payments Journal to record all cash payments transactions. In this way only one line is required to record a transaction. Furthermore, only the total need be posted to the credit side of the Cash account at the end of the month.

To illustrate how cash payments may be recorded in a Cash Payments Journal, suppose Dr. Johnson's dental practice issued the cheques as summarized on the next page for the month of January, 19-2. In all cases, assume that the basic measures to control all cash payments have been followed.

Summary of Cash Payments Transactions

19-2

Jan. 2 Issued Cheque No. 301 for $1 000 to Central Realty Ltd. for January's rent of the office building.

3 Issued Cheque No. 302 to Denco Supply for $8 000 in full settlement of account.

4 Issued Cheque No. 303 to Mardan Business Systems Ltd. for $2 000 in full settlement of account.

5 Issued Cheque No. 304 for $200 to Dr. J.H. Johnson for his personal use.

14 Cheque No. 305 was spoiled and promptly voided.

14 Issued Cheque No. 306 for $94.70 to Denco Supply in payment of Invoice No. 92524.

18 Issued Cheque No. 307 for $61.75 to Public Utilities Commission in payment of utility bill number 010950818402.

18 Issued Cheque No. 308 for $85.33 to Bell Canada in payment of telephone bill 981390 due "Now."

20 Issued Cheque No. 309 for $200 to Dr. J.H. Johnson for his personal use.

22 Issued Cheque No. 310 to The Royal Trust Co. for $500 in part payment of the 5-Year Note Payable.

30 Issued cheques to pay monthly salaries as follows: Cheque No. 311 for $1 000 to Lynn Fortier, front-office person; Cheque No. 312 for $1 200 to Kathy Lewis, dental assistant/hygienist.

31 Received a lab fee bill, number 68741, from Edwards Laboratory, dated January 30; total lab fees, $700; terms: "Now Due." Issued Cheque No. 313 in full payment.

31 Purchased an office copier from Office Products Ltd. Special exhibition price of $1 800 if purchased for cash. Issued Cheque No. 314 in full payment.

31 Issued Cheque No. 315 for $75 to A. Gilmore for delivery and installation charges to the new office copier purchased from Office Products Ltd.

Analysis: Look at how the cheques have been recorded in the Cash Payments Journal illustrated next. Are the cheque numbers in sequence? Here are other key points to remember in a careful analysis of the recorded transactions:

- The name of the special journal appears on the top line along with the journal page number.
- Journal page numbers are numbered consecutively beginning with "1."
- The main headings for each column in this special journal

CASH PAYMENTS JOURNAL **Page 1**

Date 19-2	Cheque No.	Cheque Paid To	Accounts Payable Post. Ref.	Accounts Payable Amount DR.	Other General Ledger Accounts Account Title	Post. Ref.	Amount DR.	Cash CR.
Jan. 2	301	Central Realty Ltd.			Rent Expense		1 000 00	1 000 00
3	302	Denco Supply		8 000 00				8 000 00
4	303	Mardan Business Systems Ltd.		2 000 00				2 000 00
5	304	Dr. J.H. Johnson			J.H. Johnson, Drawing		200 00	200 00
14	305	VOID		—			—	—
14	306	Denco Supply		94 70				94 70
18	307	Public Utilities Commission		61 75				61 75
18	308	Bell Canada			Telephone Expense		85 33	85 33
20	309	Dr. J.H. Johnson			J.H. Johnson, Drawing		200 00	200 00
22	310	The Royal Trust Co.			5-Year Note Payable		500 00	500 00
30	311	Lynn Fortier			Salaries Expense		1 000 00	1 000 00
30	312	Kathy Lewis			Salaries Expense		1 200 00	1 200 00
31	313	Edwards Laboratory			Lab Fees Expense		700 00	700 00
31	314	Office Products Ltd.			Office Equipment		1 800 00	1 800 00
31	315	A. Gilmore			Office Equipment		75 00	75 00

Note: *In practice, the number of columns will vary with the needs of the accounting system.*

are: (1) A *Date* column to record the transaction date appearing on the source document (in this case the date would be the date of the cheque, because the cheque stub would also have this date); (2) A *Cheque No.* column to record the pre-numbered cheque; (3) A *Cheque Paid To* column to record the name of the payee named on the cheque; (4) An *Accounts Payable* column for checking off future posting references and the amount debited to Accounts Payable; (5) A section to identify those General Ledger accounts other than Accounts Payable. Here, there is a GL *Account Title* column, a *Post. Ref.* column for future posting, and an *Amount DR.* column.

Before recording any transaction in this special journal, analyze the transaction in either T-account form or General Journal form. For example, on January 2, Cheque No. 301 was issued in payment of the monthly rent so you would debit Rent Expense and credit Cash. Use appropriate account titles as offered from the firm's chart of accounts. If no account name is available, use

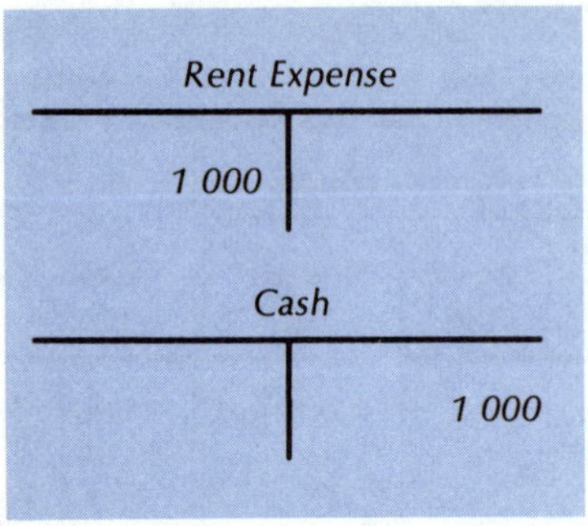

one that would be added in support of the accounting policies followed by the firm. Since the Cash account is credited, the transaction must be recorded in the Cash Payments Journal. And since no Accounts Payable is involved, Rent Expense is shown in the space for other GL account titles. Of course, the cheque amount is placed in the *Cash CR.* column. You have recorded the complete double entry across one line.

- Look at how an accounts payable transaction is recorded. For example, on January 3, Cheque No. 302 has been issued to Denco Supply in full settlement of account. Before recording this payment, think of the entry in T-account form or General Journal form as follows:

19-2			
Jan. 3	*Accts. Pay./Denco Supply*	*8 000*	
	Cash		*8 000*
	To record Cheque No. 302.		

Since Denco Supply is an account payable, enter the amount in the *Accounts Payable DR.* column. Of course, the cheque amount goes to the *Cash CR.* column. Once again, the complete double entry has been recorded on one line.

- The transaction to record Cheque 304 on January 5 is easy. The owner of a business is allowed to withdraw cash for personal use, but good internal control requires that a cheque be issued even to the owner. Remember, all personal withdrawals must be debited to the owner's Drawing account rather than to an expense account.
- On January 14, a solid line is shown under appropriate columns to illustrate how a voided cheque is recorded. A sound measure of internal control requires that all cheques be accounted for; thus, show a recording of every spoiled cheque to account for all cheque numbers.
- The last two cheques issued have been recorded in accordance with the *cost principle.* To ready the copier for its intended use, the firm had to pay the cost of the machine plus delivery and installation charges. The cost principle requires you to debit both these "costs" to the Office Equipment account.
- On any line, the debit amount equals the credit amount. Thus, the double entry is recorded on one line only.

Posting from the Cash Payments Journal

As with any special journal, postings from the Cash Payments Journal occur in two stages: one during the month, and a second at the end of the month.

During the Month All accounts that appear in a subsidiary ledger should be posted *daily.* Since the subsidiary ledger to be posted from the Cash Payments Journal deals with individual creditor accounts, all postings to these accounts must come from the *Accounts Payable DR.* money column. Because the individual creditor accounts are filed alphabetically, a check mark is placed in the *Post. Ref.* column of the Cash Payments Journal next to the *Accounts Payable* column. This shows that the amount has been transferred to the subsidiary ledger. The source of posting also appears in the *Post. Ref.* column of each individual creditor's account. Examine the illustrations below.

CASH PAYMENTS JOURNAL **Page** 1

Date 19-2	Cheque No.	Cheque Paid To	Accounts Payable Post. Ref.	Accounts Payable Amount DR.	Other General Ledger Accounts Account Title	Other General Ledger Accounts Post. Ref.	Other General Ledger Accounts Amount DR.	Cash CR.
Jan. 2	301	Central Realty Ltd.			Rent Expense		1 000 00	1 000 00
3	302	Denco Supply	√	8 000 00				8 000 00
4	303	Mardan Business Systems Ltd.	√	2 000 00				2 000 00

Accounts Payable Ledger

Name Denco Supply
Address Don Mills, Ontario M3C 3G1

DATE 19-2		EXPLANATION	POST. REF.	DEBIT	CREDIT	BALANCE	
Jan.	2	Balance forward	✓			8000–	CR.
	3	Cheque 302 CPJ	1	8000–		-0-	
	5	Inv. 92524; due Jan. 14 GJ	2		94.70	94.70	

Name Mardan Business Systems Ltd.
Address 48 Preston Street, Kitchener, Ontario N2G 3W4

DATE 19-2		EXPLANATION	POST. REF.	DEBIT	CREDIT	BALANCE	
Jan.	2	Balance forward	✓			2000–	CR.
	4	Cheque 303 CPJ	1	2000–		-0-	

At Month-End Post information to all *General Ledger accounts* only at the end of the month. Why? The GL provides the balances of accounts needed for the future preparation of financial statements. Since financial statements are prepared monthly, postings to the GL occur monthly.

Before such postings occur, these actions should be taken:

- Total the Cash Payments Journal.

- Double-check the totals (use the footing procedure or an adding-machine check).
- Prove the double-entry theory within the special journal: *The total debits must be equal to the total credits.*

The illustration below shows how this double entry works.

Total of Accounts Payable DR. column	*$10 156.45*	
Total of Other GL Accounts DR. column	*6 760.33*	
Total of All Debits	*$16 916.78*	← **These totals**
Total of Cash CR. Column	*$16 916.78*	← **must agree.**

Remember this important point: *Never post to the GL until the columns are proved to show that the total debits are equal to the total credits.* Once this proof is obtained, postings can occur as illustrated below. The total of Accounts Payable DR. is posted from the Cash Payments Journal to the controlling account and the total of Cash CR. is transferred to the Cash account. Then the journal is ruled off for the month.

CASH PAYMENTS JOURNAL **Page 1**

Date 19-2	Cheque No.	Cheque Paid To	Accounts Payable Post. Ref.	Accounts Payable Amount DR.	Other GL Account Title	Other GL Post. Ref.	Other GL Amount DR.	Cash CR.
Jan. 2	301	Central Realty Ltd.			Rent Expense	501	1 000 00	1 000 00
3	302	Denco Supply	√	8 000 00				8 000 00
4	303	Mardan Business Systems Ltd.	√	2 000 00				2 000 00
…								
31	314	Office Products Ltd.			Office Equipment	112	1 800 00	1 800 00
31	315	A. Gilmore			Office Equipment	112	75 00	75 00
31				10 156 45			6 760 33	16 916 78
				(202)			(√)	(101)

Double line to rule off the journal for the month.

GL account number shows the total posted to the controlling account.

Check mark indicates this total is not to be posted.

GL account number shows the total posted to the Cash account.

General Ledger

Cash — Account No. 101

DATE 19-2		EXPLANATION	POST. REF.	DEBIT	CREDIT	BALANCE	
Jan.	2	Balance forward	✓			20000 —	Dr.
	31	Total Cash Receipts CRJ	1	2093 —		22093 —	
	31	Total Cash Payments CPJ	1		16916 78	5176 22	

Accounts Payable — Account No. 202

DATE 19-2		EXPLANATION	POST. REF.	DEBIT	CREDIT	BALANCE	
Jan.	2	Balance forward	✓			10000 —	CR.
	4	G.J.	2		642 —	10642 —	
	5	G.J.	2		94 70	10736 70	
	6	G.J.	2		61 75	10798 45	
	31	C.P.J.	1	10156 45		642 00	

John H. Johnson, Drawing — Account No. 302

DATE 19-2		EXPLANATION	POST. REF.	DEBIT	CREDIT	BALANCE
Jan.	5	CPJ	1	200 —		200 —
	20	CPJ	1	200 —		400 —

Cash Short and Over Transactions

In systems using a cash register, differences commonly occur when a cash proof is prepared. A cash proof may show that the amount of cash in the drawer is less or more than the amount shown on the locked-in tape. When the reason for the cash difference cannot be identified, it is assumed that human error occurred when making change. In most businesses, therefore, the supervisor authorizes a cash proof form with a cash shortage or a cash overage.

Analyzing Cash Shortages If the cash proof shows *less* cash in the drawer than there should be, the cash is said to be *short* or there is said to be a cash *shortage*. For example, the February 21 cash proof illustrated in the margin on page 270 shows that the net cash received is $600 while the net amount of cash counted in the drawer after the change fund is deducted is only $595.

CASH PROOF

Date February 21, 19--

Register No. 2

Cash Sales	600	00
Received on Account	—	
Total Cash Received	—	
Less: Cash Paid Out	—	
Net Cash Received	600	00
Cash in Drawer	615	00
Less: Change Fund	20	00
Net Cash Handled	595	00
Cash Short ~~or Over~~	5	00

Clerk Coleen Brown

Supervisor Pat Kelly

Assuming that the money making up the difference cannot be found, accounting personnel will use the authorized cash proof as a source document to record the shortage of $5. Two entries will be analyzed as follows:

DR. Cash	*600*	
CR. Sales Revenue		*600*
To record cash sales on Feb. 21.		
(Since Cash is debited, the entry would be recorded in the Cash Receipts Journal.)		

DR. Cash Short and Over	*5*	
CR. Cash		*5*
To record the cash shortage as per cash proof for Register 2, Feb. 21.		
(Since Cash is credited, the entry would be recorded in the Cash Payments Journal.)		

Cash Short and Over: a GL account whose DR. balance is an expense and whose CR. balance is miscellaneous revenue.

To understand why a special account called Cash Short and Over is debited in the Cash Payments Journal for the shortage, let's review the cash receipts transaction. From Entry 1, notice that Cash would be debited for $600 and Sales Revenue credited for $600 as per the source document (the cash register tape).

However, the net cash handled is only $595, so the Cash account must be decreased by the $5 — credited. And since there is a cash shortage approved by the supervisor, an expense of operating the business is recognized and appears as a debit to the special account Cash Short and Over.

To summarize any recognized "cash shortage," remember that two steps are required:

- Record the debit entry to Cash in the Cash Receipts Journal using the information on the source document (cash register tape, sales slip, etc.).
- Record the credit entry to Cash in the Cash Payments Journal to recognize the expense of the cash shortage.

After postings occur at month-end, the balance in the Cash account will reflect the correct net amount of cash handled.

Analyzing Cash Overages If the cash proof shows *more* cash in the drawer than there should be, the cash is said to be *over,* or there is said to be a cash *overage.* When such an overage is authorized by the supervisor, correct accounting analysis requires that the excess amount of cash be credited to the Cash Short and Over account.

Suppose that the actual cash counted on the next day, February 22, is $499, but the register tape shows cash sales of $497. In this case, the entry may be analyzed in General Journal form as follows:

DR. Cash ($497 + $2)	499	
CR. Sales Revenue		497
CR. Cash Short and Over		2
To record the cash sales from Register 2 on Feb. 22 and the $2 cash overage as per the cash proof of Register 2.		

The Cash Receipts Journal must be used here, because there is an inflow of cash. Cash is debited for the net cash handled (the cash received from sales plus the overage). Since there are two credits, the entry requires two separate lines, as shown below in a special journal which may be used for businesses using a cash register system.

CASH RECEIPTS JOURNAL **Page** 3

Date 19-2		Account Credited	Explanation	Post. Ref.	Amount
Feb.	22	Sales Revenue	Daily cash sales		497 00
	22	Cash Short and Over	Cash overage		2 00

Analyzing the Balance After all cash shortages and overages are posted to the Cash Short and Over account at month-end, the balance in the account will be identified as an expense or a revenue balance. In the case of the previous examples, there would be a debit balance of $3. This net difference for the month is an expense, because the debit balance causes a decrease to *OE* in the accounting equation. If statements are prepared at month-end, the expense would be reported as "Cash Shortage" or "Miscellaneous Expense" in the income statement.

Cash Short and Over 515			
Feb. 21 (Expense)	5	Feb. 22 (Misc. revenue)	2

If the monthly balance in the account is greater on the credit side, the balance must be identified as revenue. On the income statement, the credit balance figure should not be included in the sales amount (the main source of revenue), but as a separate item described as "Miscellaneous Revenue."

Cash shortages will likely be greater than the amounts of cash overage, so the account Cash Short and Over is generally given an account code under *Expenses* in the Chart of Accounts. This special account is used only when differences in cash cannot be traced to errors. Remember, a supervisor or someone other than the clerk receiving the cash must authorize all cash shortages.

Kelly's Office Services
Chart of Accounts

EXPENSES
515 Cash Short and Over

Advantages of a Cash Payments Journal

The main advantages of using a special journal to record all cash payments may be summarized as follows:

- Most entries take up only one line instead of three or four lines.
- A special column for recording cheque numbers helps to account for all cheques issued. This special journal helps to strengthen the internal control of cash payments.
- Since only the monthly total is posted to the credit of Cash, much time is saved. Also, the frequency of human error in posting is automatically reduced when only the total is transferred to the Cash account.
- The task of maintaining the cash payments journal may be assigned to a single clerk. This is also in accordance with the control measure called division of responsibility.

Summarizing the Cash Payments System

Seven very basic measures for controlling cash payments in any firm may be summarized in the form of an accounting systems

FLOWCHART OF A CASH PAYMENTS SYSTEM

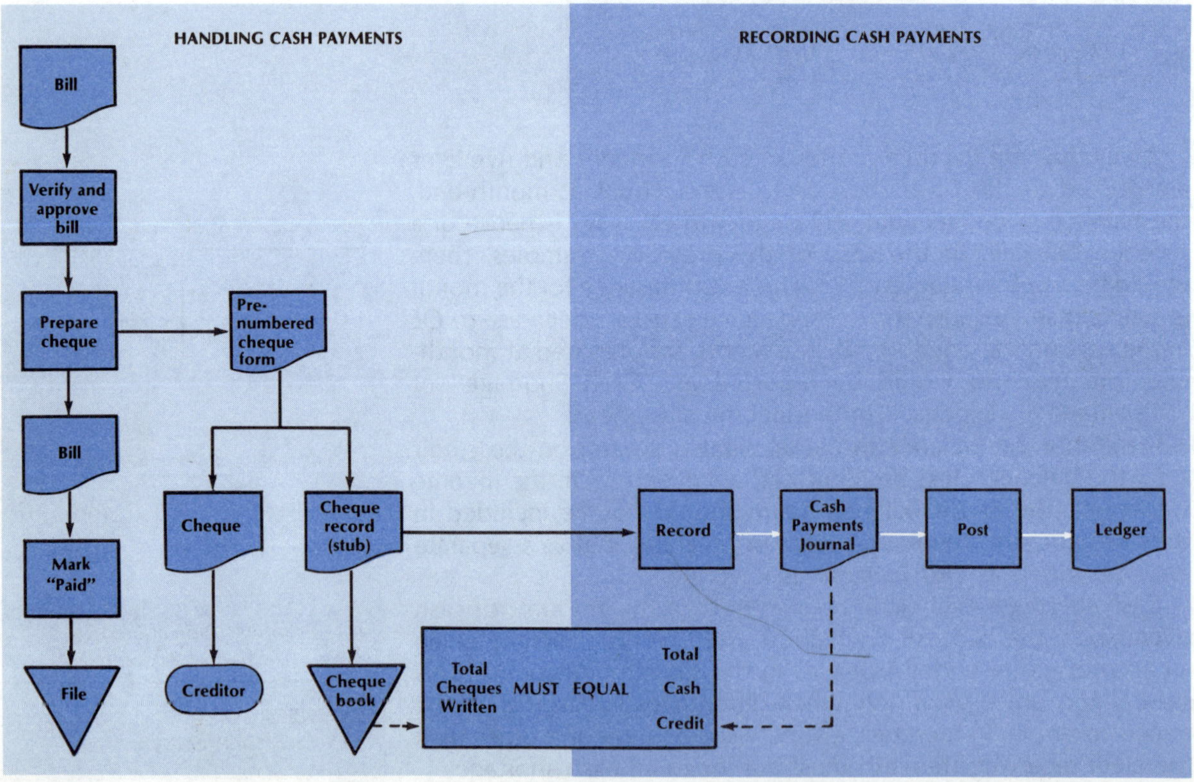

flowchart. Examine the flowchart on page 272. Can you identify those control measures?

TOPIC 3 PROBLEMS

8-9 The following cheques were issued by Dr. Penny Thornton's dental practice for the month of December, 19-1:

Dec. 1 Cheque 001 issued to City Realty Co. for $600 for rent of office and dental examining room.
3 Cheque 002 issued to Denco Equipment Supply for $500 on account.
4 Cheque 003 issued to Mardan Business Systems Ltd. for $200 on account.
8 Cheque 004 issued to Bell Canada for Invoice 4987 (installation of telephone) now due for $65.
9 Cheque 005 was spoiled and voided.
9 Cheque 006 was issued to City Dry Cleaners for $36 for cleaning of uniforms (Cleaning Expense, No. 510).
12 Cheque 007 issued to Wright Office Ltd. for $1 500 (special cash price for purchase of office equipment, exclusive of installation).
13 Cheque 008 to A.J. Holt for $100 for installing office equipment obtained on December 12.
15 Cheque 009 issued to Dr. Penny Thornton for her personal use, $500.
16 Cheque 010 issued to Denco Equipment Supply for $500 on account.
17 Cheque 011 issued to Mardan Business Systems Ltd., $200 on account.
18 Cheque 012 was spoiled and voided.
22 Cheque 013 issued to Dr. Penny Thornton for $1 000 for her personal use.
27 Cheque 014 to Public Utilities Commission for $47.50 in payment of Bill 16250 due today. *Note:* Recorded as an account payable on December 12.
30 Cheque 015 to Pat Davis, front-office person, monthly salary, $1 000.
31 Cheque 016 to the Royal Bank of Canada, $500, in part payment of demand loan.
31 Cheque 017 to Central Finance Co., $635, for monthly payment of 5-Year Note Payable.

a Record the above cheques in a Cash Payments Journal, Page 1. Use a form similar to the one illustrated on page 268.

b Set up individual accounts payable accounts as follows: Denco Equipment Supply, Don Mills, Ontario, M3C 3G1 (Balance Forward, Dec. 29, $11 070); Express Dental Inc., Downsview, Ontario (Balance Forward, Dec. 5, $1 414.01); Mardan Business Systems Ltd., 48 Preston Street, Kitchener, Ontario, N2G 3W4 (Balance Forward, Dec. 7, $3 321); Public Utilities Commission, Box 3060, Any Town, Canada (Balance Forward, Dec. 12, $47.50). *Note:* These account balances are carried forward from the solution solved for Problem 8-6.

c Post the data from the Cash Payments Journal to the individual accounts set up for the Accounts Payable Ledger.

d Total the money columns in the Cash Payments Journal. Then check the double-entry theory from these totals.

e Post the data from the Cash Payments Journal to those General Ledger accounts affected by the special journal. Show balances forwarded in the following accounts: Cash (101), December 31, $10 874; Office Equipment (112), December 1, $4 000; Bank Loan Payable (201), December 1, $5 000; Accounts Payable (202), December 29, $15 852.51; 5-Year Note Payable (220), December 1, $38 000. Set up appropriate account titles and numbers for all other accounts affected by the special journal.

Key Check Figure Balance of Accounts Payable, Dec. 31 = $14 405.01 CR.

f Rule off the Cash Payments Journal for the month.

8-10 Bernice Obierski is the owner-manager of a mailing service. A cash register system is used to control cash receipts. This firm follows the accounting policy of debiting Supplies Expense for all supplies purchased. You have been asked to perform the following:

a Open General Ledger accounts and record March 1 balances as follows: Cash (101), $8 500; Equipment (110), $2 500; Bank Loan Payable (201), $1 000; Accounts Payable (202), $1 400; Bernice Obierski, Capital (301), $8 600; Bernice Obierski, Drawing (302); Rent Expense (501); Telephone Expense (502); Utilities Expense (503); Salaries Expense (504); Supplies Expense (505); Cash Short and Over (506).

b Open an Accounts Payable Ledger with the following accounts and their balances forward as of March 1: Maritime Supply Co., 17 Upper Queen St., Charlottetown, P.E.I., C1A 4C1 ($400); Jane Sands, 27 Central St., Summerside, P.E.I., C1N 3K8 ($1 000).

c Make the appropriate entries for the following transactions in a Cash Payments Journal similar to the one illustrated on page 268. You are starting on page 2 of the journal.

Mar. 1 Issued Cheque 28 for $400 for March rent to City Realty Co.
10 Issued Cheque 29 for $400 to Jane Sands on account.
15 Issued Cheque 30 for $500 to Northern Equipment Co. for cash purchase of additional equipment.
18 Issued Cheque 31 for $50 to Maritime Supply Co., on account.
22 Issued Cheque 32 for $100 to Bernice Obierski, the owner, for personal use.
24 Issued Cheque 33, but later voided it.
25 Issued the following cheques: No. 34 to Maritime Telephone, $28 for March telephone bill; and No. 35 to City Stationery, $80 for office supplies.
26 The cash proof of the cash register showed a shortage of $8.
27 Issued Cheque 36 for $80 to Public Utilities Commission for March utilities.
28 Issued Cheque 37 for $100 in part payment of the bank loan to the Royal Bank of Canada.
31 Issued Cheque 38 to Marjorie Ross for $1 500 for monthly salary.

d Post the appropriate entries from the Cash Payments Journal to the Accounts Payable Ledger.

e Check the addition (using an adding machine tape or the footing procedure) and prove the double-entry theory against the totals of the journal.

f Post the entries from the Cash Payments Journal to the General Ledger.

g Rule the special journal for the month.

Key Check Figure Total of Cash CR. Column in Cash Payments Journal = $3 246

8-11 Challenge Problem The following cheques were issued by Dr. John Reddon's dental practice for the month of September:

Sept. 1 Cheque 001 issued to Alberta Telephone Co., $40 for installation of telephone.

5 Cheque 002 issued to City Dry Cleaners, $46 for cleaning of uniforms.

7 Cheque 003 was spoiled and promptly voided.

7 Cheque 004 issued to Edmonton Dental Supply, $500 on account.

8 Cheque 005 issued to Wright Dental Ltd., $2 000 for new dental equipment acquired for cash.

9 Cheque 006 to Dr. John Reddon, $100 for his personal use.

10 Cheque 007 to Office Specialty Co. for $170 for office supplies. *Note:* Refer to Problem 8-8 for accounting policy.

13 Cheque No. 008 was spoiled and promptly voided.

14 Issued the following bimonthly salary cheques: No. 009 to Pamela Brown, dental hygienist, $600; No. 010 to Jill Murray, front-office person, $500.

17 Issued Cheque No. 011 for $65 to Alberta Power Ltd. in full settlement of account balance due today.

18 Issued Cheque No. 012 to Dr. John Reddon, $100 for his personal use.

19 Cheque No. 013 to City Dental Supplies, $80 for dental supplies. *Note:* Check back to Problem 8-8 for accounting policy.

21 Cheque No. 014 to City Treasurer, $75 for business licence fee.

23 Cheque No. 015 to Edmonton Dental Supply, $500 on account.

26 Cheque No. 016 to Dr. John Reddon, $100 for personal use.

28 Cheque No. 017 issued to Edmonton Dental Supply, $500, on account.

30 Issued the following bimonthly salary cheques: No. 018 to Pamela Brown, $600; No. 019 to Jill Murray, $500.

30 Issued Cheque No. 020 to the Royal Bank of Canada, $1 000, in part payment of the demand loan.

30 Issued Cheque No. 021 to City Properties Ltd., $1 200 for the monthly payment of the mortgage as follows: $500 applied to the principal (chief part) of the mortgage payable; the remaining $700 to be charged to Mortgage Interest Expense.

a Record the above cheques in a Cash Payments Journal, beginning on page 1.

b Post the data from the Cash Payments Journal to the Accounts Payable Ledger used in Problem 8-8. *Note:* No new accounts are required.

c Total the money columns in the Cash Payments Journal. Then check the double-entry theory from these totals.

d Post the data from the Cash Payments Journal to those General Ledger accounts affected by this special journal. Use the GL solved for Problem 8-8 and add the following accounts: Telephone Expense (503); Cleaning Expense (504); John Reddon, Drawing (302); Salaries Expense (505); Licence Fees Expense (506); Mortgage Interest Expense (520).

Key Check Figure Total of Cash CR. Column in CPJ = $8 676

e Rule off the Cash Payments Journal for the month.

TOPIC 4 MONTH-END PROCEDURES

So far, you have learned these important parts of the accounts payable application:

- originating accounts payable data through various purchase invoices
- journalizing and posting accounts payable data in appropriate journals and ledgers
- issuing cheques for appropriate payments
- journalizing and posting cheque record information in appropriate journals and ledgers

This final Topic involves the last part of the accounts payable application — preparing monthly trial balances.

Since management often wants a summary of cash receipts and cash payments you will also prepare a special report called the Statement of Cash Flows.

Preparing Monthly Trial Balances

The preparation of monthly trial balances is similar to the preparation of the ones introduced in Chapter 7. The only difference here is that the subsidiary ledger is for accounts payable.

In a large firm with an efficient division of responsibility, a General Ledger clerk prepares the monthly trial balance for the General Ledger. The accounts payable clerk, a person not connected with direct work with the General Ledger, prepares the monthly schedule of accounts payable. With this division of responsibility, the General Ledger balance of accounts payable controls the listing of individual creditor account balances. How is this control achieved? The accountant responsible for the General Ledger has the balance of accounts payable. He or she asks for the total of the accounts payable subsidiary ledger as provided by the Schedule of Accounts Payable. If this total does not agree with the balance of Accounts Payable in the General Ledger, the accounts payable clerk must recheck posting information to come up with the right answer.

Schedule of Accounts Payable: a list of individual creditors with their month-end balances.

If trial balances for Dr. Johnson's dental practice were taken from the combined accounts receivable and accounts payable applications covered in Chapters 7 and 8, they would appear as follows:

John H. Johnson, D.D.S.
Trial Balance
January 31, 19-2

Cash	101	$ 5 176.22	
Bank Deposit Receipts	102	15 680.00	
Accounts Receivable	103	2 892.00	
Dental Equipment	110	70 642.00	
Office Equipment	112	5 875.00	
Accounts Payable	202		$ 642.00
5-Year Note Payable	210		29 500.00
John H. Johnson, Capital	301		70 000.00
John H. Johnson, Drawing	302	400.00	
Professional Fees Earned	401		4 665.00
Rent Expense	501	1 000.00	
Salaries Expense	502	2 200.00	
Dental Supplies Expense	503	94.70	
Telephone Expense	505	85.33	
Utilities Expense	506	61.75	
Lab Fees Expense	507	700.00	
		$104 807.00	$104 807.00

John H. Johnson, D.D.S.
Schedule of Accounts Payable
January 31, 19-2

IBM Canada Ltd.	$642.00
Total of Accounts Payable	$642.00

John H. Johnson, D.D.S.
Schedule of Accounts Receivable
January 31, 19-2

B. Campbell	$ 45.00
H. Chan	557.00
R. Diloreto	65.00
Ms. A. Gomes	500.00
D. Gray	110.00
Ms. C. Lee	70.00
S. Lesniak	65.00
Ms. B. Toy	800.00
Ms. G. Tuck	400.00
Ms. C. Zander	280.00
Total of Accounts Receivable	$2 892.00

Statement of Cash Flows

Many businesses rely on an efficient accounting system to provide management and other interested parties with a statement summarizing the main sources of cash receipts and cash payments. This statement is called the Statement of Cash Flows.

Statement of Cash Flows: a financial statement reporting the main sources of cash, the main uses of cash, and the net increase or decrease of cash over a specific time period.

The Statement of Cash Flows can be prepared from several different sources of information. It can also take different forms. We'll use a simple form in this chapter.

Look at the illustration on page 278. It shows how a Statement of Cash Flows may be prepared for Dr. Johnson's dental practice.

Analysis: These points will help you understand the Statement of Cash Flows and how to prepare one.

- As in all financial statements, two main parts are the heading and the body.
- The heading consists of three lines: Line 1 reports the name of the firm; Line 2, the name of the statement; Line 3, the time period for reporting the inflow of cash and the outflow of cash.
- The time period in our illustration is one month. However, statements are usually prepared along with the income statement and the balance sheet. As you now know, financial statements are prepared at least once a year.

John H. Johnson, D.D.S.
Statement of Cash Flows
For the Month Ended January 31, 19-2

CASH WAS PROVIDED BY:		
Remittances from accounts receivable	$ 2 093.00	
Total Sources of Cash		$ 2 093.00
CASH WAS USED FOR:		
Monthly office rent	$ 1 000.00	
Telephone calls	85.33	
Personal withdrawals	400.00	
Part payment on 5-Year Note Payable	500.00	
Salaries	2 200.00	
Lab fees	700.00	
New office equipment	1 875.00	
Payment to creditors for utilities service, dental equipment, and office and dental supplies	10 156.45	
Total Uses of Cash		16 916.78
NET INCREASE (DECREASE) IN CASH FOR JANUARY		($14 823.78)
Cash balance at beginning of January		20 000.00
Cash balance at end of January		$ 5 176.22

General Ledger

Cash — Account No. 101

DATE 19-2		EXPLANATION	POST. REF.	DEBIT	CREDIT	BALANCE	
Jan.	2	Balance forward	✓			20000 –	DR.
	31	Total Cash Receipts CRJ	1	2093 –		22093 –	
	31	Total Cash Payments CPJ	1		16916 78	5176 22	

● The body contains these important subsections: the sources of cash as reported under a subheading such as *Cash Was Provided By;* the main uses of cash as reported under a subheading such as *Cash Was Used For;* the net increase (or decrease) in cash for the period; and the cash balance for the end of the period.

● Only one source of cash is shown in Dr. Johnson's statement — the cash received from patients during January. This information was obtained from the Cash Receipts Journal.

● Eight different uses of cash are reported in the statement. Of course, this information is obtained by analyzing the data in the Cash Payments Journal.

● Since more cash was used than received, the statement

shows a net decrease in cash flow during the month. This is reported *in parentheses* to indicate a negative figure.

- The beginning balance of Cash for January is added to the net decrease to report the Cash balance at the end of the month. This balance must agree with the Cash account in the GL.
- The statement ends with the double line below the final figure.
- Since the statement of Cash Flows is a formal report, dollar signs and completeness in reporting are required.

Why prepare the Statement of Cash Flows when the same information is available from two special journals and General Ledger accounts? The answer is that it is desirable to combine the information so that the statement may be used by the owner and other interested parties outside the firm. For example, a bank manager may request such a statement before granting a loan.

TOPIC 4 PROBLEMS

8-12 Refer to Problems 8-6 and 8-9.

a Prepare the General Ledger trial balance as at December 31 from the solutions for these problems. You will need two more accounts for this trial balance: Accounts Receivable (103), balance $1 614; Professional Fees Earned (401), balance $2 488.

b Prepare the Schedule of Accounts Payable from the subsidiary ledger solved for Problem 8-9.

Key Check Figure Trial Balance Total = $152 758.01

8-13 Assume that Dr. Penny Thornton requests a Statement of Cash Flows for her dental practice for the month of December, 19-1. Use the Cash Receipts Journal (solved for Problem 7-14), Cash Payments Journal (solved for Problem 8-9), and the General Ledger (solved for Problem 8-9) to prepare the statement in a form similar to that illustrated on page 278.

Key Check Figure Net Decrease in Cash for Dec. = $6 509.50

8-14 The Cash Receipts and Cash Payments Journals, along with General Ledger information, for MacPherson Plumbing & Heating of Fredericton, N.B. revealed the following data:

(i) Total cash received from customers during the year: $58 750.80
(ii) Cash received from sale of Government of Canada Bonds: $20 000.00
(iii) Cash received from sale of an old office desk: $150.00
(iv) Total cash paid to creditors for purchases of heating and plumbing supplies: $19 680.70
(v) Total cash paid for salaries and wages: $ 30 120.40
(vi) Total cash paid for rent of building: $7 200.00
(vii) Total cash paid for telephone: $604.08
(viii) Total cash paid for utilities: $812.80

(ix) Total cash paid for truck repairs: $920.10
(x) Beginning year's balance (January 1, 19-2) in Cash account: $4 870.10

Key Check Figure Net Increase in Cash for Year = $19 562.72

Prepare a Statement of Cash Flows for MacPherson Plumbing and Heating for the year.

8-15 Dr. John Reddon (Problem 8-11) asks you to prepare a Statement of Cash Flows for the month ended September 30, 19-1. Assume that the Cash Receipts Journal reported total cash received from patients during September of $12 480.

Key Check Figure Net Increase in Cash for Sept. = $3 804

From the above information and the solutions for Problem 8-11, prepare a Statement of Cash Flows in good form.

Case Study 8

In a large business with 250 office clerks, a single clerk was given the responsibility of approving all invoices for payment, making out the cheque in payment of each invoice, signing the cheque for each payment, and recording the disbursement in the accounting records.

a Do you approve of this arrangement? Why or why not?
b If your answer is no, what duties would you give this clerk?

CHAPTER 9

PETTY CASH AND BANKING APPLICATIONS

In explaining the accounts receivable and accounts payable applications, great care was taken to point out the importance of internal measures to control cash. This chapter presents measures taken to control "petty" expenditures and to prepare monthly bank reconciliation statements. With this background, you should be able to apply your knowledge to personal-use banking applications.

- Topic 1 deals with establishing and maintaining the petty cash system.
- Topic 2 deals with the preparation of bank reconciliation statements and personal use banking applications.

TOPIC 1 THE PETTY CASH SYSTEM

In Chapter 8 you learned that making payments by cheque helps businesses control the outflow of cash. However, for many small expenditures, issuing cheques is both time-consuming and costly. Imagine the time and cost involved if a busy owner-manager had to verify, approve, issue, and record cheques for the payment of postage due on incoming mail or for a small freight bill on incoming goods. To take care of these and other *petty* (small) expenditures, many firms set up a petty cash system. The chief features of this system may be analyzed through an accounting systems flowchart as shown on page 282.

Petty cash system: a system designed to control small (petty) expenditures.

A petty cash system, like any other cash system, illustrates the control measure of dividing the responsibilities of handling petty cash and recording it. The flowchart also shows that the petty cash system can be analyzed into three main parts: (1) establishing the petty cash fund, (2) making petty cash disbursements, and (3) replenishing the petty cash fund.

PETTY CASH SYSTEM

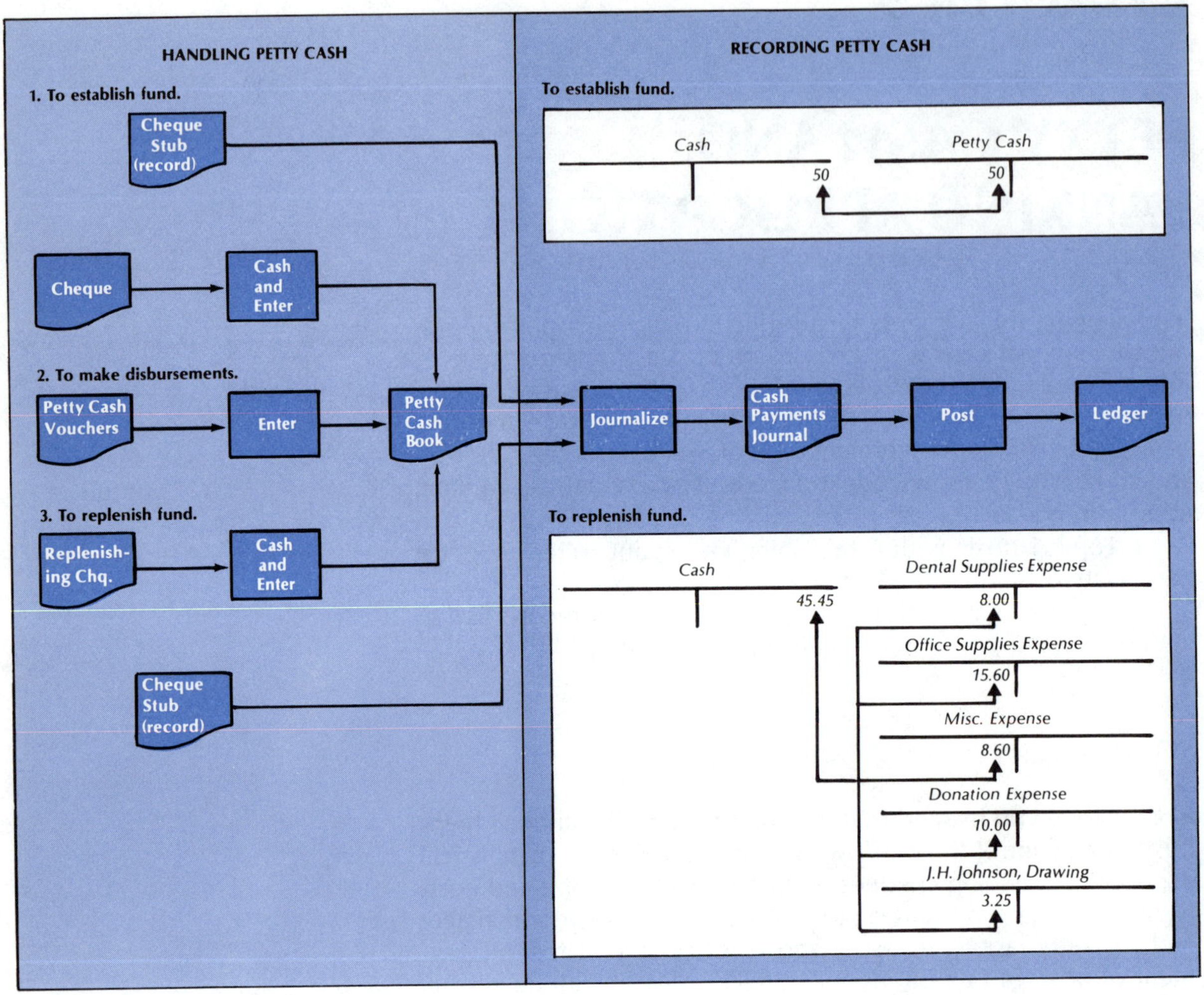

Establishing the Petty Cash Fund

The flowchart shows that, to establish the petty cash fund, a cheque is issued for an amount which will cover minor payments for a week or two, but usually not for more than one month. Suppose Dr. Johnson's dental practice issued a cheque in the second month of 19-2 as shown in the next illustration.

Analysis:

- The amount of the petty cash fund is determined by the owner-manager.
- The amount is some constant *round* number. For example, the owner-manager may decide that the size of the fund will be

DATE Feb. 1, 19-2 No. 316
ORDER OF Lynn Fortier
To establish the petty cash fund.
$50.00

DEPOSITS		JOURNAL		
		BALANCE	5176	22
		ADD DEPOSIT(S)	-0-	
		BALANCE	5176	22
		DEDUCT CHEQUE	50	00
TOTAL		BALANCE	5126	22

THE ROYAL BANK OF CANADA
MAIN BRANCH
ANY TOWN, CANADA
No. 316 Feb. 1 19-2
PAY TO THE ORDER OF Lynn Fortier $50.00
Fifty 00/100 DOLLARS
DR. JOHN H. JOHNSON
⑆0000 2⑈00 3⑆

$25, $50, or $75. Within this, a cut-off must be identified to control the individual payments. For example, the owner-manager may decide to use petty cash only for items costing $10 or less; above that, a cheque would be issued. In the case of Dr. Johnson's practice, we will assume that a $10 limit per item is used.

- The cheque is issued to an individual employee — the petty cashier, who is appointed the sole custodian of the fund.
- The following question may occur to you: Why should this cheque not be issued to "Cash" or "Petty Cash"? The answer is that if a cheque made payable to "Cash" or "Petty Cash" becomes lost or stolen, any person finding or holding it can cash it. The bank would not question the transaction because the cheque is not made out to any particular person. As a precaution against loss, always issue the cheque to the petty cashier. Since the payee must endorse it on the back with a proper signature, only the person to whom the cheque is made out can cash it.
- The petty cashier takes the cheque to the bank, endorses it, and obtains the $50 in cash.
- The currency should be kept in a locked petty cash box or drawer back at the office.
- For the convenience of the petty cashier, the amount of the fund is entered in a Petty Cash Book by some firms. The Petty Cash Book is only for the use of the petty cashier. It is *not* an accounting journal. In the case of Dr. Johnson's dental practice, assume that a Petty Cash Book is used.
- The cheque record is used to record the establishment of the fund in the accounting records. In a large business, this entry would be done by an accounting clerk or accountant working in the accounts payable department. In a small business, the entry may be done by the person assigned the responsibility of issuing the cheque or some person other than the petty cashier. Accounting entries affecting petty cash should *not* be recorded by the petty cashier.

In the case of Dr. Johnson's practice, assume that the entry to establish the petty cash fund is made by Dr. Johnson's wife in the Cash Payments Journal. This is illustrated on the next page.

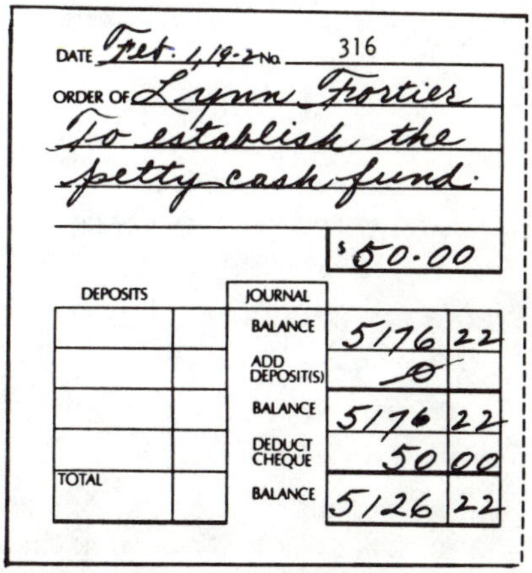

DATE Feb. 1, 19-2 No. 316
ORDER OF Lynn Fortier
To establish the petty cash fund.
$50.00

DEPOSITS		JOURNAL		
		BALANCE	5176	22
		ADD DEPOSIT(S)	-0-	
		BALANCE	5176	22
		DEDUCT CHEQUE	50	00
TOTAL		BALANCE	5126	22

CASH PAYMENTS JOURNAL **Page** 2

Date 19-2		Cheque No.	Cheque Paid To	Accts. Payable Post. Ref.	Accts. Payable Amount DR.	Other GL Accounts Account Title	Other GL Accounts Post. Ref.	Other GL Accounts Amount DR.	Cash CR.
Feb.	1	316	Lynn Fortier			Petty Cash	102	50 00	50 00

Petty Cash — Account No. 102

Date		Explanation	Post. Ref.	Debit	Credit	Balance
Feb.	1	To establish.	CPJ 2	50 00		50 00

Petty Cash (account): a current asset.

Analysis: Recording and posting the entry to establish the petty cash fund creates a current asset — an account — called Petty Cash. Of course, the credit side of the entry decreases the current asset Cash. In other words, a transfer of $50 has been made from Cash (in the bank) to a current asset called Petty Cash. Think of this action as borrowing $50 from the main source of the firm's cash — the current bank account.

Chart of Accounts

CURRENT ASSETS
101 Cash
102 Petty Cash
103 Bank Deposit Receipts
104 Accounts Receivable

The balance of the Petty Cash account does not normally change. Two changes, however, may occur:

(1) When the total of the fund must be increased, a second cheque is issued (debiting Petty Cash) to record the extra amount.

(2) When the fund must be closed, the amount is deposited in the bank and the accounting records are filled in to show a reversing entry to debit Cash and credit Petty Cash.

Making Petty Cash Disbursements

Petty cash vouchers: pre-numbered documents showing evidence of a petty cash payment.

Individual petty cash payments do not go through the accounting records. As the flowchart clearly shows, petty cash vouchers must be issued for all disbursements and a record of these vouchers is made only in the Petty Cash Book. Study the petty cash voucher illustrated in the margin on the next page.

Analysis:

- The vouchers are numbered consecutively so that all can be accounted for. (Pre-numbering is either requested when the form is ordered from the printer or done by someone other than the petty cashier.)

- Two signatures appear on the voucher. One identifies the person who received the cash; therefore, the voucher is also a receipt. The other signature identifies the person who approved the payment.
- The petty cashier places the signed voucher in the box or drawer as each payment is made. In effect, the cashier substitutes the receipted and approved voucher for the cash disbursed. This document *vouches for* (gives evidence for) the payment. Since the voucher is numbered and contains two signatures, it becomes a control document: at any time, the total payments approved on the vouchers and the remaining cash in the box (drawer) *must* equal the established amount of the petty cash fund.

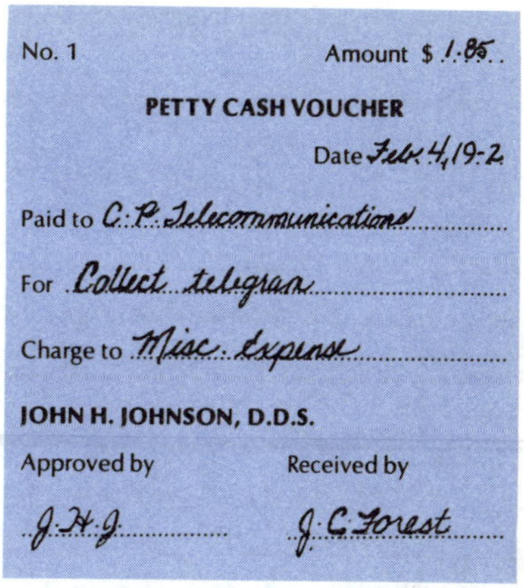
No. 1 Amount $ 1.85

PETTY CASH VOUCHER

Date Feb 4, 19-2

Paid to C.P. Telecommunications

For Collect telegram

Charge to Misc. Expense

JOHN H. JOHNSON, D.D.S.

Approved by J.H.J. Received by J.C. Forest

- Sometimes a bill of sale (sales slip, cash register tape) is obtained for the petty cash expenditure. In this case the bill paid is stapled to the back of the petty cash voucher.
- As a way of controlling petty cash expenditures, management should place a dollar limit on each item to be paid out of petty cash.
- Management should also announce a written policy regarding the cashing of personal cheques from the petty cash fund, to protect the petty cashier.

Petty Cash Book: a non-accounting record for the use of the petty cashier to summarize petty cash transactions.

As the flowchart shows, every paid voucher is entered into the Petty Cash Book. In the illustration of this record on page 286, notice that all voucher numbers (abbreviated *Vo. No.*) must be accounted for. This means that all spoiled vouchers must be recorded and kept on file. Refer to the illustration as you read the analysis.

Analysis: The analysis of transactions recorded in the Petty Cash Book is quite straightforward.

- This *book* is not a journal, so no attempt is made to provide for double entries. The Petty Cash Book is only for the use of the petty cashier. It is merely a convenient way of recording the individual transactions.
- The Petty Cash Book must contain a record of every voucher — all numbers should be accounted for.
- In the *Distribution of Payments* column, various names of ledger accounts are identified so that these accounts may be easily summarized when a request is made to replenish the fund. The account names are taken from the firm's chart of accounts.
- When the cash in the box or drawer is low, the petty cashier totals, balances, and rules off the Petty Cash Book for a period of time. In the illustration, this period is from February 1 to February 14.

PETTY CASH BOOK Page 1

Date	Explanation	Vo. No.	Petty Cash Fund: Received	Petty Cash Fund: Paid Out	Distribution of Payments: Dental Supplies Expense	Office Supplies Expense	Misc. Expense	Name of Other Account	Amount
19-2									
Feb. 1	Chq. 316 to establish fund	—	50 00						
4	Collect telegram	1		1 85			1 85		
5	No. 2 liquid cement	2		4 00	4 00				
6	Window washing	3		4 50			4 50		
7	Postage stamps	4		1 60		1 60			
8	United Way	5		10 00				Donation Expense	10 00
11	Refills for writing pens	6		7 50		7 50			
12	Paper clips	7		75		75			
13	Finishing burs	8		4 00	4 00				
14	Proprietor's lunch	9		3 25				J. H. Johnson, Drg.	3 25
15	Envelopes	10		5 75		5 75			
15	Messenger service	11		2 25			2 25		
			50 00	45 45	8 00	15 60	8 60		13 25
15	Totals		50 00	45 45	8 00	15 60	8 60		13 25
15	Cash on hand			4 55					
			50 00	50 00					
Feb. 15	Cash on hand	—	4 55						
15	Chq. 325 to replenish	—	45 45						

● Before the Petty Cash Book is ruled off, a check should be made that the totals of the columns under *Distribution of Payments* agree with the total shown in the *Paid Out* column. This check or proof may be done on a separate sheet of paper as follows:

Proof of Petty Cash Book

Dental Supplies Expense	*$ 8.00*
Office Supplies Expense	*15.60*
Miscellaneous Expense	*8.60*
Other Accounts	*13.25*
Total Paid Out	*$45.45*
Cash on Hand	*4.55*
Amount of Fund	*$50.00*

● The double line shows that one petty cash period has been

completed. A petty cash period is usually not longer than one month — the time it takes for the fund to get low.

• Notice how the next petty cash period is begun. The cash on hand is first brought down to the first writing available line below the double line. On the line below, the replenishing cheque is recorded so that the combination of the cash on hand and the replenishing cheque equals the original amount of the petty cash fund.

Some firms do not use a petty cash book. Instead, they use pre-numbered vouchers, a petty cash box or drawer, and a petty cashier who is responsible for preparing a summary of petty cash payments each time a replenishment is requested.

Replenishing the Petty Cash Fund

When the petty cash fund gets low, the petty cashier usually summarizes the expenditures on a form called the *petty cash requisition,* which requests that the fund be replenished. If a form is not available, the petty cashier can prepare the requisition on a separate sheet of paper. While the exact procedure for making a request varies from firm to firm, the following steps are usually quite common:

(1) The petty cashier totals the amount of the paid vouchers.

(2) The petty cashier proves the cash. (The totals of the vouchers plus the balance of cash in the box or drawer must equal the original amount of the fund.)

(3) The petty cashier completes the Petty Cash Book, if one is used.

(4) The petty cashier prepares a petty cash requisition for a cheque for the precise amount of the paid vouchers.

(5) The requisition and paid vouchers are submitted to the person responsible for issuing the replenishing cheque. This person must not be the petty cashier. Once the cheque is issued to the petty cashier and approved, the vouchers must be *cancelled* so that they cannot be used again. To cancel a voucher, a rubber stamp may be used to imprint *Paid* and the date of the cheque issued.

(6) After receiving the cheque, the petty cashier will cash it, place the money in the petty cash box or drawer, and enter a record of the replenishment in the Petty Cash Book. The system can then operate for another period.

After the replenishing cheque has been issued, the cheque record (the stub in this case) and accompanying documents (petty cash requisition and paid vouchers) serve as the source of information for recording the replenishment in the accounting records. Since a cheque has been issued, the entry is made in the Cash Payments Journal. The petty cash system, therefore, delays journalizing the petty cash payments until a replenishing cheque is issued.

JOHN H. JOHNSON, D.D.S.
Petty Cash Requisition

REQUEST TO REPLENISH PETTY CASH

FOR PERIOD: Feb. 1 to Feb. 15, 19-2

Petty Cash Summary:

Dental Supplies Expense	$ 8.00
Office Supplies Expense	15.60
Miscellaneous Expense	8.60
Donation Expense	10.00
J.H. Johnson, Drawing	3.25
Total Disbursements	$45.45
Cash on Hand	4.55
Amount of Petty Cash Fund	$50.00

Lynn Fortier
(Petty Cashier)

CASH PAYMENTS JOURNAL — **Page** 2

Date 19-2		Cheque No.	Cheque Paid To	Accounts Payable Post. Ref.	Accounts Payable Amount DR.	Other General Ledger Accounts Account Title	Post. Ref.	Amount DR.		Cash CR.	
Feb.	15	325	Lynn Fortier			Dental Supplies Exp.		8	00		
						Office Supplies Exp.		15	60		
						Misc. Expense		8	60		
						Donation Expense		10	00		
						J.H. Johnson, Drg.		3	25	45	45

The various debits identify the actual ledger accounts which have been summarized on the requisition. Since ledger accounts are affected only when the replenishing stage is reached, the petty cash must be reimbursed at the end of each accounting period as well as when the fund is low.

Note that the cheque for $45.45 covers all of the expenses resulting from the replenishment of petty cash. Notice too that the double entry cannot be recorded on one line because there are five accounts to be debited for the one credit to Cash. In this situation, one line has to be given for each debit. However, the total of these individual debits will add up to the one credit, $45.45.

The Petty Cash System as an Imprest System

Imprest system: a loan or advance of money from the main Cash (chequing) account.

The petty cash fund is a fixed sum which has been *loaned* or *set aside* from the regular cash in the bank. Accountants call this system of lending money the imprest system of petty cash. The imprest system is widely used because the amount borrowed can be redeposited at any time into the bank account. From a cash control viewpoint, accountants support the imprest system because it is controlled by both a cheque payment to create the fund and a cheque payment to replenish it.

Reporting Petty Cash on the Balance Sheet

Although the petty cash account is classified as a current asset in a firm's chart of accounts, the question usually arises: *Why is petty cash not given its own heading in the balance sheet?*

Cash (as defined in accounting): any item acceptable for deposit in the firm's chequing account.

To answer that question, you must first learn the meaning of cash to an accountant: coins, currency (paper money), and negotiable instruments which are accepted by banks for deposit, such as cheques.

That last idea is important. In accounting, always think of "Cash" as any item which the bank accepts for deposit in the firm's chequing account. Since well-run businesses deposit intact all their "cash" into their chequing (current) account, "cash" means "cash in the current account at the bank."

You may want to ask: Are postage stamps cash? valuable paintings? "blue-chip" stocks? The answer is no, because each fails to meet the "bank deposit" test. Bankers will not deposit the value of postage stamps into a current account. (Stamps form part of office supplies.) A valuable painting is not cash because no banker will deposit its so-called value into any chequing account. The same is true for the best "blue-chip" stock on any stock market. These must first be sold for cash, which then can be deposited.

Are balances in "pure" savings accounts cash? No, because accountants always think of cash as amounts readily available to meet current operating expenses and to pay off current liabilities. Savings accounts are more like temporary investments whose sole purpose is to earn interest revenue.

All of the above now leads to the question of petty cash. Is it cash in the accounting sense? Yes, because the petty cash fund was created from the current bank account. Also, the petty cash fund is used primarily to meet current "minor" operating expenses. Since petty cash meets the accountant's broad definition of cash, accountants prefer to report both *cash in the bank* and *petty cash* as one total figure under *Cash* in the firm's balance sheet.

TOPIC 1 PROBLEMS

9-1 The transactions below represent the petty cash events on behalf of Dr. P. Mazzone's dental practice.

19-2

Jan. 2 Issued Cheque 150 for $50 to establish the petty cash fund. Miss M. Toth has been employed as the front-office clerk.

3 Paid $4.40 to City Stationery Co. for office stationery.

4 Paid $6.50 to City Dry Cleaners for drycleaning of uniforms. (Drycleaning Expense.)

5 Paid $4.25 to C.P. Telegraph for collect telegram.

8 Paid $6.65 to City Drug Supplies for cotton pellets. (Dental Supplies Expense.)

9 Paid to City Stationery Co. $1.25 for a box of paper clips.

10 Paid $8 for tickets to Community Church Fair. (Donation Expense.)

11 Paid $8.60 to City Drug Supplies for denture paste.

12 Paid $4.50 to Dr. Mazzone for personal use.

Jan. 12 Paid $5.00 to Tom Smith for window washing. (Miscellaneous Expense.)

a Illustrate how the cheque on January 2 would be issued to establish the fund. Assume the dental practice has a current account with the Royal Bank of Canada. Also assume that the balance on Cheque Stub 150 is $2 496.40.

b Show how the entry to establish the petty cash fund would appear in the Cash Payments Journal, Page 28.

c Assume that the petty cashier is required to use petty cash vouchers (beginning with Vo. No. 1) and a Petty Cash Book similar to the ones illustrated in this chapter. Show how the petty cash transactions would appear on the vouchers and in the Petty Cash Book. Print the following account titles in the three special *Distribution of Payments* money columns: *Dental Supplies Expense, Office Supplies Expense,* and *Misc. Expense.* Assume that Dr. Mazzone is to approve each voucher. Invent a second personal name for the other signature.

d Assume that petty cash is to be replenished on January 12. Show a proof of the Petty Cash Book. Then illustrate how the petty cash requisition form would look.

e Assume that Cheque 175 is issued to replenish the fund. Show how the cheque would look. Assume the balance on the stub is $2 850.75.

f Show how the entry to replenish the fund would look in the Cash Payments Journal.

Key Check Figure Total Petty Cash Paid Out = $49.15

g Complete the Petty Cash Book for the petty cash period. Then show the cash on hand and the cheque to replenish in order to begin the new period.

9-2 The events summarized below continue the petty cash transactions for Dr. Mazzone's dental practice.

Jan. 15 Paid $4.85 for office envelopes.
16 Paid $3.20 for postage stamps.
18 Paid $5.50 for drycleaning of uniform.
19 Paid $3.25 for collect telegram.
22 Paid $6.40 for amalgam vibrator tips.
24 Paid $3.85 for pencils for the office.
26 Paid $8.00 for Dr. Mazzone's personal use.
28 Paid $0.40 for postage due. (Miscellaneous Expense.)
31 Paid $5.95 for cotton-tip applicators.

a Assume that petty cash vouchers have been issued correctly for each petty cash transaction. Use the Petty Cash Book for Problem 9-1. Leave one blank line near the bottom, to show *Totals Forward.* Then continue the record on a second page.

Key Check Figure Total Petty Cash Paid Out – $41.40

b Assume that the fund is to be replenished on January 31 through the issue of Cheque 201. Show a petty cash requisition to replenish the fund. Complete the Petty Cash Book for the period, bring down the balance of the cash on hand, and record the replenishing cheque for the new period.

c Record the replenishing cheque in the Cash Payments Journal. Continue on the journal form from Problem 9-1.

9-3 Explain briefly why each of the separate items listed below would or would not be included in the accountant's definition of cash.

a Postage stamps.
b A bank money order.
c A retail credit card.
d A cheque received from a customer.
e A stock (share) certificate.
f A valuable diamond.
g A $500-dollar bill.
h A $1000-dollar bill.
i A bank's "pure" savings account.
j A petty cash fund.
k A Canada Savings Bond interest coupon now due.

Key Check Figure A Retail Credit Card: No

9-4 Challenge Problem Frank Joyce Co. established a petty cash fund and appointed Elizabeth Condos petty cashier. The company then completed the transactions summarized below.

Oct. 1 Received, cashed, and placed into the petty cash box the $30 proceeds of Cheque 71.
2 Paid $5 to have the office windows washed.
3 Bought carbon paper and paper clips, $3.85.
4 Paid $4.65 for an advertisement in the local newspaper.
5 Bought postage stamps, $1.60.
8 Paid $4.25 for minor repairs to an office chair.
9 Paid the proprietor, Frank Joyce, $2.00 for his own use.
12 Gave $5.00 to the United Way Campaign.
12 After giving the donation to the United Way canvasser, the petty cashier found that she had only $2.65 in money in her petty cash box. Her cash proof of the Petty Cash Box, however, showed that she should have had $3.65. After checking in vain to locate the money, Elizabeth prepared a petty cash voucher for the amount of the shortage, had it approved by her employer, and recorded it in her Petty Cash Book. She then prepared a petty cash requisition and exchanged this form together with the paid vouchers for the replenishing cheque. (Cheque number 84 was issued.)

a Record the above transactions in the appropriate journal and in the Petty Cash Book. For the *Distribution of Payments* section, show *Adv. Expense, Office Expense* and *Misc. Expense.*

b Prepare the Petty Cash Book for the next petty cash period.

Key Check Figure Total Petty Cash Paid Out = $27.35

TOPIC 2 BANK RECONCILIATION AND PERSONAL-USE APPLICATIONS

In Chapters 7 and 8 you learned of several important measures for controlling cash receipts and cash payments. The two most important ones are:

- All cash receipts should be deposited intact into the firm's bank account.
- All cash payments should be made by cheque. (Even petty cash payments are controlled by cheque — a cheque is required to replenish the fund.)

Both measures identify the support which a banker gives its depositors who use a bank current (chequing) account. In Chapter 7 you learned that a banker provides current account depositors with a monthly statement showing the accounting of the depositor's receipts and payments from the banker's point of view. The bank statement allows the depositor to check information against his or her own records to make sure that any disagreement is accounted for. By having this separate accounting, the business gains one more check on the accuracy of its system.

The Bank Statement: An Illustration

Some banks prepare the monthly statement for the middle of the month; others, for the end of the month. Suppose that the bank statement on page 293 is prepared for Dr. Johnson's dental practice as at February 28, 19-2. *Note:* At the time of this writing, the Royal Bank of Canada has not considered the introduction of the International System of Units (SI); consequently, the comma appears as the triad separator in dollar amounts in the printout, as programmed by the bank's computer.

Interpreting a Bank Statement Refer to the illustrated bank statement as you read each of the following points:

- The top portion of the statement identifies the depositor by name, address, and account number. This section also indicates the month-end period for which the statement is prepared, and the number of enclosures returned with the statement.
- The balance forward ($7 376.22) from the previous statement (January 31, 19-2) is shown.
- The column headings follow the three-column account form: debits at the left, credits at the right, and a balance column to print a *running* balance after each set of postings. Royal Bank's form, however, contains three debit columns so that up to three debit entries can be printed by computer on one line. This reduces printing and paper costs. (Some banks and trust companies still use one debit column, one credit column, and a running balance column.)

Bank statement (in accounting language): a copy of a current liability on the banker's books.

- The individual debits listed on the bank statement repre-

THE ROYAL BANK OF CANADA

STATEMENT OF ACCOUNT

JOHN H JOHNSON DDS
ANY STREET
ANY TOWN OR CITY

ACCOUNT NO.	PAGE
110-134-4	
28 FEB 19-2	17
PERIOD ENDED	ENCLOSURES

'–' IF OVERDRAWN
BALANCE

CURRENT ACCOUNT

BALANCE FORWARD FROM PREVIOUS STATEMENT 7,376.22

DESCRIPTION – DEBITS / CHEQUES			DEPOSITS / CREDITS	DATE M D	BALANCE
50 00	1,000 00	1,200 00		2 01	5,126.22
DEBIT MEMO	--	6 39	600 00	2 04	5,719.83
		47 30	150 00	2 06	5,822.53
DEBIT MEMO	--	3 00		2 08	5,819.53
			1,140 00	2 10	6,959.53
100 00	48 70	19 40		2 13	6,791.43
RETURNED ITEM	--	45 00		2 14	6,746.43
		45 45	75 00	2 15	6,775.98
37 10	35 00	140 00	125 00	2 17	6,688.88
SAFEKEEPING/SDB	--	17 00		2 20	6,671.88
	200 00	1,500 00		2 24	4,971.88
			375 00	2 26	5,346.88
SERVICE CHARGES	--	2 16	100 00	2 27	5,444.72
CREDIT MEMO			193 31	2 28	5,638.03

NO. DEBITS	TOTAL AMOUNT-DEBIT	NO. CREDITS	TOTAL AMOUNT-CREDIT	
18	4,496.50	8	2,758.31	LAST STMT 31 JAN 19-2

PLEASE CHECK THIS STATEMENT WITHOUT DELAY
THE BANK MUST BE NOTIFIED IN WRITING OF ANY ERROR OR OMISSION WITHIN 30 DAYS.

sent deductions from the previous account balances; these debits are decreases to the depositor's account, because the current account (chequing account) represents a *liability* on the bank's books. Similarly, the individual credits are added to the previous running balance, because credits to a liability account *increase* the amount owing by the banker to the depositor.

Suppose you deposit $500 into a personal chequing account in your name. Using the accounting equation, the transaction would be analyzed as follows:

- The banker receives $500, so the equation must show an increase in the banker's assets.
- The increase in the banker's assets is shown by a debit Cash account.
- Any increase in the left side of the equation must be balanced by a similar increase on the right side. Why? Assets must

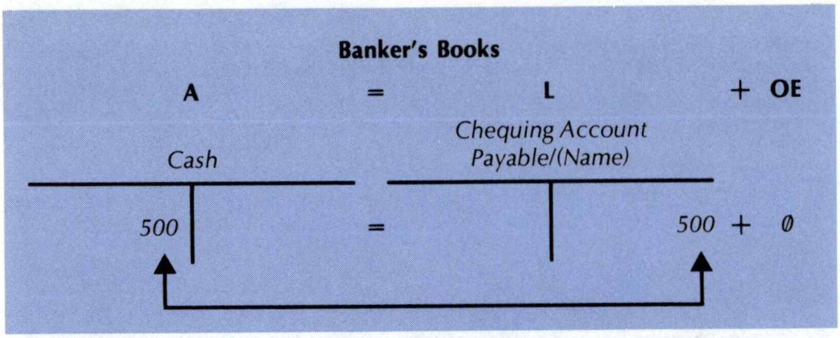

always be equal to the claims against those assets.

- The claim against the $500 belongs to the depositor. Thus, this claim must be shown as an increase under *L* (liabilities) in the accounting equation.
- The increase to *L* is recorded by crediting a liability account called Chequing Account Payable/(Name of Depositor).
- Although the banker has the use of $500, the banker has no claim on this money, so a slashed zero is placed under *OE* in the accounting equation.
- The accounting equation balances — *A* for $500 equals *L* for $500.

Now consider issuing a cheque ordering the bank to pay $100 to a party named on a cheque. When the payee presents the cheque for payment, the bank, through a computer, will analyze the transaction as follows:

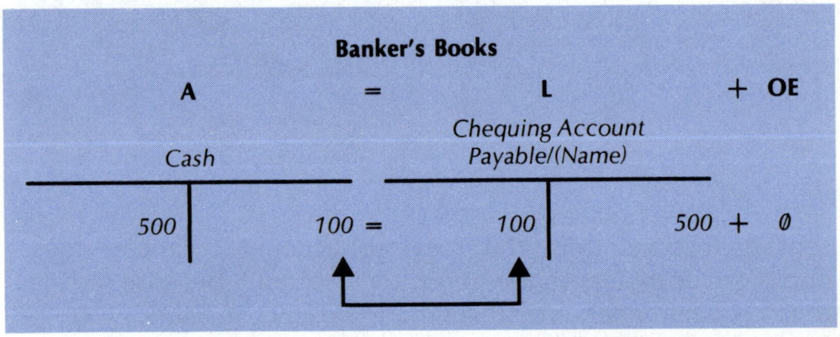

- The bank pays out $100, so the asset Cash must decrease on the left side of the accounting equation.
- This decrease is recorded by crediting the banker's Cash account.
- On the right side of the equation, the banker's debt to the depositor decreases. *L* must be decreased by $100.
- The decrease to *L* is recorded by debiting the liability account Chequing Account Payable/(Name of Depositor).
- After posting this credit, the bank still has $400 left in its Cash account. But the bank still owes this $400, because the balance in the liability account will be $400.

Date	Item	Withdrawal	Deposit	Balance

A savings account is also a liability on the books of the bank. Usually the depositor is not allowed to write cheques on such an account and no bank statement is provided. Instead, a savings account passbook is the statement of account. This passbook shows the usual three money columns: a left column (debit) to record withdrawals, a right column (credit) to record deposits, and a far-right column to show the running balance.

- To check the accuracy of a *running* balance, follow the horizontal line to total all debits, deduct the total debit(s) from the last balance, and add any credits to this figure.
- The bank shows the date of each line's transactions according to the bank's records (the bank's dates for debiting and crediting the depositor's current account).
- The bank statement explains the nature of certain transactions by means of various descriptive words. For example, the words *Debit Memo* appear on date lines 2/04 and 2/08, *Returned Item* on 2/14, *Safekeeping/SDB* on 2/20, *Service Charges* on 2/27, and *Credit Memo* on 2/28. (Some banks use only letter codes such as DM, RI, SC, and CM on their statements.) These descriptive transactions are explained below.

Debit Memo refers to an enclosed note explaining the deduction from the depositor's account. Several transactions can result in a bank debit memo. Two common examples to explain the entries on Dr. Johnson's bank statement appear below.

Bank debit memo: a source document decreasing (debiting) the depositor's account on the banker's books.

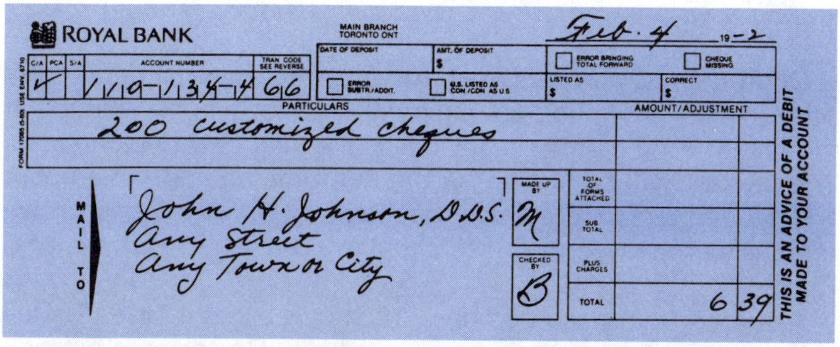
ROYAL BANK
MAIN BRANCH TORONTO ONT
Feb. 4 19-2
C/A PCA S/A | ACCOUNT NUMBER | TRAN CODE SEE REVERSE
4 | 1119-1134-14 | 66
DATE OF DEPOSIT | AMT. OF DEPOSIT $ | ERROR BRINGING TOTAL FORWARD | CHEQUE MISSING
ERROR SUBTR./ADDIT. | U.S. LISTED AS CDN./CDN. AS U.S. | LISTED AS $ | CORRECT $
PARTICULARS | AMOUNT/ADJUSTMENT
200 customized cheques
MAIL TO
John H. Johnson, D.D.S.
Any Street
Any Town or City
MADE UP BY M
CHECKED BY B
TOTAL OF FORMS ATTACHED
SUB TOTAL
PLUS CHARGES
TOTAL 6 39
THIS IS AN ADVICE OF A DEBIT MADE TO YOUR ACCOUNT

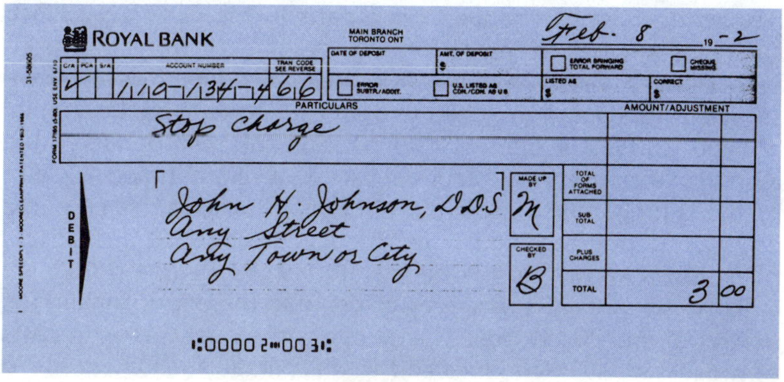
ROYAL BANK
MAIN BRANCH TORONTO ONT
Feb. 8 19-2
C/A PCA S/A | ACCOUNT NUMBER | TRAN CODE SEE REVERSE
4 | 1119-1134-1466
DATE OF DEPOSIT | AMT. OF DEPOSIT $ | ERROR BRINGING TOTAL FORWARD | CHEQUE MISSING
ERROR SUBTR./ADDIT. | U.S. LISTED AS CDN./CDN. AS U.S. | LISTED AS $ | CORRECT $
PARTICULARS | AMOUNT/ADJUSTMENT
Stop charge
DEBIT
John H. Johnson, DDS
Any Street
Any Town or City
MADE UP BY M
CHECKED BY B
TOTAL OF FORMS ATTACHED
SUB TOTAL
PLUS CHARGES
TOTAL 3 00
⑆00002⑈003⑆

The first debit memo has been issued by the bank to record the charge (fee) for 200 customized cheques. The word *debit* means that the bank has decreased (debited) its liability in the depositor's current account.

The second debit memo has been issued to record the charge for a *stop payment* on a cheque issued by the depositor. The $3.00 fee for this service would be shown in the debit column of the bank statement.

To explain stop payment: When you issue a cheque and then wish to prevent its being cashed, you must complete a "Stop Payment" form at the bank, giving a good reason for asking the bank to stop payment. Acceptable reasons would be that the cheque has been stolen or that you bought something and then found that the good or service was not satisfactory.

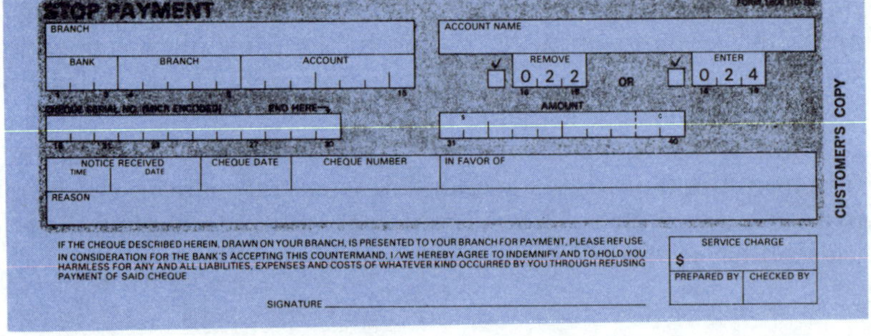
STOP PAYMENT
BRANCH
ACCOUNT NAME
BANK | BRANCH | ACCOUNT
REMOVE 0 2 2 OR ENTER 0 2 4
AMOUNT
END HERE
NOTICE RECEIVED TIME DATE | CHEQUE DATE | CHEQUE NUMBER | IN FAVOR OF
REASON
CUSTOMER'S COPY
IF THE CHEQUE DESCRIBED HEREIN, DRAWN ON YOUR BRANCH, IS PRESENTED TO YOUR BRANCH FOR PAYMENT, PLEASE REFUSE. IN CONSIDERATION FOR THE BANK'S ACCEPTING THIS COUNTERMAND, I/WE HEREBY AGREE TO INDEMNIFY AND TO HOLD YOU HARMLESS FOR ANY AND ALL LIABILITIES, EXPENSES AND COSTS OF WHATEVER KIND OCCURRED BY YOU THROUGH REFUSING PAYMENT OF SAID CHEQUE
SERVICE CHARGE $
PREPARED BY | CHECKED BY
SIGNATURE

Debit memos may be issued for any other unusual debit entry on the bank statement. For example, interest will be charged at the end of each month on any balance owing on a demand loan. The interest will be shown on the debit memo and the amount will be debited on the bank statement. Memos and descriptive terms accompany only those cheques which need an explanation.

NSF cheque: a cheque marked "Not Sufficient Funds."

Returned Item on date line 2/14 shows a debit of $45. One common returned item is an NSF cheque. Dr. Johnson's dental practice received a cheque from a patient, Mr. G.A. Jack. When Dr. Johnson's bank tried to collect the amount from Mr. Jack's bank, it was discovered that Mr. Jack's account did not have sufficient funds and the cheque *bounced,* coming back stamped *NSF* (not sufficient funds). Dr. Johnson's bank then deducted the amount from Johnson's current account. Sometimes a debit memo is prepared to explain the returned item; in this case, the original cheque received is returned (marked *NSF*) and an explanation is shown on the bank statement as *Returned Item.*

Bankers charge a service fee against both the depositor and the drawer of an NSF cheque. The charge is to cover the extra costs of processing such cheques and to discourage such cheques. At the time of this writing, most bankers charge a *minimum* of $2.00 against the depositor of a cheque which becomes NSF and $7.50 against the drawer of such a cheque. These charges are subject to review and may be increased.

Safekeeping/SDB shows a debit of $17. This is the bank's fee for renting a *safety deposit box* (SDB) to the depositor. Businesses and individuals rent these boxes to store their valuable documents. Sometimes a bank prepares a debit memo in addition to showing the descriptive entry.

Service Charges is self-explanatory. The bank has charged $2.16 for the service of preparing the bank statement, and returning cancelled cheques, debit memos, one credit memo, and the returned item. Sometimes (but not normally) the bank will prepare a debit memo to explain the service charge.

Bank credit memo: a source document increasing (crediting) the depositor's account on the banker's books.

Credit Memo refers to the form illustrated below, a bank credit memo:

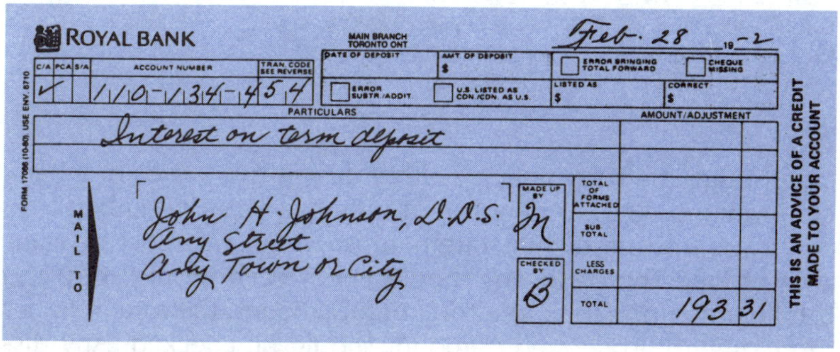
ROYAL BANK
MAIN BRANCH TORONTO ONT
Feb. 28 19-2
C/A ✓ PCA S/A
ACCOUNT NUMBER 1110-134-454
TRAN. CODE SEE REVERSE
DATE OF DEPOSIT
AMT. OF DEPOSIT $
ERROR BRINGING TOTAL FORWARD
CHEQUE MISSING
ERROR SUBTR./ADDIT.
U.S. LISTED AS CDN./CDN. AS U.S.
LISTED AS $
CORRECT $
PARTICULARS
Interest on term deposit
AMOUNT/ADJUSTMENT
MAIL TO
John H. Johnson, D.D.S.
Any Street
Any Town or City
MADE UP BY M
CHECKED BY B
TOTAL OF FORMS ATTACHED
SUB TOTAL
LESS CHARGES
TOTAL 193 31
FORM 17066 (10-80) USE ENV. 6710
THIS IS AN ADVICE OF A CREDIT MADE TO YOUR ACCOUNT

Term deposit receipt: a source document issued by the bank, giving evidence of a short-term investment.

As the memo explains, the bank has credited the depositor's current account with interest earned from a term deposit receipt — a short-term investment taken out by the depositor for 30, 60, 90, or 120 days. Such an investment usually earns a higher rate of interest than a pure bank savings account. But the depositor must invest a minimum amount of money — usually $10 000 or more. As the memo shows, the depositor's special instructions are to credit his current account with all interest earned.

A hypothetical Royal Bank term deposit receipt is shown on page 298. *Note:* A comma is shown as the triad separator for the reason explained earlier.

Bank credit memos may also be issued for other unusual items credited to the depositor's current account. For example, a loan granted by the bank would be credited to the depositor's account and may be shown on a special credit memo. Another example would be for interest earned from securities held by the bank on behalf of the depositor. For a personal-use example, an employee's regular payroll may be transferred from the employer's bank to the employee's bank account. Only unusual

NON-TRANSFERABLE
THE ROYAL BANK OF CANADA

DR JOHN H JOHNSON
ANY STREET
ANY TOWN CANADA

Branch
00003

110-134-4
Account Number

TERM DEPOSIT

************ $15,680.00 ************

INTEREST RATE PA 7.5000%	MATURITY DATE FEB 28/-2
INTEREST PAID MATURITY	ISSUED DATE DEC 30/-1
CREDIT INTEREST 110-134-4	CREDIT PRINCIPAL SPEC INSTRUCT
RENEWAL PRINCIPAL	WITHDRAWAL PRIVILEGE YES
REDEMPTION RATES PRIOR TO MATURITY	
0-29 DAYS NIL	OVER 29 DAYS 4.0000%

credit items are supported by either descriptive words or a bank credit memo. Regular deposits of money are not described.

• The bottom of the statement provides a number of valuable proofs. The depositor should check each proof listed: the total number of debits, the total debit amount, the total number of credits, the total credit amount should be checked. Any discrepancy should be reported to the bank immediately. The totals are obtained by the bank's computer but you can check them by using an adding machine. The final balance reported on the statement is the beginning balance ($7 376.22) plus the total credit ($2 758.31) less the total debit ($4 496.50), or $5 638.03.

The Need for a Bank Reconciliation

A bank statement reports an independent accounting of (1) the depositor's inflow of cash (cash receipts intact), (2) the outflow of cash (cash payments made by cheque), and (3) the cash balance of the depositor's current account as at a certain date.

The firm keeps its own record of cash transactions by maintaining a cheque record (the cheque stub) and the Cash account in the General Ledger. In theory, an identical amount for the firm's cash balance should appear in the bank's books and in the firm's cheque record and Cash account. In practice, however, the balance reported on the bank statement seldom agrees with the firm's cheque record balance and the Cash account balance. For example, Dr. Johnson's records, illustrated next, do not agree with the final balance reported by the bank statement.

DR. JOHNSON'S RECORDS

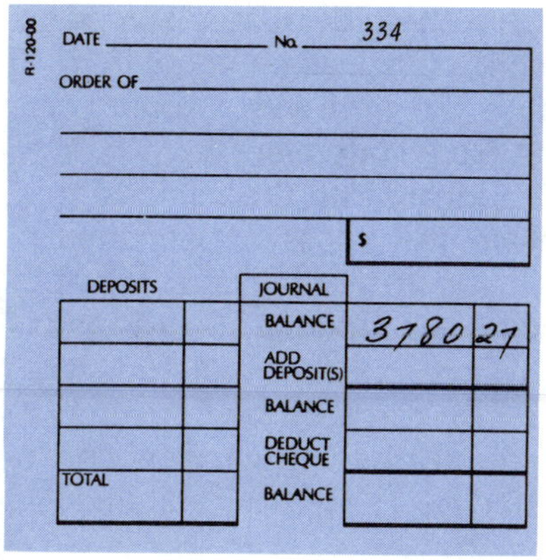

Bank statement balance as of February 28 reports $5 638.03.

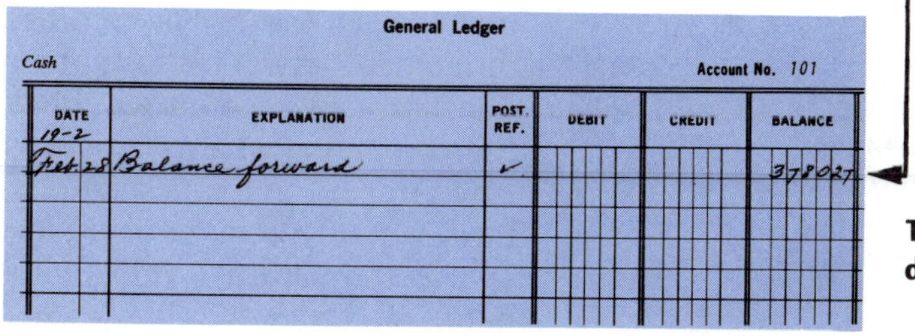

These balances do NOT agree.

Why may a bank statement balance not agree with the depositor's records for the same date? Here are six good reasons.

(1) The firm has issued one or more cheques that have yet to be cancelled by the bank. These outstanding cheques will make the bank statement balance greater than the firm's Cash account balance, because these cheques have not been listed on the bank statement. Obviously, this discrepancy represents a mere difference of timing because the bank will eventually receive these cheques and cancel them after making payment.

Outstanding cheques: cheques issued but not as yet "cashed" (cancelled) by the bank.

(2) The firm may have deposited an amount which is shown in the firm's record (cash receipts debited to Cash and the deposit recorded on the cheque stub) but the amount has yet to appear on the bank statement. This can happen when the deposit is made on the final day of preparing the bank statement. This late deposit is called a deposit in transit. It means that the bank statement balance will be lower than the firm's cheque book balance and Cash account balance. This discrepancy is another timing difference, which will be set right once the bank receives the deposit and accounts for it.

Deposit in transit: a deposit not yet credited by the bank on the books of the banker.

(3) The bank may have enclosed one or more bank debit memos with the bank statement. These memos have decreased the firm's current account balances in the bank's books, but they have yet to be treated in the firm's records. As a result, these debit memos, again, represent timing differences, because the firm will account for them once they are received with the bank statement.

(4) The bank may have enclosed one or more bank credit memos with the statement. These memos have increased the firm's current account balances in the bank's books, but they have yet to be treated in the firm's records. As a result, these credit memos represent timing differences, and the firm will account for them once they are received with the bank statement.

(5) The bank may have deducted (debited) items such as service charges on the bank statement, but these decreases have yet to be recorded in the firm's cash records. Once again, these items represent timing differences, because the firm will account for them once it identifies them on the bank statement.

(6) Errors or omissions may have appeared on the bank statement or in the firm's records. These will cause a permanent difference between the firm's balance and the bank statement. The firm can account for them only by comparing records and then preparing what is known as a bank reconciliation statement. Any error or omission made by the firm can then be corrected; however, any bank error or omission must be corrected by contacting the bank in writing within 30 days of the bank statement date.

Bank reconciliation statement: a monthly statement bringing the depositor's Cash account balance into agreement with the bank statement balance as at a certain date.

To control the accounting of the firm's most valuable asset — *Cash* — all of the above causes of difference (due to timing and possible errors or omissions) should be reconciled (made to agree) to prove that the differences are temporary and will be self-correcting. The procedure for bringing the balance as reported by the firm's records (Cash account and cheque book) and the balance as reported by the bank statement into agreement is known as *preparing a bank reconciliation statement.*

Preparing a Bank Reconciliation Statement

Bank statements should be reconciled by employees who do *not* handle cash or cash records, or sign cheques. These employees should receive the statements in the original and unopened envelopes sent by the bank.

There are at least three ways of preparing bank reconciliation statements in accounting practice. Only one will be illustrated in this chapter.

Before you can prepare such a statement, it will be necessary to compare the bank statement and enclosures with the firm's accounting records so that all discrepancy items (items of difference) can be identified and listed. The following order may be used to locate and list discrepancy items.

(1) Check all items enclosed with the bank statement against similar amounts reported on the bank statement. The banker usually encloses all documents (cheques, memos) in the order in which they have been posted to the bank statement. Simply check each one in order against the statement. Any bank errors or omissions at this point should be listed on a separate sheet of paper (you can call this paper your working paper). In the case of Dr. Johnson's bank statement, assume that all cheques and memos are correct as reported.

(2) Arrange all cancelled cheques in numerical order. Then compare each cheque with the corresponding entry in the Cash

Payments Journal. Place a check mark opposite the cheque number and cheque amount. Then list on the working paper all unchecked cheque numbers and their cheque amounts. These amounts represent outstanding cheques. In the case of Dr. Johnson's practice, assume that the following cheques are outstanding:

No. 331 (to Denco Supply)	$ 50
No. 332 (to Lynn Fortier)	1 000
No. 333 (to Kathy Lewis)	1 200

Special Note: Since the cheque record (stub) balance agrees with the Cash ledger account balance, it is not necessary to check the items with both the cheque stub and the accounting records. In some acounting practices, however, a double-check is made by comparing the cheque record as well.

(3) Compare the deposits reported by the bank statement with the receipted copy of the bank deposit slip. In some accounting practices, a double check of these deposits is made by also comparing amounts recorded in the Cash Receipts Journal and/or the cheque book. Then list on the separate sheet (the working paper) any deposits in transit. For Dr. Johnson's dental example, assume that a deposit of $512 was made on February 28 — too late for the amount to appear in the *Credit* column of the bank statement.

(4) List all debit memos, returned items, and any other identified debits on the bank statement which have not been recorded in the firm's accounting records. In the case of Dr. Johnson's bank statement, the following items would be listed on the working paper:

Debit Memo (fee for customized cheques)	$ 6.39
Debit Memo (stop payment fee)	3.00
Returned Item (NSF cheque of G.A. Jack)	45.00
Safekeeping/SDB (annual fee for renting safety deposit box)	17.00
Service Charges	2.16

(5) List all credit memos and any other identified credits on the bank statement which have not been recorded in the firm's accounting records. In the case of Dr. Johnson's bank statement, there is only one credit item: the credit memo for depositing $193.31 from the interest earned on bank deposit receipts.

(6) Check all reported calculations on the bank statement, including the various proof totals indicated at the bottom. Any errors should be listed as bank errors. In the example of Dr.

Johnson's bank statement, assume that all calculations are correct.

Once all of the discrepancy items have been identified and listed, an actual reconciliation of the bank statement balance and the Cash account balance can be made. Before this statement is illustrated, let's summarize the various discrepancy items for Dr. Johnson's example. Assume that the following information appears on your working paper:

Bank statement balance, Feb. 28, 19-2	*$5 638.03*
Cash account balance, Feb. 28, 19-2 (agrees with balance shown on Cheque Stub No. 334)	*3 780.27*
Outstanding Cheques:	
No. 331	*50.00*
No. 332	*1 000.00*
No. 333	*1 200.00*
Deposit of Feb. 28 not recorded on bank statement (deposit in transit)	*512.00*
Debit Memo (customized cheques)	*6.39*
Debit Memo (stop payment fee)	*3.00*
Returned Item (NSF cheque of G.A. Jack)	*45.00*
Safekeeping/SDB Charge	*17.00*
Service Charges	*2.16*
Credit Memo (interest earned from deposit receipts)	*193.31*

From the above summary of discrepancy items, identify which items would be added to, or subtracted from, the bank statement balance or the Cash account balance. The following two guides may help you to make a reconciliation of each item:

(1) Except for discovered errors, treat each discrepancy item according to the way in which the known party has recorded the item in his or her records.

(2) Treat all discovered errors according to their effect on the appropriate cash balance to be adjusted.

For example, the deposit not recorded by the bank must be added to the bank statement balance, because the item has already been added to the Cash account balance. Since the three outstanding cheques have not yet been cashed, the bank has not yet deducted them from Dr. Johnson's account. Therefore, they must be subtracted from the bank statement balance, because they have already been recorded in the Cash Payments Journal and are part of the total posting to Cash CR. The two debit memos, the Safekeeping/SDB fee, the NSF cheque, and the bank service charges have already been deducted from the bank statement balance. This means that these items must be deducted from the Cash account balance to make both records agree. Finally, the bank added money when it credited the interest shown on the credit memo. Since the depositor did not know this until after the bank statement was received, a similar amount must be added to the Cash account balance to make the two records agree.

If a bank error were discovered, this error would be adjusted to the bank statement balance. Suppose, for example, that the bank decreased the depositor's account with a cheque that belonged to someone else. This amount would be added back to the bank statement balance to make the two records agree. You would immediately report such an error to the bank.

If an error were discovered in the depositor's records, this error would have to show an adjustment under the Cash account balance. For example, suppose a depositor issued a cheque for $75 but recorded the amount as $57. This means that the difference ($75 − $57 = $18) must be subtracted from the Cash account balance to make the two records agree. In the case of Dr. Johnson's records and the bank statement received, assume no errors were discovered.

Study the bank reconciliation statement illustrated below. Then read the analysis.

John H. Johnson, D.D.S.
Bank Reconciliation Statement
As at February 28, 19-2

Balance as per bank statement, Feb. 28		*$5 638.03*
Add: Deposit of Feb. 28 not recorded by bank		*512.00*
		6 150.03
Deduct Outstanding Cheques:		
No. 331	*$ 50.00*	
No. 332	*1 000.00*	
No. 333	*1 200.00*	*2 250.00*
Adjusted bank statement balance		*$3 900.03*
Balance as per Cash account, Feb. 28		*$3 780.27*
Add: Bank credit memo for interest earned from bank deposit receipts		*193.31*
		3 973.58
Deduct:		
Debit Memo (customized cheques)	*$ 6.39*	
Debit Memo (stop payment fee)	*3.00*	
N.S.F. Cheque of G.A. Jack	*45.00*	
Safekeeping/SDB Charge	*17.00*	
Service Charges	*2.16*	*73.55*
Adjusted book balance of cash		*$3 900.03*

These amounts must agree.

Analysis: Here are the important points to remember when preparing a formal bank reconciliation statement.

- Begin with the traditional three-line heading: Line 1 shows the name of the firm; Line 2, the name of the statement; Line 3, the date of bringing the two cash balances into agreement.

Since the balance shown by the bank statement is the balance on February 28, reconciliation occurs as of this date and not as of the date of actually preparing the bank reconciliation statement.

- The body of the statement consists of: (1) one section for reconciling discrepancy items that affect the bank statement balance; (2) another for reconciling discrepancy items that affect the depositor's records of the month-end Cash account balance.

Note: Do not be concerned about which section to begin with. Although the illustration shows the reconciliation of the bank statement balance first, it would be just as correct to begin with the section that shows the reconciliation of the depositor's cash balance. The important thing is that discrepancy items must be related to the correct section in reconciliation; otherwise, the two cash balances cannot possibly be made to agree.

- Each section begins with the balance reported by its records as of a common date. This means that you will remove the timing difference in order to make the two balances agree.
- Additions are shown before deductions in reconciling the bank statement balance. This procedure allows you to group items so that subtotals can easily be added and then subtracted from the balance.
- Each section is shown as being completed by a double line which ends each section.
- The two adjusted balances must agree. This adjusted figure ($3 900.03) represents the *true* or *correct* balance of cash on February 28 if both the bank and the depositor had known of all discrepancy items and had accounted for them.

Adjusting the Cash Records after Reconciliation

From the depositor's point of view, two cash records must be adjusted after the bank reconciliation:

- The balance on the latest cheque stub must be brought into agreement with the adjusted book balance of cash on the bank reconciliation statement.
- The Cash account in the General Ledger must be updated by journalizing and posting appropriate entries to bring the ledger account into agreement with the adjusted book balance of cash on the bank reconciliation statement.

These adjustments will now be examined in separate sections.

Adjusting the Latest Cheque Stub

After a bank reconciliation is prepared, the latest cheque stub should be adjusted to reflect the changes shown by the reconciliation of the depositor's discrepancy items. For Dr. Johnson's dental practice, Cheque Stub 334 would show a total addition of

$119.76. This addition is the net result of the $193.31 from the bank credit memo less the total deductions of $73.55. With the addition of $119.76, the former cash balance is brought into agreement with the adjusted book balance of cash on the bank reconciliation statement. This adjustment may be made on the latest stub as illustrated in the margin.

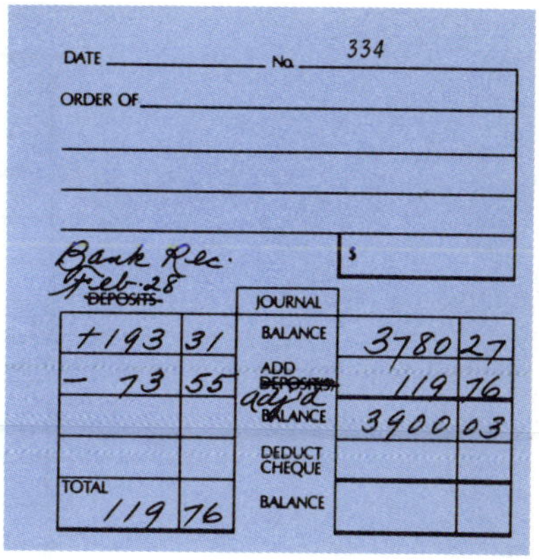

Adjusting the Cash Account in the General Ledger

To update the Cash account, appropriate *adjusting entries* must be made in the General Journal because the most adjustments in accounting take place at month-end and at the end of the financial year. You will learn more about adjusting entries in Part III of this book.

You might ask: From where do you get the information to prepare the adjusting entries? The objectivity principle in accounting requires evidence of these adjustments. The answer is: You get it from the section of the bank reconciliation statement that reconciles the cash balance of the depositor and not of the bank. For Dr. Johnson's practice, this would mean five journal entries:

- one to record the credit memo for $193.31 for interest earned from bank deposit receipts
- one to record the debit memo for $6.39 for the customized cheques
- one to record the debit memo for $3.00 for the stop payment fee
- one to record the fee of $17 for the annual rental of the safety deposit box
- one to record the bank service charges of $2.16

For the first adjustment above, the Cash account must be debited and an appropriate revenue account must be credited.

For each of the remaining adjustments, an appropriate account must be debited, and Cash must be credited.

Since Cash is debited in the first entry, and Cash is credited in each of the remaining entries, why not use the Cash Receipts Journal to record Cash DR. and why not use the Cash Payments Journal to record Cash CR.? There are two good reasons. (1) Both special journals would normally be ruled off for the month by the time a reconciliation statement is prepared. (2) All adjusting entries are normally recorded in the General Journal.

For Dr. Johnson's practice, the General Journal entries for making those adjustments resulting from bank reconciliation may be illustrated as on page 306.

The first adjusting entry records the revenue earned from the interest credited to the depositor's current account. Remember, any amount credited to the depositor's chequing account is defined as cash. Therefore, the asset Cash is debited correctly.

The second adjusting entry shows the fees for customized cheques and stop payment. Both amounts have been charged to

GENERAL JOURNAL Page 55

DATE 19-2		ACCOUNT TITLE AND EXPLANATION	POST. REF.	DEBIT	CREDIT
Feb.	28	Cash		193 31	
		Interest Revenue			193 31
		To record the bank credit			
		memo for interest earned			
		from bank deposit receipts.			
	28	Miscellaneous Expense		9 39	
		Cash			9 39
		To record the bank debit			
		memos for customized			
		cheques ($6.39) and the			
		stop payment fee ($3.00).			
	28	Accts. Rec./G.A. Jack		45 00	
		Cash			45 00
		To record the NSF cheque			
		of G.A. Jack.			
	28	Safety Deposit Box Rental Expense		17 00	
		Cash			17 00
		To record the annual			
		rental charge on the SDB.			
	28	Bank Service Charges Expense		2 16	
		Cash			2 16
		To record the service			
		charges reported on the bank			
		statement of Feb. 28.			

Note: *As an alternative to the last four entries, one compound adjusting entry may be made recording four debits and one credit to Cash for the total ($73.55).*

the Miscellaneous Expense account because the amounts are so small and similar charges would be infrequent.

The third entry debiting Accts. Rec./G.A. Jack and crediting Cash for $45 may cause some confusion. To understand why Accts. Rec./G.A. Jack must be debited for the NSF cheque, let's review the background of all transactions that led to the NSF cheque.

In the first place, the dental firm must have rendered services to G.A. Jack. This would suggest that Accts. Rec./G.A. Jack was debited for $45 and that Professional Fees Earned was credited for a similar amount.

Next, the patient remitted his cheque for $45 in full payment of his account. The result would have debited Cash and credited Accts. Rec./G.A. Jack for $45. The cheque would have been endorsed *For Deposit Only* and the dentist's bank would have credited the current account with the amount of the cheque.

However, when the cheque was returned NSF to Johnson's bank, the bank promptly deducted the amount from the current account. The adjusting entry on Johnson's books, therefore, must debit the patient's account and credit Cash. Johnson will have to wait for another cheque from G.A. Jack before the patient's account will be brought down to zero.

Once the adjusting entries have been posted to the appropriate ledger accounts, the Cash account balance will be in agreement with the adjusted book balance of cash shown on the bank reconciliation statement. Thus, the business has once more gained effective control over its most valuable asset, Cash.

General Ledger

Cash — Account No. 101

DATE		EXPLANATION	POST. REF.	DEBIT	CREDIT	BALANCE
19-2						
Feb.	28	Balance forward	✓			3 780 27
	28		G.J. 55	193 31		3 973 58
	28		G.J. 55		9 39	3 964 19
	28		G.J. 55		45 00	3 919 19
	28		G.J. 55		17 00	3 902 19
	28		G.J. 55		2 16	3 900 03

Personal-Use Applications

Bank reconciliation can also be applied to any individual's need to control personal cash. Here's a brief summary of the key measures to control anyone's most valuable asset.

- Open a personal-use chequing account or business current account at a nearby bank or trust company. (You do not have to be in business to open a business account.) A chequing account provides you with the return of *all* cancelled cheques and a monthly bank statement.
- Open a pure (true) savings account. This will earn a higher rate of interest than you can receive from a combination chequing and savings account. Also, you can better control your cash if you have only *one* chequing account.

Deposit intact *all* cash receipts into your chequing account. Arrange to have your main source of cash receipts — your pay — deposited directly into this chequing account. When you get paid by cheque, always endorse the cheque *For Deposit Only* to the credit of your chequing account.

- Leave only enough cash in the chequing account to pay your bills. Any extra amounts should always be transferred to your savings account for later investments such as bank deposit receipts, bonds, long-term guaranteed savings certificates, and stocks of business corporations.
- Rent a safety deposit box to store your valuable documents.
- Check all bills before making payment.
- Use consecutively pre-numbered cheques to pay all bills. You can order customized cheques from your banker for a very reasonable fee.
- Always record every cheque *before* completing the main cheque form. Bankers provide cheque stub forms or records in booklet form.
- Void all spoiled cheques and keep these cancelled cheques in a *Cheques Returned* file.
- Avoid carrying large amounts of cash on your person. Instead, obtain a recognized credit card for your personal expenditures. That way your purchases will eventually be controlled by a cheque payment. Where it is necessary to have actual currency, make out the cheque to *Cash* only at your bank so you won't lose it.
- Always pay your bills on time and avoid paying interest on overdue bills. Use a tickler file system if necessary.
- Always cancel every bill after issuing the cheque. Keep all cancelled bills in a file. Keep these papers for at least *six* years. That's the length of time Revenue Canada — Taxation expects individual Canadians to keep documents just in case the individual has to have a tax audit of his or her personal income tax return.
- Always prepare a bank reconciliation statement immediately after receiving your monthly bank statement.
- Keep on file for *five* years all bank statements, cancelled cheques, and bank memos.

TOPIC 2 PROBLEMS

9-5 Assume that the bank statement as of February 28, prepared for Paul W. Black, D.D.S. shows a final balance of $384.00, while Black's Cash account (and cheque book balance) as of February 28 shows $399.20. After having compared all items shown on the bank statement with the accounting records, Black writes down the following information:

Outstanding cheques: No. 110, $25.40; No. 115, $67.10; No. 123, $125.80; No. 140, $18.50.

Deposit of February 28 not recorded by bank: $250.

Bank service charges reported on the bank statement: $2.

a Prepare a bank reconciliation statement from the above information.
b Prepare in the General Journal any entries that the depositor should make as a result of having prepared the bank reconciliation.

Key Check Figure Adjusted Bank Statement Balance = $397.20

9-6 Assume that the bank statement as of March 31, prepared for Bonnie Flood, D.D.S. shows a final balance of $596.12, while Flood's Cash account (and cheque book balance) as of March 31 shows $1 758.42. Assume Flood writes down the following information after comparing all items shown on the bank statement with the accounting records.

(i) Outstanding cheques: No. 45, $35.80; No. 47, $76.10; No. 50, $225.80.
(ii) Deposit in transit, March 31: $1 485.
(iii) Debit memo for annual safety deposit box rental: $12.
(iv) Bank service charges: $3.

a Prepare a bank reconciliation statement from the above information.
b Prepare General Journal entries that the depositor should make after preparing the bank reconciliation.

Key Check Figure Adjusted Cash Account Balance = $1 743.42

9-7 The information below results from identifying and listing the discrepancy items for L.M. Munro, D.D.S. as of the February 28 bank statement.

Bank statement balance, February 28	$1 263
Cash account balance, February 28	1 510
Deposit in transit, February 28	425
Outstanding Cheques:	
No. 210	50
No. 212	65
No. 219	85
Bank service charges	4

Cheque No. 218, returned with the cancelled cheques, was correctly drawn for $42 in payment of the telephone bill. However, this cheque was accidentally recorded on the cheque record and in the Cash Payments Journal as $24.
a Prepare a bank reconciliation statement from the above information.
b Prepare General Journal entries to adjust the Cash account following a bank reconciliation.

Key Check Figure Adjusted Cash Account Balance = $1 488

9-8 Challenge Problem Assume that you work in the accounting department of a local banker. The separate transactions below, pertaining to a current depositor called Dolly's Flowers, have come to your attention for a complete analysis.
(i) Dolly's Flowers, a current account depositor, deposits cash receipts totalling $500.
(ii) The bank cashes cheques drawn by Dolly's Flowers to the amount of $200.
(iii) The bank agrees to a demand loan for Dolly's Flowers in the amount of $1 000. In turn, Dolly's Flowers deposits the amount of the loan into its current account.

Key Check Figure (iii), Demand Loans Receivable: DR.

(iv) The bank receives a cheque for $200 from Dolly's Flowers in part payment of the demand loan.

(v) The bank issues a debit memo to Dolly's Flowers showing $5 interest on the demand loan for one month.

(vi) The bank issues a debit memo to Dolly's Flowers showing that $7.50 had been charged against the depositor's account for the rental of a safety deposit box.

(vii) Dolly's Flowers has a cheque for $1 200 certified at the bank. The certified cheque is promptly mailed to the payee.

Note: A certified cheque is first made out by the depositor in the regular way. It is then presented at the depositor's bank where the banker checks the chequing account to see if there is sufficient cash to certify the cheque. If there is, the banker immediately takes out the amount from the depositor's account and keeps the funds in a special account. When the certified cheque is cashed, the bank uses the funds from this special account and not from the depositor's account. Remember, the banker has already debited the depositor's account with the amount of the certified cheque immediately after certifying it. For this service, most bankers now charge a small amount which is shown as part of the regular bank service charges on the monthly bank statement.

(viii) The bank prepares a debit memo informing Dolly's Flowers that its current account has been decreased by $100 as a result of an NSF cheque drawn by H. Hunt, an accounts receivable customer of the depositor.

(ix) The bank prepares a credit memo notifying Dolly's Flowers that its current account has been credited for $46.50 interest on Canada Savings Bonds held for the depositor.

(x) The bank deducts $2.40 from the current account of Dolly's Flowers for monthly bank service charges.

Show your analysis of each transaction in General Journal form. Remember to do this from the banker's viewpoint. Make up appropriate General Ledger titles for each entry. *Hint:* Think of the effects of each event on the banker's accounting equation before you show the double entry in General Journal form.

Key Check Figure (iii), Bank Loan Payable: CR.

9-9 Rewrite the accounting entries for each transaction in Problem 9-8, but analyze each transaction from the viewpoint of the *depositor's* records. Use the two-column General Journal form. Suggest appropriate titles for each accounting entry.

9-10 The following information was available to reconcile the firm of Mary R. Macdonald:

(i) The ledger account for Cash showed a balance on June 30 of $4 252.90.

(ii) The June bank statement showed a closing balance of $3 918.70.

(iii) The cash received on June 30 amounted to $490.75. This amount was deposited intact at the bank into the night depository chute after banking hours on June 30, so the deposit was not recorded by the bank on the June statement.

(iv) Among the cancelled cheques returned by the bank with the June bank statement was one issued by an "R. Mary McDonald" for $270. The bank erroneously charged this cheque to the account of "Mary R. Macdonald."

(v) Also included with the June bank statement was a debit memo from the bank for $10.75 representing the bank charge for renting a safety deposit box to the depositor.

(vi) Examination of the paid cheques revealed that these cheques, all issued in June, had not been cancelled by the bank: No. 540 for $187.50; No. 561 for $43.80; No. 570 for $195.25; No. 574 for $99.25; a certified cheque No. 580 for $750.

(vii) Included with the bank statement was a $75.00 cheque drawn by Judy White, a customer of Mary R. Macdonald. This cheque was marked NSF. It had been included in the deposit of June 27, but had been charged back on the bank statement on June 30.

(viii) The bank statement showed a service charge of $4.50 for operating the account during June.

(ix) Cheque No. 510, issued and cancelled correctly for $43.75, had been erroneously recorded as $34.75 on the cheque record and in the cash payments journal. This cheque was issued in payment of Utilities Expense.

a Prepare a bank reconciliation statement for Mary R. Macdonald.

b After completing the bank reconciliation, prepare adjusting entries to correct the Cash account as at June 30.

Key Check Figure Adjusted Bank Statement Balance = $4 153.65

9-11 Challenge Problem Martin Flowers Ltd. has a current account with the Northern Bank of Canada. The company last reconciled its book and bank statement balances on July 31 with two cheques, No. 310 for $118 and No. 311 for $265, outstanding. The July 31 reconciliation showed that a deposit in transit on July 31 for $298.75 had not been recorded by the bank. The following information has been supplied in order to do the August 31 reconciliation.

MARTIN FLOWERS LTD
5 ALGONQUIN AVE N
THUNDER BAY ONT P7A 6E1

CURRENT ACCT NO 107-247-6

STATEMENT OF ACCOUNT WITH

THE NORTHERN BANK OF CANADA

EXPLANATION OF SYMBOLS

CC Certified Cheque
DM Debit Memo
CM Credit Memo
IN Interest—Dr. or Cr.
RT Returned Item
SC Service Charge

DATE	DEBITS		CREDITS	BALANCE
AUG 1	BALANCE BROUGHT FORWARD			1,572.15
1			298.75	1,870.90
2	265.00		600.00	2,205.90
3	195.70	216.85	375.40	2,168.75
5	402.00			1,766.75
9	89.40			1,677.35
12	60.00		412.75	2,030.10
14	417.65	375.10	1,000.00	2,237.35
18	500.00CC			1,737.35
21			296.25	2,033.60
22	28.75		78.90	2,083.75
26	9.80DM		53.75	2,127.70
30	53.75RT			2,073.95
31	5.00IN	3.50SC	174.70CM	2,240.15

NO. ENCLOSURES	FULL PAGE	TOTAL AMOUNT-DEBIT	NO. DEBITS	TOTAL AMOUNT-CREDIT	NO. CREDITS	TOTAL SERVICE CHARGE
13		2,622.50	14	3,290.50	9	3.50

CASH RECEIPTS JOURNAL Page 16

DATE		POST. REF.	AMOUNT
Aug.	2	201	600 00
	3	401	375 40
	12	401	412 75
	14	301	1 000 00
	21	401	296 25
	22	103	78 90
	26	105	53 75
	31	401	448 95
	31	101	3 266 00

CASH PAYMENTS JOURNAL Page 21

CHEQUE NO.	POST. REF.	AMOUNT
315	202	195 70
316	519	216 85
317	203	89 40
318	112	420 00
319	520	217 40
320	302	60 00
321	104	127 90
322	516	417 65
323	107	500 00
324	110	375 10
325	205	59 40
326	505	28 75
327	502	17 90
	101	2 726 05

Cash ACCOUNT NO. 101

DATE		EXPLANATION	POST. REF.	DEBIT	CREDIT	BALANCE	
Aug.	1	Balance	✓			1 487 90	DR.
	31	Total Cash Receipts	CR 16	3 266 00		4 753 90	
	31	Total Cash Payments	CP 21		2 726 05	2 027 85	

Included with the bank statement was an NSF cheque drawn by a customer, Peter Gruhn. The cheque was charged back to the depositor's account on August 30. Its return is unrecorded.

Cheque No. 318 was correctly issued for $402 in payment of Office Equipment. An examination of the cash records showed that the accounting clerk entered it as $420.

The credit memo resulted from the banker's clipping of bond interest coupons on Canada Savings Bonds held for the depositor at the bank.

Two debit memos were included with the bank statement: one for the monthly interest charged on the bank loan of August 2, the other for the annual fee for renting a safety deposit box.

Key Check Figure Adjusted Bank Statement Balance = $2 148.50

a Compare the bank statement with the depositor's cash records; then locate and list all discrepancy items.

b Prepare an August 31 bank reconciliation for the company.

c Prepare the General Journal entries needed to adjust the book balance of cash to the reconciled balance.

9-12 Personal-Use Application A London, Ontario couple recently received their electricity and water bill from that city's Public Utilities Commission (PUC) as shown in the first illustration on page 313.

Before issuing the cheque, the couple checked the accuracy of the bill. They could not believe that $70.25 more was needed over the last bill, as illustrated in the second illustration.

PUBLIC UTILITIES COMMISSION D
BOX 3060 LONDON, ONT N6A 4J8

INQUIRIES - 8:15 TO 4:30 - MONDAY TO FRIDAY
TELEPHONE 679-5503

01 905 08184 02 843 DRIFTWOOD RD

READING DATE 29 AUG 19-3
ELECTRIC READING 1994
WATER READING 1283

29 ELECTRIC 4322 KWH 181.38
WATER 3919 CU FT 31.40

THIS BILL MAY BE PAID ON OR BEFORE THE DUE DATE AT ANY LONDON BANK OR TRUST COMPANY.

AMOUNT DUE IF PAID AFTER 22 SEPT .... 223.43 E & OE

AMOUNT DUE IF PAID BY 22 SEP 19-3 ... 212.78

PUBLIC UTILITIES COMMISSION D
BOX 3060 LONDON, ONT N6A 4J8

INQUIRIES - 8:15 TO 4:30 - MONDAY TO FRIDAY
TELEPHONE 679-5503

01 905 08184 02 843 DRIFTWOOD RD

READING DATE 27 JUN 19-3
ELECTRIC READING 7672
WATER READING 1172

Cheque 318
July 18, 19-3

29 ELECTRIC 2724 KWH 117.46
WATER 2930 CU FT 25.07

THIS BILL MAY BE PAID ON OR BEFORE THE DUE DATE AT ANY LONDON BANK OR TRUST COMPANY.

AMOUNT DUE IF PAID AFTER 19 JUL .... 149.66 E & OE

AMOUNT DUE IF PAID BY 19 JUL 19-3 . 142.53

A close look at the electricty reading showed 7672 on reading date June 27, 19-3, while the reading on August 29, 19-3 showed a lower number, 1994. How could it go from a higher to a lower number? They agreed there must be a computer error.

They also looked at the water reading. The June 27 bill showed a reading of 1172, while the current bill showed 1283 — a difference of only one hundred eleven. But the current bill shows 3919 cubic feet of water used.

Before calling to make an inquiry, the couple checked the Bills Paid file for Sept. 19-2. The total electricity and water bill for a similar period one year ago showed $167.85. They were convinced errors were made in the current bill.

A call to the PUC office revealed the following:

(i) The maximum reading on all electric meters in the city is 9999; after that, the meter begins again at 0000.

(ii) The current rate for electricity is: (a) for the first 500 kW·h (kilowatt hours), $0.0570 per kW·h (5.70 cents per kW·h); (b) the remainder at $0.04 per kW·h.

(iii) Water meters are to be read in cubic *metres.*

(iv) Water rates are based on cubic feet, so you must convert the water readings to cubic feet (the conversion is 35.31 cubic feet = 1 cubic metre).

(v) Current water rates: (a) for the first 200 cubic feet, $3.80 per 100 cubic feet; (b) for the next 5000 cubic feet, $0.64 per 100 cubic feet.

(vi) According to the PUC representative, the commission's computer is correct.

You have been asked to verify the accuracy of the current bill. Would you advise the London couple to issue the cheque or to file a letter of protest? Show calculations to support your answer.

9-13 Personal-Use Application Assume that you have acquired a full-time position after completing your education. You have also taken out a current account with a nearby branch of the Royal Bank of Canada. The transactions that follow represent your personal-use banking application for the month of July.

July 1 Deposited $1000 into the current account.
1 Issued Cheque 001 to City Properties Ltd. for $400 for one month's rent.
3 Issued Cheque 002 to *The Canadian Consumer* for $18.00 for one year's subscription.
6 Issued Cheque 003 for $45 to Bell Canada for installation of telephone.
7 Issued Cheque 004 for $65 to A & P Foods Ltd. for weekly groceries.
9 Received a cheque from J. Young for $100 in part payment of a loan transacted in June. Endorsed the cheque *For Deposit Only*.
12 Issued Cheque 005 for $47 to Dr. R.B. Biesenthal, D.D.S. for exam, X-ray, and cleaning of teeth.
14 Issued Cheque 006 for $70.80 to A & P Foods Ltd. for weekly groceries.
15 Received pay slip from employer stating that the net pay for two weeks, $400, was deposited to the credit of the current account.
18 Issued Cheque 007 to Cash for $50 for entertainment.
20 Issued Cheque 008 to L & X TV and Stereo Ltd., $100 as a down payment on a new TV set.
21 Issued Cheque 009 for $93.72 to A & P Foods Ltd. for weekly groceries.
25 Received a bill from Texaco Canada Ltd. for $55.55 for credit card purchases to date. Payment was due immediately. Issued Cheque 010 in full payment.
26 Issued Cheque 011 to L & X TV and Stereo Ltd. for $300 for FM/AM Stereo Cassette Corder.
27 Received a Visa Statement of Account showing a total owing of $138.70. Payment is due by August 15.
28 Issued the following cheques: No. 012 for $68.23 to A & P Foods Ltd. for weekly groceries; No. 013 for $50 to Cash for entertainment.
30 Issued Cheque 014 for $100 to L & X TV and Stereo Ltd. on account.
31 Received pay slip from employer showing $400 net pay being deposited into the bank's current account under your name.
31 Issued Cheque 015 for $120 to Eastown Chev Ltd. for car repairs.
31 Received cheque for $100 from J. Young as the final payment on loan due today. Deposited the cheque into the overnight depository.

a Assume that the Royal Bank of Canada supplied you with a current account cheque register as illustrated opposite. Show how the transactions above would be recorded in this cheque record. Remember that the cheque register records cheques issued as well as your deposits.

b Assume that the bank has mailed you the statement on page 316.

SUGGESTIONS FOR USING YOUR CHEQUE REGISTER

THE CHEQUE REGISTER IS DESIGNED TO GIVE YOU AN ACCURATE, COMPACT, AND THOROUGH RECORD OF YOUR CHEQUES AND DEPOSITS. HERE ARE SOME SUGGESTIONS FOR USE.

1. BE SURE THAT ALL INFORMATION IS INCLUDED AND ACCURATE.

2. KEEP A CURRENT RUNNING BALANCE BY SUBTRACTING THE CHEQUE OR ADDING THE DEPOSIT TO THE PREVIOUS BALANCE. DO THIS WITH EACH TRANSACTION OR AS OFTEN AS NECESSARY IN ORDER TO BE CURRENT.

3. THE ✓ COLUMN CAN BE USED FOR ONE OF TWO THINGS.

   A. TO RECONCILE BANK STATEMENTS. THE ✓ COLUMN MAY BE USED TO MARK EACH CHEQUE PAID BY THE BANK. ITEMS NOT MARKED ARE OUTSTANDING AND HAVE NOT BEEN PAID BY THE BANK AS OF STATEMENT DATE.

   B. TO INDICATE TAX DEDUCTIBLE ITEMS. THIS LETS YOU EASILY IDENTIFY THESE ITEMS AT TAX TIME.

4. WHEN THE REGISTER IS FULL, WRITE THE STARTING AND ENDING CHEQUE NUMBERS AND DATES ON THE FRONT AND FILE AWAY FOR FUTURE REFERENCE.

5. LIST AUTOMATIC DEPOSITS AND WITHDRAWALS ON THE PREAUTHORIZED CHARGES AND DEPOSITS PAGE AS A REMINDER TO RECORD THESE AT THE PROPER TIME.

DATE	CHEQUE NO	CHEQUES ISSUED TO OR DESCRIPTION OF DEPOSIT	AMOUNT	✓		✓	BALANCE FORWARD
						✓	1,000 00
		To Bank	175 00		DEDUCT CHEQUE − ADD DEPOSIT +		175 00
		For Car Loan			BALANCE ⇨		825 00
		To Visa	50 00		DEDUCT CHEQUE − ADD DEPOSIT +		50 00
		For Payment			BALANCE ⇨		775 00
		To Deposit	250 00		DEDUCT CHEQUE − ADD DEPOSIT +		250 00
		For			BALANCE ⇨		1025 00
		To Mortgage	300 00		DEDUCT CHEQUE − ADD DEPOSIT +		300 00
		For Payment			BALANCE ⇨		725 00
		To Cancer Society	20 00		DEDUCT CHEQUE − ADD DEPOSIT +		20 00
		For Donation			BALANCE ⇨		705 00
		To			DEDUCT CHEQUE − ADD DEPOSIT +		
		For			BALANCE ⇨		

DATE	CHEQUE NO.	CHEQUES ISSUED TO OR DESCRIPTION OF DEPOSIT	AMOUNT	✓		✓	BALANCE FORWARD
		To			DEDUCT CHEQUE − ADD DEPOSIT +		
		For			BALANCE ⇨		
		To			DEDUCT CHEQUE − ADD DEPOSIT +		
		For			BALANCE ⇨		
		To			DEDUCT CHEQUE − ADD DEPOSIT +		
		For			BALANCE ⇨		
		To			DEDUCT CHEQUE − ADD DEPOSIT +		
		For			BALANCE ⇨		
		To			DEDUCT CHEQUE − ADD DEPOSIT +		
		For			BALANCE ⇨		
		To			DEDUCT CHEQUE − ADD DEPOSIT +		
		For			BALANCE ⇨		

The following cheques were enclosed: 001, 002, 003, 004, 005, 006, 007, 008, 009, 010, 011, 013. No bank debit memos or bank credit memos were enclosed.

Check the accuracy of the final balance by using the various proofs at the bottom of the statement. Then, compare the cheque register with the bank statement given and make a note of any differences.

c Prepare a bank reconciliation statement.

d Update your cheque record with any adjustments.

Key Check Figure Adjusted Bank Statement Balance = $413.20

THE ROYAL BANK OF CANADA

STATEMENT OF ACCOUNT

ACCOUNT NO.	PAGE
110-134-5	
31 JUL --	12
PERIOD ENDED	ENCLOSURES

YOUR NAME
YOUR TOWN/CITY
YOUR PROVINCE, CANADA

IF OVERDRAWN

BALANCE FORWARD FROM PREVIOUS STATEMENT — BALANCE 0.00

C U R R E N T   A C C O U N T

DESCRIPTION – DEBITS/CHEQUES				DEPOSITS/CREDITS	DATE M	DATE D	BALANCE
				1,000 00	7	01	1,000.00
			400 00		7	03	600.00
		18 00	45 00		7	08	537.00
			65 00	100 00	7	09	572.00
PAYROLL				400 00	7	15	972.00
	50 00	47 00	70 80		7	18	804.20
		100 00	93 72		7	22	610.48
			55 55		7	27	554.93
		300 00	50 00		7	28	204.93
PAYROLL				400 00	7	31	604.93
STMT DELIVERY FEE			1 50		7	31	603.43
SERVICE CHARGES			2 00		7	31	601.43

NO. DEBITS	TOTAL AMOUNT-DEBIT	NO. CREDITS	TOTAL AMOUNT-CREDIT
12	1,298.57	4	1,900.00

PLEASE CHECK THIS STATEMENT WITHOUT DELAY
THE BANK MUST BE NOTIFIED IN WRITING OF ANY ERROR OR OMISSION WITHIN 30 DAYS.

Case Study 9

A friend of yours, the owner of a medium-sized company, learns that you have studied some important measures of controlling cash. He invites you to spend a few days studying the application of these control measures in his business. In your study, you found out the following:

(i) A petty cash fund of $1000 had been established to take care of small payments. Instead of a regular voucher form, the system permitted those using the petty cash to submit their own forms. Many of the forms were a variety of store receipts; some were short pieces of paper with some explanation by the user of the petty cash. A check of the petty cash book revealed that the fund was replenished weekly.

(ii) The petty cashier was permitted to issue the replenishing cheque, sign the cheque, and make the accounting record for all petty cash payments.

(iii) The petty cashier was permitted to approve payments of any amount up to and including $100.

(iv) Personal cheques of customers and employees were permitted to be cashed from the petty cash fund.

(v) One person was given the responsibility to act as the cashier and bookkeeper. Among other duties, he handled cash receipts, deposited all cash in the bank, issued and signed all cheques, and maintained the accounting records for all cash transactions other than those of a petty cash nature.

(vi) A cheque for $855 issued in payment of an account payable was erroneously listed in the cash payments journal as $585. The error was not corrected until the next month when the cancelled cheque was received from the bank.

a Assume that you were planning to present a written report of your findings. Identify the apparent cash control weaknesses for each disclosed fact.

b What changes in the overall cash control system would you recommend to improve the problem areas?

CHAPTER 10

THE PAYROLL APPLICATION (Salaried Payroll)

Employee: a person hired to work under the control of an employer.

Every business which hires one or more employees is required by the laws of Canada and of the province to keep payroll records. The system for collecting payroll data, recording payroll data, accounting for the resulting payroll remittances, and preparing annual tax slips makes up the *payroll application.* Some interesting jobs are found in payroll accounting.

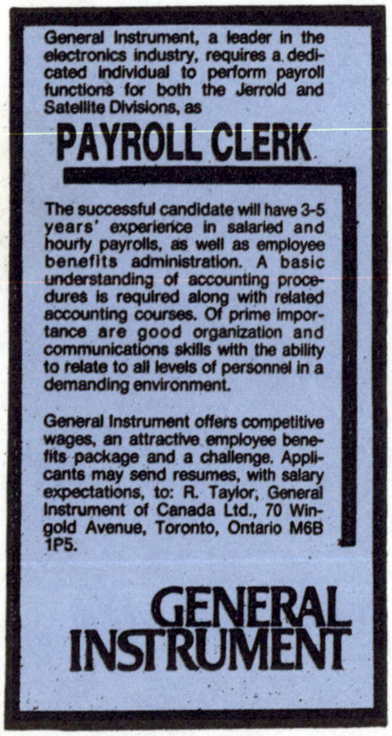

This chapter will introduce the basic items that form the payroll application for salaried employees only. The salaried payroll for a small dental practice employing three employees will be used as an example. The more complicated aspects of salaried payroll, together with the payroll accounting for personnel who are hourly employed are dealt with in Chapter 14.

This chapter covers the payroll application as follows:

- Topic 1: collecting payroll data
- Topic 2: recording payroll data
- Topic 3: payroll remittances and annual tax statements

TOPIC 1 COLLECTING PAYROLL DATA

All payroll applications begin with collecting important data on each employee. This data consists of: (1) the employee's social insurance number, (2) a special completed income tax form called Tax Exemption Return TD1, (3) details of the salaried payroll plan, (4) information on the time worked, and (5) the required employee payroll deductions.

Social Insurance Number

All employees must have a card which contains a *social insurance number* (SIN). This number is important for several reasons:

- You need it to get unemployment insurance.
- You need it to start your first pension plan (the Canada Pension Plan).
- You need it to complete your first income tax form (Form TD1).

- You need it to file your personal income tax returns.
- Most important of all, you need a SIN to receive your first pay cheque. No employer will process your pay without having your SIN.

If you haven't a SIN, go to the nearest Canada Employment Centre and make out an application; you do not have to be employed. Your SIN identifies you for the rest of your life, and will be useful in many other situations.

Tax Exemption Return TD1

Form TD1 is the first income tax paper normally completed by employees who begin their first full-time job.

Look closely at the front of Form TD1, shown on page 320.

Analysis: Here are the important points to remember about completing Form TD1.

- The first boxes are for your name and address, SIN, and date of birth.
- The box below *Address* requires you to print a dollar amount called the *net claim.* This is your claim for exemptions as calculated on the other side of Form TD1. See page 321.
- Everyone required to pay income taxes in Canada receives a Basic Personal Exemption. The form shows $3 960 on the top line. This is the basic amount everyone was allowed in 1984 to reduce his or her net income before calculating the income tax to be paid. The federal government calculates the basic personal exemption each year for you.
- The next exemption is available to a married person who supports a spouse or to a single, divorced, separated or widow(er)ed person who supports a dependant. In our example, Kathy Lewis checks off box 3 because she supports a niece whose net income will not exceed $490. Therefore, Kathy is able to claim an additional $3 960 to further reduce the amount of income tax she will have to pay.
- The next section is for claiming the exemption for wholly dependent children. In our example, no lines have been used because Kathy Lewis cannot claim her niece twice. The original claim was made in box 3 above.
- Although there are other possible claims for exemptions, as the form shows, Kathy has none.
- The larger the amount of the exemptions, the *smaller* the amount of the income tax which the employer will deduct from the employee's pay. The individual exemption amounts are added and entered on the *Total* line. Our example shows $7 430.
- If an employee receives family allowance cheques for support of the children claimed for exemptions above, the total amount of the family allowance payments received in the current year must be entered under *Deduct.* Kathy Lewis will not receive any family allowance cheques.

Basic Personal Exemption: the first deduction from a taxpayer's net income before calculating amounts subject to income tax.

Revenue Canada Taxation / Revenu Canada Impôt

TAX EXEMPTION RETURN
DÉCLARATION D'EXEMPTIONS D'IMPÔT

TD·
Rev. 198

- **A duly completed copy of this return must be filed by an individual with an employer on commencement of employment, and**
  - (a) you are in receipt of salary, wages, commissions or other remunération

  or filed with the payor, if
  - (b) you are in receipt of a superannuation or pension benefit (including an annuity payment) made pursuant to or under a superannuation or pension fund or plan, or
  - (c) you are in receipt of a benefit under the Unemployment Insurance Act, 1971, or
  - (d) you are in receipt of a training allowance paid under the National Training Act except to the extend that it was paid as or on account of an allowance for personal or living expenses while living away from home,

  and in any case,
  - (e) within **seven** days of any change in your exemptions.
- **This return need not be filed by employees claiming the "Basic Personal Exemption" only.**
- If you do not file this return, as required, income tax will be deducted as though you were a single person without dependants.
- If you believe there are other exemptions that you could claim on your income tax return you may ask your District Taxation Office whether they may be taken into account in arriving at your tax deduction.
- Do not claim a child or other dependant whose net income for the year will exceed $3,960.
- Net income of your spouse or dependants includes any pension or supplement under the Old Age Security Act or any similar Act of a province, benefits under the Canada or Quebec Pension Plan and the Unemployment Insurance Act, 1971.

- **Vous êtes tenu de remettre un exemplaire dûmen rempli de la présente déclaration à votre employeu au début de votre emploi,**
  - a) si vous recevez un traitement, un salaire, des commissions o toute autre rémunération;

  ou de la remettre au payeur,
  - b) si vous recevez des prestations de retraite ou de pension (compris des paiements de rente) en vertu d'un fonds ou d'u régime de pensions ou de retraite;
  - c) si vous recevez des prestations en vertu de la Loi de 1971 su l'assurance-chômage; ou
  - d) si vous recevez une allocation de formation en vertu de la Lc nationale sur la formation, sauf si elle est versée comme frais d subsistance ou frais engagés à l'extérieur;

  vous devez aussi remettre cette déclaration
  - e) dans les **sept** jours suivant tout changement dans vos exemp tions.
- **Les employés qui ne demandent que l'«Exemption personnell de base» n'ont pas besoin de remplir cette déclaration.**
- Si vous omettez de remplir cette déclaration, votre impôt sur le revenu ser retenu à la source comme pour un contribuable célibataire n'ayar personne à sa charge.
- Si vous croyez avoir droit à d'autres exemptions dans votre déclaratio d'impôt sur le revenu, demandez à votre bureau de district si vous pouve en tenir compte dans le calcul de vos retenues d'impôt.
- Vous ne pouvez demander d'exemption pour un enfant ou une autr personne à charge dont le revenu net pour l'année dépassera 3 960 $.
- Le revenu net de votre conjoint ou des personnes à votre charge compren toute pension ou tout supplément en vertu de la Loi sur la sécurité de l vieillesse ou de toute loi provinciale semblable, et les prestations d Régime de pensions du Canada, du Régime de rentes du Québec ou d la Loi de 1971 sur l'assurance-chômage.

FAMILY OR LAST NAME (Print) — *NOM DE FAMILLE (en majuscules)*	USUAL FIRST NAME AND INITIALS — *PRENOM USUEL ET INITIALES*	EMPLOYEE NO. - *NUMÉRO DE L'EMPLOYÉ*
LEWIS	KATHY	
ADDRESS — *ADRESSE*		SOCIAL INSURANCE NUMBER *NUMÉRO D'ASSURANCE SOCIALE*
ANY TOWN / CITY		425/27511
CANADA		DATE OF BIRTH - *DATE DE NAISSANCE* Day-Jour 14 Month-Mois JAN. Year-Année 19--

Complete the "Claim for Exemptions" area on the reverse side and enter your "Net Claim". ▶ $ 7430 ◀ Remplissez la section «Exemptions demandées» au verso et inscrivez la «Demande nette».

Refer to the "Table" below and enter the applicable "Net Claim Code". ▶ 8 ◀ Consultez la «Table» ci-dessous et inscrivez le «Code de demande nette» approprié.

Table of Net Claim Codes 1984 ***Table des codes de demande nette***

Net Claim – *Demande nette* Exceeding – Not exceeding *Excédant – N'excédant pas*	Net Claim Code *Code de demande nette*	Net Claim – *Demande nette* Exceeding – Not exceeding *Excédant – N'excédant pas*	Net Claim Code *Code de demande nette*
$3,959 — 4,010	1	$ 7,410 — 8,130	8
4,010 — 4,640	2	8,130 — 8,890	9
4,640 — 5,330	3	8,890 — 9,720	10
5,330 — 5,920	4	9,720 — 10,540	11
5,920 — 6,690	5	10,540 — 11,320	12
6,690 — 7,050	6	11,320 — 11,920	13
7,050 — 7,410	7	11,920 and up – *et plus*	X
Exemption from Tax Deduction as claimed below — *Exemptions des retenues d'impôt demandées ci-dessus*			0

- Your "Net Claim Code" is used by the employer or the payor to determine the tax deduction required from payments received as listed in (a) to (d) above.
- L'employeur ou le payeur utilise votre «Code de demande nette» pou calculer l'impôt à retenir sur les paiements indiqués en a) à d) ci-dessu

Claim for Exemption from Tax Deduction — *Valid for current calendar year only.*

This area is to be completed by an individual who is receiving remuneration that is subject to tax deduction but who wishes to claim exemption because "Total estimated income from all sources for the year" including taxable benefits but excluding Family Allowance payments, will be less than the "Net Claim" above. No claim may be made here by a person not resident in Canada for the whole year unless your earnings in Canada will be less than your exemptions apportioned to the period of residence in Canada. If you qualify for this exemption, your "Net Claim Code" is "O".

Demande d'exemption de retenues d'impôt — *Valable seulement pou l'année civile en cours.*

Section à remplir par un particulier qui désire être exempté des retenues à la sourc prélevées sur sa rémunération parce que le «Total de ses revenus estimatifs c toutes provenances pour l'année», y compris les avantages imposables, ma excluant les allocations familiales, sera inférieur à la «Demande nette» ci-dessu Si vous ne résidez pas au Canada pendant toute l'année, vous ne pouvez demand cette exemption, sauf si votre revenu au Canada sera inférieur à la fraction de vc exemptions correspondant à votre période de résidence au Canada. Si vous avı droit à l'exemption, votre «Code de demande nette» est «O».

Income to date this year from all sources — *Revenu de toutes provenances jusqu'ici cette année*	$
Estimated income for remainder of year from all sources — *Revenu estimatif de toutes provenances d'ici la fin de l'année*	$ 20 800
Total estimated income from all sources for the year — *Total des revenus estimatifs de toutes provenances pour l'année*	$ 20 800

Certification
I HEREBY CERTIFY that the information given in this return is true, correct and complete to the best of my knowledge and belief.

Attestation
J'atteste par les présentes que les renseignements donnés dans cet déclaration sont vrais, exacts et complets pour autant que je sache.

Signature *Kathy Lewis* Date *January 2* 19--

It is a serious offence to make a false return – *Faire une fausse déclaration constitue une infraction grave.*

Warning: An employer or payor should refer a form TD1 containing doubtful statements to the District Taxation Office. Any person who knowingly accepts a form TD1 containing false or deceptive statements commits a serious offence. Employers and payors must retain completed forms TD1 for inspection by officers of the Department of National Revenue, Taxation.

Avertissement: L'employ . . le payeur doit soumettre au bureau de district d'impı toute formule TD1 renfermant une déclaration douteuse. Quiconque accepte sciemment un formule TD1 renfermant une déclaration fausse ou douteuse commet une infraction grave Les employeurs et les payeurs doivent conserver les formules TD1 dûment remplies pou inspection par les agents de Revenu Canada, Impôt.

Form authorized and prescribed by order of the Minister of National Revenue

Formule autorisée et prescrite sur l'ordre du Ministre du Revenu national

Claim for Exemptions—*Exemptions demandées*

Basic Personal Exemption—***Exemption personnelle de base*** ▶ $ 3,960

Married or Equivalent Exemption—***Exemption de marié(e) ou l'équivalent***

If applicable, claim only one of these 4 items—*Demandez, selon votre cas, une seule des possibilités suivantes:*

Married and supporting spouse—***Marié(e) et soutien de son conjoint***

☐ 1. whose net income while married, will not exceed / *dont le revenu net dans l'année pendant le mariage ne dépassera pas* } $490 — Claim—*Demandez* $3,470

☐ 2. whose net income while married, will exceed / *dont le revenu net dans l'année pendant le mariage dépassera* } $490 but not / *sans dépasser* $3,960

Less: spouse's net income—*Moins le revenu net du conjoint* $ ______

Claim—*Demandez* $ ______ ▶ $ 3470

Single, divorced, separated or widow(er)—***Célibataire, divorcé(e), séparé(e) ou veuf(veuve)***

(See information in item A below) If the dependant's net income for the year—
Si vous êtes soutien d'une personne à charge (Voir dans la note A, au bas de la page, les renseignements sur les personnes à charge)

* ☒ 3. Supporting dependant whose net income will not exceed / *dont le revenu net pour l'année ne dépassera pas* } $490 — Claim—*Demandez* $3,470

* ☐ 4. Supporting dependant whose net income will exceed / *dont le revenu net pour l'année dépassera* } $490 but not / *sans dépasser* $3,960

Less: dependant's *net income—*Moins le revenu net de la personne à votre charge** $ ______

Claim—*Demandez* $ ______

*Name and relationship to you:
Nom et lien de parenté avec vous:

Exemption for Wholly Dependent Children—***Exemption pour enfants entièrement à charge***

See information in item B below. Provide details below.
Voir dans la note B, au bas de la page, les renseignements sur les enfants à charge. Donnez les précisions demandées.

Under age 18 at December 31st—If net income will not exceed $2,540, claim $710. If net income will exceed $2,540 but not $3,960 claim $710 minus one-half the amount in excess of $2,540.

Age 18 or over at December 31st—If net income will not exceed $2,600, claim $1,360. If net income will exceed $2,600 but not $3,960, claim $1,360 minus the amount in excess of $2,600.

Moins de 18 ans le 31 décembre—*Si son revenu net ne dépassera pas 2 540 $, demandez 710 $. Si son revenu net se situera entre 2 540 $ et 3 960 $, demandez 710 $ moins la moitié de la fraction qui dépassera 2 540 $.*

18 ans ou plus le 31 décembre—*Si son revenu net ne dépassera pas 2 600 $, demandez 1 360 $. Si son revenu net se situera entre 2 600 $ et 3 960 $, demandez 1 360 $ moins la fraction qui dépassera 2 600 $.*

Name of child (Attach list if space is insufficient)—*Nom de l'enfant (Faute d'espace, annexez une liste)*	Estimated annual net income—*Revenu net annuel estimatif*	Date of birth *Date de naissance* Day *Jour*	Month *Mois*	Year *Année*	If over 21, state school attended or whether infirm—*S'il a plus de 21 ans, indiquez l'école fréquentée ou dites s'il est infirme.*	
						▶ $
						▶ $
						▶ $

Exemption for Other Dependants—***Exemption pour autres personnes à charge***

Parents, Grandparents, Brothers, Sisters, Aunts or Uncles Resident in Canada (including in-laws).
Père, mère, grands-parents, frères, soeurs, tantes et oncles résidant au Canada (et ceux du conjoint).

See information in item C and provide details below.
Voir dans la note C, au bas de la page, les renseignements sur les autres personnes à charge. Donnez les précisions demandées.

Name and address of dependant *Nom et adresse de la personne à charge* (Attach list if space is insufficient) *(Faute d'espace, annexez une liste)*	Dependant's - *Personne à charge* Net income *Revenu net*	Year of birth *Année de naissance*	Estimated cost to you of support of dependant - *Montant estimatif pour l'entretien de la personne à charge*	If over 21, state school attended or whether infirm - *Si elle a plus de 21 ans, indiquez l'école fréquentée ou dites si elle est infirme.*	
					▶ $
					▶ $

Age Exemptions—***Exemption en raison d'âge***

If you are 65 years of age or over—*Si vous avez 65 ans ou plus* — Claim—*Demandez* $2,480 ▶ $

If your spouse is 65 years of age or over you may claim any unused balance of the exemption amount (maximum $2,480)—*Si votre conjoint a 65 ans ou plus, vous pouvez demander la fraction inutilisée de son exemption jusqu'à concurrence de 2 480 $.* — Unused Balance *Fraction inutilisée* ▶ $

Pension Income or Qualified Pension Income Exemption—***Exemption relative au revenu de pensions ou au revenu de pensions admissible***

If you are 60 years of age or over and have qualified pension income or are 65 years of age or over and have pension income, or if under age 60 and no contribution has been made to a registered retirement savings plan or registered pension plan from a qualified pension income, claim the lesser of $1,000 or the amount received.
Si vous avez 60 ans ou plus et avez un revenu de pensions admissible, ou si vous avez 65 ans ou plus et avez un revenu de pensions, ou si vous avez moins de 60 ans et n'avez fait aucune contribution provenant d'un revenu de pensions admissible dans un régime enregistré d'épargne-retraite ou un régime enregistré de pensions, demandez le montant de la pension reçu jusqu'à concurrence de 1 000 $. ▶ $

Disability Exemptions—***Exemption pour invalidité***

For persons blind at any time in the year, or confined to a bed or wheelchair for a substantial period each day throughout any 12 month period ending in the year.—*Pour les personnes aveugles à une date quelconque de l'année et pour celles qui doivent garder le lit ou demeurer dans un fauteuil roulant une grande partie de la journée, tous les jours, pendant au moins 12 mois consécutifs se terminant dans l'année.*

For yourself—*Pour vous-même* — Claim—*Demandez* $2,480 ▶ $

You may claim any unused balance of the disability exemption (maximum $2,480) to which your spouse, child, grandchild or supported individual (see item A below) is entitled.—*Vous pouvez demander la fraction inutilisée (maximum 2 480 $) de l'exemption pour invalidité à laquelle ont droit votre conjoint, vos enfants, petits-enfants ou personnes à votre charge (voir note A au bas de la page).* — Unused Balance *Fraction inutilisée* ▶ $

Student Exemptions—***Exemption pour les étudiants***

1. Claim $50 for each month in the year you will be a student in full-time attendance at only the following: a university or college or an institution offering job retraining courses. *Demandez 50 $ pour chaque mois de l'année où vous fréquenterez à plein temps une université, un collège ou un établissement dispensant des cours de rééducation professionnelle.* ▶ $
2. Claim your tuition fees less the total amount of all scholarships, fellowships or bursaries exceeding $500 which you will receive during the calendar year.—*Demandez vos frais de scolarité moins la fraction qui dépasse 500 $ du total de toutes les bourses d'études, de perfectionnement (fellowships) ou d'entretien que vous recevrez au cours de l'année civile.* ▶ $

Total—***Total*** ▶ $ 7430

Deduct: Taxable Family Allowance Payments (To be received in year for children claimed above.)
Soustraire: les allocations familiales imposables *(À recevoir au cours de l'année pour les enfants nommés ci-dessus.)* ▶ $ NIL

Net Claim—(Will not be less than $3,960. Enter this amount on reverse side.)
Demande nette—*(Ne doit pas être inférieure à 3 960$. Inscrire ce montant au verso.)* ▶ $ 7430

A—Claim exemption for a relative (a) wholly dependent on you or you and one or more other persons and (b) domiciled with you, in a dwelling maintained by you or by you and other persons to whom the dependant is related. (Claim **only** if there is agreement that no other person claims for the same dependant or for the same residence.)

B—Claim exemption for a wholly dependent son, daughter, grandchild, niece or nephew under 21, or any age if in full-time attendance at school, university, or infirm. Claim only for a niece or nephew if (a) you have complete custody and control or (b) the child resides in Canada and the mother is also widowed, separated or divorced and receives no alimony or allowance for child maintenance, or the father is mentally or physically infirm. Do not claim here for a child claimed in item 3 or 4.

C—Do not claim over the maximum described in the "Wholly Dependent Children" area. If any other person contributes to the support of the dependant, the aggregate claimed by you and the other person must not exceed the allowable maximum. No claim may be made here for a dependant over age 21 who is not mentally or physically infirm (except a brother or sister in full-time attendance at a school or university) or a dependant claimed in item 3 or 4.

A—Demandez une exemption pour un parent a) entièrement à votre charge ou a vo charge et à celle d'une ou de plusieurs autres personnes; et b) résidant avec vous dans logement tenu par vous ou par vous et d'autres personnes apparentées à la personne charge. (Ne demandez cette exemption que s'il est entendu que personne d'autre ne demandera pour la même personne à charge ou pour le même logement).

B—Demandez une exemption pour un fils, fille, petit-enfant, neveu ou nièce de moins 21 ans entièrement à votre charge; ou de tout âge s'il fréquente l'école à plein temps est infirme. Un neveu ou nièce ne peut être à votre charge que a) si vous en avez la gar et la responsabilité entière; ou b) si l'enfant demeure au Canada et sa mère est veu séparée ou divorcée et ne touche aucune pension alimentaire ou allocation pour l'entret de l'enfant, ou le père est atteint d'infirmité physique ou mentale. Ne faites pas de deman ici pour un enfant nommé en 3 ou 4.

C—Ne demandez pas plus que le maximum indiqué dans la section «Enfants entièreme à charge». Si quelqu'un d'autre aide à subvenir aux besoins de la personne à charge, montant total demandé par vous et l'autre personne ne doit pas dépasser le montant a missible. Ne faites pas de demande ici pour une personne à charge de plus de 21 ans n'est pas atteinte d'infirmité physique ou mentale (sauf un frère ou une soeur qui fréque à plein temps l'école ou l'université), ou pour une personne à charge nommée en 3 ou

- The last line is *Net Claim.* The net claim will never be less than the amount of the basic personal exemption.
- The net claim amount is now entered on the front of the form. Look again at the illustration of the first side of Form TD1.
- Once the net claim amount is entered, the small box labelled *Net Claim Code* can be completed. To find the taxpayer's Net Claim Code, look at the "Table of Net Claim Codes." In Kathy Lewis's case, code 8 is entered, because her total exemptions equal $7 430.
- The Table of Net Claim Codes shows that the higher the net claim, the higher the code. All payroll applications require a Net Claim Code for every employee to calculate accurately the amount of income tax to be withheld from the employee's pay.
- Once the Net Claim Code has been entered, the employee must certify the accuracy of the completed form. This is done by filling in the bottom portion under *Certification.*
- If an employee does not complete a TD1 form, the employer must deduct income taxes as though that person had Net Claim Code 1 (the lowest amount of exemption). This means that a larger deduction will be made for income tax from the employee's pay. Although the front of the form says "This return need not be filed by employees claiming the 'Basic Personal Exemption' only," most employers ask new employees to complete the form in order to collect important payroll data.

The Salaried Payroll Plan

A common payroll plan pays each employee a stated amount at the end of a fixed payroll period. This is his or her *salary.* All salaried payrolls are organized around a variety of fixed payroll periods. Study the following table of common salary pay periods.

Type of Pay Period	*Duration of Pay Period*	*No. of Pay Periods Per Yr. (= No. of Pay Days)*
Weekly	*At the end of one work week,* usually ending Friday.	52
Bi-Weekly	*At the end of two work weeks,* usually every second Friday.	26
Semi-Monthly	*Twice a month,* at the half-point and at the end of each month.	24
Monthly	*Once a month,* e.g. the 28th if this is chosen as the pay day.	12

For Dr. Johnson's dental practice, beginning in March of 19-2, three employees have been hired on a bi-weekly salaried plan as follows:

(1) Kathy Lewis, dental hygienist, at $400 per week; bi-weekly salary, $800.

(2) Lynn Fortier, receptionist/office manager, at $200 per week; bi-weekly salary, $400.

(3) Mildred Casey, dental assistant, at $175 per week; bi-weekly salary, $350.

Once an employee's salary plan is established, the information on the plan and other important employee data are recorded in the top portion of an employee's individual earnings record. This may be in the form of a card or a computer printout sheet. A typical example of a record card is shown below for Kathy Lewis.

Employee's individual earnings record: a payroll record showing an individual employee's payroll details for each pay period.

EMPLOYEE'S INDIVIDUAL EARNINGS RECORD FOR THE YEAR *19—*

Employee's Name: *Lewis, Kathy* SIN: *425-127-511* Tel. No. *679-3734*

Address: *Any Town/City* *Canada* *N6H 4H9*

Date of Birth: *January 14, 19—* Date Employed: *June 15, 19-1* Date of Termination:

Position: *Dental Hygienist* Salary Plan: *Bi-weekly* Rate of Pay: *$400 per week*

Net Claim Code per TD1: *8* UI Insurable Earnings: Minimum: *$170 bi-weekly* Maximum: *$850 bi-weekly* Maximum UI Yearly Premium: *$508.30*

CPP Year's Maximum Earnings *$20 800.00* Year's Basic Exemption *$2 000.00* Maximum Earnings for Contributions *$18 800.00* Maximum Yearly CPP *$338.40*

Pay Period Ending	Time Worked		Rate /Wk.	Earnings			Deductions				Net Pay	Year-to-Date			
	Weeks	OT Days		Regular	OT Excess	Gross Pay	CPP	UI	Inc. Tax	Total		Gross Pay	CPP	UI	Inc. Tax

Salaried payroll plans can be made much more complicated than the above by including overtime pay, bonus payments, and vacation pay. These will be examined in Chapter 14.

Attendance Record

A payroll based on a salary is a fixed sum payable after an employee works a certain length of time. This fixed sum becomes the employee's earned gross pay unless that person loses some pay because of non-excused time off.

Gross pay: amount before payroll deductions.

Small businesses usually allow each salaried person to keep track of his or her own days worked. Towards the end of a payroll period, the payroll accounting clerk checks with each employee to verify the time worked. In many firms, employees lose a day's pay for each day off work without being excused. For example, if a salaried person earns $100 per week for working five days, a day off without permission means a pay loss of the $20 for that day. In disputed cases the owner-manager makes all final decisions on each person's salary before the payroll application is processed.

In firms with several offices and many salaried employees, management may use a formal Payroll and Absentee Report to keep track of salaried attendance. The office manager signs this record before sending it to payroll accounting. An example of a Payroll and Absentee Report used by one large firm is shown below.

PAYROLL AND ABSENTEE REPORT

Department Gregg

Completed by L. Taylor

From Monday (day) 26 (date) April 19-6 (month)

To Friday (day) 30 (date) April 19-6 (month)

NAME	MONDAY absent	TUESDAY absent	WEDNESDAY absent	THURSDAY absent	FRIDAY absent	SATURDAY absent	TOTAL DAYS ABSENT	EXPLANATIONS Reasons for absence, vacations etc.
Scott Aplin	x						1	Virus cold
Ray Butler								
Henry Conway								
John Davis	x	x	x	x	x		5	Vacation

The attendance record checks off only the days absent. Reasons for absence are placed in the *Explanations* column. Any unmarked items would indicate to payroll accounting that the person's regular salary should be processed. Thus, accounting for the time worked for salaried persons is quite simple: payroll accounting assumes the regular salary is to be paid unless management instructs the payroll department to deduct an amount from the regular employee's salary.

Here, in processing Dr. Johnson's salaried bi-weekly payroll, we will assume no days lost by his employees.

Payroll Deductions

Net (or take-home) pay: amount after payroll deductions.

After an employee's gross pay is identified, payroll accounting must collect information on the deductions from that gross pay. This leaves the employee with the net pay, sometimes called the "take-home pay." The three most common payroll deductions — the Canada Pension Plan, unemployment insurance, and income tax — will be studied in the sections which follow. Other common payroll deductions will be examined in Chapter 14.

The Canada Pension Plan In all provinces except Quebec, if you are 18 years old and working as an employee, your employer must deduct from each payroll an amount which is the employee's contribution to the Canada Pension Plan (CPP). Employers in Quebec must deduct a similar amount but the contribution goes into the Quebec Pension Plan.

Canada Pension Plan (CPP): a compulsory employee's pension plan administered by the Canadian government.

Pensionable employment: employment for which CPP contributions are required.

The Canada Pension Plan is not a company pension plan. It is a fund set up by the federal government for all employees who have pensionable employment. Employees have to make contributions as long as they work right up to the age of 69. No deduction is made after an employee reaches 70. However, most employees retire at age 65, because that is when they can receive their first monthly CPP cheque.

Employees aged 65 and over may, if they wish, apply for and receive a CPP retirement pension, even though they continue to work and receive benefits. *Note:* CPP contributions are required up to the month before the month in which the pension becomes payable.

People who choose to work after the age of 65 may prefer to postpone their application for a CPP retirement pension. In that case, contributions are required until the employee applies for and receives the retirement pension, or until the end of the month in which the employee becomes 70, whichever comes first.

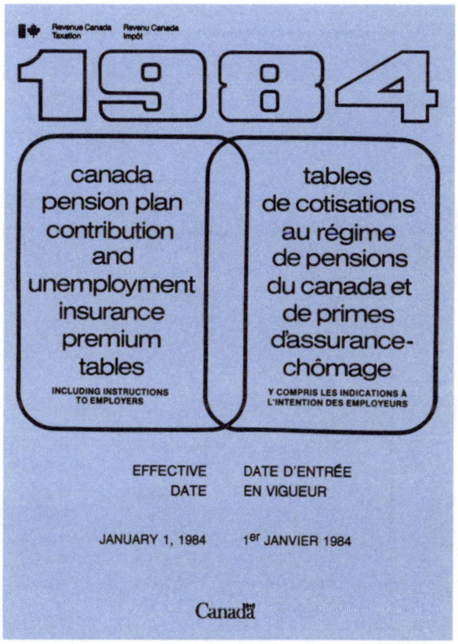

For example, if $5.00 were deducted from the employee's bi-weekly salary, the employer must contribute $5.00. That way, the Canadian government can invest $10 on behalf of the employee to build up a reasonable pension.

The federal government's tax department, called *Revenue Canada — Taxation,* administers the fund. To help employers calculate the correct deduction, the department publishes a booklet each January called *Canada Pension Plan Contribution and Unemployment Insurance Premium Tables.* As the name suggests, this booklet also contains unemployment insurance premium tables.

The contribution tables are set up according to the type of pay period plan adopted by the employer. There is also a special section giving instructions on how to calculate the employee's contribution when the table method cannot be used.

The sections of CPP tables on page 326 illustrate the deductions for Dr. Johnson's three bi-weekly employees.

Calculating the amount of the contribution is easy with the tables. Check the following examples for Dr. Johnson's dental practice.

Kathy Lewis, bi-weekly salary $800: Look up the page in the table corresponding to the pay period. Here, it would be page 34, showing tables for a bi-weekly salary range of $716.65 – $1 485.53. (Only part of the page is shown.) Next, look down the *Remuneration* column for the bracket which includes the employee's pay — in this case, $799.98 – $800.53. The amount in the adjoining column headed *Canada Pension Plan* is the amount of contribution to withhold from the employee's pay.

34

CANADA PENSION PLAN CONTRIBUTIONS — **COTISATIONS AU RÉGIME DE PENSIONS DU CANADA**

BI-WEEKLY PAY PERIOD — *PÉRIODE DE PAIE DE DEUX SEMAINES*

716.65 — 1485.53

Remuneration *Rémunération* From-*de*	To-*à*	C.P.P. *R.P.C.*	Remuneration *Rémunération* From-*de*	To-*à*	C.P.P. *R.P.C.*	Remuneration *Rémunération* From-*de*	To-*à*	C.P.P. *R.P.C.*	Remuneration *Rémunération* From-*de*	To-*à*	C.P.P. *R.P.C.*
716.65 -	717.19	11.52	756.65 -	757.19	12.24	796.65 -	797.19	12.96	1125.54 -	1130.53	18.92
717.20 -	717.75	11.53	757.20 -	757.75	12.25	797.20 -	797.75	12.97	1130.54 -	1135.53	19.01
717.76 -	718.30	11.54	757.76 -	758.30	12.26	797.76 -	798.30	12.98	1135.54 -	1140.53	19.10
718.31 -	718.86	11.55	758.31 -	758.86	12.27	798.31 -	798.86	12.99	1140.54 -	1145.53	19.19
718.87 -	719.41	11.56	758.87 -	759.41	12.28	798.87 -	799.41	13.00	1145.54 -	1150.53	19.28
719.42 -	719.97	11.57	759.42 -	759.97	12.29	799.42 -	799.97	13.01	1150.54 -	1155.53	19.37
719.98 -	720.53	11.58	759.98 -	760.53	12.30	799.98 -	800.53	13.02	1155.54 -	1160.53	19.46
720.54 -	721.08	11.59	760.54 -	761.08	12.31	800.54 -	805.53	13.07	1160.54 -	1165.53	19.55
721.09 -	721.64	11.60	761.09 -	761.64	12.32	805.54 -	810.53	13.16	1165.54 -	1170.53	19.64
721.65 -	722.19	11.61	761.65 -	762.19	12.33	810.54 -	815.53	13.25	1170.54 -	1175.53	19.73
722.20 -	722.75	11.62	762.20 -	762.75	12.34	815.54 -	820.53	13.34	1175.54 -	1180.53	19.82
722.76 -	723.30	11.63	762.76 -	763.30	12.35	820.54 -	825.53	13.43	1180.54 -	1185.53	19.91
723.31 -	723.86	11.64	763.31 -	763.86	12.36	825.54 -	830.53	13.52	1185.54 -	1190.53	20.00
723.87 -	724.41	11.65	763.87 -	764.41	12.37	830.54 -	835.53	13.61	1190.54 -	1195.53	20.09
724.42 -	724.97	11.66	764.42 -	764.97	12.38	835.54 -	840.53	13.70	1195.54 -	1200.53	20.18
724.98 -	725.53	11.67	764.98 -	765.53	12.39	840.54 -	845.53	13.79	1200.54 -	1205.53	20.27
725.54 -	726.08	11.68	765.54 -	766.08	12.40	845.54 -	850.53	13.88	1205.54 -	1210.53	20.36
726.09 -	726.64	11.69	766.09 -	766.64	12.41	850.54 -	855.53	13.97	1210.54 -	1215.53	20.45
726.65 -	727.19	11.70	766.65 -	767.19	12.42	855.54 -	860.53	14.06	1215.54 -	1220.53	20.54
727.20 -	727.75	11.71	767.20 -	767.75	12.43	860.54 -	865.53	14.15	1220.54 -	1225.53	20.63
727.76 -	728.30	11.72	767.76 -	768.30	12.44	865.54 -	870.53	14.24	1225.54 -	1230.53	20.72
728.31 -	728.86	11.73	768.31 -	768.86	12.45	870.54 -	875.53	14.33	1230.54 -	1235.53	20.81
728.87 -	729.41	11.74	768.87 -	769.41	12.46	875.54 -	880.53	14.42	1235.54 -	1240.53	20.90
729.42 -	729.97	11.75	769.42 -	769.97	12.47	880.54 -	885.53	14.51	1240.54 -	1245.53	20.99
729.98 -	730.53	11.76	769.98 -	770.53	12.48	885.54 -	890.53	14.60	1245.54 -	1250.53	21.08
730.54 -	731.08	11.77	770.54 -	771.08	12.49	890.54 -	895.53	14.69	1250.54 -	1255.53	21.17
731.09 -	731.64	11.78	771.09 -	771.64	12.50	895.54 -	900.53	14.78	1255.54 -	1260.53	21.26

Calculation of CPP remittance for Kathy Lewis ($800 earnings):

Employee's contribution	**$13.02**
Employer's contribution	**13.02**
Total	**$26.04**

Here, it is $13.02. To this amount, add an *equal* amount as the employer's contribution. The amount to remit to Revenue Canada — Taxation will be $26.04.

Lynn Fortier, bi-weekly salary $400: See page 32. Look down the *Remuneration* column to where the salary range is $399.98–$400.53. The amount of CPP for this range is $5.82. Add an equal amount for the employer's contribution. The amount to remit to Revenue Canada — Taxation will be $11.64.

Remuneration *Rémunération* From-*de*	To-*à*	C.P.P. *R.P.C.*
396.65 -	397.19	5.76
397.20 -	397.75	5.77
397.76 -	398.30	5.78
398.31 -	398.86	5.79
398.87 -	399.41	5.80
399.42 -	399.97	5.81
399.98 -	400.53	5.82
400.54 -	401.08	5.83
401.09 -	401.64	5.84

Mildred Casey, bi-weekly salary $350: This salary would be found on page 31. See the illustration in the margin. The *Remuneration* column shows the range $349.98 – $350.53 with $4.92 as the CPP amount for the employee's contribution. Add the employer's contribution and the total to remit to Revenue Canada — Taxation will be $9.84.

346.65 -	347.19	4.86
347.20 -	347.75	4.87
347.76 -	348.30	4.88
348.31 -	348.86	4.89
348.87 -	349.41	4.90
349.42 -	349.97	4.91
349.98 -	350.53	4.92
350.54 -	351.08	4.93
351.09 -	351.64	4.94

These deductions are made for each pay period until a certain limit is reached. This maximum amount of employee contribution per year varies with each calendar year; it is always shown at the beginning of the booklet. As you see below, in 1984 the booklet showed the maximum to be $338.40.

The following are in effect for 1984 — Les éléments suivants sont en vigueur en 1984

CANADA PENSION PLAN		**RÉGIME DE PENSIONS DU CANADA**
—Year's maximum pensionable earnings —*Maximum des gains annuels ouvrant droit à pension*		$20,800.00
—Year's basic exemption —*Exemption de base de l'année*		2,000.00
—Maximum earnings on which contributions are based —*maximum des gains sur lequel se fonde le calcul des cotisations*		18,800.00
—Maximum Employee Contribution —*Cotisation maximale de l'employé*	*1.8% of/de $18,800.00*	338.40
—Maximum Employer Contribution —*Cotisation maximale de l'employeur*	*1.8% of/de $18,800.00*	338.40

The above table also shows how the maximum contribution per employee (and, of course, the matching employer's amount) is arrived at. It points out that for 1984, the maximum amount of pensionable earnings was $20 800.00, and that no pension contribution is made unless you made $2 000.00 or more. This latter amount (the year's basic exemption) is subtracted from the year's maximum pensionable earnings to arrive at the maximum earnings on which contributions are based. In 1984, the figure was $18 800.00. A percentage is taken of that maximum to arrive at the maximum employee contribution. In 1984, the percentage was 1.8% of $18 800, or $338.40.

This data will always be provided by the tax department. What you yourself must do is to set up a payroll record so that the employee's contribution does not go *beyond* the year's maximum. For example, the bi-weekly pay system will have 26 pay days. In the case of Kathy Lewis, a deduction of $13.02 is made for each pay period. If deductions of $13.02 were made for 26 pay periods, this totals $338.52 — above the year's maximum of $338.40.

To make sure that only the year's maximum is deducted, payroll accounting usually designs the individual employee's record card (or computer printout) to show the maximum employee's pension contribution for the current year. In some systems, the employee's earnings record also contains a special column to report the accumulation of CPP contributions. This column is normally called *CPP to Date*. When this year-to-date figure gets close to the maximum, the remaining amount is deducted from that pay period to reach the maximum. Then no further deductions are made for the rest of the pay periods. An employee's earnings record card is illustrated on page 323.

Perhaps some employees will not contribute to the year's maximum, because their salary does not reach the maximum level of pensionable earnings. For example, Mildred Casey makes $350 every two weeks for 26 weeks. Her pay period's CPP equals only $4.92. For 26 weeks, that totals only $127.92, which is well below the maximum of $338.40. To reach the maximum, the employee must earn the maximum earnings as quoted by Revenue Canada — Taxation each year.

By law, the employer must keep records and books of account for CPP contributions. These must include enough information to determine the correct contributions to deduct from each employee's pay. This means payroll accounting must keep records of each employee's total earnings, contributory earnings if different from total earnings, and correct CPP contributions for the year. The individual employee's earnings record thus becomes an important document in every payroll application. This important payroll record must be kept for six years unless the tax department grants permission to destroy it earlier.

Legal time limit for keeping payroll records: six years.

Unemployment Insurance Most Canadian workers are required to contribute premiums to unemployment insurance. This entitles them to collect UI benefits when they're out of work.

UI: unemployment insurance.

There are some exceptions. Workers reaching their 65th birthday do not pay for unemployment insurance. Also, some part-time and a few classes of other full-time workers do not pay. Nor do those who are self-employed pay. Of course, if you do not contribute, you cannot collect UI benefits.

UI premiums: the required contributions to unemployment insurance.

UI premiums are not like deposits in a bank account where you put in and take out money whenever you wish. It is more like fire insurance; you pay a premium for protection against a fire in your home or business. If you do have a fire, you collect money to replace the items lost. If you do not have a fire, you do not collect anything. Your premiums help pay for the person who does have a fire and qualifies to receive some money. Insurance involves sharing the risk. It's the same with UI. If you qualify, you can collect. If you don't, you can't.

Insurable earnings: the amount of earnings upon which UI premiums are calculated.

Every year, the minimum and maximum limits of insurable earnings are set by the Canada Employment and Immigration Commission. These insurable earnings are the amounts upon which premiums are calculated.

In 1984, the minimum amount of insurable earnings was $85.00 per week or $170 on a bi-weekly pay system. This means that any employee who worked one week and earned at least $85 must have an amount (called the premium) deducted from his or her pay for UI. An employee who did not earn $85 per week but worked at least 15 hours in that week must also contribute to UI. The first rule in calculating an employee's deduction for UI is to find out that person's minimum amount of insurable earnings. In 1984, any employee who worked at least 15 hours a week or who made at least $85 per week was required to pay a premium for UI.

In 1984, the maximum insurable earnings for those working on a weekly basis was $425. Based on that amount, the maximum premium was $9.78. On a bi-weekly basis, maximum insurable earnings were $850, with the maximum premium set at $19.55. The booklet of tables also gives maximum insurable earnings and the related maximum premiums for semi-monthly, monthly, and other common pay periods in a year.

About 95% of Canadian workers must have payroll deductions for UI premiums. Each year, these premiums are based on insurable earnings. Payroll clerks must keep records of individual earnings and time records for each employee. They should make no deductions until the employee either earns $85 in any week (or 20% of the maximum weekly insurable earnings), or is employed 15 hours or more.

How much does an employee pay for UI? At the time of writing, the premium for employees in insurable employment was calculated at a rate of 2.3% of insurable earnings. Thus, your premium would be $2.30 for every $100 of insurable earnings.

By law, the employer is also required to pay an employer's

premium on behalf of each employee. It is set at a fixed rate of 1.4 times the employee's premium (140% of the employee's premium). For example, if the required employee's premium for a month totalled $90.72, the employer's premium would be 1.4 × $90.72 = $127.01 (140% of $90.72). All this means is that the employer is forced by law to contribute *more* than a dollar for each dollar paid by the employee.

Normally, payroll clerks use the tables in the booklet to find the amount of UI premiums to deduct for each employee's salary, wage, or other remuneration. Let's see how the UI tables work for Dr. Johnson's three employees.

- Kathy Lewis earned a bi-weekly salary of $800. Look up the bi-weekly period tables to find the salary range which covers $800. In 1984, this range is on page 79. Here's what part of that page looks like.

79

UNEMPLOYMENT INSURANCE PREMIUMS **PRIMES D'ASSURANCE-CHÔMAGE**

BI-WEEKLY PAY PERIOD — *PÉRIODE DE PAIE DE DEUX SEMAINES*

702.39 — 827.60

Remuneration *Rémunération* From-*de*	To-*à*	U.I. Premium *Prime d'a.-c.*	Remuneration *Rémunération* From-*de*	To-*à*	U.I. Premium *Prime d'a.-c.*	Remuneration *Rémunération* From-*de*	To-*à*	U.I. Premium *Prime d'a.-c.*	Remuneration *Rémunération* From-*de*	To-*à*	U.I. Premium *Prime d'a.-c.*
702.39 -	702.82	16.16	733.70 -	734.12	16.88	765.00 -	765.43	17.60	796.31 -	796.73	18.32
702.83 -	703.25	16.17	734.13 -	734.56	16.89	765.44 -	765.86	17.61	796.74 -	797.17	18.33
703.26 -	703.69	16.18	734.57 -	734.99	16.90	765.87 -	766.30	17.62	797.18 -	797.60	18.34
703.70 -	704.12	16.19	735.00 -	735.43	16.91	766.31 -	766.73	17.63	797.61 -	798.04	18.35
704.13 -	704.56	16.20	735.44 -	735.86	16.92	766.74 -	767.17	17.64	798.05 -	798.47	18.36
704.57 -	704.99	16.21	735.87 -	736.30	16.93	767.18 -	767.60	17.65	798.48 -	798.91	18.37
705.00 -	705.43	16.22	736.31 -	736.73	16.94	767.61 -	768.04	17.66	798.92 -	799.34	18.38
705.44 -	705.86	16.23	736.74 -	737.17	16.95	768.05 -	768.47	17.67	799.35 -	799.78	18.39
705.87 -	706.30	16.24	737.18 -	737.60	16.96	768.48 -	768.91	17.68	799.79 -	800.21	18.40
706.31 -	706.73	16.25	737.61 -	738.04	16.97	768.92 -	769.34	17.69	800.22 -	800.64	18.41
706.74 -	707.17	16.26	738.05 -	738.47	16.98	769.35 -	769.78	17.70	800.65 -	801.08	18.42
707.18 -	707.60	16.27	738.48 -	738.91	16.99	769.79 -	770.21	17.71	801.09 -	801.51	18.43
707.61 -	708.04	16.28	738.92 -	739.34	17.00	770.22 -	770.64	17.72	801.52 -	801.95	18.44
708.05 -	708.47	16.29	739.35 -	739.78	17.01	770.65 -	771.08	17.73	801.96 -	802.38	18.45
708.48 -	708.91	16.30	739.79 -	740.21	17.02	771.09 -	771.51	17.74	802.39 -	802.82	18.46
708.92 -	709.34	16.31	740.22 -	740.64	17.03	771.52 -	771.95	17.75	802.83 -	803.25	18.47
709.35 -	709.78	16.32	740.65 -	741.08	17.04	771.96 -	772.38	17.76	803.26 -	803.69	18.48
709.79 -	710.21	16.33	741.09 -	741.51	17.05	772.39 -	772.82	17.77	803.70 -	804.12	18.49
710.22 -	710.64	16.34	741.52 -	741.95	17.06	772.83 -	773.25	17.78	804.13 -	804.56	18.50
710.65 -	711.08	16.35	741.96 -	742.38	17.07	773.26 -	773.69	17.79	804.57 -	804.99	18.51
711.09 -	711.51	16.36	742.39 -	742.82	17.08	773.70 -	774.12	17.80	805.00 -	805.43	18.52
711.52 -	711.95	16.37	742.83 -	743.25	17.09	774.13 -	774.56	17.81	805.44 -	805.86	18.53
711.96 -	712.38	16.38	743.26 -	743.69	17.10	774.57 -	774.99	17.82	805.87 -	806.30	18.54
712.39 -	712.82	16.39	743.70 -	744.12	17.11	775.00 -	775.43	17.83	806.31 -	806.73	18.55
712.83 -	713.25	16.40	744.13 -	744.56	17.12	775.44 -	775.86	17.84	806.74 -	807.17	18.56
713.26 -	713.69	16.41	744.57 -	744.99	17.13	775.87 -	776.30	17.85	807.18 -	807.60	18.57
713.70 -	714.12	16.42	745.00 -	745.43	17.14	776.31 -	776.73	17.86	807.61 -	808.04	18.58

Since Kathy Lewis earned less than the maximum bi-weekly salary covered by insurable earnings, her UI premium must be $18.40, as the table shows. To calculate the employer's share, add an amount 1.4 times that. The total amount to remit to Revenue Canada — Taxation on behalf of Kathy Lewis will be $18.40 + $25.76 = $44.16.

Calculation of UI premium for Kathy Lewis ($800, bi-weekly salary period):

Employee's UI	**$18.40**
Employer's share:	
1.4 x $18.40	**25.76**
Total	**$44.16**

- Lynn Fortier earned a bi-weekly salary of $400. The UI premium table covering $400 in 1984 is found on page 76. As the next table shows, Lynn's UI premium would be $9.20. The employer must contribute 1.4 times $9.20, or $12.88. The total premium on behalf of Lynn Fortier is $9.20 + $12.88 = $22.08.
- Mildred Casey earned a bi-weekly salary of $350. In 1984, page 76 of the UI premium tables also covered this amount, as shown in the partial page on the right. According to this table,

Remuneration *Rémunération* From-*de*	To-*à*	U.I. Premium *Prime d'a.-c.*
397.18 -	397.60	9.14
397.61 -	398.04	9.15
398.05 -	398.47	9.16
398.48 -	398.91	9.17
398.92 -	399.34	9.18
399.35 -	399.78	9.19
399.79 -	400.21	9.20
400.22 -	400.64	9.21
400.65 -	401.08	9.22

Remuneration *Rémunération* From-*de*	To-*à*	U.I. Premium *Prime d'a.-c.*
346.31 -	346.73	7.97
346.74 -	347.17	7.98
347.18 -	347.60	7.99
347.61 -	348.04	8.00
348.05 -	348.47	8.01
348.48 -	348.91	8.02
348.92 -	349.34	8.03
349.35 -	349.78	8.04
349.79 -	350.21	8.05

Mildred's UI premium is \$8.05. The employer's required premium is 1.4 times \$8.05, or \$11.27. The total amount remitted to Revenue Canada — Taxation would be \$8.05 + \$11.27 = \$19.32.

Record of Employment: a key document proving work in insurable employment.

Under the Unemployment Insurance Act, a Record of Employment must be given to you by your employer within five days after an interruption of earnings. This form is the piece of paper that gets the unemployed person into the UI system and starts his or her payments. As a guide to filling it out, the Employment and Immigration Commission gives details in a booklet called *How to Complete the Record of Employment.* The booklet gives information for each type of pay period. One example given in the booklet covering bi-weekly pay periods is shown opposite.

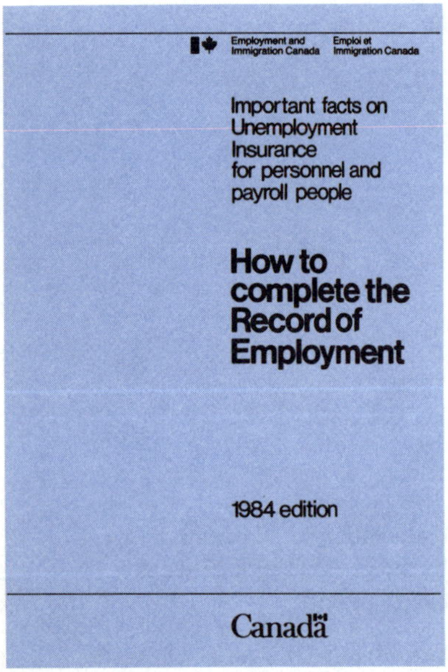

The essential information in this important record are: the employee's SIN, the employee's first day of work, the employee's last day of work, the last day for which the employer paid UI premiums for this employee, the number of weeks of insurable employment for a bi-weekly pay period, the reason for issuing the Record of Employment, and a list of insurable earnings by pay period.

Finally, by law, the employer must keep records and books of account for all UI premiums. These records must be kept for *six years,* unless the tax department grants permission to destroy them earlier.

Income tax deductions at source: income tax taken off employee's pay.

Income Tax Since 1917, all Canadians have had to pay income tax on their earnings. Employers must deduct income tax from each employee's salary, wages and commissions, bonuses, vacation pay, and any other type of earnings. Such deductions are called income tax deductions at source.

Both the federal and the provincial government enforce income tax acts which require income taxes to be deducted.

To simplify collection and remittances, all the provinces except Quebec have agreed to allow the Canadian government to collect from employers both the federal and the provincial income tax. In Quebec, separate collections and remittances are required: one to the Receiver General for Canada for federal tax

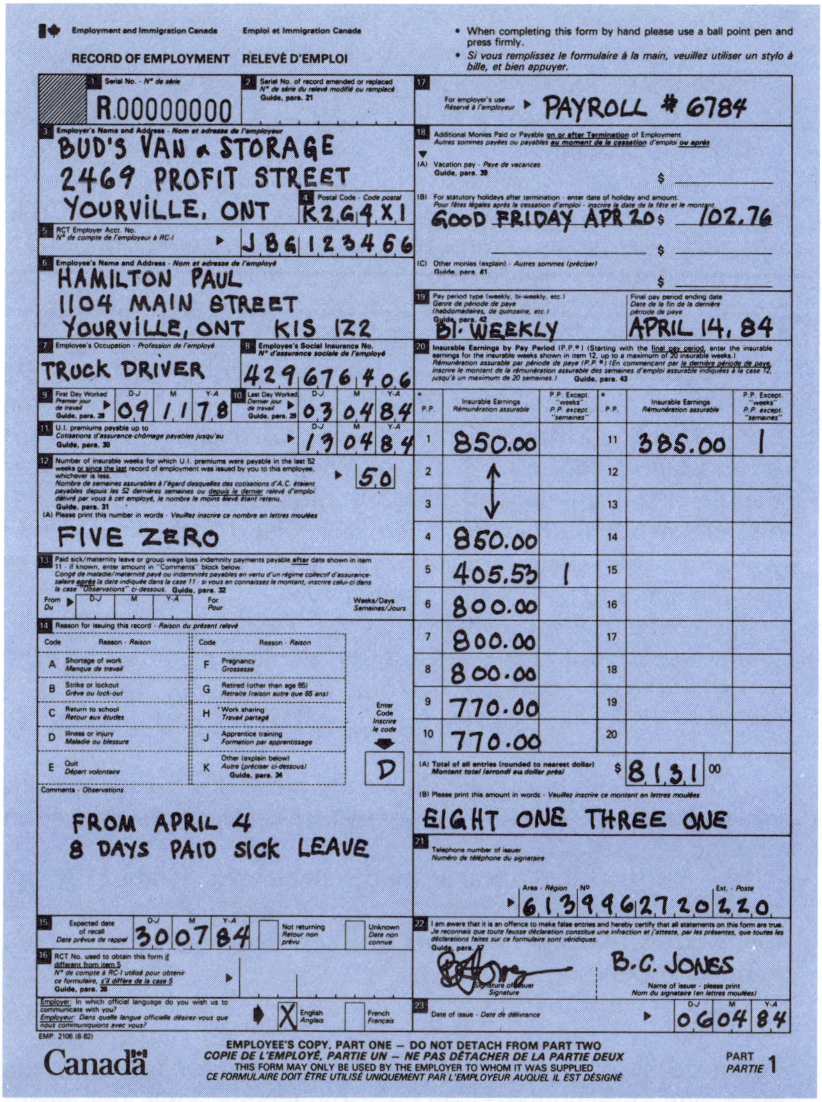

Employment and Immigration Canada — Emploi et Immigration Canada

RECORD OF EMPLOYMENT — RELEVÉ D'EMPLOI

- When completing this form by hand please use a ball point pen and press firmly.
- *Si vous remplissez le formulaire à la main, veuillez utiliser un stylo à bille, et bien appuyer.*

1 Serial No. - *N° de série*: R.00000000

2 Serial No. of record amended or replaced - *N° de série du relevé modifié ou remplacé* - Guide, para. 21

17 For employer's use - *Réservé à l'employeur* ▶ PAYROLL # 6784

3 Employer's Name and Address - *Nom et adresse de l'employeur*: BUD'S VAN & STORAGE, 2469 PROFIT STREET, YOURVILLE, ONT

4 Postal Code - *Code postal*: K2G 4X1

5 RCT Employer Acct. No. - *N° de compte de l'employeur à RC-I* ▶ JBG123466

6 Employee's Name and Address - *Nom et adresse de l'employé*: HAMILTON PAUL, 1104 MAIN STREET, YOURVILLE, ONT K1S 1Z2

7 Employee's Occupation - *Profession de l'employé*: TRUCK DRIVER

8 Employee's Social Insurance No. - *N° d'assurance sociale de l'employé*: 429 676 406

9 First Day Worked - *Premier jour de travail* - Guide, para. 28 ▶ D-J 09 M 11 Y-A 78

10 Last Day Worked - *Dernier jour de travail* - Guide, para. 28 ▶ D-J 03 M 04 Y-A 84

11 U.I. premiums payable up to - *Cotisations d'assurance-chômage payables jusqu'au* - Guide, para. 30 ▶ D-J 13 M 04 Y-A 84

12 Number of insurable weeks for which U.I. premiums were payable in the last 52 weeks or since the last record of employment was issued by you to this employee, whichever is less. *Nombre de semaines assurables à l'égard desquelles des cotisations d'A.C. étaient payables depuis les 52 dernières semaines ou depuis le dernier relevé d'emploi délivré par vous à cet employé, le nombre le moins élevé étant retenu.* Guide, para. 31 ▶ 50

(A) Please print this number in words - *Veuillez inscrire ce nombre en lettres moulées*: FIVE ZERO

13 Paid sick/maternity leave or group wage loss indemnity payments payable **after** date shown in item 11 - if known, enter amount in "Comments" block below. *Congé de maladie/maternité payé ou indemnités payables en vertu d'un régime collectif d'assurance-salaire après la date indiquée dans la case 11 - si vous en connaissez le montant, inscrire celui-ci dans la case "Observations" ci-dessous.* Guide, para. 32

From - *Du* ▶ D-J M Y-A — For - *Pour* — Weeks/Days - *Semaines/Jours*

14 Reason for issuing this record - *Raison du présent relevé*

Code	Reason - *Raison*	Code	Reason - *Raison*
A	Shortage of work - *Manque de travail*	F	Pregnancy - *Grossesse*
B	Strike or lockout - *Grève ou lock-out*	G	Retired (other than age 65) - *Retraite (raison autre que 65 ans)*
C	Return to school - *Retour aux études*	H	Work sharing - *Travail partagé*
D	Illness or injury - *Maladie ou blessure*	J	Apprentice training - *Formation par apprentissage*
E	Quit - *Départ volontaire*	K	Other (explain below) - *Autre (préciser ci-dessous)* Guide, para. 34

Enter Code - *Inscrire le code*: D

Comments - *Observations*: FROM APRIL 4 — 8 DAYS PAID SICK LEAVE

18 Additional Monies Paid or Payable on or after Termination of Employment - *Autres sommes payées ou payables au moment de la cessation d'emploi ou après*

(A) Vacation pay - *Paye de vacances* - Guide, para. 39 $ ______

(B) For statutory holidays after termination - enter date of holiday and amount. *Pour fêtes légales après la cessation d'emploi - inscrire la date de la fête et le montant.* GOOD FRIDAY APR 20 $ 102.76

(C) Other monies (explain) - *Autres sommes (préciser)* - Guide, para. 41 $ ______

19 Pay period type (weekly, bi-weekly, etc.) - *Genre de période de paye (hebdomadaires, de quinzaine, etc.)* - Guide, para. 42: BI-WEEKLY

Final pay period ending date - *Date de la fin de la dernière période de paye*: APRIL 14, 84

20 Insurable Earnings by Pay Period (P.P.*) (Starting with the final pay period, enter the insurable earnings for the insurable weeks shown in item 12, up to a maximum of 20 insurable weeks.) *Rémunération assurable par période de paye (P.P.*) (En commençant par la dernière période de paye, inscrire le montant de la rémunération assurable des semaines d'emploi assurable indiquées à la case 12, jusqu'à un maximum de 20 semaines.)* Guide, para. 43

* P.P.	Insurable Earnings - *Rémunération assurable*	P.P. Except. "weeks" - *P.P. except. "semaines"*	* P.P.	Insurable Earnings - *Rémunération assurable*	P.P. Except. "weeks" - *P.P. except. "semaines"*
1	850.00		11	385.00	1
2	↑		12		
3	↓		13		
4	850.00		14		
5	405.53	1	15		
6	800.00		16		
7	800.00		17		
8	800.00		18		
9	770.00		19		
10	770.00		20		

(A) Total of all entries (rounded to nearest dollar) - *Montant total (arrondi au dollar près)* $ 8131 00

(B) Please print this amount in words - *Veuillez inscrire ce montant en lettres moulées*: EIGHT ONE THREE ONE

21 Telephone number of issuer - *Numéro de téléphone du signataire* ▶ Area - *Région* 613 N° 946 2720 Ext. - *Poste* 220

22 I am aware that it is an offence to make false entries and hereby certify that all statements on this form are true. *Je reconnais que toute fausse déclaration constitue une infraction et j'atteste, par les présentes, que toutes les déclarations faites sur ce formulaire sont véridiques.* Guide, para. 47

Signature of issuer - *Signature* — Name of issuer - please print - *Nom du signataire (en lettres moulées)*: B.C. JONES

15 Expected date of recall - *Date prévue de rappel*: D-J 30 M 07 Y-A 84 — Not returning - *Retour non prévu* — Unknown - *Date non connue*

16 RCT No. used to obtain this form if different from item 5 - *N° de compte à RC-I utilisé pour obtenir ce formulaire, s'il diffère de la case 5* - Guide, para. 36 ▶

Employer: In which official language do you wish us to communicate with you? *Employeur: Dans quelle langue officielle désirez-vous que nous communiquions avec vous?* ▶ [X] English - *Anglais* [ ] French - *Français*

23 Date of issue - *Date de délivrance* ▶ D-J 06 M 04 Y-A 84

EMP. 2106 (8-82)

Canada

EMPLOYEE'S COPY, PART ONE — DO NOT DETACH FROM PART TWO
COPIE DE L'EMPLOYÉ, PARTIE UN — NE PAS DÉTACHER DE LA PARTIE DEUX
THIS FORM MAY ONLY BE USED BY THE EMPLOYER TO WHOM IT WAS SUPPLIED
CE FORMULAIRE DOIT ÊTRE UTILISÉ UNIQUEMENT PAR L'EMPLOYEUR AUQUEL IL EST DÉSIGNÉ

PART - *PARTIE* 1

and one to the Treasurer of Quebec for provincial tax.

Both levels of government set their own rates of income tax. For that reason, Revenue Canada — Taxation produces each year a booklet of tax tables for each province. Separate booklets are produced for people who report for work to an employer in Ontario, in Nova Scotia, and in every other province. Covers of two such booklets are shown on the next page.

Except in Quebec, the booklet of tables combines the income taxes to be collected for the federal government and for the province. Payroll clerks must be sure to use the correct booklet of tax tables; otherwise, incorrect "deductions at source" will be made.

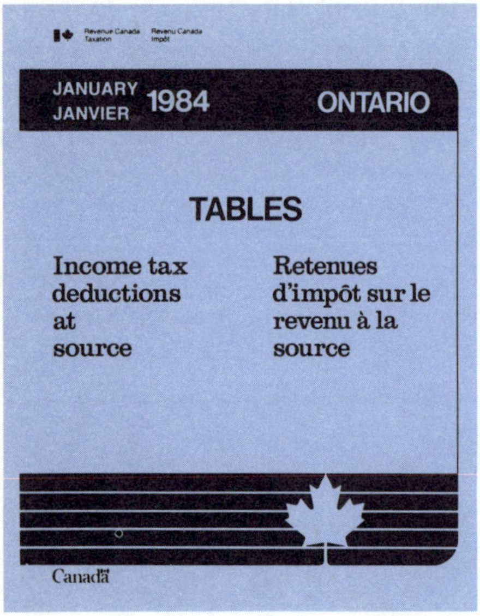

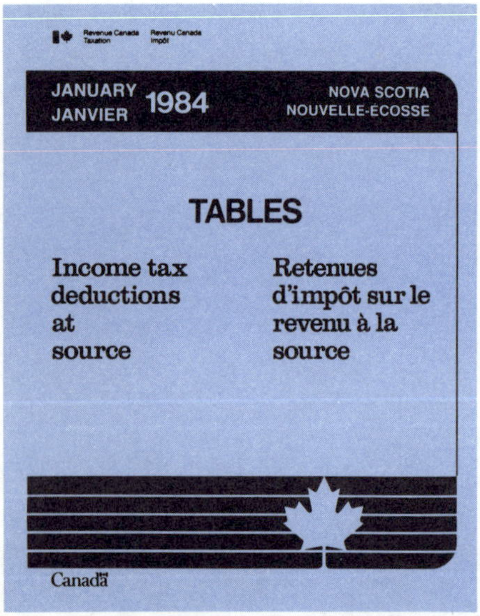

If an employer uses a computer to process the payroll, Revenue Canada — Taxation allows him or her to use a specific formula adaptable for use on the equipment rather than the tax tables. However, most employers across Canada still use the booklet of tax tables.

To find out how much a payroll clerk should deduct from each employee for income tax, check the employee's Net Claim Code on Form TD1. If the employee has not completed Form TD1, Revenue Canada — Taxation requires that the employee be treated as having Net Claim Code 1 (the code for deducting the highest amount from the employee's pay).

No deductions are made if the employee certifies on Form TD1 that the total remuneration received and receivable during the calendar year will not exceed the exemption claimed (this means a Net Claim Code of 0). Thus, in 1984, if an employee certifies that he or she will not make $3 960 (the amount of the basic exemption in 1984), then the table of Net Claim Codes (see below) will show a Net Claim Code of 0. This employee will not have to pay any income tax for that calendar year.

But most employees will make more than the basic exemption. Therefore, payroll clerks will use the booklet of tables and the Net Claim Code as shown by Form TD1. Naturally, the booklet will have separate tables for the type of pay period used by the employer.

Table 3 on the next page shows the bi-weekly tax deductions which would be used if Dr. Johnson's practice were located in Ontario.

Let's use this table to calculate the amount of income tax to be deducted from Kathy Lewis's pay. (The same procedure is followed in the other provinces, except that each has its own deduction tables.)

Kathy Lewis earned a bi-weekly salary of $800. But, before using the tax table, remember to deduct the amounts previously deducted from the employee's contribution to CPP and the employee's premium to UI. In the case of Kathy Lewis, this means making a calculation as shown below.

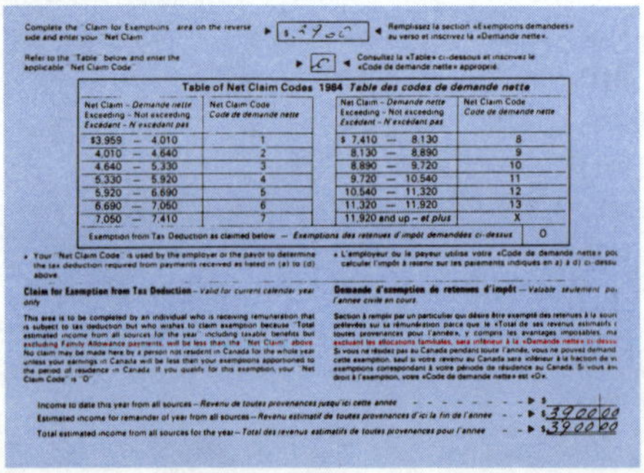

Complete the "Claim for Exemptions" area on the reverse side and enter your "Net Claim" ▶ $ 7,900 ◀ Remplissez la section «Exemptions demandees» au verso et inscrivez la «Demande nette».

Refer to the "Table" below and enter the applicable "Net Claim Code" ▶ 8 ◀ Consultez la «Table» ci-dessous et inscrivez le «Code de demande nette» approprié.

Table of Net Claim Codes 1984 ***Table des codes de demande nette***

Net Claim – *Demande nette* Exceeding – Not exceeding *Excédant – N'excédant pas*	Net Claim Code *Code de demande nette*	Net Claim – *Demande nette* Exceeding – Not exceeding *Excédant – N'excédant pas*	Net Claim Code *Code de demande nette*
$3,959 — 4,010	1	$ 7,410 — 8,130	8
4,010 — 4,640	2	8,130 — 8,890	9
4,640 — 5,330	3	8,890 — 9,720	10
5,330 — 5,920	4	9,720 — 10,540	11
5,920 — 6,690	5	10,540 — 11,320	12
6,690 — 7,050	6	11,320 — 11,920	13
7,050 — 7,410	7	11,920 and up – *et plus*	X
Exemption from Tax Deduction as claimed below — *Exemptions des retenues d'impôt demandées ci-dessus*			0

• Your "Net Claim Code" is used by the employer or the payor to determine the tax deduction required from payments received as listed in (a) to (d) above.

• L'employeur ou le payeur utilise votre «Code de demande nette» pour calculer l'impôt à retenir sur les paiements indiqués en a) à d) ci-dessus.

Claim for Exemption from Tax Deduction – *Valid for current calendar year only*

This area is to be completed by an individual who is receiving remuneration that is subject to tax deduction but who wishes to claim exemption because "Total estimated income from all sources for the year" including taxable benefits but excluding Family Allowance payments, will be less than the "Net Claim" above. No claim may be made here by a person not resident in Canada for the whole year unless your earnings in Canada will be less than your exemptions apportioned to the period of residence in Canada. If you qualify for this exemption, your "Net Claim Code" is "0".

Demande d'exemption de retenues d'impôt – *Valable seulement pour l'année civile en cours*

Section à remplir par un particulier qui désire être exempté des retenues à la source prélevées sur sa rémunération parce que le «Total de ses revenus estimatifs de toutes provenances pour l'année», y compris les avantages imposables, mais excluant les allocations familiales, sera inférieur à la «Demande nette» ci-dessus. Si vous ne résidez pas au Canada pendant toute l'année, vous ne pouvez demander cette exemption, sauf si votre revenu au Canada sera inférieur à la fraction de vos exemptions correspondant à votre période de résidence au Canada. Si vous avez droit à l'exemption, votre «Code de demande nette» est «0».

Income to date this year from all sources – *Revenu de toutes provenances jusqu'ici cette année* ▶ $

Estimated income for remainder of year from all sources – *Revenu estimatif de toutes provenances d'ici la fin de l'année* ▶ $3900 00

Total estimated income from all sources for the year – *Total des revenus estimatifs de toutes provenances pour l'année* ▶ $3900 00

Kathy Lewis
Net Claim Code 8
Bi-Weekly Salary

Gross pay		*$800.00*
Less: CPP	*$13.02*	
UI	*18.40*	*31.42*
Amount subject to taxation		*$768.58*

ONTARIO
BI-WEEKLY TAX DEDUCTIONS
Basis — 26 Pay Periods per Year

TABLE 3

ONTARIO
RETENUES D'IMPÔT DE DEUX SEMAINES
Base — 26 périodes de paie par année

BI-WEEKLY PAY Use appropriate bracket — PAIE DE DEUX SEMAINES Utilisez le palier approprié	IF THE EMPLOYEE'S "NET CLAIM CODE" ON FORM TD1 IS — SI LE «CODE DE RÉCLAMATION NETTE» DE L'EMPLOYÉ SELON LA FORMULE TD1 EST DE													See note on page 23 Voir remarque p. 23
	1	2	3	4	5	6	7	8	9	10	11	12	13	
	DEDUCT FROM EACH PAY — *RETENEZ SUR CHAQUE PAIE*													Column A Colonne A
$ 659.00 - 668.99	116.15	111.95	104.70	97.70	90.20	84.00	80.05	74.10	66.00	57.25	48.65	40.35	33.15	7.20
669.00 - 678.99	119.15	114.95	107.60	100.55	93.05	86.85	82.90	76.95	68.85	60.10	51.40	43.05	35.85	7.20
679.00 - 688.99	122.20	117.95	110.45	103.40	95.95	89.70	85.75	79.85	71.70	62.95	54.10	45.75	38.55	7.20
689.00 - 698.99	125.20	120.95	113.35	106.25	98.80	92.60	88.60	82.70	74.55	65.80	56.80	48.45	41.30	7.20
699.00 - 708.99	128.20	123.95	116.35	109.10	101.65	95.45	91.50	85.55	77.40	68.65	59.60	51.15	44.00	7.20
709.00 - 718.99	131.20	127.00	119.35	111.95	104.50	98.30	94.35	88.40	80.25	71.55	62.45	53.90	46.70	7.20
719.00 - 728.99	134.20	130.00	122.35	114.95	107.35	101.15	97.20	91.25	83.10	74.40	65.30	56.60	49.40	7.20
729.00 - 738.99	137.20	133.00	125.35	117.95	110.20	104.00	100.05	94.10	86.00	77.25	68.20	59.40	52.10	7.30
739.00 - 748.99	140.25	136.00	128.35	120.95	113.10	106.85	102.90	96.95	88.85	80.10	71.05	62.25	54.80	7.45
749.00 - 758.99	143.25	139.00	131.40	123.95	116.10	109.70	105.75	99.85	91.70	82.95	73.90	65.10	57.50	7.60
759.00 - 768.99	146.25	142.00	134.40	127.00	119.10	112.60	108.60	102.70	94.55	85.80	76.75	67.95	60.35	7.60
769.00 - 778.99	149.25	145.05	137.40	130.00	122.10	115.60	111.50	105.55	97.40	88.65	79.60	70.80	63.25	7.60
779.00 - 788.99	152.25	148.05	140.40	133.00	125.15	118.60	114.45	108.40	100.25	91.55	82.45	73.65	66.10	7.60
789.00 - 798.99	155.25	151.05	143.40	136.00	128.15	121.60	117.45	111.25	103.15	94.40	85.30	76.55	68.95	7.60
799.00 - 808.99	158.25	154.05	146.40	139.00	131.15	124.60	120.45	114.20	106.00	97.25	88.20	79.40	71.80	7.60
809.00 - 818.99	161.30	157.05	149.40	142.00	134.15	127.60	123.45	117.20	108.85	100.10	91.05	82.25	74.65	7.60
819.00 - 828.99	164.30	160.05	152.45	145.05	137.15	130.60	126.45	120.20	111.70	102.95	93.90	85.10	77.50	7.60
829.00 - 838.99	167.30	163.05	155.45	148.05	140.15	133.65	129.45	123.20	114.65	105.80	96.75	87.95	80.40	7.60
839.00 - 848.99	170.40	166.10	158.45	151.05	143.20	136.65	132.45	126.25	117.65	108.70	99.60	90.80	83.25	7.60
849.00 - 858.99	173.85	169.10	161.45	154.05	146.20	139.65	135.50	129.25	120.65	111.55	102.45	93.65	86.10	7.60
859.00 - 868.99	177.30	172.45	164.45	157.05	149.20	142.65	138.50	132.25	123.70	114.50	105.30	96.55	88.95	7.60
869.00 - 878.99	180.75	175.90	167.45	160.05	152.20	145.65	141.50	135.25	126.70	117.50	108.20	99.40	91.80	7.60

Why make this calculation in the first place? Revenue Canada — Taxation permits taxpayers to subtract the payroll deductions for both CPP and UI from their earnings so as to pay a lower income tax amount. These amounts are called tax-deductible items.

Tax-deductible items: CPP contributions, UI premiums, and other approved items which can lower the taxpayer's income on which income tax rates are based.

What would happen if payroll clerks did not take the first step to deduct from the employee's gross pay those tax-deductible items? Most employees across Canada would pay too much income tax by the end of December. Then the Canadian government would have to prepare refunds to all those taxpayers affected. And preparing and mailing refunds is very costly.

Kathy Lewis's salary subject to taxation is $768.58. Look down the left-hand column on Table 3 until you come to the correct bracket, $759.00 – $768.99. Follow this line across to the column headed by the employee's Net Claim Code. For Kathy Lewis, this is column 8. The amount of income tax to withhold is $102.70.

The same steps are followed to find the amounts of income tax to deduct for Lynn Fortier and Mildred Casey. First, subtract from their gross pays the amounts deducted for their CPP and UI. The results are the amounts subject to the tax tables, as shown in the margin on page 334.

For Lynn Fortier, the amount subject to income tax is $384.98. Use the correct page of Table 3 to find the page showing the biweekly pay bracket for $384.98. In 1984, this bracket was $381.00 – $384.99, as shown in the table.

If Lynn Fortier's Net Claim Code is 1, the amount of income tax to deduct is $36.85.

Mildred Casey's amount subject to tax deductions is $337.03. The bracket for this amount in 1984 was $337.00 – $340.99. If her

Lynn Fortier
Net Claim Code 1
Bi-Weekly Salary

Gross pay		*$400.00*
Less: CPP	*$ 5.82*	
UI	*9.20*	*15.02*
Amount subject to taxation		*$384.98*

Mildred Casey
Net Claim Code 2
Bi-Weekly Salary

Gross pay		*$350.00*
Less: CPP	*$ 4.92*	
UI	*8.05*	*12.97*
Amount subject to taxation		*$337.03*

ONTARIO
BI-WEEKLY TAX DEDUCTIONS
Basis — 26 Pay Periods per Year
TABLE 3

BI-WEEKLY PAY Use appropriate bracket — PAIE DE DEUX SEMAINES Utilisez le palier approprié		IF THE EMPLOYEE'S "NET CLAIM CODE" ON FORM TD1 IS — SI LE «COD					
		1	2	3	4	5	6
		DEDUCT FROM EACH PAY					
Under-Moins de	253.00	.00					
$ 253.00 -	256.99	1.25					
257.00 -	260.99	4.20					
261.00 -	264.99	6.00					
265.00 -	268.99	6.95					
269.00 -	272.99	7.90	2.70				
273.00 -	276.99	8.95	5.50				
277.00 -	280.99	9.95	6.50				
281.00 -	284.99	11.00	7.45				
285.00 -	288.99	12.00	8.40				
289.00 -	292.99	13.05	9.45				
293.00 -	296.99	14.05	10.45	1.70			
297.00 -	300.99	15.10	11.50	4.65			
301.00 -	304.99	16.10	12.50	6.15			
305.00 -	308.99	17.15	13.55	7.10			
309.00 -	312.99	18.15	14.55	8.05			
313.00 -	316.99	19.15	15.60	9.10			
317.00 -	320.99	20.20	16.60	10.10	1.25		
321.00 -	324.99	21.20	17.65	11.15	4.20		
325.00 -	328.99	22.25	18.65	12.15	6.00		
329.00 -	332.99	23.25	19.65	13.20	6.95		
333.00 -	336.99	24.30	20.70	14.20	7.90		
337.00 -	340.99	25.30	21.70	15.25	8.95		
341.00 -	344.99	26.35	22.75	16.25	9.95		
345.00 -	348.99	27.35	23.75	17.25	11.00	2.60	
349.00 -	352.99	28.40	24.80	18.30	12.00	5.50	
353.00 -	356.99	29.40	25.80	19.30	13.00	6.45	
357.00 -	360.99	30.40	26.85	20.35	14.05	7.40	
361.00 -	364.99	31.45	27.85	21.35	15.05	8.40	
365.00 -	368.99	32.50	28.90	22.40	16.10	9.40	1.35
369.00 -	372.99	33.60	29.90	23.40	17.10	10.45	4.30
373.00 -	376.99	34.70	30.90	24.45	18.15	11.45	6.00
377.00 -	380.99	35.75	31.95	25.45	19.15	12.45	7.00
381.00 -	384.99	36.85	33.05	26.50	20.20	13.50	7.95
385.00 -	388.99	37.95	34.15	27.50	21.20	14.50	8.95
389.00 -	392.99	39.00	35.20	28.50	22.25	15.55	10.00
393.00 -	396.99	40.10	36.30	29.55	23.25	16.55	11.00
397.00 -	400.99	41.20	37.40	30.55	24.25	17.60	12.05
401.00 -	404.99	42.25	38.45	31.60	25.30	18.60	13.05
405.00 -	408.99	43.35	39.55	32.65	26.30	19.65	14.10

Net Claim Code is 2, the amount of income tax to withhold is $21.70, as shown in the tax table.

After making deductions for CPP, UI, and employee's income taxes, the result is the employee's net or take-home pay. The calculation of net pay for Dr. Johnson's three employees may be summarized as follows:

Employee	*Gross Pay*	*Deductions*				*Net Pay*
		CPP	*UI*	*Inc. Tax*	*Total*	
Kathy Lewis	$800.00	$13.02	$18.40	$102.70	$134.12	$665.88
Lynn Fortier	400.00	5.82	9.20	36.85	51.87	348.13
Mildred Casey	350.00	4.92	8.05	21.70	34.67	315.33

TOPIC 1 PROBLEMS

10-1 Dr. F. Greco, D.D.S. has three employees who assist in revenue-making activities in the dental practice, located in British Columbia. The doctor prefers to use a bi-weekly salary pay period plan. At the end of two weeks, the payroll clerk provided the following data: S.R. Anderson, SIN 387-211-811, Net Claim Code 3, bi-weekly salary of $700, CPP contribution of $11.35, UI premium of $16.10, and income tax deduction of $109.15; J.L. Haney, SIN 436-918-200, Net Claim Code of 1, bi-weekly salary of $500, CPP contribution of $7.75, UI premium of $11.50, and income tax deduction of $60.80; W.F. Tse, SIN 679-480-190, Net Claim Code of 2, bi-weekly salary of $400, CPP contribution of $5.95, UI premium of $9.20, and income tax deduction of $33.40.

a What is the gross pay for each employee?
b Calculate and show the net pay for each employee.
c What is the total gross pay for this payroll?
d What is the total net pay for this payroll?

Key Check Figure
Total Net Pay =
$1 334.80

10-2 Using a table with headings as shown below, record the following employees' names and their bi-weekly earnings in columns 1 and 2 respectively: Anne Attridge, $765; Rose Geimer, $800; James Jessup, $770; Mark Ryan, $1 200.

	Employee (1)	*Bi-Weekly Gross Earnings (2)*	*Employee Contribution to CPP (3)*	*Employer Contribution to CPP (4)*	*Combined Contribution to CPP (5)*
EXAMPLE:	Anne Attridge	$765			

Now calculate and record the CPP contribution for each employee (column 3) and for the employer (column 4), and the total CPP contribution to be remitted (column 5). Assume that the employees work in your province. You may use the CPP contribution tables shown in this chapter. Or, you may use the latest figures supplied by Revenue Canada — Taxation.

Complete the table by totalling all money columns.

Key Check Figure
Total Employee Contribution =
$58.07

10-3 Using the information in Problem 10-2 above and a similar table, calculate the UI premium for each employee, the employer's premium for each employee, and the total premium to be remitted to Revenue Canada — Taxation. Use the UI tables given in this chapter and on the next page, or the latest information supplied by the government.

Remuneration *Rémunération* From-*de*	To-*à*	U.I. Premium *Prime d'a.-c.*
847.18 -	847.60	19.49
847.61 -	848.04	19.50
848.05 -	848.47	19.51
848.48 -	848.91	19.52
848.92 -	849.34	19.53
849.35 -	849.99	19.54
850.00 -	AND UP *ET PLUS*	19.55

Key Check Figure Total Employer Contribution = $102.56

10-4 Assume the following Net Claim Codes for the employees named in Problems 10-2 and 10-3: Attridge, 2; Geimer, 3; Jessup, 0; Ryan, 8.

Using a table with headings as illustrated, show the amount of income tax to be withheld from each employee's pay. Use the tax deduction tables given in this chapter and below.

ONTARIO
BI-WEEKLY TAX DEDUCTIONS
Basis – 26 Pay Periods per Year

TABLE 3

OI
RETENUES D'IMP(
Base – 26 péric

BI-WEEKLY PAY Use appropriate bracket — PAIE DE DEUX SEMAINES Utilisez le palier approprié	IF THE EMPLOYEE'S "NET CLAIM CODE" ON FORM TD1 IS — SI LE «CODE DE RÉCLAMATION NETTE» DE L'EMPLOY									
	1	2	3	4	5	6	7	8	9	10
	DEDUCT FROM EACH PAY – *RETENEZ SUR CHAQUE PAIE*									
$1109.00 - 1128.99	268.10	262.85	253.30	244.05	234.30	226.80	222.00	214.85	205.00	194.40
1129.00 - 1148.99	275.65	270.35	260.80	251.55	241.70	233.70	228.95	221.75	211.90	201.35
1149.00 - 1168.99	283.15	277.85	268.30	259.05	249.25	241.05	235.85	228.65	218.80	208.25
1169.00 - 1188.99	290.65	285.40	275.85	266.60	256.75	248.60	243.40	235.60	225.75	215.15
1189.00 - 1208.99	298.20	292.90	283.35	274.10	264.25	256.10	250.90	243.10	232.65	222.10

Calculation of Employees' Income Taxes

	Employee (1)	*Net Claim Code (2)*	*Bi-Weekly Gross Pay (3)*	*Deductions CPP (4)*	*UI (5)*	*Total (6)*	*Taxable Earnings (3)–(6)*	*Income Tax (7)*
EXAMPLE:	A. Attridge	2	$765	$12.39	$17.60			

Key Check Figure Attridge's Income Tax = $133.00

10-5 Using a summary table similar to the one on the bottom of page 334, show the amount of net pay for each employee in Problems 10-2, 10-3, and 10-4.

Key Check Figure Attridge's Net Pay = $602.01

TOPIC 2 RECORDING PAYROLL DATA

The next part of any payroll application is to make an accounting record of the pay period. Actually, this accounting record is divided into three parts:

- preparing a payroll summary known as the payroll register
- preparing the employee's individual earnings record
- journalizing and posting the payroll so that ledger accounts affected by the payroll can be updated

Preparing the Payroll Register

After calculating the details of gross earnings, deductions, and the net pay for each employee for a particular payroll period, the complete payroll is summarized in an accounting record. This record is called the payroll summary or payroll register.

Payroll register: an accounting record summarizing the details of a pay period.

In some accounting systems, a payroll register is prepared for each different payroll plan. Thus, separate hourly payroll registers are used to summarize the payroll for hourly-rated employees and for salaried employees. Other accounting systems combine the payroll summaries. In this chapter, a basic salary payroll register will be used to summarize the payroll for Dr. Johnson's dental firm.

The design and form of payroll registers will vary from one business to another and with the actual method of processing the payroll. For example, a register prepared by hand requires a design quite different from that of one prepared by a computer. Every payroll register, however, will contain columns to record at least:

- the names and SINs of employees
- the details of the employees' gross earnings
- the details of the employees' payroll deductions
- the employees' net pay

The payroll register shown on page 338 shows how Dr. Johnson's payroll is summarized for the payroll data collected in Topic 1. Study this illustration closely. Then read the analysis.

Analysis: These are the main points to remember about the contents and preparation of any payroll register:

- The pay ending period is found in the heading part of the payroll register. Since payroll is handled on a bi-weekly basis, the heading is *For the Two Weeks Ending March 12, 19—*.
- Record in the heading the date of the employees' cheques. This date will always be the date of the payday.
- The body of the register contains the columns *Employee Data, Earnings, Deductions,* and *Net Pay*. Of course, the information entered into these columns has already been collected and checked in Topic 1.
- The deductions are added and the total is entered into the

SALARY PAYROLL REGISTER **For the Two Weeks Ending** *March 12 19—* *Paid* ________ *19* ____

Employee Data			Time Worked			Earnings			Deductions					
SIN	Name	NC Code	Weeks	OT Days	Rate Per Wk.	Regular	OT Excess	Gross Pay	CPP	UI	Income Tax	Total	Net Pay	Cheque No.
425-127-511	*Lewis, Kathy*	*8*	*2*	—	*400 00*	*800 00*	—	*800 00*	*13 02*	*18 40*	*102 70*	*134 12*	*665 88*	
447-231-135	*Fortier, Lynn*	*1*	*2*	—	*200 00*	*400 00*	—	*400 00*	*5 82*	*9 20*	*36 85*	*51 87*	*348 13*	
438-120-720	*Casey, Mildred*	*2*	*2*	—	*175 00*	*350 00*	—	*350 00*	*4 92*	*8 05*	*21 70*	*34 67*	*315 33*	
						1 550 00	—	*1 550 00*	*23 76*	*35 65*	*161 25*	*220 66*	*1 329 34*	

Proof of Salary Payroll Register

Earnings:		
Regular	*$1 550.00*	
Overtime	*—*	
Total Gross Pay		*$1 550.00*
Deductions:		
CPP	*$ 23.76*	
UI	*35.65*	
Income Tax .	*161.25*	
Total		*220.66*
Net Pay		*$1 329.34*

Total column of the *Deductions* section. This step is important for calculating the net pay for each employee.

- There is a special column at the far right where the number of the cheque paid to the employee is later recorded.

Observe on page 338 how the payroll is proved. After the data for every employee is entered and *before the employees are paid,* the various columns must be totalled. Payroll registers are proved by adding and subtracting the appropriate column totals across the register. In some methods of data processing, the proof is done automatically by means of a computer. In manual methods, it is done with an adding machine or a calculator.

Preparing the Employee's Earnings Record

After the payroll register has been prepared and proved, the details of each employee's earnings may be posted to the employee's individual earnings record. This individual record is especially important for the following reasons.

Employee's individual earnings record: a payroll record showing the details of an employee's pay periods.

- For each employee it shows in one place a full year's summary of his or her pay periods, gross earnings, deductions, net pay, and important year-to-date totals.
- It serves as a basis for preparing tax slips so that the employer may complete an income tax return.
- It helps determine when the employer has reached the maximum points of contributions to UI and CPP.

Below is an example of how Kathy Lewis's individual earnings would be prepared. Remember that the individual earnings

EMPLOYEE'S INDIVIDUAL EARNINGS RECORD FOR THE YEAR *19—*

Employee's Name: *Lewis, Kathy* SIN: *425-127-511* Tel. No. *679-3734*

Address: *Any Town/City* *Canada* *N6H 4H9*

Date of Birth: *January 14, 19—* Date Employed: *June 15, 19-1* Date of Termination: ______

Position: *Dental Hygienist* Salary Plan: *Bi-weekly* Rate of Pay: *$400 per week*

Net Claim Code per TD1: *8* UI Insurable Earnings: Minimum: *$170 bi-weekly* Maximum: *$850 bi-weekly* Maximum UI Yearly Premium: *$508.30*

CPP Year's Maximum Earnings *$20 800.00* Year's Basic Exemption *$2 000.00* Maximum Earnings for Contributions *$18 800.00* Maximum Yearly CPP *$338.40*

Pay Period Ending	Time Worked		Rate /Wk.	Earnings			Deductions				Net Pay	Year-to-Date			
	Weeks	OT Days		Regular	OT Excess	Gross Pay	CPP	UI	Inc. Tax	Total		Gross Pay	CPP	UI	Inc. Tax
Feb. 28	2	2	400	800	160	960	15.86	19.55	150.30	185.71	774.29	3 360	55.44	70.84	513.52
Mar. 12	2	—	400	800	—	800	13.02	18.40	102.70	134.12	665.88	4 160	68.46	89.24	616.22

record for a given pay period must agree with the payroll register for the same period.

Three final points are worth noting:

- The *Earnings, Deductions* and *Net Pay* sections are in the same order as they appear on the payroll register. This is so that the amounts can be posted easily to the employee's individual earnings record. In some short-cut methods of processing the payroll, this order is important because the payroll register and the individual employee's earnings record are both prepared in one writing. (This one-write system is studied in Chapter 17.)
- An additional section, *Year-To-Date,* has been added to the earnings record. This contains columns to show the total gross pay, the total CPP, the total UI, and the total income tax to the date of posting the latest entry. From these columns, the payroll clerk can easily see when the employee has reached the maximum amount for CPP and UI, and can prepare a tax summary known as the T4 tax slip. (The T4 slip will be examined in Topic 3 of this chapter.)
- The employee's individual record becomes a payroll subsidiary ledger account. This means that each individual's earnings are accounted for in a separate payroll ledger. The total of the individual employees' gross pays will be added to show a total which must agree with the balance shown for *Salaries Expense* in the General Ledger. The same idea applies to each employee's deduction. The totals of the individual employees' deductions for UI, CPP, and income tax must agree with the amount recorded in the General Ledger accounts for *UI Payable, CPP Payable,* and *Employees' Income Tax Payable.* And the total of each employee's net pay must add up to the balance shown in the General Ledger for *Salaries Payable.* Each General Ledger account, then, becomes the control account to control by one figure the total of all employees' amounts shown in the payroll subsidiary ledger.

Payroll ledger: a subsidiary ledger containing individual employees' earnings records.

Journalizing and Posting to the General Ledger

The payroll data is now ready to be recorded and posted to appropriate accounts in the General Ledger.

In some accounting systems, the totals of the payroll register are posted directly. This means that account numbers are placed beneath each total posted to show that the transfer has occurred. Under this system, the payroll register becomes the "book of original entry." Since any book of original entry is a journal, the "book" showing the original payroll entries is known as the payroll journal. Most payroll applications using the one-write system use a payroll journal.

Payroll journal: the payroll register used as the book of original entry.

On the other hand, many accounting systems prefer to "journalize" the various totals of the payroll summary in the General Journal. In this case, the payroll summary is known as the *payroll register* because no postings occur from a register. Most computer systems print payroll registers. The totals of the payroll register are summarized in the form of a compound entry and recorded in the General Journal. In this chapter, assume that the totals of the payroll register are recorded in the General Journal.

Two classes of entries must be recorded in the General Journal:

- a compound entry recording the totals of the payroll register
- another compound entry recording the employer's additional expenses resulting from each payroll.

Let us examine each of these entries separately.

The Payroll Register Totals It is useful to return to the proof of the payroll register and analyze the key figures reported. Examine the proof below.

Earnings:			
Regular	*$1 550.00*		
Overtime	—		
Total Gross Pay		*$1 550.00*	← **A Debit to an Expense Account** (Salaries Expense)
Deductions:			
CPP	*$ 23.76*		← **Credits to Appropriate Current Liability Accounts** (CPP Contributions Payable, UI Premium Payable, Income Tax Deductions Pay.)
UI	*35.65*		
Income Tax ...	*161.25*		
Total		*220.66*	
Net Pay		*$1 329.34*	← **A Credit to a Current Liability Account** (Salaries Payable)

Analysis:

- The total of gross earnings from the payroll register must be debited to an appropriate expense account. Since this register records a salary payroll, the total of the *Gross Pay* column may be debited to an expense called Salaries Expense.
- For each of the payroll deductions, an appropriate current liability account must be credited, because the amounts withheld do not belong to the employer; they must be paid to the federal government. Until these amounts are paid, they must be treated as current liabilities on the books of the employer.
- The total amount in the *Net Pay* column is also a current liability until the employees are paid. An appropriate liability account in this case would be Salaries Payable.

The entry to record the payroll register for Dr. Johnson's dental practice is shown next. After this entry is posted to the General Ledger, the various liability accounts will show the amounts owed to the federal government and the employees.

John H. Johnson, D.D.S.
Chart of Accounts

CURRENT LIABILITIES
205 Salaries Payable
206 CPP Contributions Payable
207 UI Premium Payable
208 Income Tax Deductions Payable

EXPENSES
502 Salaries Expense
510 Payroll Taxes Expense

Mar. 12	Salaries Expense	1 550.00	
	CPP Contributions Payable		23.76
	UI Premium Payable		35.65
	Income Tax Deductions Payable		161.25
	Salaries Payable		1 329.34
	To record the bi-weekly payroll for salaried employees for the two weeks ended on March 12.		

The Employer's Additional Payroll Expenses All employers are obliged by law to contribute to the Canada Pension Plan and to unemployment insurance. To the CPP they must contribute dollar amounts equal to the employees' contribution, and they must also contribute 1.4 times the employee's share of UI. These represent additional expenses resulting from the payroll, and so they must be journalized and posted to appropriate General Ledger accounts. Study the General Journal entry shown below.

Mar. 12	Payroll Taxes Expense	73.67	
	CPP Contributions Payable		23.76
	UI Premium Payable		49.91
	To record payroll taxes resulting from the bi-weekly payroll ended March 12.		

Payroll Taxes Expense: an account used to record the additional employer's expense resulting from the payroll.

An account called Payroll Taxes Expense is commonly used to record the total debit of the various employer's additional payroll expenses. Do not misunderstand the word *taxes* in this account title; it does not mean the income taxes withheld from employees and accounted for in the current liability account. Here the word is used to suggest that the additional amounts are regarded as levies against the employer by the government, like property taxes or licence fees required for doing business — "taxes" related to payroll expense.

To complete the double entry, separate current liability accounts are used to show the dollar amounts that must be paid on behalf of the employer for the Canada Pension Plan and Unemployment Insurance. Once these amounts are posted, the balance in the current liability accounts will show how much must be paid to the federal government. This remittance will be examined in Topic 3.

TOPIC 2 PROBLEMS

10-6 Refer to your solution for Problem 10-1. Assume the end of the payroll period is February 14 of this year.

a Prepare a salary payroll register similar to the one illustrated on page 338.
b Total and prove the register.
c Show how the payroll entries would appear in the General Journal.

Key Check Figure Payroll Taxes Expense = $76.57

10-7 You will require the information for Problems 3, 10-4 and 10-5. Assume the payroll period ends March 17. Make up appropriate SIN numbers.

a Prepare a salary payroll register similar to the one illustrated on page 338.
b Total and prove the register.
c Show how the payroll entries would appear in the General Journal.

Key Check Figure Payroll Taxes Expense = $160.63

10-8 Anne Attridge has been employed as a dental assistant since the beginning of this year. She resides at 400 Main Street, Your City/Town, Canada. Her telephone number is 587-4000. Her Form TD1 shows her date of birth as June 4, 19—. Below are her past payroll periods to March 3.

Pay Period	*Earnings*			*Deductions*		
Ending	*Regular*	*OT*	*Gross Pay*	*CPP*	*UI*	*Inc. Tax*
Jan. 14	$600	—	$600	$ 9.55	$13.80	$ 92.60
Jan. 28	600	$60	660	10.63	15.18	104.35
Feb. 4	650	—	650	10.45	14.95	101.40
Feb. 18	650	50	700	11.35	16.10	116.35
Mar. 3	710	—	710	11.53	16.33	119.35

a From the information given in Problems 10-4 and 10-5, and from the added information above, complete an individual employee's earnings record for Anne Attridge to the end of March 3.

b Post the current payroll from the register prepared in Problem 10-7 to Attridge's account in the payroll subsidiary ledger.

Key Check Figure Year-to-Date Gross Pay to Mar. 17 = $4 085

TOPIC 3 PAYROLL REMITTANCES AND ANNUAL TAX STATEMENTS

As a result of journalizing the payroll, several current liabilities have been recorded in appropriate ledger accounts. These current liabilities represent the amounts owing to the employees and to the federal government. All payroll applications must include procedures for paying off these current liabilities. These payments are called payroll remittances.

Payroll remittances: payments to employees and the federal government resulting from a payroll.

The payroll application must also include procedures for preparing annual tax statements for the employees and the federal government.

Paying the Employees

In a large business, paying employees on a regular pay day involves important measures to control cash payments. This is especially true when the payroll involves both hourly-rated employees and salaried personnel. (These measures will be looked at in Chapter 14.)

For a small business such as Dr. Johnson's dental practice, employees are usually paid by issuing cheques drawn against the regular bank current account. Of course, these cheques would be recorded in the cash payments journal as illustrated below.

CASH PAYMENTS JOURNAL — **Page** *3*

Date 19-2		Cheque No.	Cheque Paid To	Accounts Payable Post. Ref.	Accounts Payable Amount DR.	Other General Ledger Accounts Account Title	Post. Ref.	Amount DR.	Cash CR.
Mar.	12	350	Kathy Lewis			Salaries Payable	205	665 88	665 88
	12	351	Lynn Fortier			Salaries Payable	205	348 13	348 13
	12	352	Mildred Casey			Salaries Payable	205	315 33	315 33

Analysis: These points will help you understand the accounting of the separate cheques issued to the employees:

- Each cheque must be analyzed as a debit to Salaries Payable and a credit to Cash.
- After the entries are posted to the GL, the Salaries Payable account would show *no balance* as follows:

General Ledger

Salaries Payable — **Account No.** 205

DATE 19-2		EXPLANATION	POST. REF.	DEBIT	CREDIT	BALANCE
Mar.	12	G.J.	5		1 329 34	1 329 34
	12	CPJ	3	665 88		663 46
	12	CPJ	3	348 13		315 33
	12	CPJ	3	315 33		– 0 –

There's one more step involved in making payroll remittances to employees — preparing the employee's pay statement. This statement may be attached to a special payroll cheque or it may be a separate form. In the case of Dr. Johnson's practice, assume that the employee's pay statement is done on a separate form:

Pay statement: an employee's statement of earnings and deductions for a pay period.

NAME	PAY PERIOD ENDING	Weeks	OT Days	PER WEEK	Regular	OT Excess	Gross Pay	CPP	UI	INC. TAX	TOTAL	NET PAY
		TIME WORKED			EARNINGS			DEDUCTIONS				
Kathy Lewis	*Mar. 12*	*2*	—	*400.00*	*800.00*	—	*800.00*	*13.02*	*18.40*	*102.70*	*134.12*	*665.88*

PAY STATEMENT

Retain this statement. It is a record of your earnings and deductions.

Analysis:

- All pay statements show the important details of the employee's pay period.
- Compare the main columns of the pay statement with those on the payroll register and the individual employee's earnings record. Do you see any similarities?
- The arrangement of columns for *Earnings, Deductions* and *Net Pay* is identical to that for the form shown on both the Payroll Register and the Employee's Individual Earnings Record. Since the order is identical, some payroll applications will prepare all three payroll forms in one writing. (This feature will be examined in Chapter 17.)

Paying the Federal Government

Before the payroll remittance to the federal government is examined, it is useful to study the liability accounts created by the payroll. This study will determine how much should be paid. Consider, for example, the General Ledger in T-account form of Dr. Johnson's practice immediately after the payment of employees' salaries, shown on page 346.

Analysis:

- The GL shows three current liability accounts with balances. These are CPP Contributions Payable for $47.52; UI Premium Payable for $85.56; and Income Tax Deductions Payable for $166.15.

General Ledger in T-Account Form

Cash 101

		Mar. 12	1 329.34

Salaries Payable 205

Mar. 12	665.88	Mar. 12	1 329.34
12	348.13		
12	315.33		
	Ø		

CPP Contributions Payable 206

		Mar. 12	23.76
		12	23.76
		Balance	47.52

UI Premium Payable 207

		Mar. 12	35.65
		12	49.91
		Balance	85.56

Income Tax Deductions Payable 208

		Mar. 12	161.25

Salaries Expense 502

Mar. 12	1 550		

Payroll Taxes Expense 510

Mar. 12	73.67		

- Under federal law, the balances shown by these three liability accounts must be remitted on Form PD7AR, called "Tax Deduction/Canada Pension Plan/Unemployment Insurance Remittance Return."
- Form PD7AR, along with a certified cheque or money order made payable to the Receiver General for Canada, must be paid at the bank where the business has an account, or mailed to the appropriate Taxation Centre, by the 15th of the month following that in which the payroll is recorded. Look closely at Form PD7AR, illustrated opposite.

Analysis:

- The data to complete the necessary blocks is obtained from the balances of General Ledger accounts.
- As the individual blocks require, the payroll clerk must show the amounts for CPP Contributions Payable (employer's and employees' combined), the UI Premium Payable (employer's

Revenue Canada Taxation — Revenu Canada Impôt

PD7AR REV. 80

REMITTANCE FORM - *FORMULE DE VERSEMENT*

NAME, ADDRESS AND OWNERSHIP CHANGES
CHANGEMENTS DE NOM, D'ADRESSE ET DE PROPRIÉTAIRE
Please enter details of any changes not reported previously.
Prière d'indiquer le détail des changements non signalés antérieurement.
New name
Nouveau nom ______
New Address
Nouvelle adresse ______
Postal Code
Code postal ______
If ownership of business has changed enter effective date.
Si la propriété de l'entreprise a changé, en indiquer la date de prise d'effet. ______

6

FOR MONTH OF: / *POUR LE MOIS DE:* March 19-2

ENTER AMOUNT OF PAYMENT / *INSCRIRE LE MONTANT DU PAIEMENT* $ 294.33

DISTRIBUTION OF REMITTANCE (INCL. EMPLOYER C.P.P. & U.I. SHARES)
RÉPARTITION DU VERSEMENT (Y COMPRIS PARTS PATRONALES DU RPC ET DE L'A.-C.)

TAX DEDUCTIONS	C.P.P. CONTRIBUTIONS	U.I. PREMIUMS
$ 161.25	$ 47.52	$ 85.56
DÉDUCTIONS D'IMPÔT	*COTISATIONS AU RPC*	*PRIMES D'A.-C.*

SIGNAL	L.P. CODE / *CODE P.P.T.*	NO. OF PAYTS. / *NBRE VERS.*	MONTH / *MOIS*	YEAR / *ANNÉE*
	1			

JOHN H. JOHNSON, D.D.S.

ANY TOWN/CITY

PROVINCE

CANADA

N6H 4H9

Your payment may be made where you bank or to:
Vous pouvez faire le paiement à votre institution bancaire ou à:
Taxation Centre - *Centre fiscal*

See reverse — *Voir au verso*

Revenue Canada Taxation — Revenu Canada Impôt

PD7A REV. 80

TAX DEDUCTION - CANADA PENSION PLAN - UNEMPLOYMENT INSURANCE REMITTANCE RETURN
DÉCLARATION DE VERSEMENTS CONCERNANT LES DÉDUCTIONS AU TITRE DE L'IMPÔT, DU RÉGIME DE PENSIONS DU CANADA ET DE L'ASSURANCE-CHÔMAGE

JOHN H. JOHNSON, D.D.S.
ANY TOWN/CITY
PROVINCE
CANADA N6H 4H9

EMPLOYER NO. / *No DE L'EMPLOYEUR* 4500
DATE April 15
YEAR / *ANNÉE* 19-2
REMITTANCE / *VERSEMENT* $
TOTAL TO DATE / *TOTAL À CE JOUR* $

TAX DEDUCTIONS	C.P.P. CONTRIBUTIONS	U.I. PREMIUMS	CURRENT REMITTANCE
$161.25	$47.52	$85.56	$ 294.33
DÉDUCTIONS D'IMPÔT	*COTISATIONS AU R.P.C.*	*PRIMES D'A.-C.*	*VERSEMENT COURANT*

IMPORTANT—SEE REVERSE
RETAIN THIS PART FOR YOUR RECORDS

BRUCE A. MACDONALD
DEPUTY MINISTER, DEPARTMENT OF NATIONAL REVENUE, TAXATION
SOUS-MINISTRE, MINISTÈRE DU REVENU NATIONAL, IMPÔT

IMPORTANT – VOIR AU VERSO
CONSERVEZ CETTE PARTIE

and employees' combined), and Income Tax Deductions Payable.

- The total of all these account balances represents the amount to be remitted to the federal government.

In the case of Dr. Johnson's practice, a cheque for $294.33 would be issued, recorded, and analyzed as shown below.

Apr. 15	*CPP Contibutions Payable*	*47.52*	
	UI Premium Payable	*85.56*	
	Income Tax Deductions Payable	*161.25*	
	Cash		*294.33*
	To record cheque issued to Receiver General for Canada as per Form PD7AR.		
	(This entry would be recorded in the Cash Payments Journal.)		

After the remittance is received, the bank teller or the Taxation Centre returns (1) the lower part of Form PD7AR as a receipt and (2) a blank remittance form to process next month's returns.

Preparing Annual Payroll Tax Statements

All payroll applications must include the preparation of annual payroll tax statements.

On or before the last day of February of each year, employers must submit two important returns:

Statement of Remuneration Paid (T4 slip): a yearly statement of earnings and deductions for income tax purposes.

1. Annual Tax Statements to Employees Employers must give their employees a report of their yearly earnings and deductions on a form known as the T4 Supplementary form, the Statement of Remuneration Paid, or simply the *T4 slip*.

This is Kathy Lewis's T4 slip.[1]

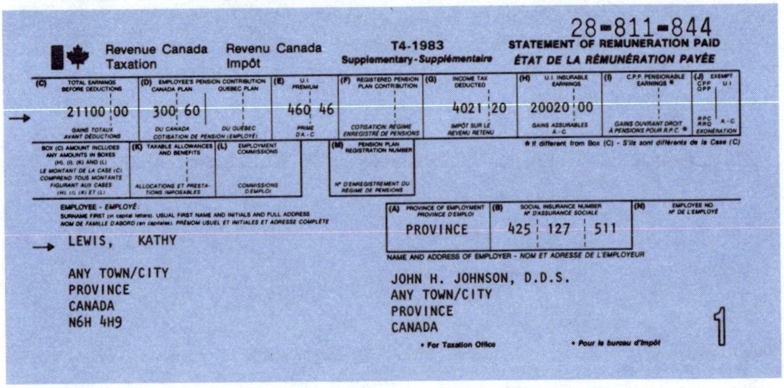

- The employer must fill out the *Total Earnings Before Deductions,* the *Employee's Pension Contribution — Canada Plan,* the *UI Premium,* the *Income Tax Deducted,* and the *UI Insurable Earnings* sections. To do this, the payroll clerk refers to the individual employee's earnings record.
- After completing the four-copy set of T4 slips for all employees, the employer must mail or deliver copy 1 of each T4 Supplementary to Revenue Canada—Taxation by no later than February 28 of each year.
- Copies 2 and 3 must also be given to the employee by no later than February 28. Copy 2 is attached to the employee's income tax return, which must be mailed by no later than April 30. Copy 3 is kept by the employee for his or her income tax records.
- Copy 4 is retained by the employer and must be kept on file, together with all other payroll records, for at least six years.

1. At the time of writing, the T4-1984 form was not available.

2. Annual Tax Statement to Revenue Canada Employers must also submit a detailed payroll summary to Revenue Canada — Taxation. This summary is called the T4-T4A Return.[2]

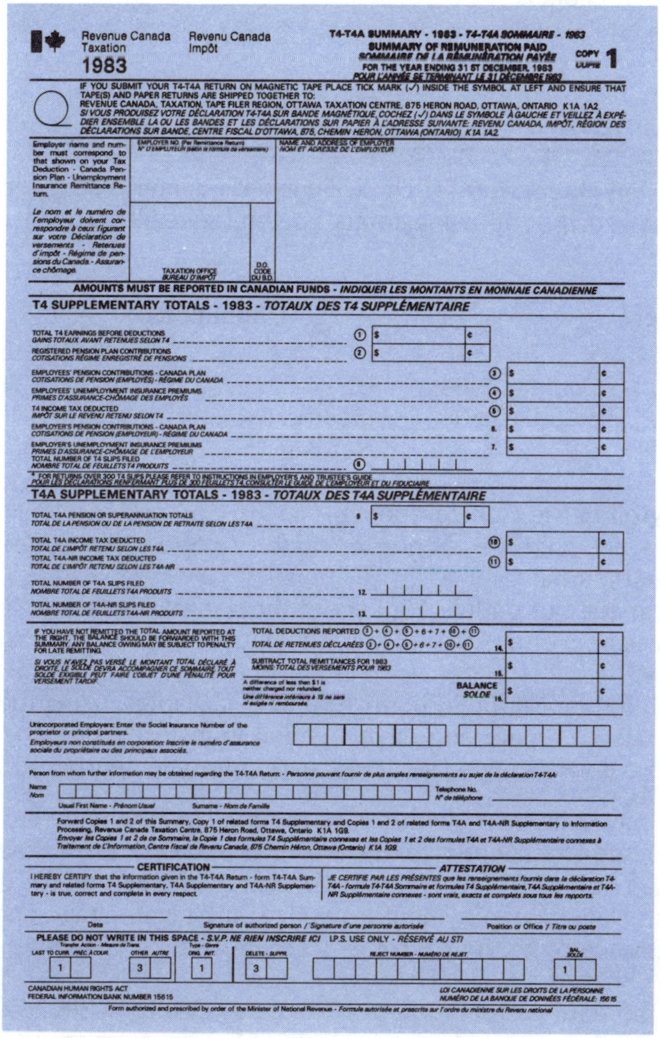

Revenue Canada Taxation Revenu Canada Impôt
1983

T4-T4A SUMMARY - 1983 - T4-T4A SOMMAIRE - 1983
SUMMARY OF REMUNERATION PAID
SOMMAIRE DE LA RÉMUNÉRATION PAYÉE
FOR THE YEAR ENDING 31 ST DECEMBER, 1983
POUR L'ANNÉE SE TERMINANT LE 31 DÉCEMBRE 1983
COPY COPIE 1

IF YOU SUBMIT YOUR T4-T4A RETURN ON MAGNETIC TAPE PLACE TICK MARK (✓) INSIDE THE SYMBOL AT LEFT AND ENSURE THAT TAPE(S) AND PAPER RETURNS ARE SHIPPED TOGETHER TO:
REVENUE CANADA, TAXATION, TAPE FILER REGION, OTTAWA TAXATION CENTRE, 875 HERON ROAD, OTTAWA, ONTARIO K1A 1A2
SI VOUS PRODUISEZ VOTRE DÉCLARATION T4-T4A SUR BANDE MAGNÉTIQUE, COCHEZ (✓) DANS LE SYMBOLE À GAUCHE ET VEILLEZ À EXPÉDIER ENSEMBLE LA OU LES BANDES ET LES DÉCLARATIONS SUR PAPIER À L'ADRESSE SUIVANTE: REVENU CANADA, IMPÔT, RÉGION DES DÉCLARATIONS SUR BANDE, CENTRE FISCAL D'OTTAWA, 875, CHEMIN HERON, OTTAWA (ONTARIO) K1A 1A2

Employer name and number must correspond to that shown on your Tax Deduction - Canada Pension Plan - Unemployment Insurance Remittance Return.

Le nom et le numéro de l'employeur doivent correspondre à ceux figurant sur votre Déclaration de versements - Retenues d'impôt - Régime de pensions du Canada - Assurance chômage.

EMPLOYER NO. (Per Remittance Return) / Nº D'EMPLOYEUR (selon la formule de versement)
NAME AND ADDRESS OF EMPLOYER / NOM ET ADRESSE DE L'EMPLOYEUR
TAXATION OFFICE / BUREAU D'IMPÔT
D.O. CODE / CODE DU B.D.

AMOUNTS MUST BE REPORTED IN CANADIAN FUNDS - INDIQUER LES MONTANTS EN MONNAIE CANADIENNE

T4 SUPPLEMENTARY TOTALS - 1983 - TOTAUX DES T4 SUPPLÉMENTAIRE

TOTAL T4 EARNINGS BEFORE DEDUCTIONS / GAINS TOTAUX AVANT RETENUES SELON T4	①	$	¢
REGISTERED PENSION PLAN CONTRIBUTIONS / COTISATIONS RÉGIME ENREGISTRÉ DE PENSIONS	②	$	¢
EMPLOYEES' PENSION CONTRIBUTIONS - CANADA PLAN / COTISATIONS DE PENSION (EMPLOYÉS) - RÉGIME DU CANADA	③	$	¢
EMPLOYEES' UNEMPLOYMENT INSURANCE PREMIUMS / PRIMES D'ASSURANCE-CHÔMAGE DES EMPLOYÉS	④	$	¢
T4 INCOME TAX DEDUCTED / IMPÔT SUR LE REVENU RETENU SELON T4	⑤	$	¢
EMPLOYER'S PENSION CONTRIBUTIONS - CANADA PLAN / COTISATIONS DE PENSION (EMPLOYEUR) - RÉGIME DU CANADA	6.	$	¢
EMPLOYER'S UNEMPLOYMENT INSURANCE PREMIUMS / PRIMES D'ASSURANCE-CHÔMAGE DE L'EMPLOYEUR	7.	$	¢
TOTAL NUMBER OF T4 SLIPS FILED / NOMBRE TOTAL DE FEUILLETS T4 PRODUITS	⑧		

* FOR RETURNS OVER 300 T4 SLIPS PLEASE REFER TO INSTRUCTIONS IN EMPLOYER'S AND TRUSTEE'S GUIDE
POUR LES DÉCLARATIONS RENFERMANT PLUS DE 300 FEUILLETS T4 CONSULTER LE GUIDE DE L'EMPLOYEUR ET DU FIDUCIAIRE

T4A SUPPLEMENTARY TOTALS - 1983 - TOTAUX DES T4A SUPPLÉMENTAIRE

TOTAL T4A PENSION OR SUPERANNUATION TOTALS / TOTAL DE LA PENSION OU DE LA PENSION DE RETRAITE SELON LES T4A	9	$	¢
TOTAL T4A INCOME TAX DEDUCTED / TOTAL DE L'IMPÔT RETENU SELON LES T4A	⑩	$	¢
TOTAL T4A-NR INCOME TAX DEDUCTED / TOTAL DE L'IMPÔT RETENU SELON LES T4A-NR	⑪	$	¢
TOTAL NUMBER OF T4A SLIPS FILED / NOMBRE TOTAL DE FEUILLETS T4A PRODUITS	12.		
TOTAL NUMBER OF T4A-NR SLIPS FILED / NOMBRE TOTAL DE FEUILLETS T4A-NR PRODUITS	13.		

IF YOU HAVE NOT REMITTED THE TOTAL AMOUNT REPORTED AT THE RIGHT, THE BALANCE SHOULD BE FORWARDED WITH THIS SUMMARY. ANY BALANCE OWING MAY BE SUBJECT TO PENALTY FOR LATE REMITTING.

SI VOUS N'AVEZ PAS VERSÉ LE MONTANT TOTAL DÉCLARÉ À DROITE, LE SOLDE DEVRA ACCOMPAGNER CE SOMMAIRE. TOUT SOLDE EXIGIBLE PEUT FAIRE L'OBJET D'UNE PÉNALITÉ POUR VERSEMENT TARDIF.

TOTAL DEDUCTIONS REPORTED ③ + ④ + ⑤ + 6 + 7 + ⑩ + ⑪ / TOTAL DE RETENUES DÉCLARÉES ③ + ④ + ⑤ + 6 + 7 + ⑩ + ⑪	14.	$	¢
SUBTRACT TOTAL REMITTANCES FOR 1983 / MOINS: TOTAL DES VERSEMENTS POUR 1983	15.	$	¢
BALANCE / SOLDE	16.	$	¢

A difference of less than $1 is neither charged nor refunded.
Une différence inférieure à 1$ ne sera ni exigée ni remboursée.

Unincorporated Employers: Enter the Social Insurance Number of the proprietor or principal partners.
Employeurs non constitués en corporation: Inscrire le numéro d'assurance sociale du propriétaire ou des principaux associés.

Person from whom further information may be obtained regarding the T4-T4A Return: - Personne pouvant fournir de plus amples renseignements au sujet de la déclaration T4-T4A:
Name / Nom — Usual First Name - Prénom Usuel — Surname - Nom de Famille — Telephone No. / Nº de téléphone

Forward Copies 1 and 2 of this Summary, Copy 1 of related forms T4 Supplementary and Copies 1 and 2 of related forms T4A and T4A-NR Supplementary to Information Processing, Revenue Canada Taxation Centre, 875 Heron Road, Ottawa, Ontario K1A 1G9.
Envoyer les Copies 1 et 2 de ce Sommaire, la Copie 1 des formules T4 Supplémentaire connexes et les Copies 1 et 2 des formules T4A et T4A-NR Supplémentaire connexes à Traitement de L'Information, Centre fiscal de Revenu Canada, 875 Chemin Héron, Ottawa (Ontario) K1A 1G9.

CERTIFICATION
I HEREBY CERTIFY that the information given in the T4-T4A Return - form T4-T4A Summary and related forms T4 Supplementary, T4A Supplementary and T4A-NR Supplementary - is true, correct and complete in every respect.

ATTESTATION
JE CERTIFIE PAR LES PRÉSENTES que les renseignements fournis dans la déclaration T4-T4A - formule T4-T4A Sommaire et formules T4 Supplémentaire, T4A Supplémentaire et T4A-NR Supplémentaire connexes - sont vrais, exacts et complets sous tous les rapports.

Date — Signature of authorized person / Signature d'une personne autorisée — Position or Office / Titre ou poste

PLEASE DO NOT WRITE IN THIS SPACE - S.V.P. NE RIEN INSCRIRE ICI I.P.S. USE ONLY - RÉSERVÉ AU STI
Transfer Action - Mesure de Trans. LAST TO CURR. PRÉC. À COUR. 1 — OTHER AUTRE 3 — Type - Genre ORIG. INIT. 1 — DELETE - SUPPR. 3 — REJECT NUMBER - NUMÉRO DE REJET — BAL. SOLDE 1

CANADIAN HUMAN RIGHTS ACT
FEDERAL INFORMATION BANK NUMBER 15615
LOI CANADIENNE SUR LES DROITS DE LA PERSONNE
NUMÉRO DE LA BANQUE DE DONNÉES FÉDÉRALE: 15615

Form authorized and prescribed by order of the Minister of National Revenue - Formule autorisée et prescrite sur l'ordre du ministre du Revenu national

This return reports important totals related to the employer's payroll of the preceding calendar year. These would include:

- the total gross earnings of all employees
- the total employees' contribution to the Canada Pension Plan
- the total employer's contribution to the Canada Pension Plan
- the total employees' premium to unemployment insurance

2. At the time of writing, the T4-T4A Return for 1984 was not available.

- the total employer's premium to unemployment insurance
- the total income tax deducted from employees

These totals are obtained from appropriate accounts in the General Ledger.

TOPIC 3 PROBLEMS

10-9 The salary payroll register for Dr. R. Schenck's dental practice in Winnipeg, Manitoba showed the following totals for the bi-weekly payroll ending June 30:

Earnings		**Deductions**	
Regular	$3 516	CPP	$ 62.10
Overtime	84	UI	70.84
Gross Pay	3 600	Income Tax	611.40
		Net Pay	2 855.66

a Record the payroll in the General Journal.

b The employees are paid by cheque on June 30. Show the payment to employees in General Journal form.

c Form PD7AR is made out on July 15. Record the remittance to the Receiver General for Canada as per Form PD7AR. Show the entry in General Journal form.

Key Check Figure Remittance to Receiver General = $905.62

10-10 Refer to the solution for Problem 10-6 of this chapter. Using the information of Problem 10-6, prepare entries in General Journal form for the transactions summarized below. Show a brief explanation for each entry.

a Feb. 14 Issued pay statements with salary cheques to all employees.

b Mar. 15 Issued certified cheque to the Receiver General for Canada and enclosed Form PD7AR to return the required amounts for Canada Pension Plan, unemployment insurance, and income taxes. *Note:* In this instance only, the payroll is to be treated as bi-weekly.

Key Check Figure Remittance to Receiver General = $341.77

10-11 Refer to the solution for Problem 10-7 of this chapter. Using the information of Problem 10-7, prepare entries in General Journal form for the transactions summarized below. Show a brief explanation for each entry.

a Mar. 17 Issued pay statements with salary cheques to all employees.

b Apr. 15 Issued certified cheque to the Receiver General for Canada and enclosed Form PD7AR to return the required amounts for Canada Pension Plan, unemployment insurance, and income taxes. *Note:* Reference to additional payrolls in March has been omitted to simplify this problem.

Key Check Figure Remittance to Receiver General = $788.01

10-12 Challenge Problem Refer to Problem 10-8 where you prepared an individual employee's earnings record for Anne Attridge.

a The last payroll entry posted to Attridge's earnings record (March 17) is repeated for all remaining bi-weekly payroll periods to the end of December. Show how her earnings record would appear to the end of the calendar year. The maximum yearly contribution to CPP is $338.40, and the maximum yearly UI premium is $508.30. *Hint:* There should be 26 line entries in the earnings record. The last pay ending period is December 29. Use two earnings record sheets to do this part of the problem.

b Prepare the yearly T4 slip for Anne Attridge. Improvise a slip similar to the one illustrated in this chapter.

Key Check Figure Total Income Tax Deducted for Year = $3 327.05

Case Study 10

A payroll clerk was rushed to hospital for an emergency operation. Before leaving he collected the following information on the payroll for the New Brunswick Manufacturing Company, which had not been completed:

(i) Payroll period was for the month ending September, current year.

(ii) Total gross pay for the month of September was $350 000. Of this amount, $225 000 represented amounts paid in excess of $18 800 (year to date) to certain employees.

(iii) The amount paid to employees in excess of $1 668.33 (the maximum monthly insurable earnings for unemployment insurance) was $200 000.

(iv) Income taxes totalling $58 000 were to be withheld from employees' earnings.

(v) Union dues totalling $9 000 were to be deducted from employees' earnings.

(vi) Unemployment insurance premiums related to insurable earnings are 1.8% for the employee. The employer is required to contribute 1.4 times the employees' premium.

(vii) The current Canada Pension Plan contribution rate on pensionable earnings is 1.8% for the employees. The employer is required to contribute an equal amount to the employees' CPP.

(viii) The company's chart of accounts shows General Ledger accounts for: Salaries and Wages Payable, 210; CPP Contributions Payable, 211; UI Premiums Payable, 212; Income Tax Deductions Payable, 213; Union Dues Payable, 214; Salaries and Wages Expense, 515; and Payroll Taxes Expense, 516.

You have been called in to complete the accounting entries for the monthly payroll ending September 30.

a Prepare the entry in General Journal form to record the salaries and wages expense.

b Prepare the employer's additional expense resulting from the September payroll.

PART 3

ACCOUNTING CYCLE FOR A MERCHANDISING FIRM

CHAPTER 11

ACCOUNTING CONCEPTS FOR MERCHANDISING FIRMS

Merchandising firm: a business that buys finished goods and sells them at increased prices.

This chapter will take you through the basic accounting ideas that apply to a firm which sells a product. Such a business is called a merchandising firm and the products it sells are called *merchandise* or *goods*.

A merchandising firm buys finished products and sells them at higher prices to make a profit. A *wholesaler* is a merchandising firm which buys finished goods from manufacturers or producers and sells them to other merchandising firms known as *retailers*. Retailers, in turn, sell these goods at marked-up prices to *consumers* (the final users of the goods).

- Topic 1 of this chapter deals with the financial statements of merchandising firms.
- Topic 2 presents the analysis of merchandising transactions.

TOPIC 1 FINANCIAL STATEMENTS

Merchandise inventory: merchandise or goods acquired for resale; a current asset on a balance sheet of a merchandising firm.

A merchandising firm has only one more asset than a service firm — goods (merchandise) acquired for resale. This asset is called merchandise inventory or simply *inventory*.

At the end of any accounting period, the inventory becomes a valuable asset and is *always* reported in the *Current Assets* section of the year-end balance sheet. You will notice this in the partial balance sheet illustrated here.

Any Merchandising Firm
Partial Balance Sheet
as at A Certain Date

ASSETS

Current Assets:	
Cash	*$15 000*
Accounts Receivable	*20 000*
Inventory (at cost)	*40 000*

Analysis:

- At the end of any accounting period (one month, three months, etc.) the merchandise on hand (not sold) is an asset of the business.
- Since the merchandise is expected to be sold within a short time (certainly within the year of the balance sheet date), you must report the inventory as *a current asset.*
- The current asset Inventory is placed after Accounts Receivable to follow the liquidity order of reporting these assets. Cash is listed first because it is the most "liquid" current asset. Then comes Accounts Receivable, because customers usually pay the firm within 30 days. Inventory would come next because it may be sold on credit (Accounts Receivable) before the goods are converted into cash.
- If the firm had investments in Canadian Bonds, or in stocks that trade every day (*Marketable Securities*), these would be placed ahead of Accounts Receivable. See the margin illustration.
- Notice the phrase *at cost* in parentheses after *Inventory.* This phrase tells readers that inventory is reported on the basis of what the asset costs, not on the basis of the selling price or the cost of replacement. Always show the words *at cost* after *Inventory* when it is reported in the balance sheet.

Current Assets:	
Cash	*$15 000*
Marketable Securities	*50 000*
Accounts Receivable	*20 000*
Inventory (at cost)	*40 000*

A business that sells a product earns most of its revenue by selling merchandise from its inventory. Once the goods are sold, the cost of these goods is used up. Any cost used up to earn revenue for the business becomes an expense to be matched against revenue. This allows the business to determine whether it has made a profit (net income) or incurred a net loss. The expense of the goods sold is called Cost of Goods Sold.

Cost of Goods Sold: a large expense of any merchandising firm.

Some accountants include *Cost of Goods Sold* with all of the other expenses (called Operating Expenses) in the income statement to report the net income or net loss for the accounting period. See the illustration of a condensed income statement below.

Any Merchandising Firm
Condensed Income Statement
For a Definite Accounting Period

Revenue:		
Sales of Goods		*$80 000*
Expenses:		
Cost of Goods Sold	*$40 000*	
Operating Expenses	*20 000*	
Total Expenses		*60 000*
Net Income		*$20 000*

Analysis:

- *Condensed* means that only the key parts of the statement are shown. Details of the cost of goods sold and operating expenses are eliminated, so that the important parts can be examined quickly.
- The main source of revenue for any merchandising firm is the sale of goods (merchandise), reported under *Revenue* as *Sales of Goods* or simply *Sales.*
- Cost of Goods Sold is an expense of the business because it shows the cost of acquiring the goods sold by the firm. This expense is usually larger than all other expenses.

Other accountants prefer to report the previous information in a slightly different way. Examine carefully the illustration below.

Any Merchandising Firm
Condensed Income Statement
For a Definite Accounting Period

Revenue:	
Sales	*$80 000*
Cost of Goods Sold	*40 000*
Gross Profit from Sales	*40 000*
Operating Expenses	*20 000*
Net Income	*$20 000*

Analysis:

Gross Profit from Sales: the result of matching sales revenue with the cost of goods sold.

- Cost of Goods Sold (an expense) is matched against sales revenue to report the Gross Profit from Sales. This method shows how much profit is made before deducting the regular operating expenses.

Important: In this book, you will be asked to report the Gross Profit from Sales. Remember, however, that the Cost of Goods Sold is still an expense in any income statement.

- Gross Profit from Sales becomes the first level of income because the other operating expenses must be deducted to report the final net income or net loss. Because there are two levels of income to report, the first is called *gross* and the second *net.* (As you recall, the word *net* means that *all* expenses have been matched with *all* revenue.)
- When reporting the Gross Profit from Sales, make sure you use the *complete* term so that readers know that this figure is the difference between Sales Revenue and the expense called Cost of Goods Sold. Do not use an abbreviation.
- Although the Cost of Goods Sold is matched separately with the Sales Revenue, this cost is an expense. Why? Because all income statements follow the matching principle. Under this prin-

ciple, revenues are matched with related expenses. If the sales of goods give the revenue figure, the cost of the goods sold becomes the expense to be matched against Sales Revenue. Always remember that Cost of Goods Sold is an expense no matter where it is reported in any income statement.

• Inventory is an unexpired cost, because its cost has not been used up. Hence, it is reported as a current asset on the balance sheet. The Cost of Goods Sold becomes the cost of the goods used up — the expired cost — and must be matched against sales revenue in the income statement.

Calculating the Cost of Goods Sold

Although this calculation is essential in the preparation of financial statements, it is not a very difficult task.

Some businesses require an accurate and immediate count of inventory. What type of product would you count at the end of each day to ensure that every item sold has been recorded? If you answer "cars on a car lot" or "diamond rings in a jewelry store," you understand the initial concept of perpetual inventory.

Perpetual inventory: a system of calculating the cost of each good sold immediately after the sale of the inventory item.

The second method of inventory calculation is periodic inventory. As its name suggests, in this method the staff of a store counts the remaining inventory periodically. Then by using the purchase cost records, they can determine the cost of the merchandise on hand or the cost of the inventory.

Periodic inventory: a system of calculating the cost of all goods sold at the end of an accounting period.

Suppose that the business accounting records of your firm (Hawkeye's Medical Supply Wholesale) shows the following information for the month of August:

1.	*Cost of the goods on hand at the beginning of August (beginning inventory)*	*$ 5 000*
2.	*Cost of the goods purchased throughout the month*	*7 000*
3.	*Sale of medical supplies to various retailers throughout the month*	*13 000*

You can easily calculate the cost of the goods that were available for sale. Then you can calculate the cost of the goods that were sold. (Remember that the business "marks up" the goods it sells, so the $13 000 sales figure contains the potential profit of the business.)

• *What did you have on hand at the beginning of the month?*

Beginning Inventory = $5 000

- *What did you purchase during the month in addition to what was already there?*

Purchases = $7 000

- *What then is available for the business to sell?*

Beginning Inventory + Purchases = Cost of Goods Available for Sale

Physical inventory: the actual counting of inventory items at the end of an accounting period.

Because we have not maintained any records concerning the cost of the goods that were sold, you must calculate this figure. But stop your calculation long enough to take physical inventory This is a count, on August 31 at the close of business, of all the items not sold during the month. By using the purchase records and multiplying the cost of each item times the number of items counted, you will discover the cost of the goods on hand at the end of the month (Ending Inventory). Now calculate the cost of the goods that you sold.

Let's assume that your calculation came to $6 500. Subtract what is left from what you had available to sell. That is the Cost of the Goods Sold.

Cost of Goods Available for Sale – Ending Inventory
= Cost of Goods Sold

Hawkeye's Medical Supply Wholesale
Partial Income Statement
For the Month Ended August 31, 19—

Revenue from Sales		$13 000
Cost of Goods Sold:		
Inventory, August 1	$ 5 000	
Purchases	7 000	
Cost of Goods Available for Sale	12 000	
Inventory, August 31	6 500	
Cost of Goods Sold		5 500
Gross Profits from Sales		$ 7 500

To summarize your calculation:

(1) Determine the Beginning Inventory.

(2) Determine the amount you purchased during the month.

(3) Add the two together to generate the Cost of Goods Available for Sale.

(4) At the end of the period determine, through a physical inventory count, the number of units remaining, and use purchase records to get the dollar value of those units — the Ending Inventory.

(5) Subtract the Ending Inventory from the Cost of Goods Available for Sale to get the Cost of Goods Sold.

(6) Finally, subtract the Cost of Goods Sold from the Revenue to get Gross Profit from Sales.

Factors affecting Sales Revenue

Every merchandising business, and especially a wholesaler, faces three different factors which can affect the final reporting of sales revenue.

- returns of merchandise sold to customers
- allowances off the sales price granted to customers
- sales discounts granted to customers

Ordinarily, the first two factors are grouped under the heading *Sales Returns and Allowances,* and the third under *Sales Discounts.*

Sales Returns and Allowances Most retail and wholesale firms allow their customers to return merchandise that is unsatisfactory — damaged, broken, or the wrong size, shape, or colour. The amount of this sales return is deducted from the customer's outstanding balance. In some cases, the customer may be willing to keep the merchandise if the seller reduces the price. This sales allowance reduces the amount of the customer's account in the same way that a sales return would affect the account. The seller reduces the customer's bill by the appropriate amount unless the goods were paid for with cash, in which case the customer gets a cash refund.

Sales return: return of merchandise by a customer to the seller.

Sales allowance: reduction from original sales price for slightly inferior or unsuitable goods.

Sales Discounts In order to encourage credit customers to pay their bills ahead of the usual credit deadline, many merchandising firms, especially wholesalers, will offer their customers what is called a sales discount. If Evergreen Nurseries offers credit terms to its retailers of "1/10, n/30," this tells customers that if they pay the nursery within 10 days of the date of the invoice, 1% of the sales amount is deducted from the total purchase price of the invoice, and that if they do not choose to pay within the discount period, they must pay the total amount of the invoice within 30 days of the date of the invoice. Both Sales Returns and Allowances and Sales Discounts decrease the amount of the original sales revenue.

Sales discount: cash discount deducted from the sales invoice.

Revenue from Sales:		
Gross Sales		*$20 000*
Less: Sales Returns and Allowances	*$200*	
Sales Discounts	*100*	*300*
Net Sales		*$19 700*

As you can see in the margin, the Net Sales (net revenue from sales) consists of the original amount of the sales revenue, called *Gross Sales* less any sales returns, allowances, and sales discounts.

Factors affecting Cost of Goods Sold

Merchandising firms that use the periodic inventory method face several factors that will affect the final calculation of Cost of Goods Sold. These factors include:

- *transportation-in* or freight charges resulting from the movement of goods from the location of the supplier to the purchaser
- *returns* of purchases to the supplier
- *allowances* granted to the buyer of merchandise
- *purchases discounts* taken by the buyer

Note: In what follows, all factors affecting the *Cost of Goods Sold* section will be explained from the point of view of the buyer.

Purchases	*$5 000*
Transportation-in	*300*
Cost of Delivered Goods	*$5 300*

Transportation-in A buyer of merchandise is often required to pay the cost of transportation. These costs, called Transportation-in or *Freight-in,* must be added directly to the purchase price. This total results in a dollar value called the *Cost of Delivered Goods.* For example, if your business contracts for the purchase of merchandise costing $5 000 from a firm in Calgary, Alberta and the shipping costs from Calgary to Red Deer, your store's location, are $300, then the cost of the delivered goods equals $5 300.

On the other hand, if you pay the cost of transporting the goods from *your* place of business to *your* customer, it is an operating expense called *Delivery Expense* or *Transportation-out* or *Freight-out.* Transportation-in and Transportation-out are totally different accounts and are not interchangeable.

Cost of Delivered Goods	**$5 300**
Purchases Returns and Allowances	**200**
Net Purchases	**$5 100**

Purchases Returns and Allowances A firm may find that the goods sent to them are damaged or that the quantity is not as ordered. They may then choose to return all the goods or negotiate with the supplier for an allowance on the original price. Depending upon the course of action taken, the business will have to record a purchases return or an allowance. These will decrease the cost of the goods purchased.

Cost of Delivered Goods		**$5 300**
Purchases Returns and Allowances	**$200**	
Purchases Discounts	**300**	**500**
Net Purchases		**$4 800**

Purchases Discounts Many suppliers will encourage buyers to pay their bills early by offering favourable credit terms. This is common practice between manufacturers and wholesalers, and between wholesalers and retailers. When a buyer accepts the credit terms and pays early, the total purchase price is reduced.

For example, a chemical company offers credit terms to one of its customers as 3/10, 1/15, n/60. If the customer, who owes

$10 000, pays within ten days of the invoice date, his or her payment equals $9 700 ($10 000 − $300). If he or she pays within fifteen days, the payment is $9 900 ($10 000 − $100). Finally, if the company chooses not to accept any discount whatsoever, the customer must pay the full $10 000 within sixty days.

The reporting of Purchases Returns and Allowances and Purchases Discounts as part of the *Cost of Goods Sold* section of an income statement is illustrated below. Notice that the final purchase cost is called *Net Purchases.*

The following illustrations of an income statement and a balance sheet show the format used by all merchandising firms that follow the periodic inventory method.

Redrock Paper Products
Income Statement
For the Year Ended December 31, 19—

Revenue from Sales:				
Sales			$65 500.00	
Less: Sales Returns and Allowances		$ 285.00		
Sales Discounts		215.00	500.00	
Net Sales				$65 000.00
Cost of Goods Sold:				
Inventory, January 1			$15 600.00	
Purchases		$48 870.00		
Add: Transportation-in		630.00		
Cost of Delivered Goods		49 500.00		
Less: Purchases Returns and Allowances	$1 250.00			
Purchases Discounts	500.00	1 750.00		
Net Purchases			47 750.00	
Cost of Goods Available for Sale			63 350.00	
Less: Inventory, December 31			14 860.00	
Cost of Goods Sold				48 490.00
Gross Profit from Sales				16 510.00
Operating Expenses:				
Advertising Expense			$ 150.00	
Salesperson's Salaries Expense			3 200.00	
Heat and Power Expense			4 000.00	
Telephone Expense			860.00	
Delivery Expense			1 110.00	
Payroll Tax Expense			630.00	
Total Operating Expenses				9 950.00
Net Income				$ 6 560.00

Redrock Paper Products
Balance Sheet
as at December 31, 19—

ASSETS

Current Assets:		
Cash	$ 5 200.00	
Marketable Securities	2 500.00	
Accounts Receivable	8 000.00	
Inventory (at cost)	14 860.00	
Supplies on Hand	1 200.00	
Total Current Assets		$31 760.00
Fixed Assets (at cost):		
Land	$10 000.00	
Building (security for the mortgage)	35 000.00	
Equipment	8 000.00	
Delivery Truck	6 500.00	
Total Fixed Assets		59 500.00
Total Assets		$91 260.00

LIABILITIES AND OWNER'S EQUITY

Current Liabilities:		
Bank Loan Payable	$ 2 800.00	
Accounts Payable	4 050.00	
Current Portion of Mortgage Payable	5 000.00	
Total Current Liabilities		$11 850.00
Long-Term Liabilities:		
Mortgage Payable, due 20— (secured by building)	$25 000.00	
Less: Current Portion due within year	5 000.00	
Total Long-Term Liabilities		20 000.00
Total Liabilities		$31 850.00
Owner's Equity:		
Capital, R. Robturn	$55 350.00	
Add: Net Income	6 560.00	
	61 910.00	
Less: Drawings, R. Robturn	2 500.00	
Total Owner's Equity		59 410.00
Total Liabilities and Owner's Equity		$91 260.00

TOPIC 1 PROBLEMS

11-1 Calculate the net sales figure under each of the following conditions. Prepare the *Revenue* section of the income statement for **d** and **e.** Gross Sales = $5 000 for **a** to **e.**

a No Sales Returns and Allowances, no Sales Discounts
b Sales Returns and Allowances = $800
c Sales Discounts = $202
d Sales Returns and Allowances = $770, Sales Discounts = $280
e Sales Returns = $285, Sales Allowances = $310, Sales Discounts = $250

Key Check Figures
Net Sales = (a) $5 000, (d) $3 950, (e) $4 155

11-2 During the year, Wildwood Products Company purchased merchandise costing $400 000. State the Cost of Goods Sold under each of the following unrelated assumptions. *Hint:* Do each of these problems in a format similar to the *Cost of Goods Sold* section of the income statement.

a No Beginning Inventory, Ending Inventory = $100 000
b Beginning Inventory = $65 000, Ending Inventory = $75 000
c Beginning Inventory = $50 000, Ending Inventory = $35 000
d Beginning Inventory = $37 000, no Ending Inventory
e Beginning Inventory = $88 000, Ending Inventory = $150 000

Key Check Figures
Cost of Goods Sold = (a)$300 000, (c) $415 000, (e) $338 000

11-3 Compute the amount of Cost of Goods Sold given the following information:

(i) Beginning Inventory, $10 000
(ii) Purchases, $65 000
(iii) Transportation-in, $560
(iv) Purchases Returns and Allowances, $250
(v) Ending Inventory, $11 000

Key Check Figure
Cost of Goods Sold =$64 310

11-4 Find the Gross Profit (Loss) from Sales for the month ended June 30, 19— from the following information.

(i) Sales, $8 000
(ii) Inventory, June 1, $5 000
(iii) Purchases, $7 500
(iv) Inventory, June 30, $3 200

Note: You are preparing a partial income statement for the XYZ Company. Include *Revenue* and *Cost of Goods Sold* sections. A heading is also required.

Key Check Figure
Gross Loss =$1 300

11-5 Prepare a partial income statement for the year ended December 31, 19— for the Skyview Plane Sales Company given the following information:

(i) Sales, $5 950
(ii) Sales Returns and Allowances, $241
(iii) Sales Discounts, $123
(iv) Inventory, January 1, 19—, $3 385
(v) Purchases: February, $2 800, June, $3 000, October, $1 800
(vi) Purchases Returns and Allowances, $100
(vii) Purchases Discounts, $85
(viii) Freight-in, $195
(ix) Inventory, December 31, 19—, $4 110

Key Check Figure
Gross Loss = $1 299

11-6 From the following information, prepare an income statement for The Halifax Novelty Company for the year ended December 31, 19—. *Note:* Expenses are summarized to save space.

(i) Inventory, January 1, $24 000
(ii) Sales, $200 000
(iii) Sales Discounts, $900
(iv) Purchases Returns and Allowances, $900
(v) Inventory, December 31, $21 000
(vi) Sales Returns and Allowances, $1 200
(vii) Purchases, $118 000
(viii) Purchases Discounts, $600
(ix) Transportation-in, $1 400
(x) General and Administrative Expenses, $18 000
(xi) Selling Expenses, $21 000

Key Check Figure
Net Income = $38 000

11-7 Yukon Auto Sales & Service Company is owned and operated by Harold Beetont. He has collected the information given below and requested that you prepare for him **a** an income statement and **b** a classified balance sheet for the year ended December 31, 19—.

(i) Sales, $280 500
(ii) Sales Returns and Allowances, $1 535
(iii) Sales Discounts, $950
(iv) Purchases, $155 000
(v) Purchases Returns and Allowances, $2 123
(vi) Purchases Discounts, $1 240
(vii) Inventory, January 1, $47 000
(viii) Inventory, December 31, $52 500
(ix) Transportation-in, $2 700
(x) Salesperson's Salaries, $18 000
(xi) Office Salaries, $12 000
(xii) Utilities Expense, $550
(xiii) Telephone Expense, $360
(xiv) Property Tax Expense, $1 755
(xv) Payroll Tax Expense, $1 255
(xvi) Insurance Expense, $1 495
(xvii) Shop Supplies Expense, $4 560
(xvii) Cash, $10 800
(xix) Accounts Receivable, $87 600
(xx) Office Supplies on hand, $763
(xxi) Land, $21 000
(xxii) Building, $25 000
(xxiii) Equipment, $5 675
(xxiv) Accounts Payable, $10 500
(xxv) Property Tax Payable, $480
(xxvi) Bank Loan Payable, $8 500
(xxvii) Mortgage Payable, $27 000 (current portion due within year, $7 000; security: Land and Building)
(xxviii) H. Beetont, Capital, January 1, $85 655
(xxix) H. Beetont, Drawings, $18 000

Key Check Figure
Total Equity = $156 858

11-8 Determine the amount of the missing item in each of the following unrelated sets of information.

a Beginning Inventory, $12; Ending Inventory, $14; Cost of Goods Sold, $85; Transportation-in, $4; Purchases, ?

b Beginning Inventory, $4; Purchases, $65; Purchases Returns and Allowances, $3; Ending Inventory, $3; Cost of Goods Sold, $63; Transportation-in, ?; Purchases Discounts, $2

c Cost of Goods Sold, $100; Purchases, $80; Purchases Returns and Allowances, $2; Sales Returns and Allowances, $1; Sales Discounts, $1; Beginning Inventory, $110; Ending Inventory, ?; Sales, ?; Gross Profit from Sales, $98

TOPIC 2 MERCHANDISING TRANSACTIONS

Much of what you have learned about analyzing service firm transactions is also true for a merchandising firm. In Part 1 of this book, you learned that there are three basic rules for debiting and crediting accounts.

(1) If an account increases, always record on the side on which the element is found in the equation. When an asset increases, record the amount on the left (debit) side, because assets are found on the left side of the accounting equation. The same is true for both liabilities and owner's equity accounts. Since both of these elements are found on the right side of the equation, increases in liability and owner's equity accounts must be recorded on the right (credit) side. Since revenue causes the element Owner's Equity to increase, and since Sales is a revenue account, all sales of merchandise will result in a credit entry to the Sales account.

A = L + OE
Assets originate on the left side, Liabilities and Owner's Equity on the right side.

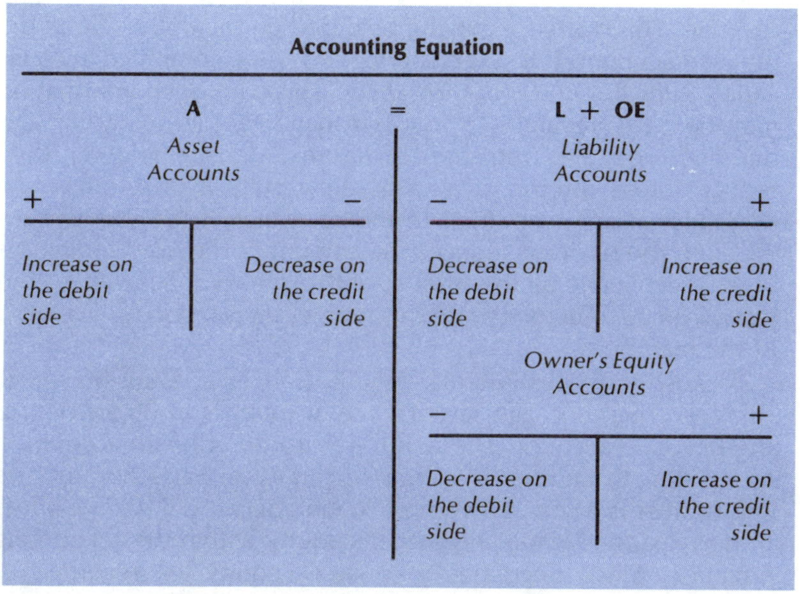

(2) If an account decreases, record on the side opposite to that on which the element is found in the equation. Thus, when an asset is to be decreased, record that amount on the right (credit) side of the account. When liabilities and owner's equity accounts decrease, the entry must be made on the left (debit) side. Because expenses cause a decrease in Owner's Equity, expenses are recorded on the debit side of the account.

(3) Normal balances in the accounts are identified on the side on which the elements are found in the equation. Therefore, we would expect asset accounts to have debit balances and

liabilities to have credit balances. Capital and revenue accounts, and those owner's equity accounts that record increases in the element, have credit balances. Drawings and expense accounts, and those owner's equity accounts which record decreases in the element, have debit balances.

With these concepts in mind, we can now analyze any merchandising firm transaction.

Cash Sales vs. Credit Sales

May 4	Cash	500	
	Sales		500
	To record the day's cash sales.		

When a business sells merchandise for cash, one entry completes the entire transaction; this is illustrated in the margin. But when extending credit, the business sells goods to the customer for a promise of cash in the future. The next example in the margin shows the sale, and later the receipt of cash.

May 1	Accts. Rec./Eastside Variety	1 500	
	Sales		1 500
	To record the sale of goods to Eastside Variety on account. Terms 2/10, n/30.		
May 31	Cash	1 500	
	Accts. Rec./Eastside Variety		1 500
	To record payment in full.		

Sales Returns and Allowances

Sales Returns and Allowances have the effect of decreasing revenue. This decrease may be recorded on the debit side of the revenue account, but it is customary to use a combined account called *Sales Returns and Allowances.* This way, such information may be kept separate to assist management in analyzing the number, type, and frequency of returns. Management can then reduce future returns. If a cash sale results in a return or an allowance, cash is returned to the customer. If the sale was on account, the business reduces the amount of the outstanding accounts receivable by the amount of that return or allowance. The journal entry to demonstrate this type of transaction is illustrated in the margin.

May 4	Sales Returns and Allowances	200	
	Accts. Rec./Eastside Variety		200
	The customer returned unsatisfactory goods.		

Because the Sales Returns and Allowances account decreases sales revenue, one can say that the account is in opposition to the Revenue account. The word used to describe an account in opposition to another is *contra.* In this case, Sales Returns and Allowances is a contra revenue account, because it has the effect of decreasing revenue and owner's equity within the accounting equation. Since decreases to owner's equity are recorded as debits in accounts that cause the decrease, all Sales Returns and Allowances are recorded as debits in the contra account.

Sales Discounts

May 10	Cash	1 470	
	Sales Discounts	30	
	Accts. Rec./Eastside Variety		1 500
	To record payment of May 1 sale less 2% discount.		

Study the margin illustration of a credit sale on May 1 for $1 500. If there were no returns and if the company pays according to the credit terms, 2/10, n/30, a cheque for $1 470 would pay the outstanding invoice in full. A 2% discount on $1 500 is equal to $30 and this would be recorded in the Sales Discounts account as a debit entry because the discount is reducing the total revenue earned.

The total of the debits, cash and sales discounts equals the credit entry for Accounts Receivable/Eastside Variety. The debit entry to Sales Discounts reduces the total amount of the Sales revenue account and therefore owner's equity. Sales Discounts is also a contra revenue account. The credit entry to Accounts Receivable/Eastside Variety is equal to the full amount of the invoice, $1 500. The credit terms permit customers to pay two percent less if they pay within ten days of the date of the invoice. Since these conditions were fulfilled, the total amount of the invoice has been paid and must be recorded by means of the Cash and Sales Discounts entries. If the discounted amount were recorded to the account receivable, there would be an outstanding balance in that account. This would be incorrect, as the invoice has been paid in full.

Consider the accounting problem that exists when a customer who is sold goods on credit returns some of them or is granted an allowance on the sale. When the discount period arrives, what figure is used to calculate the amount of the allowable discount? Return to the first transaction for Eastside Variety. The initial sale was $1 500. The return of goods was $200. The net amount sold to the customer was $1 500 – $200 = $1 300. The sales discount is to be taken on the net sale *after* any returns and allowances; therefore, the discount is 2% of $1 300 or $26. The second entry, dated May 10, shows the resulting entry after the return and discount.

May 10	Cash	1 274	
	Sales Discounts ..	26	
	Accts. Rec./ Eastside Variety		1 300
	To record payment of the May 1 sale less the return and discount.		

Both Sales Returns and Allowances and Sales Discounts are *contra revenue* accounts, and therefore must show debit entries. Also, since both are related to the revenue classification, in a chart of accounts, code them to follow the revenue account immediately, as shown in the margin.

Chart of Accounts

REVENUE
401 Sales
402 Sales Returns and Allowances
403 Sales Discounts

Transactions Affecting Cost of Goods Sold

Let's review the concept of cost of goods sold before examining the entries that account for it.

In Topic 1, the cost of goods sold was matched with the related sales revenue for an accounting period to determine the gross profit from sales. In accounting for a service firm, expenses are matched against related revenue to determine the net profit (net income) for an accounting period. For the accounting of a merchandising firm, the match-up of cost of goods sold must be regarded as one of the expenses of carrying on a merchandising business.

As illustrated in Topic 1, the cost of goods sold should be matched alone under revenue to disclose the difference (margin) between the sale and the cost of the sale. (The cost of goods sold is an expense to be matched against revenue.)

An analysis of a sales transaction and its effect within the accounting equation supports cost of goods sold as an expense of a merchandising business. Assume a beginning accounting equation as follows:

Assets			=	Liabilities	+	Owner's Equity
Cash	Inventory	Equipment		Accounts Payable		J. Hill, Capital
$5 000 +	$20 000 +	$5 000	=	$12 000	+	$18 000
$30 000			=	$30 000		

Now consider the effects of selling some of the goods on hand (inventory) costing $1 000 for $4 000 cash. The inflow of cash resulting from the sale is analyzed as shown in the following illustration.

	Assets			=	Liabilities	+	Owner's Equity	
	Cash	Inventory	Equipment		Accounts Payable		J. Hill, Capital	Revenue (Sales)
	$5 000 +	$20 000 +	$5 000	=	$12 000	+	$18 000	
(1)	+$4 000							+ $4 000
	$9 000 +	$20 000 +	$5 000	=	$12 000	+	$18 000	+ $4 000
	$34 000			=	$34 000			

Since $1 000 cost of the inventory has been sold, naturally the firm no longer has this amount of inventory. Thus, the total assets on the left side of the equation must decrease by $1 000, because there is $1 000 less inventory on hand — any total decrease on the left side of the equation must be balanced by a similar amount on the right side. Since Liabilities is not affected, some other item must cause a $1 000 decrease to Owner's Equity. Because both capital and revenue increase Owner's Equity through investments and sales, an expense must have caused a $1 000 decrease to Owner's Equity. This expense is the cost of the asset inventory used to produce the sales revenue or, in short, the cost of goods sold. The effect of the cost of the goods sold within the equation is as follows:

	Assets			=	Liabilities	+	Owner's Equity		
	Cash	Inventory	Equipment		Accounts Payable		J. Hill, Capital	Revenue	Cost of Goods Sold (Expense)
	$9 000	+ $20 000	+ $5 000	=	$12 000	+	$18 000	+ $4 000	
(2)		−1 000							− $1 000
	$9 000	+ $19 000	+ $5 000	=	$12 000	+	$18 000	+ $4 000	− $1 000
	$33 000			=	$33 000				

By matching the cost of goods sold under the revenue, the equation may be rearranged to disclose the gross profit from sales as follows:

Assets					=	Liabilities	+	Owner's Equity			
Cash		Inventory		Equipment		Accounts Payable		J. Hill, Capital			
										$4 000	Sales Revenue
										− 1 000	Cost of Goods Sold
$9 000	+	$19 000	+	$5 000	=	$12 000	+	$18 000	+	$3 000	Gross Profit from Sales
$33 000					=	$33 000					

Now if the various items shown in the accounting equation are replaced by account names, it is easy to follow the analysis of debits and credits to account for the cost of goods sold. This step suggests that an asset account called Inventory would be credited and an expense called Cost of Goods Sold would be debited. These accounts are, in fact, used by merchandising firms that follow the perpetual inventory method but not for the firms that use the periodic inventory method. Under the periodic inventory method, the cost of goods sold is calculated only once — at the end of the accounting period for all of the goods sold. Refer to the examples in Topic 1 as you study the analysis of transactions that follow.

Inventory Changes

Inventory is an asset account in both the perpetual and periodic methods of valuing inventory. In the perpetual system, inventory is always changing. In the periodic system, inventory changes are made only at the end of an accounting period, when a physical inventory count is made.

Analysis of Inventory Changes

- The *beginning inventory* figure has the same value as the ending inventory figure from the previous period. This same value can be obtained from the Inventory account in the General Ledger.

Inventory	
Beginning inventory is the cost of the unsold inventory carried forward from the last accounting period.	

- This inventory value can be added to the net purchase figure to calculate the "cost of goods available for sale" figure on the income statement of the accounting period. In this sense, the beginning inventory is no longer an asset but part of the cost of goods sold at the end of the accounting period.

- At the end of the accounting period, a physical count determines the cost of the inventory unsold. This ending inventory becomes a current asset shown on the balance sheet as at the last date of the accounting period. In addition, the cost of the ending inventory is deducted from the cost of goods available for sale to calculate the cost of goods sold.
- At the very end of the accounting cycle, General Journal entries called closing entries replace the beginning inventory figure with the ending inventory figure.

Purchase of Merchandise

Jun. 15 Purchases	*2 000*	
Accts. Pay./ Yellow Paint Store		
or		
Cash		*2 000*
Purchased merchandise on credit terms 1/10, n/30 (or buy for cash).		

Under the periodic inventory method, the cost of merchandise purchased for resale is accumulated in an account called *Purchases.* The Purchases account is debited whether the merchandise is bought with cash or on credit. See the margin illustration.

Analysis: Three points must be stressed in the analysis of the debit entry to Purchases.

(1) The Purchases account is used only for merchandise bought for resale. Assets such as trucks, supplies, or equipment, that are not for resale, must not be placed in the Purchase account. Entry of these assets is to their specific asset accounts.

(2) The Purchases account is not an inventory or asset account. It does not show if goods have been sold or are still on hand; it only indicates the total amount of goods acquired during the period of time being measured.

(3) Since the Purchases account has only the above function (so that the cost of goods available for a sale can be calculated), it must be regarded as a part of the cost of goods sold. The cost of goods sold is an expense; so is the Purchases account.

Because purchases is an expense account, it is placed under the broad heading "Costs and Expenses" in the Chart of Accounts.

Chart of Accounts

COSTS AND EXPENSES
501 Purchases

Transportation-in Freight costs must be added to the cost of purchases to determine the cost of delivered goods. An accounting entry similar to the one shown in the margin results when a transport company is paid or gives credit terms. It is important to classify the Transportation-in (or freight-in) account as part of the cost of goods sold. This makes the Transportation-in account an expense account, so make debit entries to it.

Jun. 16 Transportation-in	*55*	
Accts. Pay./ CP Express		
or		
Cash		*55*
To record freight charges on merchandise purchased on June 15.		

Merchandise purchased from other countries may be charged a tax called *duty* before such goods are allowed to cross the border. Duty would also have to be added to the cost of purchases. It is common to debit only one account — called *Transportation-in* or *Transportation-in and Duty-in* — with the cost of duties. If a firm purchases large amounts of its merchandise from a foreign firm, it is more likely to use two accounts. *Note:* In the chart of accounts shown in the margin, Transportation-in is numbered very closely to the Purchases account(s).

Purchases Returns and Allowances When merchandise received from suppliers is not acceptable, it may be returned or an allowance off the purchase price may be granted. In either case, the cost of the purchased goods must be decreased by the cost of the returned goods or by the allowance granted. The journal entry for such a transaction is shown in the margin.

In our analysis of such a transaction it must be noted that the return or allowance causes the quantity and dollar amount of the purchase to *decrease*. In theory, this causes the Purchases account to be credited (the correct entry to decrease the Purchases account). Once again, accountants have decided to isolate such transactions for future management consideration by using a separate account called *Purchases Returns and Allowances*. Furthermore, a separate account allows more complete disclosure on the income statement. Since the Purchases Returns and Allowances account has an affect opposite to that of the purchases account with which it is associated, it is proper to call the Purchases Returns and Allowances account a contra account. This association with purchases places the Purchases Returns and Allowances account in the chart of accounts as illustrated in the margin.

Purchases Discounts When a supplier offers credit terms that include a cash discount, the buyer should take advantage of them in order to decrease the cost of purchases. In our example, the credit terms offered by the Yellow Paint Store were 1/10, n/30. Under normal situations the buyer would mail a cheque for $1 683. The accounting journal entry is illustrated below.

Jun. 16	*Accts. Pay./ Yellow Paint Store*	*1 700*	
	Purchases Discounts		*17*
	Cash		*1 683*
	Cheque No. 417 in payment of the June 15 purchase, less a 1% cash discount.		

Purchases Discounts is a contra expense account and causes owner's equity to increase. We know that to increase an owner's equity account, a credit entry is required as in the illustration. To

Chart of Accounts

501 Purchases
502 Transportation-in

Jun. 16	*Accts. Pay./ Yellow Paint Store*	*300*	
	Purchases Returns and Allowances		*300*
	To record the return of defective merchandise bought on June 15 on account (or for cash).		

Chart of Accounts

501 Purchases
502 Transportation-in
503 Purchases Returns and Allowances

Chart of Accounts

501 Purchases
502 Transportation-in
503 Purchases Returns and Allowances
504 Purchases Discounts

Purchases	**$2 000**
Less Return	**300**
Net Purchase	**$1 700**
Less Discount	**17**
Amount of Cheque	**$1 683**

summarize, then, the main points in calculating the cost of goods sold under a periodic inventory method:

- The Inventory account will supply the cost of the goods available at the beginning of the accounting period, the cost of the beginning inventory.
- Add net purchases to the beginning inventory to arrive at the cost of all goods available for sale. The information to calculate the net purchases will be found in the Purchases account, the Transportation-in account, and the two contra accounts Purchases Returns and Allowances and Purchases Discounts.
- At period end, physical stock-taking is performed to learn the cost of the goods unsold (the cost of the ending inventory). Deduct ending inventory from the cost of goods available for sale to calculate the expense called Cost of Goods Sold.
- Finally, this expense may be matched against the sales revenue to determine the gross profit from sales for the accounting period.

TOPIC 2 PROBLEMS

11-9 Record the transactions below in General Journal form. Show a brief explanation for each entry.

Nov. 2 Cash sales for the day were $856.
4 Purchased merchandise from Clifford Clock Works totalling $3 000. Terms 2/10, n/30.
8 Sold merchandise on account to Black's Construction Co. Terms 1/15, n/60. $1 800.
10 Bought a new truck for $12 500. Paid $2 500 down. Remainder due in 30 days to Green Truck Company.
14 Paid Clifford Clock Works in full. (Don't forget the discount.)
16 $300 of damaged goods were returned by Black's Construction Co.
18 Purchased merchandise from Pete's Paper Products on account. Terms 2/10, n/30. $750.
20 Some of the merchandise from Pete's Paper Products was incorrect, but was kept after negotiating an allowance for $50.
23 Received payment in full from Black's Construction Co.
27 Paid invoice from Pete's Paper Products in full.

11-10 Use the transactions listed below as your source information for a merchandising firm operating under the periodic inventory method, as you do exercises **a** to **c.**

Mar. 1 The beginning inventory is $7 000. *Note:* No journal entry is required for this. Put a debit balance for this amount into the Inventory account.
4 Purchased merchandise for cash. $800.

Mar. 7 Purchased merchandise on credit from Hillsborough Mack Comp. Terms 2/10, n/60. $4 500.
7 Paid Saint John Express Company freight charges on the above purchase. $50. Used cheque No. 217.
8 Purchased new equipment from Moncton Sales & Service. Total cost $10 200. Paid $2 200 cash, remainder due in 30 days.
9 Returned for full refund $500 of the goods purchased from Hillsborough Mack Comp.
11 Purchased merchandise on credit from Fredericton Wholesalers. Terms 4/5, 2/15, n/30. $6 600.
15 Purchased merchandise for cash from Chatham Manufacturers Inc. $3 100.
17 Paid Hillsborough Mack Comp. in full with cheque No. 218. *Hint:* Don't forget the return and discount.
22 Paid the monthly utility bill with cheque No. 219. $250.
26 Paid Fredericton Wholesalers in full with cheque No. 220. *Hint:* Remember the sales discount.

a Analyze each of the transactions in General Journal form. Briefly explain each entry.

b Post each of the journal entries to T-accounts using the account names introduced in this chapter.

c Assume that on March 31, month-end physical inventory is taken and the cost of the unsold goods equals $8 700. From the information in the problem and the T-accounts ledger, calculate the Cost of Goods Sold for the month of March. The name of the company is Dalhousie Mfg. Co.

Key Check Figure Cost of Goods Sold = $12 638

11-11 Mr. A. Johnson owns and operates a print shop called A-1 Printers. He uses the periodic inventory method to calculate the Cost of Goods Sold. The financial transactions for the month of January are listed below. On January 1, Mr. Johnson's business had the following balances in the listed accounts: Cash, $1 500; Inventory, $3 500; Equipment, $2 700; Bank Loan Payable, $3 000; Accounts Payable/London Supply Comp., $700. (HINT: Calculate the amount for the owner's equity.)

Jan. 2 Paid rent on building for January. $500. The next cheque to be used by the business is No. 677.
3 Purchased merchandise on credit from Good Paper Products. Terms 2/10, n/30. $1 500.
5 Issued a cheque to London Supply Comp. for $500 on account.
6 Sold merchandise on credit to J. Kofmen. Terms net 30 days. $600.
7 Cash sales for the week totalled $2 400.
8 Purchased additional printing equipment from Boston Press Manufacturing Ltd. Terms net 60 days. $1 200.
10 Sold merchandise on credit to T. Curtis. Terms net 30 days. $500.
11 Received a shipment of paper supplies from H.G. Paper Wholesalers at a cost of $4 400. Terms 1/15, n/60.

Jan. 11 Freight of the shipment received totalled $120. Paid CN Express by cheque.
13 Issued a cheque to Good Paper Products, payment in full less the discount.
14 Cash sales for the week totalled $3 200.
15 Returned damaged goods received from H.G. Paper Wholesalers totalling $200.
16 A. Johnson invested additional cash into the business. $2 000.
18 Acquired a new cash register for the business for cash. $390.
19 Received payment in full from J. Kofmen. $600.
21 Cash sales for the week totalled $2 900.
22 Issued a cheque to pay the monthly telephone bill. $22.
23 Received a shipment of printer's ink from Graphics Supply Comp. Terms 1/15, n/30. $500.
24 Received an advertising bill from The Herald for $65. Terms net 30 days.
25 Issued a cheque in payment of an invoice with H.G. Paper Wholesalers, less return, less discount.
28 Paid for adjustment and repairs to the printing equipment. $160.
28 Cash sales for the week totalled $3 000.
29 A. Johnson withdrew $250 for personal use.
30 A. Johnson took home, for personal use, paper and envelopes valued at $100 cost. *Hint:* Don't use Inventory; the account that was originally debited must be changed.
30 Issued separate cheques for the following items: Part payment of the bank loan, $1 000; monthly hydro bill, $75; part payment to Boston Press Manufacturing Ltd., $400.

a Journalize each of the transactions in the General Journal, Page 35. Include a brief explanation.

b Post to the three-column ledger. (If you are not using the workbook, set aside 20 lines for Cash, 8 lines for Sales, and 15 lines for Accounts Payable Control.)

c Post to the Accounts Receivable and Accounts Payable subsidiary ledgers. Then prepare schedules for each to verify the control accounts in the General Ledger.

Key Check Figure Total Assets = $14 295

d Physical inventory count on January 31 showed unsold goods at $3 000. Prepare a month-end income statement and related balance sheet.

Case Study 11

In taking a physical inventory at the end of the accounting year, a stock clerk failed to count all the merchandise remaining on one complete shelf. Consequently, the year-end financial statements were prepared without a complete listing of the cost of goods unsold. A few days after the viewing of the financial statements, the omission of inventory was discovered and reported to the manager. In analyzing the omission, the manager estimated that the cost of inventory not reported was $2 000.

a Explain the effect of the inventory omission on the income statement and balance sheet.

b Assume that management did nothing to correct the omission and permitted the error to be carried into the next accounting year. Would there be any serious effect on the financial statements prepared at the end of the next accounting year? Explain your answer.

CHAPTER 12

INTRODUCING THE ACCOUNTING CYCLE

In Part 1 you learned the four steps in the accounting cycle: (1) preparing source documents, (2) making debit and credit entries from the source documents, (3) posting the financial entries to the ledger, and (4) preparing the trial balance from a listing of ledger accounts to make sure that the debits equal the credits. After calculating the trial balance, you prepared the worksheet. From this, you prepared the income statement and the balance sheet in good form.

These steps will now be applied to an accounting system that can be used by any merchandising firm.

- Topic 1 deals with the journalizing and posting of credit sales.
- Topic 2 deals with purchases of merchandise on account.
- Topic 3 deals with purchases of merchandise for cash.
- Topic 4 deals with a time-saving record called the Combination Journal.

TOPIC 1 JOURNALIZING AND POSTING DOCUMENTS AFFECTING SALES

As you know, sales transactions in a business firm may be on a cash or credit basis. This Topic will deal with journalizing and posting credit sales only.

A Flowchart Analysis

Sales invoice: a source document capturing the dollar results of a credit sale of merchandise.

When a business sells merchandise on account or for credit, a source document called a sales invoice is prepared. By studying the entire sales system for a merchandising firm, you will understand how the source document originates the transaction. A flowchart is a good method for understanding a credit sale. Although the procedures vary from business to business, a basic pattern similar to the one shown opposite is followed.

As you can see, there are many forms and procedures within a complete credit sales system. These are organized for the purpose of receiving and approving the order, packing and shipping the merchandise, billing, and accounting for the transaction. One

FLOWCHART OF A CREDIT SALES SYSTEM

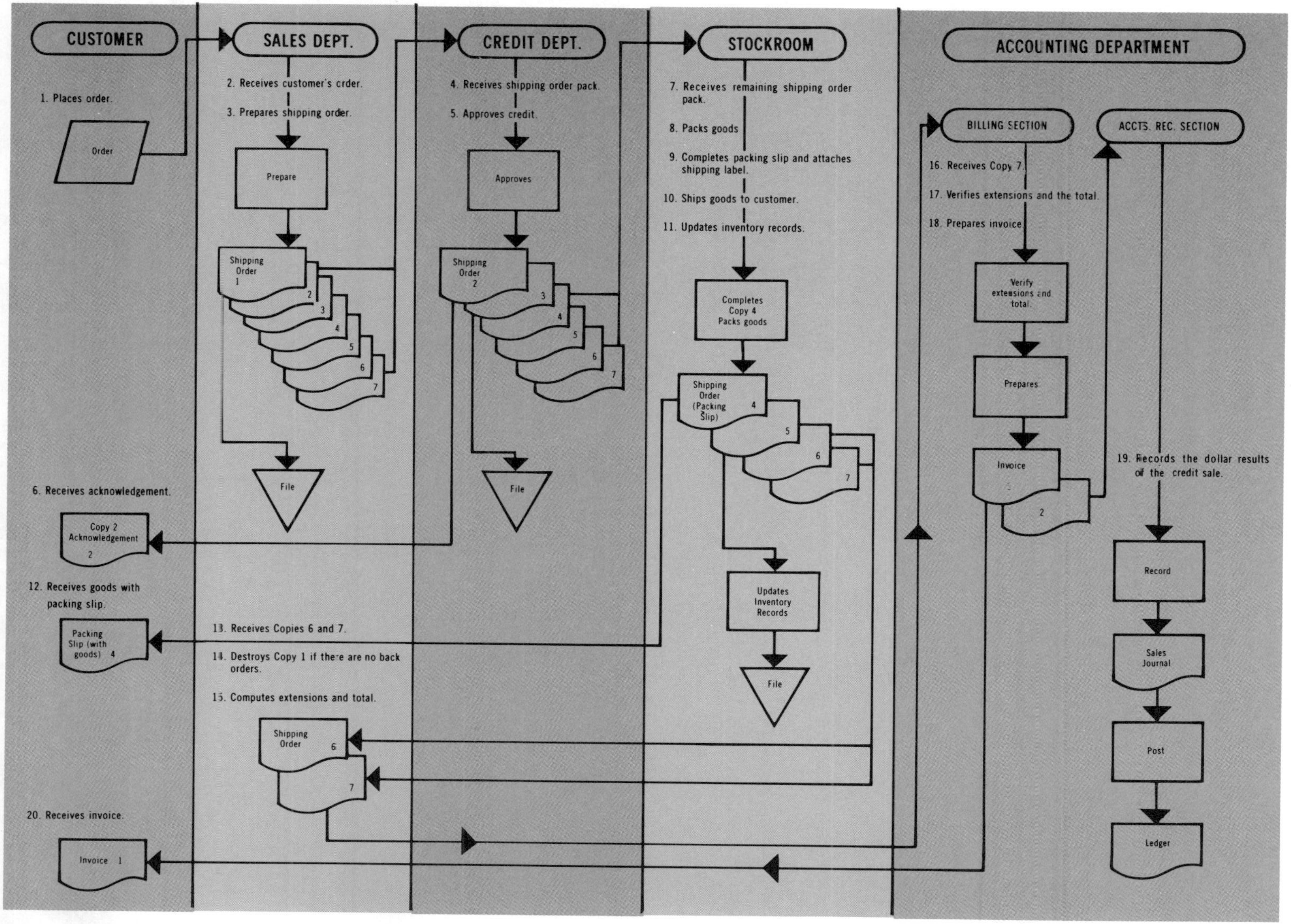

very important idea of internal accounting control is stressed. The systems flowchart emphasizes the idea that responsibility within the company should be divided. For example, the person making the sale should not be the person who records or who approves the sale. Similarly, the person who packs the goods must not be involved with the accounting records.

Detailed Analysis: Study these points as you follow the credit sales system in the chart:

Receiving the Customer's Order A sale begins when a customer places an order. The order may be received in any one of a number of ways: perhaps a sales order form is completed by a travelling salesperson making calls on a customer; or a clerk takes a customer's order over the telephone, or in person; or a standard purchase form is sent by a customer; or a letter is sent on the customer's letterhead (letter form). A typical purchase order is illustrated below.

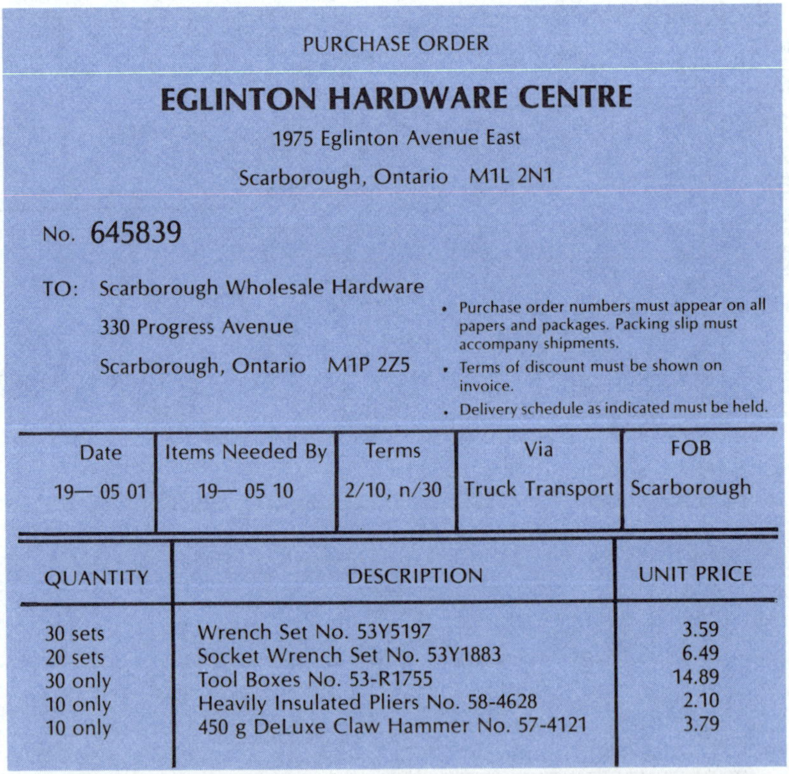
PURCHASE ORDER

EGLINTON HARDWARE CENTRE
1975 Eglinton Avenue East
Scarborough, Ontario M1L 2N1

No. 645839

TO: Scarborough Wholesale Hardware
330 Progress Avenue
Scarborough, Ontario M1P 2Z5

- Purchase order numbers must appear on all papers and packages. Packing slip must accompany shipments.
- Terms of discount must be shown on invoice.
- Delivery schedule as indicated must be held.

Date	Items Needed By	Terms	Via	FOB
19— 05 01	19— 05 10	2/10, n/30	Truck Transport	Scarborough

QUANTITY	DESCRIPTION	UNIT PRICE
30 sets	Wrench Set No. 53Y5197	3.59
20 sets	Socket Wrench Set No. 53Y1883	6.49
30 only	Tool Boxes No. 53-R1755	14.89
10 only	Heavily Insulated Pliers No. 58-4628	2.10
10 only	450 g DeLuxe Claw Hammer No. 57-4121	3.79

Preparing the Shipping Order The next document, prepared in the sales department, is the *shipping order.* This document is necessary to avoid having a variety of forms on which orders are received. Since, in a large merchandising firm, shipping orders will be used by several departments, many copies of a shipping order are made. The next illustration shows seven copies labelled for various departments. The number of copies is determined by the requirements of the business. When you examine the systems flowchart in detail, be sure that you follow the pathway of all seven copies.

SCARBOROUGH WHOLESALE HARDWARE
SHIPPING ORDER

330 Progress Avenue
Scarborough, Ontario M1P 2Z5

NO. **SO-101**
DATE 19— 05 02

SOLD TO: Eglinton Hardware Centre
1975 Eglinton Avenue East
Scarborough, Ontario M1L 2N1

SHIP TO: Same as above

P.O. No. 645839 | P.O. Date 19— 05 01

FOB Scarborough | Ship Via Barr Transport | Terms 2/10, n/30 | Date Wanted 19— 05 10

QUANTITY ORDERED	STOCK NUMBER	DESCRIPTION	UNIT PRICE	QUANTITY SHIPPED		QUANTITY BACK-ORDERED
30 sets	53Y5197	Wrench Set	3.59			
20 sets	53Y1883	Socket Wrench Set	6.49			
30 only	53-R1755	Tool Boxes	14.89			
10 only	58-4628	Heavily Insulated Pliers	2.10			
10 only	57-4121	450 g DeLuxe Claw Hammer	3.79			
		TOTAL				

COPY 1 - SALES DEPARTMENT (Control)
COPY 2 - ACKNOWLEDGEMENT
COPY 3 - CREDIT DEPARTMENT
COPY 4 - PACKING SLIP
COPY 5 - STOCKROOM (Inventory)
COPY 6 - SALES DEPARTMENT (Shipped)
COPY 7 - ACCOUNTING DEPARTMENT

Approving the Customer's Credit Rating Before merchandise is sent out to any customer, that customer's credit rating must be approved. In a large business, this is usually handled by the credit department. If the credit rating is poor, this department will prepare an explanatory note and return it to the sales department along with the shipping order. If the customer's credit rating is good, a copy of the shipping order is sent to the customer to acknowledge that the order is being processed. The credit department is also responsible for approving the terms of credit (such as "2/10, n/30, n/60," and so on).

Handling the Shipping Order in the Stockroom Once the order has been approved, the credit department keeps one copy of the shipping order on file and forwards the rest to the stockroom. The stockroom packs the customer's order and prepares it for shipment. The quantity shipped and any *back orders* — items not yet available for shipment — are identified on the shipping order copies. One copy of the order is included along with the customer's merchandise as a *packing slip*. See the next illustration.

SCARBOROUGH WHOLESALE HARDWARE
SHIPPING ORDER

330 Progress Avenue
Scarborough, Ontario M1P 2Z5

NO. **SO-101**
DATE 19— 05 02

SOLD TO:	Eglinton Hardware Centre 1975 Eglinton Avenue East Scarborough, Ontario M1L 2N1	Shipped by J. Miller 5/2/--	
SHIP TO:	Same as above	Mass 40 kg	No. of Packages 3
		P.O. No. 645839	P.O. Date 19— 05 01
FOB Scarborough	Ship Via Barr Transport	Terms 2/10, n/30	Date Wanted 19— 05 10

QUANTITY ORDERED	STOCK NUMBER	DESCRIPTION		QUANTITY SHIPPED		QUANTITY BACK-ORDERED
30 sets	53Y5197	Wrench Set		30		0
20 sets	53Y1883	Socket Wrench Set		20		0
30 only	53-R1755	Tool Boxes		30		0
10 only	58-4628	Heavily Insulated Pliers		10		0
10 only	57-4121	450 g De Luxe Claw Hammer		10		0
		TOTAL				

COPY 4 - PACKING SLIP

After the stockroom files its copy of the shipping order, copy 5 in the illustration, the two copies remaining are forwarded to the sales department. This is necessary to make sure that no changes have been made from the original order. If the entire order was filled, copy 1 is then destroyed. Otherwise, back orders are noted on copy 1 and put in the back-order file. Thus, when new stock arrives, a new shipping order is completed from copy 1. The process can then go back to step 5 on the systems flowchart.

Notice that copy 6 remains in the sales department. Copy 7 is sent to the accounting department, where activities are subdivided between the billing section and the accounts receivable section.

Preparing the Bill of Sale Copy Copy 7 is received by the billing section of accounting to prepare the customer's bill of sale. Here, all calculations are checked and the billing procedure begins. Billing ends with the important document called the *sales invoice* or simply the *invoice.*

In practice, two or more copies of the invoice are produced. The original is sent to the customer; the second copy is used by the business as the source document to prove that a credit sales transaction has occurred.

Accounting for the Sales Invoice Finally, copy 2 of the invoice is used by the accounts receivable department to account for the credit sale. Copy 2 of the sales invoice is illustrated below.

SCARBOROUGH WHOLESALE HARDWARE

330 PROGRESS AVENUE INVOICE NO. **101**

SCARBOROUGH, ONTARIO M1P 2Z5

SOLD TO: Eglinton Hardware Centre
1975 Eglinton Avenue East
Scarborough, Ontario M1L 2N1

SHIP TO: Same

INVOICE DATE: 19— 05 02

TERMS: 2/10, n/30

Purchase Order No.	Date	Shipped Via	FOB	No. of Packages
645839	19— 05 01	Barr Transport	Scarborough	3

QUANTITY	STOCK NO.	DESCRIPTION	UNIT PRICE	AMOUNT
30 sets	53Y5197	Wrench Set	3.59	107.70
20 sets	53Y1883	Socket Wrench Set	6.49	129.80
30 only	53-R1755	Tool Boxes	14.89	446.70
10 only	58-4628	Heavily Insulated Pliers	2.10	21.00
10 only	57-4121	450 g DeLuxe Claw Hammer	3.79	37.90
		TOTAL		743.10

COPY 2 - ACCOUNTING

Analysis: In Part 1, you learned that two important basic accounting principles are involved in the analysis of the sales invoice. These are the *revenue principle* and the *objectivity principle.*

The Revenue Principle As you may recall, the revenue principle (1) defines revenue and (2) pinpoints the timing of revenue recognition.

(1) Revenue may be defined as an inflow of assets (accounts receivable coming in) resulting from the sale of merchandise.

(2) The invoice is dated May 2, 19—. Therefore, revenue is recognized at the point of the sale (the date on the invoice).

The Objectivity Principle The sales invoice is a source document giving proof that a sale on account has taken place. In the language of accounting, this evidence supports the basic accounting principle of objectivity. Once objective evidence is available, accounting can proceed to account for the sale.

In summary, all credit sales systems result in a copy of the sales invoice which will be accounted for. As the systems flowchart shows, the accounting copy is recorded in a special journal, as will be explained below. Once journalized, the debits and credits can be posted to the ledger.

The Sales Journal

An efficient accounting system uses a special journal to record all highly repetitive transactions. For example, all cash inflows (debits to Cash) are recorded in the cash receipts journal. Similarly, all cash outflows (credits to Cash) are recorded in the cash payments journal.

Sales Journal: a chronological record of credit sales.

If a firm makes most of its sales of merchandise on credit to its customers, a special journal called the sales journal is used to record them. The information needed to complete the journal comes from the sales invoice.

There are many forms of sales journals. A very simple one records only credit sales as illustrated below.

SALES JOURNAL Page 1

DATE		INVOICE NO.	ACCOUNT DEBITED	TERMS	POST. REF.	AMOUNT	
19—							
May	2	101	Eglinton Hardware Centre	2/10, n/30		743	10
	5	102	Plaza Home Hardware	2/10, n/30		642	80
	9	103	Woodbridge Hardware	1/20, n/30		975	30
	14	104	Summers Hardware Limited	1/15, n/60		1 439	25
	17	105	Markham Home Hardware	2/10, n/30		832	15
	24	106	Eglinton Hardware Centre	2/10, n/30		534	40
	27	107	Hyland Hardware	1/20, n/30		890	17
	30	108	Thornhill Home Hardware	2/10, n/30		738	29

Invoice No. 101
743.10
Copy 2—Accounting

Analysis:

- The name of the journal and the page number are found at the top on the page.
- Special columns are provided to record the details of a sales transaction. This information comes from the accounting copy of the invoice.

- *Only credit sales* are recorded in this sales journal.
- The date entered in the journal, the date of the sales invoice, recognizes revenue from the point of sale.
- Since this sales journal contains only one money column, every recorded sales invoice must be analyzed as a debit to Accts. Rec./(Customer's Name), and a credit to Sales. And since only the debit side of the entry is shown, the credit to the Sales account must be understood each time the figure is entered in the *Amount* column.
- At month-end, the *Amount* column is totalled. This total is posted to the accounts receivable controlling account and the Sales account in the General Ledger. The single posting of the total results in time saved, because only the total is posted to the General Ledger at month-end.

The Need for the Accounts Receivable Ledger

A modern accounting system uses a separate accounts receivable ledger to account for changes in individual customer accounts. (This idea was introduced in Part 2 for the accounts receivable application of a dental service firm.) The need for a separate accounts receivable ledger is equally important for merchandising firms. Here's a brief review of the main reasons for a separate accounts receivable ledger.

- If a business were to list all its individual customer accounts in the General Ledger, it would become overloaded. There would be too many individual customer accounts mixed in with other GL accounts.
- Including many individual customer accounts in the GL would make this ledger cumbersome and unwieldy.
- Only one person could post at any one time.
- The trial balance would require several pages.
- If the trial balance did not "work" (balance), it could take a great deal of time to find the error.
- The *Current Assets* section of the balance sheet would be extremely long.

To eliminate these problems, the majority of merchandising firms remove the individual customer accounts from the General Ledger and replace them with one accounts receivable controlling account. Individual accounts are filed in a separate ledger called the Accounts Receivable Subsidiary Ledger or *Customer Ledger.* The process of pulling out the individual customer accounts to replace them with one account is shown on page 384.

Accounts Receivable Subsidiary Ledger: the file of all individual customer accounts.

Analysis: Keep these points in mind as you study the illustration:

- A second ledger, the *Accounts Receivable Ledger* (a subsidiary ledger), now contains all the individual accounts receivable. The individual accounts have been replaced by one

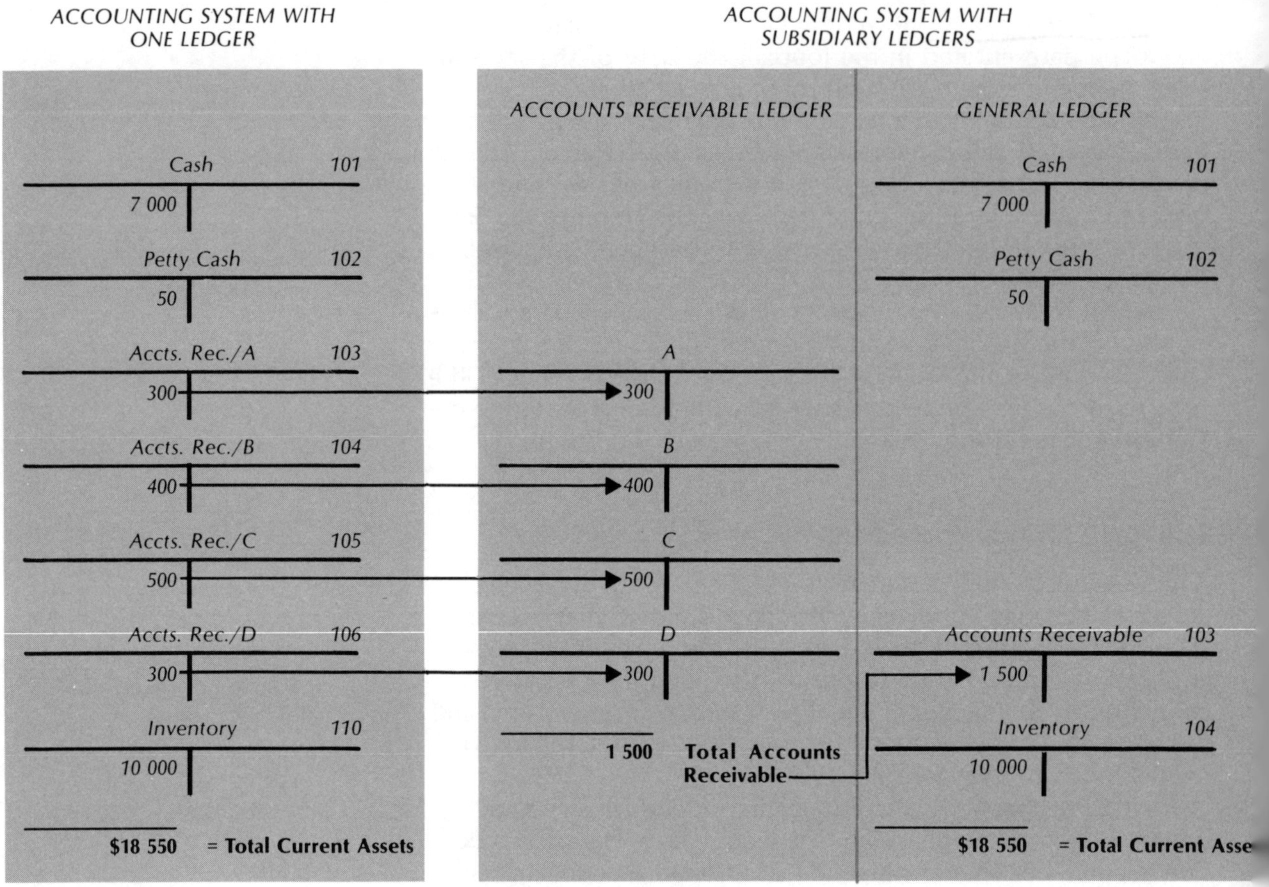

controlling account called Accounts Receivable (Accts. Rec. Control) in the General Ledger.

- Note that the amount in the GL Accounts Receivable account is the sum of all the individual accounts receivable accounts now found in the Accounts Receivable Ledger.
- The word *Control* is always understood for Accounts Receivable in the General Ledger. The Accounts Receivable account "controls" all the individual accounts in the subsidiary ledger, because the total of these individual customer accounts must agree with the debit balance shown in the control account. In this sense, Accounts Receivable in the GL controls all individual customer accounts filed in the subsidiary ledger.
- The term *subsidiary* also has a special meaning in accounting. Because the General Ledger controls *all* the business accounts for the purposes of preparing financial statements, the Accounts Receivable Ledger must become the secondary or subsidiary ledger. This idea also applies to other subsidiary ledgers like the accounts payable ledger. Subsidiary ledgers contain only individual accounts making up only one class of account. They do not contain the accounts required to prepare a set of financial

statements. All accounting systems will have a General Ledger, but only the larger firms need one or more subsidiary ledgers to go along with their GL.

- Subsidiary ledger accounts usually do not have account numbers as do accounts in the GL. Instead, they are filed alphabetically by customer name.
- One final point: With an accounting system that uses a General Ledger and one or more subsidiary ledgers, accounting clerks may work full-time in a department that is given the responsibility for a particular ledger. You may come across advertisements as illustrated in the margin here and below.

It is important to remember that the system of dividing the work among different ledgers not only speeds up the processing of accounting information, but also supports the internal control measure of division of responsibility.

Accounts Receivable CLERK

We have an opening in our accounts receivable department for a clerk.

Qualifications should include at least one years experience in accounts receivable, ability to operate calculator and some typing.

We are willing to consider two permanent part-time applicants for this position. Good company benefits, flexible working hours, own transportation necessary, northeast location.

Please reply in confidence stating salary expectations and experience to:

BOX K1347 FREE PRESS

Posting Credit Sales

The posting of credit sales is done in two stages: first, posting to the accounts receivable ledger on a daily basis; second, posting to the General Ledger at the end of the month.

Stage 1: Post daily to individual accounts in the accounts receivable subsidiary ledger.

Daily Posting Study the related illustrations on page 386. They show how posting is done to the customer's account in the subsidiary ledger.

Analysis:

- Note that Eglinton Hardware Centre has no account number. Usually, all customer accounts are filed in the subsidiary ledger in alphabetical order.
- Note the additional information in the heading of the customer's account: name and complete mailing address; telephone number; and the credit limit.
- Posting is done from the sales journal to individual customer accounts on a *daily* basis. This is necessary to get accurate, up-to-date information concerning the account at any time.
- Since individual customer accounts are filed alphabetically, a check mark (√) in the *Post. Ref.* column indicates that the information has been posted. The illustration of the sales journal shows two check marks because the entries on May 2 and May 24 have been posted.
- Note the use of the *Explanation* column in the customer's account. Unlike General Ledger accounts, individual customer accounts show detailed explanations of all entries. This information can be very important in checking the discount dates the business has allowed.

ACCOUNTING CLERK

Required by a well established pharmaceutical firm located in the Pointe Claire Industrial Park.

The applicants must have high school education, with some experience in general accounting.

This position offers good working conditions in a modern office, excellent fringe benefits, including educational assistance and a good starting salary.

Please forward complete resume, including salary requirements to:

PERSONNEL MANAGER

SCHERING CORPORATION LIMITED

3535 TRANS CANADA HIGHWAY

PTE. CLAIRE 730, QUE.

Before month-end postings are explained, it is useful to point out that some firms will use a direct posting system when transferring information to the accounts receivable ledger. This means that these firms will post *directly* from source documents

Direct posting: transferring information from the source document directly to the subsidiary ledger account.

SALES JOURNAL — Page 1

DATE		INVOICE NO.	ACCOUNT DEBITED	TERMS	POST. REF.	AMOUNT
19—						
May	2	101	Eglinton Hardware Centre	2/10, n/30	√	743 10
	5	102	Plaza Home Hardware	2/20, n/30		642 80
	9	103	Woodbridge Hardware	1/20, n/30		975 30
	14	104	Summers Hardware Limited	1/15, n/60		1 439 25
	17	105	Markham Home Hardware	2/10, n/30		832 15
	24	106	Eglinton Hardware Centre	2/10, n/30	√	534 40
	27	107	Hyland Hardware	1/20, n/30		890 17
	30	108	Thornhill Home Hardware	2/10, n/30		738 29
	31		Accounts Receivable Debit/Sales Credit			6 795 46

ACCOUNTS RECEIVABLE LEDGER

Name *Eglinton Hardware Centre* **Credit Limit** *$2 000*

Address *1975 Eglinton Ave. E., Scarborough, Ont. M1L 2N1* **Telephone** *293-1810*

DATE		EXPLANATION	POST. REF.	DEBIT	CREDIT	BALANCE
19—						
May	2	Inv. 101; 2/10, n/30	S1	743 10		743 10
	24	Inv. 106; 2/10, n/30	S1	534 40		1 277 50

to the accounts receivable ledger. Under this short-cut system, one copy of the sales invoice will go to the accounts receivable department to be totalled and then posted to the control accounts in the General Ledger.

Stage 2: Posting credit sales; post the monthly total to the General Ledger accounts.

Month-End Posting The month-end total of the sales journal is posted to the General Ledger in the form of a double entry: a debit to the accounts receivable control account, and a credit to the Sales account. Study the next illustration.

Analysis: The illustration shows the month-end total posted to the General Ledger.

- The total sales is first posted to the debit side of the Accounts Receivable account. First, the date, May 31, the posting reference, S1 (standing for 'Sales Journal, Page 1"), the amount of the debit ($6 795.46), and the new balance in the account. Since no previous balance existed, the new balance is the same as the total debit posted, $6 795.46.
- Notice how the sales journal receives the account number of the account which has just been posted. In the *Post. Ref.* column of the sales journal, the account number 103 is shown in the upper part of the column as *103/.* The slash after the number shows that something will follow. In this case, a second number, the account number for Sales, will be shown immediately after posting the total to the Sales account.

SALES JOURNAL — **Page 1**

DATE		INVOICE NO.	ACCOUNT DEBITED	TERMS	POST. REF.	AMOUNT
19— May	2	101	Eglinton Hardware Centre	2/10, n/30	√	743 10
	31		Accounts Receivable/Debit Sales Credit		103/ 401	6 795 46

GENERAL LEDGER

Accounts Receivable — **Account No.** 103

DATE		EXPLANATION	POST. REF.	DEBIT	CREDIT	BALANCE
19— May	31		S1	6 795 46		6 795 46

Sales — **Account No.** 401

DATE		EXPLANATION	POST. REF.	DEBIT	CREDIT	BALANCE
19— May	31		S1		6 795 46	6 795 46

- The same total is posted to the Sales account in the manner shown for Accounts Receivable. Of course, Sales is a revenue account; therefore, the total must be posted to the credit column. After completing the posting, the account number for Sales is cross-referenced by placing the number 401 in the *Post. Ref.* column of the sales journal.
- Once the total is posted to both accounts, the sales journal shows the two posting references *103/401*.

Columnar Sales Journals

In your first look at the sales journal you studied a one-column type. In practice, however, such a simple journal is rare. For most merchandising businesses, special money columns are added to take care of management's need for additional sales information and provincial sales tax when needed.

Columnar sales journal (multi-columned sales journal): a sales journal with several money columns.

For the sake of clarity, a columnar sales journal will be illustrated without a special column for sales taxes. (The accounting for sales taxes is a special item dealt with in Chapter 13.)

Sales Journal with Sales Analysis Most merchandising firms require some form of sales analysis, that is, a breakdown of their sales by product line, by department, or by some other feature. Suppose, for example, management wanted monthly sales figures in the income statement broken down into two distinct product lines, say "Hardware Sales" and "Electrical Sales." The earlier sales journal could easily be expanded with special money columns as illustrated below.

SALES JOURNAL **Page 1**

DATE		INVOICE NO.	ACCOUNT DEBITED	TERMS	POST REF.	ACCOUNTS RECEIVABLE DR.	HARDWARE SALES CR.	ELECTRICAL SALES CR.
19—								
May	2	101	Eglinton Hardware Centre	2/10, n/30		743 10	722 10	21 00
	5	102	Plaza Home Hardware	2/20, n/30		642 80	153 20	489 60
	9	103	Woodbridge Hardware	1/20, n/30		975 30	975 30	
	14	104	Summers Hardware Limited	1/15, n/60		1 439 25	962 93	476 32
	17	105	Markham Home Hardware	2/10, n/30		832 15		832 15
	24	106	Eglinton Hardware Centre	2/10, n/30		534 40	434 30	100 10
	27	107	Hyland Hardware	1/20, n/30		890 17	250 16	640 01
	30	108	Thornhill Home Hardware	2/10, n/30		738 29	590 73	147 56
	31		Totals			6 795 46	4 088 72	2 706 74
						(103)	(401)	(402)

Sales Journal Proof
May 31, 19—

Hardware Sales credit	*$4 088.72*
Electrical Sales credit	*2 706.74*
Accounts Receivable debit	*$6 795.46*

GENERAL LEDGER

Accounts Receivable *103*

May 31	*6 795.46*		

Hardware Sales *401*

		May 31	*4 088.72*

Electrical Sales *402*

		May 31	*2 706.74*

Analysis: Here are the important points of analysis in the study of the columnar sales journal:

- This columnar sales journal contains three money columns: one for recording the debit to Accounts Receivable, one for recording the credit to Hardware Sales, if applicable, and one for recording the credit to Electrical Sales, if applicable.
- Every sales invoice would be recorded as a debit to Accounts Receivable and a credit to one of the two categories of the sales revenue.
- During the month, daily posting may be done from the amounts recorded in the *Accounts Receivable* column of the sales journal, or directly from the source documents to the individual customer accounts filed in the subsidiary ledger.
- At the end of the month, the column totals of this *Columnar Sales Journal* (sometimes called the *Multi-Column Sales Journal*) would be verified to prove that the total debit to Accounts Receivable agrees with the total credits of the individual sales columns. See the margin illustration.
- When the sales journal proof is obtained, the column totals are posted to appropriate General Ledger accounts. In the case of the wholesale hardware example, the totals of the sales columns would be posted to the credit side of Hardware Sales and Electrical Sales. The total of the *Accounts Receivable* column would be posted to the debit side of the accounts receivable controlling account. See the margin illustration again.
- After posting the column totals to the General Ledger, account numbers of the accounts posted are placed in parentheses directly below each column total. These numbers are important

because they indicate that the totals have been posted to the General Ledger.

Since the General Ledger now contains the monthly totals of sales analyzed by product line, a monthly income statement may be prepared as shown in the partial income statement below. (Assume that all sales for the month have been on a credit basis only.)

Scarborough Wholesale Hardware
Partial Income Statement
For the Month Ended May 31, 19—

Revenue from Sales:		
Hardware Sales	*$4 088.72*	
Electrical Sales	*2 706.74*	
Total Gross Sales		*$6 795.46*

The above example illustrates how additional information in the journal and in the ledger assist the eventual preparation of more useful financial statements for management decision-making. In the very large firms which are organized around many product lines and around many departments, the accounting system would probably use a computer to produce the columnar (multi-column) sales journal. The computer would also be used to update individual customer accounts in the subsidiary ledger and appropriate accounts in the General Ledger. And with the aid of special instructions, the computer would be used to produce month-end financial statements for management.

Recording Sales Returns and Allowances

If a customer of the business finds it necessary to return part or all of an order of merchandise, the business uses the contra revenue account called Sales Returns and Allowances (often abbreviated *Sales R & A*). Under certain conditions, the customer may keep the goods but request some adjustment to the invoice price. If the customer claim and/or return is in order, the seller will issue a source document called a credit memo. A credit memo granting an allowance to Eglinton Hardware Centre is illustrated next.

Credit memo: a statement issued by the seller, granting a reduction in the invoice price for damaged or returned goods.

This document gives rise to a General Journal entry and postings as illustrated at the bottom of page 390.

Analysis: These points relate to the General Journal and related postings resulting from the credit memo issued to Eglinton Hardware Centre.

- The original copy of the credit invoice would normally be sent to the customer notifying the buyer that the claim has been allowed.

SCARBOROUGH WHOLESALE HARDWARE
CREDIT MEMO
330 PROGRESS AVENUE
SCARBOROUGH, ONTARIO M1P 2Z5

NO. **CM-01**

To: Eglinton Hardware Centre
1975 Eglinton Avenue East
Scarborough, Ontario M1L 2N1

DATE: 19— 05 25

Your Order No. 645890	Our Invoice No. 106

We have credited your account as follows:

Allowance granted for three No. 53Y5171 wrench sets received in damaged condition:

3 sets $9.50 Total $28.50

• Another copy will be used by the accounting department to produce the General Journal entry illustrated below.

• The General Journal has been used because such entries are usually infrequent. Therefore, no special journal is used.

• The General Journal entry reduces the amount in the account receivable of the customer by the amount authorized on the credit memo.

• The credit entry must be *double-posted:* once to the accounts receivable controlling account in the General Ledger, and once to the customer's account in the subsidiary ledger. (In practice, the update of the customer's account in the accounts receivable ledger could be posted directly from the source document.)

• The check mark in the *Post. Ref.* column of the General Journal shows that daily posting has taken place to the individual

GENERAL JOURNAL **Page 3**

DATE		ACCOUNT TITLE AND EXPLANATION	POST. REF.	DEBIT	CREDIT
19—					
May	25	Sales Returns and Allowances	402	28 50	
		Accounts Receivable/Eglinton Hardware Centre	103/√		28 50
		Credit Memo CM-01.			

Double-posting: posting to the controlling account in the General Ledger and also to the individual account in the subsidiary ledger

GENERAL LEDGER *SUBSIDIARY LEDGER*

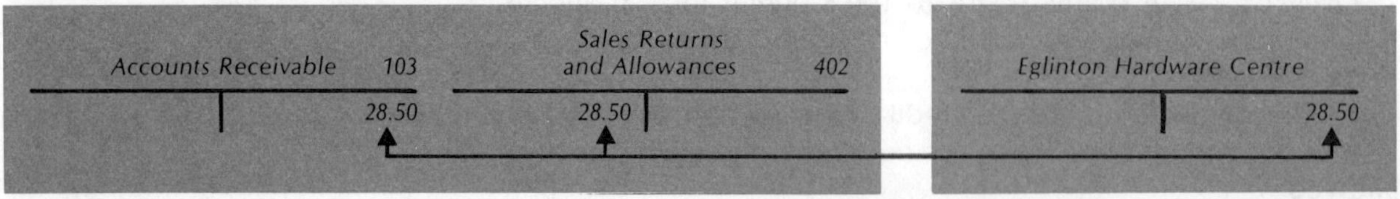

customer's account in the subsidiary ledger. Daily posting is required in this situation because the General Journal, if totalled, produces no meaningful number.

- Although General Ledger accounts are not normally updated until the end of the month, some accounting systems do update the GL accounts affected by the General Journal on a daily basis as well.
- In summary, General Ledger accounts must be updated at the end of each month to produce balances for the preparation of monthly financial statements. All subsidiary ledger accounts must be posted daily to provide very current information on these accounts. When a General Journal is used, posting from this journal may occur daily to make sure that *all* accounting information is transferred from this journal to accounts affected.

Preparation of Monthly Trial Balances

The Trial Balance is an important accounting check before financial statements can be prepared. This check determines if the sum of the debits of the General Ledger equals the sum of the credits. In order to determine the accuracy of these ledgers, trial balances or schedules of accounts must be prepared. In the case of Scarborough Wholesale Hardware, a Schedule of Accounts Receivable is prepared from monthly balances of all customer accounts in the subsidiary ledger, as illustrated on page 392.

Schedule of Accounts Receivable: a list of all customers' account balances, the total of which must agree with the controlling account balance.

A look at the accounts receivable control account in the GL should show agreement between the two figures. A great deal of confidence can be placed in this proof, since the figures were arrived at from different directions.

Here is a useful summary of preparing trial balances under the five-journal system:

General Ledger Trial Balance All accounts with balances are listed in the order in which they are found in the GL. The only difference is the replacement of several individual accounts receivable and accounts payable accounts with one accounts receivable control and one accounts payable control.

Subsidiary Ledger Trial Balances (Schedules of Accounts) A separate alphabetical listing of all subsidiary ledger accounts with outstanding balances is what accountants call a *Schedule of Accounts.* There will be a schedule for every separate subsidiary ledger. Two common subsidiary ledgers are for accounts receivable and accounts payable. Therefore, there will be a schedule of accounts receivable and a schedule of accounts payable. The totals of these two schedules must agree with the corresponding control account balances in the GL. This agreement is essential before the next step of the accounting cycle — the preparation of the worksheet — is taken.

In large firms, different persons would prepare the trial balances. For example, an accounts receivable clerk may prepare the

Scarborough Wholesale Hardware
Schedule of Accounts Receivable
May 31, 19—

Eglinton Hardware Centre	$1 249.00
Hyland Hardware	890.17
Markham Home Hardware	832.15
Plaza Home Hardware	642.80
Summers Hardware Limited ...	1 439.25
Thornhill Home Hardware	738.29
Woodbridge Hardware	975.30
Total of Accounts Receivable	$6 766.96

GENERAL LEDGER

Accounts Receivable		103
	6 795.46	28.50
Balance	6 766.96	

ACCOUNTS RECEIVABLE LEDGER

Eglinton Hardware Centre		
	743.10	28.50
	534.40	
Balance	1 249.00	

Hyland Hardware	
890.17	

Markham Home Hardware	
832.15	

Plaza Home Hardware	
642.80	

Summers Hardware Limited	
1 439.25	

Thornhill Home Hardware	
738.29	

Woodbridge Hardware	
975.30	

Schedule of Accounts Receivable; and a General Ledger clerk (or junior accountant) would prepare the General Ledger Trial Balance. Therefore, when totals agree, one important internal control measure has been used, namely the division of duties.

TOPIC 1 PROBLEMS

12-1 The following are transactions for the month of October for the Red Bay Woodsman Company.

Oct. 3 Sold cord wood to A. Loude on account. Invoice No. 101. Terms 2/10, n/30. $75.00.

10 Sold timber logs to Cody Lumber Mills on account. Invoice No. 102. Terms 1/15, n/60. $500.00.

20 Sold on account, Invoice No. 103, to Churchill Wood Products Limited, 400 bags of cedar wood chips. These chips cost $2.00/bag and the terms offered were n/30.

29 Sold cord wood to Bob Brown on account. Invoice No. 104. Terms 2/10, n/30. $60.00.

a In a one-column Sales Journal, Page 67, record each of the transactions.

b Total the journal correctly, checking to ensure that the debit and credit totals are equal (journal proof or cross-footing).

c Indicate all daily postings by placing *DP* in the *Post. Ref.* column. Indicate which accounts will be posted monthly by placing *MP* under those accounts.

Key Check Figure Sales Journal Total = $1 435.00

12-2 Pete's Pants Palace in St. John's, Newfoundland specializes in workpants and workshirts. Pete uses a multi-columned sales journal to record all credit sales. He offers terms of 1/10, n/30 to all customers.

a Pete has the following columns in his Sales Journal: Accounts Receivable — DR.; Sales Workpants — CR.; Sales Workshirts — CR. Set up the appropriate sales journal similar to the example on page 388. Journalize the following transactions:

19-3

May 1 Sold to Henry Killroy, 10 pairs of workpants at $12.50/pair. Invoice No. 773.

5 Sold to Martha Hanks, 5 pairs of workpants at $13.00/pair and 5 workshirts at $10.00/each. Invoice No. 774.

10 Sold to George Jotter, 25 pairs of workpants at $12.00/pair and 10 workshirts at $10.00/each. Invoice No. 775.

15 Sold to Liz Arts, 3 pairs of workpants at $11.00/pair and 3 workshirts at $10.00/each. Invoice No. 776.

b Total your journal and prepare a journal proof (cross-footing) to check the accuracy of the debits and credits.

Key Check Figure Accounts Receivable Total = $703.00

12-3 W. Passington owns and operates a small printing business called A-1 Printing in Medicine Hat, Alberta. The transactions affecting credit sales for the month of June are illustrated below.

SALES JOURNAL **Page** *15*

Date *19-5*	**Invoice No.**	**Account DR.**	**Terms**	**Post. Ref.**	**Accounts Rec. DR.**	**Sales Fliers CR.**	**Sales Documents CR.**	**Sales Other CR.**
June 1	*9876*	*Peter's Ltd.*	*n/15*		*85*		*85*	
4	*9077*	*ABC Ads Ltd.*	*n/15*		*150*	*150*		
7	*9878*	*A. Deler*	*n/15*		*25*			*25*
12	*9879*	*Talbot Ford Car Sales*	*n/15*		*550*		*400*	*150*
19	*9880*	*Peter's Ltd.*	*n/15*		*100*	*100*		
25	*9881*	*ABC Ads Ltd.*	*n/15*		*245*	*245*		
28	*9882*	*ABC Ads Ltd.*	*n/15*		*480*	*480*		
30		*Totals*			*1 635*	*975*	*485*	*175*

GENERAL JOURNAL **Page** *10*

Date *19-5*	Account Title And Explanation	Post Ref.	Debit	Credit
June 21	*Sales Returns and Allowances*		*20*	
	Accounts Receivable/Peter's Ltd.			*20*
	Allowance made for several poorly printed fliers. Invoice 9880.			

a Open a partial General Ledger with the following accounts: Accounts Receivable Control (120), Sales — Fliers (401), Sales — Invoices (402), Sales — Other (403), Sales Returns and Allowances — Fliers (405). *Note:* Sales returns and allowances accounts for Invoices and Other would also be found, if they were made necessary by the question.

b Open an Accounts Receivable Ledger with the following customer accounts: ABC Ads Ltd., 860 Redcliff Drive, Medicine Hat, Alberta, T1A 3E3; A. Deler, 444 13th Ave., Medicine Hat, Alberta, T1A 4F2; Peter's Ltd., 900 7th Street, Medicine Hat, Albera, T1A 3B4; Talbot Ford Car Sales, 3300 13th Ave., Medicine Hat, Alberta, T1A 4F9.

c Prepare a journal proof of the sales journal before any posting is completed.

Key Check Figure Accounts Receivable Control = $1 615.00

d Prepare the necessary postings to the General Ledger and the subsidiary accounts receivable ledger using the information presented above.

e Prepare an appropriate schedule at the end of the month to check the accuracy of the control account.

12-4 W.J. Stoddard's Wholesale Plumbing Supply uses a one-column Sales Journal similar to the one illustrated in the text. April's transactions involving sales and returns were as follows:

19-1

Apr. 2 Sold on account to ABC Plumbers, Invoice No. 280, goods totalling $310.00. Terms 2/10, n/30.

5 Sold on account to Ace Plumbing, Invoice No. 281, $500.00. Terms 2/10, n/30.

8 Sold on account to A-1 Plumbing Comp., Invoice No. 282, goods totalling $637. Terms 2/10, n/30.

10 Issued a credit memo on Invoice No. 281 for $50.00

15 Sold on account to Hill Street Hardware merchandise totalling $7 600.00. Invoice No. 283; terms 3/10, n/60.

17 Sold on account to Carl's Contracting service $5 000 of merchandise. Invoice No. 284; terms 3/10, n/60.

20 Issued a credit memo to Carl's Contracting Service for incorrect items. $300.00

28 Sold to ABC Plumbers, Invoice No. 285, additional merchandise totalling $750.00. Terms the same as our other entry with this firm.

a Open Accounts Receivable Control, Sales, and Sales Returns and Allowances accounts in the General Ledger.

b Open the following accounts in the Accounts Receivable Subsidiary Ledger: A-1 Plumbing Comp., ABC Plumbers, Ace Plumbing, Carl's Contracting Service, Hill Street Hardware.

c Journalize the transactions to the appropriate journal. *Note:* You may require a General Journal.

d Make all necessary daily postings as you complete the journal entries. Proof your sales journal and make the necessary monthly postings.

e Verify the control account by preparing a schedule for the accounts receivable subsidiary ledger.

Key Check Figure Total of Sales Journal = $14 797

TOPIC 2 JOURNALIZING AND POSTING DOCUMENTS AFFECTING COST OF GOODS SOLD

Return to Chapter 11 and carefully review the accounting of Cost of Goods Sold for a merchandising firm that uses the periodic inventory method. Remember that the periodic inventory method does *not* use the Inventory account to record the purchase of merchandise. Instead, the Purchases account is used, along with other, related purchases accounts in the General Ledger. This Topic will deal strictly with purchases of merchandise on account. Topic 3, involving the cash payments journal, will deal with the purchase of merchandise for cash.

A Flowchart Analysis

When firms buy something on account, they expect to receive an invoice from the seller. To the seller of those goods this source document is a "sales invoice." To the company buying the goods, this business paper becomes their purchase invoice. The systems flowchart on page 398 traces a purchase on account from beginning to end.

Purchase invoice: a bill received by the buyer for merchandise purchased on credit.

Note that no one person is permitted to control all four of the operations involved. Management would insist on supporting the basic internal control measure of *division of responsibility.* In a large business, there would be one person assigned to each of the following duties: (1) ordering the merchandise, (2) receiving the merchandise, (3) storing the merchandise, and (4) accounting for the merchandise.

Analysis: Study these points as you follow the credit purchases system on the chart:

Preparing the Purchase Requisition A *purchase requisition* is required from the department requesting the purchase. In larger firms, a *stockroom inventory card* would be maintained on each product in order to determine how many of the product are presently available for sale. The margin illustration shows

FLOWCHART OF A CREDIT PURCHASES SYSTEM

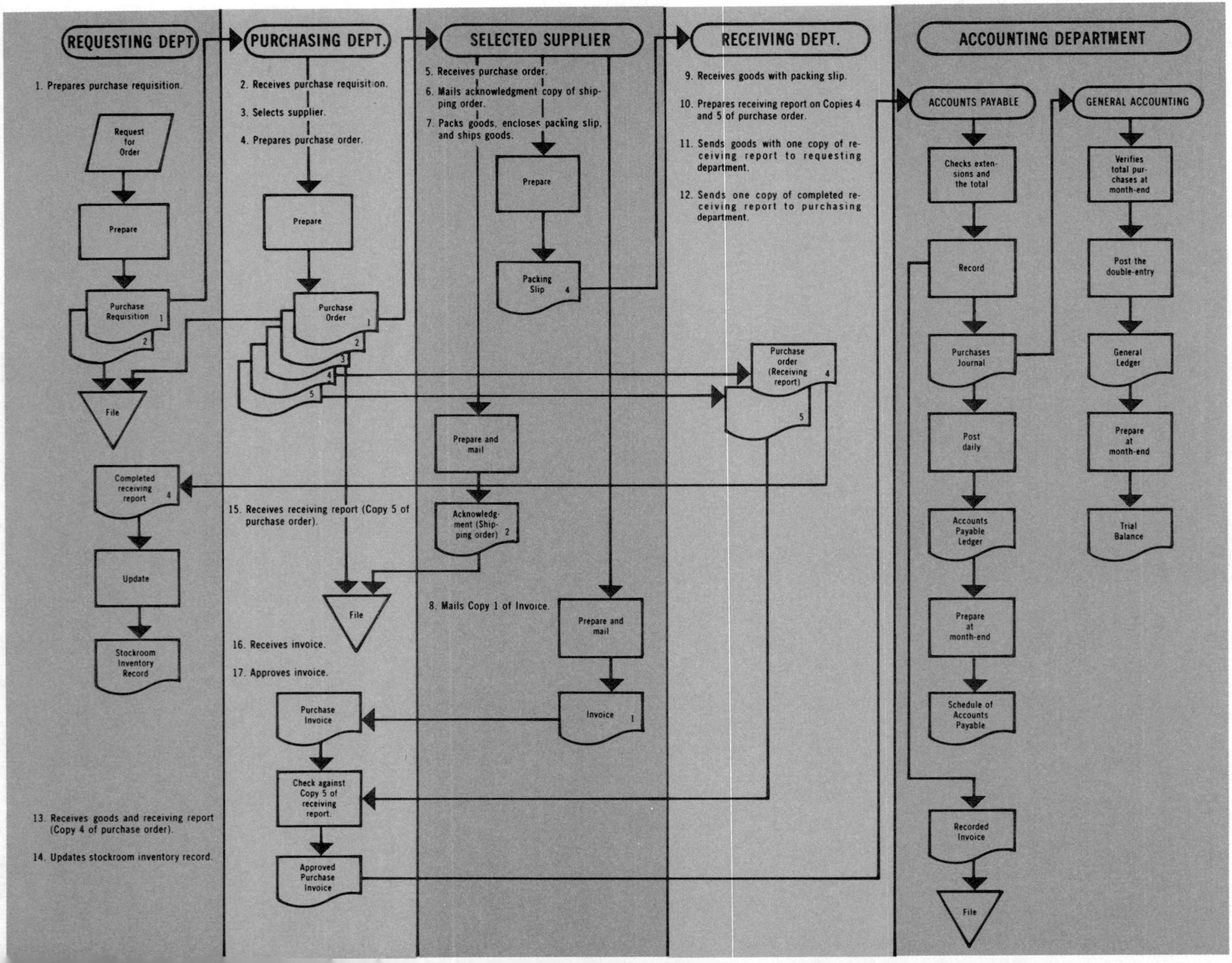

this idea. When the number of units reaches the minimum, a purchase requisition, requesting the re-order of enough units to return the stock to the maximum, is completed.

Preparing the Purchase Order In a larger firm, the requisition would be presented to the purchasing department. This department is responsible for finding a supplier of the product requested for the best purchase conditions (price, delivery, credit terms). This department completes the *purchase order.* The purchase order is prepared in several copies, as illustrated on page 398. Of course, the first copy is mailed to the supplier. If the firm is small, it is the owner-manager who usually prepares the purchase order. In any case, management will divide duties so that there is internal control over the purchase function.

STOCKROOM INVENTORY CARD

No. 53Y5197
Item Wrench Set
Location: Aisle 12 Bin 5
Maximum 100 Minimum 10

Date	Quant. Rec'd	Unit Cost	Quant. Sold	Balance
Jan 10	100	2.59		100
20			10	90
Feb 3			30	60
12			15	45
Mar 8			35	10
10	90			100
Apr 10			20	80
25			25	55
30			15	40
May 2			30	10

Note that five copies of the purchase order have been prepared in our illustration. Special instructions are often entered on the form. These include shipping instructions as in the illustration: "Via Inter-City Express Ltd., FOB Winnipeg, Manitoba." In accounting language, this means the supplier has been requested to ship the order by a specific trucking company (Inter-City Express Ltd.) and it is stated that the purchaser is willing to pay the shipping costs from Winnipeg, the shipping point, to its own place of business in Scarborough, Ontario, the destination. Because the buyer is paying the freight, the supplier can quote a price without adding in any shipping costs. Remember, this is referred to as FOB Shipping Point and the buyer is responsible for the freight charges. The account affected by freight charges, under a periodic inventory system, is Transportation-in or Freight-in. As you recall from Chapter 11, this account is part of the expense called Cost of Goods Sold. Therefore, you would show a debit entry for any Transportation-in.

FOB Shipping Point: buyer agrees to pay the shipping charges from the shipping point to his or her place of business.

Sometimes, the purchase order may state FOB Destination This means that the freight charges are to be left with the supplier. The buyer would have no freight charges to record at all. *Note:* If the shipping terms are FOB Destination, the supplier usually chooses the type of transportation to be used (truck, train, air). If the buyer requested "FOB Scarborough" (free on board to the destination Scarborough), the supplier would normally quote a price including the shipping costs.

FOB Destination: seller agrees to pay the carrier for all transport costs from the shipping point to the buyer's place of business.

Receiving the Merchandise The supplier will ship the goods with a packing slip. The actual sales invoice is usually mailed under separate cover. In the hands of the buyer, this invoice becomes the purchase invoice.

The receiving department will use two copies of our purchase order, stamped as illustrated on page 399 (the box at upper right) to verify the order when it is received. One copy becomes a Receiving Report, which enables the ordering department to update its stockroom inventory card. The other is forwarded to the purchasing department and is used to verify the invoice when it arrives.

PURCHASE ORDER **PO-0078**

SCARBOROUGH WHOLESALE HARDWARE Req. No. R-0051

330 PROGRESS AVENUE
SCARBOROUGH, ONTARIO M1P 2Z5

Small Tools Limited
229 Kearney Street
Winnipeg, Manitoba R2M 4B5

Purchase order number must appear on all letters and packages.

Date Issued	Date Needed	Terms
19— 05 03	19— 05 10	2/10, n/30

Via Inter-City Express Ltd. FOB Winnipeg, Manitoba

	QUANT. ORDERED	STOCK NO.	DESCRIPTION	UNIT PRICE
	90 sets	53Y5197	Wrench Set	2.59
	80 sets	53Y1883	Socket Wrench Set	4.25
	50 only	53-R1755	Tool Boxes	8.75

SCARBOROUGH WHOLESALE HARDWARE

By G Morrison
Purchasing Agent

Copy 1 – Supplier
Copy 2 – Requesting Department
Copy 3 – Purchasing Department
Copy 4 – Receiving Report: Inventory
Copy 5 – Receiving Report: Purchasing

Receiving the Purchase Invoice When the purchase invoice is received, it is sent to the purchasing department. Why? Because it is their responsibility to check the order against the invoice before passing it on to the accounting department (accounts payable division) for payment. If differences occur between the purchase order and the purchase invoice and the shipping report, the supplier must be contacted to clear up any difficulties. Once approval has been given, which is usually indicated with a special stamp, the invoice is forwarded to the accounting department for recording and future payment. An approved purchase invoice is illustrated on page 400.

STOCKROOM INVENTORY CARD

No. 53Y5197
Item Wrench Set
Location: Aisle 12 Bin 5
Maximum 100 Minimum 10

Date	Quant. Rec'd	Unit Cost	Quant. Sold	Balance
	100	2.59		100
			10	90
			30	60
			15	45
			35	10
	90	2.59		100
			20	80
			25	55
			15	40
			30	10
	90	2.59		100

PURCHASE ORDER

PO-0078

SCARBOROUGH WHOLESALE HARDWARE

Req. No R-0051

330 PROGRESS AVENUE
SCARBOROUGH, ONTARIO M1P 2Z5

Small Tools Limited
229 Kearney Street
Winnipeg, Manitoba R2M 4B5

Goods Received 5/8/–
Quantity Checked RS
Quality Checked RS

Date Issued	Date Needed	Terms
19— 05 03	19— 05 10	2/10, n/30

Via Inter-City Express Ltd. FOB Winnipeg, Manitoba

QUANT. REC'D	QUANT. ORDERED	STOCK NO.	DESCRIPTION	UNIT PRICE
	90 sets	53Y5197	Wrench Set	2.59
	80 sets	53Y1883	Socket Wrench Set	4.25
	50 only	53-R1755	Tool Boxes	8.75

SCARBOROUGH WHOLESALE HARDWARE

By G Morrison
Purchasing Agent

Copy 4 – Receiving Report: Inventory

SMALL TOOLS LIMITED

229 KEARNEY STREET
WINNIPEG, MANITOBA R2M 4B5 INV. NO. **0387**

SOLD TO: Scarborough Wholesale Hardware
330 Progress Avenue
Scarborough, Ontario M1P 2Z5

SHIP TO: Same as above

INVOICE DATE: 19— 05 09

TERMS: 2/10, n/30

Customer Order No.	Date	Shipped Via	FOB	No. of Cartons
PO-0078	19— 05 03	Inter-City Express Ltd.	Winnipeg	3

QUANTITY SHIPPED	STOCK NO.	DESCRIPTION	UNIT PRICE	AMOUNT
90 sets	53Y5197	Wrench Set	2.59	233.10
80 sets	53Y1883	Socket Wrench Set	4.25	340.00
50 only	53-R1755	Tool Boxes	8.75	437.50
		SUB TOTAL		1 010.60
		FEDERAL SALES TAX 12.00%		121.27
		TOTAL AMOUNT PAYABLE		1 131.87

APPROVED	DATE 5/10/—
QUANTITIES RECEIVED	G. Morrison
PRICES CHARGED	G. Morrison
EXTENSIONS & TOTALS	S. Davies
DATE PAID	
CHEQUE NO.	

Analysis:

- Accounting now has objective evidence that a purchase of merchandise has occurred. The approved invoice becomes the source document to prove that the transaction is a real one. This concept supports the *objectivity principle.*
- Note that the federal sales tax of 12% has been added to the invoice price. This is required by law on any goods produced or manufactured in Canada or imported into Canada. For the buyer, this is an added cost of purchasing the goods. As the invoice total shows, the tax is added to show the total amount payable.
- The total amount payable becomes the total cost of obtaining the merchandise. This concept supports the *cost principle.* Here, the cost of the merchandise is the seller's price plus the federal sales tax — in other words, the total amount payable on the invoice.
- In Chapter 8, you learned that the cost principle defined what "cost" to use when an invoice offered discount terms. In that chapter, a utility bill was used offering 30 days' credit for the

gross amount and 15 days' credit for the net amount. You learned that, in strict accounting theory, the cost to record for that invoice should be the *cash equivalent price* on the invoice as of the day the invoice is received and approved. In other words, cost is the net amount payable after removing the amount of the cash discount.

Accounting systems which remove the amount of the cash discount before making payment follow the strict application of the cost principle. Under this system, all invoices are accounted for on their *net amounts;* therefore, these accounting systems are said to use the net amount method when accounting for invoices.

Net amount method: a method of accounting for invoices wherein all cash discounts are removed to account for the net cash equivalent price of invoices.

In practice, however, many merchandising firms use the gross amount method to account for invoices. This means that the total amount payable on the invoice would be recorded. No accounting of the cash discount would take place until the future cash was transacted. At this time, the amount of the cash discount would be accounted for as a contra account to the invoice. By showing the cash discount as contra (a deduction) to the original gross amount of the invoice, the net cash equivalent price would be reported on financial statements.

Gross amount method: a method of accounting for invoices wherein the total amount owing shown on the invoice is recorded, and all cash discounts are accounted for only when the cash is transacted.

Here, we will use the gross amount method to account for all invoices. This means that the cost of the invoice to be recorded will be the total amount payable on the invoice. This also means that all cash discounts will be accounted for only when the future cash transaction is identified. (The accounting of cash discounts will be examined in Topic 3.) (The net amount method of accounting for invoices is best learned in more advanced courses of financial accounting.)

- Since Scarborough Wholesale Hardware uses the periodic inventory system, the cost principle measures the amount of purchases as equal to the total amount payable on the invoice. Here, the total cost is $1 131.87.
- Since, under the periodic inventory system, Purchases is an expense (part of the total expense called Cost of Goods Sold), the expense must be recognized according to the *expense principle.* As you know, an expense is recognized when it is incurred and not necessarily when payment is made. Here, the expense is incurred on the stamped approved date: 5/10/—. Accounting can recognize the debit to the Purchases account on that date.

Accounting for the Purchase Invoice As previously indicated, the purchasing department will forward approved invoices to an accounting department called Accounts Payable. It is the responsibility of the accounts payable department to:

(1) Record the dollar amount in accordance with the cost principle. (Since the cost of purchasing merchandise under the periodic inventory system becomes an expense, accounting must recognize the expense Purchases according to the expense principle.)

(2) Record the expense Purchases in a special journal designed to accept credit purchases.

(3) Post purchases transactions to a subsidiary ledger to maintain accurate information in individual creditor accounts.

(4) Maintain a file on each of the suppliers to ensure that payment is made by the stated due dates and that all available purchases discounts are taken.

(5) Update the General Ledger so that amounts are posted at the end of the month to Purchases and to Accounts Payable (control).

Accounts Payable Clerk

To perform accounts reconciliation, coding of invoices and miscellaneous clerical functions. High school leaving. 2 to 3 years experience in general accounting.
Excellent working conditions and salary. Better than average fringe benefits.
Apply in person or in writing to:

PERSONNEL DEPARTMENT

AVIATION ELECTRIC LTD.

Bendix 200 Laurentian Blvd. St. Laurent, Quebec

744-2811

In tracing the systems flowchart you will have noted that several individuals have been involved at different stages. This improves not only internal control, but also the efficiency of the purchasing system. In large merchandising firms, several accounts payable clerks are often required to work in the accounts payable department.

In summary, all credit purchases systems result in a source document called the purchase invoice, which will be accounted for. As the systems flowchart shows, the purchase invoice is recorded in a "Purchases Journal," which we will discuss next. Once journalized, the debits and credits can be posted to the ledger.

The Purchases Journal

Purchases Journal: a chronological record of merchandise purchases on credit.

A special journal called the Purchases Journal is often used to record credit merchandise purchases. A simplified, one-column purchases journal is illustrated opposite. In practice, each business will design the journal to best fulfill its needs.

Analysis: Note the similarity of this to the one-column sales journal in Topic 1. Both journals operate in the same way. Here are some special points of analysis about the purchases journal:

- When using the one-column purchases journal, only credit merchandise purchases are recorded. The one money column serves to record the debit to the Purchases account and the credit to the individual accounts payable identified on the explanation line. Where would you expect to record the purchase of an asset, such as equipment, bought on credit? Since it cannot go into the purchases journal and it certainly is not a sale and no cash is involved, the choice, by elimination, must be the General Journal.
- In the purchases journal, the first column is the date the purchase invoice is approved by the purchasing department. This date is usually stamped on the invoice copy to be sent to the accounts payable department.
- The next column accepts the supplier's name.
- Each of these accounts is a part of the Accounts Payable Subsidiary Ledger. This ledger must be posted daily to ensure up-to-date balances in each separate creditor's account.

Accounts Payable Subsidiary Ledger: the file of all individual creditor accounts.

PURCHASES JOURNAL — Page 1

DATE		ACCOUNT CREDITED	INVOICE NO.	INVOICE DATE	TERMS	POST. REF.	AMOUNT
19— May	10	Small Tools Limited	0387	5/9/—	2/10, n/30	✓	1 131.87
	15	Northern Electrical Co.	6140	5/10/—	1/15, n/60	✓	210.13
	19	F. Milsom Limited	P390	5/19/—	2/10, n/30	✓	475.90
	21	Steel Co. of Canada, Ltd.	S498	5/20/—	2/10, n/30	✓	750.00
	25	Small Tools Limited	0600	5/24/—	2/10, n/30	✓	495.70
	29	Wark Electronics	W174	5/28/—	1/15, n/60	✓	895.30
	31	Purchases Debit/ Accts. Pay. Credit				501/202	3 958.90

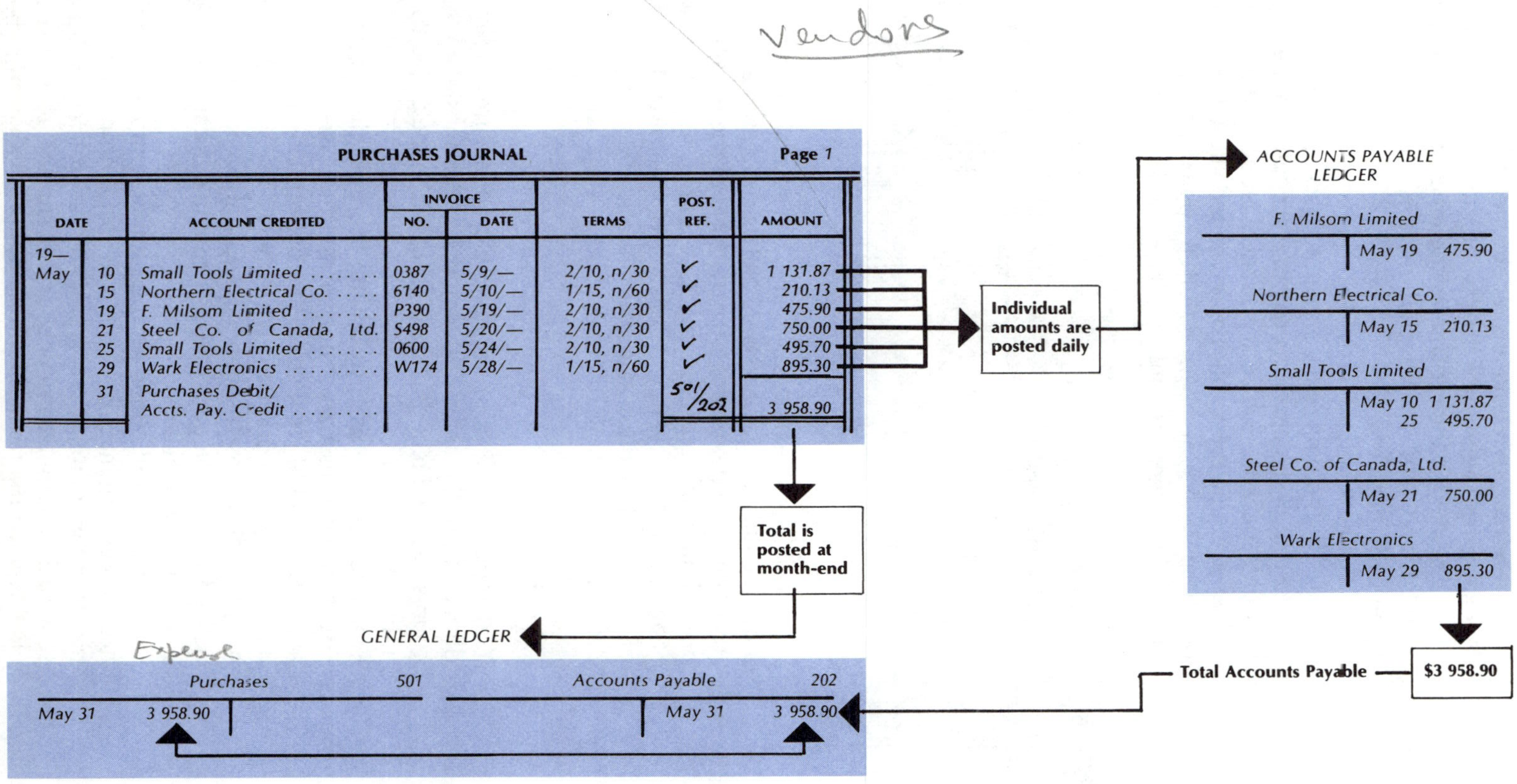

• The next two columns record the invoice number and the invoice date. The invoice date is the billing date of the supplier.

• The next column contains the credit terms granted by the supplier and tells the buyer if there is any discount available upon early payment.

• The next column is the *Post. Ref.* column. In the purchases journal, this column will contain a check mark (√) to indicate the posting of the accounts payable accounts to the appropriate accounts payable subsidiary ledger. Notice, in the subsidiary ledger account for Small Tools Limited illustrated below, that purchase invoice numbers are often copied into the explanation line of the ledger account.

Name *Small Tools Limited*

Address *229 Kearney Street, Winnipeg, Manitoba R2M 4B5*

DATE		EXPLANATION	POST. REF.	DEBIT	CREDIT	BALANCE
19—						
May	10	Inv. 0387	P1		1 131 87	1 131 87
	25	Inv. 0600	P1		495 70	1 627 57

• Finally, the money column in the special journal represents a double entry: a debit to the Purchases account and a credit to Accounts Payable. Notice that the total of the money column is posted monthly to those two GL accounts. At the month-end, a Schedule of Accounts Payable is taken. (See page 405.) The total of this schedule must agree with the accounts payable control account before any further accounting work is carried out.

Schedule of Accounts Payable: a list of all creditor account balances, the total of which must agree with the controlling account balance.

Direct Posting of Accounts Payable

You should recall from Topic 1 that some firms prefer to post directly from the source documents to the subsidiary ledger accounts. When direct posting is followed to the accounts payable ledger, two copies of the invoice are requested from the seller. One copy will be used to update the individual customer's account in the subsidiary ledger. If the firm uses a computer, the accounts payable clerk codes the appropriate information to be inputted by the computer department. The second copy of the invoice will go to the general accounting division to be journalized for the preparation of a monthly total in the accounts payable control account.

Some firms will eliminate the journal completely and merely make an adding machine tape of the totals from all invoice documents. At month-end, the subsidiary ledger clerk will produce a schedule of all outstanding payables and the general accounting clerk will list the totals of the accounts payable from the journal

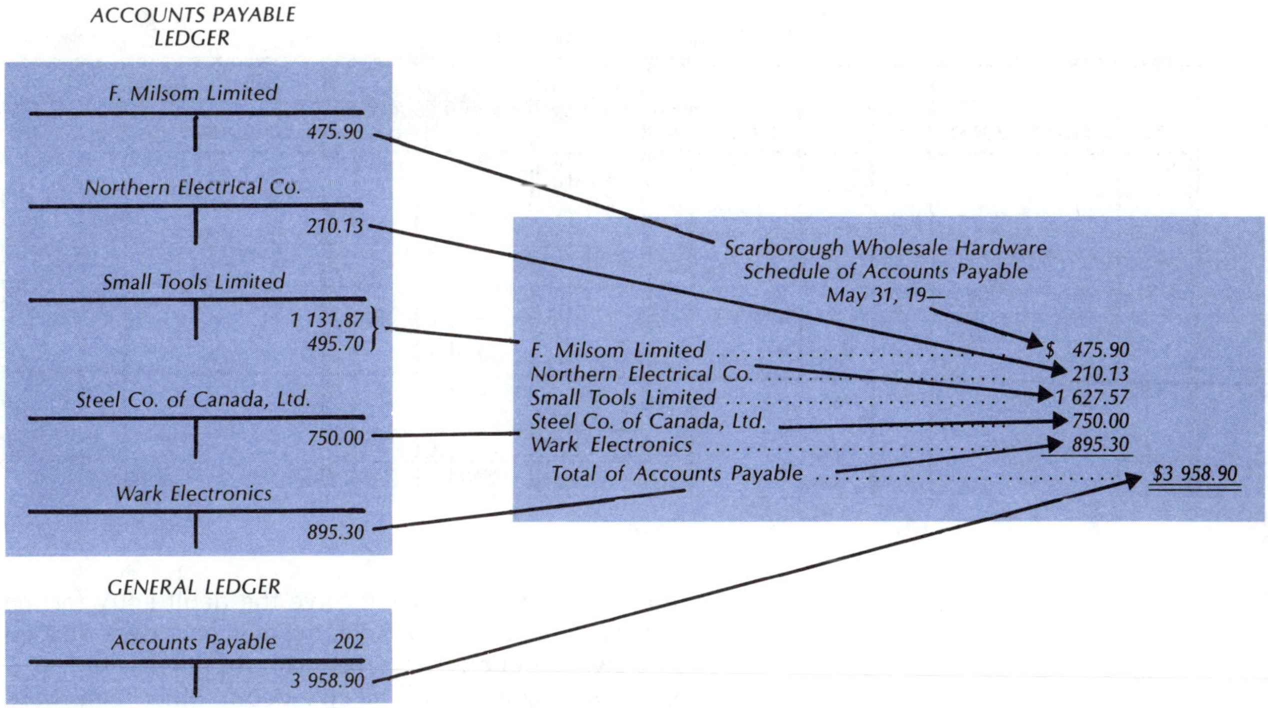

or from the tape, whichever is available. A comparison of the two sets of numbers then takes place before any further accounting steps occur. This illustrates another common internal control measure used by business.

Columnar Purchases Journal

You have seen a one-column purchases journal. In modern accounting there is little need or application for such a simplified journal. Instead, a *columnar purchases journal* is used. Such a journal permits separate identification of different merchandise purchases. Furthermore, this type of journal accepts expenses, and assets other than merchandise purchases that may be acquired *on account*. Thus, the columnar purchases journal may be used to record all transactions for which there is a credit to Accounts Payable. The columnar purchases journal illustrated next identifies these various entries.

Analysis: The first four columns are similar to those used in the one-column purchases journal. Study the points for the other columns.

- The first money column is headed *Accounts Payable CR*. The columnar purchases journal records all transactions that result in an increase in accounts payable.
- The offsetting debit will be distributed either in the *Purchases* column or in the *Sundries* column.

COLUMNAR PURCHASES JOURNAL Page 1

DATE	ACCOUNT CREDITED	INVOICE NO.	INVOICE DATE	TERMS	POST. REF.	ACCOUNTS PAYABLE CR.	PURCHASES HARDWARE DR.	PURCHASES ELECTRICAL DR.	SUNDRIES ACCOUNT DEBITED	SUNDRIES POST. REF.	SUNDRIES AMOUNT DR.
19—											
May 2	Bell Canada	81390	5/1/—	net 30 days	✓	17 05			Telephone Expense	515	17 05
10	Small Tools Limited	0387	5/9/—	2/10, n/30	✓	1 131 87	1 131 87				
10	Inter-City Express Ltd.	4187	5/10/—	net 30 days	✓	24 15			Hardware Transport-in	503	24 15
15	Northern Electrical Co.	6140	5/10/—	1/15, n/60	✓	210 13		210 13			
16	Public Utilities Co.	4X20	5/16/—	net 10 days	✓	45 80			Utilities Expense	516	45 80
19	F. Milsom Limited	P390	5/19/—	2/10, n/30	✓	475 90	200 00	275 90			
21	Steel Co. of Canada, Ltd.	S498	5/20/—	2/10, n/30	✓	750 00	750 00				
25	Small Tools Limited	0600	5/24/—	2/10, n/30	✓	495 70	495 70				
29	Wark Electronics	W174	5/28/—	1/15, n/60	✓	895 30		895 30			
30	Craig Motors, Ltd.	X200	5/28/—	net 60 days	✓	5 000 00			Delivery Equipment	112	5 000 00
31	Totals					9 045 90	2 577 57	1 381 33			5 087 00
						(202)	(501)	(502)			(✓)

• The *Purchases* column will receive the debit entry for the type of merchandise purchased. Here, the merchandise is divided between hardware and electrical merchandise purchases.

• The *Sundries* column will receive debits other than those analyzed for merchandise purchases.

• Each line of the journal will analyze a complete double entry: a credit to Accounts Payable, and a debit to Purchases or some other account in the *Sundries* column.

• To ensure accuracy of the debits and credits, the totals of all debit columns will be compared to the accounts payable total before any posting to the General Ledger occurs. This technique is called a purchases journal proof or simply *cross-footing*.

Purchases Journal Proof

Hardware Purchases DR.	**$2 577.57**
Electrical Purchases DR.	**1 381.33**
Sundries DR.	**5 087.00**
Accounts Payable CR.	**$9 045.90**

• Posting to individual creditor accounts is done daily. Proof of postings are shown by check marks in the first *Post. Ref.* column.

• Posting to General Ledger occurs at the end of the month. For each money column headed by a GL account, the account number is shown below the total. This account number proves that the total has been transferred to the General Ledger.

• For each GL account shown under the *Sundries* column, there must be a separate posting to the GL. The illustration shows account numbers placed in the *Post. Ref.* column next to the *Amount* column. Since the total of this *Amount* column is not posted, a simple check mark is shown below the total.

Recording Transportation-in

You have learned that an FOB shipping point quoted on a purchase order means that the buyer is prepared to pay the carrier the charges involved in transporting the goods from the seller's location to the buyer's place of business. If the carrier's bill is paid at the time of delivery, the entry debiting Transportation-in (or Freight-in) and crediting Cash is recorded in the cash payments journal.

On the other hand, if the carrier's bill allows credit terms such as net 30 days, an account payable must be credited. As you have seen, this entry could easily be recorded in a columnar purchases journal under *Sundries*. In an accounting system using a one-column purchases journal, however, the entry to record the transportation-in and accounts payable must be shown in the General Journal as illustrated below.

GENERAL JOURNAL — **Page** 2

DATE		ACCOUNT TITLE AND EXPLANATION	POST. REF.	DEBIT	CREDIT
19— May	10	*Transportation-in*	502	24 15	
		Accts. Pay./Inter-City Express Ltd.	202/✓		24 15
		Freight charges payable in 30 days.			

Analysis:

- The debit is to an expense account called Transportation-in. This expense is part of the future calculation of the expense called Cost of Goods Sold.
- The credit half of the entry is to Accounts Payable.
- The credit must be double-posted: once to the accounts payable controlling account in the GL, and once to the individual creditor's account filed in the accounts payable ledger.
- A check mark is placed in the *Post. Ref.* column of the General Journal to indicate that posting has taken place to the individual creditor's account in the subsidiary ledger.

Recording Purchases Returns and Allowances

Sometimes a firm finds it necessary to return purchased goods because they are unsuitable or damaged. In other cases, the units may still be useable, so an allowance off the purchase price is requested. Or perhaps upon receipt of the invoice a mathematical error is found, or there is a shortage of units in the shipment. To handle such cases, many of the larger merchandising firms prepare a source document called a debit memo that is sent to the seller. Study the illustration of a debit memo on page 408.

Debit memo: a source document created by the buyer to notify the seller that the account payable has been decreased by the amount of the purchase return or allowance requested.

Analysis:

- Usually, a minimum of two copies is made.
- The original is sent to the seller, and the second to the firm's accounting department.
- The word *debit* in *debit memo* means that the firm is notifying the seller that the seller's accounts payable account will be decreased as a result of the return or requested allowance.

SCARBOROUGH WHOLESALE HARDWARE

330 PROGRESS AVENUE
SCARBOROUGH, ONTARIO M1P 2Z5

DEBIT MEMO
DM-14

DATE: 19— 05 26

TO: Small Tools Limited
ADDRESS: 229 Kearney Street
Winnipeg, Manitoba R2M 4B5

WE DEBIT YOUR ACCOUNT AS FOLLOWS:

Return of merchandise. 10 only Tool Boxes No. 53-R1755 arrived badly damaged and are being returned via Inter-City Express Ltd.

10 @ $8.75 .... $87.50

References: Your Invoice No. 0600, dated 19— 05 24

Our Order No. PO-0091, dated 19— 05 20

Purchasing Agent

- The debit memo has a complete explanation.
- It is signed by the purchasing agent.

Because transactions involving returns and allowances are few, it is unusual to record these in a special journal. Instead, the firm uses a General Journal entry similar to that in the following illustration.

GENERAL JOURNAL **Page 2**

DATE		ACCOUNT TITLE AND EXPLANATION	POST. REF.	DEBIT	CREDIT
19— May	26	*Accts. Pay./Small Tools Limited*	202/✓	87 50	
		Purchases Returns and Allowances	503		87 50
		Issued DM-14 for return of damaged goods.			

Analysis:

- The debit entry must be double-posted: once to the accounts payable controlling account in the GL and once to the individual creditor's account in the subsidiary ledger.
- Double posting is completed when the *Post. Ref.* column shows the account number of the GL account and a check mark for the individual creditor's account.
- The credit to Purchases Returns and Allowances is posted to the GL. The effect of this posting is to decrease the original cost of Purchases. Therefore, Purchases Returns and Allowances is contra to the Purchases account.

Upon receipt of the purchaser's debit memo, the seller will

prepare a credit memo similar to that discussed in Topic 1. When the purchaser receives this, it will be attached to the related debit memo and filed. *Note:* No entry is required under this arrangement.

Some firms will not prepare a debit memo, but send the goods back to the seller and wait for the seller's credit memo. Once received, the credit memo will be used as the source document to record the purchase return and allowance. Regardless of which method is used, the books must be adjusted to decrease the original cost of the merchandise purchased.

Having recorded and posted the Purchases Returns and Allowances to the GL, you have now examined all but one account necessary to prepare the Cost of Goods Sold figure. These include: Inventory (beginning balance only), Purchases, Purchases Returns and Allowances, and Transportation-in. The other account, Purchases Discount, affects the payment of cash and is dealt with in Topic 3.

TOPIC 2 PROBLEMS

12-5 A.J. Lauton Company is a wholesale firm that uses the one-column purchases journal. The following journal illustrates some typical business transactions.

PURCHASES JOURNAL **Page** *34*

Date 198-		Account Credit	Invoice No.	Invoice Date	Terms	Post. Ref.	Amount
Apr.	2	Nathan Supplier	1214	Apr. 1	2/10, n/30		8 000
	5	M. & M. Wholesaler	6334	Apr. 3	1/15, n/60		12 000
	10	Key Works Ltd.	A-663	Apr. 10	n/30		5 500
	13	Nathan Supplier	1383	Apr. 12	2/10, n/30		7 500
	15	Purchases—DR./Accts. Pay.—CR.					33 000

a Open General Ledger accounts for Purchases (501) and Accounts Payable (207).

b Open a subsidiary ledger for accounts payable accounts for Key Works Ltd., M. & M. Wholesaler, and Nathan Supplier.

c Complete the appropriate daily postings and then the mid-month postings for A.J. Lauton Company.

Key Check Figure
Accounts Payable Control = $33 000

12-6 No Drips Plumbing Supply Company uses a one-column purchases journal to record the purchase of any merchandise on account. The transactions which follow represent the approved purchasing activities of the company for the month of February.

Feb. 4 The firm bought merchandise from D.W. Enterprises, dated Feb. 1, Invoice No. 10830; terms 2/10, n/30. Total invoice, $7 200.
7 The firm bought small parts from Ryan Wholesalers dated Feb. 6. Invoice No. 782; terms n/30. Total invoice, $4 500.
12 The firm bought 10 000 metres of copper pipe at $1.00/metre from Copper Works Ltd. The invoice number is 27673 and the invoice date is Feb. 9. Terms offered are 2/10, 1/15, n/30.
22 The firm bought glues and adhesives from Sticky Stuff Company totalling $8 000. Invoice No. 12-02-87 is dated Feb. 12 and the terms offered are 2/10, n/60.
27 The firm bought general-purpose plumbing supplies from XYZ Plumbers Wholesalers. Invoice No. 781, dated Feb. 25. The total amount of the invoice is $5 200. Terms are 2/10, n/30.

a In the General Ledger, open accounts for Purchases and Accounts Payable Control. Assign an appropriate number to each account.

b Open the following accounts payable subsidiary ledger accounts: Copper Works Ltd., D.W. Enterprises, Ryan Wholesalers, Sticky Stuff Company, XYZ Plumbers Wholesalers.

c Complete the journalizing in a journal similar to the one used in Problem 12-5.

Key Check Figure Accounts Payable Schedule = $34 900

d Post the daily entries to the appropriate accounts.

e Post the month-end totals.

f Prepare a schedule of accounts payable to prove the accuracy of the accounts payable control account.

12-7 Challenge Problem Martin Greenhouses Company uses a General Journal, a multi-column Purchases Journal, a General Ledger, and an Accounts Payable Subsidiary Ledger. Their product line is as follows: Evergreen Trees, Bulbs & Seeds, Box Plants, and Fertilizers and Other Chemicals. The business purchases all items except the box plants, which they grow in their greenhouses. The company's major suppliers all offer credit terms as follows:

B.C. Tree Farms: 2/10, n/30, free shipping on all orders over $1 000. Otherwise, n/60, FOB shipping point.

CIL Canada Ltd.: 1/15, n/60, FOB shipping point.

Dow Chemical of Canada Limited: n/45, FOB Destination.

Holland Bulb and Seed Suppliers: n/30 on all orders under $450, and 2/10, n/30 on any order $450 or more. FOB shipping point.

a Open the following GL accounts and assign an appropriate account number; Accounts Payable Control; Purchases — Evergreen Trees; Purchases — Bulbs & Seeds; Purchases — Fertilizers and Other Chemicals; Purchases Returns and Allowances; Transportation-in; Utilities Expense; Gas Expense.

b Open a subsidiary ledger for accounts payable for: B.C. Tree Farms, 175 Broadway E., Vancouver, B.C., V5T 1W2; CIL Inc., Courtright, Ontario; CP Express, P.O. 1674, Don Mills, Ontario, M3C 2H8; Dow Chemical of Canada Limited, Modeland Road, Sarnia, Ontario, N7S 4X4; Holland Bulbs & Seed Suppliers, 921 Erie E., Windsor, Ontario; Newton PUC, Newton, Ontario; Union Gas Limited, Chatham, Ontario.

c Record the following transactions for the month of March in the Purchases Journal or General Journal. Use the following columns in the columnar purchases journal.

		Invoice			Post.		Purchases			Sundry		
Date	Account Credit	No.	Date	Terms	Ref.	Account Pay.				Account DR.	PR	Amount

Mar. 1 Purchased from B.C. Tree Farms, Invoice No. 0083, dated March 1, 100 1.5-metre spruce trees, $1 100.

1 Purchased from Holland Bulbs & Seed Suppliers, Invoice No. M-1111, dated Feb. 26, 5 000 tulip bulbs at $0.50 each, 12 000 dozen daffodil bulbs at $0.25/doz. and 15 000 seed packets at $0.10/packet.

4 Purchased from CIL, Invoice No. 82-074, dated March 2, 700 22-kg bags of lawn fertilizer. $10.00/bag.

7 Union Gas billed Martin Greenhouses for natural gas used to heat the greenhouses during February. Due date: April 2. $8 800. Invoice No. 7733 dated March 2.

11 CP Express delivered order, Invoice No. M-1111. Offered terms of n/30. $46.00.

15 Purchased from Dow Chemical, 150 10-kg bags of broadleaf weed killer, $18/bag; 10 dozen cans of all-purpose insecticide $36/dozen. Invoice No. DZ-1234, dated March 15.

20 CP Express delivered the CIL order. $107. Terms n/30.

24 Received an invoice No. BC-1135, dated March 15, from Newton PUC. Terms n/25 from billing date. $247.00.

30 Received order from B.C. Tree Farms by CN Express. On examination of the shipment, it was found that 16 trees were 1 metre or less in height and cost a total of $48.00 less than the invoice price. The firm intends to keep the trees but is requesting the adjustment outlined. A debit memo No. DM-143 was prepared.

d Post all daily items as they occur to the appropriate ledger account.

e Total the purchases journal, prepare a journal proof, and post the month-end totals.

f Prepare a schedule of accounts payable to verify the General Ledger control account.

Key Check Figure
Accounts Payable Schedule = $25 062

TOPIC 3 JOURNALIZING AND POSTING DOCUMENTS AFFECTING CASH

Much of this Topic will be review, since the account for Cash was discussed in Part II. The new account you will now study is cash discounts offered to credit customers.

Receiving Cash from Credit Customers

SCARBOROUGH WHOLESALE HARDWARE
Remittance Slip No. RS-75
Name *Thornhill Home Hardware*

Amount	Cheque Number	Cheque Date
$723.52	*170*	*June 7, 19--*

Explanation
Customer's payment of invoice 108

Date *June 18, 19--* Received By *ST*

Earlier you learned two important points:

- Many merchandising firms mail a bill or invoice to the customer, offering credit terms such as 2/10, n/30; 1/15, n/60; n/30; n/60; etc.
- Many firms require a *remittance slip* to be prepared every time a cheque is received. This acts as a control device and becomes a source document. A typical remittance slip is illustrated in the margin.

Analysis:

- Each remittance slip is pre-numbered. The numbers allow accounting to control all incoming cheques because all remittance slips must be accounted for.
- The clerk opening the mail would fill out the slip, entering the name of the drawer (the party who has signed the cheque), the amount on the cheque, the cheque number, the cheque date, a simple explanation for the cheque, the date of receiving the cheque, and his or her initials.
- After the remittance slip has been made out, the cheque would be endorsed *For Deposit Only* and included for the day's deposit.
- The slip would be sent to the accounting department for recording.

In the accounting department, the remittance slip becomes the source document for proper accounting analysis. Since a cheque was received, Cash must be debited for the full amount on the cheque. Since the customer has paid for Invoice 108, Accounts Receivable must be credited for the amount owing on the invoice. And since the customer's cheque has been received within the discount period, the account Sales Discount must be debited for the amount of the cash discount. The entire entry would be recorded in the cash receipts journal as follows.

CASH RECEIPTS JOURNAL Page 3

DATE		ACCOUNT CREDITED	EXPLANATION	POST. REF.	GENERAL LEDGER CREDIT	ACCOUNTS RECEIVABLE CREDIT	SALES DISCOUNT DEBIT	NET CASH DEBIT
19—								
June	8	Thornhill Home Hardware	For Invoice 108	✓		738 29	14 77	723 52

Analysis:

- Special money columns are used to allow the clerk to record the double entry on a single line.
- The *Cash* column records the actual amount of the cheque.
- The *Sales Discount* column records the calculated cash discount. See the margin for this calculation.
- The total amount owing on the invoice is recorded in the *Accounts Receivable* money column.
- A check of the complete double entry on one line shows that the debit to Cash and the debit to Sales Discount ($723.52 + $14.77) equal the one credit to Accounts Receivable ($738.29). The double entry balances.
- The first money column, *General Ledger Credit,* would be used to credit a General Ledger account other than Accounts Receivable. Examples are given in the illustration on page 414.

Discount Calculation

$738.29
×0.02
$14.7658, rounded to $14.77

Posting the Cash Receipts Journal During the Month

A complete set of entries recorded in a columnar cash receipts journal is illustrated on page 414.

Analysis:

- The special money columns *Cash DR., Accounts Receivable CR.,* and *Sales Discount DR.* will produce meaningful month-end totals. The posting of these totals will be discussed later.
- The *General Ledger Credit* column contains many different, unrelated accounts, so the total, while useful in cross-footing at month-end, cannot be used for posting.
- Each entry in the *General Ledger Credit* column must be posted separately on the day it is recorded. The evidence of this posting is given by the account numbers in the *Post. Ref.* column next to the first money column.
- Daily postings are also required of all amounts entered in the *Accounts Receivable Credit* column. Of course, these postings will be made to individual customer accounts filed in the accounts receivable subsidiary ledger. Evidence of such postings is shown by the check mark in the *Post. Ref.* column. The corresponding posting reference in the ledger accounts will be the journal name and page number.

Posting from the Cash Receipts Journal at Month-End

Before any month-end posting is completed, all money columns must be verified to prove the equality of the debit and the credit entries. This can be done by listing and totalling the debits and the credits as shown in the margin illustration below the completed cash receipts journal.

Analysis:

- As soon as the equality of the money columns has been

CASH RECEIPTS JOURNAL — **Page** 3

DATE		ACCOUNT CREDITED	EXPLANATION	POST. REF.	GENERAL LEDGER CREDIT	ACCOUNTS RECEIVABLE CREDIT	SALES DISCOUNT DEBIT	NET CASH DEBIT
19—								
June	1	Cash Balance	$10 600	—				
	6	Sales	Cash sales for week	401	490 00			490 00
	8	Thornhill Home Hardware	For Invoice 108	✓		738 29	14 77	723 52
	10	Howard Capes, Capital	Additional investment	301	500 00			500 00
	12	Sales	Cash sales for week	401	469 00			469 00
	16	Office Equipment	One calculator sold at cost	115	100 00			100 00
	17	Hyland Hardware	For Invoice 107	✓		890 17	8 90	881 27
	18	Sales	Cash sales for week	401	875 00			875 00
	20	Eglinton Hardware Centre	For Invoice 106	✓		534 40		534 40
	24	Plaza Home Hardware	For Invoice 115	✓		649 75	13 00	636 75
	25	Sales	Cash sales for week	401	590 00			590 00
	28	Miller Home Centre	For Invoice 117	✓		718 20	7 18	711 02
	30	Sales	Cash sales for week	401	370 00			370 00
	30	Bank Loan	Royal Bank demand note	201	1 000 00			1 000 00
					1	2	3	3
	30	Totals			4 394 00	3 530 81	43 85	7 880 96
					(✓)	(103)	(403)	(101)

1
Credits posted during the month to accounts in the General Ledger.

2
Credits posted during the month to customers' accounts in subsidiary ledger. But the total is posted at month-end to the accounts receivable control account in the General Ledger.

3
Amounts in these two columns are not posted separately during the month.

verified, the journal can be ruled off for the month as illustrated next.

- The totals of the money columns represented by account titles are then posted to the appropriate General Ledger accounts.
- Note that the *General Ledger Credit* column has only a check mark instead of a posting reference number. The mark simply indicates that the total is not to be posted because each of the entries in the column has been posted previously on a daily basis.
- Note that the *Accounts Receivable Credit* column has a posting reference number. Although the individual entries in this column were posted daily to the subsidiary ledger, the total of this column must be posted to the General Ledger.

CASH RECEIPTS JOURNAL — **Page** 3

DATE		ACCOUNT CREDITED	EXPLANATION	POST. REF.	GENERAL LEDGER CREDIT	ACCOUNTS RECEIVABLE CREDIT	SALES DISCOUNT DEBIT	NET CASH DEBIT
19								
June	30	Bank Loan	Royal Bank demand note	201	1 000 00			1 000 00
	30	Totals			4 394 00	3 530 81	43 85	7 880 96
					(✔)	(103)	(403)	(101)

● Finally, notice that all other totals are posted to their appropriate General Ledger accounts because account numbers have been placed beneath their totals.

Cash Receipts Journal
Zero Proof
June 30, 19--

0.00T

4 394.00-
3 530.81-
43.85
7 880.96

0.00T

Preparing Monthly Statements to Credit Customers

Many merchandising firms mail a monthly statement of account to their credit customers. This statement usually shows the opening balance (last month's closing balance), purchases during the month made in chronological order, the payments received during the current month, and the final balance owing at the end of the current month.

Two common forms of statements may be prepared. One is the *non-descriptive* form, shown below.

SCARBOROUGH WHOLESALE HARDWARE
330 Progress Avenue
Scarborough, Ontario M1P 2Z5

STATEMENT OF ACCOUNT

Date: 19— 06 30

To: Thornhill Home Hardware
67 Grandview Avenue
Thornhill, Ontario L3T 1H3

Amount Enclosed $ ______

Please return this stub with your cheque.

Date	Reference	Charges	Credit	Balance
Balance Forwarded: 19— 05 30				738.29
June 8	RS-75		738.29	.00
25	120	1 000.00		1 000.00
27	CM-08		100.00	900.00

In the non-descriptive form, no details are shown of each individual entry. Note that the form has a tear-off portion which is returned by the customer with the appropriate payment.

MAY'S DEPARTMENT STORE

AMOUNT ENCLOSED $

PLEASE ENTER AMOUNT OF PAYMENT ABOVE.

MRS H J KELLER
843 DRIFTWOOD RD
LONDON ONT N6H 4H9

BRANCH AND	ACCOUNT NUMBER
457	740-351-40
	TORONTO

PLEASE DETACH THIS PORTION OF STATEMENT AND RETURN WITH YOUR PAYMENT

YOUR ACCOUNT NUMBER: 740-351-40 YOUR BRANCH NUMBER: 457

STATEMENT DATE	PREVIOUS BALANCE	TOTAL CHARGES	TOTAL CREDITS	NEW BALANCE	PAYMENT REQUIRED
SEP 1/—	40.03	32.11	40.03	32.11	32.11

DATE	REFERENCE	GENERAL DESCRIPTION	AMOUNT
		CREDITS	
AUG 14	1870073		
	BOX4000	PAYMENT - THANK YOU	40.03CR
		CHARGES	
AUG 22	5271645		
	LONDON	MISSES CO ORDINATES	16.67
AUG 22	5271645		
	LONDON	MISSES CO ORDINATES	13.34
AUG 22	5271645	SALES TAX	2.10

A second form of statement is the *descriptive,* illustrated above.

In the descriptive form, the details for each transaction are spelled out. Note that this form also has a tear-off portion. Before the customer sends payment, he or she should make a detailed comparison between the statement and his or her own records. If there are differences, these should be resolved as quickly as possible with the seller's accounts receivable department.

Cycle billing: billing according to alphabetical sequence of last names at designated dates during the month.

Many large businesses such as department stores and utility companies practice cycle billing. Simply, cycle billing divides the firm's customers into alphabetical groups. The company processes those groups on different days throughout the month. For example, customers with surnames falling between A and F may be billed on the 10th of each month; those between G and N on the 15th of the month; those between O and S on the 20th of the month; and those between T and Z on the 25th of the month. This system eliminates a massive volume of work at month-end.

Making Payments to Creditors

Credit terms outline the terms and dates when payment is due. In large firms an accounts payable department is responsible for the payment of *all* invoices within a certain time period. This department becomes even more important when sellers offer discount terms such as 2/10, n/30.

A filing system often called a *tickler file system* enables the department to file invoices according to their discount due date. By filing an approved invoice at the date when an invoice must be paid to get a discount, the firm ensures that all invoices will be paid in time to take advantage of such offers.

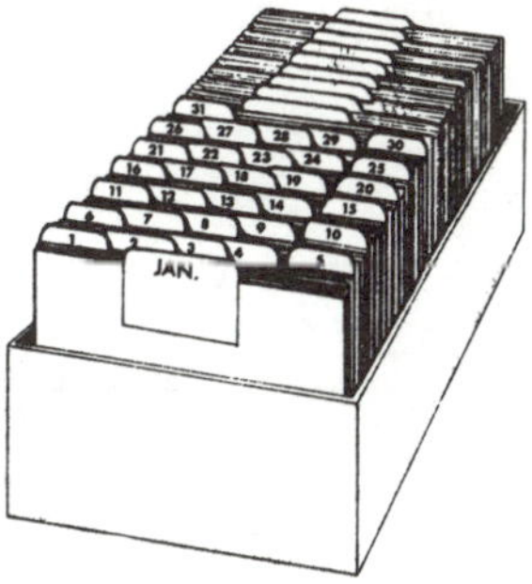

Tickler File

When these invoices are pulled on the appropriate date, a responsible person decides whether or not the discount should be taken. If the decision is to delay payment, the invoice is refiled on the last day of the credit period. If, however, approval is given, the invoice can then be paid in full with a cheque equal to the full amount less the cash discount.

Good internal control requires that all cash payments be made using serially numbered cheques. The cheque record, or cheque voucher, should be checked for accuracy before the transaction is journalized. The journal entry should include:

- a debit entry for the *full* amount on the account payable
- a credit entry to Purchases Discount for the amount of the cash discount
- a credit entry to Cash for the exact amount on the cheque

A well-designed cash payments journal would permit the above compound entry to be recorded on one line. The journal should also be designed to record a variety of debit transactions resulting from cheques' being issued. Look closely at the cash payments journal illustrated here:

CASH PAYMENTS JOURNAL — **Page 3**

DATE		ACCOUNT DEBITED	EXPLANATION	CHEQUE NO.	POST. REF.	GENERAL LEDGER DEBIT	ACCOUNTS PAYABLE DEBIT	PURCHASES DISCOUNT CREDIT	NET CASH CREDIT
19—									
June	1	Mortgage Payable ..	June mortgage	612	220	250 00			250 00
	4	Small Tools Limited .	Invoice 0600	613	✓		408 20	8 16	400 04
	5	Office Equipment ..	Typewriter	614	115	600 00			600 00
	7	Transportation-in ...	Reimer Transport ..	615	402	40 00			40 00
	12	Wark Electronics ...	Invoice W174	616	✓		895 30	8 95	886 35
	16	Telephone Expense .	June bill	617	518	18 95			18 95
	18	R. Stone Limited ...	On account	618	✓		100 00		100 00
	20	Advertising Expense	City Press	619	519	175 00			175 00
	23	Northern Electrical Co.	Invoice 6270	620	✓		750 90	7 51	743 39
	26	Utilities Expense ...	Gas & electricity ...	621	520	38 50			38 50
	28	J. Thompson Ltd. ...	Invoice A25K30	622	✓		800 00	16 00	784 00
	30	Howard Capes, Drawing	Personal withdrawal	623	302	100 00			100 00
	30	Totals	....			1 222 45	2 954 40	40 62	4 136 23
						(✓)	(202)	(504)	(101)

Analysis:

- The four money columns allow the clerk to record any cash payments transaction on one line.
- Every line entry in the journal must show an equal debit for a credit entry.
- Every entry in the journal requires a cash payment; therefore, a cheque number will support each entry.
- Posting from the cash payments journal has two phases: daily and month-end.
- Daily postings occur from the *Accounts Payable Debit* column to individual creditor accounts filed in the subsidiary ledger. Evidence of such posting is found by showing a check mark in the *Post. Ref.* column of the journal.
- Daily postings also occur from the *General Ledger Debit* column to appropriate accounts in the General Ledger. These are named in the *Account Debited* column. Evidence of this posting is found by showing the account number in the *Post. Ref.* column. Since figures from the *General Ledger Debit* column have been posted on an individual basis, the total of the column is not posted at the end of the month. This fact is shown by placing a check mark in parentheses below the total of the column.
- Before posting at month-end occurs, the journal should be totalled and the columns should be checked to make sure that the total debits equal the total credits. This journal proof is essential before any column totals are posted to the General Ledger. Once this proof is obtained, the journal can be ruled off for the month.
- Column totals, except for *General Ledger Debit,* are posted to appropriate accounts in the General Ledger. Evidence of such posting is found by placing the account number in parentheses below the column total.

Summary of Transactions Affecting Sales and Cost of Goods Sold

Remember that the Inventory account has not been affected during the accounting period because a periodic inventory system is followed. Also keep in mind that the gross amount method of recording invoices has been used. This means that the accounting of the cash discount for sales and for purchases will be done when the cash is received or paid out.

Study the chart that follows. In particular, try to relate the transaction with the correct journal.

TRANSACTION	SOURCE DOCUMENT	RECORDED IN	POSTING PRINCIPLES
Sales for cash.	Cash proof	Columnar Cash Receipts Journal	Cash debit is posted as part of the total at month-end. Individual Sales credits are posted during the month unless a special column is provided for Sales Credit.
Sales returns or allowance for cash.	Cash proof	Columnar Cash Payments Journal	Individual Sales Returns and Allowances are posted from General Ledger Debit column during the month. Cash credit is posted as part of the total Net Cash Credit at month-end.
Sales on credit.	Sales invoice	One-column Sales Journal	Individual customer accounts are posted daily to Accounts Receivable Ledger. Column total is posted at month-end to debit of Accounts Receivable and to the credit of Sales in the General Ledger.
		Columnar Sales Journal	Daily posting from Accounts Receivable Debit column to subsidiary ledger. Column totals are posted at month-end to appropriate accounts of the General Ledger.
Sales returns or allowance for credit.	Credit memo	General Journal	Daily posting as transaction occurs. Debit is posted to Sales Returns and Allowances in General Ledger; credit is double-posted: once to the customer's account in the subsidiary ledger, and once to Accounts Receivable controlling account in the General Ledger.
Customer's cheque received	Remittance slip	Columnar Cash Receipts Journal	Daily posting from Accounts Receivable Credit column to customer accounts filed in subsidiary ledger. At month-end the column totals are posted to General Ledger for Accounts Receivable Cr., Sales Discount Dr., and Cash Dr.
Merchandise purchases for cash.	Cheque record (Stub or voucher)	Columnar Cash Payments Journal	Individual Purchases debit is posted during month unless a special column is provided for Purchases Debit. Cash credit is posted as part of the total Cash Credit column at month-end.
Purchases returns or allowances for cash.	Remittance slip	Columnar Cash Receipts Journal	Cash debited is posted as part of the total at month-end from special money column for Cash Debit. Purchases Returns and Allowances are posted during the month from the General Ledger Credit column.

(cont.)

Merchandise purchases for credit.	Purchase invoice	One-column Purchases Journal	Daily posting to credit of individual creditors' accounts filed in subsidiary ledger. Double-entry to General Ledger for total posted at month-end to debit of Purchases and to the credit of Accounts Payable controlling account.
		Columnar Purchases Journal	Daily posting from Accounts Payable Credit column to individual accounts in subsidiary ledger. All column totals are posted at month-end to appropriate accounts in the General Ledger.
Purchases returns or allowances for credit.	Debit memo (Some firms wait for seller's credit memo.)	General Journal	Daily posting as transaction occurs. Double-posting of debit entry: once to individual creditor's account in subsidiary ledger, and once to Accounts Payable controlling account in General Ledger. The credit entry is posted to Purchases Returns and Allowances in the General Ledger.
Cheque issued in payment of purchase invoice.	Cheque record (Stub or voucher)	Columnar Cash Payments Journal	Daily posting of amounts recorded in Accounts Payable Debit column to individual accounts in subsidiary ledger. Column totals are posted at month-end to debit of Accounts Payable, to credit of Purchases Discount, and to credit of Cash.

TOPIC 3 PROBLEMS

12-8 Ted's Shoe Repairs is in the business of fixing shoes and other leather items. The firm also sells shoe-care products.

a In a journal similar to the one illustrated, record the cash inflow transactions listed below. *Note:* Ted extends terms on *all* credit sales of 2/10, n/30.

CASH RECEIPTS JOURNAL **Page** *21*

	Date	Account Credit	Explanation	Post. Ref.	General Ledger CR.	Accounts Receivable CR.	Sales Discount DR.	Cash DR.
EXAMPLE:	*July 1*	*Cash Balance*	*$550*					

July 5 Velvet Furniture Repair Shop paid their account in full after the discount date. $120.
7 Cash sales for the week totalled $850.
10 Sold an extra piece of machinery for cash at its book value. $480.
14 Cash sales for the week totalled $900.
16 Potter's Book Binders sent a cheque for $245 to pay Invoice No. 373 in full. The invoice was billed at $250.

July 30 Borrowed from the Royal Bank of Canada, $1 000. The loan is a demand loan.

b Total the journal at month-end. Proof the journal and indicate in the *Post. Ref.* column with a *DP* those items that should be posted daily assuming a subsidiary accounts receivable ledger. Place an *MP* in the correct locations to indicate where any monthly posting takes place.

Key Check Figure Cash Total = $3 595

12-9 Eric Street Hardware Store uses a cash payments journal similar to the one illustrated on page 417.

Using a similar cash payments journal, record the following cash outflow transactions:

Aug. 3 Paid Trenton Hardware Suppliers in full. Invoice No. 1876 for $1 000 offered terms of 2/10, n/30. Cheque No. 123 for $980 was dated on the last day of the discount period and sent to Trenton Hardware Suppliers.

8 Paid our monthly mortgage payment of $553 with cheque No. 124. *Note:* All further payments will be made with consecutively numbered cheques.

15 Paid Taylor Suppliers in full. Invoice No. 0141 amounted to $758; terms n/30.

21 Paid Northern Electric for Invoice No. 4473. $92.

27 The owner, P. Donovan, withdrew funds for personal use. $150.

31 Paid *The National Edition,* a newspaper, $280 for advertising. The invoice number was No. 00721 and no terms of discount were offered.

Key Check Figure Cash Total = $2 813

12-10 World of Toys, located in Edmonton, Alberta, uses a cash receipts journal and a cash payments journal similar to those illustrated on pages 414 and 417. The following transactions took place during the month of February. Credit terms for the firm are 2/10, n/60 for all customers.

Feb. 1 Cash balance $9 200.

2 Received from A. Bateman $225, payment in full on his account. No discount was taken by Bateman.

3 Paid the utility bill to PUC for the month of January. Issued cheque No. 807 for $590.

6 Cash sales for the week totalled $4 500.

8 The owner, Fran Bentlea, invested an additional $3 500 into the business.

10 The firm purchased new office equipment from Coleman Ltd. for cash. Issued cheque No. 808, $1 000.

12 Issued cheque No. 809 for $980 to pay Mattel Toys Ltd. in full. The total of the invoice was $1 000. The firm took advantage of a 2% discount.

13 Cash sales for the week totalled $6 350.

15 Issued cheque No. 810 for $2 700 to pay the firm's employees.

Feb. 18 Received on account from Tellman Company, $2 352. This represents payment in full of their account which totalled $2 400. *Note:* Make sure you account for the $48 difference.
20 Cash sales for the week totalled $5 200.
24 The owner issued cheque No. 811 to pay her personal rent. $350.
27 Cash sales for the week totalled $4 900.
28 The company sold some of the old office equipment at cost for $220.
28 Issued cheque No. 812 to Hartley Realty Co. This cheque for $750 represents the rent on the company building for the month of March.
28 Issued cheque No. 813 for $2 700. This is the amount of the payroll for the employees.

a Journalize the above cash transactions in the cash receipts journal and the cash payments journal.

b By placing *DP* in the *Post. Ref.* column, indicate in both journals which items must be posted daily.

Key Check Figure Cash (DR.) Total = $27 247

c Total the journals and prepare journal proofs to ensure equality of the debits and the credits.

12-11 Challenge Problem W. Keeper Wholesale Jewelry Ltd. used the five-journal system, a General Ledger, and accounts receivable and accounts payable subsidiary ledgers in maintaining its accounting records. It is company policy to take all discounts offered to the firm. Sales data is broken down under four headings: *Diamond Jewelry, Other Jewelry, Watches,* and *Other.* Also:

Credit terms: 2/10, n/30 to all credit customers.

Next cheque to be written: No. 432 (All cash outflow is by cheque.)

Next sales invoice to be used: No. S2001

a Open a sales journal with the following headings: Date, Invoice No., Account Debited, Terms, Post. Ref., Accounts Receivable, Diamond Jewelry, Other Jewelry, Watches, Other. Page number: 66.

b Open a purchases journal with the following headings: Date; Account Credited; Invoice Number and Date; Terms; Post. Ref.; Accounts Payable; Purchases Accounts: Diamond Jewelry, Other Jewelry, Watches, Other; Sundry Items: Account Debit, Post. Ref., Amount. Page number: 54.

c Open a cash receipts journal with the following headings: Date, Account Credited, Explanation, Post. Ref., General Ledger, Accounts Receivable, Sales Discounts, Sales Accounts: Diamond Jewelry, Other Jewelry, Watches, Other, Cash. Page number: 98.

d Open a cash payments journal with the following headings: Date, Account Debited, Explanation, Cheque Number, Post. Ref., General Ledger, Accounts Payable, Purchases Discounts, one blank column, Cash. Page number: 78.

e Open a General Journal. Page number: 12.

f Open the General Ledger accounts from the trial balance provided opposite.

g Open the accounts receivable subsidiary ledger accounts from the information provided opposite.

h Open the accounts payable subsidiary ledger accounts from the information provided below.

W. Keeper Wholesale Jewelry Ltd.
Trial Balance
June 30, 198-

Cash	101	10 200	
Accounts Receivable Control	110	7 500	
Inventory	112	8 000	
Office Supplies	125	800	
Land	140	25 000	
Building	145	85 000	
Vault and Storage Equipment	150	30 000	
Delivery Equipment	155	8 500	
Bank Loan Payable	201		15 000
Accounts Payable Control	210		6 500
Mortgage Payable (due 1995)	240		45 400
W. Keeper, Capital	301		100 010
W. Keeper, Drawings	302	2 600	
Sales:			
Diamond Jewelry	401		18 000
Other Jewelry	402		6 000
Watches	403		3 000
Other	404		2 500
Sales Returns and Allowances	406	1 200	
Sales Discounts	407	3 200	
Purchases:			
Diamond Jewelry	501	6 000	
Other Jewelry	502	2 000	
Watches	503	600	
Other	504	1 000	
Purchases Returns and Allowances	506		350
Purchase Discounts	507		170
Transportation-in	510	420	
Property Tax Expense	520	980	
Telephone Expense	525	650	
Delivery Expense	530	900	
Utilities Expense	535	2 010	
Office Supplies Expense	540	370	
		196 930	196 930

Accounts Receivable Information

Miller Jewels	$1 500
Northland Gems Ltd.	2 000
Sabrina's Precious Stones	3 000
Treasures by Taylor	1 000
	$7 500

Accounts Payable Information

Diamond Discount Dealers	$4 000
Precious Gems Wholesale	2 400
Wholesale Watches Ltd. ..	100
	$6 500

i Journalize the following information in the appropriate journals. Post daily as required. Note: property taxes are expensed as they are paid.

Cash Inflow Transactions

July 3 Received payment in full from Northland Gems Ltd. within the discount period.
9 Sold a watch for $85 cash.
14 Received $980, payment in full from Treasures by Taylor.
20 Sold an Opal Bracelet. $360.
25 Received payment in full from Miller Jewels. $1 500. They failed to meet the discount date.

Cash Outflow Transactions

July 2 Paid the second installment of property taxes. $985.
5 Paid Diamond Discount Dealers in full. The firm is within the discount period. Discount allowed: 3%.
10 Paid wages to the employees. $2 400.
14 Paid CN Express $45 for freight charges from a delivery.
18 Paid $150 to the local bank. The total amount is to be subtracted from the loan.
20 Paid the telephone bill. $124.
25 Bought five crystal vases from a local manufacturer after obtaining an approved purchase order. P-1025. $250.
30 Paid the employees. $2 400.
30 Paid the monthly mortgage installment. $950: $300 to mortgage payable, $650 to Mortgage Interest Expense.

Sales Transactions

July 5 Sabrina's Precious Stones: 3 diamond pins, $200 each; 8 digital watches, $22 each.
9 Miller Jewels: 6 crystal vases, $47 each; 15 pairs of pearl earrings, $21 each; 4 self-wind watches, $77 each.
22 Treasures by Taylor: 3 diamond broaches, $250 each; 4 men's diamond rings, $175 each; 7 women's diamond rings, $225 each.

Purchases Transactions

July 3 Purchase Order No. P-1023: Precious Gems Wholesale; 12 digital watches, $10 each; 3 diamond pendants, $125 each; 10 high-school rings, $5 each. Invoice No. 123. Dated July 2, 198-.
18 Purchase Order P-1024: Wholesale Watches Ltd.; Terms 1/10, n/30; 5 self-wind watches, $44; 18 digital watches, $15 each. Invoice No. W-222, dated July 15. Terms 2/10, n/30.

General Information

July 12 Miller Jewels returned one self-wind watch, for which the firm granted Miller full credit.
22 The firm returned all five watches ordered from Wholesale Watches Ltd. P-1024. The goods were damaged and would not operate.

j Total and prepare the necessary proofs for the journals.
k Post all the journals.

l Prepare schedules for both of the subsidiary ledgers to ensure the accuracy of the General Ledger control accounts.

m Prepare a trial balance at the end of July.

Key Check Figure
Trial Balance = $198 786

TOPIC 4 THE COMBINATION JOURNAL

You have now been introduced to the use of the four very specialized journals, the General Journal, and the subsidiary ledger system. These techniques are extremely valuable for a large business that processes enough transactions to require separate people working in each of these areas. The division of duties is very important to maintain a good system of internal control.

In many small businesses, however, the number of transactions involved does not require the use of more than one employee to maintain a set of books. In fact, often the owner does all the bookwork. One might resign oneself to the use of the General Journal, but that would be a very time-consuming job and require multiple postings. To solve this difficulty, accountants have combined all five journals into one called the Combination Journal. It is sometimes referred to as the *Synoptic* or *Multi-Columned Journal.* (*Synoptic* means "presenting a general view of the whole.") Its job is to receive the entry of all types of transactions. This is accomplished by including separate columns for those accounts used on a repetitive basis, such as Cash, Accounts Payable, and Accounts Receivable. A sundry or general ledger account section looks after all other less frequently encountered transactions. The illustration on page 426 demonstrates how these columns can be arranged to allow all the transactions to be recorded in the one journal.

Combination Journal: a multi-columned journal that takes the place of the entire five-journal system.

Analysis: Let us examine now a series of transactions in the General Journal and compare them to similar entries in the Combination Journal. (See the margin for the General Journal format.)

- *The owner invests $500 cash into the business.*

The General Journal entry would appear as shown in the margin. Note that the entry requires three lines: one for the debit entry to Cash, one for the credit entry to Capital, and one for the explanation. Now refer back to the illustration of the Combination Journal. Note that the entire transaction is recorded on just one line and requires only one posting. The General Journal required two postings.

General Journal Format

19—			
Sept. 25			
Cash	*101*	*500*	
P. Bet, Capital	*301*		*500*
*Owner invested cash into the business.**			

Let's try another. Once again refer to the two illustrations to observe the actual entries in each case.

- *The company buys land for $2 000 and a building for $6 000. It agrees to pay $1 000 in cash and the rest in the form of a mortgage.*

Land	*130*	*2 000*	
Building	*132*	*6 000*	
Cash	*101*		*1 000*
Mtg. Pay.	*250*		*7 000*
*Bought land and building with cash and mortgage.**			

**Normally an explanation requires only one line in the General Journal.*

COMBINATION JOURNAL

Page 3

	Date 19—	Account Title and Explanation	Post. Ref.	General Ledger Debit	General Ledger Credit	Accounts Receivable Debit	Accounts Receivable Credit	Accounts Payable Debit	Accounts Payable Credit	Purchases Debit	Purchases Discount Credit	Sales Credit	Cash Debit	Cash Credit	Chq. No.	
1	Sept. 1	Cash Balance $5 600	—													1
2	3	J. Ball Invoice No. 106	√			100 00						100 00				2
3	5	Postage Expense (Replenish	512	32 00												3
4		Transportation-in Petty	508	55 00												4
5		P. Bet, Drawings Cash)	303	100 00												5
6		Supplies Expense	520	23 00										210 00	736	6
7	7	Cash Sales for Week	—									400 00	400 00			7
8	10	J. Ball Payment rec'd	√				100 00						100 00			8
9	12	M.&C. Ltd. 2/10,n/30	√						580 00	580 00						9
10	14	Parkview Motors—Truck	140	10 000 00					10 000 00							10
11	14	Bank Loan Payable	202		10 000 00								10 000 00			11
32	19	Carried Forward		10 210 00	10 000 00	100 00	100 00		10 580 00	580 00		500 00	10 500 00	210 00		32

Page End — Daily Posting

COMBINATION JOURNAL

Page 4

	Date 19—	Account Title and Explanation	Post. Ref.	General Ledger Debit	General Ledger Credit	Accounts Receivable Debit	Accounts Receivable Credit	Accounts Payable Debit	Accounts Payable Credit	Purchases Debit	Purchases Discount Credit	Sales Credit	Cash Debit	Cash Credit	Chq. No.	
1	Sept. 19	Balance Brought Forward	—	10 210 00	10 000 00	100 00	100 00		10 580 00	580 00		500 00	10 500 00	210 00		1
2	19	Cash Sales for Week	—									200 00	200 00			2
3	20	Telephone Expense	530	85 00										85 00	737	3
4	25	P. Bet, Capital (Investment)	301		500 00								500 00			4
5	25	Land	130	2 000 00												5
6	25	Building	132	6 000 00												6
7	25	Mortgage Payable	250		7 000 00									1 000 00	738	7
8	25	XYZ Company	√			7 000 00						7 000 00				8
9	30	Wages Expense	528	500 00										500 00	739	9
10	30	Totals		18 795 00	17 500 00	7 100 00	100 00		10 580 00	580 00		7 700 00	11 200 00	1 795 00		10
11				(√)	(√)	(110)	(110)		(205)	(501)		(401)	(101)	(101)		11

The General Journal requires five lines and four postings; the Combination Journal three lines and three postings, as shown.

● *The company sells goods on account to the XYZ Company for $7 000.*

The General Journal requires three lines of journal space and three postings. Remember that the accounts receivable must be posted twice; once to the subsidiary ledger account and once to the control account. The Combination Journal shows its best performance yet in this transaction: it requires only one line of journal space and only one posting to the subsidiary ledger. The sales entry is under its own column heading, and it and the accounts receivable control can both be posted once only as monthly totals.

Accts. Rec./ XYZ Co.	*210/✓*	*7 000*	
Sales	*401*		*7 000*
*Sold goods on account to XYZ Company.**			

**Normally an explanation requires only one line in the General Journal.*

Advantages of the Combination Journal

● The Combination Journal saves time because it requires fewer daily postings. Many items can be posted as totals at month-end.

● It requires less space for the same information.

● Less posting is required because columns are used for highly repetitive transactions. There is thus less chance for error.

● Since all journal entries are combined, a business can be easily reviewed from this type of journal. No other sources need to be consulted.

● Because all the journal information is on a single page, one person can easily handle all of the journalizing for a small business without the necessity of contending with a number of journals.

● In the developmental stages of a new business, the Combination Journal may be ideal because it readily lends itself to expansion into the five-journal system.

Disadvantages of the Combination Journal

● When there are many columns to work with, the frequency of error increases.

● The journal must be physically large, making it awkward and cumbersome.

● The recording of some entries requires several lines of journal space.

● The internal control measure for the division of duty is violated, because one person handles *all* the journal entries. This permits easy manipulation of the records. *Note:* This may not be a problem if the owner is the bookkeeper or if the owner regularly reviews the journal entries of the employee.

● This type of journal is best done by hand. It does not lend itself to automated data processing methods.

More about the Combination Journal

Referring once again to the illustration, examine each of the following points:

- The journal has its name, the month(s) of operation, and the page number across the top.
- The column headings, although they will vary from company to company, according to its specific needs, highlight the key accounts in a business. They include: Date, Explanations (which may include terms of sale), a Posting Reference column for the General Ledger debit and credit columns to follow, debit and credit columns for both Accounts Receivable and Accounts Payable, Purchases, Purchases Discounts, Sales, Sales Tax and Sales Discounts, and debit and credit columns for Cash. There is also a column to record cheque numbers. A business may change the number of columns in order to meet its individual needs.
- Daily posting is required from the General Ledger columns to the General Ledger accounts, and daily posting to the accounts receivable and accounts payable if the business maintains subsidiary ledgers for either of those items. Since all other accounts are listed in their own separate columns, they can be totalled at the end of the month. The total only is posted to the General Ledger accounts at that time.
- At the end of each page of work, the columns are totalled using "pinhead totals" — very tiny pencilled totals at the ends of columns to ensure accuracy before use at the top of the page. The journal should also be proofed to check the accuracy of the debit and credit entries. *Note:* Pinhead totals are omitted in later illustrations of the Combination Journal.
- After this check is done, the pinhead totals are transferred to the top of the next page and identified with the words *Brought Forward.* (See page 426.)
- When the Combination Journal is being closed, a procedure similar to the one described above is employed. The columns are totalled showing pinhead totals. Then, the totals of each column are added to prove that the total debits equal the total credits in the Combination Journal. When this has been done, the totals are copied in ink and the date column and *all* money columns are double-underlined.

Note that as the column totals are posted, the General Ledger account number is recorded beneath the total in parentheses. It is important to notice too that the General Ledger column totals are not posted, because each of the individual items was posted daily, and therefore check marks in parentheses are put below the double-underlined totals. (See page 426.)

TOPIC 4 PROBLEMS

12-12 Refer back to the illustration of the Combination Journal on page 426 and then answer the following questions regarding that illustration.

a Why is the cash balance of $5 600 not recorded in the Cash debit account column?

b Why are four lines used to record the transaction on September 5?

c What is the purpose of the debit and credit *General Ledger* columns?

d Under what circumstances would a transaction be recorded, not in the Combination Journal, but in the General Journal?

e Are there any numbers that should be posted under the circumstances in **d**?

f Outline briefly what steps you would take to complete the journal at month-end.

g Find a transaction that would normally have been a multiple-line General Journal entry that the Combination Journal records on one line.

12-13 David Bradford practices law under the company name D. Bradford, Lawyer. He has a receptionist who also maintains his accounting records. These records consist of a Combination Journal (refer to the illustration on page 426 as a sample) and a General Ledger. (Not used in this problem.)

a Complete the necessary journal entries in the Combination Journal for the month of July 19—. Read all transactions first and decide what accounts you will put in your journal column headings.

July
1 Opening cash balance equaled $1 250.
3 Received on account from Bawin Comp. Ltd. $800.
6 D. Bradford invested an additional $1 000 into the practice.
6 Paid CCH Canadian Limited $950 for taxation books to be added to the law library. Cheque No. 251. (Cheque numbers now follow in order.)
7 Paid receptionist weekly pay. $250.
10 Performed legal services for J. Parson on account. $1 200.
12 Purchased office supplies from Hay Stationery Ltd. on account. Terms n/30. $250.
15 Paid receptionist weekly pay. $250.
16 Paid the monthly telephone bill. $52.
20 Performed legal services for A. Brackett for cash. $325.
21 Paid receptionist weekly pay. $250.
23 D. Bradford withdrew cash (write a cheque) for personal use. $100.
24 Arranged a loan for $1 000 with Royal Bank of Canada. Cash was deposited to chequing account.
27 Bought additional office furniture from Steelcase Office Furniture Company on account. Terms 2/10, n/60. $1 010.
28 Paid receptionist weekly pay. $250.

July 30 Paid PUC Invoice No. 1616 in full. $332.
30 Paid Round the World Realty Ltd. August rent. $750.

Key Check Figure Cash (DR.) Total = $3 125

b Total the journal, check the totals to prove that the debits equal the credits and rule the journal off for month-end.

12-14 Whitehead Photo Studios provides portrait sittings and all types of photographic equipment and supplies. The firm uses a Combination Journal, a General Ledger, an accounts receivable subsidiary ledger, and an accounts payable subsidiary ledger. The owner's husband, Jack Whitehead, does all the bookkeeping. This allows Jane to concentrate on the photographic end of the business. An employee handles the daily counter sales and reservations. All cash outflow is paid by cheque. The firm offers credit terms of n/30 to all customers.

a Open General Ledger accounts as follows: Cash $8 700; Accounts Receivable Control; Inventory; Processing Supplies; Equipment; Accounts Payable Control; Jane Whitehead, Capital, $10 000; Jane Whitehead, Drawings; Photo Services; Photographic Sales; Photographic Sales Returns and Allowances; Purchases; Purchases Returns and Allowances; Purchases Discounts; Rent Expense, $1 300; Telephone Expense; Wages Expense.

b Open the following accounts receivable subsidiary ledger accounts: B. Hall, M. Thomas, C. Woo.

c Open the following accounts payable subsidiary ledger accounts: Fuji Films Ltd., Kodak Ltd., S. & P. Photo Services.

d Journalize the following transactions for the month of October. The page is 23.

Oct. 2 Bought photographic supplies from Kodak Ltd. on account. $250. These will be resold.
4 Took family portraits for M. Thomas. Invoice No. 2639 $150.
5 Sold camera equipment to C. Woo on account. Sale price totalled $375. Prepared Invoice No. 2640.
8 Paid the monthly rent to Randolph Realty Ltd. $450. Cheque number 735 was used.
10 Paid Bell Canada's monthly telephone bill. Issued cheque number 736 for $42.
13 Received an invoice No. T-332 dated October 12 from S. & P. Photo Services. It was for services performed for the business and totalled $300. (Use Purchases account.)
15 Purchased from Kodak, on account, processing supplies needed for the business. $325.
19 Paid S. & P. Photo Services in full. Terms offered on invoice No. T-332 stated 1/10, n/30.
20 Took wedding pictures for B. Hall. Invoice No. 2641. $575.
21 Sent to C. Woo finished pictures left previously for development. The firm included invoice No. 2642. $27.
25 Purchased store supplies on account from Fuji Ltd. These goods are for resale. $280.
27 J. Whitehead withdrew $150 for personal use.

e Complete all necessary daily postings. Total and prove the accuracy of the Combination Journal.

f Post the necessary totals.

g Prepare schedules of the subsidiary ledgers to verify the accuracy of the control accounts.

h Prepare a trial balance for the end of October.

Key Check Figure
Trial Balance =
$11 985

Case Study 12

The TMW Company uses the five-journal system to record all transactions. Upon completion of all journalizing and posting at the end of March 198-, the company accountant cannot obtain a successful trial balance. She begins checking to determine where the error might be. She has asked for your assistance and has provided you with the following information:

Sales Journal totals: Accts. Rec. $10 000, Sales $9 500.

Purchases Journal totals: General Ledger $400, Accts. Pay. $8 200, Purchases $7 800.

Cash Receipts Journals totals: General Ledger $150, Sales $500, Sales Tax Payable $50, Accts. Rec. $8 000, Cash $8 700.

Cash Payments Journal totals: General Ledger $650, Accts. Pay. $6 500, Purchase Discounts $100, Cash $7 050.

GENERAL JOURNAL

March 10	Sales R & A	403	100	
	Accts. Rec./Woodwell Ltd.	✓		100
20	Accts. Pay./Petertown Comp.	✓	50	
	Purchases R & A	505		50

Accounts Receivable Ledger

ABC Comp.	
8 000	8 000
0	

Woodwell Ltd.	
2 000	100
1 900	

Accounts Payable Ledger

B-1 Ltd.	
3 500	4 000
	500

Petertown Comp.	
50	4 200
3 000	
	1 150

General Ledger

Accts. Rec. Control	
10 000	8 000
2 000	

Accts. Pay. Control	
6 500	8 200
	1 700

a List the checks you believe should have occurred before the trial balance was attempted.

b What check has the accountant forgotten?

c Why is there an error?

d Indicate what must be done to produce the correct balance.

CHAPTER 13

ACCOUNTING FOR SPECIAL ITEMS

The last two chapters covered common transactions of merchandising firms. This chapter deals with transactions covering what are known as *special items*. Two special items are the accounting of federal and provincial sales tax and the accounting of credit card transactions.

- Topic 1 deals with federal and provincial sales tax.
- Topic 2 deals with credit card transactions.

Percentage Rates of Provincial Sales Tax

Alberta	No tax
Saskatchewan	5%
Manitoba	6%
British Columbia	7%
Ontario	7%
Quebec	9%
New Brunswick	10%
Nova Scotia	10%
Prince Edward Island	10%
Newfoundland	11%

Courtesy of Clarkson Gordon

TOPIC 1 FEDERAL AND PROVINCIAL SALES TAX

In Canada, there are two levels of sales taxation.

(1) *Retail sales tax* is added to the purchase price of most items in most provinces. (At the time of writing, retail sales tax was levied in all provinces except Alberta.) It is "visible" tax, because it is seen by the consumer (and paid by him or her) when a purchase is made. The table in the margin shows the retail rate for each of the provinces.

(2) *Federal sales tax* is "hidden," because it is charged at the manufacturer's level and thus included within the purchase price paid by the consumer. GST

Federal Sales Tax

Manufacturer's and/or Wholesaler's Sales Tax Licence holder: a business that makes or sells a product to another party who will resell those goods to the public.

This tax applies to the selling price of Canadian manufactured goods and on the duty-paid value of most imported goods. Producers of goods subject to federal sales tax are required to obtain a *Manufacturer's* and/or a *Wholesaler's Sales Tax Licence*. The holder of this licence is a business that makes or sells a product to another party who will resell those goods to a consumer.

A non-licence holder is a business that resells goods to the consumer. The goods are bought from a holder of a manufacturer's or a wholesale sales tax licence. This means if goods are to be sold to a business that resells the products, unchanged, to the general consuming public, a sales tax is levied on the manufacturer. If, however, the goods are to be sold to a firm, another licence holder, that would add to the product purchased (thus producing a new or changed product) then the tax would not be applied on the first sale described. When the second manufacturer sells its product to a non-licence holder, the federal sales tax would then be included.

Federal sales tax is charged at a rate of 9% on all items except building and certain construction materials. Tax is paid on these materials at a rate of 5%.

Federal sales tax produces revenue for the federal government of about six to seven billion dollars annually. This tax has been under study for over 40 years and changes have again been suggested as recently as 1981 in the form of draft legislation from the federal government.

Retail Sales Tax

This book will use Ontario forms and procedures to illustrate the retail sales tax system. Remember that there are differences from the retail sales tax procedures used in other Canadian provinces, though they are minor.

Taxable sales: the sale or rental of all goods except those exempt under the Retail Sales Tax Act.

Collection of Retail Sales Tax Persons who regularly make taxable sales — all sales or the rental of goods except those exempt under the Retail Sales Tax Act — are required to collect retail sales tax. For sales tax purposes, you are a "person" if your business is:

- a proprietorship (one owner)
- a partnership (more than one owner)
- a corporation (an incorporated business with shareholders)
- an association (a group; e.g., the Lions Club or the YWCA)

Retail Sales Tax Vendor's Permit: an identification document issued by the provincial government to all businesses required to collect retail sales tax.

A business required to collect Retail Sales Tax is allowed to conduct sales only after applying for a Retail Sales Tax Vendor's Permit. This is an identification document issued by the provincial government to all businesses that are required to collect retail sales tax. It is available free of charge through any of the retail sales tax branch offices in your province.

A Vendor's Permit is required for those businesses that sell the following products or services: alcoholic beverages, cigarettes, hotels, restaurants, snack bars, telecommunications, automobile maintenance, and clothing alterations.

Businesses that do not charge taxable sales, but consume or use taxable goods, also require a vendor's permit — for example, a person who sells goods or services at a flea market.

In Ontario, the retail sales tax rate is 7%. Therefore, for every dollar of taxable sales, the seller must collect seven cents for the Ontario government. To help sellers collect and calculate these amounts, the government supplies businesses with a chart showing the amount of sales tax to be charged. See the first illustration on page 434.

Computerized cash register systems are programmed to automatically calculate the tax and determine the final total.

Let us use the schedule to determine the amount of tax to be charged if the taxable amount totals $10.51.

Ontario Ministry of Revenue

SALES TAX SCHEDULE AT 7%

AMOUNT $ $	TAX $	AMOUNT $ $	TAX $
.21	.01	6.50 to 6.64	.46
.22 to .35	.02	6.65 to 6.78	.47
.36 to .49	.03	6.79 to 6.92	.48
.50 to .64	.04	6.93 to 7.07	.49
.65 to .78	.05	7.08 to 7.21	.50
.79 to .92	.06	7.22 to 7.35	.51
.93 to 1.07	.07	7.36 to 7.49	.52
1.08 to 1.21	.08	7.50 to 7.64	.53
1.22 to 1.35	.09	7.65 to 7.78	.54
1.36 to 1.49	.10	7.79 to 7.92	.55
1.50 to 1.64	.11	7.93 to 8.07	.56
1.65 to 1.78	.12	8.08 to 8.21	.57
1.79 to 1.92	.13	8.22 to 8.35	.58
1.93 to 2.07	.14	8.36 to 8.49	.59
2.08 to 2.21	.15	8.50 to 8.64	.60
2.22 to 2.35	.16	8.65 to 8.78	.61
2.36 to 2.49	.17	8.79 to 8.92	.62
2.50 to 2.64	.18	8.93 to 9.07	.63
2.65 to 2.78	.19	9.08 to 9.21	.64
2.79 to 2.92	.20	9.22 to 9.35	.65
2.93 to 3.07	.21	9.36 to 9.49	.66
3.08 to 3.21	.22	9.50 to 9.64	.67
3.22 to 3.35	.23	9.65 to 9.78	.68
3.36 to 3.49	.24	9.79 to 9.92	.69
3.50 to 3.64	.25	10.00	.70
3.65 to 3.78	.26	20.00	1.40
3.79 to 3.92	.27	30.00	2.10
3.93 to 4.07	.28	40.00	2.80
4.08 to 4.21	.29	50.00	3.50
4.22 to 4.35	.30	100.00	7.00
4.36 to 4.49	.31	200.00	14.00
4.50 to 4.64	.32	300.00	21.00
4.65 to 4.78	.33	400.00	28.00
4.79 to 4.92	.34	500.00	35.00
4.93 to 5.07	.35		
5.08 to 5.21	.36		
5.22 to 5.35	.37		
5.36 to 5.49	.38		
5.50 to 5.64	.39		
5.65 to 5.78	.40		
5.79 to 5.92	.41		
5.93 to 6.07	.42		
6.08 to 6.21	.43		
6.22 to 6.35	.44		
6.36 to 6.49	.45		

Use these computations in calculating larger amounts.

For Example

Sale $134.00

Tax on $100.00 7.00

30.00 2.10

4.00 .28

$9.38

For sales tax rate @ 10% see reverse side

GV-13 0418P (83-08)

On ten dollars, the chart indicates tax of $0.70. For $0.51 the tax is $0.04. The tax is thus $0.70 + $0.04 = $0.74. Check this by multiplying: $10.51 × 7% = $0.7357 = $0.74.

Sales tax is collected by the business on behalf of the provincial government. The account used to record the provincial sales tax is usually called Sales Tax Payable and is a current liability. The reason for this classification will be explained later.

To account for a sales tax amount is relatively simple. Assume that on April 2, 19—, Walter Frameton sells taxable goods for cash, $800. The accounts affected would be Cash, Sales and the new account Sales Tax Payable. The entry in the General Journal would appear as shown below.

GENERAL JOURNAL **Page 6**

Date 19—	Account Title and Explanation	Post. Ref.	Debit	Credit
Apr. 2	Cash		856 00	
	Sales			800 00
	Sales Tax Payable	205		56 00
	To record the sale of goods plus the collection of sales tax at 7%.			

Analysis:

- The transaction results in a credit entry to Sales of $800.
- Sales tax is calculated at 7%; therefore the tax to be collected is $800 × 7% = $56.
- A liability has increased. Credit Sales Tax Payable $56.
- The asset increases by $800 + $56 = $856. Debit cash $856.

On April 4, goods totalling $100 are sold to J. Arland on account. The journal entry would appear as follows:

GENERAL JOURNAL **Page 6**

Date 19—	Account Title and Explanation	Post. Ref.	Debit	Credit
Apr. 4	Accounts Receivable/J. Arland		107 00	
	Sales			100 00
	Sales Tax Payable	205		7 00
	To record the sale of goods on account plus sales tax at 7%. Terms n/30.			

Walter Frameton's business now owes the Ontario government $63, as shown in the T-account in the margin. Each time the business makes a sale of taxable goods, the sales tax owing to the government increases.

Analysis: Examine the cash sale and the credit sale illustrated in the General Journal, and then examine the other two systems.

- Notice on April 2 the cash sale for $800. Because the firm must collect sales tax, a special column, Sales Tax Payable/Credit, has been prepared to collect these amounts.
- Remember, if a separate column is used, no posting is required until month-end. The entry is easier than the General Journal entry in the illustration on page 434. It requires only one line and each item has a column heading.
- The credit sale to J. Arland is shown next. Compare the Combination Journal entry on page 436 to the General Journal entry on page 434. Finally, look at the receipt of funds from J. Arland on April 30 in the Combination Journal.

Note: Posting references are shown only for entries under discussion.

Now examine the same set of entries in the cash receipts journal of the five-journal system shown on page 437.

Analysis:

- In the cash receipts journal entry of April 2, the entry is on one line.
- By expanding the journal and including one more column, *Sales Tax Payable — Credit*, each account has its own column. This reduces the amount of posting.

Examine the sales journal for the sale on account. At month-end, the sales tax payable account would appear as in the next illustrations in each of the three systems.

No matter which system is used, the firm has collected sales tax totalling $178.50 for the provincial government. The method of submitting this amount will be given later.

Sales Tax Payable

Debit	Credit	
	19—	
	April 2	56
	4	7
		63

Sales Tax Pay.

General Journal Example

Sales Tax Payable **Account No.** *205*

19—		Post. Ref.	Debit	Credit	Balance
Apr. 2	Cash Sale	GJ6		56.00	56.00
4	J. Arland	GJ6		7.00	63.00
10	P. Frameton			14.00	77.00
20	Cash Sale			70.00	147.00
25	P. Marvel			31.50	178.50

(cont. on page 438)

COMBINATION JOURNAL

	Date 19—	Account Title and Explanation	Post. Ref.	General Ledger Debit	General Ledger Credit	Accounts Receivable Debit	Accounts Receivable Credit	Accounts Payable Debit	Accounts Payable Credit	Purchases Debit	Purchases Discount Credit	Sales Credit	Sales Tax Payable Credit	Cash Debit	Cash Credit	Chq. No.	
1	Apr. 1	Cash Balance $5 400	—														1
2	2	Cash Sale	—									800 00	56 00	856 00			2
3	4	J. Arland Terms n/30	—			107 00						100 00	7 00				3
4	6	Bought Merchandise	—							650 00					650 00	73	4
5	10	P. Frameton Terms n/30	—			214 00						200 00	14 00				5
6	13	PUC Expense Inv. T-1173	—	85 00											85 00	74	6
7	18	Paid M.&D. Ltd. in Full	—					312 00							312 00	75	7
8	20	Cash Sale	—									1 000 00	70 00	1 070 00			8
9	25	P. Marvel Terms n/30	—			481 50						450 00	31 50				9
10	29	Bought Equipment on Acct.															10
11		J. Rosand Ltd.	—	2 000 00					2 000 00								11
12	30	Paid Rent Expense	—	480 00											480 00	76	12
13	30	Rec'd from J. Arland	—				107 00							107 00			13
14	Apr. 30	Totals		2 565 00		802 50	107 00	312 00	2 000 00	650 00		2 550 00	178 50	2 033 00	1 527 00		14
15													(205)				15

SALES JOURNAL Page 3

Date 19—	Invoice Number	Account Debited	Terms	Post. Ref.	Accounts Receivable Debit	Sales Credit	Sales Tax Payable Credit
Apr. 4	V-111	J. Arland	n/30		107 00	100 00	7 00
10	V-112	P. Frameton	n/30		214 00	200 00	14 00
25	V-113	P. Marvel	n/30		481 50	450 00	31 50
Apr. 30					802 50	750 00	52 50
							(205)

CASH RECEIPTS JOURNAL Page 10

Date 19—	Account Credited	Explanation	Post. Ref.	Other Accounts Credit	Accounts Receivable Credit	Sales Credit	Sales Tax Payable Credit	Sales Discounts Debit	Cash Debit
Apr. 1	Cash Balance	$5 400							
2		Cash sale.				800 00	56 00		856 00
20		Cash sale.				1 000 00	70 00		1 070 00
30	J. Arland	On account.			107 00				107 00
Apr. 30					107 00	1 800 00	126 00		2 033 00
							(205)		

(cont. from page 435)

Combination Journal Example

Sales Tax Payable **Account No.** *205*

19—		Post. Ref.	Debit	Credit	Balance
Apr. 30	Total	CJ11		178.50	178.50

Five-Journal System Example

Sales Tax Payable **Account No.** *205*

19—		Post. Ref.	Debit	Credit	Balance
Apr. 30	Sales Journal Total	SJ3		52.50	52.50
30	Cash Receipts Journal Total	CRJ10		126.00	178.50

Accounting for Sales Tax and Sales Returns and Allowances

Whenever a sale is made, there is a chance that the item sold will be returned for some reason. What happens when sales tax is involved?

Assume that on April 3, $25 worth of the April 2 sale is returned because the goods are damaged. The firm agrees to refund the $25 plus the applicable sales tax. The tax totals $1.75 ($25 × 7%), so the total cash refund would be $26.75 ($25.00 + $1.75). The General Journal entry appears as on page 440. Compare the entry of April 3 in the other two systems, illustrated opposite.

The issuing of a cheque for the cash refund has been analyzed in General Journal form for the five-journal system. Normally it would be placed in the cash payments journal.

Assume that on April 26 P. Marvel returns $10 of her goods. After negotiations, she agrees to keep the goods and receive an allowance equal to $5.00. Study the treatment of this transaction under the three systems, as illustrated opposite.

Analysis:

- Because the price was reduced, the sales tax is reduced accordingly.
- Note the increased number of entries in the General Ledger accounts. This is because neither the Combination Journal nor

GENERAL JOURNAL

Page 6

Date 19—		Account Title and Explanation	Post. Ref.	Debit	Credit
Apr.	3	Sales R & A		25 00	
		Sales Tax Payable	205	1 75	
		Cash			26 75
		Cash Refund for Goods Returned.			
	26	Sales R & A		5 00	
		Sales Tax Payable	205	35	
		Accts. Rec./P. Marvel			5 35
		To record an allowance.			

COMBINATION JOURNAL

Page 11

Date 19—	Account Title and Explanation	Post. Ref.	General Ledger Debit	General Ledger Credit	Accounts Receivable Debit	Accounts Receivable Credit	Accounts Payable Debit	Accounts Payable Credit	Purchases Debit	Purchases Discount Credit	Sales Credit	Sales Tax Payable Credit	Cash Debit	Cash Credit	Chq. No.
Apr. 1	Cash Balance $5 400	—													
2	Cash Sale	—									800 00	56 00	856 00		
3	Sales Returns and														
	Allowances	—	25 00												
	Sales Tax Payable	205	1 75											26 75	72
4	J. Arland (n/30)	—			107 00						100 00	7 00			
6	Bought Merchandise	—							650 00					650 00	73
10	P. Frameton (n/30)	—			214 00						200 00	14 00			
13	PUC Expense Inv. T-1173	—	85 00											85 00	74
18	Paid M.&D. Ltd. in Full	—					312 00							312 00	75
20	Cash Sale	—									1 000 00	70 00	1 070 00		
25	P. Marvel (n/30)	—			481 50						450 00	31 50			
26	Sales R&A/P. Marvel	—	5 00												
	Sales Tax Payable	205	35			5 35									
29	Bought Equip. (J. Rosand Ltd.)	—	2 000 00					2 000 00							
30	Paid Rent Expense	—	480 00											480 00	76
30	Rec'd from J. Arland	—				107 00							107 00		
Apr. 30	Totals		2 597 10		802 50	112 35	312 00	2 000 00	650 00		2 550 00	178 50	2 033 00	1 553 75	
												(205)			

GENERAL JOURNAL **Page** 6

Date 19—	Account Title and Explanation	Post. Ref.	Debit	Credit
Apr. 3	Sales R & A		25.00	
	Sales Tax Payable	205	1.75	
	Cash			26.75
	To record the refund on the April 2 sale. Cheque No. 72.			
26	Sales R & A		5.00	
	Sales Tax Payable	205	.35	
	Accounts Receivable/ P. Marvel			5.35
	To record an allowance of $5 on merchandise.			

the five-journal system has a special debit column for sales tax payable. In the five-journal system, the sales allowance and returns transaction involving a transaction on account must go into the General Journal.

General Journal Example

Sales Tax Payable **Account No.** 205

19—		Post. Ref.	Debit	Credit	Balance
Apr. 2	Cash Sale			56.00	56.00
3	Sales Return	GJ6	1.75		54.25
4	J. Arland			7.00	61.25
10	P. Frameton			14.00	75.25
20	Cash Sale			70.00	145.25
25	P. Marvel			31.50	176.75
26	Sales Allowance— Marvel	GJ6	.35		176.40

Combination Journal Example

Sales Tax Payable **Account No.** 205

19—		Post. Ref.	Debit	Credit	Balance
Apr. 3	Sales Return	CJ11	1.75		1.75 DR.
26	Sales Allowance— Marvel	CJ11	.35		2.10 DR.
30	Total			178.50	176.40

Five-Journal System Example

Sales Tax Payable					Account No. *205*
19—		Post. Ref.	Debit	Credit	Balance
Apr. 3	*Sales Return*	*GJ6*	*1.75*		*1.75 DR.*
26	*Sales Allowance— Marvel*	*GJ6*	*.35*		*2.10 DR.*
30	*Sales Journal Total*			*52.50*	*50.40*
30	*Cash Receipts Total*			*126.00*	*176.40*

Sales Discounts and Sales Tax Payable Discounts are taken *only* on the amount of the sale, *not* the total amount owing. Refer to the transaction involving J. Arland. If terms of 2/10, n/30 had been offered and J. Arland had paid within the discount period, the discount would have totalled $2 ($100 × 2%). The discount must be taken on only the $100 sale price. Remember how purchases discounts were taken when transportation-in was involved? The sales discount procedure is exactly the same.

Finally, note from the illustration that the Combination Journal does not have a special sales discount column. Therefore, the sales discount would have to be recorded in the General Ledger debit column. The cash receipts journal does contain the Sales Discount — Debit column, and should be used whenever possible.

Remitting Sales Tax to the Provincial Government Normally, at the end of each month, businesses must submit to the provincial government the retail sales tax collected during that month. *Note:* Some businesses can submit their collections less frequently if their sales tax collections are small enough.

You should now understand why sales tax payable is considered a current liability. Since even the smallest businesses submit their collections at least every six months, the liability is paid within one year, and so sales tax payable must be a current liability.

To make the submission, the business must complete a Registered Vendor Retail Sales Tax Return form, as illustrated on page 442. To complete this form you would use the following information:

- Total of sales (in Ontario) was $2 550.
- Tax collected on sales was $176.40.
- Tax on purchases for own consumption amounted to zero.
- Payment is being made on time.
- Compensation falls between $16.01 and $400 ($176.40). Therefore compensation is $16.00.
- There are no adjustments.

Condensed Compensation Table

If line two is:

$0.00 to $16.00 compensation is nil

$16.01-$400.00 compensation is $16.00

$400.01 or more compensation is 4% of line 2

Registered Vendor Retail Sales Tax Return: the form used for submission of retail sales tax to the provincial government.

- Tax to be paid is $176.40 — $16 = $160.40.

Let us follow the illustration to see where each number came from:

Line 1:	$2 550.00	Total sales
Line 2:	$ 176.40	Sales tax collected on sales
Line 3:	Ø	(No tax on purchases)
Line 4:	$ 176.40	Total of lines 2 and 3
Line 5:	Ø	(No late payment penalty)
Line 6:	$ 176.40	Subtotal
Line 7:	$ 16.00	Compensation
Line 8:	$ 160.40	Subtotal
Line 9:	Ø	(No adjustments)
Line 10:	$ 160.40	Tax to be paid

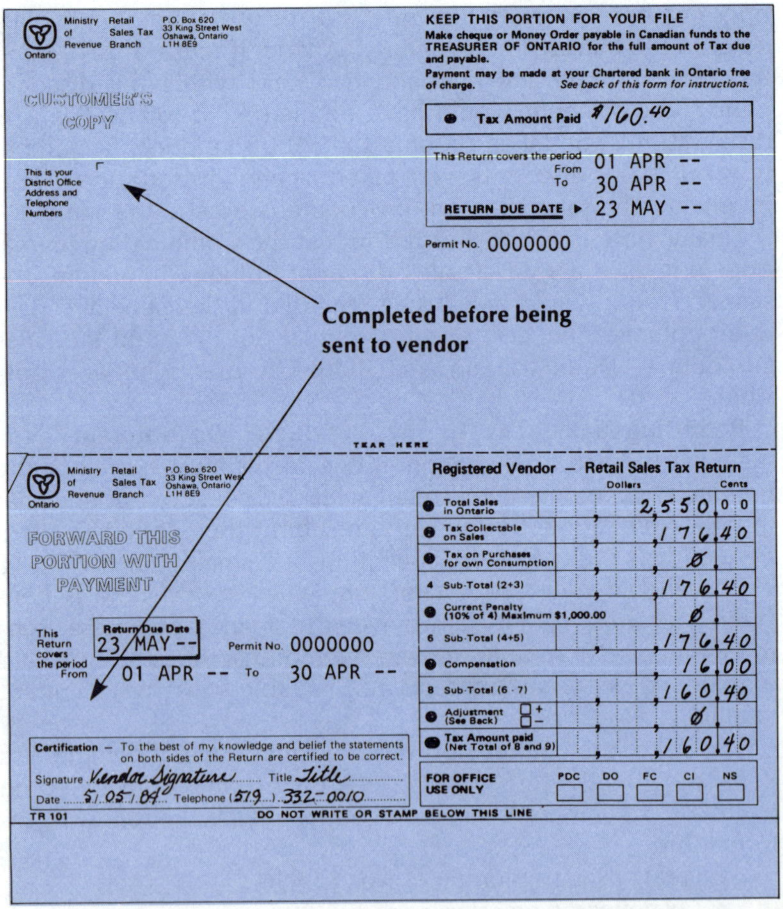
Ministry of Revenue Ontario — Retail Sales Tax Branch — P.O. Box 620, 33 King Street West, Oshawa, Ontario L1H 8E9

CUSTOMER'S COPY

KEEP THIS PORTION FOR YOUR FILE

Make cheque or Money Order payable in Canadian funds to the TREASURER OF ONTARIO for the full amount of Tax due and payable.

Payment may be made at your Chartered bank in Ontario free of charge. See back of this form for instructions.

Tax Amount Paid $160.40

This is your District Office Address and Telephone Numbers

This Return covers the period From 01 APR -- To 30 APR --

RETURN DUE DATE ▸ 23 MAY --

Permit No. 0000000

Completed before being sent to vendor

TEAR HERE

Ministry of Revenue Ontario — Retail Sales Tax Branch — P.O. Box 620, 33 King Street West, Oshawa, Ontario L1H 8E9

FORWARD THIS PORTION WITH PAYMENT

This Return covers the period From 01 APR -- To 30 APR --

Return Due Date 23 MAY --

Permit No. 0000000

Registered Vendor — Retail Sales Tax Return

	Dollars	Cents
1 Total Sales in Ontario	2,550	00
2 Tax Collectable on Sales	176	40
3 Tax on Purchases for own Consumption	Ø	
4 Sub-Total (2+3)	176	40
5 Current Penalty (10% of 4) Maximum $1,000.00	Ø	
6 Sub-Total (4+5)	176	40
7 Compensation	16	00
8 Sub-Total (6 - 7)	160	40
9 Adjustment (See Back) + −	Ø	
10 Tax Amount paid (Net Total of 8 and 9)	160	40

Certification — To the best of my knowledge and belief the statements on both sides of the Return are certified to be correct.

Signature Vendor Signature Title Title

Date 51.05.1.84 Telephone (519) 332-0010

FOR OFFICE USE ONLY PDC DO FC CI NS

TR 101 DO NOT WRITE OR STAMP BELOW THIS LINE

Due dates: the date by which the vendor must submit the retail sales tax collected to the provincial government.

The date by which the vendor must submit the retail sales tax to the provincial government is called the due date. Due dates are shown on the front of every return. Failure to meet this deadline results in a penalty (see line 5 of the above illustration) and the loss of any compensation for that period. Returns are mailed to firms approximately three weeks before their due date.

Payments can be made in three ways:

(1) *Mail payment* by cheque or money order to the ministry, with the envelope provided. You must allow delivery time in the mail to ensure arrival before the due date.

(2) *Bank payment* to any chartered bank before the due date. Late payments must be mailed or delivered to the District Retail Sales Tax Office. There is no charge for this bank service.

(3) *Cash payment* by cheque or money order to a District Retail Sales Tax Office.

If a business has not made sales or collected tax during the period, *Nil* is written in the appropriate places and the form is returned to the District Retail Sales Tax Office. (Banks cannot accept this type of form.) Only the owner or an authorized person may provide the information for the certification box of the form: (1) the signature, (2) the signing officer's title, (3) the date, and (4) the business telephone number.

Certification box: a location on the Retail Sales Tax Return which the owner or authorized person completes to certify the accuracy of the information on the form.

Finally, any corrections needed because of changes in operation, ownership, business, trade, legal name, or business mailing address must be reported. This can be done on a notification-of-change form, which again is mailed to the District Retail Sales Tax Office.

Once the form is complete, the firm must account for the information produced. A cheque or money order for $160.40 must be sent to the Treasurer of Ontario. The sales tax payable account must be reduced to zero and $16.00 of compensation revenue must be recorded. The entry, in General Journal format, would appear as shown below. Depending upon the amount of revenue earned in the form of compensation, a firm may open a "Compensation Revenue" account or use a "Miscellaneous or Other Revenue" account.

19—			
May 10	*Sales Tax Payable*	*176.40*	
	Cash		*160.40*
	Compensation Revenue		*16.00*
	To record payment of the sales tax less sales tax compensation. Cheque No. 84.		

This same entry could be made in either of the other two systems discussed in this chapter.

Maintenance of Records The provincial government requires that every business keep complete and up-to-date records of all business transactions. Records may not be destroyed until a set of strict conditions are met in accordance with regulations in

3 000 units at $2.00	$6 000
Trade Discount ($6 000 × 5%)	300
Taxable Sale Amount	$5 700

each province. These records may be examined — "audited" — at any time.

Sales Tax on Net Sales Sales tax need be charged only on the net sales total. For example, say ABC Company sells taxable items at $2.00 a unit. If the buyer orders more than 1 000 units, ABC Company offers a trade (quantity) discount of 5%. Therefore, if WDW Ltd. orders 3 000 units, the taxable selling price would be as calculated in the margin.

Similarly, if ABC offers a 6% discount for immediate payment in cash, and if WDW Ltd. pays cash for the 3 000 units they ordered, the taxable sale amount would be as shown in the first illustration below.

3 000 units at $2.00	$6 000
Cash Discount ($6 000 × 6%)	360
Taxable Sale Amount	$5 640

If both discounts were taken:

	$6 000	
Less:	300	Trade Discount
Less:	360	Cash Discount
	$5 340	

Dinner Bill	$25.00
Less: Coupon	5.00
Taxable Amount	20.00
Tax at 7%	1.40
Total Bill	$21.40

Orange Soda	$0.79
Tax	0.06
Pre-Coupon Price	0.85
Coupon Value	0.25
Net Price	$0.60

Retail store coupons: printed forms offering a specified reduction (discount) at a specific store on a particular product.

Restaurant coupons: printed forms offering some sort of reduction in the price of a meal or a combination of meals.

Manufacturers' coupons: printed forms offering a reduction on the price of a certain product at any store that sells the product.

Money coupons: printed forms representing money, given to customers at the time of a purchase to lower the cost of a future purchase at that store.

Discount Coupons Retail stores and restaurants may issue coupons, called retail store coupons and restaurant coupons, that provide a discount on specific products when presented for redemption. Since this is considered a discount, the retail sales tax is charged on the net sale price, the total less the discount (coupon). For example, if a customer presents a $5.00 restaurant coupon when paying a $25.00 dinner bill, the tax is calculated as shown in the second illustration above.

Do not confuse retail store and restaurant coupons with manufacturers' coupons and money coupons: manufacturers' coupons reduce the price of a specific product at any store, and money coupons give a customer the chance to reduce the price of a future purchase at a specific store. They give the customer a reduction in price, but tax must be paid on the price before the discount. For example, a customer has a manufacturer's coupon for orange soda for $0.25. The store price for the soda is $0.79. The cost to the customer is calculated as shown above.

Some of the other rules and regulations which affect retail sales tax are: Status Indians, Purchase Exemption Certificates, Tax-Included Pricing, and Rentals.

Since tax laws are always changing in all the provinces, you are well advised to get the latest information from the retail sales tax office in your province.

TOPIC 1 PROBLEMS

13-1 Calculate the retail sales tax that must be charged on each of the items 1 to 10. Find the amount charged in Ontario (7% rate); then find the amount charged in your own province. If you live in Ontario, use New Brunswick as the other province. Do the calculations in a chart like the one shown below.

Item	*Amount*	*Retail Sales Tax*	
		Ontario	*Your Province*
(1) New car	$9 500.00		
(2) Soft drink	0.79		
(3) Chocolate bar	0.40		

(4) Refrigerator, $959.00; (5) Living room suite, $4 850.00; (6) Television set, $675.00; (7) Roast of beef, $12.80; (8) Repairs to your car, $125.00; (9) Bird feeder, $10.95; (10) Lawn fertilizer, $23.70.

13-2 Refer to the illustration of a sales tax return form shown in the text on page 442.

a Given the following information, calculate the amount of the cheque to be sent to the Treasurer of Ontario by completing the return.

b Complete the necessary General Journal entry to record the results of this source document.

Information

Total Sales for the Month	$15 585.00
Sales Tax Collected	972.15
Tax on Own Purchases	27.55

Key Check Figure
Tax Amount Paid = $960

13-3 A customer enters a local department store in Vancouver, B.C. Calculate the final amount to be paid in the following situation:

(i) Bought 1 lawnmower, $327.00; 3 brooms at $2.50 each; 1 case of pop, $5.99; all items are taxable.
(ii) Store coupon on pop = $1.00.
(iii) Money coupon = $3.75.
(iv) Manufacturer's coupon for the lawnmower = $55.00.

Key Check Figure
Total = $304.50
(if using 7% sales tax)

13-4 Rose's Flower Shop sells cut flowers and household plants. Rose uses a multi-columned sales journal which includes British Columbia retail sales tax of

7% in a separate column. The following were the transactions affecting credit sales for November. Calculate retail sales tax on all sales. Terms for all sales are n/60.

19—

Nov. 1 Invoice No. A-710 for cut flowers was issued to L. Star. Amount, $20 on account.

3 Invoice No. A-711 for a household plant was issued to B. Dart. Amount, $35 on account.

4 Invoice No. A-712 for cut flowers was issued to D. Ball. Amount, $18 on account.

Note: Invoices will now proceed in numerical order.

8 Sold one dozen carnations to L. Star on account. $20.

9 Credit memo to L. Star, No. CM-010, re Invoice No. A-713. $14.

11 Sold on account to L. Star one dozen yellow roses. $32.

12 Sold to Ingrid Berg on account, a cut flower arrangement totalling $54.

14 D. Ball bought a potted plant on account for $28.

15 Credit memo No. CM-011 to Ingrid Berg re Invoice No. A-715. $18.

Key Check Figure Total of Accounts Receivable Schedule = $187.25

a Open General Ledger accounts as necessary.

b Open accounts receivable ledger accounts for L. Star, B. Dart, D. Ball, and Ingrid Berg. *Hint:* Don't forget subsidiary order.

c Journalize the transactions and post daily as necessary.

d Total the journals and cross-foot as of November 30.

e Post month-end totals and verify the control account in the appropriate manner.

13-5 Spence's Athletic Footwear specializes in athletic shoes (running, football, basketball, etc.). The business has two employees in addition to the owner. It uses a Combination Journal similar to the illustration given earlier. The business operates a General Ledger, an accounts receivable subsidiary ledger, and an accounts payable subsidiary ledger. The owner does all the ordering and bookkeeping.

a Open General Ledger accounts for: Cash, $12 500; Accounts Receivable Control; Truck; Office Equipment; Bank Loan Payable; Accounts Payable Control; Sales Tax Payable; Mortgage Payable, $3 000; Capital, P. Spence, $9 500; Drawings, P. Spence; Shoe Sales; Sales R & A; Sales Discounts; Purchases/Shoes; Purchases R & A; Purchases Discounts; Transportation-in; Salaries Expense; Interest Expense; Mortgage Interest Expense.

b Open the following accounts receivable ledger accounts: R.D. Atlas, A.X. Chopping, R.P. Minute, V.F. Runner.

c Open the following accounts payable ledger accounts: Addidas Outlets, Converse Suppliers.

d Complete in the Combination Journal the following transactions for the month of March 19-4. (One invoice number and one cheque number will be given. All others follow in numerical order. *Note:* Sales terms are identical for all companies.)

Mar. 1 Record the cash balance.
1 Sold to V.F. Runner, four pairs of football boots at $42 a pair plus 5% sales tax. Terms 2/10, n/30. Invoice No. T-1123.
2 Purchased from Addidas Outlets 85 pairs of various shoes. Total of Invoice No. P-7082 was $1 215. Terms 1/15, n/60. FOB Destination.
2 Arranged a bank loan with the Royal Bank of Canada. Principal was $10 000, interest rate was 12%, due date was March 2, 19-5. Total interest payable in advance. Do not use a cheque. Use a direct deduction from the amount borrowed.
5 Bought office equipment from National Equipment Producers for cash. $1 500. Cheque No. 414.
6 The owner invested personal van for the use of the business. It was appraised at $3 600 by a local automobile dealership.
10 Received payment in full from Invoice No. T-1123.
11 Sold three pairs of jogging shoes at $31 a pair, two pairs of soccer boots at $47 a pair, and one pair of boxing boots for $83. (*Note:* Remember the sales tax.) Issued invoice to R.D. Atlas for the full amount.
12 Sold 12 pairs of basketball runners at $27 a pair to R.P. Minute. (*Note:* Don't forget the tax and terms and invoice number.)
15 Paid two employees $400 each to meet semi-monthly salary obligations.
17 Issued a cheque to Addidas Outlets, $1 202.85.
18 Purchased from Converse Suppliers 55 pairs of shoes at $22 a pair. Invoice No. T-6717. Terms 2/10, n/30. FOB Shipping Point.
19 Paid to Fidelity Trust Company the monthly mortgage payment, $650. The interest portion was $400.
21 Received from R.D. Atlas payment in full. (*Hint:* Don't forget discount.)
21 Received the order from Converse Suppliers. Delivery was made by CN Express. Their invoice No. D-1123 was for $45. Prepared and gave the driver a cheque to cover this amount.
22 After having examined the Converse order, a clerk discovered two faulty pairs of shoes. Prepared a debit memo, No. DM-021, totalling $44, and returned the goods with the memo.
23 The owner withdrew $75 for personal use. (Use a cheque.)
24 Sold 28 pairs of golf shoes, $1 120 to A.X. Chopping.
26 Prepared and sent a credit memo, CM-0111, to A.X. Chopping for 3 pairs of golf shoes. (Return to entry of the 24th to determine unit cost.)
26 Received a credit memo, CM 671, from Converse Suppliers for $44. Attached this to debit memo.
28 Paid Converse Suppliers in full, less discount, less return.
29 Paid semi-monthly salaries to employees. $400 each.

e Total the journal, verify those totals, and post.

f Prepare the appropriate schedules to verify the General Ledger control accounts.

Key Check Figure
Cash = $15 535.61

g If a calculator with paper tape is available, prepare a zero-proof trial balance of the General Ledger.

TOPIC 2 CREDIT CARD TRANSACTIONS

"Plastic money" — everyone has heard that description of credit cards. There are bank credit cards (e.g., VISA and MasterCard), gasoline company cards (Esso, Texaco, Shell, Petrocan), department store cards (Sears, Woolco, Eatons, K-Mart, The Bay), credit service company cards (Carte Blanche, American Express, Diner's Club), and finally very specialized service cards (Bell Canada, whose card enables one to make long-distance calls).

This book will discuss only VISA credit cards with illustrations from the Royal Bank of Canada. In most cases, the ideas will be similar no matter which card is considered.

To apply for a VISA card, pick up an application form at your local bank or from almost any store merchant who accepts the card.

Study this sample application form below.

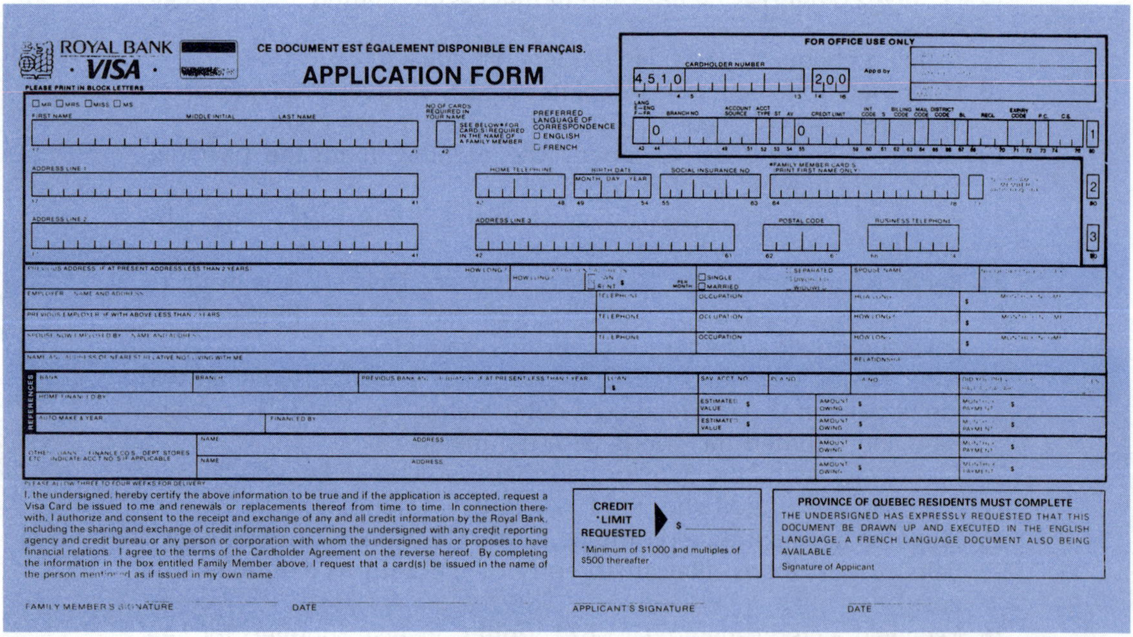

ROYAL BANK · VISA ·

CE DOCUMENT EST ÉGALEMENT DISPONIBLE EN FRANÇAIS.

APPLICATION FORM

FOR OFFICE USE ONLY

PLEASE PRINT IN BLOCK LETTERS

☐ MR ☐ MRS ☐ MISS ☐ MS

FIRST NAME — MIDDLE INITIAL — LAST NAME

NO OF CARDS REQUIRED IN YOUR NAME — SEE BELOW* FOR CARD(S) REQUIRED IN THE NAME OF A FAMILY MEMBER

PREFERRED LANGUAGE OF CORRESPONDENCE ☐ ENGLISH ☐ FRENCH

ADDRESS LINE 1 — HOME TELEPHONE — BIRTH DATE (MONTH, DAY, YEAR) — SOCIAL INSURANCE NO — *FAMILY MEMBER CARD'S (PRINT FIRST NAME ONLY)

ADDRESS LINE 2 — ADDRESS LINE 3 — POSTAL CODE — BUSINESS TELEPHONE

PREVIOUS ADDRESS (IF AT PRESENT ADDRESS LESS THAN 2 YEARS) — HOW LONG? — SINGLE — MARRIED — SEPARATED — SPOUSE NAME

EMPLOYER (NAME AND ADDRESS) — TELEPHONE — OCCUPATION — HOW LONG

PREVIOUS EMPLOYER (IF WITH ABOVE LESS THAN 2 YEARS) — TELEPHONE — OCCUPATION — HOW LONG

SPOUSE NOW EMPLOYED BY (NAME AND ADDRESS) — TELEPHONE — OCCUPATION — HOW LONG

RELATIONSHIP

REFERENCES: BANK — BRANCH — SAV. ACCT. NO. — HOME FINANCED BY — ESTIMATED VALUE $ — AMOUNT OWING $ — MONTHLY PAYMENT $ — AUTO MAKE & YEAR — FINANCED BY — ESTIMATED VALUE $ — AMOUNT OWING $ — MONTHLY PAYMENT $

OTHER LOANS (FINANCE COS., DEPT. STORES, ETC.) INDICATE ACCT NO.'S IF APPLICABLE — NAME — ADDRESS — AMOUNT OWING $ — MONTHLY PAYMENT $

PLEASE ALLOW THREE TO FOUR WEEKS FOR DELIVERY

I, the undersigned, hereby certify the above information to be true and if the application is accepted, request a Visa Card be issued to me and renewals or replacements thereof from time to time. In connection therewith, I authorize and consent to the receipt and exchange of any and all credit information by the Royal Bank, including the sharing and exchange of credit information concerning the undersigned with any credit reporting agency and credit bureau or any person or corporation with whom the undersigned has or proposes to have financial relations. I agree to the terms of the Cardholder Agreement on the reverse hereof. By completing the information in the box entitled Family Member above, I request that a card(s) be issued in the name of the person mentioned as if issued in my own name.

CREDIT *LIMIT REQUESTED $ ____
*Minimum of $1000 and multiples of $500 thereafter

PROVINCE OF QUEBEC RESIDENTS MUST COMPLETE
THE UNDERSIGNED HAS EXPRESSLY REQUESTED THAT THIS DOCUMENT BE DRAWN UP AND EXECUTED IN THE ENGLISH LANGUAGE. A FRENCH LANGUAGE DOCUMENT ALSO BEING AVAILABLE.
Signature of Applicant

FAMILY MEMBER'S SIGNATURE — DATE — APPLICANT'S SIGNATURE — DATE

After completing the form, mail it to the Royal Bank VISA Centre. Unless there is an error or omission or further questions regarding the application, you will then receive your credit card, usually by registered mail.

The card displays your name, an expiry date (in most cases), and an identification number in raised lettering. This information is automatically recorded onto source documents. Also printed on the card will be the name *VISA* and the name of the bank.

With the card will be some information and instructions such as: your assigned credit limit (usually from $700 to $1 500 to start), where to sign your name on the card (usually on the back), what to do if your card is lost or stolen, how and when payment is required, and information on minimum payments and interest charges.

If the card is lost or stolen, the cardholder is responsible for up to $50 even after notification of loss or theft. When payment falls due, the cardholder must pay a minimum of $10 or 10% of the outstanding balance, whichever is greater.

When these cards first came into existence and until one year before the writing of this text, there was no user charge for the privilege of having and using the card. Furthermore, if the cardholder paid the total outstanding monthly balance within 25 days of the date of the statement there was no interest charge. This is still true for some types of credit cards.

The banks now charge a user fee for the use of the card. The basis of these fees varies from charges per transaction to flat monthly or even yearly charges.

At present, the interest charges on the outstanding balance have remained the same, except that some banks have reduced the number of days before payment is due. The only exception now occurs when the cardholder borrows money (a "cash advance") using the card. Then interest is charged immediately and daily.

Interest rate charges can and do change according to economic conditions. The law requires that they be stated not only as a monthly rate, but as an annual percentage as well.

Credit cards are used as a form of payment for many reasons. Two basic reasons are:

- The consumer need not carry large sums of cash.
- Both the merchant and the consumer use the credit card as a method of introduction. The consumer has an established credit rating if he or she has been issued a card. The merchant can accept the credit card and know that payment is assured.

Before accepting the customer's VISA card, the merchant must check that the card is not a stolen one. Regularly updated lists are sent to merchants, listing the numbers of the cards not to be accepted or to be withheld from the customer for one reason or another. This may be because the card is stolen or that the customer's right to use the card has been withdrawn. The merchant must also obtain the necessary five-digit authorization number from VISA Centre if the amount to be charged is greater than the store's floor limit. A "floor limit," $75 for example, is an amount agreed upon between VISA and the merchant. If the amount of the purchase is greater than the floor limit, the merchant must phone the VISA Centre and obtain an authorization number. This call ensures that the customer is not over his or her credit limit and that VISA will guarantee payment to the merchant.

Finally, VISA Centre acts as a clearing house for all transactions.

Accounting for a Credit Card Transaction

On June 10, 19—, Martha J. Roberts, of 1812 Elm Street, Somewhere, Ontario takes her Royal Bank VISA card to Rockstone Clothing Ltd., a local clothing store. Mrs. Roberts makes a few purchases for herself and her husband. The total bill is:

Blouse	$42.00
Shirt	35.00
Tie	10.00
Total	$87.00

Mrs. Roberts presents her VISA card for payment. The owner, Ms. Rockstone, prepares a sales slip similar to the illustration below.

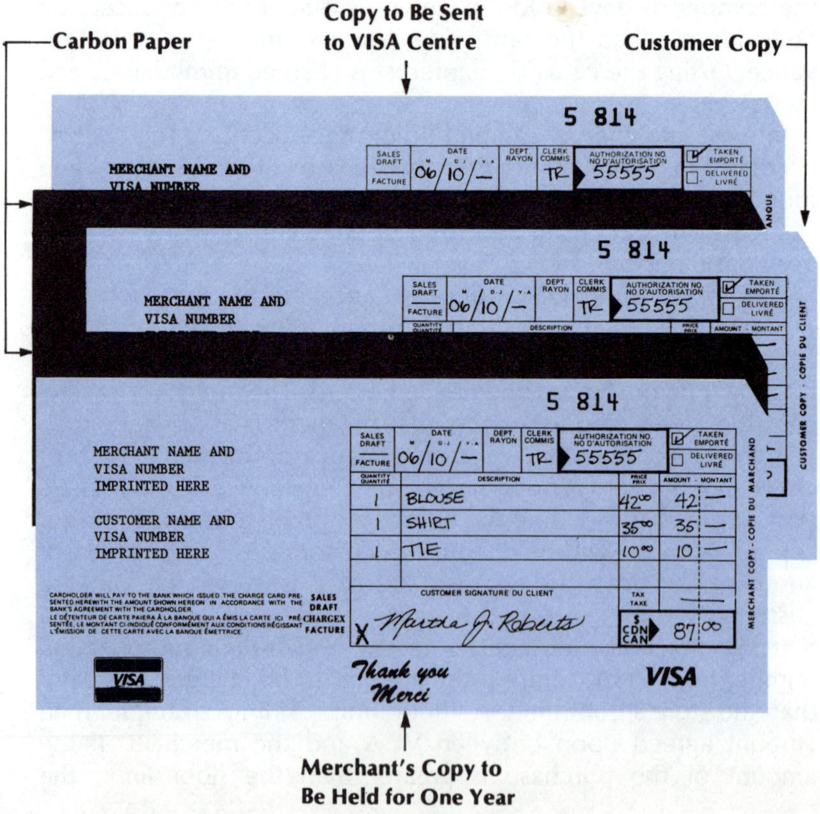

Each item is listed and the list totalled. In most provinces sales tax would be added, but to simplify this illustration sales tax will be omitted, so the total will be $87.

Once the purchase has been authorized, Mrs. Roberts will receive the copy marked *Customer Copy* and the transaction is complete.

The accounting entry for the merchant appears in the cash receipts journal, if one is used, under *Cash — Debit* and *Sales — Credit.* The transaction is considered the same as a cash transaction. Often a special money column for VISA is also used to identify credit card transactions.

In the General Journal the transaction appears as below.

Left Side

CASH RECEIPTS JOURNAL

Date 19—	Account Credited	Explanation	Post. Ref.	General Ledger CR.
June 10	*Sales*	*VISA — Mrs. Roberts*		

Right Side

ROCKSTONE CLOTHING LTD. **Page** *6*

Accounts Receivable CR.	Sales CR.	Sales Tax Payable CR.	Cash DR.	Distribution to Bank Credit Cards	
				VISA	MasterCard
	87 00		*87 00*	*87 00*	

GENERAL JOURNAL **Page** *10*

Date 19—	Account Title and Explanation	Post. Ref.	Debit	Credit
June 10	*Cash (VISA)*		*87 00*	
	Sales			*87 00*
	To record the sale of a blouse, a tie, and a shirt. Paid by VISA.			

The merchant makes up a deposit slip at the end of the day with *Cash: $573.25* (this does not include the VISA sales) and *Cheques: $217.20.* Check this information on the deposit slip below:

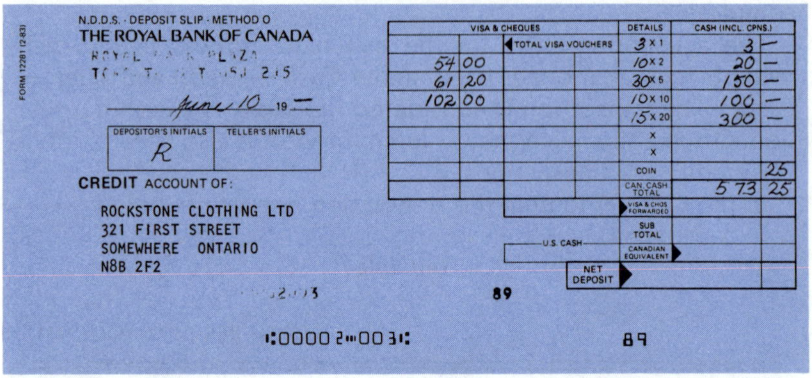

Now the credit card sales information must be dealt with. In addition to the sale to Mrs. Roberts, Ms. Rockstone made two additional VISA sales of $65 and $49. Also, a customer returned unsatisfactory merchandise totalling $15. Since the customer had paid with a VISA card, a VISA credit slip was completed similar to the one shown opposite.

Sales Slips
June 10, 19—

	$ 87.00
	65.00
	49.00
	$201.00

The slip must be run through the imprinting machine and all necessary information completed. Once all the slips are collected together, Ms. Rockstone totals all the sales slips and completes a merchant "recap slip." This is done by recording the amount of each slip, first the sales drafts and then the credit slips in the appropriate locations. (See illustration below.) Next the date is recorded, and the net sales figure is calculated. (Total of the sales slips less the total of the credit slips: $201 − $15 = $186.) This figure is recorded in the *Sales — Net* box.

Discount fee: the dollar amount paid to the bank by the merchant in order that the merchant may accept payment with a VISA card. This is usually a percentage (4% - 8%) of the sale price of an item.

Now, because Ms. Rockstone is a Royal Bank VISA merchant, she multiplies the subtotal by her business discount fee. The

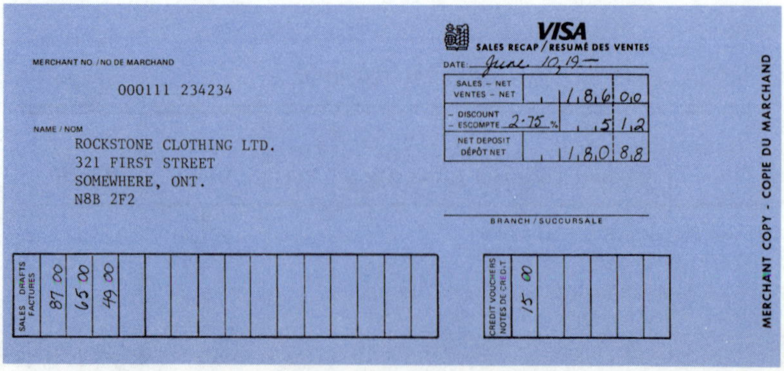

CREDIT SLIP

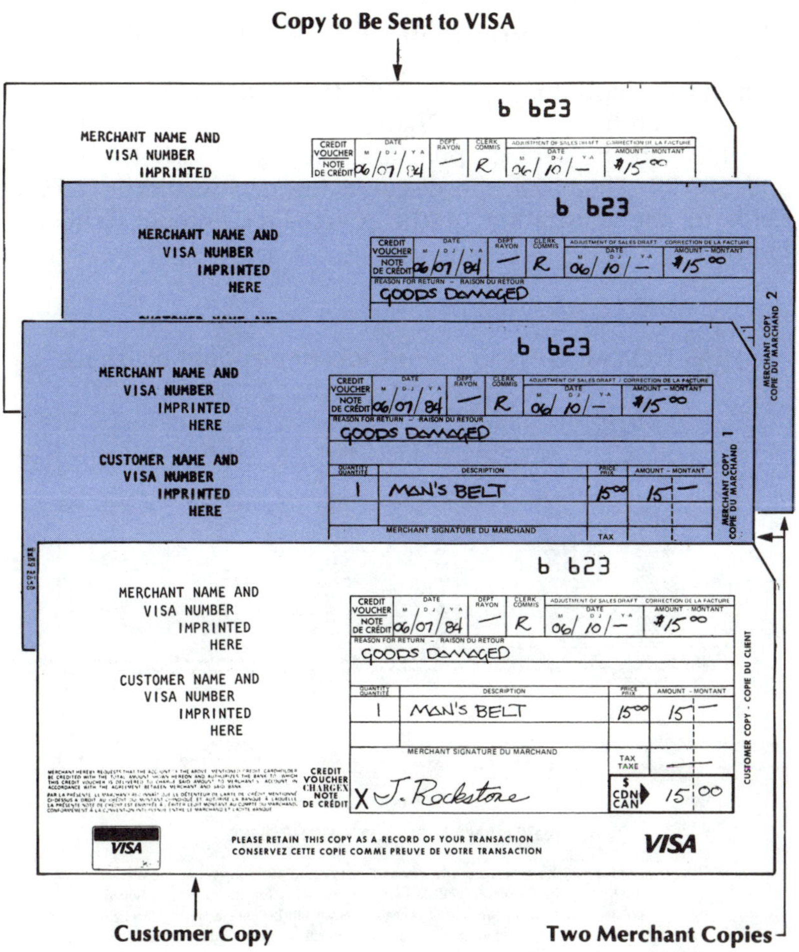

discount fee is the amount that VISA charges the business for allowing the company to handle VISA credit sales. This fee is outlined in the contract between the merchant and VISA and is usually based upon the volume of business conducted with VISA cards. In the case of Rockstone Clothing Ltd., the discount fee is 2.75%. Ms. Rockstone, therefore, must multiply $186 by 2.75% to get a total discount fee of $5.12. This amount is listed on the recap slip and deducted from the $186 subtotal for a net VISA deposit of $180.88.

This completes the sales recap slip. Other banks offering VISA and MasterCard services have slightly different forms and require their customers to record a net sales figure without the discount fee calculated or deducted. This calculation is made by VISA Centre and a discount fee is levied against the merchant's bank account once a month. The calculation of discount fees and the agreements as to the amount and the review dates of this fee may vary from bank to bank. All references made in this book are to the methods used by the Royal Bank of Canada at the time of writing.

In our example for Rockstone Clothing Ltd., assume that the average monthly volume of VISA sales is between $5 000 and $12 499 and the average purchase (draft size) is between $50 and $99.99. Therefore, the discount fee rate would be 2.75%. Refer to the illustration of the Merchant Discount Schedule below.

Front

ROYAL BANK

VISA
MERCHANT DISCOUNT SCHEDULE

* Average Monthly Volume	Average Draft Size			
	Under $30.00	$30.00 to $49.99	$50.00 to $99.99	$100.00 and Over
	%	%	%	%
$ 1- $ 999	5.50	4.50	3.50	3.25
1,000- 2,499	4.75	4.00	3.25	2.75
2,500- 4,999	4.50	3.75	3.00	2.75
5,000- 12,499	4.25	3.50	2.75	2.50
12,500- 19,999	4.00	3.25	2.50	2.25
20,000- 29,999	3.75	3.00	2.25	2.25
30,000- 49,999	3.50	2.75	2.25	2.00
50,000- 74,999	3.25	2.75	2.00	2.00
75,000- 149,999	3.00	2.50	2.00	2.00
150,000- 299,999	2.50	2.25	2.00	2.00
300,000- and over	2.00	2.00	2.00	2.00

*Average Monthly Volume is calculated March 31 and September 30 of each year based on preceding 12 months' sales. Rate change if warranted to be implemented May 1 and November 1 and will apply to the future six month period (See over for further particulars).

FORM 3202 (3-81)

Back

VISA
MERCHANT DISCOUNT SCHEDULE

Discount rates will be reviewed and revised semi-annually during the months of April and October using monthly VISA volume statistics for the previous twelve months. When a change in rate is warranted a letter will be sent advising the new rate and the date it is effective. No advice is forwarded if a change in rate is not in order.

For further information regarding discount policy ask your Service Representative or contact your VISA Centre.

Ms. Rockstone now places the back of the sales slip, the back of the credit slip, and the back of the recap slip into the deposit envelope, with the recap slip on top, and the envelope is sealed. The deposit is now complete. (See the next illustration.)

Now Ms. Rockstone can complete the deposit slip. On the current account deposit slip you will find a spot set aside for these deposits. The final (net) amount calculated on the recap slip is recorded on the deposit slip. (See opposite.) The total of all cash, cheques, and VISA is recorded and Ms. Rockstone goes to the bank to make her deposit.

ROYAL BANK BANQUE ROYALE

VISA DEPOSIT ENVELOPE
ENVELOPPE DE DÉPÔT

NOM
ROCKSTONE CLOTHING LTD.
321 FIRST STREET
SOMEWHERE, ONT.
N8B 2F2

SALES RECAP / RÉSUMÉ DES VENTES
June 10, 19—

NET	11,8	6 00
2.75 %		
DEPOSIT	11,80	8.8

Net amount to be deposited to merchants account subject to terms and conditions of agreement between merchant and bank.

Prière de déposer au compte du marchand le montant net, sujet aux termes et conditions de l'entente intervenue entre le marchand et la banque.

List and total the amount of sales drafts and credit vouchers on a recap form. Enclose sales drafts, credit vouchers, adding machine listing if used, and one completed recap form in this envelope, so that Merchant Identification, discount amount and net deposit show through the window.

Faire la liste et établir le total des factures et des notes de crédit en utilisant la formule de récapitulation. Insérer dans cette enveloppe, les factures, les notes de crédit, la bande de calcul de la machine à additionner (s'il y a lieu) ainsi qu'une formule de récapitulation dûment remplie et disposée de telle sorte que le numéro d'identification du marchand, le montant de l'escompte et le montant net du dépôt apparaissent dans la fenêtre.

At the bank Ms. Rockstone presents her cash, cheques, and VISA package to the teller. The teller checks the various items against the deposit slip and updates the current account of Rockstone Clothing Ltd. by the amount of the deposit.

FORM 12281 (2-83)

N.D.D.S. - DEPOSIT SLIP - METHOD O
THE ROYAL BANK OF CANADA
ROYAL BANK PLAZA
TORONTO, ONT M5J 2J5

June 10 19—

DEPOSITOR'S INITIALS	TELLER'S INITIALS
R	

CREDIT ACCOUNT OF:

ROCKSTONE CLOTHING LTD
321 FIRST STREET
SOMEWHERE ONTARIO
N8B 2F2

VISA & CHEQUES	
180	88
54	00
61	20
102	00
TOTAL VISA VOUCHERS 398	08

DETAILS	CASH (INCL. CPNS.)	
3 × 1	3	—
10 × 2	20	—
30 × 5	150	—
10 × 10	100	—
15 × 20	300	—
×		
×		
COIN		25
CAN. CASH TOTAL	573	25
VISA & CHQS FORWARDED	398	08
SUB TOTAL	971	33
U.S. CASH — CANADIAN EQUIVALENT	Ø	
NET DEPOSIT	$971	33

00002003 89

⑆00002⑈003⑆ 89

The bank collects all the VISA deposit envelopes and forwards them to VISA Centre by courier at the end of each banking day.

After Ms. Rockstone returns to the store, she will use the sales recap as a source document in order to record the amount of the VISA discount. This entry is illustrated in General Journal form below.

VISA Discount Expense	*5.12*	
Cash		*5.12*
To record the VISA discount as shown on the deposit envelope of June 10.		

Processing a VISA Transaction

VISA Centre The Royal Bank of Canada has VISA Centres in Vancouver, Toronto, and Montreal. Each office handles designated areas of the country. Once a deposit envelope arrives at a

Centre, the information on the recap slip is verified against the sales and credit slips and the information is inputted to the computer. Since the first five digits of a customer account number identify the bank that issued the card, the computer can rapidly sort the information for each of the various banks and then record that information on magnetic tape. The appropriate pieces of tape are physically exchanged between the various VISA Centres, allowing easy and accurate updating of customer accounts.

Merchant account numbers are also recorded from the slips and internal banking memoranda are issued between the VISA Centre and the local bank branches that service the merchant's accounts.

Now that the sorting and exchange procedures have been carried out, the Centre has the computer update each customer's account. The account is identified by its number, and all charges are listed, including the transaction date, the store, and the dollar amount. It must be remembered that payments on account received directly at the Centre and through bank branches must be recorded in the customer's account as well. On set dates throughout the month, the computer will be instructed to produce totals of the charges and payments received, and the difference between these two amounts. If a balance has been outstanding more than twenty-five days, interest will be charged and added to the total billing figure. Then the computer will be instructed to produce a customer statement which will be mailed to the customer. This statement will be examined shortly.

It is reasonable to say that the offering of such services would not be practical unless computers were available to process the massive volume of information generated every day. Later, a study of some uses of computers in accounting will be made.

Customer Statements Throughout the month *cyclic billing* takes place. (Recall this term from Chapter 12.) The computer will generate a customer statement similar to the one in the next illustration. Therefore, depending on the billing date of Mrs. Roberts's account, within a month the purchase she made at Rockstone Clothing Ltd. will appear on her VISA statement. Note the information presented on the statement.

The statement is in two parts. The top part, retained by the customer, is a list of the purchases made, giving the name and location of the store, the date of the purchase, and the total dollar amount. Included here will be the date and amount of any payments made during the past period as well as interest charged on any past due amounts. Immediately after this information is the customer account number, and the balance from the last statement less the total credits (payments) plus the total debits (new purchases or charges) — in other words, the new balance. Next is the statement date, the remaining credit limit, the total of any amount past due and the due date. (This should be 25

ROYAL BANK
· VISA ·

VISA Centre
325 Front St. West,
Toronto, Ontario M5V 2V5

Date	Particulars	Debits/Credits
27 MAY --	PAYMENT - THANK YOU	140.77CR
10JUNE--	ROCKSTONE CLOTHING LTD SOMEWHERE, ONT	87.00
15JUNE--	TRANSACTION FEE	0.15

Account Number	Balance On Last Statement		Total Credits		Total Debits		Your New Balance
4444 333 111 999	140.77	−	140.77	+	87.15	=	87.15

Statement Date	Credit Limit
15 JUN --	2000
Past Due	**Due Date**
.00	10 JUL --
Amount Paid	**Minimum Payment**
$87.15	10.00

MARTHA J ROBERTS
1812 ELM ST
SOMEWHERE ONT
N0N 1K1

If your address shown above is incorrect or you are moving, fill in the tear slip attached to your return payment envelope.

Payments must reach the Visa Centre by due date in order to appear on your next statement.

Retain this portion for your records.

---

001 0018 4444333111999 000000000000 000000 000000 005000

ROYAL BANK
· VISA ·

VISA Centre
325 Front St. West
Toronto, Ontario M5V 2V5

MARTHA J ROBERTS

Payment of this account may be made without service charge:

- at any Royal Bank branch;
- at any Personal Touch Banking machine; or
- by returning this portion with your remittance (payable to Royal Bank - VISA) in the return payment envelope provided.

Statement Date	Page	Account Number	Payments Must Reach The VISA Centre by	Enter amount of Payment
15 JUN --	1	4444 333 111 999	10 JUL --	$87.15

⑆00032⑈003⑆ 000⑈001⑈8⑈ 96

days after the statement date.) Finally, there is a place to record the amount the customer will decide to pay to VISA, and the minimum payment due this month is stated.

The bottom part is returned to VISA with the payment. This section contains the customer's name, the statement date, the page number, the customer's account number, the date by which payment must reach the VISA Centre to avoid interest charges, and the amount of the payment being made.

If Mrs. Roberts sends a cheque to VISA Centre or pays her local bank in time for the payment to be processed at the VISA Centre before the due date, she will be able to pay her account in full without any interest payment. In addition to the $87 charge there would be a $0.15 transaction or user fee levied that the customer would have to pay. Thus Mrs. Roberts could pay her account in full by preparing a cheque for $87.15, recording that amount on both portions of the customer statement, and returning the cheque and lower portion of the statement to VISA Centre by the due date shown.

We have now covered (1) the procedures for obtaining a VISA card and for using the card and paying for purchases made by a customer; (2) the procedures followed by the merchant to make a sale and to deposit the funds; and (3) the procedures used for recording merchants' submissions, keeping individual customers' accounts, and billing individual customers. However, it is important for the student to realize that some of the details may change when bank procedures are revised. For accurate information, students should try to get current samples of blank VISA statements, sales slips, and credit slips.

TOPIC 2 PROBLEMS

13-6 Refer to the customer statement on page 457 and answer the following questions:

a When was the last payment received at VISA?
b How much was sent?
c How many transactions took place this month?
d What was the total dollar value of these transactions?
e Mrs. Roberts owes $87.15. Account for the discrepancy regarding $87.15 and the answer of **d.**
f When was this statement prepared?
g What is the due date?
h What is Mrs. Roberts's credit limit?
i What is her account number?
j Was Mrs. Roberts charged any interest on her previous balance? Where would this show up on her statement?

13-7 Given the following information, complete the VISA sales draft.

On August 30, 19—, Mr. Henry Walty bought two pairs of men's shoes at $52.50 each, and shoe polish for $1.75. All this merchandise was purchased at F. & B. Shoes Ltd. The store's floor limit is $100, so the clerk, Phil Times, had to phone for an authorization number (No. 65435). The store is located in Regina,

Saskatchewan and sales tax (5%) was charged on the total amount. Mr. Walty's VISA number is 1111 222 333 444. The clerk works in Department 6 and Mr. Walty takes the goods with him.

Key Check Figure Total on Slip = $112.09

13-8 On September 3, 19—, Mr. Henry Walty returned the shoe polish and requested a refund because the store did not have shoe polish to replace the faulty tin. Mr. Bill Loft, an owner, signs the form.

Complete a Credit Slip similar to the one illustrated on page 453.

Key Check Figure Credit Slip Total = $1.84

13-9 Complete the sales recap form and then a deposit form for Petty Hardware Supplies given the following information:

(i) Sales slips: $85.50, $210.50, $105.00, $65.23.

(ii) Credit slips: $10.25, $17.20.

(iii) The firm's monthly VISA volume has been approximately $23 000 per month and the average draft size was $73.45.

(iv) Cash for the day is in the form of: 11 ones, 17 twos, 2 fives, 6 tens, 21 twenties, and $5.83 in change.

(v) Two cheques were accepted: $287.25 and $27.30.

(vi) Use today's date and your initials as the depositor.

Key Check Figure VISA and Cheque Total = $743.46

13-10 Use an expanded cash receipts journal which includes additional columns to distribute the VISA and MasterCard purchases.

a Complete the transactions which will be entered into the Cash Receipts Journal, Page 120. Year, 198-.

Apr. 2 Cash balance = $10 200.
5 Cash sales for the week totalled $5 800; sales tax $348.
9 Sold goods to B. Pilot for $400 plus 10% sales tax. Mr. Pilot used his VISA card to pay the bill.
11 Sold goods to Mary Waters for $290 plus 10% sales tax. She used her VISA card as payment.
15 Borrowed $6 000 from the bank on a demand loan.
19 Cash sales for the past two weeks totalled $9 200 plus sales tax of $900.
22 Sold goods to Helen Powers for $350 plus 10% sales tax. She paid for her goods with MasterCard.
27 Sold goods to M. Narthwood for $670 plus 10% sales tax. He used his VISA card to make payment.
30 Weekly sales totalled $7 000. Sales tax totalled $685.

b Total the journal and cross-foot to ensure accuracy.

c Total the distribution columns and determine what percentage of total cash sales VISA and MasterCard account for.

d In chart form, prepare a list of the VISA discount expense amounts for each of the VISA transactions. Prepare the journal entry for April 9 in General Journal form. The business average monthly volume totals $1 700 and the average draft size is greater than $100.

Key Check Figure VISA % = 6.3%

13-11 Farley Company has just completed the sales recap slip for VISA transactions for May 2, 19-4. Net sales totals, $817.00. The average monthly volume is $38 500 and the average draft size is $167.

a Determine the discount percentage for Farley Company.

b Record in General Journal form the entry to show the VISA discount expense for the day.

Case Study 13

Fred Cutter owns a tract of land in northern Manitoba. During the summer months he explores this land and collects colourful rocks, unusually shaped pieces of driftwood, and unique fungi. This used to be a hobby for him, but in the past two years he has found people willing to pay reasonable prices for these articles. As a result, Mr. Cutter has been selling them from his home for the past six months. He never bothers keeping any records, but simply pockets the cash. Recently, talking to a close friend, Cutter realized that he may have some problems with both provincial and federal authorities.

What considerations has Cutter totally ignored and what must be done to fulfill these obligations?

CHAPTER 14

PAYROLL ACCOUNTING FOR HOURLY AND OTHER SALARY-EMPLOYED PERSONNEL

This chapter will discuss payroll for hourly paid personnel, other salaried employees and several government, contractual, and voluntary deductions which are often faced by employers and which were not discussed in Chapter 10. These last include: company pension plans, medical plans, union dues, garnishments and government demands, group insurance, Canadian Savings Bonds, credit unions, community service, and miscellaneous deductions.

Special items such as vacation pay, commissions, salary-commissions, piece-rate, and Workers' Compensation will also be examined.

- Topic 1 deals with the collection of payroll data.
- Topic 2 deals with the recording and disbursing of the payroll.
- Topic 3 deals with vacation pay and Workers' Compensation.

TOPIC 1 COLLECTING PAYROLL DATA

Timekeeping and Computing Earnings

Applicants for a position are usually interviewed to determine their suitability. In a small business this is often done by the owner; in a larger firm, a *personnel department* is assigned this task. In either circumstance, the hired person is hired under a contract of employment, or, in more legal terms, a contract of service. This is not to be confused with a contract *for* service.

Contract of service: an employment contract binding employer and employee, whereunder the employer directs the employee's work.

A contract *of* service is an agreement between two parties, an employer and an employee, to have the employee perform work for the employer for some agreed-upon amount of pay. For example, Joan Doe, a lawyer, may be hired by XYZ Company as its solicitor. XYZ dictates the type of jobs Doe will undertake, and agrees to pay her an annual salary of $40 000.

Contract for service: an employment contract whereunder an individual doing work for a firm bills the firm for the services, and the employee directs his or her own activity.

On the other hand, a contract for service results when a person bills a firm for services he or she performs on behalf of the firm, but the firm does *not* direct how the job is to be done. For example, if a lawyer sets up a private practice and is hired by XYZ Company to undertake legal work for it, the lawyer will perform the job as he or she sees fit and will bill the firm.

If a person is hired under a contract of service, then by law the employee must have a social insurance number, and must fill out a TD-1 form, obtained from the federal government. Some kind of contract to dictate the wage or salary to be paid is also required.

SIN
TD1

Common Salary and Wage Plans

Every business has different salary or wage plans. The details are usually outlined in the employee contracts. Five of the more commonly used plans to determine the employee's pay will now be discussed.

1) **The Hourly-Rate Plan** In this plan, the employee's gross earnings is based on the number of hours worked at a set rate per hour. For example, if the employee is paid at $5.00 per hour and has worked 40 hours during the week, that employee's gross earnings will equal $200.00 ($5 × 40). Usually, the term *wages* is used to describe this type of earnings.

Overtime: the amount of time worked beyond the normally-agreed-upon work day.

Overtime rate: the rate of pay at which overtime hours are calculated.

After an employee works more than a stated or agreed-upon amount of time, the employer must pay overtime at an overtime rate. Overtime rates vary from *time-and-a-half* to *double time*, and sometimes to *triple time*. For example, if an employee has worked 42 hours during the week, and the contract states that overtime is anything over 40 hours and that overtime will be paid at double time (twice the regular rate), then the following calculation is required:

Overtime Pay = Overtime Hours × Overtime Rate

Regular hours worked	=	40		
Regular rate of pay	=	$5.00/h		
Regular pay	=	40 × $5.00	=	$200.00
Overtime hours worked	=	2		
Overtime rate of pay	=	$5.00 × 2 = $10.00/h		
Overtime pay	=	2 × $10.00	=	20.00
Gross earnings			=	$220.00

2) **The Salary Plan** The salary plan is also based on time worked. The time period is normally stated as a day, a week, a month, or a year. The amount to be paid is stated as $100 per day or $30 000 per year. A salary amount is a fixed amount and it is common to call persons paid under such a plan *salaried employees.*

3) **The Commission Plan** Many businesses such as real estate brokers, life insurance companies, and car dealers will create an

incentive for their salespersons to increase sales by agreeing to pay a commission. Under the commission plan, the employee will receive gross earnings based on some agreed-upon percentage of his or her total dollar value of sales. For example, if a car salesperson receives a 4% commission on the sale price of each automobile that he or she sells, and if that person's total sales for the week amount to $30 000, his or her gross earnings will be $1 200 for the week ($30 000 × 4%). As added incentive, an employer may offer 6% on all sales over $30 000 per week, and 10% on all sales over $50 000 per week.

Commission: a stated percentage of the total dollar value sold by an employee.

The Salary-Commission Plan This is a combination of the salary and the commission plans. It might mean that a car salesperson receives $250 per week no matter what the amount sold and 2% on all sales. The incentive plan might be added to this plan as well.

The Piece-Rate Plan Any business that manufactures a product may pay its employees on the basis of the number of units of the product that they produce. For example, an employee who produces a certain part of a radio may be paid $0.10 per piece made. If the employee produces 2 000 pieces during the week, his or her gross earnings will then be $200 (2 000 × $0.10). This is, of course, an incentive plan.

The Constitution permits each province to enact its own legislation regarding the maximum hours of work and minimum wages. Generally, overtime is paid at one and a half times the regular rate of pay on any hours in excess of 40 to 44 per week. Furthermore, any hours over 8 in a 24-hour period are traditionally considered to be overtime. (*Note:* Many firms, in agreement with their employees, work ten- or twelve-hour shifts in order to accommodate an extra day off each week.)

The minimum wage changes regularly and so cannot be identified here, even in a general way.

Provincial laws set only *maximum* hours of work and *minimum* wages. Many employers and employees have negotiated contracts with *fewer* hours and *higher* rates of pay. This basic agreement between the employer and the employees is referred to as the *contract of employment*. Here are some main points of the contract of employment between a major Canadian industry and a large international union.

Basic agreement: the contract of employment between an employer and a union.

Hours of Work:

(a) The normal work day shall be eight (8) hours of work in a 24-hour period.

(b) The normal work week shall be any five (5) normal work days within a work week.

Overtime rates shall be paid for:

(a) Time worked in excess of eight (8) hours in a work day.

(b) Time worked in excess of forty (40) hours in a work week.

(c) Time worked on the sixth (6th) or seventh (7th) working day of a work week during which work was performed on five (5) other working days.

(cont.)

> *(d) Time worked before his regular starting time when an employee is called in before the regular starting time of any shift of eight (8) hours.*
>
> *(e) Time worked after his regular quitting time when an employee is held after the regular quitting time of any shift of eight (8) hours.*
>
> *(f) Time worked on statutory holidays (Christmas Day, New Year's Day, etc.)*
>
> **Overtime Rates:**
>
> *All overtime worked shall be paid for on regular paydays at one and one-half times the regular rate of pay except that time worked in excess of eight (8) hours on a statutory holiday shall be paid for at double the regular rate of pay.*

Finally, under the law in each province and the federal government, every employer is required to keep complete records of the hours worked by each employee. Generally, permits are required to allow employees to work more than 48 hours per week. In order to conform to legislation, every accounting system must keep accurate and reliable records.

Timekeeping: the accounting of time spent on the job for each employee.

Timekeeping

The responsibility for preparing daily records of time worked by each employee is often given to an employee or to a department. Each method or plan of work requires a different type of timekeeping The chart on page 465 gives the various (non-commission) methods of recording employee hours, the internal control procedures to verify those hours, and the location for submission to ensure that employees are paid.

Name ______________ Employee No. ______

Social Insurance No. ______________

Week Ending ______________

CLOCK CARD

	Regular				Extra		
Days	In	Out	In	Out	In	Out	Hours
Thur.							
Fri.							
Sat.							
Sun.							
Mon.							
Tue.							
Wed.							

	Hours	Rate	Earnings
Regular			
Overtime			
Total Hours		Gross Earnings	

Computation of Gross Earnings

In a larger firm, the payroll department will have the responsibility of verifying and reconciling timekeeping submissions. Once this is done, the department is responsible for the computation of the gross earnings.

Hourly-Rated Employees With the aid of time clocks, clock cards, and daily report of time forms (see margin illustration), the payroll department can verify the hours worked, the regular pay, and the overtime pay, and finally determine the gross earnings of the employee.

It is important to note that this is a manual or mechanical method of computation done by a payroll employee. If, on the other hand, a computer is used to calculate the payroll, the payroll department would complete the verification and then submit the payroll data produced to data processing, where the gross pay of each employee would be calculated automatically. Many payroll programs are commercially available if computer assistance is desired, but at this point, you will be asked to calculate by hand or with an office calculator.

To begin the calculation of an hourly-rated employee's gross earnings, it is first important to check the contract of employment regarding working hours. For example, hourly-rated

Wage or Salary Plan	*Internal Control*	*Payroll Department Activity*
Hourly-Rate Plan: Daily time records are produced with the assistance of a time clock. Employees are required to punch in and out to verify time on the job.	The hourly employees' clock cards are checked by a supervisor preparing the *daily report of time* form, based on the supervisor's observations.	Clock cards and daily report of time forms are submitted to the payroll department for comparison and verification. Discrepancies are reconciled and the gross earnings calculated.
Salary Plan: Usually a fixed (annual) amount is paid to the employee monthly or semi-monthly.	Some type of attendance record is maintained by supervisory personnel. (See illustration on page 324.) The immediate supervisor must sign the attendance record sheet.	Attendance forms are submitted to payroll. If major discrepancies exist, the employee's supervisor will be contacted to determine the course of action.
Piece-Rate Plan: Departmental reports show details of production numbers.	The piece-rate report must be signed by a responsible head prior to submission to payroll.	Payroll can check individual submissions with total production figures to verify piece-rate figures.

employees may be required to work from 8:00 a.m. to 12:00 noon and from 1:00 p.m. to 5:00 p.m.[1] Some rules must be made regarding tardiness and the computation of time. Here are the rules followed by some employers. They will be used for the margin illustration of calculating the gross earnings of one employee:

- Time before 8:00 a.m. and 1:00 p.m. is not counted.
- Daily time is computed in hours and quarter hours. Fractions of an hour less than 15 minutes are not counted when calculating either the regular or the overtime hours.
- For lateness, the employee loses 15 minutes for each 15 minutes, or portion thereof, of lateness in the morning or afternoon. In the clock card for John Blair (illustrated in the margin on page 466), a penalty of 15 minutes is charged on Thursday and Tuesday mornings for clocking in at 8:01 and 8:05 respectively,

1. At the time of writing, most Canadian industries using a time clock system do not use the 24-hour clock.

Name John Blair Employee No. 3

Social Insurance No. 425-127-511

Week Ending June 30, 19—

CLOCK CARD

Days	Regular In	Regular Out	Regular In	Regular Out	Extra In	Extra Out	Hours
Thur.	8:01	12:00	1:00	5:01			7¾
Fri.	7:59	11:59	1:00	5:00			7¾
Sat.							
Sun.							
Mon.	7:55	12:02	12:58	5:05	6:00	8:00	8+2
Tue.	8:05	12:03	12:59	5:01	6:00	7:01	7¾+1
Wed.	7:59	12:01	1:16	5:02	5:57	8:01	7½+2

	Hours	Rate	Earnings
Regular	38¾	$6.00	$232.50
Overtime	5	9.00	45.00
Total Hours	43¾	Gross Earnings	$277.50

and a penalty of 30 minutes is charged on Wednesday afternoon for clocking in at 1:16.

- The same penalties apply for clocking out early. On Friday, Blair is penalized 15 minutes for clocking out at 11:59 a.m.
- Overtime is calculated in quarter hours only. The employee must work a full quarter-hour period (15, 30, 45 min., etc.).
- In computing the total hours for an employee's pay period, the regular hours are calculated separately from the overtime period.

Other Employees Attendance records must be kept for both piece-rated and commission-based employees. The records sent to the payroll department must contain the necessary information for the department to calculate the gross earnings.

Deductions from Gross Earnings

An employee does not take all that he or she earns home in the form of *net pay* or *take-home pay*. Instead, before pay is given to an employee, deductions are made from the gross earnings. Some of these are required by law: for example, unemployment insurance premiums, Canada Pension Plan contributions, and income taxes. Other deductions are a direct result of contract agreements between the employer and the employees, usually a union. Still other deductions are voluntary: for example, deductions that the employee has requested the employer to make.

Priority of Payroll Deductions

The following is a list of some typical deductions from an employee's gross earnings. It also indicates the priority assigned to each deduction.

Required by Law

(1) Unemployment insurance
(2) Canada Pension Plan (in Quebec, the Quebec Pension Plan)
(3) Federal and provincial income taxes
(4) Provincial health insurance plan
(5) Garnishments and government demands

Required by Collective Bargaining Agreements

(6) Union initiation fees
(7) Union dues

Voluntary

(8) Group insurance
(9) Company pension plan
(10) Canada Savings Bonds
(11) Credit union
(12) Community services (United Way, etc.)
(13) Miscellaneous deductions: safety shoes, glasses, badges, tools, etc.

Unemployment Insurance

With a few exceptions, all persons employed under a contract of service are subject to unemployment insurance premium deductions. The law also requires that the employer contribute to the plan.

Employee Contribution "The premium for employees in insurable employment is calculated at a rate of 2.3%, that is, $2.30 for every $100 of insurable earnings." The illustration below shows the minimums and maximums of insurable earnings. At the time of writing, as the above quotation from the government employment insurance booklet states, the employee must contribute 2.3% of his or her insurable earnings. In the case of John Blair, the employer is obliged to deduct $6.38 (2.3% × $277.50) from his gross earnings. This calculation can also be made by referring to the above-mentioned booklet. The desired column for this calculation is also illustrated.

UNEMPLOYMENT INSURANCE — **ASSURANCE-CHÔMAGE**

SCHEDULE OF MINIMUM HOURLY AND PERCENTAGE THRESHOLDS AND MAXIMUM INSURABLE EARNINGS FOR VARIOUS PAY PERIODS

TABLEAUX DES SEUILS MINIMUMS D'HEURES ET DE POURCENTAGES ET DU MAXIMUM DE LA RÉMUNÉRATION ASSURABLE POUR DIVERSES PÉRIODES DE PAIE

Under Regulation 13 employees' earnings are insurable when one of the two following conditions is met; (i) they have cash earnings of 20% of the maximum weekly insurable earnings or (ii) worked 15 hours in a week. As long as an employee is employed in each week or part week of the pay period and the cash earnings or hours worked in the pay period are equal to or exceed the minimum for the pay period as in the table below, earnings for the whole pay period are insurable.

En vertu de l'article 13 du Règlement la rémunération d'un employé est assurable quand une des deux conditions suivantes est remplie: (i) sa rémunération en espèces est égale à 20% du maximum de la rémunération hebdomadaire assurable, ou (ii) il a travaillé quinze heures dans une semaine. Tant qu'un employé travaille au cours de chaque semaine ou partie de semaine de la période de paie et que sa rémunération en espèces ou les heures de travail dans la période de paie sont égales au minimum ou le dépassent pour la période de paie selon la table ci-dessous, la rémunération pour toute la période de paie est assurable.

Pay Period *Période de paie*	Note*: It is necessary to fall below both of the minimum requirements specified in U.I. Regulation 13 in order to be in EXCEPTED employment for U.I. purposes. *Remarque: Pour qu'un emploi soit EXCLU aux fins de l'A.-C., l'employé ne doit atteindre aucun des deux minimales énoncées dans l'article 13 du. Règlement sur l'A.-C.*	Minimum* *Minimum* Hours *d'heures*	Minimum* *Minimum* Earnings *rémunération*	Maximum Insurable Earnings *Maximum de la rémunération assurable*	Maximum Premium *Prime maximum* Per Period @ 2.3% *Pour période @ 2.3%*	Maximum Premium *Prime maximum* Per Annum see Note(1) *Par année voir remarque(1)*
Weekly—*Hebdomadaire*	(52 P.P.)	15	85.00	425.00	9.78	508.56(1)
Bi-Weekly—*Quinzaine*	(26 P.P.)	30	170.00	850.00	19.55	508.30(1)
Semi-Monthly—*Bi-mensuelle*	(24 P.P.)	33	184.16	920.83	21.18	508.32
Monthly—*Mensuelle*	(12 P.P.)	65	368.33	1,841.66	42.36	508.32
10 Pay Periods Per Year—*10 périodes de paie par année*		78	442.00	2,210.00	50.83	508.30
13 Pay Periods Per Year—*13 périodes de paie par année*		60	340.00	1,700.00	39.10	508.30
22 Pay Periods Per Year—*22 périodes de paie par année*		35	200.90	1,004.54	23.10	508.20
Yearly—Annuelle			4,420.00	22,100.00		508.30

—Employee Premium Rate 2.3% Note(1) See "Additional weekly or bi-weekly premiums"
—*Taux de la prime ouvrière* 2.3% Remarque(1) Voir «Primes hebdomadaires ou de quinzaine supplémentaires».

—Employer Premium Rate 1.4 times employee's premium (unless a reduced rate applies) see "Employer's premium rate reduction".
—*Taux de la prime patronale* *1,4 fois le montant de la prime ouvrière (à moins qu'un taux réduit ne s'applique) voir «Reduction du taux de la prime patronale».*

Note: Should this issue be received after deductions have been made for some 1984 periods, those deductions will have to be recalculated using the new 1984 rates contained in this publication.

Remarque: *Si des retenues ont été effectuées pour des périodes de paie en 1984 avant que la présente brochure ait été reçue, elles devront être recalculées suivant les nouveaux taux de 1984 qui y sont indiqués.*

Remuneration *Rémunération* From-*de*	To-*à*	U.I. Premium *Prime d'a.-c.*
272.39 -	272.82	6.27
272.83 -	273.25	6.28
273.26 -	273.69	6.29
273.70 -	274.12	6.30
274.13 -	274.56	6.31
274.57 -	274.99	6.32
275.00 -	275.43	6.33
275.44 -	275.86	6.34
275.87 -	276.30	6.35
276.31 -	276.73	6.36
276.74 -	277.17	6.37
277.18 -	277.60	6.38
277.61 -	278.04	6.39
278.05 -	278.47	6.40
278.48 -	278.91	6.41
278.92 -	279.34	6.42
279.35 -	279.78	6.43
279.79 -	280.21	6.44
280.22 -	280.64	6.45
280.65 -	281.08	6.46
281.09 -	281.51	6.47
281.52 -	281.95	6.48
281.96 -	282.38	6.49
282.39 -	282.82	6.50
282.83 -	283.25	6.51
283.26 -	283.69	6.52
203.70 -	284.12	6.53

As the illustration for maximums and minimums indicates, John Blair is not yet at the maximum weekly pay. If he were to earn more than $277.50 in any one week, the premium would be greater. If he were to receive less than the $277.50 in any one week, the deduction would be correspondingly lower. If he were to earn in any one week less than $85.00 there would be no premium deduction that week. If he were to earn more than $425.00, only the maximum deduction of $9.78 would apply.

The weekly tables are illustrated above.

Employer Contribution By law, the employer is required to make contributions to the unemployment insurance fund. This contribution is calculated at 1.4 times the employee contribution. If John Blair earned $277.50 during the week, his contribution would equal $6.38. The employer's contribution would then equal $8.93 ($6.38 × 1.4). This amount will become a payroll expense which you will learn to account for in the next Topic of this chapter.

Canada Pension Plan (or Quebec Pension Plan)

The Canada Pension Plan was established under federal law in 1965. This plan operates in all parts of Canada except Quebec, which has its own pension plan. Employee deductions have been compulsory since 1966 and the plan covers almost everyone who works. Stated briefly, the plan provides seven benefits:

- a pension for you when you retire
- a pension for you if you have to stop working because you are disabled
- benefits for your children if you are disabled and cannot work
- a pension for your wife if you die
- benefits for your children if you die
- pensions for disabled widowers
- a lump-sum payment to your estate on your death

Pensionable earnings: the amount upon which the pension rate is applied.

Calculating the Employee's Contribution Every employee covered by the Canada Pension Plan is required to make contributions at the rate of 1.8% of his or her pensionable earnings. The first calculation to be made is the appropriate deduction based on the type of pay. From the first illustration on page 469, you can see that for John Blair, who is paid weekly, the first $38.46 is subtracted from gross earnings to produce his pensionable earnings. Then this figure is multiplied by 1.8% to determine the deduction to be made for Canada Pension Plan. For John Blair this deduction is $4.30 ($239.04 × 1.8%). For determining the contributions, the Department of National Revenue — Taxation supplies employers with charts similar to those used for unemployment deductions. From the second illustration on page 469, you can determine John Blair's deduction on the chart. As was the case with unemployment insurance, there is a maximum deduction or contribution that any one employee is required to submit. From the third illustration, you can see that this amount is equal to $338.40.

The contribution for any pay period can be calculated from

Calculation Method

From the employee's pay, first deduct the appropriate basic exemption for the pay period as follows:

Annual	$ 2,000.00
Semi-Annual	1,000.00
Quarterly	500.00
Monthly (12 pp)	166.66
Semi-Monthly (24 pp)	83.33
10 Pay periods a year	200.00
13 Pay periods a year (quadri-weekly)	153.84
20 Pay periods a year	100.00
22 Pay periods a year	90.90
Bi-Weekly (26 pp)	76.92
Weekly (52 pp)	38.46

and where an employee is employed on a non-continuous basis,

Daily (240 pp)	8.33
Hourly (2000 hours)	1.00

Multiply the remainder by 1.8%, keeping in mind that the maximum for the year is $338.40. The result is the amount of employee contribution to withhold, to which you must add an equal amount as the employer contribution.

Remuneration *Rémunération* From-*de*	To-*à*	C.P.P. *R.P.C.*
268.19 -	268.73	4.14
268.74 -	269.29	4.15
269.30 -	269.84	4.16
269.85 -	270.40	4.17
270.41 -	270.95	4.18
270.96 -	271.51	4.19
271.52 -	272.07	4.20
272.08 -	272.62	4.21
272.63 -	273.18	4.22
273.19 -	273.73	4.23
273.74 -	274.29	4.24
274.30 -	274.84	4.25
274.85 -	275.40	4.26
275.41 -	275.95	4.27
275.96 -	276.51	4.28
276.52 -	277.07	4.29
277.08 -	277.62	4.30
277.63 -	278.18	4.31

The following are in effect for 1984 — Les éléments suivants sont en vigueur en 1984

CANADA PENSION PLAN		RÉGIME DE PENSIONS DU CANADA
—Year's maximum pensionable earnings —*Maximum des gains annuels ouvrant droit à pension*		$20,800.00
—Year's basic exemption —*Exemption de base de l'année*		2,000.00
—Maximum earnings on which contributions are based —*maximum des gains sur lequel se fonde le calcul des cotisations*		18,800.00
—Maximum Employee Contribution —*Cotisation maximale de l'employé*	*1.8% of/de $18,800.00*	338.40
—Maximum Employer Contribution —*Cotisation maximale de l'employeur*	*1.8% of/de $18,800.00*	338.40

these charts. For example, if a salesperson has worked 64 days and earned $650.00, the deduction would be calculated as follows:

Exemption: $2 000 × 64/365 = $350.68
Pensionable earnings: $650 − $350.68 = $299.32
Pension Plan deduction: $299.32 × 1.8% = $5.39

It is important to remember that the maximum deduction for the year is $338.40. When that amount has been paid no further deductions are required. *Note:* All chart material is prepared from the 1984 booklets.

Calculating the Employer's Contribution Remember that the employer is required to match the employee deduction.

Company Pension Plans

Although the company pension plan was shown in the earlier priority chart under the "voluntary" class of deductions, it is treated here to help you understand the next legal deduction — income taxes. The term *voluntary deduction* simply refers to the idea that the employee agrees, usually in writing, to have a certain amount deducted from his or her gross earnings. In this case, the employee would agree to contribute to a company pension plan.

In general, the federal government permits employers to offer a company pension plan so that employees may build up an overall pension plan for themselves. It is important to remember these points about any company pension plan:

- The company pension plan is *not* a substitute for the required contributions to the Canada Pension Plan. Any company plan is only a supplement to the Canada Pension Plan.
- Most company pension plans are *registered pension plans* because the Income Tax Act provides for such registration. This means that the employer has submitted the plan first for approval by the Department of National Revenue—Taxation. Once approval has been given, the plan is registered and the employer must abide by the provisions of the National Revenue Department. Most company pension plans are registered because they offer the best security for the employees' savings invested in such plans.
- As in the Canada Pension Plan, contributions to a registered company pension plan must be made by both employee and employer. Of course, the employer's share will be identified as an additional payroll expense and must be accounted for.
- As in the Canada Pension Plan, contributions by the employee to a registered company pension plan are deductible from the employee's income tax. This last point must be considered in the next section, where we examine the method of calculating the amount of income taxes to be withheld from an employee's gross earnings.

Federal and Provincial Tax Deductions

Review the necessary information about federal income tax deductions in Chapter 10. Then review the illustration of John Blair in this Topic. John Blair's Net Claim on the TD1 for personal exemptions is \$8 140.00. His Net Claim Code, therefore, is 9. See the TD1 illustration on page 320 of Chapter 10.

To illustrate how the tax tables should be used, we will consider the case of John Blair and his weekly pay of \$277.50:

(1) Add the employee's individual contributions to unemployment insurance (\$6.38), the Canada Pension Plan (\$4.30), and his registered company pension plan (assume it to be \$14.10).

ONTARIO
WEEKLY TAX DEDUCTIONS
Basis — 52 Pay Periods per Year

TABLE 2

ONTARIO
RETENUES D'IMPÔT PAR SEMAINE
Base — 52 périodes de paie par année

WEEKLY PAY Use appropriate bracket — PAIE PAR SEMAINE Utilisez le palier approprié	IF THE EMPLOYEE'S "NET CLAIM CODE" ON FORM TD1 IS — SI LE «CODE DE RÉCLAMATION NETTE» DE L'EMPLOYÉ SELON LA FORMULE TD1 EST DE													See note on page 23 — Voir remarque p. 23
	1	2	3	4	5	6	7	8	9	10	11	12	13	
	DEDUCT FROM EACH PAY — *RETENEZ SUR CHAQUE PAIE*													Column A Colonne A
$ 205.00 - 206.99	22.35	20.45	17.00	13.80	10.45	7.70	5.90	3.30						
207.00 - 208.99	22.90	21.00	17.55	14.30	10.95	8.20	6.40	3.80						
209.00 - 210.99	23.45	21.55	18.10	14.80	11.50	8.70	6.95	4.25						
211.00 - 212.99	23.95	22.05	18.65	15.35	12.00	9.20	7.45	4.80						
213.00 - 214.99	24.50	22.60	19.20	15.85	12.50	9.70	7.95	5.30						
215.00 - 216.99	25.05	23.15	19.70	16.40	13.00	10.25	8.45	5.80	1.35					
217.00 - 218.99	25.60	23.70	20.25	16.95	13.50	10.75	9.00	6.30	2.75					
219.00 - 220.99	26.15	24.25	20.80	17.45	14.05	11.25	9.50	6.85	3.25					
221.00 - 222.99	26.70	24.80	21.35	18.00	14.55	11.75	10.00	7.35	3.70					
223.00 - 224.99	27.20	25.30	21.90	18.55	15.05	12.30	10.50	7.85	4.20					
225.00 - 226.99	27.75	25.85	22.45	19.10	15.55	12.80	11.00	8.35	4.75					
227.00 - 228.99	28.30	26.40	22.95	19.65	16.10	13.30	11.55	8.90	5.25					
229.00 - 230.99	28.85	26.95	23.50	20.20	16.65	13.80	12.05	9.40	5.75	.40				
231.00 - 232.99	29.40	27.50	24.05	20.70	17.20	14.30	12.55	9.90	6.25	1.90				
233.00 - 234.99	30.00	28.05	24.60	21.25	17.70	14.85	13.05	10.40	6.75	2.95				
235.00 - 236.99	30.55	28.55	25.15	21.80	18.25	15.35	13.60	10.90	7.30	3.40				
237.00 - 238.99	31.15	29.10	25.65	22.35	18.80	15.85	14.10	11.45	7.80	3.90				
239.00 - 240.99	31.70	29.70	26.20	22.90	19.35	16.40	14.60	11.95	8.30	4.40				
241.00 - 242.99	32.25	30.25	26.75	23.45	19.90	16.95	15.10	12.45	8.80	4.90				
243.00 - 244.99	32.85	30.85	27.30	23.95	20.45	17.50	15.60	12.95	9.35	5.40				
245.00 - 246.99	33.40	31.40	27.85	24.50	20.95	18.05	16.15	13.50	9.85	5.95	.50			
247.00 - 248.99	34.00	32.00	28.40	25.05	21.50	18.55	16.70	14.00	10.35	6.45	2.00			
249.00 - 250.99	34.55	32.55	28.90	25.60	22.05	19.10	17.25	14.50	10.85	6.95	2.95			
251.00 - 252.99	35.15	33.15	29.50	26.15	22.60	19.65	17.80	15.00	11.35	7.45	3.45			
253.00 - 254.99	35.70	33.70	30.05	26.65	23.15	20.20	18.30	15.50	11.90	8.00	3.90			
255.00 - 259.99	36.70	34.70	31.05	27.60	24.10	21.15	19.25	16.45	12.80	8.85	4.80			
260.00 - 264.99	38.15	36.15	32.50	28.95	25.45	22.50	20.60	17.80	14.05	10.15	6.10	1.35		
265.00 - 269.99	39.55	37.55	33.95	30.40	26.80	23.85	21.95	19.15	15.35	11.45	7.35	3.45		
270.00 - 274.99	41.00	39.00	35.35	31.85	28.15	25.20	23.35	20.50	16.65	12.70	8.65	4.70		
275.00 - 279.99	42.40	40.40	36.80	33.25	29.55	26.55	24.70	21.85	18.00	14.00	9.95	6.00	2.60	2.60
280.00 - 284.99	43.85	41.85	38.20	34.70	30.95	27.90	26.05	23.20	19.35	15.25	11.20	7.25	3.90	3.35
285.00 - 289.99	45.30	43.25	39.65	36.15	32.40	29.30	27.40	24.60	20.70	16.60	12.50	8.55	5.15	3.40
290.00 - 294.99	46.70	44.70	41.05	37.55	33.80	30.70	28.75	25.95	22.10	17.95	13.75	9.85	6.45	3.40
295.00 - 299.99	48.15	46.15	42.50	39.00	35.25	32.15	30.15	27.30	23.45	19.30	15.05	11.10	7.70	3.40
300.00 - 304.99	49.55	47.55	43.95	40.40	36.70	33.55	31.60	28.65	24.80	20.65	16.35	12.40	9.00	3.40
305.00 - 309.99	51.00	49.00	45.35	41.85	38.10	35.00	33.00	30.05	26.15	22.00	17.70	13.65	10.25	3.40
310.00 - 314.99	52.40	50.40	46.80	43.25	39.55	36.45	34.45	31.50	27.50	23.35	19.05	14.95	11.55	3.40
315.00 - 319.99	53.85	51.85	48.20	44.70	40.95	37.85	35.90	32.90	28.85	24.70	20.40	16.25	12.85	3.40
320.00 - 324.99	55.30	53.25	49.65	46.15	42.40	39.30	37.30	34.35	30.25	26.05	21.75	17.60	14.10	3.50
325.00 - 329.99	56.75	54.70	51.05	47.55	43.80	40.70	38.75	35.75	31.70	27.40	23.10	18.95	15.40	3.55

Gross Earnings	**$277.50**
Less	**24.78**
Taxable Earnings	**$252.72**

(2) Deduct the sum of these contributions, $24.78, from the gross earnings of $277.50 to arrive at Blair's taxable earnings. (If this procedure is not followed, the employee will be paying too much income tax when the deduction tables are applied.)

(3) Refer to the pages of the table appropriate to the pay period. In this case, you would have to refer to the *Weekly* pages.

(4) Look down the appropriate *Weekly Pay* column for the bracket containing the employee's pay (taxable earnings). For John Blair, you would find the bracket *$251.00—252.99.*

(5) Follow this line to the exemption column that reflects the Net Claim Code identified for the employee on form TD1. John Blair's Net Claim Code is 9, so the amount of income tax to be withheld is $11.35. Check this by referring to the table illustrated.

Provincial Health Insurance Plan

Most provinces have legislated compulsory payroll deductions to cover the payment of the premium for their respective provincial health insurance plans. Of course, the plan and the employee's premium vary from province to province. In John Blair's case, assume that a weekly payroll deduction of $12.50 covers the employee and his family under the Ontario Health Insurance Plan. The accounting of this deduction and the subsequent remittance are dealt with in the next Topic of this chapter. The point here is to remember that the employer is obliged by provincial law to deduct the required premium from the employee's gross earnings and to make periodic remittances to the provincial government.

Garnishments and Government Demands

In addition to the compulsory deductions for unemployment insurance, the Canada Pension Plan, income taxes, and provincial health insurance plans, employers must be aware of two other deductions that may be ordered by law.

Garnishments In order to recover money owed to him or her, a creditor may obtain, in all Canadian provinces, a court order from the Small Claims Court called a *garnishment*. A garnishment requires an employer to withhold a portion of the debtor's wages each payday and surrender it to the court. This action is called *garnisheeing* an employee's wages. Most provinces have regulations limiting the percentage of wages that may be garnisheed (usually to 30%) so that the debtor will have some wages to live on. Moreover, only one garnishment may be made against any one source of income of the debtor. On the other hand, the creditor can continue to garnishee until the debt has been satisfied.

Government Demands on Employee's Earnings An order in writing from the federal Department of National Revenue or the Quebec Income Tax Service requiring the payment of a lump sum or designated payments in settlement of outstanding income tax arrears is known as a tax demand. In addition, demands from the federal Unemployment Insurance Commission for withheld payments to recover an overpayment of unemployment insurance benefits can also be applied.

Union Initiation Fees and Union Dues

Generally, the payment of an initiation fee and of union dues is a condition of employment for all employees who are members of a union. As part of the basic agreement, the employer is obliged to withhold from an employee's earnings an amount for union dues.

Because deductions for union dues are not covered by law, the employer is required to have a written authorization from the employee before making any such deduction. However, as part of the basic agreement between union and employer, all employees covered by the agreement are generally required, as a condition of employment, to sign such an authorization.

Voluntary Deductions

In addition to the compulsory deductions required by law or covered in a basic agreement, the employee may request the employer to make special deductions for such items as safety shoes, group life insurance, a registered company pension plan, Canada Savings Bonds, donations to community services, and savings in a credit union. These optional deductions are computed individually for each employee and are handled in the same manner as compulsory deductions.

Computation of Net Pay

Once the various compulsory and voluntary deductions have been calculated, the sum of these deductions can be subtracted from the employee's gross earnings. As you now know, the remainder is known as the employee's net pay, or simply take-home pay.

The net pay of John Blair for the weekly pay period ending June 30 may be computed as follows:

Gross Earnings		*–*	*Total Deductions*		*=*	*Net Pay*
Regular 38¾ h × $6.00 =	*$232.50*		*Unemployment Insurance*	*$ 6.38*		
Overtime 5 h × $9.00 =	*45.00*		*CPP*	*4.30*		
			Company Pension Plan	*14.10*		
			Income Tax	*11.35*		
			Medical Plan	*12.50*		
			Group Insurance	*6.00*		
	$277.50	*–*		*$54.63*	*=*	*$222.87*

TOPIC 1 PROBLEMS

14-1 R. Manta works for the Beta Corporation as an electrical engineer. She is a salaried employee earning $36 000 per year. If she is paid monthly, calculate her gross earnings per pay. (Show your work.)

14-2 Refer to the two clock cards illustrated opposite.

a Determine the total number of hours worked each day by Potter and Steven. Compute the daily time in hours and quarter-hours. Regular hours are 7:30 a.m. to 11:30 a.m. and 12:00 noon to 4:00 p.m. daily, 40 hours per week. For lateness, the employee is docked 15 minutes for each 15 minutes or portion thereof of lateness in the morning or the afternoon. A similar rule applies to clocking out early.

b Determine the total number of hours worked during the week.

c Compute regular, overtime, and total gross pay. Potter's regular rate is $6.00 an hour and Steven's regular rate is $7.00 an hour. Consider all hours in excess of eight per day, and on Saturdays and Sundays, as overtime. Overtime is calculated only on quarter-hours and is paid at double the regular rate.

Key Check Figure
Potter: $295.50

14-3 The Fun-Time Toy Company pays its employees on the piece-rate plan. For each piece produced from 1 to 250 the rate of pay is $0.15; from 251 to 500, $0.20; and over 500, $0.25.

Determine the gross earnings for the following employees:

Employee	Total Number of Pieces	Employee	Total Number of Pieces
a F. Milsom	330	**e** J. Lewis	255
b M. Prost	240	**f** K. Sutherland	405
c H. Brooks	315	**g** J. Miller	503
d M. Toddal	145	**h** L. Laidlaw	287

Key Check Figure
Total = $401.90

Name Callo Potter **Employee No.** 12
Social Insurance No. 444-545-697
Week Ending May 10, 19—

CLOCK CARD

	Regular				Extra		
Days	**In**	**Out**	**In**	**Out**	**In**	**Out**	**Hours**
Thur.	7:28	11:30	12:00	4:02			8
Fri.	7:29	11:31	12:11	4:01			7 3/4
Sat.							
Sun.			11:59	4:04			4
Mon.	7:31	11:32	12:00	5:01			7 3/4 +1
Tue.	7:28	11:25	11:58	4:04			7 3/4
Wed.	7:27	11:33	11:57	4:06			8

	Hours	Rate	Earnings
Regular	39 1/4	6	235.50
Overtime	5	12	60
Total Hours	44 1/4	**Gross Earnings**	295.50

Name John Steven **Employee No.** 8
Social Insurance No. 565-878-001
Week Ending May 10, 19—

CLOCK CARD

	Regular				Extra		
Days	**In**	**Out**	**In**	**Out**	**In**	**Out**	**Hours**
Thur.	7:28	11:31	12:00	4:00	5:00	6:17	
Fri.	7:28	11:32	11:59	4:02			
Sat.	7:29	11:30					
Sun.							
Mon.	7:28	11:31	11:58	4:00			
Tue.	7:24	11:33	12:05	4:08			
Wed.	7:29	11:30	12:00	4:01	4:49	6:31	

	Hours	Rate	Earnings
Regular		7	
Overtime			
Total Hours		**Gross Earnings**	

14-4 Raid Rattles Manufacturers makes three different types of rattles and pays workers a different piece rate for each as follows: Rattle J: $0.08 per piece; Rattle XL: $0.12 per piece; Deluxe Rattle: $0.15 per piece. Calculate the gross earnings of employee James Baddin for the following work:

Day of the Week	Number and Kind of Products Assembled	
Monday	412	J
	223	XL
	45	Deluxe
Wednesday	334	J
	202	XL
	299	Deluxe
Friday	54	J
	489	XL
	387	Deluxe

Key Check Figure
Total = $283.33

14-5 The Edmonton A-1 Car Sales Company pays all of its sales staff on a commission plan with terms of 6% of total sales. Calculate the gross earnings of each of these employees if they made sales as follows during the month of July:

Key Check Figure
Banks: $885

a Frank Doogan $12 000
b George Jackson $18 800
c Ruth Corver $13 000
d Martha Banks $14 750

14-6 Baker Bippy Company pays its sales staff on a salary-commission plan. Each salesperson receives $300 salary per month and then commissions on total sales above $1 000 as follows: $1 000 – $2 500, 4%; $2 501 – $4 000, 6%; more than $4 000, 10%. M. Jacques sold $3 570 in total this month; T. Ronald sold $6 750; M. Lawly sold $750. Calculate each employee's salary, commission, and total gross pay.

Key Check Figure
Jacques: $424.20

14-7 Suppose four employees have weekly gross earnings as follows: P. Banner, $197.23; L. Swift, $274.89; M. Rooden, $241.00; K. Teepes, $238.87.

a Calculate the unemployment insurance premiums to be deducted from each.

b Calculate the amount the employer is required to submit and produce in a properly titled T-account the total amount to be paid to the Receiver General.

c Show your calculation based on the number percentages provided in the text and then verify your calculation for L. Swift by finding the amount in the tables on page 467. *Note:* If you have more up-to-date materials for your province available in your school, use that information. If you have the tables, check all the calculations.

Produce a chart similar to the following in order to record your work:

Key Check Figure
Total UI = $52.54

	Employee	*Gross Earnings*	*Calculation*
EXAMPLE:	P. Banner	$197.23	

14-8 Calculate the Canada Pension Plan deductions for the employees in the previous problem. Calculate the employee's, then the employer's contribution. Finally, total the amount to be paid to the Receiver General and record the amount in a properly titled T-account.

a Show your calculation based on the number percentages provided in the text and then verify your calculation for L. Swift by finding the amount in the tables found on page 469. *Note:* If you have more up-to-date materials available in your school, use that information.

b Produce a chart similar to the one in the previous problem in order to record your work.

Key Check Figure
Total CPP = $28.76

14-9 Calculate the company pension plan deductions for each of the employees found in Problem 14-7. The deduction is based on 5% of the gross earnings figure provided. The company matches the employee deduction.

a Show the calculations based on the number percentages shown above for both the employee and the employer.

b Prepare a T-account, properly titled, and record the total amount to be paid to the insurance company providing the company pension plan.

Key Check Figure Company Pension = $95.18

14-10 Calculate the income tax deduction for each of the employees listed in Problem 14-7 using the table found on page 471. Think carefully about Banner. Their Net Claim Codes are as follows: Banner, 9; Swift, 1; Rooden, 4; Teepes, 3. Using a chart like the one shown below, and the information you have calculated from the previous three questions, complete the chart for each of the employees. *Note:* The employees should be listed in alphabetical order.

Calculation of Employee's Income Taxes

	Employee (1)	Net Claim Code (2)	Weekly Gross Earnings (3)	Deductions				Taxable Earnings 3 — 7 (8)	Inc. Tax (9)
				UI (4)	CPP (5)	Co. P. Plan (6)	Total of 4,5,&6 (7)		
EXAMPLE:	P. Banner	9							

Key Check Figure Teepes Income Tax = $20.25

TOPIC 2 RECORDING AND DISBURSING THE PAYROLL

A complete recording of payroll involves:

- preparing a summary known as the payroll register
- preparing a summary of the details of each employee's earnings — an employee's individual earnings record
- journalizing and posting the payroll so that ledger accounts affected by the payroll may be updated

Preparing the Payroll Register

The method of recording all of the payroll information is usually a record known as the payroll summary or the payroll register. Some firms will maintain a separate register for each different payroll plan: a firm may have an hourly payroll register to summarize the hourly-rated employees and a salary payroll register to summarize the salaried employees.

Study the illustrations of an hourly payroll register and a salary payroll register on page 478, then examine the analysis that follows the second illustration.

Analysis: Here are the main points to remember when analyzing the contents and the preparation of any payroll register.

- Each summary identifies the type of payroll and the pay ending period. The hourly employees are paid on a weekly basis, while the salary payroll register indicates that these employees

HOURLY PAYROLL REGISTER

For the Week Beginning *June 24* 19 — and Ending *June 30* 19 — Paid ________ 19 ___

No.	SIN	Name	Net Claim Code	Hours	Rate of Pay	Regular	Overtime	Gross Pay	UI	CPP	Company P. Plan	Income Tax	Prov. H.I.P.	Group Ins.	Other	Total	Net Pay	Chq. No.
	Employee Data					Earnings			Deductions									
1	387-430-193	Abel, Paul	3	40	6.00	240.00		240.00	5.52	3.63	13.12	20.25	12.50	6.00		61.02	178.98	
2	214-617-119	Agar, Ben J.	5	40	5.50	220.00		220.00	5.06	3.27	12.80	8.40	12.50	6.00		48.03	171.97	
3	425-127-511	Blair, John	9	43¼	6.00	232.50	45.00	277.50	6.38	4.30	14.10	11.35	12.50	6.00		54.63	222.87	
4	391-715-110	Calvert, Peter	4	42	7.00	280.00	21.00	301.00	6.92	4.73	14.90	31.85	12.50	6.00		76.90	224.10	
5	425-218-187	Ford, Robert	8	39	6.50	253.50		253.50	5.83	3.87	13.95	9.40	12.50	6.00		51.55	201.95	
						1 226.00	66.00	1 292.00	29.71	19.80	68.87	81.25	62.50	30.00		292.13	999.87	

SALARY PAYROLL REGISTER

For the Two Weeks Ending *June 30* 19 — Paid 19

SIN	Name	Net Claim Code	Base Salary /Wk.	Regular	Overtime	Gross Pay	UI	CPP	Comp. P. Plan	Income Tax	Medical Plan	Group Ins.	Other	Total	Net Pay	Chq. No.
Employee Data				Earnings			Deductions									
425-187-873	Baxter, Della	1	250	500.00		500.00	11.50	7.62	23.00	57.40	25.00	6.00		130.52	369.48	
128-345-876	DuBois, Susan	2	300	600.00	100.00	700.00	16.10	11.22	34.00	103.40	25.00	6.00		195.72	504.28	
458-214-489	Gare, Ellen	2	320	640.00		640.00	14.72	10.14	31.00	89.10	25.00	6.00		175.96	464.04	
763-092-982	Long, Henry	3	260	520.00	180.00	700.00	16.10	11.22	34.00	96.15	25.00	6.00		188.47	511.53	
231-344-779	North, Rose	1	350	700.00		700.00	16.10	11.22	34.00	107.40	25.00	6.00		199.72	500.28	
				2 960.00	280.00	3 240.00	74.52	51.42	156.00	453.45	125.00	30.00		890.39	2 349.61	

are paid bi-weekly (once every two weeks). This pay method is common practice.

- Both summaries show that the pay period ends on June 30. The *Cheque No.* column and the *Paid* date line are not filled out because the payroll department will require one or two days after the end of the pay period to prepare the payroll for distribution. The date that will be filled in at the top of the summary will be the same date as that found on the employee's cheques. Sometimes in other accounting systems, especially with salaried personnel, the payroll may be processed one or two days before the pay ending period, but the cheques will be dated for the last day of the pay ending period. Should adjustments be required due to absences or overtime on those last two days, an adjustment will be made to the next payroll period.
- Internal control procedures were implemented for both hourly and salaried employees. This control was represented by the supervisor's daily time report on the hourly employees and the supervisor's signature on the attendance reports of the salaried employees. Both of these control procedures enable the payroll department to check and ensure the accuracy of the timekeeping information.
- After the gross earnings have been calculated, notice the method of recording the deductions. The unemployment insurance, the Canada Pension Plan, and the company pension plan are listed first. The total of these three items must be subtracted from the gross earnings before the income tax calculation is made. The next item listed, the medical plan, is the last of the compulsory deductions. Finally, all remaining deductions are listed.
- In the earnings and the deductions sections of both summaries, *Total* columns are provided in order to highlight these calculations. By subtracting the total deductions from the total gross earnings you can calculate the net pay and record it in its own column on the extreme right-hand side of the summary.
- Both registers have a special column at the right to record the number of the cheque used to pay the employee.
- Observe, in both registers, how the payroll is proved. After all the data is entered for all employees, but before the payroll is paid, the various columns must be totalled. The proof is completed by adding and subtracting the appropriate column totals across the register. If the computer is used, the register proof is obtained automatically. In your classroom, use an adding machine or electronic calculator to prove the payroll register similar to the proofs shown in the margin. All payroll registers must be proved before payment is made to employees and before journal entries are made to record the dollar results of each payroll.

Register Proofs

Proof of Hourly Payroll Register

Earnings:		
Regular	$1 226.00	
Overtime	66.00	
Total		$1 292.00
Deductions:		
UI Premiums	$ 29.71	
CPP	19.80	
Company Pension Plan	68.87	
Income Tax	81.25	
Medical Plan	62.50	
Group Insurance	30.00	
Other	—	
Total		$ 292.13
Net Pay		$ 999.87

Proof of Salary Payroll Register

Earnings:		
Regular	$2 960.00	
Overtime	280.00	
Total		$3 240.00
Deductions:		
UI Premiums	$ 74.52	
CPP	51.42	
Company Pension Plan	156.00	
Income Tax	453.45	
Medical Plan	125.00	
Group Insurance	30.00	
Other	—	
Total		$ 890.39
Net Pay		$2 349.61

Preparing the Employee's Individual Earnings Record

After a payroll register is prepared and proved, the details of each individual's earnings must be posted to the employee's individual earnings record card. This record is very important for the following reasons:

- The record provides a full year's summary of each employee's pay periods, gross earnings, deductions, and net pay.
- It serves as a basis for the preparation of the employee's T4 slips so that he or she can complete an income tax return.
- It helps the employer to prepare the year-end summaries of unemployment insurance premium payments and Canada Pension Plan payments.

An earnings record card for John Blair is shown below. Notice that all of the columns are set up exactly in the same order as they appear in the register. This has been done for two reasons. First, it makes the transfer from a manual or computer method easier to accomplish. Second, some firms use a one-write system. This system lets the payroll department prepare the employee's cheque, the earnings record card, and the payroll register all at the same time.

Finally, note that there is an extra column, *Accumulated Earnings,* at the end of the card. This column enables the firm to maintain a running total of the gross earnings so that the payroll clerk can easily notice when the employee has earned the

EMPLOYEE'S INDIVIDUAL EARNINGS RECORD FOR THE YEAR 19—

Employee's Name *Blair, John* S.I. No. *425-127-511* Employee No. *2*

Address *843 Driftwood Rd.* *London, Ontario N6H 4H9* Phone No. *471-8622*

Date of Birth January 14, 1930 Date of Reaching 65 January 14, 1995

Date Employed *January 2, 1968* Date of Termination Reason

Position *Stockroom Clerk* Salary or Wage Plan *Hourly-Rate Plan* Rate of Pay *$6.00/h*

Net Claim Code per TD 1 *9* U.I. Insurable Earnings *Minimum: $85.00 per week; Maximum: $425.00 per week*

PAY PERIOD ENDING	RATE PER HOUR	HOURS	EARNINGS Regular	Overtime	Gross Pay	DEDUCTIONS U.I.	C.P.P.	Company P.P.	Inc. Tax	O.H.I.P.	Group Ins.	Other	Total	NET PAY	ACCUMULATED EARNINGS
															5 360 40
June 2	6 00	40	240 00		240 00	5 52	3 63	10 40	3 25	12 50	6 00		41 30	198 70	5 600 40
June 9	6 00	41	240 00	9 00	249 00	5 73	3 79	10 52	5 25	12 50	6 00		43 79	205 21	5 849 40
June 16	6 00	$43\frac{1}{2}$	240 00	31 50	271 50	6 24	4 19	13 98	10 35	12 50	6 00		53 26	218 24	6 120 90
June 23	6 00	38	228 00		228 00	5 24	3 41	10 26	∅	12 50	6 00		37 41	190 59	6 348 90
June 30	6 00	$43\frac{3}{4}$	232 50	45 00	277 50	6 38	4 30	14 10	11 35	12 50	6 00		54 63	222 87	6 626 40

maximum amount for the Canada Pension Plan. It also assists in the year-end reporting of the gross earnings.

Journalizing and Posting the Payroll

When the payroll register has been totalled and proved, the payroll data must then be recorded and posted to the appropriate ledger accounts. In some accounting systems this data is posted directly to the ledger accounts. Then, the payroll register becomes the book of original entry and is then called the payroll journal. Other accounting systems summarize the data from the payroll register in the form of a compound General Journal entry. This General Journal entry is then posted to the appropriate ledger accounts. Regardless of the system used, two distinct classes of entries are required: (1) the entry to record the dollar results of the payroll register; and (2) the entry to record the employer's additional expenses, the payroll tax expenses, resulting from each payroll. Each of these classes will now be analyzed separately.

Payroll journal: the payroll register used as the book of original entry.

Recording the Payroll Register Totals Each of the totals from the payroll register must now be debited to an appropriate expense account. In the case of the hourly payroll register, the total of gross earnings would likely go into Wages Expense. In the case of the Salary Payroll Register, the total would go into the Salaries Expense account. For each payroll deduction, the firm is obliged to set up the appropriate liability account. A liability account is necessary because the employer does not own these funds, but rather is holding them temporarily for some specific party. In the case of unemployment insurance, the Canada Pension Plan, and federal income tax, the Receiver General will receive the amounts. Still other amounts will be sent to provincial treasurers, insurance companies, and union headquarters. Each of these liabilities will have a specific payment date. For example, the amounts to be sent to the Receiver General are due by the 15th of the month following the month of collection. Until these amounts are submitted they must be treated as current liabilities. The largest amount in the register is also treated as a current liability until it is paid, namely *Net Pay*. This column total is recorded as wages or salary payable depending upon the payroll register considered.

Receiver General < UI CPP Tax

Net Pay

The General Journal entries needed to record these accounts are listed on page 480. Observe that a compound entry has been made for each of the different payroll registers. This is not necessary, but it has been done to show more clearly where the individual numbers come from. Examine the ledger account illustration to verify the totalled effect of several of the liability accounts after the posting from both sample general entries.

June 30	Wages Expense	1 292.00	
	UI Payable		29.71
	CPP Payable		19.80
	Comp. Pension Payable		68.87
	Income Tax Payable		81.25
	Medical Plan Payable		62.50
	Group Insurance Payable		30.00
	Wages Payable		999.87
	To record the payroll of the hourly-rated employees for the week ended June 30.		
June 30	Salaries Expense	3 240.00	
	UI Payable		74.52
	CPP Payable		51.42
	Comp. Pension Payable		156.00
	Income Tax Payable		453.45
	Medical Plan Payable		125.00
	Group Insurance Payable		30.00
	Salaries Payable		2 349.61
	To record the payroll of the salary-rated employees for the week ended June 30.		

June 30	Payroll Tax Expense	130.26	
	UI Payable		41.59
	CPP Payable		19.80
	Comp. Pension Payable		68.87
	To record the employer's payroll tax expense from the hourly-rated payroll from the week ended June 30.		
June 30	Payroll Tax Expense	311.75	
	UI Payable		104.33
	CPP Payable		51.42
	Comp. Pension Payable		156.00
	To record the payroll tax expense from the salaried employees' pay for the week ended June 30.		

Wages Payable

	999.87

Salaries Payable

	2 349.61

UI Payable

	29.71
	74.52
	41.59
	104.33

CPP Payable

	19.80
	51.42
	19.80
	51.42

Comp. Pen. Payable

	68.87
	156.00
	68.87
	156.00

Inc. Tax. Payable

	81.25
	453.45

Med. Plan Payable	
	62.50
	125.00

Grp. Insur. Payable	
	30.00
	30.00

Salaries Exp.	
3 240.00	

Wages Exp.	
1 292.00	

Payroll Taxes Exp.	
130.26	
311.75	

Recording the Employer's Additional Payroll Expense You will recall that, by law, the employer is obliged to contribute to the unemployment insurance premiums at 1.4 times the employee premiums and to match the employee CPP deductions. In addition, an employer may maintain a registered company pension plan. If so, any deduction withheld from the employees' pay must be at least matched by the company. This too becomes a part of the payroll taxes expense to be recorded. In practice, an account called Payroll Tax Expense is used to record these amounts paid out by the business. The use of the word "Taxes" should not be confused with the Income Taxes which are withheld from the employees and accounted for in the current liability account. Instead, the word is used as part of the "Payroll Taxes Expense" account to suggest that the additional amounts are levied against the employer by the government in much the same way as in the case of property taxes or licence fees required for doing business. Since the employer had no choice but to contribute, in the language of business, these additional levies may be regarded as taxes related to payroll expense.

Account: Payrol Tax Exp

To complete the journal entry, credit entries to the individual current liability accounts are required. The accounts affected include the unemployment insurance account, the CPP account, and the company pension plan account. Refer once again to the ledger accounts to examine the effect of these postings.

individ. current liability
UI, CPP. Cny. P. P.

Controlling Payroll Payments

Now it is time to pay the appropriate amounts to the various organizations. A separate cash payment will be required for each organization. Since the amount owing to the employees is the largest cash outflow, paying the employees will be examined first.

Paying the Employees

Employers generally designate a particular day in the week or month as the normal pay day. For the hourly employees, it might be every Friday; for the salaried employees, the 15th and the last day of every month. Generally, there are three methods by which a business may pay their employees: by cash, by cheque, or by direct deposit to a bank account in the employee's name. All three represent a very large cash payment; therefore, each must be carefully controlled.

Payment in Cash When it is necessary (because of law, union contract, etc.) to pay salaries and/or wages by cash, care must be taken to control the handling and the recording of the cash. First, the payroll clerk must determine the number of bills and coins that will be needed. As this job is carried out, a change sheet simi-

CHANGE SHEET FOR PAYROLL **Date** *June 30*

Employee No.	Net Pay		Bills					Coins				
			$20	$10	$5	$2	$1	50¢	25¢	10¢	5¢	1¢
1	178	98	6	4	3	1	1		3	2		3
2	171	97	6	5			1		3	2		2
3	222	87	9	4		1			3	1		2
4	224	10	9	4		2				1		
5	201	95	7	6			1		3	2		
6												
7												
Totals	$999	87	37	23	3	4	3		12	8		7

lar to the one illustrated above must be prepared. Then the clerk will prepare a currency requisition form. This form (see margin) requests permission to receive a cheque which will provide the clerk with the necessary bills and coins to prepare the individual pay envelopes. The total change sheet and the currency requisition sheet must agree with the net pay total from the payroll register and the amount of net pay journalized in the General Journal entry. Now the cash payments officer must issue a cheque for the amount of the currency requisition. The payroll clerk may have actually prepared the cheque for this purpose, but it will have to be signed by one or more different persons who are authorized to issue cheques. In a larger firm, the person in charge of such activities is the *paymaster.* The paymaster usually pre-

CURRENCY REQUISITION

Denomination	Quantity	Amount	
$20	37	$740	00
$10	23	230	00
$ 5	3	15	00
$ 2	4	8	00
$ 1	3	3	00
50¢			
25¢	12	3	00
10¢	8		80
5¢			
1¢	7		07
	Total	$999	87

pares the cheques and obtains the necessary signatures. Once the payroll clerk has the cheque, it can be cashed for the appropriate bills and coin. Then the pay envelopes for the employees can be prepared ready for distribution. A business may find it worthwhile to have the bank prepare the envelopes. Banks provide such a service and guarantee the correctness of the amounts inserted into each envelope.

The journal entry for the steps outlined above should not present too much difficulty for you. Check your thoughts against the illustration below. Notice the effect of this entry on the cash and two liability accounts.

From the company's standpoint, the payment of salaries and wages in cash is the least desirable method because:

- it requires more work in the preparation of payrolls
- it increases the possibility of errors in pay
- it involves a significant risk, because large amounts of cash must be transported and kept at the company

Therefore, wherever possible, accountants support the practice of making payments by cheque or by direct bank transfer to an employee's account.

July 2	*Wages Payable*	*999.87*	
	Salaries Payable	*2 349.61*	
	Cash		*3 349.48*
	To record the receipt of cash for the payroll or the transfer of funds to the special payroll bank account.		

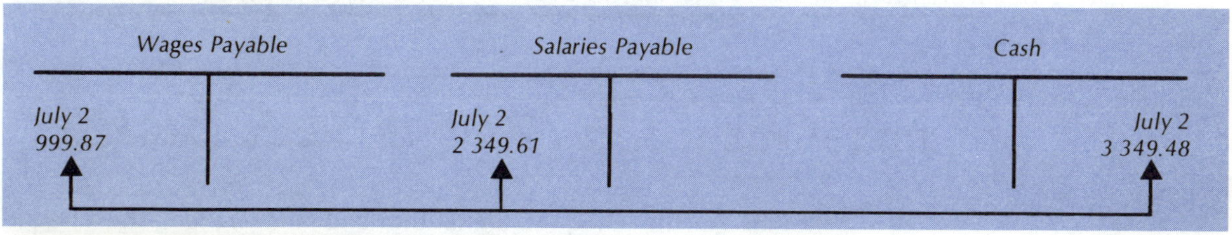

Payment by Cheque For greater internal control over cash payments, many employers prefer to issue special "payroll cheques" to pay their employees. The general procedures leading to the issuance of these payroll cheques may be outlined as follows:

(1) After the payroll register or registers are verified, the paymaster requests permission of the treasurer or of another person in charge of the cash payments to write a cheque to transfer the amount required for net pay for all employees into a separate *payroll bank account.* This bank account is like any other demand deposit account except that it is used strictly for the purpose of writing payroll cheques. The entry to transfer the cash from the

company's regular current account to the payroll account is made in the cash payments journal and analyzed in General Journal format, as the entry illustrated in the cash payment section just completed. Note how the payables are debited and reduced to zero by this entry.

(2) Next, the paymaster will issue individualized cheques to each of the employees from the payroll bank account. Usually, these cheques will be in the form of voucher cheques so that the employee may keep the detachable part as a record of the gross earnings, deductions, and net pay. A voucher cheque is illustrated below.

		Earnings			Deductions								Net Pay	
Period Ending	Hours Worked	Regular	Over-time	Total	U.I.	CPP	Comp. P.P.	Inc. Tax	OHIP	Insur-ance	Other	Total	Amount	Cheque No.
—06 30	43 3/4	232.50	45.00	277.50	6.38	4.30	14.10	11.35	12.50	6.00		54.63	222.87	503

Employees Statement of Earnings
Detach and retain for your records.

Western Sales Company
Mount Brydges, Ontario

- -

Western Sales Company
22 Adelaide North
Mount Brydges, Ontario NOL 1W0

Payroll Cheque No. 503

July 2, 19—

Pay To
The Order Of *John Blair* *$222.87*

Two Hundred Twenty-Two . . . . *87/100* Dollars

THE ROYAL BANK OF CANADA
Mount Brydges, Ontario

WESTERN SALES COMPANY

Arthur Peabody

⑆00884⑈003⑆ 110⑈134⑈4⑈

(3) As the cheques are authorized and signed, the cheque number is permanently recorded in the payroll register. (Of course, many large firms use a signature plate containing a signature facsimile to sign a great number of payroll cheques.)

(4) When these payroll cheques are all presented for payment, the amounts are deducted from the bank account. If all the cheques are cashed, the account will be reduced to zero. Since the special payroll bank account has been used, nothing happens to the general current account as the payroll cheques are cashed by the employees. The use of a separate payroll bank account simplifies the month-end bank reconciliation of both accounts. Cancelled pay cheques can be compared to the payroll register, while the general current account cheques are compared with the cash payments journal.

Payment by Bank Deposit There is now a trend among firms to pay their employees by means of a deposit to the credit of an employee in his or her account in a chartered bank located near the employer's place of business. Some of the very large firms may make arrangements to transfer the employee's deposit to a chartered bank, trust company, or credit union of his or her choice. While the exact mechanics of processing such deposits may vary from firm to firm, some businesses contract a "package deal" with their bank. In general terms, the employer provides the bank with the necessary payroll data, while the bank processes the entire payroll through its computer. In return for a processing fee, the bank provides the employer with a payroll summary and takes care of the employees' payment by bank deposit as well.

The laws of each province require that employees paid by bank deposit be provided with a statement to explain their earnings. To meet the legal requirements, employees' statement of earnings, such as the one illustrated below are usually given to each employee at work on pay day.

6706 - 1 FIN. ACCT. JAN. 75

Statement of Salary and Deductions — Ford Motor Company of Canada, Limited

NAME AND INITIALS	DEPT.	EMPLOYEE NO.	½ MONTH SALARY	½ MONTH C.O.L.A.	OVERTIME EARNINGS	SHIFT PREMIUM	GROSS PAY
BRAUN	DJ 8815	406 674 481	296.08	5.78	40.99		342.85

PAY PERIOD ENDING	QUARTERLY C.O.L.A.		VAC. DAYS REM.	OVERTIME HOURS	SHIFT PREM. HOURS	FEDERAL TAX	QUEBEC TAX	CAN. PENS. CONTRIB.	FORD PENS. CONTRIB.	BONDS	U.D.	U.I.C.
MAR 31, 19--	18.18		10	8.00		70.97		5.92	7.30			3.03

CHARITY	CREDIT UNION	TAX DEMANDS ASSIGNMENTS	SHOES	C.L.	S.	GROUP INSURANCE	CODE	MISCELLANEOUS DEDUCTION	CODE				NET DEPOSIT
1.00									00				254.63

Please direct inquiries to your supervisor

Ford Motor Company of Canada, Ltd.

Analyzing Other Payroll Disbursements

Let us now deal with the payment of all other liabilities created as a result of the payroll. First, examine the illustration showing the accounts affected by the payroll calculations. The wages and salaries payable have already been reduced to zero. As you read the points to follow, notice how each of the remaining payables will be reduced to zero.

Payment of UI, CPP, and Income Taxes You have already studied the payment of these in detail in Chapter 10. Remember that they are all payable to the Receiver General by the 15th of the month following their collection. If further review is required, return to Chapter 10.

Receiver General
U I, CPP
Inc. Taxes

Payment to the Company Pension Plan On some predetermined payment date, the company will regularly submit to the firm handling the company pension plan the funds collected to date. This requires that a cheque be prepared and the appropriate journal entry be made to record the disbursement.

Payment of Provincial Health Insurance Premiums By a certain monthly date, the company will be required to send the medical plan premiums to the treasurer of the province. This, of course, requires a cheque and an entry into the cash payments journal.

Payments of Other Amounts Owing The remaining liabilities will have to be paid according to the due dates or agreements made with those organizations. These include the group insurance, union dues and initiation fees, and other voluntary deductions.

TOPIC 2 PROBLEMS

14-11 Paper Products Limited has three salaried employees as shown below.

	Earns	Net Claim Code	SIN
Tom Terrific	$582.50	1	323-444-567
Mary Goodright	$615.00	4	544-456-778
Mark Leftly	$490.75	6	389-998-123

The company has a pension plan that deducts 6% of the employee's gross pay. The company matches the employee deduction.

Prepare the payroll register for the two weeks ending March 23, 19—. (Use the illustration on page 478 as a model.) After completing the register, check your work by means of a Proof of Salary Payroll form. *Note:* All compulsory deductions should be determined from the latest tables available to you. Don't forget to put the employees in alphabetical order.

14-12 Refer to Problems 14-7, 14-8, 14-9, and 14-10. Using the following information, prepare an hourly payroll register similar to the one illustrated on page 478. The time period is April 5 – April 11, 19—.

Employee No.	SIN	Name	Group Insurance	Other Deductions
1	333-444-555	P. Banner	$5.50	$10.00
2	434-445-778	M. Rooden	5.50	12.00
3	123-234-345	L. Swift	5.50	9.00
4	675-472-321	K. Teepes	5.50	25.00

a Prepare an hourly payroll register for the employees listed above.

b Total and prove the payroll register. Prepare a form similar to the one on page 479. (Attach a machine tape if possible.)

c Prepare all the journal entries that would result from the register. Use April 11, 19—, Page 26.

Key Check Figure
Net Pay = $717.88

14-13 The Baker Coat Company derived the following totals from its salary payroll register for the two weeks ending October 15, 19—: Gross Pay, $4 500.00; UI, $65.00; CPP, $80.00; Company Pension Plan, $250.00; Income Tax, $710.00; Medical Plan, $52.00; Group Insurance, $43.00; Net Pay, $3 300.00. The employer is required to meet the latest government requirements for unemployment insurance and the Canada Pension Plan. It has also agreed to match employee contributions to the company pension plan, the medical plan, and the group insurance.

a Prepare a proof for the salary payroll register.

b In General Journal form, record the dollar results of the payroll register.

c In General Journal form, record the additional employer's expenses as a result of the payroll calculations.

Key Check Figure
Net Pay = $3 300

14-14 Use the information from the payroll register you completed in 14-12 to prepare a Change Sheet and a Currency Requisition for the employees' net pay.

Key Check Figure
Number of Twenties = 35

14-15 The Underwood Supply Company has the following account balances in its General Ledger as a result of the past month's payroll entries. The company meets all government requirements and matches the employee contributions to the company pension plan. The company pension plan is held with Fidelity Trust Company, the medical plan funds are sent to your provincial treasurer, and the group insurance plan is held with London Life.

a In the General Journal, record the last weekly payroll tax expenses incurred by the company, and post them to the ledger account balances shown below and on the next page.

b Total the ledger accounts and make the necessary General Journal entry to transfer funds from the company's general current bank account to the payroll bank account.

c Record in the General Journal the necessary entries to pay the amounts owing to: **i** the Receiver General; **ii** Fidelity Trust; **iii** London Life; **iv** your provincial treasurer.

Key Check Figure
Receiver General:
$1 710.20

Wages Payable			*UI Payable*			*CPP Payable*		
Feb.	6	2 100.00	Feb.	6	68.00	Feb.	6	50.00
	13	2 200.00		6	95.20		6	50.00
	20	2 100.00		13	72.00		13	51.00
	27	2 150.00		13	100.80		13	51.00
				20	68.00		20	50.00
				20	95.20		20	50.00
				27	70.00		27	50.50

Comp. P. Plan Payable

	Feb. 6 35.00
	6 35.00
	13 39.00
	13 39.00
	20 35.00
	20 35.00
	27 37.00
	27 37.00

Income Tax Deduc. Payable

	Feb. 6 150.00
	13 175.00
	20 150.00
	27 165.00
	640

Med. Plan Payable

	Feb. 6 38.00
	13 38.00
	20 38.00
	27 38.00

Group Insur. Payable

	Feb. 6 25.00
	13 25.00
	20 25.00
	27 25.00

Wages Expense

Feb. 6 2 466.00	
13 2 600.00	
20 2 466.00	
27 2 535.50	

Payroll Tax Expense

Feb. 6 180.20	
13 190.80	
20 180.20	
27 185.50	

14-16 Challenge Problem Waterloo Printing Company has two salaried employees and two hourly employees. The company pays overtime to its hourly employees at a rate of time-and-a-half. Salaried employees do not receive overtime pay. The company has a registered pension plan for all its employees — 3% of gross pay — and the company contributes double the employee contribution. The company pays all of the medical plan which amounts to a flat rate of $3.50 per week. Group insurance deductions are a flat $2.50 per week and this is deducted from the employee's pay. Hourly employees are paid each week, salaried employees bi-weekly. *Hint:* Don't forget to double the weekly flat-rate deductions. Use the data in the chapter for all other deductions.

The following people are under the salary plan: David Boone, SIN 647-824-512, base salary $550/week, Net Claim Code 6; Ruth Carter, SIN 421-385-664, base salary $600/week, Net Claim Code 2.

The following people are under the hourly plan:

1. Matt Cooper, SIN 454-678-998, hourly rate $5.60, Net Claim Code 7, hours recorded the past two weeks, 40 + 4, 39 + 1.

2. Jill Farnwell, SIN 734-886-556, hourly rate $5.40, Net Claim Code 5, hours for the past two weeks, 40, 40 + 5.

a Record the necessary information into the salary payroll register and the hourly payroll register for the two weeks ending May 15, 19—.

b Total and proof the registers.

c Prepare the needed journal entries to record the employee payroll records and the payroll tax expense records.

d Show the amounts to be paid into the company payroll account, to each employee, to the federal government, to the provincial government, and to any other sources.

Key Check Figure Company Pension: $195.42

TOPIC 3 OTHER FACTORS AFFECTING PAYROLL ACCOUNTING

Vacation pay and workers' compensation require some consideration whenever payroll is discussed. Neither of these points affects payroll entries regularly, but they are legal obligations in most cases.

Vacation Pay

This is the amount of money added to an employee's base salary (50 weeks of actual productive service) so that he or she will receive regular weekly pays during his or her vacation period (minimum of two weeks).

Weekly earnings for 50 weeks	*$100/week*
Total earnings over 50 weeks	*$5 000*
Vacation pay: 4% of total earned pay ($5 000)	*$200*
Vacation pay per week ($200/50 weeks)	*$4*

After a year of service, employees are entitled to two weeks' vacation with pay. This pay must be at least four percent of the total wages for the year for which vacation is given. The employer may decide when the vacation will be taken. It may be a block of two weeks at one time or divided into two one-week periods. It must be given within ten months after the employee has earned the vacation. It should be noted that many employers pay vacation pay at greater than four percent, award more than two weeks' vacation, or allow the employee, within reason, to pick the date and the block(s) of time.

Vacation benefits must be paid within one week of termination of employment. If employment was for less than one year, the employee is entitled to vacation pay totalling four percent of total wages from the first day employed.

Accounting for Vacation Pay Vacation pay may be handled in several ways. Often, it is recorded in a liability account each week for hourly-paid personnel. The accounting entry, in General Journal form, appears below.

May 12	*Wages Expense*	*4*	
	Vacation Pay Payable		*4*
	To record the vacation pay payable for the week ended May 12 ($5 000 × 4%/50 weeks).		

Often this vacation pay payable is distributed to the employees twice a year. This entry would appear as shown below.

June 30	*Vacation Pay Payable*	*100*	
	Cash		*100*
	Issued Cheque No. 721 for semi-annual payment vacation pay payable to the hourly employees.		

If vacation pay is distributed in this way, the employee would not expect a pay cheque for either of the two weeks of vacation because the vacation pay would have already been given out as lump sums twice during the year.

Compare this with the typical treatment for a salaried employee. The salaried employee is usually presented with an annual pay figure. If this figure is $52 000, the employee will receive $2 000 bi-weekly. Assuming that the quoted $52 000 per year includes the vacation pay, the actual earned salary totals $50 000. Commonly, employees simply receive a regular pay even though they are on vacation.

Actual Earned Salary	*$50 000*
Vacation Pay (4% × $50 000)	*$ 2 000*
Total Salary	*$52 000*

July 15	*Salaries Expense*	*2 000*	
	Cash		*2 000*
	Issued Cheque No. 800 to record payment of vacation pay to Mr. Teller.		

Workers' Compensation

The Workers' Compensation Act applies to two types of industries, designated "Schedule 1" and "Schedule 2."

Generally speaking, Schedule 1 industries are manufacturers. This group contains most industries, and employers in these industries are required to pay an annual assessment. The money makes up the Workers' Compensation Board's accident fund, out of which compensation payments and medical aid are paid. Schedule 1 businesses operate under the collective liability principle. This means that payments for compensation and medical aid are made from a "pot" that all have contributed to.

Some of the businesses in Schedule 2 are railways, federal telephone companies, municipalities, and school boards.

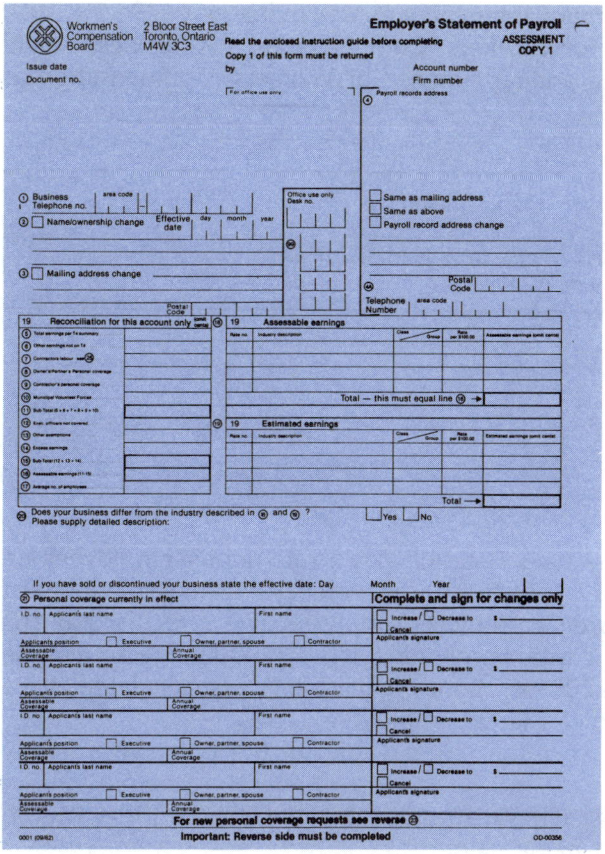

Workmen's Compensation Board 2 Bloor Street East Toronto, Ontario M4W 3C3

Employer's Statement of Payroll

Read the enclosed instruction guide before completing

Copy 1 of this form must be returned by

ASSESSMENT COPY 1

Issue date

Document no.

Account number

Firm number

Payroll records address

1 Business Telephone no. area code

2 Name/ownership change Effective date day month year

3 Mailing address change

Postal Code

Office use only Desk no.

Same as mailing address

Same as above

Payroll record address change

Postal Code

Telephone Number area code

19 Reconciliation for this account only

19 Assessable earnings

Total — this must equal line 16

19 Estimated earnings

Total

Does your business differ from the industry described in and ? Please supply detailed description:

Yes No

If you have sold or discontinued your business state the effective date: Day Month Year

Personal coverage currently in effect

Complete and sign for changes only

I.D. no. Applicant's last name First name

Increase / Decrease to $

Cancel

Applicant's signature

Applicant's position Executive Owner, partner, spouse Contractor

Assessable Coverage Annual Coverage

For new personal coverage requests see reverse

Important: Reverse side must be completed

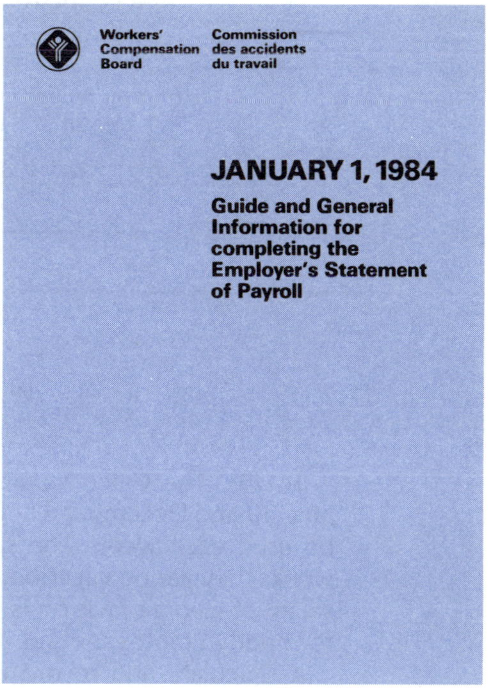

Schedule 2 industries are individually liable, under the board's direction, to pay compensation and the medical costs of every employee who has an accident or develops an industrial disease.

Industries not covered in Schedule 1 may apply to be included in Schedule 1. The board's decision on this is final.

If a business falls under Schedule 1 or 2, it is obliged by law to contribute to the fund. Employees do not contribute in any way.

Rating for Schedule 1 Before the board can accurately assess an industry, certain information is required. The board asks each business to complete an Employer's Statement of Payroll. Included with the form is a booklet with general information and a guide for completing the form. Once the board receives this form, the rate of assessment can be calculated, based on the following points:

- The assessment rate is determined annually for each industry.
- Each industry is placed into one of 27 classes according to the type of work being done.
- The assessment rate is determined by several factors that enable the board to project its future needs in every class. A statement is prepared and mailed to each business for payment.

- The minimum assessment for any industry is $25.

Accounting for Workers' Compensation A business would account for the annual expense of Workers' Compensation as follows:

Feb. 28	*Workers' Compensation Expense*	*295*	
	Cash		*295*
	Issued Cheque No. 432 to pay annual Workers' Compensation assessment.		

TOPIC 3 PROBLEMS

14-17 The Calco Company pays vacation pay to its hourly employees on June 30 and December 31. This means that a Vacation Pay Payable account must be used each week. The salaried employees simply receive a regular pay the weeks they are on vacation. The total hourly payroll is $10 000 per week and the salary of George Jackson is $4 700 per month. Vacation Pay is calculated at 4% for hourly employees and 8% for salaried employees.

a Calculate and record the vacation pay payable for the company's hourly workers.

b Calculate and record the total in vacation pay payable on June 30/—. Record the entry to show this amount being paid.

c Record the entry for G. Jackson on August 31 when he is on his month's vacation.

Case Study 14

X Company Limited is required by law to pay wages to construction workers in cash. Tom Estay, a payroll clerk, completes carefully the change sheet for payroll and the currency requisition. A cheque for $150 000 is issued to Tom, who cashes the cheque at a nearby bank. At the bank, Tom also prepares each employee's pay envelope with the correct change.

On his return from the bank, Tom is held at gunpoint by two robbers. Fortunately, the men are frightened away by a passing police car, which escorts Tom safely to his employer's place of business. Tom promptly hands over the bags containing the pay envelopes to Jack Jones, the paymaster, who quickly locks the cash in his desk drawer for overnight safekeeping.

The next day, all pay envelopes are claimed by the employees except one marked for Ed Hurst. A few hours later, a woman claiming to be Mrs. Ed Hurst appears at the paymaster's office to claim her husband's pay. After receiving an identification card, the paymaster gives the envelope to the woman, who later turns out to be an impostor.

If you were the chief accounting officer for the company, what protective steps would you include to cover the following?

a delivering funds to the company
b filling pay envelopes
c safekeeping of funds prior to payment
d issuing pay envelopes
e handling unclaimed pay envelopes

CHAPTER 15

AN INTRODUCTION TO ADJUSTING ENTRIES

As their name suggests, adjustments adjust, update, or correct accounts which change as a result of the ongoing activities of a business. The idea of *change* is the key. If the analysis of an account shows that a change has resulted, an accounting entry must be made to reflect the change. No matter what type of an adjustment you study, it is this idea of *change* which is the key to understanding it and correctly carrying it out.

Generally, there are four types of adjustments: for prepaid expenses, for accrued revenues, for accrued expenses, and for unearned revenue. In this chapter, two areas of special concern will be the accounting for bad debts and for the depreciation of fixed assets.

- Topic 1 deals with adjusting for prepaid expenses.
- Topic 2 deals with adjusting for the expenses occasioned by bad debts.
- Topic 3 deals with adjusting for depreciation expense.
- Topic 4 deals with adjusting for accrued revenues, accrued expenses, and unearned revenue.

The firm we will study will have an accounting period of one year with year-end on December 31. On December 31 a series of General Journal entries will be required in order to update the records. This will fulfill the requirements of the matching principle. These entries are called adjusting entries.

TOPIC 1 ADJUSTING FOR PREPAID EXPENSES

To understand the concept of a prepaid expense and how it is adjusted at the end of an accounting period, study these transactions of the Wawdel Company for the month of June.

June 1 Wawdel Company issued a cheque for $200 to purchase enough office supplies to last several months. The accounting policy is to record the cost in an asset account.

This transaction would result in the following T-account analysis:

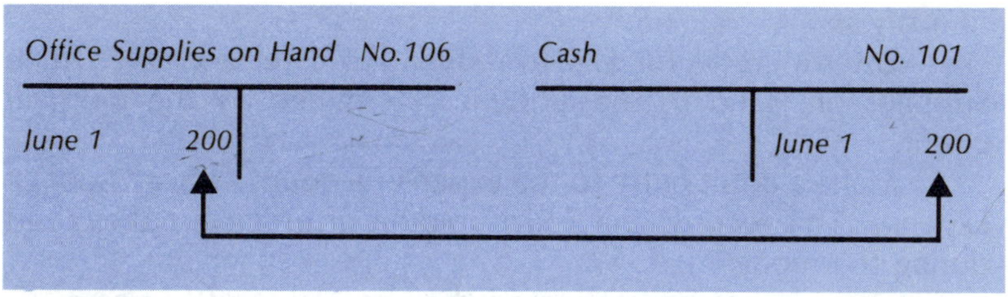

Analysis:

- Since the company issued a cheque, Cash is credited and the cash payments journal is used. The cash was used to acquire an asset, Office Supplies. Office Supplies is an asset acquired under the cost principle; therefore, it must be debited.

Could Wawdel Company use an account called Office Supplies Expense? Yes, but the supplies bought would be used in more than one accounting period. Merchandising firms usually prefer to debit an asset account. This asset is known as a prepaid expense because more than one accounting period will benefit from the expenditure. To be more exact, the prepaid expense is a current asset because its cost will be used up (expired, consumed) usually within one year of the date of the balance sheet. At the end of each period, the portion used must be determined and an adjustment made to transfer that used portion from the asset account into the appropriate expense account.

Prepaid expense: an expense payment made in advance to benefit more than one accounting period; hence, a current asset whose cost will be used up in the very near future.

Examine the following transaction.

June 30 In preparation for month-end financial statements, Wawdel Company takes a physical count of office supplies and discovers $125 of unused supplies.

The margin shows the calculation that is now required. This gives $75 of office supplies used during the month of June. The asset account Office Supplies on Hand is no longer accurate and should be adjusted to reflect its remaining cost. The necessary General Journal entry is illustrated below.

Office Supplies count, June 1	**$200**
Less: Office Supplies count, June 30	**125**
Supplies Used	**$ 75**

June 30	*Office Supplies Expense*	*75*	
	Office Supplies on Hand		*75*
	To adjust the Office Supplies on Hand account for the month ended June 30.		

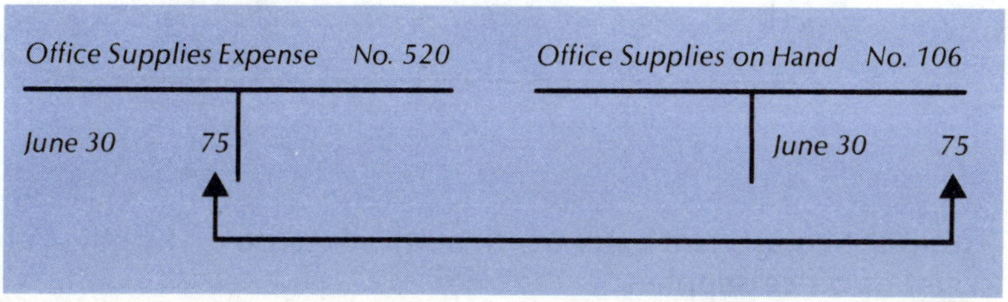

Analysis:

- Enter a credit for $75 to reduce the asset account Office Supplies on Hand to the amount determined by the physical count.
- Make a debit entry to the expense account Office Supplies Expense. This records the dollar amount of office supplies used during the month.

The adjustment has corrected the cost value of the asset so that it will reflect the unused or unexpired cost of office supplies in the current asset section of the balance sheet. The amount used, the expired cost, will also be reported, but in the expense section of the income statement. The adjustment has updated both accounts and matched the expense of the period just completed with the revenues of that period.

If the adjustment had not been made, the following conditions would have resulted:

- The revenues and expenses would be mismatched.
- Expenses would have been understated by $75, because the used portion of office supplies would not have been recorded.
- Net Income would have been overstated by $75.
- Owner's Equity, specifically Capital, would have been overstated by $75.
- The asset section of the balance sheet would have been overstated by $75, because the unused portion of the asset account would not have been reduced by the amount used during June.

Office Supplies Expense Recorded for More Than One Accounting Period

Some firms record the entire cost of office supplies as an expense. This method assumes that the entire amount will be used within an accounting period. The acquisition of these office supplies are then recorded as follows:

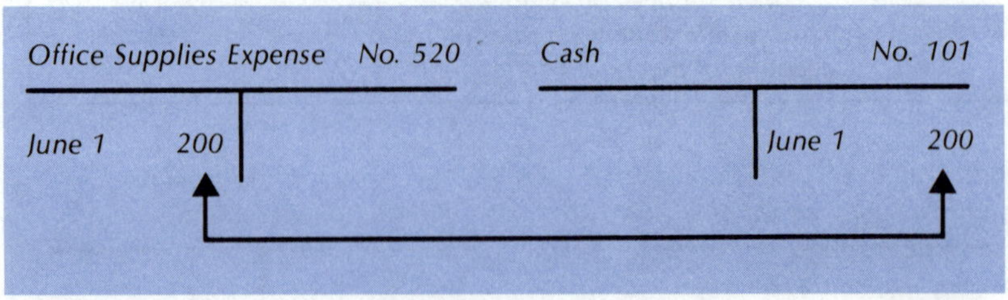

This is the adjustment entry which results because of the physical count of office supplies:

Office Supplies on Hand No. 106				*Office Supplies Expense No. 520*			
June 30	*125*			*June 1*	*200*	*June 30*	*125*

Analysis:

- Office Supplies on Hand has a debit balance of $125 and the Office Supplies Expense account has a debit balance of $75. The difference is that the expense account contains the change instead of the asset account. Because the closing of the books by means of the Revenue and Expense Summary will close the Office Supplies Expense account, bringing it to zero, any future adjustments, if they are required, will have to be carried out on the asset account Office Supplies on Hand.

The asset account tells you that the business owns so many dollars of office supplies. At the end of the accounting period, the business examines the physical asset to determine how much is still available. Any difference must now be accounted for. If the count shows that some of the asset has been used, an expense exists and must be recorded. The result of the analysis must be an accounting entry to reflect the changes.

Prepaid Insurance

Another prepaid expense in business is insurance. Insurance is purchased on assets (such as inventory, equipment, and building) to insure against loss due to theft, fire, flood, etc. Because insurance premiums must be paid in advance, usually yearly, only at the date of purchase does the asset Prepaid Insurance truly reflect an up-to-date balance. Therefore, this account should be adjusted periodically.

June 1 Wawdel Company issues a cheque for $1 200 to pay for comprehensive fire and theft insurance on the building and the contents of the business.

The entry causes the following:

June 1	*Prepaid Insurance*	*1 200*	
	Cash		*1 200*
	To pay for a one year insurance policy.		

Prepaid Insurance			*No. 105*	*Cash*			*No. 101*
June 1	*1 200*					*June 1*	*1 200*

Analysis:

- The company bought 12 months of insurance coverage for $1 200 ($100/month). The business now owns insurance coverage for one year with an unexpired cost on June 1 of $1 200.
- Since cash was paid it must be a credit entry.
- Note the change to prepaid insurance at the end of the month. The amount of protection offered is now 11 months, not 12 — 1/12th of the insurance coverage has been *used.* An expense exists, namely Insurance Expense for 1/12th of the $1 200 premium ($100). An adjustment is in order. Examine the following:

June 30	*Insurance Expense*	*100*	
	Prepaid Insurance		*100*
	To record the expired cost of one month of insurance.		

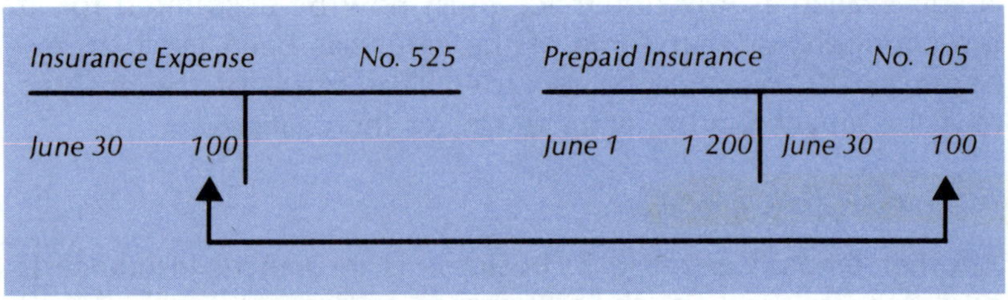

The company now owns 11 months of insurance coverage, $1 100. The current asset account Prepaid Insurance now reflects that amount, due to the adjustment illustrated above.

Other Prepaid Expenses

Other prepaid accounts are rent and advertising. Any time an expense is paid for in advance, for longer than one accounting period, it may be recorded as a prepaid expense. *Note:* If a firm pays for its rent only one month in advance, it is very unlikely that the company will call that amount prepaid rent. Instead, because it will last for less than one accounting period, it will be expensed immediately and listed as rent expense in the journal entry.

Current Assets Redefined

In Part 1, current assets were defined as cash and other assets expected to be converted into cash within one year of the date of the balance sheet. With the introduction of prepaid expenses, however, this definition must be expanded as follows:

GAAP for Defining Current Assets

Current assets are cash and other economic resources which are reasonably expected to be realized in cash, sold, or consumed during the normal operating cycle of the business.

From the above principle, note that two distinct types of assets are included in the definition of current assets.

1. • *Assets like Accounts Receivable and Inventory that are intended to be converted into cash during the normal operating cycle of the business.*

Operating cycle: the time it takes to complete the following: (1) purchase of merchandise; (2) sale of goods on credit; (3) collection of cash from accounts receivable.

The operating cycle is the average time period between the purchase of merchandise and the conversion of this merchandise back into cash. Most often this is one year (or less) from the date of the balance sheet.

2. • *Assets to be consumed during the normal operating cycle of the business.* These are identified as prepaid expenses (expenses which are unexpired costs [current assets] when they are acquired). Generally, they are expected to be consumed (their costs are to be expired) within one year of the date of the balance sheet. Remember, the expired cost of such prepaid expenses must be transferred to expense accounts by preparing adjusting entries.

In presenting the current asset section on any balance sheet, place those assets that are to be realized in cash before assets that will expire their costs while being used to support revenue-making activities. The following illustration shows that the liquidity order is shown before the listing of all prepaid expenses:

Wawdel Company
Partial Balance Sheet
June 30, 19-1

Current Assets:	
Cash	*$ 8 796.00*
Accounts Receivable	*5 400.00*
Inventory (at cost)	*4 200.00*
Supplies on Hand	*125.00*
Prepaid Insurance	*1 100.00*
Total Current Assets	*$19 621.00*

TOPIC 1 PROBLEMS

15-1 Prepare the appropriate adjustment entries in the General Journal for each of the following (unrelated) situations. Date all entries on April 30. (Include an explanation.)

a Supplies on Hand, April 1: $75; Supplies on Hand, April 30: $15.

b Supplies on Hand at the beginning of the accounting period: $410; Supplies on Hand at the end of the accounting period: $95.

c Prepaid Insurance, April 1: $960; Prepaid Insurance, April 30: $840.

d Prepaid Insurance, premium paid on February 1 for one-year policy, $600. Adjust Prepaid Insurance as of April 30.

e Prepaid Insurance at the beginning of the accounting period: $1 000; Expired Insurance as of the end of the accounting period: $400.

Key Check Figure Shop Supplies Expense = $740

15-2 The XYZ Company had shop supplies at the beginning of the year equal to $425. (Use the title *Shop Supplies.*) During the year they acquired additional supplies totalling $575. At year-end the physical count of supplies revealed a balance of $260. Prepare the necessary adjusting entry as of December 31. *Hint:* T-accounts might prove useful.

15-3 Given the following T-accounts and information, prepare adjusting entries on July 31 to update both accounts and post your journal entries to the T-accounts.

Office Supplies on Hand No. 105		
July 1	*120*	

Prepaid Insurance No. 108		
July 1	*300*	

Information

(i) A physical count of supplies indicates 200 units at $0.50 per unit.

(ii) The July 1 entry represents a one-year policy bought on that date.

15-4 Nuts and Bolts Hardware Company bought and paid for three months of advertising space at a total cost of $450 on October 1. It is company policy to prepare updated financial statements each month.

a Make the entry to show the purchase of the advertising space. Post to the appropriate T-accounts.

b Make the entry to show the adjusting entries on October 31. Post it and indicate the balance in the prepaid advertising account and in Advertising Expense in the post closing trial balance of the business.

15-5 Fresh and Clean Laundry Service bought cleaning supplies on March 1 totalling $2 400. They recorded this amount directly to Cleaning Supplies Expense and Cash. On March 31 they had used $2 100 of the supplies.

Open T-accounts for the various events. Record the postings that would occur as a result of the transactions on March 1 and March 31.

15-6 Sally's Stenographic Service rents office space by paying six months in advance. The business also rents all office equipment by paying three months in advance. The automobile that the business owns carries an insurance policy that is prepaid by the year. The trial balance illustrated below outlines the accounts of the business.

Sally's Stenographic Service
Trial Balance
May 1, 19—

Cash	101	$ 100	
Accounts Receivable	110	90	
Prepaid Office Rent	115	1 200	
Prepaid Equipment Rent	117	150	
Prepaid Car Insurance	119	840	
Bank Loan Payable	201		$ 500
S. Flood, Capital	301		280
S. Flood, Drawings	305	250	
Stenographic Service Revenue	401		5 000
Telephone Expense	510	150	
Wages Expense	520	3 000	
		$5 780	$5 780

Additional Information

(i) The Office Space Rent was last paid on May 1.
(ii) The Office Equipment Rent was last paid for on March 1.
(iii) The Car Insurance was last paid for on February 28.

a Adjust any accounts that require updating so that quarterly statements can be prepared on May 31.

b Make the necessary General Journal entries to complete the needed adjustments as of May 31. You may wish to use T-accounts to assist in organizing your figures.

c Prepare an income statement for the three months ended May 31.

d From the trial balance information and the adjustment figures, prepare a classified balance sheet.

Key Check Figure
Total Assets =
$1 820

15-7 Gorgand Company, a small retail merchandising firm, prepared the trial balance on page 504 at the end of their accounting year.

Additional Information

(i) The physical count of store supplies reveals a balance of $560.
(ii) The amount of used prepaid insurance is equal to $200.
(iii) Their physical inventory count reveals goods on hand equal to $7 700.

a Prepare the needed adjusting entries to update the business accounts.

b Prepare an income statement and a classified balance sheet for the year ended December 31, 19—.

Gorgand Company
Trial Balance
December 31, 19—

Cash	$ 1 000	
Accounts Receivable	3 000	
Inventory (January 1)	8 000	
Store Supplies on Hand	1 200	
Prepaid Insurance	900	
Store Equipment	12 000	
Office Equipment	5 000	
Bank Loan Payable		$ 8 000
Accounts Payable		1 300
P. Gorgand, Capital		15 870
P. Gorgand, Drawings	1 500	
Sales		45 500
Sales Returns and Allowances	250	
Sales Discounts	100	
Purchases	23 000	
Purchases Discounts		180
Transportation-in	1 000	
Sales Salaries Expense	10 600	
Heat, Light, and Power Expense	2 300	
Telephone Expense	250	
Advertising Expense	750	
	$70 850	$70 850

Key Check Figure
Net Income = $6 290

TOPIC 2 ADJUSTING FOR BAD DEBTS EXPENSE

Bad debts expense: the cost of granting credit to an uncollectable accounts receivable.

Many businesses sell their services and/or products on credit to make their product more attractive to the customer. Some credit customers, however, will not or cannot pay. Such an uncollectable account is called a bad debts expense or Doubtful Accounts Expense. Since this is an expense account and the bad debts situation is constantly changing, this account is a good example of a potential adjusting entry. The following illustration shows how a bad debt occurs, and how the Wawdel Company deals with it.

December 3, 19-1 Sold merchandise on credit for $200 to Company X; terms 2/10, n/30.

General Ledger | **Accts. Rec. Subsidiary Ledger**

Accounts Receivable			No. 110
Dec. 3	200		

Sales			No. 401
		Dec. 3	200

Company X			
Dec. 3	200		

Company X did not take the discount offered, so the $200 amount was in the 19-1 year-end accounts receivable and sales figures. Despite all attempts in the early months of 19-2, Wawdel Company was unable to collect the $200.

Analyzing the Direct Write-off Method

April 2, 19-2 Three months after the amount was first due, management decides to write off the $200 of Company X as a bad debt.

19-2				
April 2	*Bad Debts Expense*	*508*	*200*	
	Accts. Rec./Company X	*110/√*		*200*
	To write off the account as uncollectable.			

Accts. Rec. Subsidiary Ledger

Company X

Dec. 2	200	Apr. 2	200

General Ledger

Bad Debts Expense			*No. 508*
19-2			
Apr. 2	*200*		

Accounts Receivable			*No. 110*
		19-2	
		Apr. 2	*200*

Analysis:

- The expense is called *Bad Debts Expense* and it is a debit entry.
- The credit entry directly reduces both the Company X accounts receivable subsidiary ledger account and accounts receivable control. Company X is removed from the books and the accounts receivable control account has been reduced.

The bad debts expense is recorded in year 19-2 but the Revenue was recorded in year 19-1. Clearly there is a violation of the GAAP called the matching principle, because related revenues fail to match related expense. As a result, both years' financial statements will be incorrect. Year 19-1 will understate the expenses and thus overstate the net income. Year 19-2 will overstate the expenses, thus understating the net income. Both net income figures are in error.

Examine the comparative income statement illustrated below. (Assume that only the Bad Debts Expense numbers are different in the two years to clearly show the effect of bad debts on net income.)

Wawdel Company
Comparative Income Statement

	For the Year Ended 19-1	For the Year Ended 19-2
Revenue	*$200 000*	*$200 000*
Gross Profit from Sales	*75 000*	*75 000*
Expenses:		
Bad Debts Expense	*0*	*200*
	$ 75 000	*$ 74 800*
	Overstated	**Understated**

The owner's equity (capital) in the balance sheet will be overstated in 19-1, because net income was overstated; the Capital account in 19-2 will be understated, because net income was understated. Some accountants will argue that the direct write-off method is acceptable if the amounts processed are insignificant. This argument, however, does not alter the fact that the direct write-off method is in clear violation of the matching principle. The proper method for dealing with bad debts will now be examined in detail.

Analyzing the Matching Entry

To solve the problems created by the direct write-off method, an adjusting entry is required at year-end to record the bad debts expense. This immediately creates two problems: (1) How much should be debited to the bad debts expense account? Bad debts are not realized for several months after the actual sale, as illustrated by the Company X example. (2) Which accounts receivable accounts must be reduced?

(1) The bad debts expense must be estimated. The company studies past company default records and develops a workable policy. The exact mechanics will be examined later in this Topic.

(2) None of the accounts receivable must be reduced! The entire receivable amount is reduced, by using an "allowance" account, the *Allowance for Bad Debts*. This amount is listed immediately after the accounts receivable in the current asset

section of the balance sheet. See the illustration below. Allowance for Bad Debts contains the estimate of the accounts receivable that are expected to be lost during that period. It is a contra account, because of its effect on the accounts receivable account. To review, the term *contra* implies that the balance is contrary to the normal balance of the account that it affects. In the analysis of the journal entry below, notice that Allowance for Bad Debts is assigned the next account number.

Partial Balance Sheet
As at December 31, 19-1

Current Assets:		
Cash		*$ 6 000*
Accounts Receivable	*$14 000*	
Allowance for Bad Debts	*1 000*	
(Net Realizable Amount)		*13 000*

Wawdel Company
Chart of Accounts

CURRENT ASSETS
110 Accounts Receivable
111 Allowance for Bad Debts

Let us observe what happens as the business sets up the Allowance for Bad Debts account and makes the Bad Debts Expense entry with an adjustment in the General Journal on December 31.

WHAT HAPPENS	ACCOUNTING RULE	ENTRY
The estimated expense for bad debts decreases owner's equity by $1 000.	To decrease owner's equity, debit the account that caused the decrease.	Debit: Bad Debts Expense $1 000.
The amount realizable from Accounts Receivable decreases by $1 000.	To decrease an asset, credit the account.	Credit: Allowance for Bad Debts $1 000.

Accounts Receivable	*No. 110*
19-1	
Dec. 31 1 000	

Allowance for Bad Debts	*No. 111*
	19-1
	Dec. 31 1 000

Bad Debts Expense	*No. 508*
19-1	
Dec. 31 1 000	

December 31 Wawdel Company estimates its losses to bad debts will be $1 000 in 19-1.

Analysis:

- After the estimate of Bad Debts Expense ($1 000) has been

determined, the bad debts expense amount can be included in the income statement at year-end. See the illustration.

Wawdel Company
Income Statement
For the Year Ended December 31, 19-1

Revenue:		
Revenue from Sales		*$200 000*
Less: Cost of Goods Sold		*125 000*
Gross Profit from Sales		*75 000*
Less Operating Expenses (includes $1 000 for Bad Debts Expense)		*50 000*
Net Income	**These are estimates.**	*$ 25 000*

• Since bad debts expense is only an estimate, the net income is only a fair calculation, not an exact one.

• The allowance for bad debts is now included in the current assets section of the balance sheet (see previous illustration of Wawdel's partial balance sheet), creating a "net realizable" accounts receivable figure. No specific account receivable is affected, but accounts receivable have been reduced overall by the expected loss.

Analyzing the Write-off

What happens on April 2, 19-2 when management decides to write off Company X's account?

April 2, 19-2 Three months after the amount first became due, management decides to write off the $200 charged to Company X's account as a bad debt.

GENERAL JOURNAL — **Page** *10*

Date *19-2*	**Account Title and Explanation**	**Post. Ref.**	**Debit**	**Credit**
Apr. 2	*Allowance for Bad Debts*	*111*	*200 00*	
	Accounts Receivable, Company X	*110 ✓*		*200 00*
	To write off the Company X account as a bad debt.			

Analysis:

• After the General Journal entry has been made, the amounts are posted to the appropriate accounts. The debit entry to Allowance for Bad Debts reduces that account by $200 to $800 (the company estimate of potential bad debt losses has been reduced to $800).

- Nothing happens to bad debts expense. That account's job, to match estimated bad debts expense to the reported revenues in 19-1, has been done. The Allowance for Bad Debts account now absorbs any actual write-offs. Nothing else needs to be done with bad debts expense until the end of 19-2.
- The credit entry causes the Accounts Receivable Subsidiary Ledger account, Company X, to be closed — brought equal to zero. That is the intent of the write-off. The accounts receivable control account has also been reduced by $200.
- Accounts receivable have been reduced, by $200, but so has the Allowance for Bad Debts account. Therefore, Net Accounts Receivable has not changed. It still reflects the amount of the receivables that the company believes it can collect.

Net Accounts Receivable: Accounts Receivable less Allowance for Bad Debts.

	Before the Write-off	After the Write-off
Accounts Receivable	*$12 000*	*$11 800*
Allowance for Bad Debts	*1 000*	*800*
Net Amount of Receivables	*$11 000*	*$11 000*

At the end of the year, the Allowance for Bad Debts account will probably have some balance. If the balance is a credit, the estimate of bad debts was too high. If it is a debit, the company lost more to bad debts than estimated. In either case, the adjusting entry made at the next year-end will take this balance into account. This will be explained in the last part of this Topic.

Collection of a Debt Written Off

What happens when a customer whom the company wrote off suddenly pays, in full or in part?

May 5, 19-2 Company X sends a cheque for $200 to settle its overdue account. With the cheque is a letter of apology for the late remittance.

GENERAL JOURNAL — **Page** *12*

Date *19-2*	Account Title and Explanation	Post. Ref.	Debit	Credit
May 5	*Accounts Receivable/Company X*	*✓/110*	*200 00*	
	Allowance for Bad Debts	*111*		*200 00*
	To reverse the write-off of Company X.			

Analysis:

- Because the amount Company X owes no longer exists on the books, the write-off is reversed. This re-establishes Company X as a customer on the books.
- Record the receipt of cash in the cash receipts journal and the reduction of the Accounts Receivable/Company X account to zero. If a partial payment was received, the account, of course, would show a balance still owing. After such an entry is made, a credit report is prepared to determine the new credit standing of this customer.

Methods of Estimating Bad Debts Expense

Several methods may be used to estimate the bad debts expense for an accounting period. Two of these methods will be examined here: (1) aging the accounts receivable and (2) taking a percentage of the net sales.

Aging the Accounts Receivable

Aging of accounts receivable: classifying the balance of each account according to the age of the claim.

In Chapter 7 you learned that many firms prepare and mail a monthly statement of account in the form of an *aged* statement. Similarly, many firms, particularly large ones with many accounts receivable, use a method called aging of accounts receivable. In the past this method was long and difficult, but modern computers can do the job quickly and relatively inexpensively.

Aging requires a classification of every receivable on the company books into an aging category such as: not past due, or past due 1-30 days, 31-60 days, 61-90 days, or over 90 days — the category is determined by management's desires. The process of aging can be seen in four stages:

(1) Preparing a Schedule of Accounts by Age Each receivable is listed by name and balance. It is then categorized as *not*

Wawdel Company
Schedule of Accounts Receivable by Age
December 31, 19-2

			DAYS PAST DUE			
ACCOUNT WITH	BALANCE	NOT PAST DUE	1-30	31-60	61-90	OVER 90
Anderson Hardware	$ 600	$ 600				
Eglinton Hardware Centre	900	400	$ 500			
Hyland Hardware	700			$ 700		
Reid Home Hardware	300				$100	$200
Summers Hardware Limited	1 000	900	100			
Thornhill Home Hardware	200	200				
Young Hardware Centre	100					100
Totals	$11 500	$8 000	$1 500	$1 100	$500	$400

past due or *past due*. A typical schedule is illustrated on page 510. A customer may fall under two headings if more than one invoice is outstanding. Invoices still within the credit terms are entered in the *Not Past Due* column; all others are broken down according to the listed column headings. The schedule can be checked for accuracy by adding all the column totals and comparing that sum to the sum of the *Balance* column.

(2) Estimating the Percentage of Probable Losses Once totalled, the estimated losses are determined by multiplying the totals by some percentage. Even the *Not Past Due* column can be expected to generate some losses. Logically, the further past due, the greater the chance of loss. The percentage figures used are arrived at from past experience of actual losses. See the illustration below.

(3) Applying the Percentages Prepare a chart similar to the one shown. The amounts are multiplied by the percent and the losses are estimated and totalled. This estimate will be the basis for the year-end adjusting entry.

Percentage of Probable Losses	
Over 90 days	**50%**
61-90 days	**25%**
31-60 days	**10%**
1-30 days	**2%**
Not past due	**1%**

Age Group (in days)	Total	Estimated Percentage	Estimated Loss
Over 90	$ 400	50%	$200
61-90	500	25%	125
31-60	1 100	10%	110
1-30	1 500	2%	30
0	8 000	1%	80
	$11 500		$545

(4) Recording the Adjusting Entry The estimated loss due to bad debts is now journalized in the General Journal as an adjusting entry at year-end by debiting Bad Debts Expense and crediting Allowance for Bad Debts. One of three conditions will exist:

(1) If the Allowance for Bad Debts has a zero balance, the dollar amount calculated will be entered. For Wawdel Company this would be $545.

(2) If the Allowance for Bad Debts has a credit balance, say $100, *deduct* the credit balance from the dollar amount calculated and record $445 in the journal entry. When posted, Allowance for Bad Debts will once again show $545, the amount the business has expected to lose this past accounting period.

(3) If the Allowance for Bad Debts has a debit balance, say $155, *add* $155 to the dollar amount calculated. For Wawdel Company, the journal entry would be $700 ($155 + $545). Since the allowance for bad debts in the journal entry is a credit entry, when the $700 credit is added to the $155 debit the balance again returns to $545, the amount the firm expects to lose. If care is taken, this is a reliable and easy calculation and entry.

Percentage of Net Sales

Under this method the percentage is based on past experience within your own business and related businesses. For example, if, over the past ten years, your business has lost 0.5% of all net sales to bad debts, this trend will likely continue. Four points must be considered.

(1) The base is net sales. Sales R & A and Sales Discounts must be deducted first.

(2) Only credit sales should be examined (you cannot suffer a bad debt if the sale was paid with cash).

Sales		**$111 200**
Less:		
Sales R & A	**$700**	
Sales Disc.	**500**	
Net Sales		**$110 000**

(3) Now that the base is established (see the margin calculation), multiply that number by the percentage calculated for Wawdel Company. Thus $110 000 × 0.5% = $550 ($110 000 × .005).

(4) The amount of the adjustment will be the computed amount regardless of any previous balance in Allowance for Bad Debts. Why? Under the percentage of net sales method, the estimate is made on the basis of the relationship between bad debts and net sales for that period regardless of any entry made in previous periods, rather than on a total estimate based on bad debts expense and the year-end accounts receivable.

TOPIC 2 PROBLEMS

15-8 Make the necessary General Journal entries to record the following adjustments related to bad debts expense. Assume that management prefers to use the method of aging accounts receivable to estimate the bad debts expense in each case below.

a The aged accounts receivable at the end of December shows that $850 is estimated to be uncollectable. The Allowance for Bad Debts account has no balance.

b The aged accounts receivable at the end of October shows that $385 is estimated to be uncollectable. The Allowance for Bad Debts account shows a credit balance of $85.

c The aged accounts receivable at the end of March shows that $1 235 is estimated to be uncollectable. The Allowance for Bad Debts account shows a debit balance of $100.

15-9 Record in the General Journal the necessary entries for the following (unrelated) transactions. Use the Allowance for Bad Debts account.

a Management decides to write off the account of T. Oden. The balance owing in this account is $325.

b The company receives a cheque for $415 in the mail from D. Enders to cover his account in full. D. Enders's account had been previously written off as a bad debt. *Remember:* this takes two entries.

c The company determines that it has net sales equal to $25 000. In the past this company has lost one-half of 1% of all net sales to bad debts. The Allowance for Bad Debts account has no balance.

d The company receives a cheque in the mail from Ralph Knotter for $100. He wishes to re-establish his business with our firm. His account, totalling $350 had been written off as a bad debt some three months ago.

15-10 On December 1, 19-1, the Allowance for Bad Debts account shows a credit balance of $500. In the General Journal, make the necessary routine, adjusting, and closing entries for the following transactions. Use T-accounts.

Dec. 5 The company decides to write off the account of Mark Fatherson. Fatherson currently owes the company $210.
9 The company also decides to write off the account of G. Howe. G. Howe owes $410.
14 The company receives payment in full from P. Henderson. The Henderson account had been written off as uncollectable. Amount $125.
31 The company uses the aging of receivables method to estimate uncollectable accounts. This year's estimate is $675.
31 The company closes the books.

Jan. 10 Mark Fatherson sends a cheque to the company for $210. Accompanying the cheque is a letter of apology and an explanation for the late payment.
31 The company receives a letter stating that Betty Upbridge, a customer, has gone bankrupt. A cheque for $51 is enclosed. This is all the company can expect to receive against her outstanding balance of $510.

15-11 Suppose that, in Problem 15-10, management decided to use the percentage of sales method to estimate the accounting period's bad debts expense. On December 31, 19-1 the trial balance reported as follows: Sales, $62 525; Sales Returns and Allowances, $420; Sales Discounts, $505. The percentage of net sales believed to be uncollectable is 1%.

Prepare General Journal entries for each of the transactions in Problem 15-10 under the above circumstances.

15-12 Markham Manufacturing Company has prepared the following list of accounts receivable. The balance in the Allowance for Bad Debts account on December 31, 19-1 is $190.00 CR. The company offers all customers terms of n/30.

Customer	Invoice Date	Amount
Bakers Manufacturing	June 10, 19-1	$ 500.00
Carter Truck Bodies	July 31, 19-1	300.00
Grady Supplies	November 30, 19-1	1 500.00
Markham Production Comp.	December 4, 19-1	8 000.00
Regal Products Ltd.	November 1, 19-1	900.00
	December 1, 19-1	2 300.00

Watson Manufacturing Ltd.	October 12, 19-1	3 300.00
Others	December 22, 19-1	25 700.00

a Prepare from the list of customers a Schedule of Accounts Receivable by Age, as illustrated on page 510.

b Prepare a table showing the percentage of probable losses similar to the one shown on page 511. Use the percentages shown on page 511 to make your calculations.

Key Check Figure Over 90 Days: $800

c Prepare the necessary adjusting entry to record the Bad Debts expense for year-end. Prepare the closing entry for Bad Debts Expense.

15-13 The following data was taken from the records of Windsor Wholesale Distributors.

	Year 19-1	Year 19-2	Year 19-3
Net Credit Sales	$1 000 000	$1 250 000	$1 200 000
Collection of Receivables during the Year	895 000	1 190 500	1 183 500
Balance of Accounts Receivable at December 31	300 000	350 000	360 000
Bad Debts Written Off during Year	5 000	9 500	8 000
Bad Debts Recovered during Year	0	0	1 500

On January 1, 19-1, the accounts receivable balance was $200 000. Prior to year 19-1, the firm followed a policy of writing off bad debts under the direct write-off method. On December 31, 19-1, management decided to provide for the estimated uncollectables so that the net income would be determined more appropriately, by a better matching of the expenses and revenues. In this connection, the controller provided the following estimates under two methods:

Method of Estimating Uncollectables	19-1	19-2	19-3
Aging	$ 7 500	$ 9 000	$13 000
Percentage of Net Credit Sales	10 000	12 500	12 000

Assume that management asks you to use both methods for purposes of comparison.

a Journalize the necessary entries to record all transactions relating to bad debts (show entries under both methods for all three years).

b Use T-accounts to reconstruct ledger accounts for Accounts Receivable, Allowance for Bad Debts, and Bad Debts Expense (include the year-end adjusting entry). *Note:* Show separate ledgers for each method of estimating bad debts expense.

c Prepare partial balance sheets as at December 31, 19-2 and 19-3, showing Accounts Receivable and Allowance for Bad Debts under each method.

d What amounts should be shown as Bad Debts Expense on the income statement under each method for the years 19-1, 19-2, and 19-3? Show the solutions.

Key C
Bad D
Dec.
$10 5

TOPIC 3 ADJUSTING FOR DEPRECIATION EXPENSE

The ordinary meaning of depreciation as it is defined in common usage does not apply to the study of accounting. You must learn how this term is used in accounting and specifically how it is used in accordance with accounting principles.

One way to learn the correct accounting use of depreciation is through the analysis of why any business acquires fixed assets such as a building, equipment of various sorts, machinery, delivery truck, etc. Examine the questions and answers that follow.

- *Why does a business acquire fixed assets like a building?*

A business acquires them to carry on business.

- *What is meant by the phrase* to carry on business?

The chief purpose of any business operation is to make money. This is accomplished by generating revenue exceeding the expenses incurred in a particular accounting period.

This last answer is most important, for it leads to the acknowledgement of a very important principle in the study of accounting:

GAAP for Acquiring Fixed Assets

Fixed assets such as buildings, machinery, delivery trucks, etc. are acquired to generate revenue or to support revenue-making activities.

Think of acquiring fixed assets as services to be received by the business over a period of future years. For example:

(1) Acquiring a building may be regarded as payment in advance for several years' supply of housing services. The building "houses" the sales personnel who sell goods or services; it "houses" the equipment and office personnel required to support the operations of the business; it "houses" the inventory to be sold to customers; and it "houses" the customers who shop at the business location. The building has been acquired to *support revenue-making activities* for a number of years to come. It was not acquired for the purpose of resale. If it were, it would cease to operate the moment the building was sold.

(2) A delivery truck which has been purchased offers transportation services to the business for a period of years or so many thousands of kilometres. The purpose of acquiring a truck is to *support the revenue-making activities* of a business. It has not been acquired for resale.

Remember, fixed assets have been acquired to *generate revenue* or *support revenue-making activities* for years to come.

• *What GAAP is used to interpret the dollar amounts assigned in reporting fixed assets on a balance sheet?*
The cost principle. All fixed assets are reported in accounts and in the balance sheet on the basis of what they cost the business.

• *If a business acquires a building at a cost of $48 000, how long will the building last in order to generate revenue for the business?*
One can estimate that the building will last for 10, 15, or 20 years.

• *Won't the building last forever?*
No, because use and the outside elements (sun, wind, rain, etc.) will wear it out — a building's useful life is limited by a factor called physical deterioration.

Physical deterioration: Wear and tear resulting from use and climatic factors.

• *Are there any other factors limiting the useful life of a fixed asset like a building?*
Yes. In time, an old building may not attract so many customers, as there are those who prefer to shop in a modern store.

• *What do accountants call this factor?*
This factor is referred to as obsolescence

Obsolescence: the process of becoming out of date.

You have now learned two important accounting concepts: (1) that fixed assets are acquired by business to generate revenue or support revenue-making activities; and (2) that physical deterioration and obsolescence limit the length of time fixed assets can generate revenue. The next set of questions will introduce a third important concept.

• *Let's assume (1) management has decided that the estimated useful life of the building is 20 years and (2) the building will be worthless at the end of that time. What would management expect from the use of the building in that 20 years?*
Management would expect to obtain housing benefits to assist the revenue-making operations for the next 20 years.

• *If the building was acquired at the beginning of this year for $48 000 to generate revenue for 20 years, should the business charge this year's net income, $15 000, with the entire cost of the building? In other words, should the accountant show an expense of $48 000 in this year's income statement?*
No.

• *Why would it be wrong to match the entire cost of the building with this year's revenue?*
It would not be fair. The building will generate revenue for another 19 years. The fairest method is to spread the cost as evenly as possible over the useful life of the asset — to spread the cost of $48 000 over 20 years.

The last answer brings us to the GAAP of matching revenues and expenses within the same accounting period. Since the building is to generate revenue for 20 years, a fair proportion of the cost of the building must be matched in each of those 20 years. This important concept of spreading is illustrated through the following series of diagrams.

Diagram 1: Building costs at the beginning of the first year. (The building has yet to be used.)

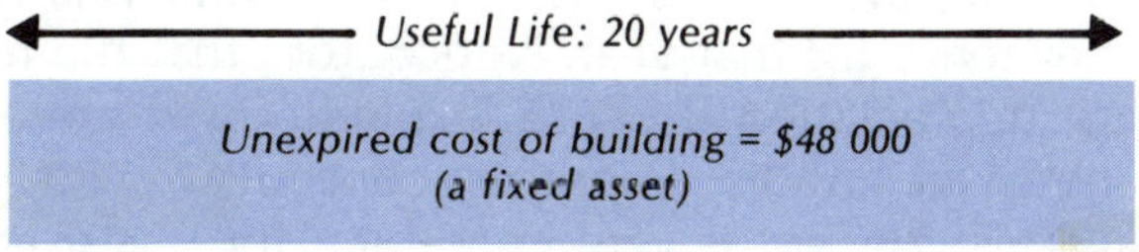

Observe from the diagram that the cost of the building is being analyzed at the beginning of year 1. *No cost of the building is charged against the revenue until the building is used.* Since the building has yet to be used, the cost is said to be *unexpired.* Any unexpired cost that will generate revenue or support revenue-making activities for a period longer than one accounting period (a year) will be reported on the balance sheet under the heading *Fixed Assets* (or *Plant and Equipment* or *Long-Lived Assets*). As you will recall, unexpired costs such as prepaid expenses are reported under *Current Assets,* because their costs are expected to expire within one year of the date of the balance sheet. Now let's examine what happens at the end of the first year of using the building to produce revenue.

Diagram 2: Building costs at the end of the first year.

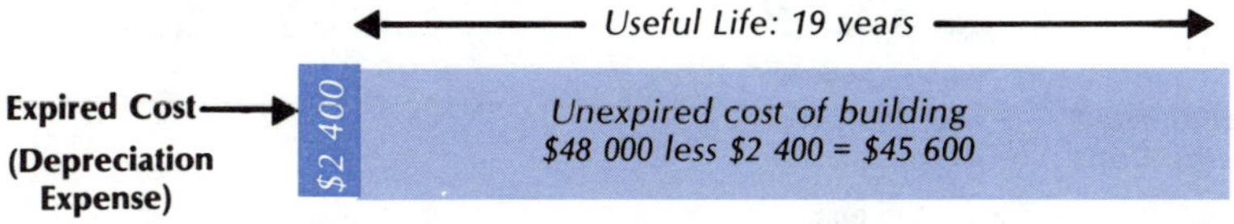

This second diagram reveals an expired cost portion of $2 400; that is, $2 400 of the cost of the building has been used up at the end of the first year. Obviously, the expired cost was calculated to be 1/20 of $48 000, since the building was estimated to have a useful life of 20 years. As you will recall from the study of prepaid expenses, the expired cost must be removed from the unexpired cost to be recognized as an expense. In the language of accounting, the expired cost of a fixed asset is known by the special name depreciation expense. It is important to emphasize that depreciation expense is the used (expired) cost portion of a fixed asset for a particular accounting period. Examine the next diagram.

Depreciation expense: the expired cost of using a fixed asset.

Diagram 3: Building costs at the end of the second year.

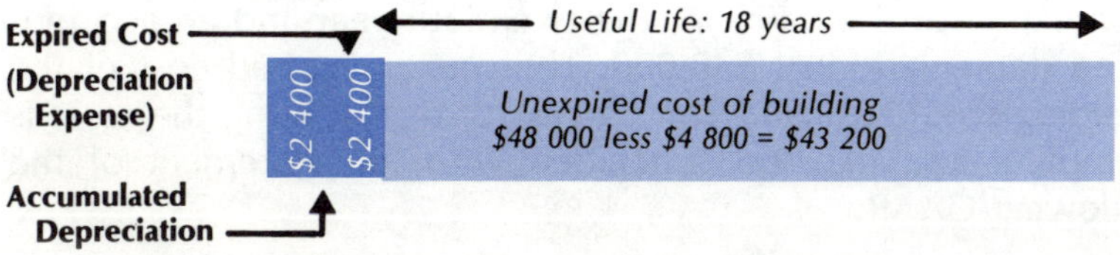

Accumulated depreciation: the total of the expired costs of any one asset.

When the building costs are analyzed at the end of the second year, two important concepts are evident. From the diagram, notice that the expired cost for the second year is the depreciation expense for that year. Notice, too, that the first and second years' depreciation expense (expired costs) are added together to introduce another important concept: accumulated depreciation. This concept is very important, for it is used to report the calculation of the unexpired cost of the building at the end of the second year. The balance sheet illustrated in the margin shows the reporting of the original cost of the building less its accumulated depreciation. In other words, the reader of the balance sheet should interpret this calculation as the original cost of the fixed asset less the accumulation of expired costs. You will find that this type of calculation is required for all fixed assets which expire their costs over their useful life. The next diagram shows the concept of depreciation expense and accumulated depreciation.

Partial Balance Sheet
(as at the end of the second year)

Fixed Assets (at cost):	
Building	*$48 000*
Less: Accumulated Depreciation	*4 800*
	$43 200

Diagram 4: Building costs at the end of the fifth year.

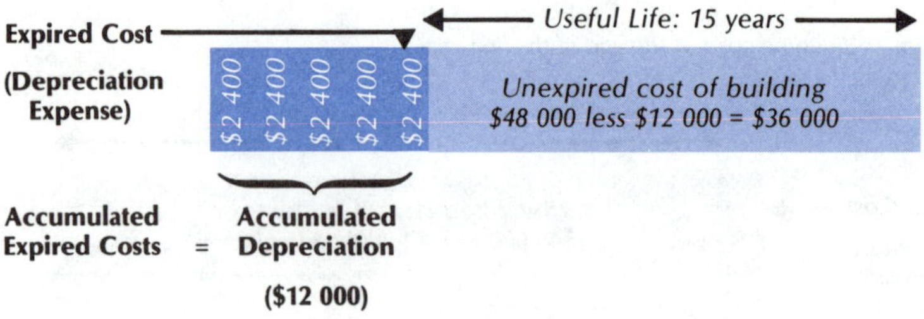

Partial Income Statement
For the Year Ended December 31, 19-5

Operating Expenses:	
Depreciation Expense on Buildings	*$2 400*

Partial Balance Sheet
as at December 31, 19-5

Fixed Assets (at cost):	
Building	*$48 000*
Less: Accumulated Depreciation	*12 000*
	$36 000

Notice that the expired cost (Depreciation Expense) is singled out for the fifth year. This calculation is no different from the previous ones, since 1/20 of the original cost has been identified. What is clearly shown, however, is the concept of accumulating the depreciation expense over five years. At the end of the fifth year, the accumulation of expired cost of the building is $12 000. This amount would be used in the reporting of the fixed asset amount on the fifth year's balance sheet. Of course, the depreciation expense of $2 400 would be matched against the revenue of the fifth year to calculate fairly the net income (or loss) for that accounting period.

The concept of spreading the cost of the building over its useful life may be illustrated in diagrams to the end of the twentieth year. Obviously, the last diagram would show a depreciation expense of $2 400 for the twentieth year and an accumulated depreciation of $48 000. Thus, no unexpired cost of the building would remain. The process of depreciating the asset is complete and may be concluded with the statement of the following GAAP:

Depreciation is a process of allocating the cost of a fixed asset over its estimated useful life. It is *not* a process of evaluation.

GAAP for Defining Depreciation

The above principle clearly defines depreciation as it applies to accounting practice. Notice that it emphasizes the process of allocation — spreading the cost of the asset over its useful life. In accounting language, depreciation must refer to the process of converting the original cost of fixed assets into expenses, that is, into expired costs. In other words, the expired cost must be matched against the revenue earned for the same accounting period. Failure to provide for depreciation expense would result in understating the total expenses of the period and consequently in overstating the net income.

There is, however, one fixed asset that does not depreciate — land. The cost of land must not be matched against the revenue of any accounting period. There are two reasons why land does not depreciate. (1) Land is acquired solely with the idea of serving as a site on which the depreciable building will be constructed. (2) Land is regarded as having unlimited life because its cost can be recovered once the building is eliminated. On any balance sheet, therefore, land is placed under *Fixed Assets* at its original cost, but there will be no accumulated depreciation. For this reason, land must be separated from Buildings on a balance sheet.

Recording Depreciation Expense

On the basis of your experience with other adjusting entries, you should have a good idea of how the depreciation entry will be recorded. Check your thoughts against the illustration on page 520.

Analysis:

- The debit entry describes a specific depreciation account.
- In the chart of accounts the company assigns a separate depreciation expense account for each asset being depreciated. Depreciation expense, like any other expense, is matched against the revenues of the period. For this reason the company must calculate the depreciation expense at year-end for that accounting period, in order to have the correct amount of depreciation expense to match against the corresponding revenues.
- The depreciation expense is, of course, closed at period-end to the Revenue and Expense Summary as part of the routine closing.
- The credit entry is an accumulation account.
- In the chart of accounts the company assigns each accumulated depreciation account to its related fixed asset account. Accumulated Depreciation/Building is the contra account of Building.

GENERAL JOURNAL — Page 20

Date 19-2	Account Title and Explanation	Post. Ref.	Debit	Credit
Dec. 31	Depreciation Expense/Building	510	2 400 00	
	Accumulated Depreciation/Building	112		2 400 00
	To record one year's depreciation on the building.			

Wawdel Company
Chart of Accounts

EXPENSES
510 Depreciation Expense/Building
511 Depreciation Expense/Warehouse Equipment
512 Depreciation Expense/Office Equipment
513 Depreciation Expense/Delivery Trucks

Wawdel Company
Chart of Accounts

FIXED ASSETS
110 Land
111 Building
112 Accumulated Depreciation/Building
113 Warehouse Equipment
114 Accumulated Depreciation/Warehouse Equipment
115 Office Equipment
116 Accumulated Depreciation/Office Equipment
117 Delivery Trucks
118 Accumulated Depreciation/Delivery Trucks

• The cost principle requires that a business always report the fixed assets at their original cost price. Only when the accumulated depreciation account value is deducted from this original price can the unexpired cost of that fixed asset be accurately presented. This accumulated depreciation will not be closed at the end of an accounting period, because it represents the accumulation of depreciation expense. Look for a related accumulated depreciation account with every fixed asset account — except, of course, Land.

Methods of Estimating Depreciation Expense

When depreciation is spread out in equal amounts over several periods, this is known as the *straight-line method.* It is very popular. The calculation is as follows:

$$\text{Straight-Line Depreciation} = \frac{\text{Asset Cost} - \text{Disposal Value}}{\text{Estimated Life}}$$

Disposal Value: estimated value of the fixed asset when it is sold, scrapped, or traded.

Asset Cost is the original cost figure of the asset. *Disposal Value* is the estimated value of the fixed asset when it is sold, scrapped, or traded. *Estimated Useful Life* is management's best determination of the useful life of the asset. Since the estimated useful life is a key part of the calculation, and is an estimate, as is the disposal value, the final calculation of depreciation can only be an estimated figure.

There are several other methods of estimating depreciation, but we will examine only one more, later on in this book.

Study the following asset from the time it is bought until it is disposed of.

January 1, 19-1 Issued a cheque for $700 to purchase an electronic typewriter for the office.

General Ledger

Office Equipment	No. 115
19-1	
Jan. 1 700	

Cash	No. 101
	19-1
	Jan. 1 700

Fixed Asset Subsidiary Ledger

Typewriter 4082611	
19-1	
Jan. 1 700	

Analysis:

- Record the entry in the cash payments journal with a debit to the fixed asset Office Equipment and a credit to Cash.
- The fixed asset ledger, which maintains a list of each individual fixed asset, must be debited for the same amount as the Office Equipment account. Most large firms own many pieces of equipment, such as typewriters, calculators, filing cabinets, desks, chairs, etc. It would not be practical to open separate General Ledger accounts for each, but it is necessary to account for all equipment collectively and individually. The General Ledger account Office Equipment fulfills the first task and the fixed asset subsidiary ledger the second.
- Within the fixed asset ledger, each asset has its own record card listing.
- Each card contains a listing of all information needed for the calculation and recording of depreciation of that asset over its useful life. Refer to page 522, and examine the ledger card.
- The total of all the individual items is identified in the General Ledger in the office equipment account. This General Ledger account acts as a control account similar to the control for accounts receivable or accounts payable.

Fixed asset ledger: a subsidiary ledger containing a card for each fixed asset.

December 31, 19-1 An adjusting entry is made to record the dollar result of using the typewriter for one year. Management has estimated a useful life of five years and a disposal value of $100 for this type of office equipment.

SUBSIDIARY FIXED ASSET RECORD

ITEM Typewriter — GENERAL LEDGER ACCOUNT Office Equipment

SERIAL NO. 4082611 — PURCHASED FROM IBM Canada Ltd.

DESCRIPTION IBM Selectric II — LOCATION Accounting Department

ORIGINAL COST $700 — AGE WHEN ACQUIRED New

ESTIMATED USEFUL LIFE 5 yrs. — ESTIMATED SCRAP OR TRADE-IN VALUE $100 — ANNUAL DEPRECIATION $120

DATE			EXPLANATION	FIXED ASSET ACCOUNT			ACCUMULATED DEPRECIATION			BOOK VALUE
Year	Mo.	Day		DEBIT	CREDIT	BALANCE	DEBIT	CREDIT	BALANCE	
19-1	01	01	*Purchased*	700 00		700 00				700 00
19-1	12	31						120 00	120 00	580 00
19-2	12	31						120 00	240 00	460 00
19-3	12	31						120 00	360 00	340 00
19-4	12	31						120 00	480 00	220 00
19-5	12	31						120 00	600 00	100 00
19-5	12	31	*Sold*		700 00	– 00	600 00		– 00	– 00

Sold, Traded, or Scrapped to: H. J. King 19-5 12 31 — Amount Received: $100

Controlling Account in General Ledger (General Ledger Account)

Depreciation Information (Annual Depreciation)

Current Unexpired Cost (Book Value)

Entries Affecting Fixed Asset Account in General Ledger (Fixed Asset Account columns)

Entries Affecting Contra Account in General Ledger (Accumulated Depreciation columns)

Balance of Fixed Asset Account Minus Accumulated Depreciation (Book Value column)

Depreciation Expense/ Office Equipment No. 512		Accumulated Depreciation/ Office Equipment No. 116	
19-1 Dec. 31 120			19-1 Dec. 31 120

Original Cost	$700
Less: Disposal Value	100
Total Depreciation	$600
Divided by: Years of Estimated Useful Life	5
Yearly Depreciation	$120

Analysis:

- Using a straight-line method of estimating the depreciation expense, calculate the figure by substituting the numbers given in the transaction into the equation shown earlier. The margin shows another method of arriving at the same figure.
- From the original price, subtract the disposal value. This represents the unexpired cost to be allocated over the next five years.
- Since all years are considered identical under the straight-line method, simply divide by 5 and your answer is one full year of depreciation for the next five years. If you wished to know the depreciation by the month, you would divide one year's depreciation by 12.
- There is no change at all to the fixed asset Office Equipment; instead, the amount is recorded, as a credit, to the contra account Accumulated Depreciation/Office Equipment.
- The current unexpired cost of office equipment or the Book Value is the difference between the two accounts. Remember that the Depreciation Expense account will be closed to the R & E Summary during the closing of the books at year-end.
- In each subsequent year, the Accumulated Depreciation/Office Equipment account will increase by $120 until at the end of year 5 the business disposes of the asset.

Book Value: Original Asset Cost less Accumulated Depreciation.

December 31, 19-5 After the adjusting entry is made to record the final year's depreciation, the typewriter is sold for $100 cash. Two entries must be analyzed.

Office Equipment No. 115		Accumulated Depreciation/ Office Equipment No. 116		Depreciation Expense/ Office Equipment No. 512	
19-1 700			19-1 120	19-5 Dec. 31 120	
			19-2 120		
			19-3 120		
			19-4 120		
			19-5 120		

Cash			No. 101
19-5			
Dec. 31	100		

Office Equipment			No. 115
19-1		19-5	
Jan. 2	700	Dec. 31	700

Accumulated Depreciation/ Office Equipment			No. 116
19-5		19-1	120
Dec. 31	600	19-2	120
		19-3	120
		19-4	120
		19-5	120

Analysis: When the unit reaches the end of its useful life, the accounts affected will appear as illustrated.

- The expense account shows only the last year's entry.
- The accumulated depreciation account clearly identifies the total of five years of accumulated expired costs for this machine.
- The difference between the unexpired cost listed in the asset Office Equipment and the total of the expired costs listed in the accumulated depreciation account of that specific asset is the disposal value of that asset.

Now examine the transaction that actually disposes of or sells that asset. There are three possible outcomes. Examine each separately as they are illustrated below.

(1) Sale for Disposal Value

19-5			
Dec. 31	Cash	100	
	Accumulated Depreciation/Office Equipment	600	
	Office Equipment		700
	To record the sale of the office equipment at book value.		

Analysis: The illustration is recorded for you in General Journal format, but properly it would be recorded in the cash receipts journal.

- The unexpired cost, the disposal value in this case, is also the amount of cash received.
- Because the asset is no longer owned by the company, it must be removed from the books. The Fixed Asset account, as you know, always has its partner, Accumulated Depreciation. Both must be brought equal to zero to close them.
- Debit $600, an equal and opposite amount, to Accumulated Depreciation/Office Equipment and credit $700 to Office Equipment. When posted, both of these accounts are closed with a zero balance.

• Finally, the subsidiary ledger account, page 522, must be posted to close it.

Notice the information that can be obtained from the completed subsidiary ledger card. Keeping a subsidiary ledger for individual fixed asset items offers these advantages:

• The individual account is identified by a complete description which includes the serial number. Consequently, a physical inventory of all fixed assets can be taken to ensure that all units of office equipment shown by the records are actually on hand. In other words, proper identification of the equipment in the subsidiary ledger ensures a degree of internal control over the fixed assets.

• The original cost of the typewriter, the estimated useful life, and the estimated disposal value are clearly indicated so that the periodic calculation of depreciation can be made.

• A complete record of both the Fixed Asset account and its related contra account are maintained on one card. At any time, therefore, the "book value" (current unexpired cost) of the asset can easily be learned.

• The individual record also supports information that will be required for tax returns, for obtaining proper insurance coverage, and for supporting claims for losses that may be made against the insurance coverage.

• Management is able to follow the useful life of the asset in order to budget for its replacement at least one year ahead of disposing of the asset.

(2) Sale for More than Disposal Value

19-5			
Dec. 31	*Cash*	*150*	
	Accumulated Depreciation/Office Equipment	*600*	
	Office Equipment		*700*
	Gain on Disposal of the fixed asset		*50*
	To record the sale of office equipment in excess of book value.		

Partial Income Statement
For the Year Ended December 31, 19-5

Sales Revenue	*$150 000*
Less: Operating Expenses	*110 000*
Net Operating Income	*40 000*
Other Revenue:	
Gain on the disposal of fixed asset	*50*
Net Income	*$ 40 050*

Analysis: Often, if equipment has been well maintained, it will sell for more than its estimated disposal value, say $150. In our example, this is $50 more than the estimated disposal value. Work from what you know. What would the journal entry be?

- You have $150 cash. Debit cash $150.
- You sold the asset. You must bring that account equal to zero with an equal and opposite entry. Credit Office Equipment $700.
- The accumulated depreciation account is not required any further; therefore, debit $600. The debits do not equal the credits. Remember you received more for the asset than you estimated. You have a *gain on the disposal of the fixed asset.* Such a gain is considered to be a *secondary source* of revenue, so you would expect a credit to gain on disposal of fixed assets of $50. Now your debits equal your credits.

Examine the journal entry once again. Note how the gain on disposal is ultimately reported.

(3) Sale for Less than Disposal Value What if you could not sell the unit for disposal value, but instead received only $75? Verify your thoughts by examining the entry below.

19-5			
Dec. 31	*Cash*	*75*	
	Accumulated Depreciation/Office Equipment	*600*	
	Loss on disposal of the fixed asset	*25*	
	Office Equipment		*700*
	To record the sale of the office equipment at a loss.		

Analysis:

- A special expense, a loss on disposal of fixed assets, of $25 occurs. You would report this loss as one of the expenses (under *Other Operating Expenses*) in the income statement and subtract it from the net income for the period.

Capital Cost Allowance Method

This is another method for determining depreciation. Under the Income Tax Act, a business may deduct the depreciation expense for most of its fixed assets in its calculation of net income. Although most firms use straight-line depreciation as the method for calculating depreciation, for income tax purposes the business must use the *capital cost allowance method.*

The Department of National Revenue — Taxation Division divides fixed assets into classes. Each is given a maximum percentage rate of depreciation. Several classes and their accompanying rates are shown in the following table.

The mathematics involved in calculating a capital cost allowance is quite easy. For example, on the typewriter, which

Class	Description of the Fixed Asset	Rate Allowed
3	A building of brick, cement, or stone	5%
6	A building of frame, log, stucco on frame, galvanized iron, or corrugated iron	10%
8	Furniture, equipment for the office, dairy plant, and equipment	20%
10	Automobiles, trucks, tractors, and automotive equipment	30%
29	Manufacturing and processing machinery and equipment	50%

costs $700, the first year's depreciation would be 20% of $700, or $140. The disposal value must not be considered under this method. In calculating the allowance (expense) for the second year, however, the first year's allowance must be deducted before applying the specified rate. The capital cost allowance in subsequent years is allowed only on the resulting balance, or the unexpired cost of the asset. For this reason, this method is known as the *fixed-percentage-on-declining-balance method.* In the illustration below, note that in applying the fixed percentage of 20% on each resulting balance, a larger amount of depreciation expense is estimated in the earlier years of the useful life of the typewriter, and a progressively smaller amount is shown in the later years.

Year	Unexpired Cost (Beginning of Year)	Amount of Capital Cost Allowance (20%)	Unexpired Cost (Resulting Balance at End of Year)
1	$700.00	$140.00	$560.00
2	560.00	112.00	448.00
3	448.00	89.60	358.40
4	358.40	71.68	286.72
5	286.72	57.34	229.38

Capital cost allowances are legal deductions permitted taxpayers as a matter of government policy. The rates of allowance are not designed to reflect a proper depreciation charge as is understood for accounting purposes. For this reason, an accountant will generally keep two sets of records in calculating depreciation:

- One to record the straight-line method of depreciation in the accounting records
- A separate record with respect to capital cost allowances for tax purposes

Comparing the Two Contra Asset Accounts

Although Allowance for Bad Debts and Accumulated Depreciation are both contra accounts and have similarities, it is very important to learn the differences between them. But first, let us examine the similarities:

- Both appear on the balance sheet as deductions: the accumulated depreciation is shown as a deduction from depreciable assets such as buildings and office equipment, and the allowance for bad debts as a deduction from Accounts Receivable.
- Both are created by adjusting entries.
- Both are based on estimates rather than on precisely determined amounts.
- Both show that the debit side of the adjusting entry affects an expense account (Depreciation Expense or Bad Debts Expense).

On the other hand, you should also note striking differences between the two contra asset accounts:

DIFFERENCES	
Accumulated Depreciation	Allowance for Bad Debts
1 This account does not reduce the related fixed asset to a realizable value. It merely shows what portion of the original cost has expired and has been recorded as expenses.	1 This account serves to reduce the accounts receivable to the amount of cash expected to be obtained through the collection of accounts receivable.
2 This account is debited only at the time the related fixed asset is disposed of.	2 This account is debited each time an individual customer account is written off.
3 This account will have only a credit balance during the lifetime of the related fixed asset.	3 This account may have either a debit or a credit balance at the end of each accounting year. The specific type of balance will depend on the extent of bad debts written off during the accounting period.

4 *This account is "contra" to a fixed asset account.*	4 This account is "contra" to a current asset account.

TOPIC 3 PROBLEMS

15-14 The T. Lookout Company bought a new electronic typewriter on January 2, 19-1 for $2 000. The company intends to sell the machine at the end of its useful life, which they estimate to be four years. They believe at that time the disposal value will be $400.

a In a chart, indicate the four years of useful life and list the amount of depreciation that will be recorded each year, assuming the firm uses the straight-line method.

b Journalize in the General Journal and then post to a three-column ledger account the purchase of the machine. (Post just the fixed asset account.)

c Journalize and post on December 31, 19-1 the necessary adjusting entries to record the depreciation expense for the machine. *Note:* You will need two more three-column ledger accounts.

Key Check Figure Depreciation per Year = $400

15-15 The Vermont Trucking Company purchases a dump truck for $27 000. They believe it will have a useful life of five years and a disposal value of $2 000. Use the straight-line method.

a Calculate and record the depreciation expense to be recorded in years 1 and 2.

b Prepare the General Journal entry to record the first year of depreciation expense. Year-end is December 31.

c In a three-column ledger account, Accumulated Depreciation/Truck, record each of the five years' depreciations.

d Prepare a General Journal entry to record the sale of the truck at the end of its useful life for its disposal value.

Key Check Figure Depreciation Expense/Truck = $5 000

15-16 The Regina Wholesale Company purchased a piece of land for $10 000 and the building for $40 000 on January 2, 19-5. The building has an estimated useful life of 20 years and there is no disposal value expected at that time. The land and building were purchased with a $5 000 down payment and the remainder with a mortgage.

a Record the General Journal entry for the purchase.

b Record the year-end adjustment entry required for the depreciation expense. Use the straight-line method.

c Indicate what the depreciation expense would be for each year and for one month.

d Prepare a partial balance sheet to record the fixed assets at the end of the second year. (Year-end is December 31.)

Key Check Figure Net Building = $36 000

15-17 The Manitoba Manufacturing Company bought a new drill press for $10 300 on January 1, 19-1. The company estimates its useful life at five years

Key Check Figure yearly depreciation $2 000

and disposal value at $300. The company uses straight-line depreciation.

a What is the depreciation expense at the end of 19-1? 19-2?

b What would the depreciation expense be per month?

c What would be the balance in the Accumulated Depreciation/Factory Equipment account at the end of 19-1? 19-3? 19-5?

d What would the unexpired cost be in the Factory Equipment account on January 1, 19-1? December 31, 19-1? December 31, 19-4?

e Prepare the General Journal entry to record the depreciation expense on December 31, 19-5.

f The drill press was sold on December 31, 19-5, for $300. Record the necessary journal entry. What would the entry be if the drill press sold for $500? $150?

15-18 The Hamilton Trucking Company bought a brick building to serve as its office for $22 000. The company estimates its useful life at 25 years with expected salvage value (same as disposal value) of $2 000. The business uses the straight-line method of depreciation but is obliged for income tax purposes to use the capital cost allowance method. The two depreciation methods are kept on separate records.

a Record in the General Journal the depreciation entry that is required each year for the straight-line method.

b Record in the General Journal the depreciation entry for the first two years. (The percentage you require is listed on page 527.)

Key Check Figure Capital Cost Allowance = $2 145

c Indicate how the accounts would appear in the balance sheet at the end of the second year if: **i** the straight-line method was used; **ii** the capital cost allowance method was used.

Key Check Figure 19-4 Book Value = $2 300

15-19 Return to Problem 15-17 and complete a fixed asset subsidiary ledger card similar to the one illustrated on page 522. Make up any information that is required to complete the top. Assume that the drill press was sold to K. Hardy for $300.

15-20 The Halifax Car Rental Company uses the straight-line depreciation method. Their year-end is December 31. On May 4, 19-1 they purchased from IBM Canada Ltd. a Selectric III typewriter, serial number 153433, for $1 265. The estimated useful life is seven years, with disposal value of $253.

On June 30, 19-1 the company purchased an Olivetti electronic calculator for $654. The estimated useful life is five years, with disposal value of $94. The serial number is 997665. On July 23, 19-1, the company bought a four-drawer, locking, legal-size filing cabinet for $380, serial number 11-343. The estimated useful life is ten years, with disposal value of $25. Bought from Steelcase Ltd.

a Open a General Ledger account for Office Equipment and another for its related contra account. Assign appropriate account numbers.

Key Check Figure Calculator, Book Value Dec. 31/-1 = $598

b Open subsidiary fixed asset ledger cards as required. Make up any details needed to complete the top.

c Prepare journal entries in the General Journal for all transactions. All purchases were made by cheque. Begin with No. 872. Post to the two ledger (general) accounts as required.

19-1
Dec. 31 Record the first year's depreciation on the office equipment. *Note:* Since depreciation is an estimate, calculate the year's depreciation to the nearest month. If the item was bought between the 1st and the 15th, record a full month. If it was bought between the 16th and the end of the month, ignore that month in your calculation.

19-2
Oct. 18 The company sold the Olivetti electronic calculator to Halifax PUC for $550. *Note:* Don't forget to record depreciation up to the date of sale.
Dec. 31 Record the depreciation on all equipment to date.

d Prepare a "Schedule of Office Equipment and Accumulated Depreciation" (a schedule of the subsidiary ledger accounts) at the end of the second year to prove that the total book value of the fixed assets in the subsidiary ledger agrees with the balance of the controlling account, and that the total of accumulated depreciation in the subsidiary ledger agrees with the Accumulated Depreciation/Office Equipment controlling account in the General Ledger.

TOPIC 4 ADJUSTING FOR ACCRUED REVENUES, ACCRUED EXPENSES, AND UNEARNED REVENUE

The reverse side of prepaid expenses is accrued expenses. The term *prepaid* means an amount has been paid in advance; thus, you record it as an unexpired cost and list it as an asset.

To be able to complete adjustments for accrued revenue and expenses, a good understanding of both the cash and the accrual bases of accounting is necessary. Read through the brief discussion of each which follows.

Cash Basis

This is by far the simpler of the two systems. The cash basis records an event only when it directly involves cash. For example, a cash sale is recorded immediately, but a sale on account is ignored because it is a revenue, and no cash has been received. It is not until cash is received or paid out that this system is concerned with an entry.

Note that this system makes calculating business profits difficult.

The cash basis is not approved under present GAAPs except in a few special cases, but these are best studied in other accounting courses.

Accrual Basis

This method lets the business account for revenue that has been earned but not yet received, and for expenses incurred but not yet paid. It requires maintenance of inventory records so that the cost of goods sold can be calculated. The cash-basis system ignores calculation of inventory. Under the accrual system an attempt to match revenues and related expense of a period can be planned and undertaken. It allows the recording of revenue and expenses when they are earned and incurred regardless of any cash received.

Accrued expense: an expense that has occurred but has not been recorded or paid.

An accrued expense is an expense which has been incurred during an accounting period, but not paid for or recorded. When you see the word "accrued," think of the word "grew" or "increased." An employee's pay grows day by day as he or she continues working. These accrued wages must be accounted for at the end of any accounting period. For example, Wawdel Company pays its hourly-rated personnel every Friday. Jane Dawson receives $50 per day, or $250 every Friday. Last Friday, June 25, the company recorded in its Cash Payments Journal: Debit — Wages Expense, Credit — Cash, Amount - $250. The next period will fall on Friday, July 2. Jane Dawson will receive $250 on that date. However, June 30, a month-end, occurred during that week. If you record the same entry into the cash payments journal on July 2, you will be violating the matching principle.

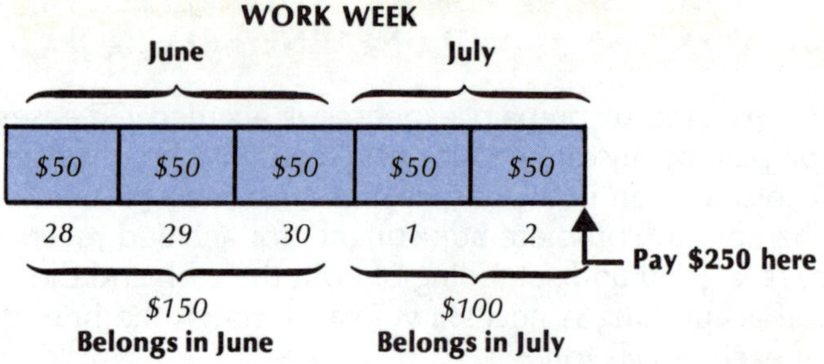

As the illustration shows, $150 of the $250 paid properly belongs to the month of June; $100 belongs to the month of July. Should Wawdel Company pay J. Dawson twice this week? No, but an adjusting entry, dated June 30, is needed to record the $150 wages expense incurred in the month of June. Since the amount owing will not be paid until July 2, the $150 must be recorded as owing in the form of a liability called Wages Payable — $150. On July 2 the wages payable for $150, and the wages expense for July 1 and 2, $100, will be recorded. A cheque for $250 will be paid to J. Dawson. Examine the following illustration for these entries.

Accrued: grown or increased, as interest on a debt (receivable or payable) increases day by day. The term applies mostly to a continuing flow of services rather than to physical assets.

Week of June 21 – 25

19-1			
June 25	*Wages Expense*	*250*	
	Cash		*250*
	To record one week's wages for J. Dawson.		

Note: *This entry would appear in the cash payments journal.*

Week of June 28 — July 2

19-1			
June 30	Wages Expense	150	
	Wages Payable		150
	To record the adjustment for wages expense for June 28, 29, 30.		

Note: *This is an adjustment and would appear in the General Journal.*

19-1			
July 2	Wages Expense	100	
	Wages Payable	150	
	Cash		250
	To record payment of five days' wages owing to J. Dawson.		

Note: *July 2 is in a new accounting period. This entry belongs in the cash payments journal.*

The June 30 entry is an adjusting entry. If the wages expense of June 28, 29, and 30 is to be included in the wages expense account for the month of June, the adjustment is absolutely necessary. If this entry were omitted, three days' wages expense would have been recorded in July. A mismatch would have occurred. Instead, J. Dawson receives her full pay on July 2. Two days' wages expense is recorded in July and the wages payable account, set up by the adjustment June 30, has been cleared. Anytime an expense has the potential of being recorded in the wrong period, an adjustment for an accrued expense is in order.

Read carefully the following situation and decide what the problem is. On May 1, 19-1, Wawdel Company borrowed $10 000 from the local bank. The interest rate was 12% per annum. Therefore, the interest expense per month was 1%. Interest payments are due November 1 and May 1. Wawdel Company's year-end is December 31. What would the interest expense equal on November 1, 19-1? What journal entry would be expected and in what journal? Is there an accrued expense December 31, 19-1? Check your thoughts against the entry that follows.

19-1			
Nov. 1	Bank Loan Interest Expense	600	
	Cash		600
	To record payment of 6 months' interest on the bank loan.		

Note: *Record in the cash payments journal.*

Adj

19-1			
Dec. 31	Bank Loan Interest Expense	200	
	Bank Loan Interest Payable		200
	To record the year-end adjustment for the bank loan interest.		

Note: *Record in the General Journal.*

There most certainly is an adjustment, as the second of the two entries illustrates. If you waited until May 1, 19-2, the next payment date, you would be creating a mismatch of bank interest expense. The $200 recorded on December 31, 19-1 belongs to year 19-1. If you recorded an entry similar to the November 1, 19-1 entry on May 1, 19-2, $200 of that $600 would be entered into the wrong year. The December 31 adjusting entry prevents that mistake. Now what would the May 1, 19-2 entry look like?

19-2			
May 1	Bank Loan Interest Expense	400	
	Bank Loan Interest Payable	200	
	Cash		600
	To record the payment of six months' interest expense on the bank loan.		

Accrued revenue: a revenue that has been earned but not recorded or received.

If an accrued expense is an expense that has occurred, but has not been recorded or paid, what then is an accrued revenue? An accrued revenue is a revenue which has been earned, but not yet recorded or the funds received. Study the following situation.

Wawdel Company has outstanding a note receivable for $12 000, paying 8% per annum. It was purchased October 31, 19-1 and pays interest annually. On December 31, 19-1 Wawdel Company's note has earned interest equal to $160 ($12 000 × 0.08 × 2/12). No interest will be paid until October 31, 19-2. Interest revenue, however, equivalent to $160 (2 months), belongs to 19-1. What type of entry is required?

Adj entry

19-1			
Dec. 31	Interest Receivable	160	
	Interest Revenue		160
	To record 2 months' interest earned on our note receivable.		

This is an adjusting entry and belongs in the General Journal. Without this adjusting entry, the 19-1 revenue would be recorded in 19-2. This would result in a mismatch of revenue and expenses in both years and violate the matching principle. The

$200 of interest revenue is recorded on December 31, 19-1 and a receivable is introduced to hold the amount on the company books until the actual receipt of cash occurs on October 31, 19-2. What then is the entry on October 31, 19-2?

19-2			
Oct. 31	*Cash*	*960*	
	Interest Receivable		*160*
	Interest Revenue		*800*
	To record 10 months' interest earned and 12 months' interest paid on our note receivable.		

Both accrued revenues and accrued expenses will result in year-end adjusting entries to ensure that there is no violation of the matching principle. Without such adjustments, there would surely be mismatches involving the revenue and expense accounts in both of the years affected by the transaction. The same is true if one examines the effect such an adjusting entry would have on the year-end financial statements.

When you consider the various methods by which a firm earns and collects its revenue, you must acknowledge two circumstances. You have just examined the situation where the firm completes all or part of the work before it receives any payment. The value of the work done is referred to as accrued revenue and a period-end adjustment is required in order to match the proper revenue of the period with related expenses. The exact opposite situation can also exist. This occurs when the firm is paid in advance of performing the actual work. For example, if Wawdel Company agrees on August 1, 19-1 to perform work for XYZ Company for the next nine months at $100 per month, the total revenue to be earned over those nine months would be $900 (9 × $100). If the XYZ Company paid Wawdel Company the full $900 fee in advance, the following entry would be recorded in the cash receipts journal. (Illustration is in General Journal format.)

19-1			
Aug. 1	*Cash*	*900*	
	Unearned Revenue		*900*
	To record receipt of $900. Payment in advance for revenue yet to be earned.		

Unearned Revenue *No. 208*

	Aug. 1 *900*

Examine the above transaction very carefully. Note that an asset, Cash, has been increased and therefore is a debit entry. The new concept is the credit entry named *Unearned Revenue.*

The key word is *unearned.* Remember the accounting equation: *A = L + OE*. In this case, cash for $900 is received. But this cash is unearned because the work has yet to be performed. Thus, the accounting equation would read:

A	=	L
Cash	=	Unearned Revenue
$900	=	$900

Wawdel Company owes XYZ Company services equal to $900. The term *owes* indicates a liability. Unearned revenue, therefore, is a current liability until Wawdel Company earns, through performance of services, the asset already received. Examine the circumstances on December 31, 19-1. The company's year-end has arrived and it is time to ensure that the matching of related revenues and expenses has taken place. Five months have passed and Wawdel Company has performed services for XYZ Company for August to December. Wawdel Company has earned five of the nine months of the unearned revenue paid for on August 1, 19-1. This revenue belongs in 19-1, so an adjustment is required. Obviously, a revenue account must be credited. What is the debit entry? You will remember that on August 1, 19-1 Wawdel Company recorded a credit to a liability, Unearned Revenue. It represented nine months of unearned revenue. You now know, however, that five of those nine months have passed and the work has been completed under the terms of the agreement. It is necessary, then, to reduce that current liability by $500 (5 months at $100 per month). A debit entry is required to reduce a liability, so the following adjustment occurs:

19-1			
Dec. 31	*Unearned Revenue*	*500*	
	Contract Revenue		*500*
	To record the adjustment of unearned revenue.		

Unearned Revenue		*No. 208*	
Dec. 31	*500*	*Aug. 1*	*900*

Contract Revenue		*No. 410*	
		Dec. 31	*500*

Note that the adjustment matches the revenue that was earned in 19-1 with the expenses of the same period. The liability has been reduced by the amount of revenue earned. The liability account now reflects the correct amount of revenue still unearned.

The change in the unearned revenue account has been identified and recorded.

This type of adjustment is the last of the four. You have examined: prepaid expenses, accrued revenues, accrued expenses, and unearned revenue. Each type of adjustment deals with a specific situation — a change — that might occur as a firm carries on its business activities. It should be noted that entries of another kind called *reversing entries* are sometimes used with adjustments, but these will be left for a more advanced course.

TOPIC 4 PROBLEMS

15-21 The Dayside Chair Manufacturing Company has an outstanding bank loan for $25 000 at 12% per annum interest. The interest dates fall due on March 1 and September 1. The loan was arranged on March 1, 19-1.

Record the General Journal entry required for March 1, 19-1, September 1, 19-1, December 31, 19-1, and March 1, 19-2. (Assume that the company year-end is December 31.)

15-22 Greenway Lawn Care Company was hired by Mr. Rich to care for his estate from April 1, 19-1 to October 31, 19-1 at a cost of $250 per month. Mr. Rich agreed to pay the entire amount at the end of the service contract, October 31, 19-1. The company year-end falls on September 30.

Record the adjusting entry required at our company year-end and then record the entry to receive payment.

15-23 The C & V Company owns a large piece of machinery that cost $300 000 when it was purchased new in 19-1. It has an estimated useful life of ten years and no disposal value. The firm uses the straight-line depreciation method and depreciation is calculated quarterly.

The machine was bought on November 1, 19-1. Record the necessary General Journal entries for the remaining period in year 19-1 and for year 19-2.

15-24 The Triple Z Company gives you the following information and asks you to prepare all the needed General Journal adjusting entries as of December 31, 19-1.

a The firm owns a building worth $50 000, with $3 000 of salvage value and an estimated life of 25 years. All depreciation is based on the straight-line method. Record one full year of depreciation.

b The company has agreed to a contract dated October 1, 19-1. The contract calls for Triple Z to perform services for three years at a rate of $4 500 per year. We receive nothing in advance but are paid every quarter.

c The firm has an outstanding loan of $10 000 with the bank. Interest payments are required every six months on April 30 and October 30. The rate of interest is 18%.

d At the end of the year, December 31, 19-1, our Allowance for Bad Debts has a debit balance of $45. The firm ages the receivables and determines that $289 will be uncollectable in 19-2.

e The firm owns Canada Savings Bonds worth $5 000. The interest rate is 10% and interest is paid on November 1. The company has owned the bonds for three years.

15-25 XYZ Company hires ABC Company to perform cleaning services for seven months. The contract is signed on September 1, 19-1 and the XYZ pays $700 in advance on that date ($100 per month). Each company has a year-end of December 31.

Key Check Figure Cleaning Services Revenue = $400

a Record the entry required on September 1, 19-1 for ABC Company.
b Prepare the necessary adjustment on December 31, 19-1 for ABC Company.
c Prepare T-accounts for all parts of **a** and **b.**
d Repeat parts **a, b,** and **c** for XYZ Company.

15-26 Sam's Snow Removal Service is hired by Balfourd Company Ltd. for snow removal from October 19-1 to April 30, 19-2. The billings are as follows:

October and April:	$500/month	= $1 000
November through March:	$750/month	= 3 750
Total		$4 750

The total of $750 was paid in advance on October 1, 19-1.

If Sam's Snow Removal prepares year-end adjustments on December 1, 19-1, what would the General Journal entry be on October 1, 19-1? What would the adjusting entry be on December 31, 19-1?

15-27 Alpha Corporation contracts to perform services for one year. Beta Electronic pays the first three months in advance, and the remainder upon completion of the job. The contract begins November 15, 19-1. Alpha Corporation has a year-end of December 31. The agreement calls for $200/month.

a Record in the General Journal, the entry on November 15, 19-1, when the advance payment is made.

b Record, in the General Journal, the year-end adjustment entry that is required on December 31, 19-1.

c Record the necessary entry on the following November 15, 19-2. *Hint:* This deals with unearned revenue.

Case Study 15

The Peter Pauling Company provides furniture cleaning and repair services for three major hotels. The firm has the following contracts with each hotel:

Hotel Deluxe: The company is required to complete all cleaning and repairs for a flat rate of $250/month. This has worked well for the company, because there is usually very little repair work to complete. The hotel pays in advance, quarterly (February 15, May 15, August 15, November 15).

12th Street Hotel: The company is called in as required. Furniture cleaning is a flat $25/piece and repairs are $20/hour which includes any needed materials. Each quarter, (January 1, April 1, July 1, October 1) the hotel makes an advance payment of $550 ($300 for cleaning, $250 for repairs). Any charges over and above must be billed.

Hotel Terrace: This is the firm's largest customer. The contract requires that the firm clean the contents of two floors every month. The firm is paid $750/month for this service on the 15th of the following month. Repairs are paid on a flat rate, one year in advance on May 1. Amount: $3 600.

Prepare all necessary General Journal adjustment entries for the company year-end, December 31, 19-4.

Additional Information

All items are paid up to date for all three hotels as you begin work.

Since October 1, the firm has cleaned 20 items and repaired 7 items at 12th Street Hotel. Each item repaired took one hour.

All accounts have the exact balances that they should have assuming everything works out perfectly.

Accounts used by the company are: Cleaning and Repairs Revenue/Hotel Deluxe, Cleaning Revenue/12th Street Hotel, Repairs Revenue/12th Street Hotel, Cleaning Revenue/Hotel Terrace, Repairs Revenue/Hotel Terrace.

CHAPTER 16

COMPLETING THE ACCOUNTING CYCLE

This chapter will cover the rest of the accounting cycle for a merchandising firm. Up to this point in Part 3 you have looked at: (1) the origination of information in the form of source documents; (2) the analysis of those documents and the subsequent recording of the transactions into the appropriate journals; (3) the posting of the journal entries to the subsidiary and general ledgers; and (4) the preparation of schedules for the subsidiary ledgers and a trial balance from the General Ledger.

Earlier, you learned how to complete the six-column worksheet, following the preparation of the trial balance. This working paper was introduced to permit a rough draft of the financial statements — the income statement and the balance sheet. From the worksheet, the firm would then prepare formal financial statements suitable for presentation to the general public. The accounting cycle was completed by the closing entries and the preparation of a postclosing trial balance.

Recall that the adjustments explained in Chapter 15 were not included in the previous discussion of the accounting cycle. This is a major addition to the cycle and results in an expanded worksheet. The first Topic of this chapter carefully outlines the changes that occur in the worksheet. Once the worksheet is completed, the closing of the accounts of the merchandising firm can be done.

- Topic 1 deals with preparing the ten-column worksheet.
- Topic 2 deals with preparing financial statements.
- Topic 3 deals with the completion of the accounting cycle.
- Topic 4 deals with the interpretation of financial statements.

TOPIC 1 PREPARING THE TEN-COLUMN WORKSHEET

Worksheet: an expanded trial balance for computing, classifying, and sorting account balances before preparing financial statements.

The worksheet is the accountant's tool for expanding the trial balance for computing, classifying, and sorting account balances in order to prepare the period-end financial statements. It is not a permanent document of the firm and is usually prepared in pencil. This is the only document where corrections by erasing are permissible. The actual process for preparing the worksheet will now be discussed.

Step 1: Complete the Trial Balance Section

The first step is to transfer the period-end General Ledger trial balance into the account-title column and the first two money columns. Refer to the illustration of a worksheet on pages 542 and 543 to examine this first job. Note that the account numbers have been included in a separate column between the account-title column and the money columns.

Let's stop here for a moment to examine the worksheet heading.

(1) The heading answers the questions *who* (the name of the company), *what* (the name of the document: worksheet), and *when* (the accounting period for the month, quarter, or year ended December 31, 19—; the appropriate date must be placed in this spot). No abbreviations may be used, and because you will be listing income statement items, the date identifies the period of time being measured (in this case For the Month Ended August 31, 19—).

(2) The six-column worksheet which you worked with earlier in Chapter 5 is now being expanded to accept the adjustments you completed in Chapter 15. Examine once again the illustration on pages 542 and 543. You will see that two more sets of columns have been added. These include the *Adjustments* and the *Adjusted Trial Balance* columns. You now have a ten-column worksheet. In practice, worksheets may contain six, eight, ten, or more columns. In this book, you will deal only with the six- and the ten-column worksheet.

(3) The worksheet trial balance section is identical to the formal preparation of the General Ledger trial balance. In fact, often the firm will dispense with the formal trial balance and prepare the trial balance in the worksheet directly from the ledger accounts. After the trial balance is prepared, it must be checked to ensure that the debits equal the credits. If they don't, the worksheet preparation stops until a balance is determined.

(4) In a merchandising firm, you must remember that there is a merchandising inventory account. Careful examination reveals that the amount listed in the trial balance is the beginning inventory. Since no year-end inventory amount is disclosed, this firm must use the periodic inventory method to calculate the figure for cost of goods sold. Be prepared to examine how the ending inventory figure will be identified as the worksheet is completed.

(5) Finally, you should be able to identify a number of accounts within the trial balance that may require adjusting entries (prepaid assets, accumulated depreciation, etc.). The lack of related expired cost (expense) accounts for any of these accounts

Wawdel Company
Worksheet
For the Month Ended August 31, 19—

	Account Title	Acct. No.	Trial Balance		Adjustments		Adj. Trial Balance		Income Statement		Balance Sheet		
			Debit	Credit	Debit	Credit	Debit	Credit	Debit	Credit	Debit	Credit	
1	Cash	101	10 700										1
2	Petty Cash	102	50										2
3	Notes Receivable	103	60 000										3
4	Accounts Receivable	104	6 400										4
5	Allowance for Bad Debts	105		20									5
6	Interest Receivable	106	500										6
7	Merchandise Inventory, Aug. 1	110	4 200										7
8	Supplies on Hand	112	400										8
9	Prepaid Insurance	114	550										9
10	Land	150	12 000										10
11	Building	155	48 000										11
12	Accum. Deprec./Building	156		700									12
13	Warehouse Equipment	160	4 000										13
14	Accum. Deprec./Whs. Equip.	161		210									14
15	Office Equipment	165	7 200										15
16	Accum. Deprec./Off. Equip.	166		550									16
17	Delivery Trucks	170	20 000										17
18	Bank Loan	201		5 500									18
19	Unearned Revenue	202		500									19
20	Accounts Payable	203		6 800									20
21	Bank Loan Interest Payable	204		75									21
22	Unemployment Insurance Payable	210		60									22
23	CPP Payable	211		120									23
24	Income Tax Payable	212		800									24
25	OHIP Payable	213		42									25
26	Group Insurance Payable	214		124									26
27	Mortgage Payable	250		50 000									27
28	R. Wawdel, Capital	301		85 530									28
29	R. Wawdel, Drawings	302	705										29
30	Sales	401		32 536									30

31	*Sales Returns & Allowances*	*402*	*220*										31
32	*Sales Discounts*	*403*	*145*										32
33	*Purchases*	*501*	*5 800*										33
34	*Transportation-in*	*502*	*150*										34
35	*Purchases Returns & Allowances*	*503*		*210*									35
36	*Purchases Discounts*	*504*		*160*									36
37	*Advertising Expense*	*510*	*185*										37
38	*Utilities Expense*	*512*	*60*										38
39	*Delivery Expense*	*514*	*180*										39
40	*Wages & Salaries Expense*	*516*	*1 600*										40
41	*Payroll Tax Expense*	*518*	*864*										41
42	*Interest Expense*	*520*	*28*										42
43			*183 937*	*183 937*									43
44													44
45													45

indicates that the trial balance values are unadjusted, beginning-of-the-year figures. As the worksheet preparation continues, be prepared to examine each of these accounts as well.

Step 2: Complete the Adjustments Section

In Chapter 15, you learned how to resolve mismatches between revenues and expenses through adjusting entries. In practice, adjusting entries are examined and recorded in the worksheet before they are journalized and posted. Remember, the trial balance provided only beginning-of-the-year figures. Since none of the information required to prepare adjustments can be obtained from the worksheet, additional information must be provided in order for the business to proceed with the adjustments. Such information might include:

- a year-end count of office and/or store supplies
- the unused portion of prepaid rent or prepaid insurance
- the amount of an accrued revenue or expense
- the total of aged receivables or a percentage of net sales taken to estimate the amount of bad debts expense for the accounting period
- the depreciation calculations for the firm's fixed assets or the change in an unearned revenue account

Each of these various adjustments will now be examined. Remember, you will be looking for a *change*. *Note:* The letters A to J in the following headings refer to the letter codes discussed.

A. Adjusting for Supplies Used Refer to the earlier worksheet illustration and look at the Supplies on Hand listing. You find a debit entry for $400. This represents the amount in supplies on August 1, 19—. Assume that the unused supplies have been counted on August 31, 19— and that the total is $300. The change is $100 ($400 − $300). Supplies worth $100 have been used up (expired) resulting in an expense, Supplies Expense. To record this change, debit $100 to Supplies Expense and reduce the Supplies on Hand account by $100 with a credit entry. Now study the illustration on pages 546 and 547. See how the two accounts identified above are illustrated. The credit column of the adjustments section accepts the supplies on hand entry. Since there is no Supplies Expense account listed, it must be recorded in the account title column, beneath the trial balance items. The debit entry for Supplies Expense is then recorded in the debit column of the adjustment section. Each adjustment, as it is recorded, should be identified with a letter of the alphabet. This will serve as a reference tool to permit easy identification of the related entries and assist in the preparation of General Journal entries in the future.

Supplies Expense			*No. 521*
(A)	*100*		

Supplies on Hand			*No. 112*
		(A)	*100*

Summary: (1) Analyze the complete double entry. T-accounts are often useful (see margin). (2) Record the entries opposite the listed accounts in the appropriate debit or credit column or open any account not previously listed in the trial balance. (3) Letter-code all adjustments for reference and ease of journalizing in the future.

B. Adjustment for Expired Insurance Assume that your insurance policy was bought on July 1, 19— for $600. The cost per month works out to $50 ($600/12). The adjustment, therefore, for August, the second month to be adjusted, is $50. The entry required is: debit Insurance Expense, credit Prepaid Insurance. Note the alphabetic letter reference B.

C. Adjustment for Bad Debts Assume that by the aged accounts receivable method, management estimated uncollectable accounts for August to be $120. The Allowance for Bad Debts amount must be considered. Because Allowance for Bad Debts shows a credit balance for $20, the adjustment, debit Bad Debts Expense and credit Allowance for Bad Debts, is equal to $100 ($120 − $20). Notice the letter code C, and that once again the expense account is listed below the trial balance listing.

D. Adjustment for the Interest Receivable The firm's note receivable pays $500 per month or $6 000 per year. Payment is received June 30 and December 31. Examine the entry on the worksheet. Coded D, the debit is to Interest Receivable, $500 and the credit is to Interest Revenue, $500.

E. Adjustment for the Accrued Interest Expense The firm's bank loan of $5 500 requires interest payments on March 31, June 30, September 30, and December 31. The interest rate of 16.36% creates interest expense of $900 per year or $75 per month. The adjustment, debit Interest Expense $75, and credit Interest Payable $75 is coded E.

F. Adjustment for Depreciation of the Building Assume management has estimated a useful life of 20 years, with no disposal value and the use of straight-line method. Annual depreciation is $2 400 ($48 000/20). Monthly depreciation is $200 ($2 400/12). The code is F and the entry reads: debit Depreciation Expense/Building $200, and credit Accumulated Depreciation/Building $200. Check this entry in the worksheet on pages 546 and 547.

G. Adjustment for Depreciation on Warehouse Equipment To deal with this adjustment, assume: (1) that the warehouse equipment was purchased at varying times; and (2) that the disposal value has varying amounts. To calculate the depreciation, therefore, you would have to examine the fixed asset subsidiary ledger and add the yearly amounts estimated for each piece of equipment. Suppose that the fixed asset subsidiary ledger shows a total depreciation of $360 to be recorded for the current year. For August, therefore, the depreciation expense must be $30.

H. Adjustment for Depreciation on Office Equipment The fixed asset subsidiary ledger cards for office equipment showed total depreciation for the year of $840. The adjustment for August is $70 ($840/12).

Wawdel Company
Worksheet
For the Month Ended August 31, 19—

	Account Title	Acct. No.	Trial Balance		Adjustments		Adj. Trial Balance		Income Statement		Balance Sheet		
			Debit	Credit	Debit	Credit	Debit	Credit	Debit	Credit	Debit	Credit	
1	Cash	101	10 700										1
2	Petty Cash	102	50										2
3	Notes Receivable	103	60 000										3
4	Accounts Receivable	104	6 400										4
5	Allowance for Bad Debts	105		20		(C) 100							5
6	Interest Receivable	106	500		(D) 500								6
7	Merchandise Inventory, Aug. 1	110	4 200										7
8	Supplies on Hand	112	400			(A) 100							8
9	Prepaid Insurance	114	550			(B) 50							9
10	Land	150	12 000										10
11	Building	155	48 000										11
12	Accum. Deprec./Building	156		700		(F) 200							12
13	Warehouse Equipment	160	4 000										13
14	Accum. Deprec./Whs. Equip.	161		210		(G) 30							14
15	Office Equipment	165	7 200										15
16	Accum. Deprec./Off. Equip.	166		550		(H) 70							16
17	Delivery Trucks	170	20 000										17
18	Bank Loan	201		5 500									18
19	Unearned Revenue	202		500	(J) 250								19
20	Accounts Payable	203		6 800									20
21	Bank Loan Interest Payable	204		75		(E) 75							21
22	Unemployment Insurance Payable	210		60									22
23	CPP Payable	211		120									23
24	Income Tax Payable	212		800									24
25	OHIP Payable	213		42									25
26	Group Insurance Payable	214		124									26
27	Mortgage Payable	250		50 000									27
28	R. Wawdel, Capital	301		85 530									28
29	R. Wawdel, Drawings	302	705										29
30	Sales	401		32 536									30

31	Sales Returns & Allowances	402	220										31
32	Sales Discounts	403	145										32
33	Purchases	501	5 800										33
34	Transportation-in	502	150										34
35	Purchases Returns & Allowances	503		210									35
36	Purchases Discounts	504		160									36
37	Advertising Expense	510	185										37
38	Utilities Expense	512	60										38
39	Delivery Expense	514	180										39
40	Wages & Salaries Expense	516	1 600										40
41	Payroll Tax Expense	518	864										41
42	Interest Expense	520	28										42
43			183 937	183 937									43
44	Supplies Expense	521			(A) 100								44
45	Insurance Expense	523			(B) 50								45
46	Bad Debts Expense	525			(C) 100								46
47	Interest Revenue	405				(D) 500							47
48	Bank Loan Interest Expense	530			(E) 75								48
49	Deprec. Expense/Bldg.	550			(F) 200								49
50	Deprec. Expense/Whs. Equip.	552			(G) 30								50
51	Deprec. Expense/Off. Equip.	554			(H) 70								51
52	Deprec. Expense/Trucks	556			(I) 300								52
53	Accum. Deprec./Trucks	171				(I) 300							53
54	Fees Earned	407				(J) 250							54
55					1 675	1 675							55
56													56

I. Adjustment for Depreciation on Delivery Trucks Assume that two delivery trucks were purchased on July 31, 19—. Each cost $10 000, will have a useful life of five years, and will have a disposal value of $1 000. Straight-line depreciation is used. Since this was a new purchase, the contra account Accumulated Depreciation/Delivery Truck is not found in the trial balance. Now that an adjustment is required, this account will be added to the bottom of the list. The next time a trial balance is prepared, it will be added into the appropriate part of the trial balance. The base cost of the trucks is $20 000 less disposal of $2 000. The annual depreciation is $3 600 ($18 000/5). Monthly depreciation is $300 ($3 600/12).

J. Adjustment for Unearned Revenue Assume that the firm contracted one month earlier, on July 2, to perform services for the R. & R. Company for three months at $250 per month. The full $750 was paid in advance and recorded in the liability account Unearned Revenue. The adjustment at the end of July reduced the unearned revenue by $250 — one month of revenue — and a similar adjustment is required in August. The entry would read: debit Unearned Revenue $250, credit Fees Earned $250. The code would be J.

With this adjustment complete, assume that there are no further adjustments necessary. A single line is now drawn across both the debit and credit columns, and the columns are totalled. The two columns must agree before you may proceed. If they do not, an error exists and must be located. The coding will now be most helpful as you check the equality of each entry step by step. Once the two columns agree, the traditional double line is ruled across both the debit and credit columns.

Step 3: Complete the Adjusted Trial Balance Section

After all adjustments are recorded and the balanced totals are completed, the next step is to correct or to update the trial balance figures by transferring them into the adjusted trial balance section after adding or subtracting the appropriate adjustment. For example, the Cash account amount of $10 700 is extended directly into the adjusted trial balance section as a debit for $10 700 because there was no adjustment to change the original trial balance figure. (See illustration on pages 550 and 551.) The same procedure is true for the petty cash account and the accounts receivable account. Note, however, the next account, Allowance for Bad Debts. This account has a balance of $20 in the trial balance section. There is a credit adjustment equal to $100. To extend this account, add the two credit amounts, $20 and $100 (likes are added, opposites are subtracted), and extend the total, $120, into the credit column of the adjusted trial balance section. Next, examine the account Supplies on Hand, opening balance $400. Subtract the credit adjustment from the debit opening balance ($400 − $100), and extend the $300 difference into the debit column of the adjusted trial balance section. Finally, if the adjustments created an additional account after the original trial balance, transfer those amounts directly into the adjusted trial balance section. Now draw a single line across both columns of the adjusted trial balance and total the debit and credit columns. Again, these two columns must agree. If they do not, locate the error before you proceed. After agreement is obtained, double-underline the two columns.

Step 4: Move the Adjusted Trial Balance Amounts into the Statement Columns

After the *Adjusted Trial Balance* columns have been proved to be correct, the individual amounts are moved to one column of either the *Income Statement* section or the *Balance Sheet* section. Here are two rules that will help you to move an amount to the correct location:

(1) If the amount is a debit in the adjusted trial balance, move the amount to the debit of the *Statement* section to which the account is related.

(2) If the amount is a credit in the adjusted trial balance, move the amount to the credit of the *Statement* section to which the account is related.

These two rules simply reinforce the idea that a debit in the adjusted trial balance must become a debit elsewhere, and a credit in the adjusted trial balance must become a credit in a related *Statement* section. These rules help you to move amounts to a correct location. They do not, however, explain why the figure must be a debit or a credit under a *Statement* section. Look closely at the section of the worksheet illustrated on pages 552 and 553; then study the important points of analysis that follow.

Analysis: Each account balance in the *Adjusted Trial Balance* section must be extended into either the debit or the credit column of its related *Statement* section. Obviously, assets, liabilities, and the owner's equity capital and drawing accounts must be moved to the *Balance Sheet* columns. Similarly, revenue, contra revenue, costs (cost of goods sold), expense, and contra expense accounts must be extended to the correct *Income Statement* columns.

One group of accounts requires careful analysis. A merchandising firm using a periodic inventory method does not calculate the cost of each good sold as the sale is made. That is why no account for Cost of Goods Sold will be found in either the trial balance or the adjusted trial balance. Instead, a group of "costs" is used to make an indirect calculation of the cost of goods sold. These accounts are (1) Inventory (showing the beginning amount

Wawdel Company
Worksheet
For the Month Ended August 31, 19—

	Account Title	Acct. No.	Trial Balance Debit	Trial Balance Credit	Adjustments Debit	Adjustments Credit	Adj. Trial Balance Debit	Adj. Trial Balance Credit	Income Statement Debit	Income Statement Credit	Balance Sheet Debit	Balance Sheet Credit	
1	Cash	101	10 700				10 700						1
2	Petty Cash	102	50				50						2
3	Notes Receivable	103	60 000				60 000						3
4	Accounts Receivable	104	6 400				6 400						4
5	Allowance for Bad Debts	105		20		(C) 100		120					5
6	Interest Receivable	106	500		(D) 500		1 000						6
7	Merchandise Inventory, Aug. 1	110	4 200				4 200						7
8	Supplies on Hand	112	400			(A) 100	300						8
9	Prepaid Insurance	114	550			(B) 50	500						9
10	Land	150	12 000				12 000						10
11	Building	155	48 000				48 000						11
12	Accum. Deprec./Building	156		700		(F) 200		900					12
13	Warehouse Equipment	160	4 000				4 000						13
14	Accum. Deprec./Whs. Equip.	161		210		(G) 30		240					14
15	Office Equipment	165	7 200				7 200						15
16	Accum. Deprec./Off. Equip.	166		550		(H) 70		620					16
17	Delivery Trucks	170	20 000				20 000						17
18	Bank Loan	201		5 500				5 500					18
19	Unearned Revenue	202		500	(J) 250			250					19
20	Accounts Payable	203		6 800				6 800					20
21	Bank Loan Interest Payable	204		75		(E) 75		150					21
22	Unemployment Insurance Payable	210		60				60					22
23	CPP Payable	211		120				120					23
24	Income Tax Payable	212		800				800					24
25	OHIP Payable	213		42				42					25
26	Group Insurance Payable	214		124				124					26
27	Mortgage Payable	250		50 000				50 000					27
28	R. Wawdel, Capital	301		85 530				85 530					28
29	R. Wawdel, Drawings	302	705				705						29
30	Sales	401		32 536				32 536					30

31	Sales Returns & Allowances	402	220				220						31
32	Sales Discounts	403	145				145						32
33	Purchases	501	5 800				5 800						33
34	Transportation-in	502	150				150						34
35	Purchases Returns & Allowances	503		210				210					35
36	Purchases Discounts	504		160				160					36
37	Advertising Expense	510	185				185						37
38	Utilities Expense	512	60				60						38
39	Delivery Expense	514	180				180						39
40	Wages & Salaries Expense	516	1 600				1 600						40
41	Payroll Tax Expense	518	864				864						41
42	Interest Expense	520	28				28						42
43			183 937	183 937									43
44	Supplies Expense	521			(A) 100		100						44
45	Insurance Expense	523			(B) 50		50						45
46	Bad Debts Expense	525			(C) 100		100						46
47	Interest Revenue	405				(D) 500		500					47
48	Bank Loan Interest Expense	530			(E) 75		75						48
49	Deprec. Expense/Bldg.	550			(F) 200		200						49
50	Deprec. Expense/Whs. Equip.	552			(G) 30		30						50
51	Deprec. Expense/Off. Equip.	554			(H) 70		70						51
52	Deprec. Expense/Trucks	556			(I) 300		300						52
53	Accum. Deprec./Trucks	171				(I) 300		300					53
54	Fees Earned	407				(J) 250		250					54
55					1 675	1 675	185 212	185 212					55
56													56

Wawdel Company
Worksheet
For the Month Ended August 31, 19—

	Account Title	Acct. No.	Trial Balance Debit	Trial Balance Credit	Adjustments Debit	Adjustments Credit	Adj. Trial Balance Debit	Adj. Trial Balance Credit	Income Statement Debit	Income Statement Credit	Balance Sheet Debit	Balance Sheet Credit	
1	Cash	101	10 700				10 700				10 700		1
2	Petty Cash	102	50				50				50		2
3	Notes Receivable	103	60 000				60 000				60 000		3
4	Accounts Receivable	104	6 400				6 400				6 400		4
5	Allowance for Bad Debts	105		20		(C) 100		120				120	5
6	Interest Receivable	106	500		(D) 500		1 000				1 000		6
7	Merchandise Inventory, Aug. 1	110	4 200				4 200		4 200	4 000	4 000		7
8	Supplies on Hand	112	400			(A) 100	300				300		8
9	Prepaid Insurance	114	550			(B) 50	500				500		9
10	Land	150	12 000				12 000				12 000		10
11	Building	155	48 000				48 000				48 000		11
12	Accum. Deprec./Building	156		700		(F) 200		900				900	12
13	Warehouse Equipment	160	4 000				4 000				4 000		13
14	Accum. Deprec./Whs. Equip.	161		210		(G) 30		240				240	14
15	Office Equipment	165	7 200				7 200				7 200		15
16	Accum. Deprec./Off. Equip.	166		550		(H) 70		620				620	16
17	Delivery Trucks	170	20 000				20 000				20 000		17
18	Bank Loan	201		5 500				5 500				5 500	18
19	Unearned Revenue	202		500	(J) 250			250				250	19
20	Accounts Payable	203		6 800				6 800				6 800	20
21	Bank Loan Interest Payable	204		75		(E) 75		150				150	21
22	Unemployment Insurance Payable	210		60				60				60	22
23	CPP Payable	211		120				120				120	23
24	Income Tax Payable	212		800				800				800	24
25	OHIP Payable	213		42				42				42	25
26	Group Insurance Payable	214		124				124				124	26
27	Mortgage Payable	250		50 000				50 000				50 000	27
28	R. Wawdel, Capital	301		85 530				85 530				85 530	28
29	R. Wawdel, Drawings	302	705				705				705		29
30	Sales	401		32 536				32 536		32 536			30

31	Sales Returns & Allowances	402	220				220		220				31
32	Sales Discounts	403	145				145		145				32
33	Purchases	501	5 800				5 800		5 800				33
34	Transportation-in	502	150				150		150				34
35	Purchases Returns & Allowances	503		210				210		210			35
36	Purchases Discounts	504		160				160		160			36
37	Advertising Expense	510	185				185		185				37
38	Utilities Expense	512	60				60		60				38
39	Delivery Expense	514	180				180		180				39
40	Wages & Salaries Expense	516	1 600				1 600		1 600				40
41	Payroll Tax Expense	518	864				864		864				41
42	Interest Expense	520	28				28		28				42
43			183 937	183 937									43
44	Supplies Expense	521			(A) 100		100		100				44
45	Insurance Expense	523			(B) 50		50		50				45
46	Bad Debts Expense	525			(C) 100		100		100				46
47	Interest Revenue	405				(D) 500		500		500			47
48	Bank Loan Interest Expense	530			(E) 75		75		75				48
49	Deprec. Expense/Bldg.	550			(F) 200		200		200				49
50	Deprec. Expense/Whs. Equip.	552			(G) 30		30		30				50
51	Deprec. Expense/Off. Equip.	554			(H) 70		70		70				51
52	Deprec. Expense/Trucks	556			(I) 300		300		300				52
53	Accum. Deprec./Trucks	171				(I) 300		300				300	53
54	Fees Earned	407				(J) 250		250		250			54
55					1 675	1 675	185 212	185 212	14 357	37 656	174 855	151 556	55
56										14 357			56
57	Net Income									23 299	→	23 299	57
58											174 855	174 855	58
59													59

only), (2) Purchases, (3) Transportation-in, (4) Purchases Returns and Allowances, and (5) Purchases Discount. In addition, the figure of the final inventory is needed to calculate the cost of goods sold. Analyze how each one is identified on the worksheet.

Inventory, Aug. 1			*$4 200*	
Purchases		*$5 800*		
Transportation-in		*150*		
Cost of Delivered Goods		*5 950*		
Purchases R & A	*$210*			
Purchases Discount	*160*	*370*		
Net Purchases			*5 580*	
Cost of Goods Available for Sale			*9 780*	
Inventory, Aug. 31			*4 000*	
Cost of Goods Sold				*$5 780*

(1) The beginning inventory is shown in the *Adjusted Trial Balance* section. It is shown as a debit figure, so it must be extended to the debit column of the *Income Statement* section. As a debit here, the balance is treated as part of the cost of goods sold. In other words, the effect of the debit is to decrease owner's equity in any accounting equation since the beginning inventory is assumed to have been completely sold.

(2) The amount of Purchases is a debit balance in the *Adjusted Trial Balance* section. As a debit, it must be extended to the debit side of the *Income Statement* section. Here, the balance must be considered as part of the cost of goods sold. In theory, under a periodic system, these purchases are assumed to have been completely sold; consequently, the debit indicates the effect of decreasing owner's equity in any accounting equation.

(3) Transportation-in is directly related to Purchases in order to calculate the cost of delivered goods. The account balance is a debit; therefore, it must be extended to the debit side of the *Income Statement* section. Since transportation-in adds to the cost of goods sold, and since the cost of goods sold decreases the

owner's equity in any accounting equation, the figure is correctly analyzed as a debit to the income statement.

(4) Purchases Returns and Allowances and Purchases Discounts are both contra accounts to Purchases. Both have credit balances. Since both accounts have the effect of decreasing the cost of purchases, both must decrease the cost of goods sold. Another way to express this idea is to say that both must increase owner's equity in any accounting equation; consequently, both must be credits in any income statement analysis. At this stage of the analysis, you should think of the *Income Statement* section on the worksheet as simply a method of calculating the net income (or loss) through a series of debits and credits.

(5) The ending inventory must be considered the critical part of the analysis. Under the periodic method, the final inventory balance is not shown in the *Trial Balance* section or the *Adjusted Trial Balance* section. At the end of the accounting period a physical stock-taking must occur to determine this cost figure. Assume that at the end of August the amount of final inventory is costed at $4 000. Three points of analysis must be made for this final inventory figure.

- The final inventory is acknowledged on the inventory line. Notice that the account code remains the same. You will learn how to update this account by a series of closing entries later in this chapter.
- The final inventory is an asset; therefore, the amount must be entered on the debit side of the *Balance Sheet* section.
- The final figure has the effect of decreasing the cost of goods sold; therefore, the figure is entered as a credit in the *Income Statement* section. As a credit here, the figure is correctly analyzed as contra to the "costs" entered in the debit column. To remember this point, check back to the illustration on page 554 showing the method of calculating indirectly the cost of goods sold for a firm using a periodic inventory method. It may help you to remember that the final inventory is entered on the worksheet as a double entry: a debit to the *Balance Sheet* section to indicate the correct asset amount as at the end of the accounting period, and a credit to the *Income Statement* section to indicate the effect of being contra to the cost of goods available for sale.

As an alternative, the final inventory, properly dated, may be shown on the worksheet on a separate line below the trial balance figures in the form of a double entry: debit to the balance sheet and credit to the income statement.

Wawdel Company
Worksheet
For the Month Ended August 31, 19—

	Account Title	Acct. No.	Adj. Trial Balance		Income Statement		Balance Sheet		
			Debit	Credit	Debit	Credit	Debit	Credit	
1	Cash	101	10 700				10 700		1
2	Petty Cash	102	50				50		2
3	Notes Receivable	103	60 000				60 000		3
4	Accounts Receivable	104	6 400				6 400		4
5	Allowance for Bad Debts	105		120				120	5
6	Interest Receivable	106	1 000				1 000		6
7	Merchandise Inventory, Aug. 1	110	4 200		4 200				7
54	Fees Earned	407		250		250			54
55			185 212	185 212					55
56	Merchandise Inventory, Aug. 31	110				4 000	4 000		56
57					14 357	37 656	174 855	151 556	57
58						14 357			58
59	Net Income					23 299	→	23 299	59
60							174 855	174 855	60

Step 5: Calculate the Net Income (or Loss) and Complete the Worksheet

After all amounts have been recorded into one of the two statements, the totals of the statement must be recorded. First, rule a single line across both sections after the last number recorded in either section. Second, total the debit column of the income statement (expenses and contra revenues and beginning inventory) and then total the credit column (revenues and contra expenses and ending inventory). Refer to the illustration above. Obviously, if the credit column total is larger than the debit column total, a net income exists. If the opposite situation exists, a net loss occurs. In either case, the smaller number is subtracted from the larger to calculate the net income or net loss. Identify the net income or loss in the *Account Title* column opposite the number. Next, total the debit and credit columns of the balance sheet. Finally, some accounting analysis is required. You know that net income belongs to the owner and thus causes owner's equity to increase. Therefore, net income is recorded in the balance sheet on the credit side. Conversely, net loss causes owner's equity to decrease; therefore, it should be recorded on the debit side. Regardless which of the situations exists, when the two columns are totalled they must be equal. See the illustration on page 553. If they are not equal, the error must be located.

Calculation of Net Loss

	Income Statement		Balance Sheet		
	Debit	Credit	Debit	Credit	
51	12 000	9 000	20 000	23 000	51
52	9 000				52
53	3 000 →		3 000		53
54			23 000	23 000	54
55					55
56					56

Wawdel Company
Worksheet
For the Month Ended August 31, 19—

	Account Title	Acct. No.	Trial Balance Debit	Trial Balance Credit	Adjustments Debit	Adjustments Credit	Adj. Trial Balance Debit	Adj. Trial Balance Credit	Income Statement Debit	Income Statement Credit	Balance Sheet Debit	Balance Sheet Credit	
1	Cash	101	10 700				10 700				10 700		1
2	Petty Cash	102	50				50				50		2
3	Notes Receivable	103	60 000				60 000				60 000		3
4	Accounts Receivable	104	6 400				6 400				6 400		4
5	Allowance for Bad Debts	105		20		(C) 100		120				120	5
18	Bank Loan	201		5 500				5 500				5 500	18
19	Unearned Revenue	202		500	(J) 250			250				250	19
20	Accounts Payable	203		6 800				6 800				6 800	20
21	Bank Loan Interest Payable	204		75		(E) 75		150				150	21
22	Unemployment Insurance Payable	210		60				60				60	22
23	CPP Payable	211		120				120				120	23
53	Accum. Deprec./Trucks	171				(I) 300		300				300	53
54	Fees Earned	407				(J) 250		250		250			54
55					1 675	1 675	185 212	185 212	14 357	37 656	174 855	151 556	55
56										14 357			56
57	Net Income									23 299 →		23 299	57
58											174 855	174 855	58
59													59

When they are in agreement, double-underline both statement columns.

Now the worksheet is finished, and the accountant has mathematical proof of its accuracy. We can move on to the next phase of the accounting cycle — the preparation of the financial statements.

TOPIC 1 PROBLEMS

16-1 The trial balance for Albert Hotel for the month ended October 31, 19— is illustrated.

Albert Hotel
Trial Balance
October 31, 19—

Cash	101	$ 100	
Prepaid Insurance	110	500	
Office Supplies on Hand	112	250	
Housekeeping Supplies on Hand	114	150	
Land	150	775	
Building	155	200	
Accumulated Depreciation/Building	156		$ 10
Equipment	170	175	
Accumulated Depreciation/Equipment	171		25
Accounts Payable	203		15
Unearned Revenue	205		150
Mortgage Payable*	250		260
M. Albert, Capital	301		1 455
M. Albert, Drawings	302	165	
Concession Revenue	401		150
Accommodation Revenue	405		600
Telephone Expense	510	50	
Cleaning Expense	513	70	
Wages Expense	514	210	
Miscellaneous Expense	516	20	
		$2 665	$2 665

The mortgage payable is secured by the land and the portion falling due within this current year is $12.

Given the following additional information, prepare a ten-column worksheet.

(i) An examination of the insurance policy reveals $350 of insurance still in force.

(ii) A count of the office supplies in the back room reveals that $100 of the supplies have been used up.

(iii) The custodial department counted the household supplies and determined that $80 of supplies remains unused.

(iv) The building depreciation for the period totalled $15. The Equipment Accumulated Depreciation account increased by $55.

(v) The company has earned, but not yet received, concession revenue equal to $22.

(vi) The hotel owes to its employees $31 for wages earned, but as of October 31, 19— has not yet paid.

(vii) G. Peabody, a corporation president, paid for the executive suite on October 15, 19— for the next three months. This suite rents at $50 per month.

Key Check Figure
Net Income = $26

16-2 Illustrated is the trial balance for Royal Rugs as at December 31, 19-4.

Royal Rugs
Trial Balance
December 31, 19-4

Cash	101	$ 5 500	
Accounts Receivable	105	8 000	
Allowance for Bad Debts	106		$ 40
Inventory January 1, 19-4	110	12 500	
Office Supplies on Hand	115	1 200	
Prepaid Insurance	120	2 700	
Land	150	12 000	
Building	160	53 000	
Accumulated Depreciation/Building	161		2 800
Trucks	165	25 000	
Accumulated Depreciation/Truck	166		1 500
Office Equipment	171	6 000	
Accumulated Depreciation/Equipment	172		2 800
Bank Loan Payable	210		11 000
Accounts Payable	212		2 900
Unearned Revenue	215		1 800
Property Taxes Payable	220		1 400
P. Matthews, Capital	301		88 160
P. Matthews, Drawings	302	1 100	
Carpet Sales	410		76 000
Sales Returns and Allowances	411	500	
Sales Discounts	412	2 300	
Installation Fees Earned	420		25 500
Purchases	501	62 000	
Transportation-in	502	5 800	
Purchases Returns and Allowances	503		300
Purchases Discounts	504		4 100
Wages Expense	508	18 900	
Supplies Expense	520	400	
Telephone Expense	525	1 400	
		$218 300	$218 300

Given the following information, prepare a ten-column year-end worksheet.

(i) The physical inventory count revealed $11 950 of material in the warehouse.

(ii) All but $150 of the unearned revenue had been earned by year-end. (One-third is installation; two-thirds is carpet sales.)

(iii) The staff determined that there is still $250 of unexpired insurance at year-end.

(iv) There are no office supplies left at year-end.

(v) The business uses the straight-line method of depreciation. Building: salvage $3 000, useful life 25 years. Trucks: salvage $0, useful life 5 years. Equipment: salvage $500, useful life 11 years.

(vi) The company decides to write off A. Mitchell as a bad debt: $50.

(vii) The aging of the receivables produces an estimate for bad debts for the year of $90.

(viii) Interest on the bank loan is 12% per annum. Payments are required January 31 and July 31. The last instalment was paid on July 31. Nothing has been paid or recorded since that date.

(ix) The PDQ Company had us install two rugs. The material was paid for and recorded immediately, but the instalment charges are still unrecorded and unpaid. These charges total $80.

(x) Two days' wages totalling $260 are outstanding and unrecorded.

Key Check Figure
Net Income =
$3 720

16-3 Given the trial balance illustrated and the following additional information, prepare a ten-column worksheet for the month ended July 31, 19-3.

H & P Fisheries Enterprise
Trial Balance
July 31, 19-3

Cash	101	$ 11 600	
Accounts Receivable	105	7 500	
Allowance for Bad Debts	106		$ 50
Warehouse Supplies	110	2 200	
Marine Supplies	111	6 150	
Prepaid Insurance	114	990	
Land	150	12 000	
Building	155	48 000	
Accumulated Depreciation/Building	156		10 500
Boat	160	152 000	
Accumulated Depreciation/Boat	161		47 870
Equipment	170	22 000	
Accumulated Depreciation/Equipment	171		10 110
Accounts Payable	201		1 250
Mortgage Payable	260		88 000
H. Williamson, Capital	301		49 888
H. Williamson, Drawings	302	18 000	
Fish Sales	401		96 580
Fuel Expense	505	6 700	
Maintenance Expense	510	1 580	
Depreciation Expense/Building	515	525	
Depreciation Expense/Boat	516	5 066	
Depreciation Expense/Equipment	517	3 667	
Insurance Expense	520	990	
Mortgage Interest Expense	525	5 280	
		$304 248	$304 248

(i) Insurance was purchased January 2, 19-3. The policy runs for one full year. Remember that adjustments have been recorded every month.

(ii) A review of the supplies reveals the following amounts still available: Warehouse $2 000, Marine Supplies $5 900.

(iii) Building: salvage value $6 000, useful life 40 years. Straight-line depreciation.

(iv) Depreciation for the month: Boat $884, Equipment $611.

(v) On July 30, 19-3 the company negotiated a bank loan for $10 000. It has not yet been recorded.

(vi) Mortgage interest for the month is not yet recorded. The payment was mailed out by means of a cheque, but the amount has not yet been recorded. The rate of interest is 12% per annum.

(vii) Fuel received during July but not yet recorded or paid for totals $1 100.

(viii) The mortgage payable is secured by the boat and the current portion owing is equal to $5 000.

Key Check Figure
Net Income =
$68 594.50

16-4 Challenge Problem *Note:* If the instructor so desires, this problem may be left until after Topic 3 has been covered. This will enable the student to work through the entire process.

The Hooker Wholesale Company is just finishing its second full year of operation. The company's year-end is December 31. The product line is children's toys. From the illustrated trial balance and additional information prepare all adjustments and then do the ten-column worksheet. The company draws off financial statements each month.

Additional Information

(i) The year-end inventory count reveals 52 510 units at an average cost of $1.52 per unit.

(ii) Examination of the prepaid insurance shows $600 is still unexpired.

(iii) The management decides to write off two accounts — R. Wrong $97 and R. Wright $100 — as uncollectable.

(iv) The aging of receivables indicates that $869 should be the losses due to bad debts this coming year.

(v) The company has undertaken three contracts. The details are as follows: (1) ABC Company wanted a six-month supply of "Wonderful Walkers," total cost $18 000. The contract was dated November 1, 19-1 and required full payment in advance; (2) Delta Distributors ordered 25 000 yo-yos at $0.50 per unit on December 15, 19-1. The shipment has been delivered, but to date the entry has not been recorded and no payment has been received; (3) Valarie's Variety Stores ordered $24 000 of various toys for its stores. The agreement, signed May 1, 19-1, required one-half of the payment in advance and one-half on October 1, 19-1. Hooker is to stock the variety store with equal amounts of toys each month for ten months. Both parties have fulfilled their part of the agreement to date.

(vi) Wages earned but not paid as of December 31 are as follows: gross pay $1 550, net pay (?), federal taxes $510, Canada Pension Plan $43, unemployment insurance $38. *Hint:* Don't forget the company's portion of the government expenses.

(vii) The firm uses the capital cost allowance method. The trucks were bought January 2 of the first year of operation. Warehouse: straight-line depreciation, salvage $1 000, useful life 10 years. Equipment: straight-line depreciation, no salvage, useful life 7 years.

(viii) The mortgage on the warehouse requires interest payments each month.

Hooker Wholesale Company
Trial Balance
December 31, 19-1

Cash	101	$ 6 740.00	
Accounts Receivable	104	24 850.00	
Allowance for Bad Debts	105		$ 112.00
Supplies	110	1 760.00	
Inventory January 1, 19-1	120	74 985.00	
Prepaid Insurance	125	750.00	
Land	150	24 000.00	
Warehouse	155	25 000.00	
Accumulated Depreciation/ Warehouse	156		4 600.00
Trucks	160	34 000.00	
Accumulated Depreciation/Trucks	161		16 745.00
Equipment	170	21 000.00	
Accumulated Depreciation/ Equipment	171		5 750.00
Bank Loan Payable	201		10 000.00
Accounts Payable	205		11 800.00
Unearned Revenue	210		22 200.00
Mortgage Payable	250		23 000.00
T.J. Hooker, Capital	301		117 792.08
T.J. Hooker, Drawings	302	31 500.00	
Toy Sales	401		147 600.00
Sales Returns and Allowances	403	890.00	
Sales Discounts	405	1 505.00	
Purchases	501	97 800.00	
Purchases Returns and Allowances	505		1 450.00
Purchases Discounts	506		1 043.00
Transportation-in	510	1 710.00	
Insurance Expense	520	1 050.00	
Depreciation/Warehouse	530	2 200.00	
Depreciation/Trucks	532	6 545.00	
Depreciation/Equipment	534	2 750.00	
Mortgage Interest Expense	550	3 057.08	
		$362 092.08	$362 092.08

The interest rate is 14.5% per annum and December's payment has not been recorded or paid.

Key Check Figure
Net Income = $51 243

(ix) The mortgage payable is secured by the land and the warehouse, and the portion owing this year is $12 000.

TOPIC 2 PREPARING FINANCIAL STATEMENTS

This topic will deal with the preparation of financial statements from the related worksheet you have just examined. The preparation of financial statements is Step 6 in the accounting cycle.

Preparing the Income Statement

The first statement must be the income statement. The completed worksheet contains all the necessary information to complete both the income statement and the balance sheet. All you must do is to arrange the information into the correct sequence and format of a formal statement. A popular way is to divide it into sections: Revenue from Sales, Cost of Goods Sold, and Operating Expenses. If other revenues or other expenses exist, they are added to the end of the statement under those titles. This results in the calculation of either net income or net loss. The illustration on page 564 will help you prepare the formal statement from the worksheet.

Multiple- vs. Single-Step Income Statements

The first presentation of Wawdel Company illustrates a multiple-step statement. This method allows the management to report in detail and in "multiples" — that is, breaking up revenues and breaking up expenses, in order to report partial incomes such as Gross Profit from Sales (Gross Margin from Sales) and Operating Income. The advantage of this type of statement is the amount of disclosure it provides. The main disadvantage is its complexity. Only revenue related to sales can be listed under the initial *Revenue* location. Since this type of statement reports a partial income — Gross Margin *from Sales* — no other type of revenue can be included if a meaningful comparison of numbers is to take place. To look after the other, non-operating revenues, the income statement must be expanded to include the categories *Other Revenues* and *Other Expenses* after the total of the operating income. See the illustration on page 564.

On page 565, a single-step statement is shown. The main advantage of this statement is its lack of complexity. The main disadvantage is its lack of reporting ability, because this method reports all sources of revenue under one heading. Similarly, only one heading, *Expenses*, is used, because no multiples are reported. Since all expenses are reported under this heading, cost

Wawdel Company
Worksheet
For the Month Ended August 31, 19—

	Account Title	Income Statement Debit	Income Statement Credit
1	Cash		
2	Notes Receivable		
3	Accounts Receivable		
4	Allowance for Bad Debts		
5	Revenue Receivable		
6	Merchandise Inventory	4 200 (E)	4 000 (F)
30	Sales		32 536
31	Sales R & A	220	
32	Sales Discounts	145	
33	Purchases	5 800	
34	Transportation-in	150	
35	Purchases R & A		210
36	Purchases Discounts		160
37	Advertising Expense	185	
38	Utilities Expense	60	
39	Delivery Expense	180	
40	Wages and Sal. Expense	1 600	
41	Payroll Tax Expense	864	
42	Other Interest Expense	28	(D)
43			
44	Supplies Expense	100	
45	Insurance Expense	50	
46	Bad Debts Expense	100	
47	Interest Earned		500 (B)
48	Bk. Loan Interest Expense	75	(C)
49	Deprec. Expense/Bldg.	200	
50	Deprec. Expense/Whs. Equip.	30	
51	Deprec. Expense/Off. Equip.	70	
52	Deprec. Expense/Trucks	300	
53	Accum. Deprec./Trucks		
54	Fees Earned		250 (A)
55		14 357	37 656
56			14 357
57	Net Income		23 299
58			

Wawdel Company
Income Statement
For the Month Ended August 31, 19—

Sales Revenue:				
Gross Sales				$32 536
Less: Sales Returns and Allowances			$ 220	
Sales Discounts			145	365
Net Sales				32 171
Cost of Goods Sold:				
(E) Inventory, August 1			4 200	
Purchases		$5 800		
Add Transportation-in		150		
Cost of Delivered Goods		5 950		
Less: Purchases Returns and Allowances	$210			
Purchases Discounts	160	370		
Net Purchases			5 580	
Cost of Goods Available for Sale			9 780	
(F) Less: Inventory, August 31			4 000	
Cost of Goods Sold				5 780
Gross Margin from Sales				26 391
Operating Expenses:				
Advertising Expense			185	
Utilities Expense			60	
Delivery Expense			180	
Wages and Salaries Expense			1 600	
Payroll Taxes Expense			864	
Supplies Expense			100	
Insurance Expense			50	
Bad Debts Expense			100	
Deprec. Expense/Building			200	
Deprec. Expense/Warehouse Equipment			30	
Deprec. Expense/Office Equipment			70	
Deprec. Expense/Trucks			300	
Total Operating Expenses				3 739
Operating Income				22 652
Other Revenues:				
(B) Interest Earned		500		
(A) Fees Earned		250	750	
Other Expenses:				
(C) Interest on Bank Loan		75		
(D) Other Interest Expense		28	103	647
Net Income				$23 299

Single-Step Statement

Wawdel Company
Income Statement
For the Month Ended August 31, 19—

Revenues:		
Gross Sales		*$32 536*
Less: Sales Returns and Allowances	*$220*	
Sales Discounts	*145*	*365*
Net Sales		*32 171*
Interest Earned		*500*
Fees Earned		*250*
Total Revenue		*$32 921*
Expenses:		
Cost of Goods Sold (see separate schedule)	*$5 780*	
Advertising	*185*	
Utilities	*60*	
Delivery	*180*	
Wages and Salaries	*1 600*	
Payroll Taxes	*864*	
Supplies Used	*100*	
Insurance Used	*50*	
Bad Debts	*100*	
Depreciation/Building	*200*	
Depreciation/Warehouse Equipment	*30*	
Depreciation/Office Equipment	*70*	
Depreciation/Trucks	*300*	
Interest on Bank Loan	*75*	
Other Interest Expense	*28*	
Total Expenses		*9 622*
Net Income		*$23 299*

of goods sold is also included as a single number supported by a separate schedule.

Another important point is illustrated in the single-step statement. Some accountants prefer to avoid the use of account titles on financial statements by using account names similar to those illustrated in the single-step statement expense section. Such account names are common in both single- and multiple-step statements and not exclusive to one or the other.

A Separate Cost of Goods Sold Schedule

Some firms prepare an income statement that provides only a total figure for Cost of Goods Sold. To calculate the cost of goods sold figure, the firm produces the cost of goods sold schedule. (See the illustration on page 567.) The schedule is prepared before the income statement, so that the cost of goods sold figure can be placed into the income statement as it is prepared. (See the second illustration on page 567.)

Gross margin: the difference between net sales and cost of goods sold.

The schedule provides this key figure, Net Sales less Cost of Goods Sold, permitting the calculation of *Gross Profit from Sales* or what is often called gross margin. Note that while some businesses prefer the latter term, both are used in accounting practice.

Classified Income Statement

Previously you recorded all expenses on the merchandising firm under the heading *Operating Expenses.* Many larger firms, however, require a more detailed breakdown or classification of the business operating expenses. Typically, the operating expenses are divided into two sections: *Selling Expenses* and *General and Administrative Expenses.* Note that all non-operating expenses will be recorded in a separate section below the income from operations. Examine the illustration found on page 568 carefully.

You will observe in the classified income statement that the operating expenses have been divided into two groups: *Selling Expenses* and *General and Administrative Expenses.* Note as well that the non-operating expenses — *Other Interest Expense* and *Bank Loan Interest Expense* — are reported after Income from Operations. The following are the important points of analysis for this new area of study.

Selling expenses: one class of operating expenses related directly or indirectly to the selling function of the business.

Selling Expenses In general, selling expenses include all expenses of storing and preparing merchandise for sale, advertising and promotion, and actually making sales, such as salaries for the sales personnel. In addition, the expense of delivering the goods from your business to the customer is usually regarded as a selling expense. Many of the selling expenses and general and administrative expenses — advertising, delivery, depreciation on warehouse equipment, and depreciation on delivery truck expenses — require no separate division in the General Ledger.

There are other areas that require special identification and some fair division between the two classes. For example, all the salaries and wages expense cannot be listed in one account. Clearly there are salaries paid to sales and to administrative personnel. If the company's premises house both the selling and

Wawdel Company
Schedule of Cost of Goods Sold
For the Month Ended August 31, 19—

Merchandise Inventory, August 1			$4 200	
Purchases		$5 800		
Transportation-in		150		
Cost of Delivered Goods		5 950		
Purchases Returns and Allowances	$210			
Purchases Discounts	160	370		
Net Purchases			5 580	
Cost of Goods Available for Sale			9 780	
Merchandise Inventory, August 31			4 000	
Cost of Goods Sold				$5 780

Wawdel Company
Income Statement
For the Month Ended August 31, 19—

Revenue from Sales:		
Net Sales		$32 171
Cost of Goods Sold (see separate schedule)		5 780
Gross Margin from Sales		26 391
Operating Expenses:		
Selling Expenses	$2 994	
General and Administrative	745	3 739
Operating Income		22 652
*Other Revenues and Expenses:		
Other Revenues	$750	
Other Expenses	103	647
Net Income		$23 299

*This is another presentation of the other revenues and other expenses. Compare this to the method used in the multiple-step presentation shown earlier. **Note:** Only totals were used in the above illustration, to save space. Ordinarily all items would be listed. This type of presentation is frequently referred to as a condensed statement.

administrative functions, some division, usually by a percentage of floor area occupied, must be applied. For example, if sales occupies 80% of the area, it might be fair to assign 80% of the cost

Wawdel Company
Income Statement
For the Month Ended August 31, 19—

Revenue from Sales:			
Sales		$32 536	
Sales Returns and Allowances	$220		
Sales Discounts	145	365	
Net Sales			$32 171
Cost of Goods Sold (see schedule)			5 780
Gross Margin From Sales			26 391
Operating Expenses:			
Selling Expenses:			
Advertising	$ 185		
Utilities	48		
Delivery	180		
Wages and Salaries	1 280		
Payroll Taxes	691		
Supplies	80		
Insurance	40		
Depreciation/Building	160		
Depreciation/Warehouse Equipment	30		
Depreciation/Delivery Truck	300		
Total Selling Expenses		$ 2 994	
General and Administrative Expenses			
Utilities	$ 12		
Wages and Salaries	320		
Payroll Taxes	173		
Supplies	20		
Insurance	10		
Bad Debts	100		
Depreciation/Building	40		
Depreciation/Office Equipment	70		
Total General and Administrative		745	
Total Operating Expenses			3 739
Income From Operations			22 652
Other Revenues:			
Fees Earned	$ 250		
Interest Revenue	500	$ 750	
Other Expenses:			
Other Interest Expense	28		
Bank Loan Interest Expense	75	103	647
Net Income			$23 299

for utilities, taxes, depreciation, etc. to Selling Expenses and 20% to General and Administrative Expenses.

This type of discussion is only elementary "cost accounting." Since cost accounting is an advanced-level study, this book will not deal with it in any more detail.

General and Administrative Expenses In general, this classification includes expenses involving the general office, the accounting office, and the personnel of those offices. In addition, costs involving the credit and collection departments fall under this expense classification. Examples of general and administrative expenses might include Bad Debts Expense and Depreciation Expense/Office Equipment. Other expenses will fall into a grey area as was the case with selling expenses. Office supplies, payroll taxes expense, and insurance expense will require an equitable division between selling and general and administrative expenses.

General and administrative expenses: a large class of operating expenses related to the non-selling aspects of the business.

Finally, the division of expense means that there must be a division of responsibility regarding the budgeting of these expenses. Budgeting is a coordinated plan to estimate the future transactions covering a planned time period. It is another major subdivision of accounting best dealt with in an advanced course.

Budgeting: a coordinated plan to estimate the future transactions covering a planned period of time.

Income from Operations Another addition to the classified income statement is *Income from Operations* or *Operating Income*. The statement attempts to match the revenues generated from operations and the expenses incurred in the generation of that revenue. Any other source of revenue and expense occurring within the firm is to be isolated and identified after the income from operations in the income statement. When these items are added to and subtracted from the income from operations figure, net income or net loss results. Examine the end of the classified statement on page 568 for an example of non-operating items.

Income from operations: the excess of matching revenues and expenses that are related to the main operations of the business.

Condensed Income Statement

Many firms do not wish to present a classified statement at all times. Instead, they prepare a condensed or shortened version similar to the illustration on page 567. Since the firm will still prepare a schedule of cost of goods sold, the final number is available for use in the condensed income statement. Totals for sales and for selling and general and administrative expenses can be generated relatively easily from the General Ledger accounts.

Notice that the details within each section have been omitted. The figures included will be net sales, cost of goods sold, the calculation for gross margin from sales, the selling and general and administrative expenses, income from operations, any non-operating revenues and/or expenses, and net income or loss. The condensed statements are prepared for ease of understanding by the general public. Accountants support the principle for more disclosure, and detailed statements are required by the Department of National Revenue — Taxation and by management.

Preparing the Balance Sheet The classified balance sheet is prepared, of course, after the income statement. You will recall that the two formats for the balance sheet are the account form and the report form. The account form is most popular for an annual report presentation, but the report form is far easier when the statement is in typewritten form. The report form is illustrated on page 572.

The treatment of Mortgage Payable is new and of particular importance in the balance sheet.

- It is important to tell the reader of the balance sheet as much information about the mortgage as space permits. This usually means the insertion of the following pieces of information: the type of mortgage, the due date, and the assets that are offered as security.
- There should be a notation made beside each asset used to secure a mortgage payable.
- The portion of the mortgage that falls due during this accounting year must be identified in the *Current Liabilities* section.
- The current portion must be subtracted from the total amount of the mortgage owing in the *Long-Term Liabilities* section. Examine the illustration now and take particular note of the points mentioned above.

Preparing the Statement of Owner's Equity

To reduce the size and complexity of the Balance Sheet, some firms prepare a Statement of Owner's Equity similar to the one illustrated below. This enables the detailed calculations to be completed and illustrated away from the classified balance sheet. The final amount is then placed into the balance sheet in the appropriate location. The detail still exists in the statement of

Wawdel Company
Statement of Owner's Equity
For the Month Ended August 31, 19—

R. Wawdel, Capital, August 1		*$ 85 530*
Net Income	*$23 299*	
Less: R. Wawdel, Drawings	*705*	
Increase in Capital		*22 594*
R. Wawdel, Capital, August 31		*$108 124*

Wawdel Company
Worksheet
For the Month Ended August 31, 19—

	Account Title	Acct. No.	Balance Sheet Debit	Balance Sheet Credit	
1	Cash	101	10 700		1
2	Petty Cash	102	50		2
3	Notes Receivable	103	60 000		3
4	Accounts Receivable	104	6 400		4
5	Allowance for Bad Debts	105		120	5
6	Interest Receivable	106	1 000		6
7	Merchandise Inventory, Aug. 31	110	4 000		7
8	Supplies on Hand	112	300		8
9	Prepaid Insurance	114	500		9
10	Land	150	12 000		10
11	Building	155	48 000		11
12	Accum. Deprec./Building	156		900	12
13	Warehouse Equipment	160	4 000		13
14	Accum. Deprec./Whs. Equip.	161		240	14
15	Office Equipment	165	7 200		15
16	Accum. Deprec./Off. Equip.	166		620	16
17	Delivery Trucks	170	20 000		17
18	Bank Loan	201		5 500	18
19	Unearned Revenue	202		250	19
20	Accounts Payable	203		6 800	20
21	Bank Loan Interest Payable	204		150	21
22	Unemployment Ins. Pay.	210		60	22
23	CPP Payable	211		120	23
24	Income Tax Payable	212		800	24
25	OHIP Payable	213		42	25
26	Group Insurance Payable	214		124	26
27	Mortgage Payable	250		50 000	27
28	R. Wawdel, Capital	301		85 530	28
29	R. Wawdel, Drawings	302	705		29
52	Deprec. Expense/Trucks	556			52
53	Accum. Deprec./Trucks	171		300	53
54	Fees Earned	407			54
55			174 855	151 556	55
56					56
57	Net Income			23 299	57
58			174 855	174 855	58

owner's equity and the size and complexity of the balance sheet is still reduced. Anyone requiring the details can simply refer to the statement of owner's equity. The details that might be shown include:

- the beginning capital balance
- any additional investments
- the net income or loss for the period
- the personal withdrawals of the owner

Not all the above information is available from the worksheet. Beginning capital plus additional investments would be found in

Wawdel Company
Balance Sheet
As at August 31, 19—

ASSETS

Current Assets:			
Cash		$10 750	
Notes Receivable		60 000	
Interest Receivable		1 000	
Accounts Receivable	$ 6 400		
Less: Allowance for Bad Debts	120	6 280	
Merchandise Inventory (at cost)		4 000	
Supplies on Hand		300	
Prepaid Insurance		500	
Total Current Assets			$ 82 830
Fixed Assets (at cost):			
Land (Security for Mortgage Payable)		$ 12 000	
Building (Security for Mortgage Payable)	$48 000		
Less: Accumulated Depreciation/Building	900	47 100	
Warehouse Equipment	4 000		
Less: Accumulated Depreciation/Warehouse Equipment	240	3 760	
Office Equipment	7 200		
Less: Accumulated Depreciation/Office Equipment	620	6 580	
Delivery Trucks	20 000		
Less: Accumulated Depreciation/Trucks	300	19 700	
Total Fixed Assets			89 140
Total Assets			$171 970

LIABILITIES AND OWNER'S EQUITY

Current Liabilities:		
Bank Loan Payable	$ 5 500	
Accounts Payable	6 800	
Unearned Revenue	250	
Interest Payable on Bank Loan	150	
Unemployment Insurance Payable	60	
CPP Payable	120	
Income Tax Collected from Employees Payable	800	
OHIP Payable	42	
Group Insurance Payable	124	
Current Portion of Mortgage Payable	2 000	
Total Current Liabilities		15 846
Long-Term Liabilities:		
10% Mortgage Payable, due 20— (secured by Land and Building)	50 000	
Less: Current Portion	2 000	48 000
Total Liabilities		63 846
Owner's Equity:		
R. Wawdel, Capital	$ 85 530	
Add: Net Income	23 299	
	108 829	
Less: R. Wawdel, Drawings	705	
Total Owner's Equity		108 124
Total Liabilities and Owner's Equity		$171 970

the Capital Account. The statement of owner's equity reports changes in the equity of the owner of a single proprietorship. Remember, the equity is the owner's claim against the total assets. Equity is made up of the net income and the owner's investment. Partnership equity is prepared in a Statement of Partnership Equity. Corporations prepare equity for the shareholders in the Statement of Retained Earnings.

LIABILITIES	
Total Liabilities	$ 63 846
OWNER'S EQUITY	
R. Wawdel, Capital	108 124
Total Lias. and O.E.	$171 970

STATEMENT OF OWNER'S EQUITY

Capital, January 1		$10 000
Additional Investment		1 200
Total Investment		$11 200
Net Loss for the Year	$550	
Drawings	950	
Decrease in Capital		1 500
Capital, December 31		$ 9 700

Additional Investment and Net Loss Illustrated

TOPIC 2 PROBLEMS

16-5 Refer to Problem 16-1, about Albert Hotel, and prepare the following from the completed worksheet:
a A formal income statement. (No classification is required.)
b A formal balance sheet.

Key Check Figure Total Assets = $1 747

16-6 Refer to Problem 16-2, about Royal Rugs, and prepare the following from the completed worksheet:
a Cost of goods sold schedule.
b A formal income statement. (No classification is required.)
c A formal balance sheet.

Key Check Figure Cost of Goods Sold = $63 950

16-7 Refer to the worksheet of Problem 16-3 and prepare the following:
a An income statement for the month-end.
b A classified balance sheet.

Key Check Figure Total Assets = $200 832.50

16-8 Refer to Problem 16-4 and prepare from the completed worksheet the following:
a A schedule of cost of goods sold.
b A classified income statement. *Note:* The business follows a practice that divides the selling and administrative expenses on a 90:10 split.
c A statement of owner's equity.
d A formal classified balance sheet.

Key Check Figure Cost of Goods Sold = $92 186.80, Total Assets = $201 059.20

TOPIC 3 COMPLETING THE ACCOUNTING CYCLE

Six steps of the accounting cycle have been covered to this point: (1) originating the accounting data, (2) journalizing, (3) posting, (4) preparing trial balances, (5) preparing a worksheet, and (6) preparing a set of financial statements. The last three steps will be dealt with in this Topic: (7) making the adjusting entries, (8) making the closing entries, and (9) preparing a postclosing trial balance.

Making the Adjusting Entries

Revenues and expenses in the worksheet reflect up-to-date balances, since adjustments were completed within the worksheet. Also, the formal financial statements reflect a proper match-up because the numbers used came from the worksheet. It is equally important, however, for the General Ledger accounts to reflect the same up-to-date balances. Unless the adjustments are journalized and then posted to the appropriate General Ledger accounts, this task will never be completed. Therefore, you must now return to the adjustment column of the worksheet and carefully journalize, in the General Journal, each of the adjustments. Compare the worksheet column to the illustration of the journal on page 575. Notice that the posting reference numbers have been shown, indicating that posting has taken place as soon as the journal entries were completed. In order to save space, no postings have been illustrated.

Making the Closing Entries

If you are not certain of the closing procedures, refer to Topic 1 in Chapter 6. The closing entries bring all revenue, expense, and drawings accounts to zero in order that those accounts might receive transactions from the next accounting period. Furthermore, in a merchandising firm, the beginning inventory figure must be closed and then updated with the most recently calculated figure, called *Ending Inventory*. This is accomplished with the use of a clearing account called Revenue and Expense Summary. The process is as follows:

(1) All revenue accounts are debited with equal and opposite amounts to those found in their ledger account. The R & E Summary records the single credit entry to offset the debit entries.

(2) All expense accounts are credited with equal and opposite amounts. The R & E Summary records the single debit entry to offset the total credit entries.

(3) The old merchandise inventory figure is eliminated with an equal and opposite credit entry. The R & E Summary account supplies the equal and opposite debit entry.

(4) The new inventory figure is brought into the Inventory account with a debit entry. The Summary supplies the equal and opposite credit entry.

General Journal Adjusting Entries

19—					
Aug.	31	Supplies Expense	521	100	
		Supplies on Hand	112		100
		A count of supplies revealed $300 of supplies on hand. ($400 — $300 = $100.)			
	31	Insurance Expense	523	50	
		Prepaid Insurance	114		50
		Examination of the insurance policy reveals $50 of insurance has been used up.			
	31	Bad Debts Expense	525	100	
		Allowance for Bad Debts	105		100
		The aged accounts receivable reveals $120 of uncollectable accounts for the period. The Allowance for Bad Debts accounts requires an additional $100 ($120 — $20).			
	31	Interest Receivable	106	500	
		Interest Revenue	405		500
		Interest earned on the note equals $500 per month.			
	31	Bank Loan Interest Expense	530	75	
		Bank Loan Interest Payable	204		75
		The monthly interest accrued equals $75 ($900/12.)			
	31	Depreciation Expense/Building	550	200	
		Accum. Deprec./Building	156		200
		($48 000/20 = $2 400/12 = $200.)			
	31	Deprec. Exp./Warehouse Equip.	552	30	
		Accum. Deprec./Warehouse Equip.	161		30
		*($360/12 = $30.)			
	31	Deprec. Exp./Off. Equip.	554	70	
		Accum. Deprec./Off. Equip.	166		70
		*($840/12 = $70.)			
	31	Deprec. Exp./Truck	556	300	
		Accum. Deprec./Truck	171		300
		*($18 000/5 = $3 600/12 = $300.) (Base cost $20 000 less $2 000 disposal cost = $18 000.)			
	31	Unearned Revenue	202	250	
		Fees Earned	407		250
		Each month $250 is earned by partial completion of the contract.			

*Calculation usually performed in detail on supporting schedules maintained on each separate asset.

(5) The R & E Summary is totalled and then closed to the Capital account.

(6) Finally, the Drawings account is closed directly to Capital with an equal and opposite credit entry.

When the worksheet is available, all closing information can be completed from the income statement columns, with the exception of the drawings amount. A short-cut, using two compound journal entries, will close the revenue and expense accounts and deal with the merchandise inventory amounts with only two journal entries. Simply, anything in the credit column of the worksheet must be debited and the R & E Summary will provide the offsetting credit entry. Similarly, anything in the debit column must be credited, the R & E Summary providing the debit entry. This, of course, will eventually have to be posted to each of the accounts in the General Ledger. Next the R & E Summary must be closed to Capital and finally Drawings will be closed directly to the Capital account. Although many firms use this system, it does not lend itself to a simple explanation regarding the handling of beginning and ending inventory. It does, however, save time if handled properly. The following is a step-by-step breakdown of the closing procedure. Follow the General Journal entries and examine the related T-accounts for these closing entries. All the accounts are located in the worksheet and the income statement and balance sheet of the Wawdel Company illustration.

Closing Entry 1 Transfer the revenue from the sales by closing the Sales, Interest Revenue, and Fees Earned accounts to R & E Summary. Remember, revenue accounts are considered temporary accounts because they are closed at the end of an accounting period. The R & E Summary account will now have a credit balance.

GENERAL JOURNAL **Page** *10*

Date 19—	Account Title and Explanation	Post. Ref.	Debit	Credit
Aug. 31	Sales	401	32 536	
	Fees Earned	407	250	
	Interest Earned	405	500	
	R & E Summary	399		33 286
	To close the revenue accounts.			

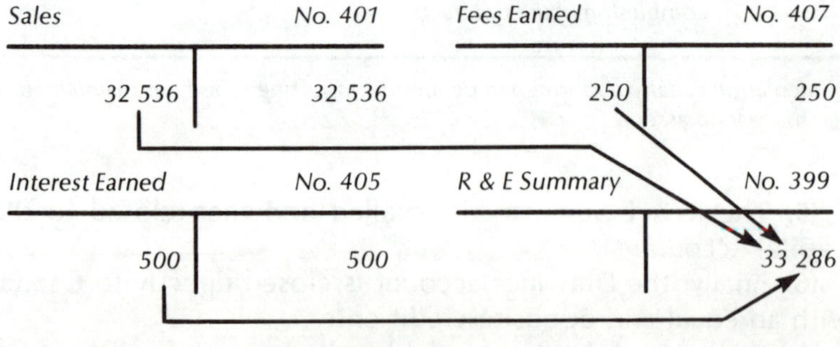

Closing Entry 2 Transfer the two contra revenue accounts Sales Discounts and Sales Returns and Allowances to the R & E Summary. After posting this entry, the balance of the Summary account will be equal to the net Sales figure plus the total of Other Revenue as reported on the income statement.

GENERAL JOURNAL **Page** *10*

Date 19—	Account Title and Explanation	Post. Ref.	Debit	Credit
Aug. 31	*R & E Summary*	*399*	*365*	
	Sales Returns and Allowances	*402*		*220*
	Sales Discounts	*403*		*145*
	To close the contra sales accounts.			

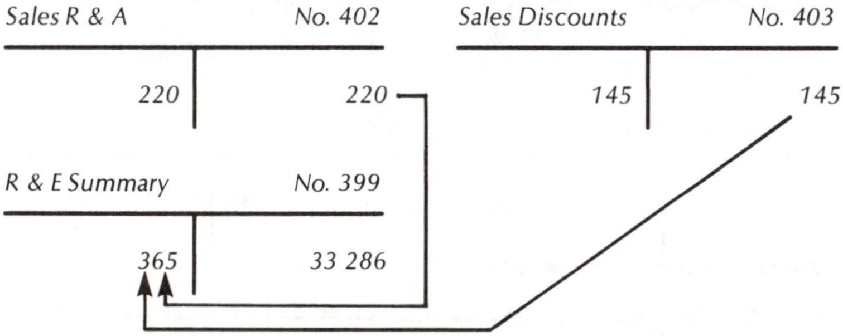

Closing Entry 3 Transfer the beginning inventory by debiting the R & E Summary and crediting the merchandise inventory account. This entry, when posted, would cause the inventory account to equal zero, thus closing the account. The R & E Summary balance would be on the side on which it is found in the worksheet of the income statement.

GENERAL JOURNAL **Page** *10*

Date 19—	Account Title and Explanation	Post. Ref.	Debit	Credit
Aug. 31	*R & E Summary*	*399*	*4 200*	
	Merchandise Inventory	*110*		*4 200*
	To close the beginning inventory figure.			

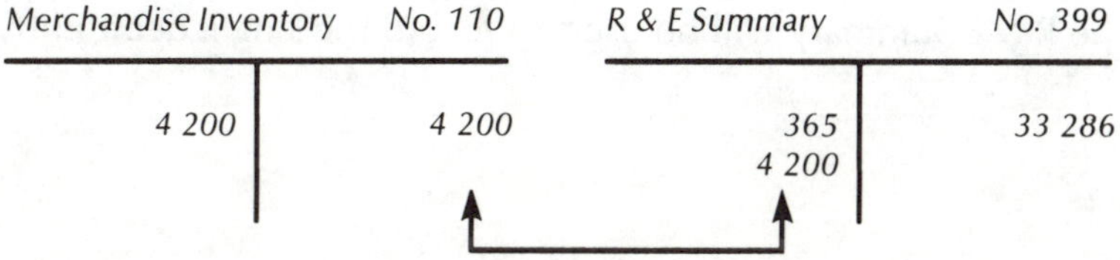

Closing Entry 4 Record the ending inventory on the debit side of that account and the credit side on R & E Summary. When posted, the Inventory account will now reflect the most up-to-date inventory amount. Note how the Summary account reflects the same position, the credit side, as it is found on the work-sheet. The debit to inventory reflects the debit found in the balance sheet.

GENERAL JOURNAL **Page** *10*

Date 19—	Account Title and Explanation	Post. Ref.	Debit	Credit
Aug. 31	Merchandise Inventory	110	4 000	
	R & E Summary	399		4 000
	To re-open the merchandise inventory.			

Merchandise Inventory No. 110

Debit	Credit
4 200	4 200
4 000	

R & E Summary No. 399

Debit	Credit
365	33 286
4 200	4 000

Closing Entry 5 A transfer of the two purchase costs, Purchases and Transportation-in, follows next. These accounts require credit entries to bring the accounts equal to zero, and the R & E Summary would therefore be a debit entry.

Closing Entry 6 Transfer the entries that cause the purchase price to be reduced. These include: Purchases Returns and Allowances and Purchases Discounts. After debiting the two accounts and then posting, the two related purchases accounts have a zero balance. The R & E Summary account would be credited for the total amount of the two previous account amounts.

Closing Entry 7 By the use of a compound entry, all the expenses (operating plus other expenses) shown on the income statement can now be closed. Each individual account requires a credit entry, which when posted will produce a zero balance. The R & E Summary will be used to record the single debit entry.

GENERAL JOURNAL — Page *10*

Date 19—		Account Title and Explanation	Post. Ref.	Debit	Credit
Aug.	31	R & E Summary	399	5 950	
		Purchases	501		5 800
		Transportation-in	502		150
		To close Purchases and Transportation-in.			

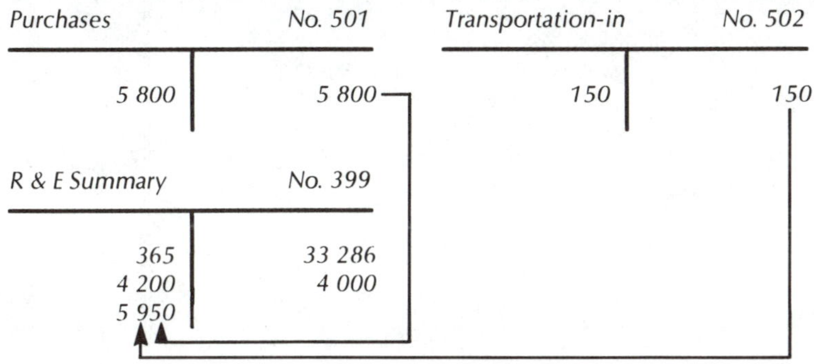

GENERAL JOURNAL — Page *10*

Date 19—		Account Title and Explanation	Post. Ref.	Debit	Credit
Aug.	31	Purchases Returns and Allowances	503	210	
		Purchases Discounts	504	160	
		R & E Summary	399		370
		To close the contra Purchases accounts.			

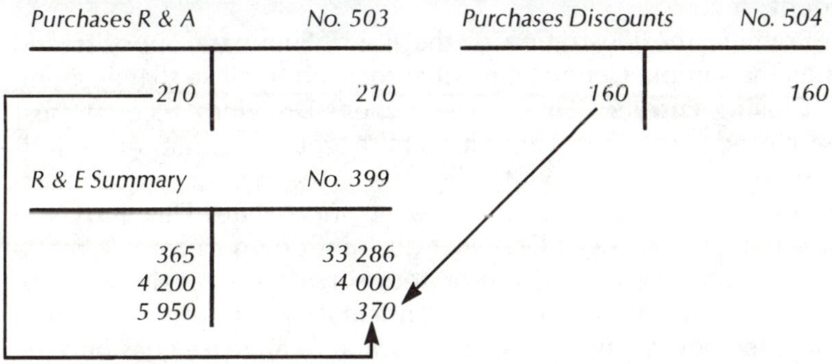

GENERAL JOURNAL — Page 11

Date 19—	Account Title and Explanation	Post. Ref.	Debit	Credit
Aug. 31	R & E Summary	399	3 842	
	Advertising Expense	510		185
	Utilities Expense	512		60
	Delivery Expense	514		180
	Wages and Salaries Expense	516		1 600
	Payroll Tax Expense	518		864
	Interest Expense	520		28
	Supplies Expense	521		100
	Insurance Expense	523		50
	Bad Debts Expense	525		100
	Bank Loan Interest Expense	530		75
	Deprec. Expense/Building	550		200
	Deprec. Expense/ Warehouse Equip.	552		30
	Deprec. Expense/ Office Equip.	554		70
	Deprec. Expense/Truck	556		300
	To close the expense accounts.			

Closing Entry 8 The balance in the R & E Summary must now be transferred into the owner's equity Capital account. The entry necessary to close the R & E Summary will be determined by the balance in that account. If the Summary account has a credit balance, then you know that an equal and opposite debit entry will be required to bring that account to zero. Since the Summary account contains all the income statement information, the balance should reflect the firm's net income or loss for the period. Furthermore, since the net income or loss belongs to the owner, the capital account is used to close the R & E Summary account. *Note:* If the R & E Summary account has a debit balance, an equal and opposite credit entry would be required to bring that account to zero.

Examine the illustration of the R & E Summary opposite and then the sample General Journal entry used to close that account.

Closing Entry 9 Finally, the owner's Drawings account must be closed into the owner's Capital account so that, at period-end, the Capital account will reflect the owner's total claim against total assets as at the balance sheet date. This entry will also bring the owner's Drawings account down to zero. Remember that owners of a single proprietorship do not receive a salary, but rather withdraw funds in anticipation of future earnings. Since the net income that causes capital to increase goes into the Capital account, drawings which reflect early withdrawals from net income should ultimately be subtracted from the income in the Capital account. This last closing entry looks after that requirement.

GENERAL LEDGER

R & E Summary — No. 399

Date 19—	Account Title and Explanation	Post. Ref.	Debit	Credit	Balance	
Aug. 31	To close the revenue accounts.	GJ10		33 286	33 286	
31	To close the contra revenues.	GJ10	365		32 921	← **Net Revenue**
31	To close beginning inventory	GJ10	4 200		28 721	
31	To open the ending inventory.	GJ10		4 000	32 721	
31	To close Purchases & Trans.-in.	GJ10	5 950		26 771	
31	To close the contra Purchases.	GJ10		370	27 141	← **Gross Margin**
31	To close the expense accounts.	GJ11	3 842		23 299	← **Net Income**
31	To close the Summary to Capital.	GJ11	23 299		0	

GENERAL JOURNAL — Page 11

Date 19—	Account Title and Explanation	Post. Ref.	Debit	Credit
Aug. 31	R & E Summary	399	23 299	
	R. Wawdel, Capital	301		23 299
	To close the R & E Summary.			

R. Wawdel, Capital — No. 301

	85 530
	23 299

GENERAL JOURNAL — Page 12

Date 19—	Account Title and Explanation	Post. Ref.	Debit	Credit
Aug. 31	R. Wawdel, Capital	301	705	
	R. Wawdel, Drawings	302		705
	To close the Drawings account.			

R. Wawdel, Capital — No. 301

705	(Beginning capital) 85 530
	(Net income) 23 299

R. Wawdel, Drawings — No. 302

705	705

Preparing the Postclosing Trial Balance

The final step in the accounting cycle is to prepare the postclosing trial balance. This is a final check to ensure that all the permanent accounts of the business found in the General Ledger are still in balance. (See illustration below.) In all, three checks occur when the postclosing trial balance is prepared:

- The debit and credit totals must be equal.
- There must be only permanent accounts listed.
- The balance in the Capital account of the postclosing trial balance must be identical to the total owner's equity in the owner's equity section of the balance sheet.

If you examine the accounts in the postclosing trial balance, you will find them identical to the accounts in the balance sheet, with one exception, Drawings. This is because both statements

Wawdel Company
Postclosing Trial Balance
August 31, 19—

Cash	10 700	
Petty Cash	50	
Notes Receivable	60 000	
Accounts Receivable	6 400	
Allowance for Bad Debts		120
Accrued Revenue Receivable	1 000	
Merchandise Inventory	4 000	
Supplies on Hand	300	
Prepaid Insurance	500	
Land	12 000	
Building	48 000	
Accumulated Depreciation/Building		900
Warehouse Equipment	4 000	
Accumulated Depreciation/Warehouse Equipment		240
Office Equipment	7 200	
Accumulated Depreciation/Office Equipment		620
Delivery Trucks	20 000	
Accumulated Depreciation/Trucks		300
Bank Loan Payable		5 500
Unearned Revenue		250
Accounts Payable		6 800
Bank Loan Interest Payable		150
Unemployment Insurance Payable		60
CPP Payable		120
Income Tax Payable		800
OHIP Payable		42
Group Insurance Payable		124
Mortgage Payable		50 000
R. Wawdel, Capital		108 124
	174 150	174 150

contain only permanent accounts. When the postclosing trial balance is complete, the accounting cycle is also complete, and the books are ready for the next accounting cycle.

TOPIC 3 PROBLEMS

16-9 Refer to the worksheet of Problem 16-1.

a Journalize the adjustments in the General Journal. Include a brief explanation for each entry.

b Open T-accounts for Capital, Drawings, R & E Summary, and Insurance Expense. Record the balance of each, taking the figure from the adjusted trial balance.

c Journalize, in the General Journal, all necessary closing entries. Include a brief explanation for each entry.

d Indicate how each of the T-accounts would appear after closing information had been posted into each account.

e Prepare a postclosing trial balance.

Key Check Figure Postclosing Trial Balance: $1 852

16-10 Refer to the worksheet of Problems 16-2 and 16-6.

a Journalize the adjustments in the General Journal. Include a brief explanation.

b Open T-accounts for Capital, Drawings, R & E Summary, and Bank Loan Interest Expense. Record the balance of each, taking the figure from the adjusted trial balance.

c Journalize, in the General Journal, all necessary closing entries. Include a brief explanation.

d Indicate how each of the T-accounts would appear after closing information had been posted into each account.

e Prepare a postclosing trial balance.

Key Check Figure Postclosing Trial Balance: $121 730

16-11 Refer to the worksheet of Problems 16-3 and 16-7.

a Journalize the adjustments in the General Journal. Include a brief explanation.

b Open T-accounts for Capital, Drawings, R & E Summary, and Marine Supplies Expense. Record the balance of each, taking the figure from the adjusted trial balance.

c Journalize, in the General Journal, all necessary closing entries. Include a brief explanation.

d Indicate how each of the T-accounts would appear after closing information had been posted into each account.

e Prepare a postclosing trial balance.

Key Check Figure Postclosing Trial Balance: $270 945

16-12 Refer to the worksheet of Problems 16-4 and 16-8.

a Journalize the adjustments in the General Journal. Include a brief explanation.

b Open T-accounts for Capital, Drawings, R & E Summary, and Wages Payable. Record the balance of each, taking the figure from the adjusted trial balance.

Key Check Figure Postclosing Trial Balance: $230 068.20

c Journalize, in the General Journal, all necessary closing entries. Include a brief explanation.

d Indicate how each of the T-accounts would appear after closing information had been posted into each account.

e Prepare a postclosing trial balance.

TOPIC 4 ANALYZING FINANCIAL STATEMENT RELATIONSHIPS

The financial statements of any business are a detailed summary of the financial position of that business. In Topic 3 of Chapter 5, information about what an income statement and a balance sheet say and do not say was presented. This Topic will briefly introduce you to several ideas and techniques used to analyze statements.

Comparisons

One of the most effective ways of examining the success of a business is to study its performance over a number of years. A

Wawdel Company
Comparative Balance Sheet
as at December 31
(in 000's of dollars)

ASSETS

	19-5	19-4	19-3	19-2	19-1
Current Assets	870	880	700	750	740
Fixed Assets	1 500	1 400	1 400	1 000	900
Total Assets	2 370	2 280	2 100	1 750	1 640

LIABILITIES AND OWNER'S EQUITY

	19-5	19-4	19-3	19-2	19-1
**Current Liabilities*	780	730	590	550	600
Long-Term Liabilities	1 000	1 000	1 000	960	800
Capital	590	550	510	240	240
Total Liabilities and Owner's Equity	2 370	2 280	2 100	1 750	1 640

**Assume that the current portion of the mortgage payable is included in this total. Mortgage Payable, under Long-Term Liabilities, has the current portion subtracted from it.*

comparative balance sheet is one such tool. Study the illustration on page 584 and then read through the analysis which follows. *Note:* The illustration which follows is not related to any previous illustration of Wawdel Company. Also, all illustrations which follow that contain current liability and long-term liability information reflect a current portion of Mortgage Payable in the current liability figures, and the total of Mortgage Payable less the current portion in the long-term liability figures.

Analysis: Such a presentation lets the reader look for trends. If a particular item changes drastically from one year to the next, or constantly over the years, more research into its cause might be indicated.

Often, an examination of dollar values reveals little. If, however, the dollars are converted to percent changes, the result may be very revealing. Study the Trend Percentages illustration below.

Wawdel Company
Trend Percentages From Base Year 19-1*

	19-5	**19-4**	**19-3**	**19-2**	**19-1 (Base Year)**
Current Assets	*118%*	*119%*	*95%*	*101%*	*100%*
Current Liabilities	*130%*	*122%*	*98%*	*92%*	*100%*

**All numbers are rounded.*

$$\text{Trend Percentage} = \frac{\text{Comparison Year}}{\text{Base Year}} \times 100\%$$

$$\text{Therefore} \quad \frac{19\text{-}2}{19\text{-}1} \times 100\% = \frac{750}{740} \times 100\% = 101.35\% = 101\%.$$

These statements permit the reader to make some kind of judgement as to the performance of the company being examined. For example, one might show some concern regarding the percent increase of current liabilities in comparison to current assets. Merely examining the related dollar amounts (Current Assets 19-5 = \$870; Current Liabilities 19-5 = \$780), might not quickly disclose a problem.

One way of simplifying the comparison is to use a *common-size* method. This means that, for example, the total asset and total liability figures are considered to be 100% and all other figures are calculated as a percentage of those totals.

Wawdel Company
Common-Size Balance Sheet
as at December 31

ASSETS

	19-5	19-4	19-3	19-2	19-1
Current Assets	37%	39%	33%	43%	45%
Fixed Assets	63%	61%	67%	57%	55%
Total Assets	100%	100%	100%	100%	100%

LIABILITIES AND OWNER'S EQUITY

	19-5	19-4	19-3	19-2	19-1
Current Liabilities	33%	32%	28%	31%	36%
Long-Term Liabilities	42%	44%	48%	55%	49%
Capital	25%	24%	24%	14%	15%
Total Liabilities and Owner's Equity	100%	100%	100%	100%	100%

The same type of comparison can be made for an income statement. Study the next two illustrations. *Note:* Other Revenues and Other Expenses have not been included in these examples in order to ensure simplicity.

The dollar values give a hint of the problem, but the percentages emphatically drive this point home.

A final method for presenting statement information is illustrated on pages 587 and 588. These comparisons show a breakdown by month for both the Income Statement and the Balance

Wawdel Company
Comparative Income Statement
Years Ended December 31

	19-3	19-2	19-1
Net Sales	1 200	900	800
Cost of Goods Sold	1 000	700	600
Gross Margin on Sales	200	200	200
Operating Expenses	50	40	30
Net Income	150	160	170

Wawdel Company
Common-Size Income Statement
Years Ended December 31

	19-3	19-2	19-1
Net Sales	100.0%	100.0%	100.0%
Cost of Goods Sold	83.3%	77.8%	75.0%
Gross Margin on Sales	16.7%	22.2%	25.0%
Operating Expenses	4.2%	4.4%	3.75%
Net Income	12.5%	17.8%	21.25%

Sheet. With both dollar and percent changes now available, the reader can collect needed information easily and quickly. All these statements can be accurately and very quickly prepared by the computer once the needed information is provided to the computer.

Scotts Company
Comparative Income Statement
For the Months Ended May 31, 19— and April 30, 19—

	Month Ended May 31, 19—	Month Ended April 30, 19—	Increase(*) or Decrease	
			Am't	%
Revenue	2 000	1 800	200*	11.1%
Cost of Goods Sold	1 800	1 620	180*	11.1%
Gross Margin from Sales	200	180	20*	11.1%
Expenses:				
Taxes	25	25	0	—
Telephone	10	12	2	16.7%
Hydro	18	16	2*	12.5%
Wages	100	100	0	—
Advertising	39	21	18*	85.7%
Total Expenses	192	174	18*	10.3%
Net Income	8	6	2*	33.3%

Scotts Company
Comparative Balance Sheet
May 31, 19—

Description	April	May	Dollar Increase(*) or Decrease	Percentage Increase(*) or Decrease
ASSETS				
Current Assets:				
Cash	50	55	5*	10%*
Accounts Receivable	60	67	7*	11.7%*
Inventory (at cost)	100	110	10*	10%*
Total Current Assets	210	232	22*	10.5%*
Fixed Assets (at cost):				
Land	400	400	0	—
Building	900	1 000	100*	11.1%*
Total Fixed Assets	1 300	1 400	100*	7.7%*
Total Assets	1 510	1 632	122*	8.1%*
LIABILITIES				
Current Liabilities:				
Bank Loan	70	55	15	21.4%
Accounts Payable	25	30	5*	20.0%*
Property Taxes Payable	15	0	15	100.0%
Current Portion of Mortgage Payable	10	10	0	—
Total Current Liabilities	120	95	25	20.8%
Long-Term Liabilities:				
Mortgage Payable less Current Portion	340	330	10	2.9%
Total Liabilities	460	425	35	7.6%
OWNER'S EQUITY				
R. Tram, Capital	1 047	1 202	155*	14.8%*
Net Income	6	8	2*	33.3%*
	1 053	1 210	157*	14.9%*
Less: Drawings	3	3	0	—
Total Equity	1 050	1 207	157*	15.0%*
Total Liabilities and Owner's Equity	1 510	1 632	122*	8.1%*

Indicators (Ratios) for Short- and Long-Term Analysis

A person may want to know more about a particular business and its probability of future success. Two major groups of people spend time analyzing financial statements: *insiders* and *outsiders*.

Insiders are owners and managers of the business. They are the primary users of the comparative and common-size statements just presented. They use that information, and some of the information gained through indicators, in making decisions on future business operations. They watch for danger signs. And of course, positive trends are noted and used to further the success of the firm.

Outsiders include creditors, potential investors, and government agencies. Outsiders use the comparative statements far less than insiders; but on the other hand, they have much greater use for the information which follows.

A series of tests called *indicators* can be applied in order to learn about various aspects of a business. This book will only touch on these. If you have further interest, consult a more advanced accounting text.

First we will discuss indicators that can be used for short-term tests.

Working Capital Working capital is the difference between the current assets and the current liabilities of a business. From Wawdel Company, Year 19-1, working capital equals $140. ($740 — $600). Once again a comparison could prove interesting: 19-2 $200, 19-3 $110, 19-4 $150, 19-5 $90.

Adequate working capital allows a company to meet its obligations on time, take advantage of valuable purchase discounts, and expand its business without the need to borrow. Lack of working capital is a major cause of business failure.

Current Ratio or Working Capital Ratio This ratio is determined as follows: Current Assets/Current Liabilities. For Wawdel Company in 19-1 the ratio equals $740/$600 or 1.23:1. This means that the company has $1.23 of current assets to pay each $1.00 of current liabilities. The rule of thumb has been that a 2:1 ratio is good. One must, however, study the type of business being examined. A high ratio might be wise for one company but very unwise for another. For example, a grocery store with a steady inflow of cash needs a much lower ratio (1.5:1) than a company that builds road graders (5:1). Finally, a strong current ratio may be misleading if a large portion of current assets is not easily converted into cash. For example, inventory is a current asset, but often generates cash slowly.

Quick Ratio (Acid Test Ratio) The last point leads us to the necessity for another test. The quick ratio indicates how quickly and easily a business is able to pay for all of its current liabilities. All current assets which cannot be readily converted into cash are removed. This usually leaves only cash, marketable securities, and accounts receivable. Inventory and prepaid expenses are not used in this calculation. Wawdel Company's current assets and quick ratio appear in the next illustration.

Current Assets, 19-1:

Cash	*$100*	**Quick Assets**
Accounts Receivable	*240*	
Inventory	*300*	
Prepaids	*100*	

$$\text{Quick Ratio} = \frac{\text{Quick Assets}}{\text{Current Liabilities}} = \frac{\$340}{\$600} = 0.57:1$$

The above means that if Wawdel Company had to pay all its current liabilities immediately it would have only $0.57 in quick assets to cover each dollar of current liabilities.

Other indicators of the short-term strengths and weaknesses of a business are:

- *Inventory Turnover:* This is how often a particular item for sale is sold and replaced in a stated period of time.
- *Accounts Receivable Turnover:* This is usually the average age of receivables in days. For example, if a firm offers terms of 2/10, n/30 and the accounts receivable turnover shows 20 days, this could be considered very favourable.

The indicators that follow can be used for long-term tests.

Wawdel Company 19-1:

$$\frac{\textbf{Total Liabilities}}{\textbf{Total Assets}} \times 100\%$$

$$= \frac{\$1\ 400}{\$1\ 640} \times 100\% = 85\%$$

Debt Ratio This ratio, usually calculated as a percentage, compares the total assets to the total liabilities. It tells the analyst what percentage of total assets is tied up in debt to outsiders, and what percentage is in the form of investment by owners.

Rate of Mark-up on Cost This last provides both short-term and long-term information. You have learned to determine Gross Margin from Sales by subtracting Cost of Goods Sold from Net Sales. These numbers can readily be converted to percentages as illustrated by the Common-Size Income Statement on page 587. Gross Margin is always expressed as a percentage of Net Sales. For example, Wawdel Company's Gross Margin in 19-1 was 25% of Net Sales and 16.7% of Net Sales in 19-3.

Mark-up generally refers to the increase added to the cost of the item purchased. The following illustration demonstrates how the percentage of mark-up is calculated.

If Selling Price	*= 100%*	**Common-Size Comparison**
then Cost Price	*= 75%*	
and Gross Margin from Sales	*= 25%*	

*The ratio of mark-up to cost price is 25/75 * 100% = 33.33%. (* is a symbol for multiplication.) If the cost price is $200, the dollar mark-up must be $200 * 33.33%, producing a selling price of $266.67 ($200 + $66.67).*

However, accountants usually prefer the following calculation.

*Selling Price = 100/75 * Cost Price*
*= 100/75 * $200 = $266.67*

A second approach: If (Cost Price) $200 = 75%, then (Selling Price) x = 100%.
*Solving for x: x = $200 * 100/75 = $266.67.*

Businesses may find it necessary to adjust their mark-ups, and therefore their gross margin from sales, to meet the competition. In the Wawdel Company example on page 587 of the text, the percentage mark-up on cost in 19-1 is 25/75 * 100% or 33.33%; in year 19-2, 22.2/77.8 * 100% or 28.5%; and in year 19-3, 16.7/83.3 or 20.0%.

Competitive businesses in the same type of business will have similar mark-up percentages. This is most likely the situation that Wawdel Company is facing, hence the constant drop of percentage mark-up. *Note:* Because the mark-up and the gross margin from sales is the same, sometimes the rate of gross margin is referred to as the *rate of mark-up on sales.* To prevent confusion, the rate of mark-up will always be based on cost and the rate of gross margin on sales on the selling price.

Many other ratios and tests could be examined for short-term and long-term analysis, but these will be left for a more advanced course. It should be further noted that this is a complex topic and requires a great deal of practice and skill in order to be able to use the information gained in an informed way.

TOPIC 4 PROBLEMS

16-13 When using comparative statements, differences between years must be calculated in dollars and often as a percentage.

a Calculate the dollar differences for each of the following examples. Indicate positive changes with *.

b Calculate the percentage for each. Indicate a positive change with *

Remember. the least recent date is the *base figure.*

Company A

	19-2	19-1
Assets	$6 000	$5 000

Company B

	19-4	19-3	19-2	19-1
Net Sales	$12 500	$11 000	$10 000	$ 9 000

Company C

	19-4	19-3	19-2	19-1
Net Sales	$28 000	$21 000	$22 500	$25 000
Operating Expenses	23 500	24 000	21 000	19 500
Net Income	?	?	?	?

Key Check Figure
Net Income 19-4 = 18.2%

16-14 Calculate the dollar difference and then the percentage change for each of the values in the comparative income statement shown here.

XYZ Company
Comparative Income Statement
For the Months Ended March 31, 19— and February 28, 19—

	Month Ended Mar. 31, 19—	Month Ended Feb. 28, 19—	Increase(*) or Decrease	
			Am't	%
Revenue from Sales	8 500	7 000		
Operating Expenses:				
Rent	2 500	2 500		
Wages	3 000	3 000		
Telephone	150	110		
Heat	600	800		
Miscellaneous	95	60		
Total Expenses	6 345	6 470		
Net Income (Loss)	2 155	530		

Key Check Figure
Net Income = $1 625

Key Check Figure
Net Income March 31 = 25.4%

16-15 Refer again to XYZ Company's comparative income statement. Prepare a common-size income statement similar to the one on page 587. Since you have only two months to compare, you will need only two columns.

16-16 From the information in PQR Company's balance sheet, given here, do the following exercises.

PQR Company
Balance Sheet
December 31, 198-

ASSETS			
Current Assets:			
Cash		$ 1 000	
Accounts Receivable		2 500	
Inventory (at cost)		2 400	
Prepaid Rent		900	
Total Current Assets			$ 6 800
Fixed Assets (at cost):			
Land		$10 000	
Building (security for mortgage)	$25 500		
Accumulated Depreciation	5 300	20 200	
Total Fixed Assets			$30 200
Total Assets			$37 000
LIABILITIES			
Current Liabilities:			
Bank Loan Payable		$ 2 700	
Accounts Payable		450	
Wages Payable		150	
Current Portion of Mortgage Payable		500	
Total Current Liabilities			$ 3 800
Long-Term Liabilities:			
Mortgage Payable (due in 30 years and secured by the building)		$15 000	
Less: Current Portion		500	14 500
Total Liabilities			18 300
OWNER'S EQUITY			
Tom Terrific, Capital		$16 500	
Net Income		5 400	
		21 900	
Less: T. Terrific, Drawings		3 200	
Total Equity			$18 700
Total Liabilities and Owner's Equity			$37 000

a Calculate **(i)** the working capital, **(ii)** the current ratio, **(iii)** the quick ratio, and **(iv)** the debt ratio.

b Could the following be calculated for PQR? **(i)** accounts receivable turnover. **(ii)** inventory turnover. If it is *not* possible to calculate any or all of these, state the reason.

Key Check Figure Quick Ratio = 0.92:1

16-17 Refer to the illustration of Scotts Company on page 587.

a Determine the rate of gross margin from sales for each month.

b Determine the rate of mark-up on cost for each month.

16-18 Answer the questions about Computing Company given below. Use a form like the following.

	Month											
	A	B	C	D	E	F	G	H	I	J	K	L
Net Sales	*$100*											
Cost of Goods Sold												
Gross Margin												

a Using the figure given for month A, determine the net sales for the other eleven months, assuming a sales increase each month of 10% to keep up with inflation.

b Determine all the cost of goods sold figures, assuming each equals 40% of net sales.

c Determine the gross margin for each month.

d Determine the rate of gross margin from sales for each month.

e Determine the rate of mark-up on cost for each month.

16-19 The Blue Bell Sales Company supplies you with the following cost figures. The company has a rate of mark-up to cost of 35%.

a Calculate the selling price for each item.

b Indicate what the rate of gross margin from sales would be for each item.

Item	*Cost Price*	*Selling Price*
A	$700.00	
B	100.00	
C	61.46	

Case Study 16

Rossanni Wholesalers had its May 31, 19— worksheet completed and ready to use for the preparation of financial statements. But then the sprinkler system accidentally went off, and the worksheet was almost destroyed.

Suppose that you have been asked to reconstruct the worksheet from what is left, which is shown opposite.

Rossanni Wholesalers
Worksheet
For the Month Ended May 31, 19—

	Account Title	Acct. No.	Trial Balance		Adjustments		Adj. Trial Bal.		Inc. Statement		Balance Sheet	
			Debit	Credit	Debit	Credit	Debit	Credit	Debit	Credit	Debit	Credit
1	Cash		10								10	
2	Accounts Receivable		25		(E) 10							
3	Allowance for Bad Debts			3		(A) 2						
4	Inventory		15								17	
5	Supplies on Hand		4									
6	Prepaid Insurance		7			(B) 4						
7	Land		20									
8	Building		35									
9	Accumulated Depreciation			15		(C)						19
10	Delivery Truck		8									
11	Accumulated Depreciation			2		(D)						3
12	Bank Loan Payable			7								
13	Accounts Payable			5								
14	Mortgage Payable			31								
15	M. Rossanni, Capital			69								69
16	M. Rossanni, Drawings		6									
17	Sales			55		(E)				65		
18	Sales Discounts		2									
19	Purchases		41									
20	Purchases R & A			1								
21	Purchases Discounts			2								
22	Transportation-in		3									
23	Heat Expense		10									
24	Delivery Expense		4									
25			190									
26	Wages Payable											10

PART 4

MODERN ACCOUNTING SYSTEMS

106-Hospital-Professional Employment

DENTAL Receptionist required to handle all bookkeeping etc., (Mardan system). Also manage appointments for dentist and hygienist. Apply to Box K1669, Free Press.

DENTAL Receptionist, modern, North London office. Mardan system experience an asset. Box K1670, Free Press.

ACCOUNTS Receivable clerk, responsible individual, exper. on One Write System. Computer experience helpful. Salary $225. 273-4565.

DATA ENTRY CLERK

To post payables, receivables, cash, etc. on a MAI IV BASIC Computer. Our accounting system is fully integrated so accuracy is a must and some knowledge of bookkeeping is essential.

Our working day is 8-5 Monday through Friday. We offer a good range of benefits, paid OHIP, group insurance including medical and dental.

Please send resume stating position desired, availability and salary requirements to:

BOX 2135 THE GLOBE & MAIL
444 FRONT ST. W.
TORONTO, ONTARIO M5V 2S9

BOOKKEEPER

South London licenced establishement requires Bookkeeper, 3-5 years' experience required. McBee or one write and computer payroll knowledge beneficial.

Please send resume in confidence to:
BOX 4705M, FREE PRESS

COST ACCOUNTANT

Maple Leaf Mills Limited, located in the Yonge-Eglinton area requires a Cost Accountant for its Flour Division.

This position will be responsible for the costing of flour products, maintaining and updating the computerized costing files for the flour mills across Canada, analyzing variances, preparing month-end schedules and special projects.

We require a mid-level RIA with strong interpersonal, organizational, analytical and documentation skills. Familiarity with computerized accounting applications would be an asset. We offer a good starting salary and a full range of company benefits. Please reply in confidence to:

Manager, Employment Services
MAPLE LEAF MILLS LIMITED
P. O. Box 710,
Station K
Toronto, Ontario
M4P 2X5

CHAPTER 17

ONE-WRITE APPLICATIONS

Traditional bookkeeping method: journalizing and posting data in separate steps.

In Parts 1, 2, and 3 you learned how to do the accounting of accounts receivable, accounts payable, and payroll applications using the traditional bookkeeping method. For example, in accounts receivable, a fee bill or invoice is prepared. The transaction is then recorded in a revenue journal like the fees earned journal or the sales journal. After this step, posting takes place from the journal to the patient's (customer's) account. And, finally, a statement of account may be prepared for the customer at month-end. Under this traditional method, each part of the accounts receivable application was done as a separate procedure. Similar separate step-by-step procedures were followed in applications for accounts payable and the payroll.

This traditional method may work reasonably well in a small business staffed with an efficient accounting clerk. However, in more complex situations it often breaks down because of these serious problems:

- Errors are often made when a clerk copies data incorrectly from one accounting form to another. For example, he or she may post the wrong debit figure from the revenue journal to the customer's account.
- Extra time is required to repeat information which has already been recorded in an earlier accounting document. For example, the charge shown on the fee bill has to be copied again to the journal and again to the customer's account. This time could have been used to perform other accounting tasks.
- When the volume of transactions grows, the clerk may not find time to post debits and credits to each customer's account for one or two days. This means that the owner or manager will not know how much each customer owes the business immediately after each accounts receivable transaction.

One-write system: a system of preparing more than one accounting document and record in a single step.

To eliminate these shortcomings, many small businesses use short-cuts. One modern manual short-cut permits the accounting clerk to combine the separate steps (stages) of creating the source document, journalizing, and posting so that these can be done at the same time. In the language of accounting, the manual method of combining the bookkeeping stages of common accounting applications such as accounts receivable, payroll, and accounts payable is known as the one-write system

Actually, you are probably familiar with the idea of preparing two or more forms at the same time. Common examples are:

(1) *Manual sales books:* The use of carbon paper between different forms, or using NCR (no carbon required) paper, permits the clerk to make copies in one writing.

(2) *Duplicators:* All duplicating machines work on the idea that you prepare the material only once. For example, once a stencil is prepared for a stencil duplicator, the clerk can run off many copies.

(3) *Photocopiers:* A number of different types exist. Again, whatever the process, once an original (the *camera-ready copy*) has been prepared, copies are automatically created.

(4) *Pegboards or one-write boards:* Also called *accounting boards,* these employ the one-write idea for several accounting applications simultaneously. The board provides a writing surface and usually has a series of evenly spaced pegs along one or two of its edges, or in the middle. Several accounting forms with corresponding punched holes can thus be positioned on the boards so that the writing lines on the top form can be lined up with appropriate lines on the forms beneath it. See the illustration on page 600.

All of these examples point to the basic idea of any one-write system: *the automatic or simultaneous preparation of more than one document or record.*

- Topic 1 (the only Topic in this chapter) deals with the application of the one-write concept to accounts receivable. To simplify matters, we will use examples taken from Dr. Johnson's dental practice in Part 2.
- Once you have learned one application like accounts receivable, you can apply this knowledge to others such as payroll and accounts payable. Consequently, only accounts receivable will be dealt with.

Sales Book

Duplicator **Courtesy of Gestetner**

Electrostatic Dry Photocopier **Courtesy of Xerox**

TOPIC 1 ACCOUNTS RECEIVABLE

Although several firms have developed excellent one-write systems, the system developed by the Canadian firm *Mardan Business Systems Limited* has been selected here.

No attempt will be made to cover every aspect of the accounts receivable application for a dental office. Instead, several common transactions will be presented to illustrate the main concepts and especially the short-cuts in journalizing and posting.

Common Dental Transactions Reviewed

After a dental service is given, one of several possible transactions may occur.

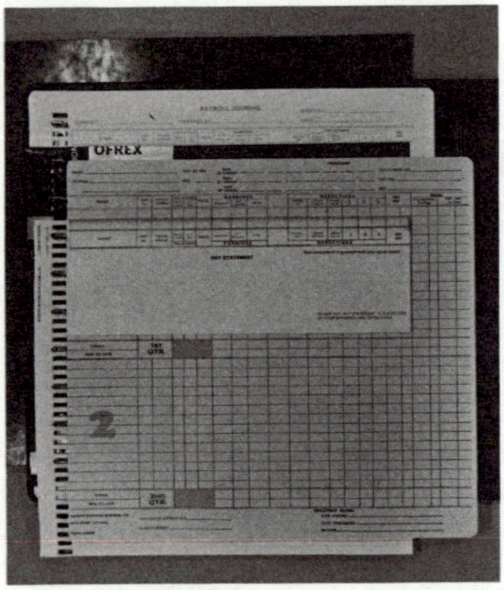

One-Write Board

- The patient may arrange to charge the service; hence, a statement (bill) is usually issued. Under traditional accounting theory, the patient's account (receivable) would be debited, and a revenue account such as Fees Earned would also be credited for the same amount. And, under traditional accounting procedures, such a transaction would be recorded in a fees earned journal. Posting would then follow either directly from the source document (the statement) or from the journal to the patient's account in the accounts receivable ledger. If a remittance is not received by the end of the month, a statement of account is usually prepared for the total amount owing as at month-end.
- When the future remittance is received, Cash is debited and the patient's account receivable credited for the amount received. Under traditional bookkeeping procedures, this entry would be recorded in the cash receipts journal, after which posting would be made to credit the patient's account in the accounts receivable ledger. A cash receipt for the amount received would also be prepared and given to the patient.
- The patient may pay cash immediately. Under traditional accounting theory, this transaction calls for a debit to Cash and a credit to Fees Earned. Also, under traditional bookkeeping, the transaction would be recorded in the cash receipts journal. A receipt is then prepared for the patient in the amount received.
- The patient may make partial payment, thus charging the remaining amount as an account receivable. Under traditional accounting procedures, the entire amount of the service is usually recorded in the fees earned journal as an Accounts Receivable debit and Fees Earned credit. Then the part payment is recorded in the cash receipts journal as a debit to Cash and a credit to Accounts Receivable for the actual amount of cash received. Posting would then follow to the patient's account to show the results of both transactions, leaving a balance owing on account. In addition, a monthly statement of account, indicating the amount owing as at month-end, is usually prepared and mailed.

Under the Mardan One-Write System, however, several shortcuts are possible in the creation of source documents, and in journalizing and posting the dollar results of common transactions. The Mardan System combines the fees earned journal and the cash receipts journal on one sheet. In addition, Mardan permits the creation of the source document, the journalizing of the transaction, and the posting to the patient's account *all in one writing*. Before the common transactions are analyzed in detail for the one-write system, it is useful to identify the components of the complete accounts receivable application.

Accounts Receivable Layout

The assembly of the accounts receivable pegboard system which is applicable to a professional dental office is illustrated on page

602. From left to right in this illustration (which is sideways on the page) the individual components are identified as follows:

- the binder
- an instruction sheet
- the pegboard with a ball-point pen on top
- the accounts receivable monthly summary sheet
- the record and distribution of charges and receipts journal
- the carbon sheet
- the patient's ledger card
- the receipt or statement of account form
- envelopes

These items are described in more detail below.

The Binder The binder is used to store the monthly summary sheets and the journal sheets, which form part of the permanent accounting records of all daily and monthly transactions of the dental practice.

The Instruction Sheet This explains details of the accounts receivable application.

The Pegboard The pegboard is a flat board containing ten pegs. The board provides a writing surface and receives the accounting forms. The pegs permit the necessary forms to be brought together in a certain order for one-writing. This is known as collating them.

Collating: putting forms together in a certain order.

The Ballpoint Pen An extra fine ballpoint pen with carbon black ink will ensure high-quality, permanent recordings. Of course, the clerk must take care to write neatly and legibly. Revenue Canada — Taxation requires all accounting records to be kept for *six* years unless permission is received to destroy them earlier.

The Accounts Receivable Monthly Summary Sheet This sheet receives the totals of the daily transactions as they have been recorded on the journal sheet. At the end of the month, it is totalled to show the monthly figures for Accounts Receivable and Fees Earned. The Accounts Receivable Monthly Summary Sheet also provides for a reconciliation (proof) of accounts receivable recordings, and for infrequent transactions such as bad debt write-offs, amounts recovered during the month on amounts formerly written off, and other adjustments related to accounts receivable. For convenience, the back of the summary sheet contains sections for preparing the monthly bank reconciliation, for summarizing out-of-pocket expenses, for summarizing convention expenses, and for listing outstanding cheques.

The Record and Distribution of Charges and Receipts Journal This is actually a *Combination Journal* which permits the journalizing of all transactions related to accounts receivable. This means the journal combines the features of the traditional fees earned journal and the cash receipts journal. In addition, it contains special sections for preparing the daily proof of postings to individual accounts receivable, for proving the accounts receivable control, and for proving the daily cash. As will be emphasized later, one journal sheet is used for each day's set of accounts receivable and related transactions.

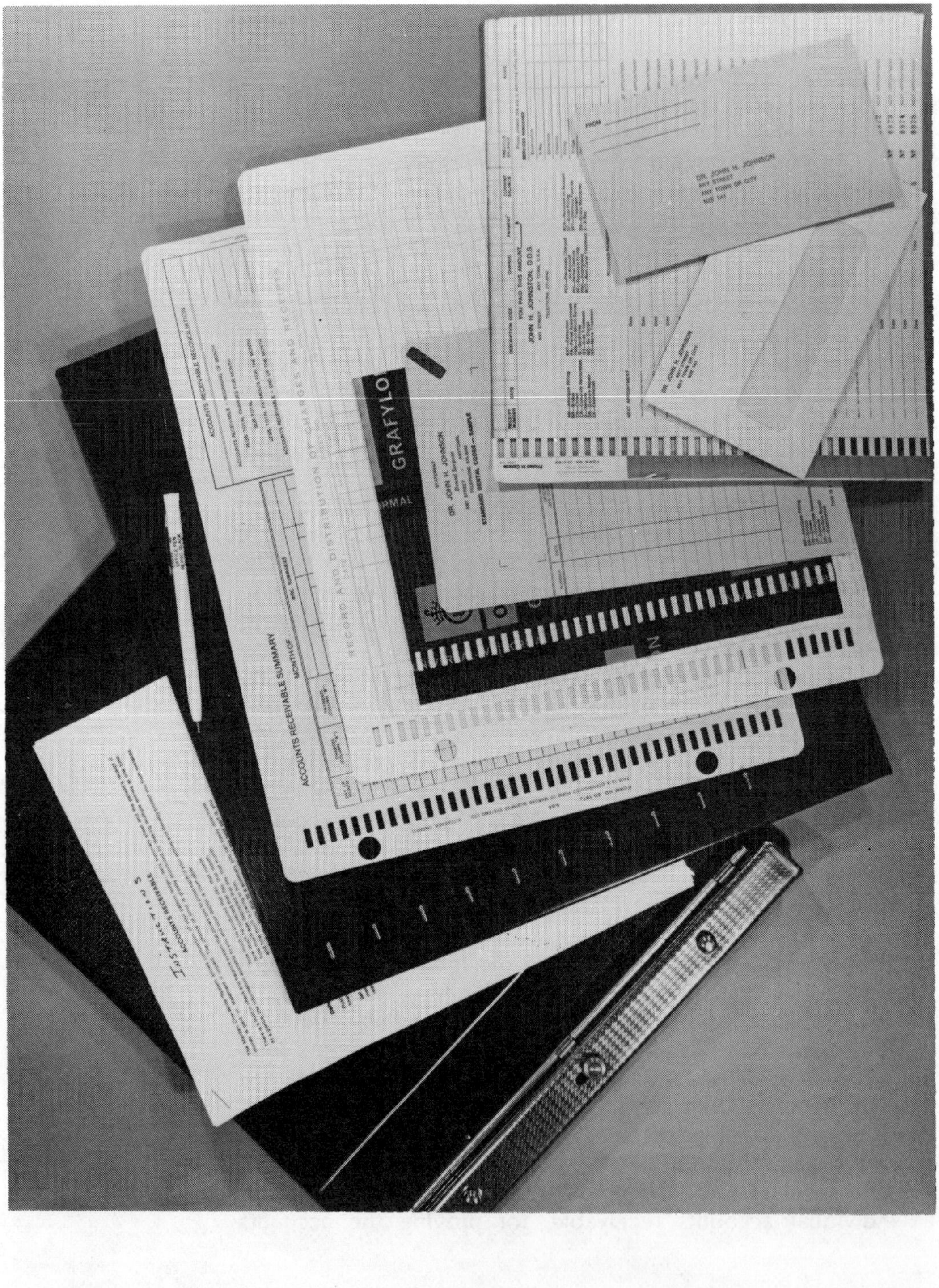

The Carbon Sheet A carbon sheet is used to allow the one-writing of transactions to the journal sheet. The carbon sheet fits over the journal sheet.

The Patient's Ledger Card The accounts receivable ledger card becomes the family financial profile (outline) showing services rendered for individual members of a family as well as the total amount owed by the family.

The family or patient's ledger card shows the traditional three-money column format: the left column to record the charge, the middle column to record the payment, and the far-right column to record the current balance. Of course, translated into accounting language, the columns are known as *Debit* (for charges), *Credit* (for payments), and *Balance* (for the running or current balance).

In dental practice, it is also common to file the family ledger cards in a ledger tray, which becomes the accounts receivable subsidiary ledger. A typical ledger tray is illustrated in the margin.

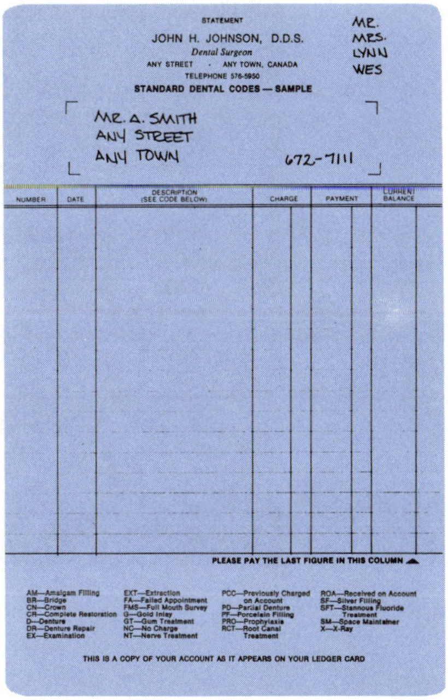
STATEMENT
JOHN H. JOHNSON, D.D.S.
Dental Surgeon
ANY STREET · ANY TOWN, CANADA
TELEPHONE 576-5950
STANDARD DENTAL CODES — SAMPLE

MR.
MRS.
LYNN
WES

MR. A. SMITH
ANY STREET
ANY TOWN 672-7111

NUMBER	DATE	DESCRIPTION (SEE CODE BELOW)	CHARGE	PAYMENT	CURRENT BALANCE

PLEASE PAY THE LAST FIGURE IN THIS COLUMN ▲

AM—Amalgam Filling
BR—Bridge
CN—Crown
CR—Complete Restoration
D—Denture
DR—Denture Repair
EX—Examination
EXT—Extraction
FA—Failed Appointment
FMS—Full Mouth Survey
G—Gold Inlay
GT—Gum Treatment
NC—No Charge
NT—Nerve Treatment
PCC—Previously Charged on Account
PD—Partial Denture
PF—Porcelain Filling
PRO—Prophylaxis
RCT—Root Canal Treatment
ROA—Received on Account
SF—Silver Filling
SFT—Stannous Fluoride Treatment
SM—Space Maintainer
X—X-Ray

THIS IS A COPY OF YOUR ACCOUNT AS IT APPEARS ON YOUR LEDGER CARD

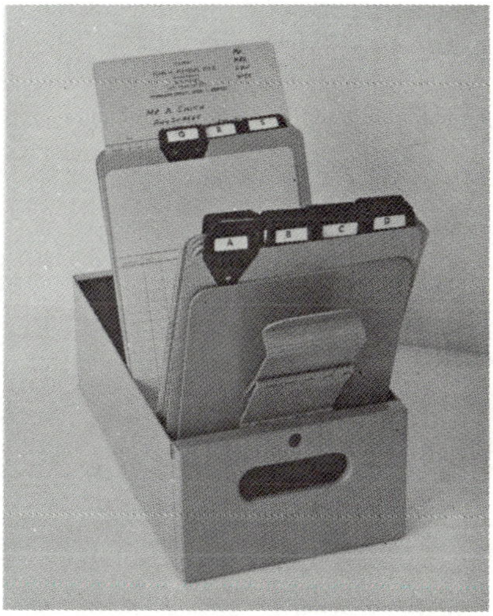

The Receipt or Statement of Account Form This final form, illustrated on page 604, is a two-part document.

Analysis:

- The left side becomes the receipt when cash is paid and the statement (bill) when a charge is transacted.
- The right side is a perforated section known as the *travelling stub*. It is detached and goes to the doctor to identify what services were rendered. The stub is then returned to the front office and serves as the source document for the one-write board.
- Note that the top edge of reverse side contains a layer of carbon to allow the transfer of what will be written on the top line of the statement and stub to appear on the ledger card and journal forms.

Envelopes Two envelopes are shown in the illustration of the accounts receivable assembly. One is self-addressed for the convenience of the patient in mailing his or her future remittance. The other is a window envelope. It is used in the month-end billing procedures.

Collating and Assembling the Forms

Look closely at the large illustration on page 605. It shows how the individual parts are put together (collated) on the Mardan pegboard. Note the order, which is important:

- *First,* the Monthly Summary Sheet is placed on top of the board. Since the side holes of the sheet fit over the pegs only in one position, no error can be made as to the placement of this first sheet.
- *Second,* the Record and Distribution of Charges and Receipts Sheet, that is, the journal, is placed on top of the Monthly Summary Sheet. Again, the side holes of the journal sheet fit over the pegs only in one position. No error can be

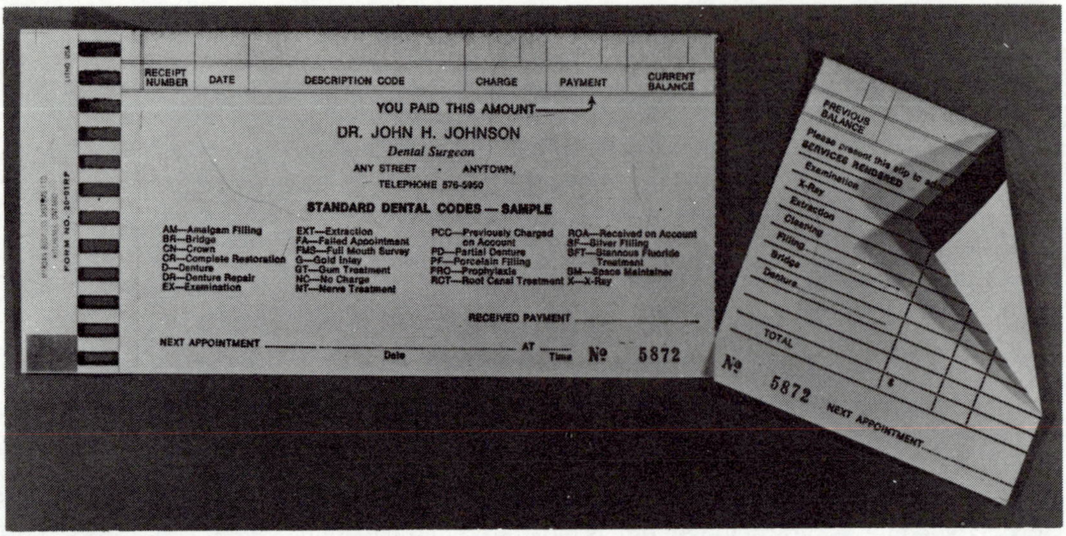

made in placement as long as the holes are positioned over all of the pegs.

- *Third,* the carbon sheet is placed on top of the journal in a position that covers everything up to, but not including, the individual column headings of the journal. Again, the holes at the side of the carbon are placed over the pegs to permit correct positioning of the carbon against the journal sheet.
- *Fourth,* the Receipt or Statement of Account forms are placed on top of the carbon so that the top line of the receipt form is lined up against the first writing line on the journal. Again, the side holes of the receipt form permit positioning of the receipt over the pegs so that a correct placement is assured. In the illustration on page 605, observe that the receipts for professional offices like dentistry come "shingled" on a sheet of 20. Of course, while the entire set of 20 receipts are on the journal, only the top one will be used for the first transaction. As one is completed, the next one can be used and so on.

It is essential to remember that the patient's ledger card is not placed in position until the first four steps have been completed. In other words, always place on the Mardan board the Monthly Summary Sheet, then the journal, the carbon sheet, and the shingled set of receipt forms.

- *Fifth,* to make an entry on a patient ledger card, simply slide the ledger card underneath the first receipt. Align the vertical lines on the ledger card with those on the receipt form as well as the column headings of the card over the journal form. With a little patience and practice, you should be able to line up the ledger card underneath the receipt form and over the journal form so that the correct writing line is automatically viewed.

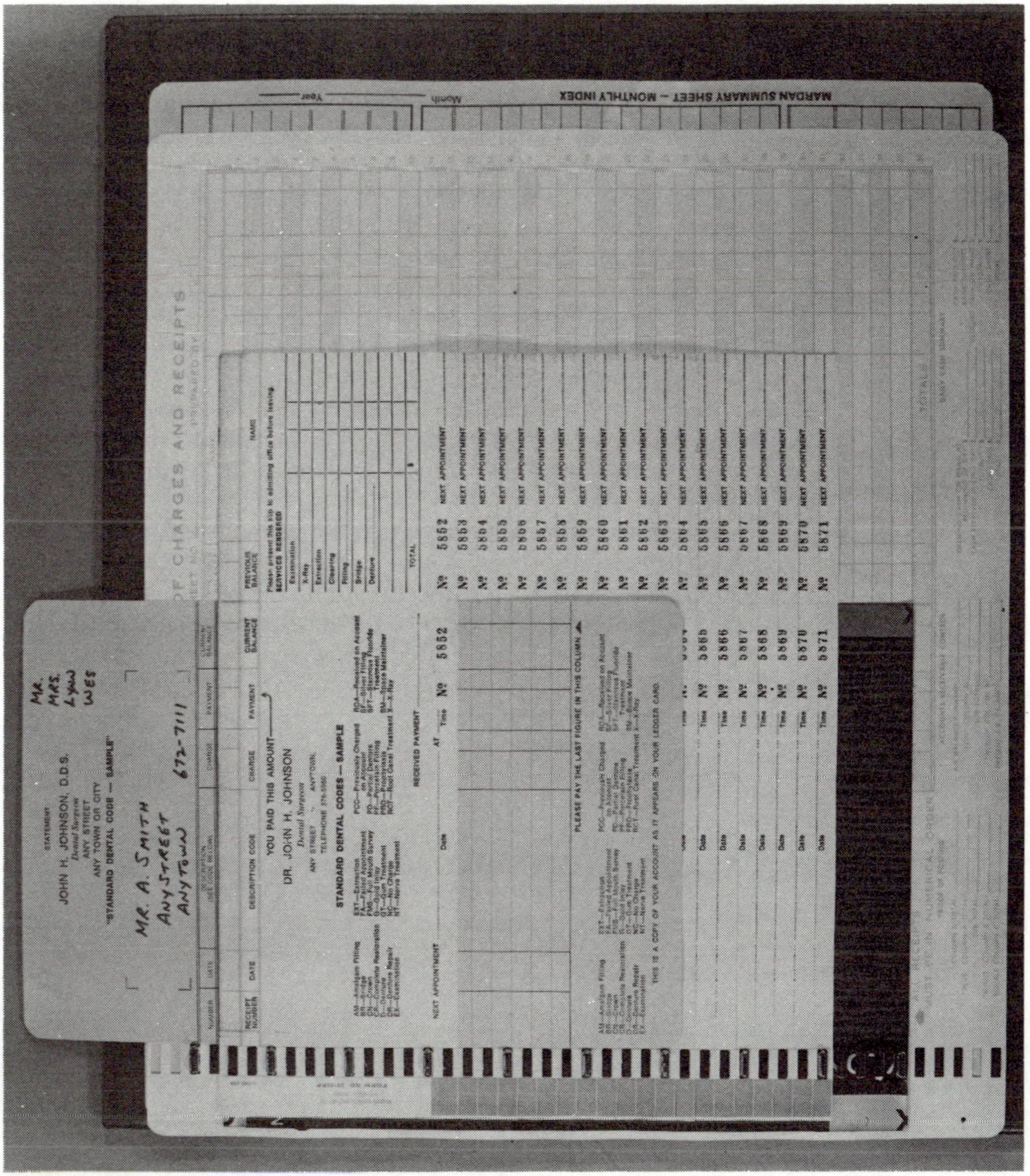

Common Transactions Analyzed

To illustrate four common accounts receivable transactions, we will use the Smith family of Any Street and Any Town, Canada. Mr. A. Smith, Any Street, Any Town, Canada would be printed, handwritten, or typewritten in the main identification section of the card. In the case of a female principal family name, such as Ms. A. Brown, that name would be entered on the card. Then, all of the family members would be indicated in the upper right corner as illustrated on page 605. Of course, other information may be entered on the card such as the family's home telephone number and dental insurance policy and certificate numbers.

Transaction 1: Entering the Zero Balance for a New Patient Suppose that Mrs. Smith is the first member of the family to be treated at Dr. Johnson's office. Since Mrs. Smith is a new patient, the first entry records a zero balance on the stub portion of the receipt form.

Assume, first of all, that the receptionist has collated correctly the one-write forms at the beginning of the day. Remember that the Monthly Summary Sheet would already be in place from yesterday's work. The only time this summary sheet is removed is following the end of the month. At the beginning of the new day, therefore, a new journal sheet is positioned over the summary sheet; then a new carbon sheet and, finally, the new set of shingled forms.

It is important to remember that the patient's ledger card is *not* used to enter the zero balance; thus, the ledger card is *not* inserted between the top receipt form and carbon sheet at this time. Only the stub portion of the receipt form is used to enter the zero balance, as illustrated below.

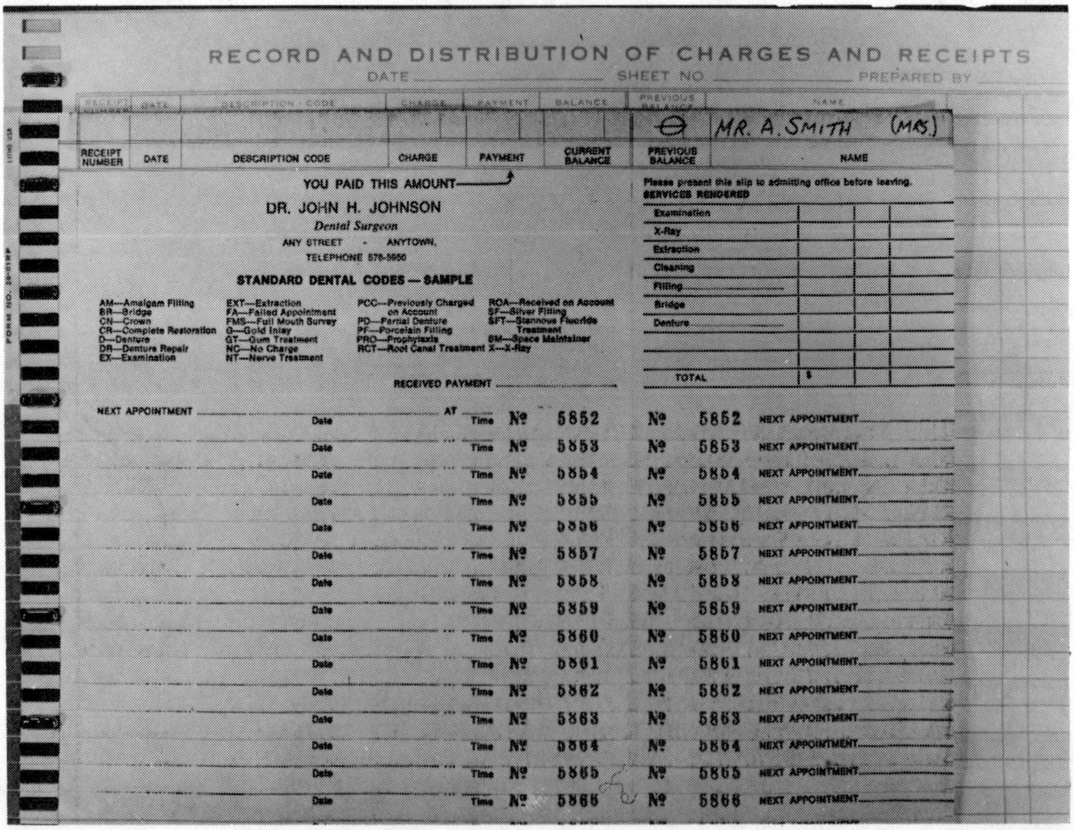

Analysis: The stub portion of the receipt form is completed in this order.

- *First,* enter the symbol Ø in the *Previous Balance* section of the stub.
- *Second,* print the family name, *Mr. A. Smith,* on the stub in the appropriate section above *Name.* As you will recall, the principal family name is identified for billing purposes.
- *Third,* print *Mrs.* to the right of that, to identify the member of the family who will receive treatment.
- *Fourth,* detach the travelling stub from the main portion of the receipt form and insert it into the large envelope containing the treatment chart.

The stub and treatment chart are taken to the dentist. Here, the travelling stub now becomes the communication document between the front office and the examining room. The dentist can quickly see who is responsible for the bill, whom he is seeing today, and how much is outstanding before proceeding with additional treatment.

Two advantages of the stub can now be identified.

- If the stub shows a large amount above *Previous Balance,* the doctor can discuss the patient's financial problem with him or her directly.
- The stub can be used as the source document from which the future accounting entry is made.

After the treatment, Dr. Johnson records the services rendered and fees charged on the stub. In addition, he can indicate the next appointment. The completed stub can then be returned to the front-office person for the accounts receivable entry. In the case of Mrs. Smith's treatment, the completed stub is illustrated in the margin.

Analysis: Three points must be learned in the analysis of the completed travelling stub.

- Note that the receipt form and detachable stub contain the same serial number. The number of the stub must always match the main receipt form in any one-write application. The use of pre-numbered documents supports the basic measure of controlling all cash receipts transactions. All firms, regardless of type, ownership, and size should create pre-numbered source documents to account for all cash receipts.
- Note that whatever was printed on the stub would also appear on the journal sheet. As you will recall, the receipt and stub form has a layer of carbon on the back to allow the transfer of printing to the journal sheet.
- In some systems, the travelling stub may *not* be detached from the main receipt form. Some dentists prefer to use the travelling stub concept, while others do not. Where the stub is not detached, it remains with the main receipt form to be completed after the doctor communicates the services rendered.

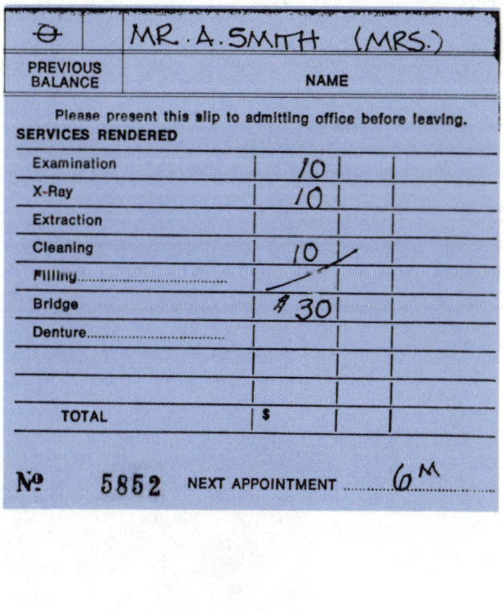

PREVIOUS BALANCE	NAME
Ø	MR. A. SMITH (MRS.)

Please present this slip to admitting office before leaving.

SERVICES RENDERED

Examination	10	
X-Ray	10	
Extraction		
Cleaning	10	
Filling		
Bridge	$30	
Denture		
TOTAL	$	

№ 5852 NEXT APPOINTMENT 6M

Transaction 2: Recording a Charge and Part Payment In the case of Mrs. Smith, assume that the dentist writes the following information on the stub: opposite *Examination,* a fee of $10; opposite *X-Ray,* a fee of $10; and opposite *Cleaning,* a fee of $10. Suppose further that the stub is totalled for $30 and that the next appointment is indicated as *6M,* the abbreviation for "six months."

At the front office, the receptionist/clerk first compares the number on the travelling stub with the number on the main portion of the receipt or statement form. This is important, because the patient would not necessarily return to the front office in the order in which he or she was admitted.

After the numbers have been checked, the patient's ledger card is inserted under the correct receipt form and lined up with the line containing the zero balance entry. Before entering the total charge, however, the receptionist should always ask the patient: "Your bill comes to $30. Will that be cash or cheque?" The reason for this form of the request is to minimize the possibility of a negative reply. If the clerk asked: "Would you like to pay your bill now?" the answer might well be no. Obviously, some payment now is better than untimely delays in the future.

Let us suppose Mrs. Smith pays $20 now and the balance later. In this case, the receptionist records the entry from left to right as follows:

- the receipt number in the *Receipt Number* section
- the current date in the *Date* column
- the description code (as interpreted from the standard dental codes in the receipt form) in the left side of the *Description Code* section
- *Mrs.* in the right side of the *Description Code* section to identify the patient
- $30— in the *Charge* column
- $20— in the *Payment* column
- $10— in the *Current Balance* column

The illustration of this entry appears above, opposite.

Analysis: The following three points should be learned in the correct analysis of the accounting entry.

- In making the entry, keep in mind that three forms are affected in one writing: the receipt or statement form, the patient's ledger card, and the journal. Print legibly and large enough to see every letter and number clearly.
- No "cent" figures should appear in any dollar amount. Dental practices prefer to use dollar amounts only, to simplify calculations so that errors may be avoided. Since no cent figures will appear in the accounts receivable application, the clerk is usually instructed to use a dash in the cents column.
- There is an important short-cut in the correct analysis of the double entry. This short-cut can be shown in three separate but related entries:

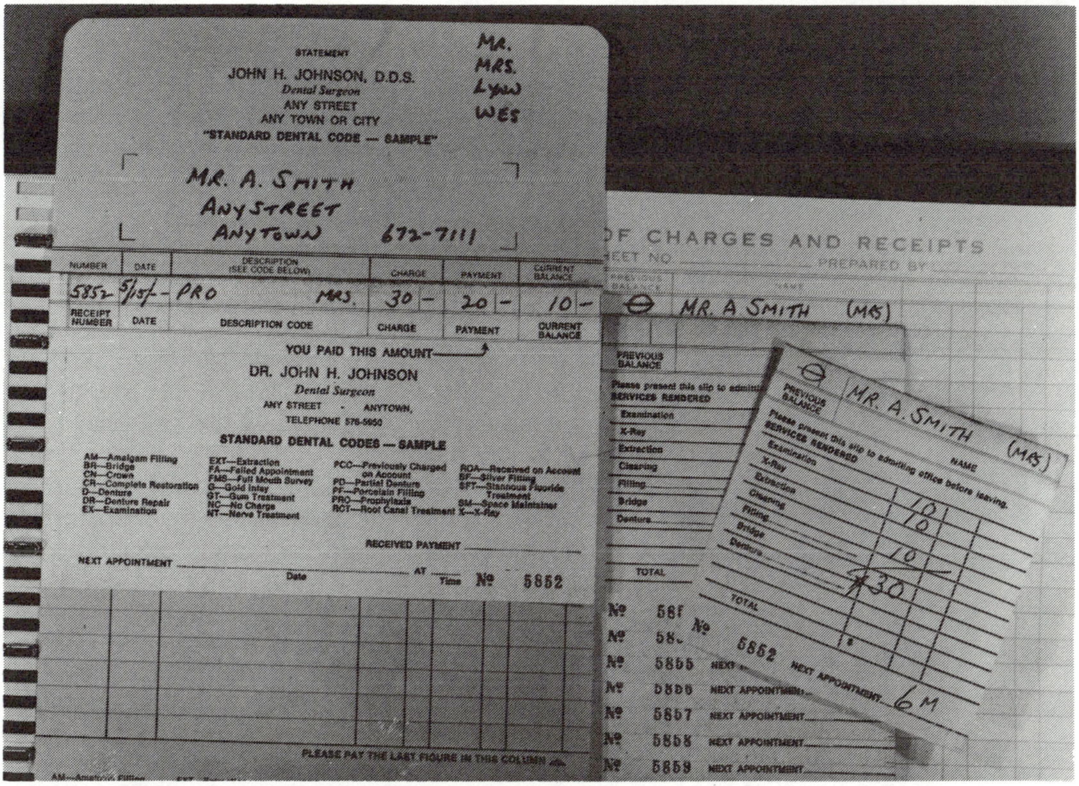

(1) By entering the $30 in the *Charge* column, you are following the accounting theory of debiting Accounts Receivable and crediting a revenue account such as Fees Earned. Think of the *Charge* column of the Combination Journal as the traditional revenue journal (fees earned journal). The entry may be analyzed in T-account form as shown below.

(2) By entering the $20 in the *Payment* column, you are following the accounting theory of debiting Cash and crediting Accounts Receivable. The *Payment* column on the journal, therefore, replaces the traditional cash receipts journal. The entry may be analyzed in T-account form as shown next.

(3) By entering the $10 in the *Current Balance* column, you are following the accounting theory of calculating the balance of the

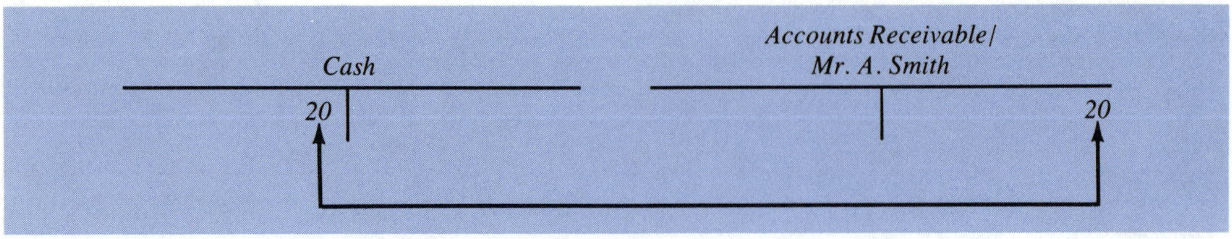

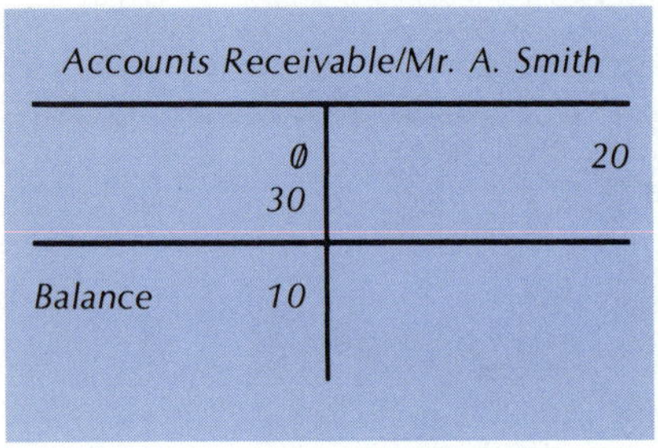

Accounts Receivable account. Accounts Receivable has received a debit for $30 and a credit for $20. Since no previous balance existed, $10 is recorded in the *Current Balance* column. The entry may be analyzed in T-account form as shown in the margin.

At this point, four advantages of the one-write system may be summarized as follows:

- The accounting clerk, in one writing, creates the receipt or statement form, the posting to the accounts receivable subsidiary ledger account (the patient's card), and the journal entry on the Combination Journal.
- Posting is performed automatically to the patient's account. If the entry is recorded correctly, no error can occur on the ledger card. This feature is contrasted with the traditional bookkeeping method of posting from the journal or source document to the customer's account. Errors are always possible when copying information from one source to another.
- The family ledger card concept contains the complete financial profile of the family. In this way, both the doctor and the responsible family member know at a glance how much is owing in total rather than having to look at individual family cards.
- The Combination Journal eliminates the need for recording separate entries in a fees earned journal and cash receipts journal. As you will recall, any entry in the *Charges* column supports the theory of recording Accounts Receivable and Fees Earned; therefore, the *Charges* column in the journal may be regarded as the theoretical revenue journal. Similarly, an entry in the *Payments* column supports the theory of recording Cash and Accounts Receivable; therefore, the *Payments* column in the journal may be regarded as the theoretical cash receipts journal.

To complete the transaction with Mrs. Smith, the receipt/statement form is detached once the entry is recorded to the end of the *Current Balance* column. Then, with the form removed from the board, the receptionist records the next appointment on the travelling stub. In this case, the appointment would be for six months from that day. In addition, *Smith* is written to identify the form for tax receipt purposes. And finally, the clerk's initials are placed opposite *Received Payment.* Of course, the reason for detaching the receipt/statement form and entering the above details away from the board is to avoid transferring the material via carbon to the journal sheet. The completed receipt/statement, together with the patient's ledger card and the stub, are illustrated below.

The completed receipt/statement form may then be inserted in a self-addressed envelope, which becomes a convenient method of returning the balance owing. Of course, the receipt/statement form shows not only what was paid, but also what is still owing "on account." As a result, by issuing both the receipt/statement form and the envelope, the receptionist can emphasize that it is the policy of the office to avoid mailing duplicate statements of account at month-end. In this way, Dr. Johnson saves time and mailing costs, and also has a positive means of controlling his accounts receivable. By giving the customer a statement and a self-addressed envelope, the dentist is assured, for the most part, an early remittance.

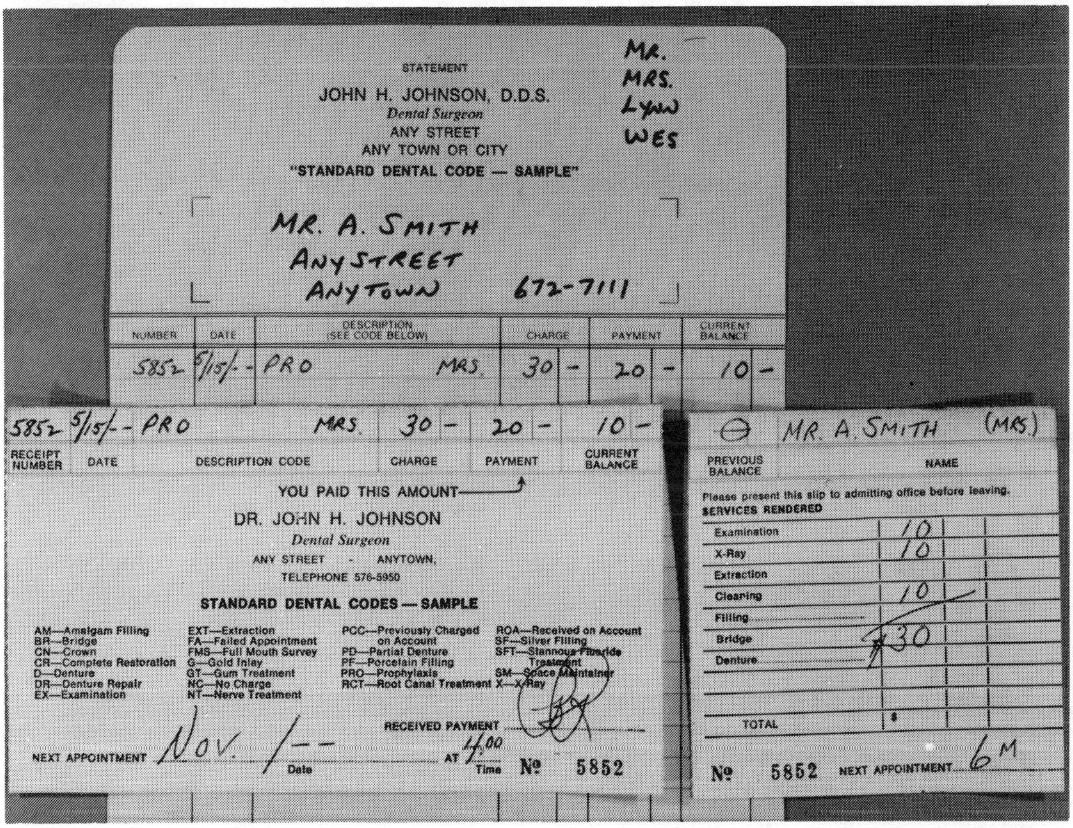
STATEMENT
JOHN H. JOHNSON, D.D.S.
Dental Surgeon
ANY STREET
ANY TOWN OR CITY
"STANDARD DENTAL CODE — SAMPLE"

MR.
MRS.
LYNN
WES

MR. A. SMITH
ANYSTREET
ANYTOWN 672-7111

NUMBER	DATE	DESCRIPTION (SEE CODE BELOW)	CHARGE	PAYMENT	CURRENT BALANCE
5852	5/15/--	PRO MRS.	30 –	20 –	10 –

RECEIPT NUMBER	DATE	DESCRIPTION CODE	CHARGE	PAYMENT	CURRENT BALANCE
5852	5/15/--	PRO MRS.	30 –	20 –	10 –

YOU PAID THIS AMOUNT
DR. JOHN H. JOHNSON
Dental Surgeon
ANY STREET - ANYTOWN,
TELEPHONE 576-5950

STANDARD DENTAL CODES — SAMPLE

AM—Amalgam Filling
BR—Bridge
CN—Crown
CR—Complete Restoration
D—Denture
DR—Denture Repair
EX—Examination
EXT—Extraction
FA—Failed Appointment
FMS—Full Mouth Survey
G—Gold Inlay
GT—Gum Treatment
NC—No Charge
NT—Nerve Treatment
PCC—Previously Charged on Account
PD—Partial Denture
PF—Porcelain Filling
PRO—Prophylaxis
RCT—Root Canal Treatment
ROA—Received on Account
SF—Silver Filling
SFT—Stannous Fluoride Treatment
SM—Space Maintainer
X—X-Ray

RECEIVED PAYMENT
NEXT APPOINTMENT Nov. 1-- Date AT 4:00 Time № 5852

PREVIOUS BALANCE	NAME
0	MR. A. SMITH (MRS.)

Please present this slip to admitting office before leaving.
SERVICES RENDERED

Examination	10		
X-Ray	10		
Extraction			
Cleaning	10		
Filling			
Bridge	$30		
Denture			
TOTAL	$		

№ 5852 NEXT APPOINTMENT 6 M

Transaction 3: Recording a Charge Only Suppose that on another day in the same month, Lynn, the daughter of Mr. and Mrs. Smith, comes to the office by appointment. In this case, the first step of this accounts receivable application would be to make out a travelling stub showing *\$10—* for the previous balance, and *Mr. A. Smith* and *Lynn* in the name section, as shown below.

Of course, the amount of the previous balance would be obtained from the family ledger card, which would have been pulled from the accounts receivable ledger tray. Keep in mind also that the information printed on the stub would appear on the journal sheet in the appropriate matching columns to the right of the *Balance* column.

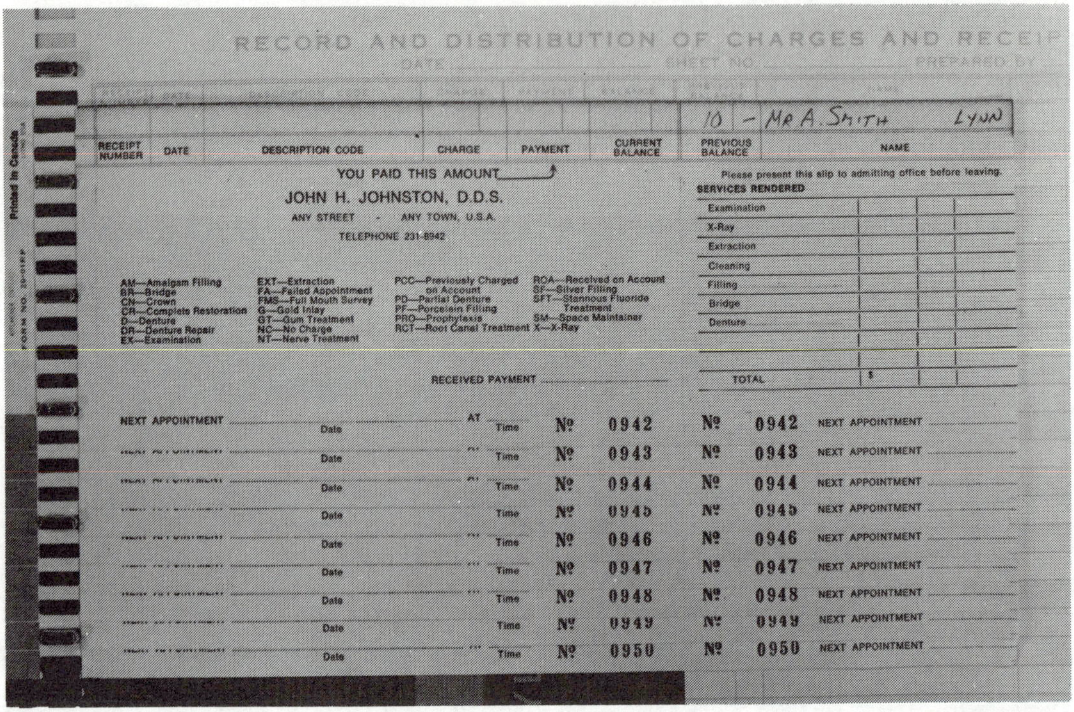

RECORD AND DISTRIBUTION OF CHARGES AND RECEIP

DATE ... SHEET NO. ... PREPARED BY

RECEIPT NUMBER	DATE	DESCRIPTION CODE	CHARGE	PAYMENT	CURRENT BALANCE	PREVIOUS BALANCE	NAME
						10 –	MR A. SMITH LYNN

YOU PAID THIS AMOUNT

JOHN H. JOHNSTON, D.D.S.
ANY STREET - ANY TOWN, U.S.A.
TELEPHONE 231-8942

AM—Amalgam Filling
BR—Bridge
CN—Crown
CR—Complete Restoration
D—Denture
DR—Denture Repair
EX—Examination

EXT—Extraction
FA—Failed Appointment
FMS—Full Mouth Survey
G—Gold Inlay
GT—Gum Treatment
NC—No Charge
NT—Nerve Treatment

PCC—Previously Charged on Account
PD—Partial Denture
PF—Porcelain Filling
PRO—Prophylaxis
RCT—Root Canal Treatment

ROA—Received on Account
SF—Silver Filling
SFT—Stannous Fluoride Treatment
SM—Space Maintainer
X—X-Ray

RECEIVED PAYMENT

NEXT APPOINTMENT ... Date AT ... Time № 0942

Please present this slip to admitting office before leaving.

SERVICES RENDERED: Examination, X-Ray, Extraction, Cleaning, Filling, Bridge, Denture, TOTAL $

№ 0942 NEXT APPOINTMENT
№ 0943 NEXT APPOINTMENT
№ 0944 NEXT APPOINTMENT
№ 0945 NEXT APPOINTMENT
№ 0946 NEXT APPOINTMENT
№ 0947 NEXT APPOINTMENT
№ 0948 NEXT APPOINTMENT
№ 0949 NEXT APPOINTMENT
№ 0950 NEXT APPOINTMENT

Printed in Canada

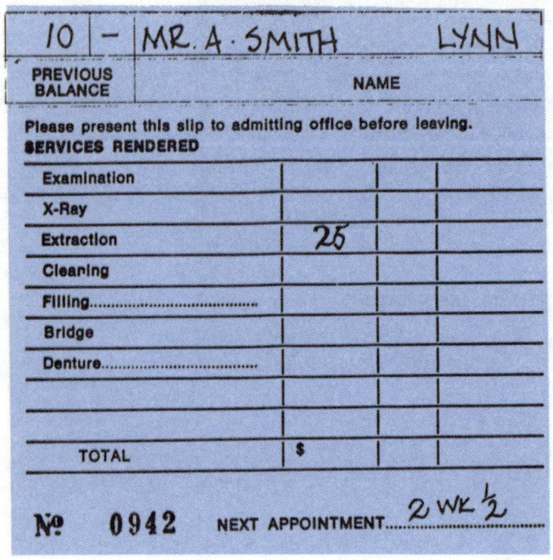

PREVIOUS BALANCE	NAME
10 –	MR. A. SMITH LYNN

Please present this slip to admitting office before leaving.

SERVICES RENDERED

Examination			
X-Ray			
Extraction	25		
Cleaning			
Filling			
Bridge			
Denture			
TOTAL	$		

№ 0942 NEXT APPOINTMENT 2 WK ½

For Lynn's treatment, suppose that Dr. Johnson completes the travelling stub as shown in the margin. A fee of $25 was recorded opposite *Extraction,* and the next appointment was marked as *2WK1/2* (two and one-half weeks from now). Suppose also that the daughter was given no money to pay for the bill. In this case, the receptionist would record the one-write entry for the charge as shown on page 613.

Analysis: These points should be read in relation to the illustration.

- The family ledger card would be inserted between the correct receipt/statement form and the carbon sheet in the correct vertical and horizontal position.
- With the aid of the black-ink ballpoint pen, the receptionist would complete the entry by printing with care the receipt number in the *Receipt Number* column; the date in numeric form in the *Date* column; the code *EXT* to describe the

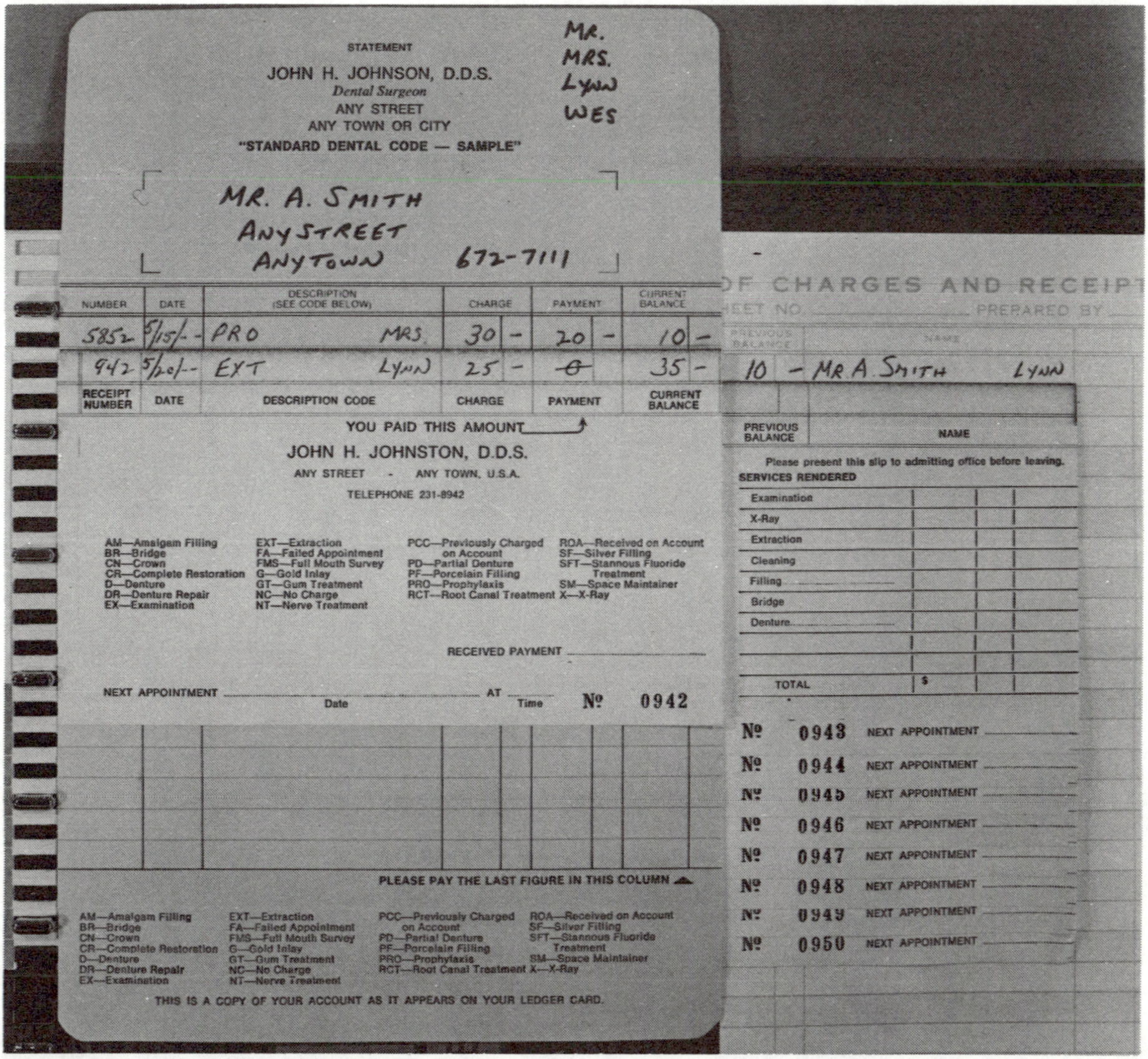

dental service at the left of the *Description Code* column; *Lynn* to the right of the *Description Code* column; *25—* in the *Charge* column; *0* in the *Payment* column; and *35—* in the *Current Balance* column. This one-write entry is clearly shown on the receipt/statement form in the above illustration.

- The statement form is then detached and placed in a position away from the board to avoid any further one-writing on the forms resting on the board. Then, the receptionist can show *Smith* on the face of the receipt/statement form as well as a stroke through the *Received Payment* part of the form, since no payment was made. In addition, he or she will print the date and time of the next appointment, as suggested by the dentist on the travelling stub. Of course, the exact date and time would be obtained from the appointments book always kept by the receptionist. The completed receipt/statement form would appear as illustrated below.

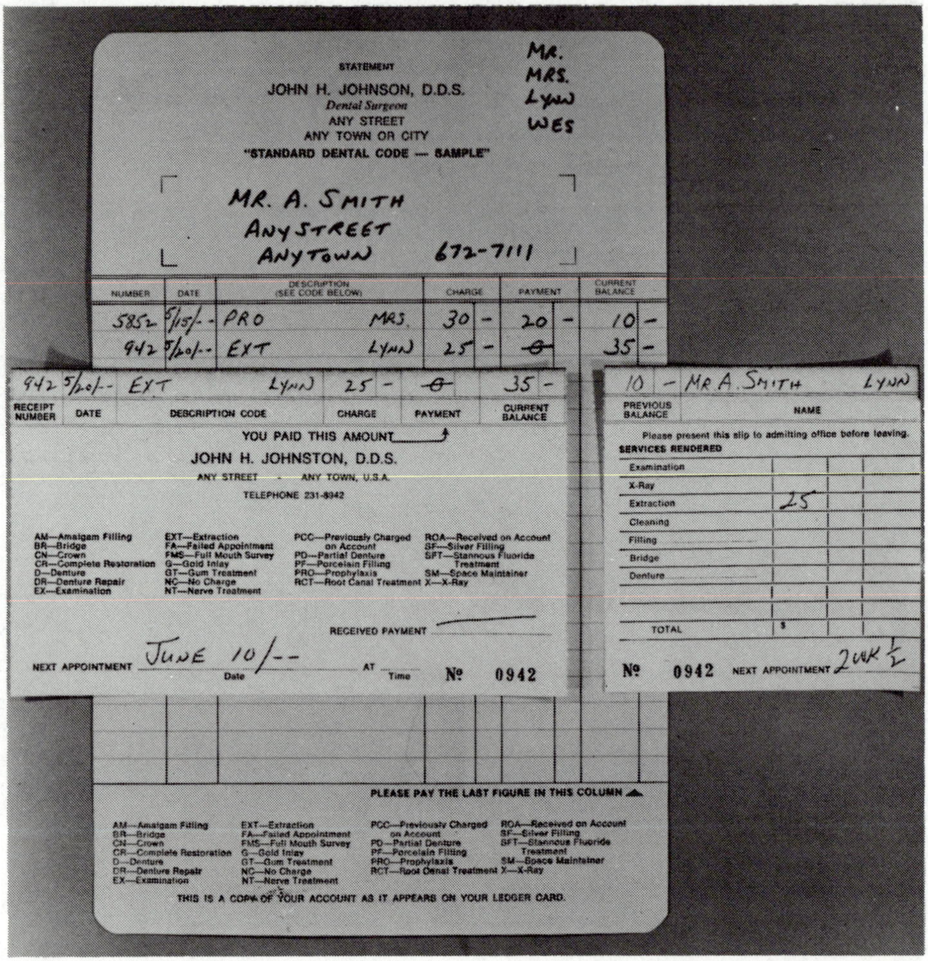
STATEMENT
JOHN H. JOHNSON, D.D.S.
Dental Surgeon
ANY STREET
ANY TOWN OR CITY
"STANDARD DENTAL CODE — SAMPLE"

MR.
MRS.
LYNN
WES

MR. A. SMITH
ANY STREET
ANYTOWN 672-7111

NUMBER	DATE	DESCRIPTION (SEE CODE BELOW)		CHARGE	PAYMENT	CURRENT BALANCE
5852	5/15/--	PRO	MRS.	30 -	20 -	10 -
942	5/20/--	EXT	LYNN	25 -	-0-	35 -

RECEIPT NUMBER	DATE	DESCRIPTION CODE		CHARGE	PAYMENT	CURRENT BALANCE
942	5/20/--	EXT	LYNN	25 -	-0-	35 -

YOU PAID THIS AMOUNT
JOHN H. JOHNSTON, D.D.S.
ANY STREET - ANY TOWN, U.S.A.
TELEPHONE 231-8942

AM—Amalgam Filling, BR—Bridge, CN—Crown, CR—Complete Restoration, D—Denture, DR—Denture Repair, EX—Examination, EXT—Extraction, FA—Failed Appointment, FMS—Full Mouth Survey, G—Gold Inlay, GT—Gum Treatment, NC—No Charge, NT—Nerve Treatment, PCC—Previously Charged on Account, PD—Partial Denture, PF—Porcelain Filling, PRO—Prophylaxis, RCT—Root Canal Treatment, ROA—Received on Account, SF—Silver Filling, SFT—Stannous Fluoride Treatment, SM—Space Maintainer, X—X-Ray

RECEIVED PAYMENT

NEXT APPOINTMENT JUNE 10/-- Date AT Time № 0942

PREVIOUS BALANCE	NAME	
10 -	MR A. SMITH	LYNN

Please present this slip to admitting office before leaving.

SERVICES RENDERED

Examination	
X-Ray	
Extraction	25
Cleaning	
Filling	
Bridge	
Denture	
TOTAL	$

№ 0942 NEXT APPOINTMENT 2 WK 1/2

PLEASE PAY THE LAST FIGURE IN THIS COLUMN ▲

THIS IS A COPY OF YOUR ACCOUNT AS IT APPEARS ON YOUR LEDGER CARD.

- The completed receipt/statement form is placed in the "convenience" envelope and handed to Lynn, with instructions to return the envelope and form to her parents. At this point, the enclosed form becomes a true statement of account which shows the services rendered, how much was charged ($25), the new balance ($35), and the date and time of the next appointment.
- Finally, the receptionist would return the family ledger card to the accounts receivable tray, filed alphabetically under the surname of the family.

Detailed Analysis: It is worth enlarging on the analysis of this transaction.

• A new journal sheet would be used since the daughter's treatment occurred on a different day from that of her mother. Remember, a new journal sheet is used for every day of the month. This means that the new journal sheet is actually the daysheet showing only the transactions for a particular day. This practice is quite different from the traditional bookkeeping method which uses a journal page until it is full, which may take several days. The daysheet system is preferred by many auditors who wish to see one day's set of transactions per sheet rather than a collection of days.

Daysheet: a journal sheet showing recorded transactions for one day only.

• The entire entry on the receipt/statement form, from left to right, is transferred by carbon to the family ledger card and the journal. This transfer is done automatically.

From an accounting theory viewpoint, the dollar entries must be analyzed as follows:

• The $25 charge is analyzed as a debit to Accounts Receivable/Mr. A. Smith and a credit to Fees Earned, as shown in the margin.

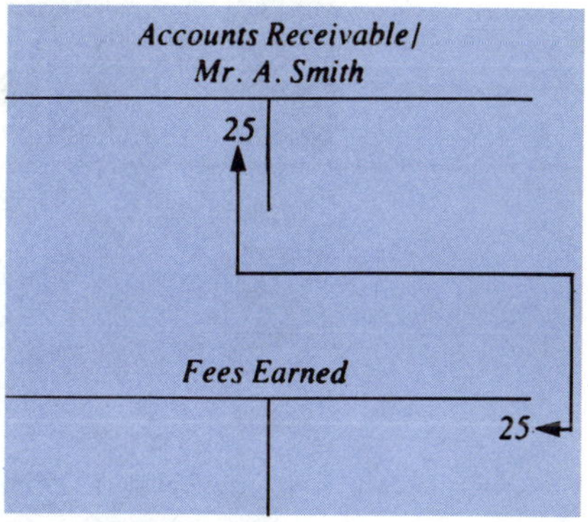

• The Ø payment is self-evident in that no accounting entry can be analyzed since no payment occurred.

• And the $35 current balance is the amount of the charge ($25) plus the previous balance ($10), as shown in the margin in T-account form.

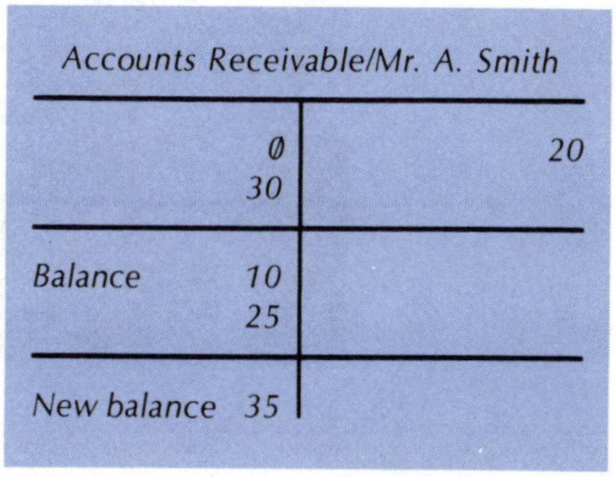

Of course, the theoretical T-account form is not used in dental practice. As you are now aware, the three-column ledger form showing the "running balance" is preferred for accounts in the accounts receivable ledger. Similarly, the three-column form is popular in the General Ledger, which is updated at the end of each month.

Transaction 4: Recording a Remittance on Account Suppose that on another day in the month a cheque is received from Mr. Smith for $15 in part payment of the balance owing on his family's account. The entry to record this remittance may be analyzed on the illustration on page 616.

Analysis: These points are related to the illustration.

• Mr. Smith's ledger card would be pulled from the ledger tray to identify the previous balance owing.

• The stub portion would first be made out as follows:

(1) In the *Previous Balance* section, the amount *35*— is entered carefully to show the balance owing after the last family transaction.

(2) *Mr. A. Smith,* the head of the household, is printed carefully in the *Name* section.

(3) The rest of the stub may be left blank. Some practices prefer to show *ROA* ("received on account") and the cheque amount, because the travelling stub is considered the source document to identify the transaction. Other practices may leave this part out since the description will appear on the main statement form.

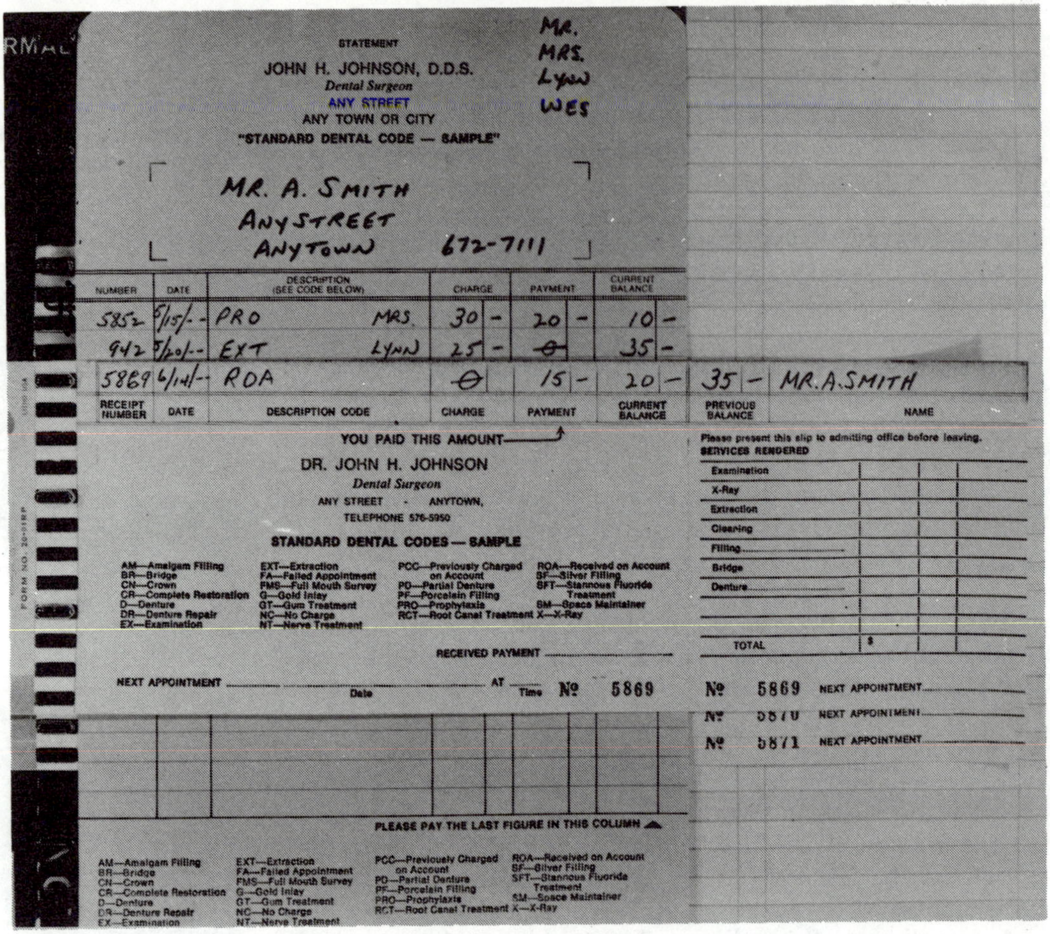

STATEMENT
JOHN H. JOHNSON, D.D.S.
Dental Surgeon
ANY STREET
ANY TOWN OR CITY
"STANDARD DENTAL CODE — SAMPLE"

MR.
MRS.
LYNN
WES

MR. A. SMITH
ANYSTREET
ANYTOWN 672-7111

NUMBER	DATE	DESCRIPTION (SEE CODE BELOW)		CHARGE	PAYMENT	CURRENT BALANCE
5852	5/15/--	PRO	MRS.	30 —	20 —	10 —
9412	5/20/--	EXT	LYNN	25 —	⊖	35 —

RECEIPT NUMBER	DATE	DESCRIPTION CODE	CHARGE	PAYMENT	CURRENT BALANCE	PREVIOUS BALANCE	NAME
5869	6/14/--	ROA	⊖	15 —	20 —	35 —	MR. A. SMITH

YOU PAID THIS AMOUNT

DR. JOHN H. JOHNSON
Dental Surgeon
ANY STREET - ANYTOWN,
TELEPHONE 576-5950

STANDARD DENTAL CODES — SAMPLE

AM—Amalgam Filling
BR—Bridge
CN—Crown
CR—Complete Restoration
D—Denture
DR—Denture Repair
EX—Examination
EXT—Extraction
FA—Failed Appointment
FMS—Full Mouth Survey
G—Gold Inlay
GT—Gum Treatment
NC—No Charge
NT—Nerve Treatment
PCC—Previously Charged on Account
PD—Partial Denture
PF—Porcelain Filling
PRO—Prophylaxis
RCT—Root Canal Treatment
ROA—Received on Account
SF—Silver Filling
SFT—Stannous Fluoride Treatment
SM—Space Maintainer
X—X-Ray

RECEIVED PAYMENT

NEXT APPOINTMENT ______ Date ______ AT ______ Time № 5869

Please present this slip to admitting office before leaving.
SERVICES RENDERED

Examination		
X-Ray		
Extraction		
Cleaning		
Filling		
Bridge		
Denture		
TOTAL	$	

№ 5869 NEXT APPOINTMENT
№ 5870 NEXT APPOINTMENT
№ 5871 NEXT APPOINTMENT

PLEASE PAY THE LAST FIGURE IN THIS COLUMN

AM—Amalgam Filling
BR—Bridge
CN—Crown
CR—Complete Restoration
D—Denture
DR—Denture Repair
EX—Examination
EXT—Extraction
FA—Failed Appointment
FMS—Full Mouth Survey
G—Gold Inlay
GT—Gum Treatment
NC—No Charge
NT—Nerve Treatment
PCC—Previously Charged on Account
PD—Partial Denture
PF—Porcelain Filling
PRO—Prophylaxis
RCT—Root Canal Treatment
ROA—Received on Account
SF—Silver Filling
SFT—Stannous Fluoride Treatment
SM—Space Maintainer
X—X-Ray

- The stub is not detached, because the transaction involves the accounting of a cheque received in part payment of an account receivable.
- The receptionist now inserts the family ledger card correctly positioned between the receipt/statement section and the carbon sheet.

The details of the transaction would now be completed on the receipt/statement form from left to right as follows:

- the receipt number corresponding to the same number at the bottom of the receipt/statement and stub portions
- the date of the transaction (in this case, the date of receiving the customer's cheque)
- *ROA* in the *Description Code* section
- *Ø* in the *Charge* column, because no fee has been involved in this transaction
- *15—* in the *Payment* column, which is the exact amount of the cheque

• *20*— in the *Current Balance* section to show the new balance on account

The receipt/statement and stub form is detached from the shingled set and placed away from the writing board, and the receipt/statement section is initialled in the usual manner. The completed receipt and ledger card are shown below.

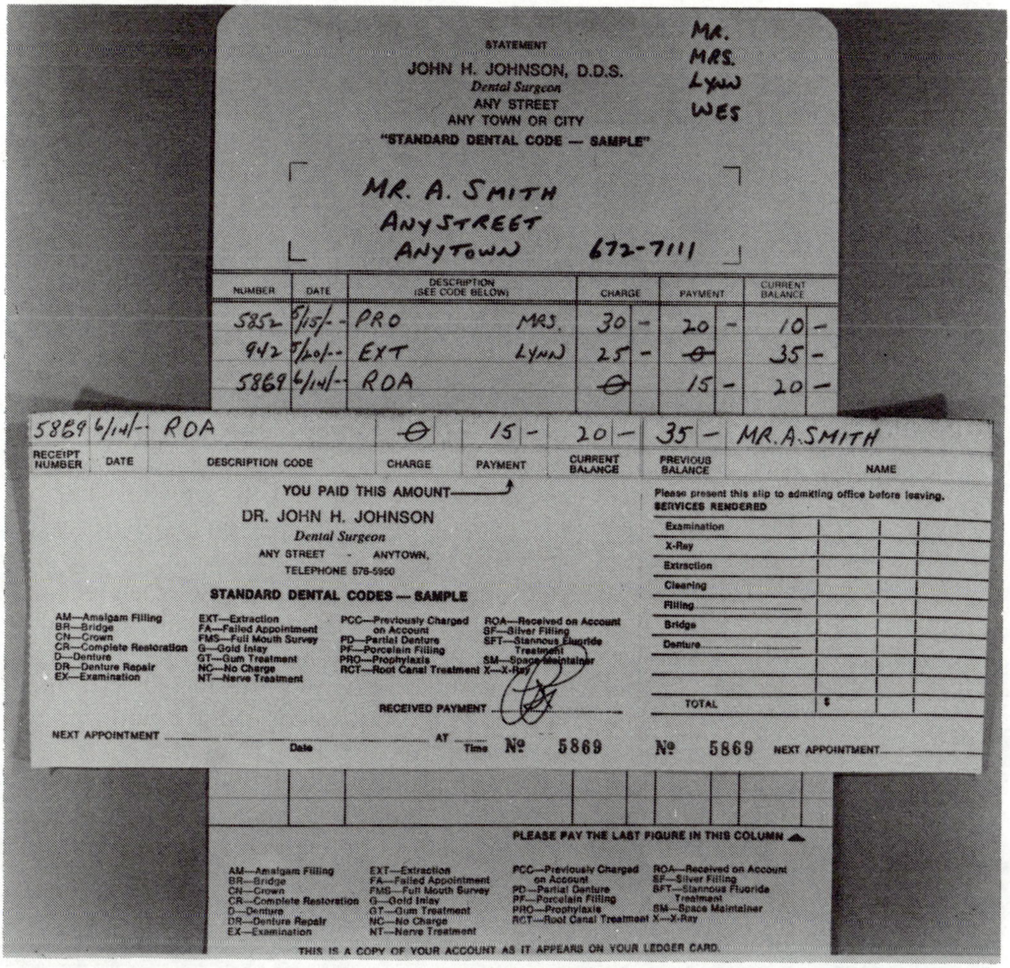

Unless the patient requests a mailed receipt, the complete receipt/statement form is attached to the back of the ledger card. Both the ledger card and attached receipt/statement form are then filed back into the accounts receivable ledger. The receipt/statement form can then be given to the member of the family who receives the next treatment together with the receipt/statement form for that new day.

Detailed Analysis: The ROA transaction may be analyzed in detail as follows:

• The record of the remittance would appear on a new

journal sheet, since the cheque was received on a day different from that of the last patient's visit.

- The entire entry shown on the top line of the stub form is transferred via carbon to the journal sheet only. Note that where the *Services Rendered* part shows *ROA* and the amount, this recording is not transferred to the journal sheet, because the carbon layer at the back of the stub appears behind the top line only.
- The entire entry on the receipt/statement portion is transferred to the family ledger card and journal. Of course, the carbon layer on the back of the receipt/statement form transfers the writing to the ledger card, while the carbon sheet transfers the one-writing to the journal sheet.

The dollar amounts entered on the journal sheet, corresponding of course to the entry on the receipt/statement form and the accounts receivable ledger card, would be analyzed as follows:

- The Ø charge is not analyzed, since no fee was transacted.
- The $15 payment is analyzed correctly as a payment on an account receivable. The *Payment* section of the journal is, in accounting theory, a cash receipts journal. Thus, the correct analysis is as shown in T-account form in the margin.

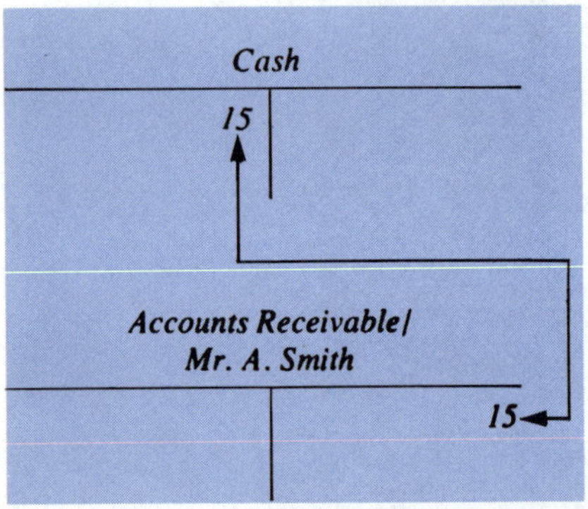

- The $20 current balance in the customer's account is the amount of the payment subtracted from the previous balance ($35), as shown in T-account form in the margin and in the actual patient's ledger account.

Accounts Receivable/Mr. A. Smith

	Ø 30	20
Balance	10 25	
Balance	35	15
New balance	20	

Note two important measures for the control of cash receipts:

- In Chapter 7 you learned that a pre-numbered source document is made out to give evidence of a cash receipts transaction. In this case, the stub portion of the receipt/statement form may be considered as the equivalent of the remittance slip showing the cheque amount received on account.
- In Chapter 7 you also learned that all cash receipts must be deposited *intact* in the firm's current bank account. This means that the back of the cheque will be endorsed *For Deposit Only* before the day's cash receipts are deposited.

Recording and Analyzing Uncommon Transactions

Together, the method of recording the opening zero balance, and the previous three transactions, represent approximately 95 percent of the common transactions for the accounts receivable application of a dental office. To complete the study of this application, several of the "uncommon" transactions affecting accounts receivable will be examined.

The only new information is to learn how each transaction is recorded on Mardan's one-write system. In the illustrations for each transaction analyzed below, only the appropriate section of the journal sheet will be shown. At this stage, you should be able to analyze what would appear on the receipt/statement/stub form and on the patient's ledger card without the aid of illustrations.

Transaction 5: Credit Balance Suppose that a patient, Mr. F. Baron, mails a cheque which "overpays" his account. In this case, all entries would be the same as for Transaction 4. In the *Balance* column, however, the new balance would be shown as a credit, as illustrated below.

RECEIPT NUMBER	DATE	DESCRIPTION • CODE	CHARGE	PAYMENT	BALANCE	PREVIOUS BALANCE	NAME
1004	*02/6/–*	*Mr. F. Baron ROA*	*∅*	*50 —*	*CR (20 —)*	*30 —*	*Mr. F. Baron*

Analysis:

- A credit balance is treated as an *abnormal* balance for any asset account.
- To show abnormal balances in accounting for assets, place brackets around the balance or write *CR.* immediately after it. The Mardan system recommends that both the brackets and letters be used to avoid any possible error in interpreting the amount. *Note:* The symbols *CR.* and *DR.* are often used without the periods, as in the illustration.
- The credit balance would generally remain on the books until the next dental treatment, when a debit entry would probably result in the elimination of the abnormal balance.

Transaction 6: Recording NSF Cheques In the section on bank reconciliation in Chapter 9, you learned that an NSF cheque resulted in an adjusting entry whereby the depositor firm charged back the amount of the cheque to the customer's account.

As you will recall, this adjusting entry, recorded in the General Journal, debited Accounts Receivable and credited Cash for the amount of the cheque. The effect of the entry, therefore, was to reverse the earlier one that recognized Cash as having been debited and Accounts Receivable as having been credited when the cheque was received from the customer and then deposited into the firm's bank account.

While the above theory also applies to the accounting of the transaction on the Mardan one-write system, slight changes are required in the bookkeeping aspects so that the one-write concept can be used. The following steps should be used when recording NSF cheques on the Mardan system.

(1) Re-enter the amount of the NSF cheque as a charge. As illustrated next, the amount is entered in the *Charge* column and in the *Balance* column, since the previous balance of the patient's account was zero.

(2) On the journal sheet, mark the amount of the charge with an asterisk (*) so that it can be found easily for later entry on the monthly summary sheet.

RECEIPT NUMBER	DATE	DESCRIPTION · CODE	CHARGE	PAYMENT	BALANCE	PREVIOUS BALANCE	NAME
1100	15/6/–	NSF	*15 —	∅	35 —	20 —	Mr. J. Doe

The asterisked amount in the *Charge* column of the journal sheet shows that an unusual entry occurred on this line. The asterisk and the *NSF* code causes the reader to analyze the qualified amount correctly as Accounts Receivable debit and Cash credit.

BAD DEBTS AND OTHER ADJUSTMENTS WRITTEN OFF THROUGH DAY SHEETS		
DATE	NAME	AMOUNT
15/6/—	Mr. J. Doe NSF	15—

(3) List all NSF cheques, including name, date, and cheque amount in the *Adjustments* section of the monthly summary sheet. This is required so that the amount can be adjusted correctly at month-end. See the margin illustration.

Of course, the receptionist would phone the patient with specific instructions as to repayment, or send the statement. When the payment arrives, the remittance is analyzed and recorded in the usual manner.

Transaction 7: Write-off Entry In some cases, it is necessary to write off part or all of the patient's account as uncollectable. This is recorded as a debit to the contra asset account Allowance for Bad Debts, and as a credit to Accounts Receivable.

Under traditional bookkeeping procedures, the entry would be recorded in the General Journal with a double posting of the credit entry: once to Accounts Receivable (Control) in the General Ledger and once to the customer's account in the accounts receivable ledger. By recording and posting the entry as uncollectable, the customer's amount owing is eliminated.

While the accounting theory of the write-off applies to the Mardan one-write system, the bookkeeping aspects must be changed to accommodate the one-write concept as described below.

(1) Enter the previous balance and name of the patient on the stub portion of the receipt/statement form in the usual manner. The illustration below shows a previous balance of $16 for a Mrs. Watson, the head of the household.

RECEIPT NUMBER	DATE	DESCRIPTION · CODE	CHARGE	PAYMENT	BALANCE	PREVIOUS BALANCE	NAME
1139	16/6/–	Mrs. Watson W/O	(16 —)	∅	∅	16 —	Mrs. Watson

(2) Record the document number and current date in the appropriate columns of the receipt/statement form.

(3) In the *Description Code* column, enter the name of the patient and *W/O* ("write-off").

(4) Enter the amount to be written off in the *Charge* column with brackets around it. As we have seen, in accounting practice an amount with brackets around it is treated as a minus quantity. In this case, Accounts Receivable must be decreased. This means that a negative entry must be shown. The brackets will also reject the amount as a credit to Fees Earned.

(5) Enter Ø in the *Payment* and *Balance* columns to complete the entry, as shown in the illustration.

(6) Remove the ledger card and place it in a position away from the accounting board; then explain on the ledger card the reason for the write-off.

(7) Finally, enter the date, the name, and *W/O,* and the amount of the write-off in the *Bad Debts and Other Adjustments* section of the monthly summary sheet. See the margin illustration. Obviously, this write-off must be adjusted at month-end to appropriate general ledger accounts. This section of the monthly summary sheet becomes the source from which the accountant will analyze the adjusting entries.

BAD DEBTS AND OTHER ADJUSTMENTS WRITTEN OFF THROUGH DAY SHEETS

DATE	NAME		AMOUNT
15/6/—	*Mr. J. Doe*	*NSF*	*15—*
16/6/—	*Mrs. Watson*	*W/O*	*16—*

Transaction 8: Bad Debt Recovered In some cases a payment is received on an amount that has been previously written off. Under traditional accounting procedures, two entries would be analyzed and recorded. The first would be an adjusting entry which would be made in the General Journal to reverse the previous write-off. This entry would debit Accounts Receivable/(Customer) and credit Allowance for Bad Debts. The second would account for the normal remittance, which would be made in the cash receipts journal. Of course, this entry would be analyzed as Cash debit and Accounts Receivable/(Customer) credit.

Under a one-write system, however, the two separate entries are combined as shown below.

RECEIPT NUMBER	DATE	DESCRIPTION • CODE	CHARGE		PAYMENT		BALANCE		PREVIOUS BALANCE		NAME
1240	*15/7/—*	*Mrs. Watson Coll. Ag. Rec'd*	**16*	*—*	*16*	*—*	*Ø*		*Ø*		*Bad Debts Recovered —Watson*

(1) Record the stub portion, showing Ø in the *Previous Balance* column, and *Bad Debts Recovered — (Patient's Name)* in the *Name* section.

(2) Enter the correct receipt number and the date of transaction in the appropriate columns of the receipt/statement section.

(3) In the *Description Code* column, enter the name of the patient and an appropriate explanation. For example, if a collection agency had been hired to recover the amount, show the name of the patient followed by *Coll. Ag. Rec'd.*

(4) Enter the amount recovered in the *Charge* and *Payment* columns. Of course, the resulting balance will be zero since Ø was shown in the *Previous Balance* column.

(5) In the *Charge* column of the journal sheet, show an asterisk beside the amount to indicate an unusual entry. Of course, the charge amount in this case must be analyzed in accordance with the explanation offered by the description code, that is, a debit to Accounts Receivable and a credit to Allowance for Bad Debts. The symbol would also suggest that Fees Earned, the revenue account, is not affected by the transaction. The amount in the *Payment* column does not have to be asterisked because it follows the normal theory of debiting Cash and crediting Accounts Receivable, as supported by the traditional cash receipts journal.

AMOUNTS RECOVERED DURING MONTH ON AMOUNTS FORMERLY WRITTEN OFF		
DATE	NAME	AMOUNT
15/7/—	*Mrs. Watson*	*16—*

(6) In the *Amounts Recovered* section of the monthly summary sheet, record the date, name, and amount of the recovery. Of course, this reference is necessary at month-end when the accountant must analyze all adjustments. See the margin illustration.

When a collection agency is involved, some dental offices prefer to use a separate ledger card entitled *Bad Debts Recovered* to record charges equal to the amount of payment, that is, the collection of accounts receivable previously written off. The use of a separate ledger card for Bad Debts Recovered would then show all amounts recovered through a collection agency on one card. On the other hand, if the patient comes in voluntarily to remit an amount previously written off, the common practice is to use the patient's ledger card for two reasons: the patient's ledger card would show a complete history of the credit transaction from beginning to end; and the patient's card would provide information to the local credit bureau so that a fair credit rating may be established.

End-of-Day Procedures

Several important procedures are recommended at the end of each day to ensure a correct accounting of accounts receivable and cash:

- the proof of posting to patients' ledger accounts
- the proof of Accounts Receivable Control
- the proof of cash through a daily cash summary
- the posting of the daily total to the monthly summary sheet

Daily Balancing and Proof of Posting At the end of office hours, a proof of the posting to patients' ledger accounts is taken from the dollar amounts recorded in the *Charge, Payment, Balance,* and *Previous Balance* columns of the journal sheet. The procedure for obtaining this proof is illustrated next and may be done in accordance with the following steps.

RECORD AND DISTRIBUTION OF CHARGES AND RECEIPTS

DATE *MAY 12, 19--* SHEET NO. *166*

RECEIPT NUMBER	DATE	DESCRIPTION CODE	CHARGE	PAYMENT	BALANCE	PREVIOUS BALANCE
ALL RECEIPTS MUST BE IN NUMERICAL ORDER			COLUMN A *450 -*	COLUMN B *200 -*	COLUMN C *750 -*	COLUMN D *500 -*

PROOF OF POSTING

COLUMN D TOTAL:	*500 -*
"PLUS" COLUMN A TOTAL:	*450 -*
SUB TOTAL:	*950 -*
"MINUS" COLUMN B TOTAL:	*200 -*
EQUALS COLUMN C TOTAL:	*750 -*

ACCOUNTS RECEIVABLE CONTROL

A.R. BALANCE FORWARD:	*3985 -*
"PLUS" COLUMN A:	*450 -*
SUB TOTAL:	*4435 -*
"MINUS" COLUMN B:	*200 -*
PRESENT A.R. BALANCE:	*4235 -*

(1) Add the dollar amounts in column A *(Charge)*, column B *(Payment)*, column C *(Balance)*, and column D *(Previous Balance)*. Often an adding machine with a tape printout is used to double-check the totals. Remember that all bracketed amounts are minus quantities; therefore, they must be treated as negative amounts in arriving at the column totals. Of course, all other amounts are considered positive.

(2) Enter each total at the bottom of each column, which is clearly marked by the letters, A, B, C, and D, as shown in the illustration.

(3) Under the section *Proof of Posting*, enter the totals as directed and follow the calculating instructions closely. For example, if column A totals $450, column B $200, column C $750, and column D $500, the proof of posting is done as shown in the illustration.

From the illustration it is evident that the proof of posting is based on the simple and yet important idea that the total of all previous balances (as revealed on the patients' ledger cards), plus the total of the *Charge* column, minus the total of the *Payment* column, must be equal to the total of the *Balance* column. Check this again by reviewing the illustration.

This proof supports the theory that at the end of the day's journalizing and posting to accounts receivable the total of beginning debit balances of accounts receivable for that day, plus the total debits recorded to accounts receivable for that day, minus the total credits to accounts receivable for that day, must be equal to the total new debit balances of those same accounts receivable used on that day.

This could easily be verified by listing the new account balances as shown by the individual ledger cards on an adding machine tape and obtaining a total. Of course, this procedure is unnecessary because the one-write feature already contains these current balances right on the journal sheet in the *Balance* column. This feature is another strong advantage of using the Mardan one-write system. As long as the column totals balance and the receptionist always places the ledger card on the daily summary sheet to make an entry, you can be almost 100 percent sure that there are no errors.

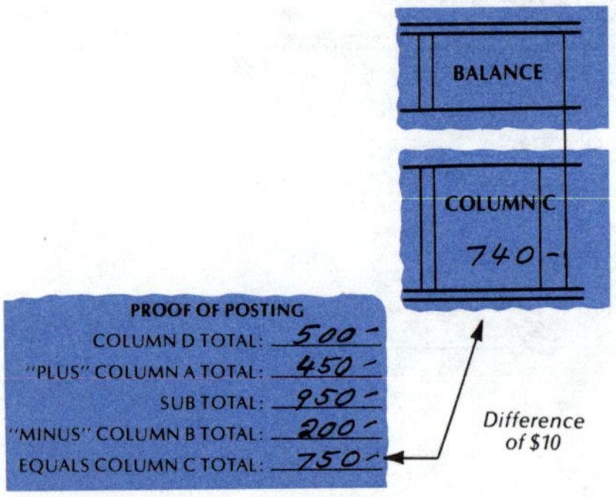

Of course, the above proof can be achieved only if the clerk has performed accurate recordings for each transaction. Suppose, for example, that an error was made in mentally calculating a new balance that should have been $25 but was recorded as $15 in the *Balance* column. Using our earlier example, the totals of the four columns would then be: column A $450, column B $200, column C $740, and column D $500. The proof of posting would now appear as shown in the margin.

Obviously, the receptionist/clerk would have to recheck the individual calculations until the error is located and corrected. Here are four key areas to check if daily balancing is not achieved.

- Recheck entries and add columns again.
- Recheck each entry across for errors or hard-to-distinguish numerals. In particular, check the calculation for the new balance in column C. Remember that this new balance is the result of combining the previous balance with the amount shown in the *Charge* column, less the amount shown in the *Payment* column.
- After the error is located, correct it on the patient's ledger card and on the journal. In the manual method, an error is corrected by drawing a single line through the entire amount; then the correction is made neatly and clearly above. Most accountants do not favour erasures since they not only eliminate a view of the original error, but also destroy part of the paper surface on which the correction is to be made.
- If all else fails, put the sheet away for a couple of hours or overnight. A fresh start can make it easier to locate the problem.

Proof of Accounts Receivable Control In earlier chapters you learned of an important monthly measure to test the accuracy of the balances of the individual customer accounts against the total of accounts receivable control in the General Ledger. This test involved preparing an independent summary of the end-of-month balances of the individual customer accounts of the subsidiary ledger, the total of which had to agree with the balance of the control account, also independently calculated. Such a control is called *"taking a trial balance of accounts receivable."*

Under the Mardan system, the concept of a trial balance of accounts receivable is also used. There is, however, a slight change. Instead of using the traditional General Ledger control account for accounts receivable, the control account is actually accounted for *daily* from the data supplied on the daily journal sheets. In other words, the balance in the theoretical accounts receivable control account is kept on a daily basis as part of the end-of-day activities. Thus, a special section at the bottom on the daily journal sheet is provided to check the accuracy of Accounts Receivable Control.

Here are the steps to follow to "post" to accounts receivable control on a daily basis. *Note:* Check back to the illustration on page 623 when reading these points.

(1) Bring forward the balance of Accounts Receivable Control from the previous day. In theory, this balance would be the total of the previous day's balances as shown by all of the individual patients' ledger cards which are filed in the accounts receivable ledger. Let us suppose that this total is $3 985.

ACCOUNTS RECEIVABLE CONTROL	
A.R. BALANCE FORWARD:	3985 -
"PLUS" COLUMN A:	450 -
SUB TOTAL:	4435 -
"MINUS" COLUMN B:	200 -
PRESENT A.R. BALANCE:	4235 -

(2) Add the total in column A of the current day sheet; that is, the total charges from today's transactions. In our previous example, this amount is $450.

(3) Show a subtotal of the results of adding the two amounts.

(4) Subtract the total in column B — that is, the total payments from today. In our previous example, this amount is $200.

(5) Calculate and show accurately the new Accounts Receivable Control balance as at the end of the current day. From the illustration, you can see that this calculation would give $4 235.

From the above calculation, therefore, the present *A.R. Balance* would, in theory, have to agree with the total of *all* individual patient ledger card balances on file in the accounts receivable ledger. Of course, this listing of individual patient account balances could easily be obtained on an adding machine with a tape printout. In practice, the "trial balance" of the subsidiary ledger is not done daily, but at the end of the month. At this point, it is important to understand that the balance in Accounts Receivable Control will be calculated daily so that, by month-end, the final day's balance will reveal the month-end balance for the Accounts Receivable Control account. By so doing, it is unnecessary to set up a formal General Ledger control account for accounts receivable.

Proving the Daily Cash The Mardan system provides for this control measure with a section at the bottom of the journal sheet called *Daily Cash Summary.*

Analysis: These points should be recalled in any analysis of the Daily Cash Summary.

- *Opening Cash on Hand at Beginning of Day* is the amount

DAILY CASH SUMMARY

		CASH PAID OUT $	
OPENING CASH ON HAND AT BEGINNING OF DAY $	25.00 (Float)	BANK DEPOSITS $	200.00 = C/A.B
CASH RECEIVED DURING DAY $	200.00	CLOSING CASH ON HAND $	25.00 = Float
TOTAL $	225.00	TOTAL $	225.00
CASH LONG $		CASH SHORT $	
TOTAL $		TOTAL $	

of currency borrowed from the main bank account to handle change in any person-to-person cash transaction. This amount becomes the change fund or "float." This change fund or petty cash fund is borrowed from the firm's main source of cash and must be accounted for.

- Although the heading *Cash Paid Out* is provided, no amount is stated opposite it. The absence of an amount of "cash" paid out is in keeping with your learning of basic measures to control cash receipts and cash payments. As you will recall, one such measure is to deposit the daily receipts intact into the firm's current account at the bank. Similarly, one basic measure for controlling cash payments is to pay by cheque all amounts other than for "petty" expenditures. And, as you recall, a petty cash system is recommended to control all such incidental expenditures.
- Notice that the Summary has included provision for *Cash Long* and *Cash Short.* As you may recall from Chapter 8, any cash overage or shortage must be accounted for.
- As an additional measure of cash control, someone other than the person handling the cash or recording the dollar results of cash transactions should be assigned to prepare the daily proof summary. In practice, therefore, the responsibility for preparing the summary may be given to the dentist, to his or her spouse, or to an assistant.

Posting the Daily Totals to the Monthly Summary Sheet One of the last end-of-day activities is to enter on the specific date line the total charges (column A) and the total payments (column B) of the yellow monthly summary sheet of accounts receivable. See the illustration below.

ACCOUNTS RECEIVABLE SUMMARY
Month of May, 19--

DAY OF MONTH	CHARGES (COLUMN "A")		PAYMENTS (COLUMN "B")		MISC. SUMMARIES							
12	*450*	–	*200*	–								

After this "posting" is completed, the journal sheet is detached and placed in the post binder for permanent filing. Of course, the clerk would also glance down the *Charge* column of the journal sheet to make sure that all adjustments, such as for NSF cheques, were also listed on the summary sheet. A new day sheet would then be placed over the monthly summary sheet in preparation for the next day's transactions.

Monthly Procedures

As has been suggested earlier, the monthly summary sheet will remain on the accounting board until the end of the month. At this month-end, at least two important procedures are followed: (1) preparing the trial balance of accounts receivable; (2) aging the accounts receivable.

Preparing the Trial Balance of Accounts Receivable Here are the recommended steps under the Mardan one-write system:

(1) Total columns A and B on the monthly summary sheet. Since the accuracy is very important, use a calculator or adding/listing machine if possible. Take time to double-check all additions.

(2) Enter the totals for the month in the boxes at the bottom of each column. Again, it is important to make neat and legible figures.

(3) In the upper right corner of the summary sheet, complete the accounts receivable reconciliation to ensure that all accounts receivable calculations for the month are correct. As you can see from the illustration below, this reconciliation is based on the formula shown in the margin.

If these totals do not balance, an error has been made and must be found and corrected.

Formula

Total A/R for the beginning of month (1st day sheet)
plus total charges for the month
minus total payments for the month
equals A/R at the end of month (last day sheet)
which equals the total outstanding balances on patient ledger cards

ACCOUNTS RECEIVABLE RECONCILIATION	
ACCOUNTS RECEIVABLE – BEGINNING OF MONTH	Ø
PLUS: TOTAL CHARGES FOR MONTH	4755
SUB-TOTAL	4755
LESS: TOTAL PAYMENTS FOR THE MONTH	4435
ACCOUNTS RECEIVABLE – END OF THE MONTH	320
ACCOUNTS RECEIVABLE TOTAL PER LEDGER CARDS	320
DIFFERENCE	Ø
ADJUSTMENT OF CONTROL APPROVED BY	HK

MAY Year 19--

(4) With the aid of an adding/listing machine or a calculator with a tape printout, list the month-end balances from each patient's ledger card. Of course, the total of this listing must equal the Accounts Receivable Control balance shown in step 3. If they agree, identify the tape and attach it to the summary sheet.

(5) If there is a difference and you have found the tape listing to be correct, adjust the control balance so that your opening balance for the next month will correspond to the total from the ledger cards. This difference must be entered on the monthly summary sheet in the section for the accounts receivable reconciliation. Finally, the difference must be approved and initialled by the practitioner.

After the monthly trial balance of accounts receivable has been completed, the monthly summary sheet is placed in the post binder on top of the last day sheet. The post binder, therefore, contains a complete set of journal sheets and the monthly summary sheet. (These journal sheets, together with the monthly summary sheet, will be required by the accountant who is usually hired to handle the audit and month-end adjustments for use in the future preparation of the annual financial statements.)

Aging the Accounts Receivable One of the remaining month-end procedures is to "age" each patient's ledger balance.

One simple yet effective method of aging is as follows:

(1) During the last week of every month, examine the balance of each patient's ledger card.

(2) If the account balance is past due by 30 days, place a green sticker in the top right corner of the card.

(3) If the account balance is past due by 60 days, place a yellow sticker in the same corner.

(4) If the account balance is past due by 90 or more days, place a red sticker in the corner.

This simple method calls attention to those accounts requiring immediate action. The red or "danger" cards would normally be considered first, then the yellow, and finally the green. In most cases, a monthly statement is mailed to the green- and yellow-labelled ledger cards. For the red-labelled cards, a collection agency may be hired to try to recover all or a portion of the outstanding balance now long past due and for which past billings have failed to bring forth a remittance.

One final comment: Suppose that the month-end review of accounts receivable reveals that the total past due amount is $1 000. If this total consists of an average outstanding amount of, say $20, then 50 billings should be required at month-end. Of course, that many billings are just too costly. To ensure an inexpensive yet efficient control of daily accounts receivable, one may use the travelling stub concept, whereby the doctor can speak directly to the patient in the examining room or train the front-office person to politely request payment following each transaction.

TOPIC 1 PROBLEMS

17-1 List the individual components that make up the accounts receivable pegboard system dealt with in this chapter. Then give a brief explanation of the main function of each item.

17-2 Answer the following questions about the processing of accounts receivable on the Mardan one-write system. Refer to the illustrations on pages 602 and 606.

a In what order should the accounting forms that comprise the accounting set for processing a dental fee be placed on the writing board?

b Is the patient's ledger card placed on the accounting board at the time the stub portion of the receipt/statement form is prepared? Explain why or why not.

c Briefly explain how the one-write concept is achieved on the Mardan one-write board.

17-3 Assume that you have been engaged as the receptionist/clerk for the dental office of John H. Johnson, D.D.S. of your town or city. Assume further that the office uses the Mardan one-write system. The transactions below are related to a new family, that of Mr. G. Swift. Perform the activities that are offered for each transaction below. *Note:* Save your solutions for use in the next problem.

a From the following data, set up the new patient's family ledger card: principal family member, Mr. G. Swift; address, your town or city; telephone number, 471-8622; other family members, Mrs. and a daughter, Heather.

b Assume that Mrs. Swift arrived at Dr. Johnson's office on May 1, current year, in response to an earlier dental appointment. Set up a zero balance on the stub portion of the receipt/statement form similar to the one illustrated in this chapter.

c Assume that the dentist has entered the following information on the travelling stub: examination $10, X-ray $10, cleaning $22, next appointment 6M. Assume further that you have placed the required forms in their correct writing position on the Mardan one-write board, and that Mrs. Swift will pay $20 of the bill today. Record the dollar results of the transaction on the receipt/statement form used in **b** above.

d Assume that the receipt/statement form has been removed from the Mardan one-write board. Show how the receipt/statement form would be receipted and indicate the next appointment for a date in accordance with the dentist's request.

e Show how the entry would appear on the ledger card used in **a** above.

Key Check Figure Current Balance = $22

17-4 Use the solutions for Problem 17-3 to continue the dental transactions as they affect the Swift family to the end of May.

May 12 Heather Swift received the following treatment: examination $10, X-ray $10, filling $15. Next appointment is for 3WK. No payment is received.

25 Mr. Swift received the following services: examination $10, X-ray 2 at $10, cleaning $15. Next appointment, 2WK1/2. Mr. Swift paid $25 cash.

May 31 Received a cheque for $77 from Mr. G. Swift in full payment of his family's account.

a Record the dollar results of each transaction on separate receipt/statement/stub forms. Where applicable, show how the travelling stub would appear as having been completed by the doctor in the examining room.

Key Check Figure Balance on May 31 = 0

b Show how the ledger card would appear posted for all transactions to the end of May. What balance should appear in the account as of May 31? How would this balance be indicated?

17-5 The transactions below, as indicated by individual receipt numbers, occurred in the dental office of John H. Johnson, D.D.S. on Monday, October 4. For each transaction:

a Show how the entry would appear in the journal sheet of the Mardan one-write system.

b After recording the transaction in the journal, use T-accounts to explain the analysis of the theory of the accounting entry for each transaction.

Note: Save the journal sheet for use in the next problem.

1000 To Sue, daughter of Mr. L. Waldock, for examination, X-ray, and cleaning. Total fee $24. No previous balance. No payment received.

1001 To Mr. A. Huston, for examination, X-ray, and temporary filling. Total fee $44. No previous balance. Received $20 cash on account.

1002 To Mrs. H. Irwin, for examination, X-ray, endo (root canal) treatment. Total fee $142. No previous balance. No payment received.

1003 To Ms. S. Bailey, new patient, exam and X-ray. Total fee $35. No previous balance. Received cheque for $35.

1004 To Mr. C. Webb, for silver filling, $28. Previous balance $35. Received $63 cash.

1005 To David, son of Mr. C. Remus, for filling, $12. Previous balance $12. No payment received.

1006 To Don, son of Mr. D. Lunau, for fillings. Total fee $41. No previous balance, no payment received.

1007 To Mrs. J. Meeuwis, for examination, 2 X-rays, and cleaning. Total fee $44. No previous balance. Received $20 cash.

1008 To Mr. T. Tighe, for examination, X-ray, and cleaning. Total fee $36. No previous balance. Cheque received for $36.

1009 To Jane and Mary, daughters of Mr. B. Speed. Jane's treatment: exam, X-ray, and cleaning, $30. Mary's treatment: exam, X-ray, cleaning, and fluoride, $34. Previous balance $36. No payment received.

1010 To Mr. P. Thornton, for exam, X-ray, and extraction. Total fee $48. Previous balance $14. Cheque received in full payment of account.

1011 To Mrs. E. Leyland, for exam, X-ray, and silver filling. Total fee $28. Previous balance, $15 CR. No payment received.

1012 To Mrs. J. Dickson, for silver filling, $14. Previous balance $56. Cheque received in full payment of account.

1013 To Mr. G. Butler, for exam, X-ray, and cleaning. Total fee $36. No previous balance. Received cheque for $36.

1014 To George Jr., son of Mr. G. Weiler, for extraction, $13. Previous balance $10. Received cheque for $23 from Mr. Weiler.

1015 To Lynda, daughter of Mr. R. Asselstine, for exam and X-ray. Total fee $20. Previous balance $20. Payment of $20 received in cash.

1016 To Mr. W. Kechnie, for exam, X-ray, and cleaning. Total fee $44. Previous balance $10. Cheque received for $54.

1017 To Mr. R. Mandel, for bridge, $110. No previous balance. Received $50 on account.

1018 To Mrs. R. Brien, for a crown, $75. Previous balance $25 CR. Cheque received for $50.

1019 To Ms. R. McGauley, for exam, X-ray, silver filling, and retentive pin. Total fee $44. No previous balance. Cheque received in full payment of account.

1020 To Paul, son of Mr. J. Pendergast, for exam, X-ray, cleaning, and fluoride. Total fee $38. No previous balance. No payment received.

1021 Cheque received in mail from Mr. H. Wallis for $41 in full payment of previous balance.

1022 Cheque received in mail from Ms. S. Kipps for $25. Previous balance $50.

1023 Cheque received from Mr. J.H. Johnstone for $100. Previous balance $70.

1024 The Welfare Insurance Agency of the town/city stated that no further coverage would be made on behalf of Mrs. W. Watson's account. The doctor advised that the balance of $16 is to be written off as uncollectable.

1025 Mr. Larry Brown's outstanding balance of $10 is to be written off as uncollectable.

1026 The Welfare Insurance Agency submitted a cheque for $5 to apply to the outstanding balance of Mr. F. Milsom's account. The previous balance is $10. The agency also advised that no further statements can be sent to the patient; thus, the balance is to be written off as uncollectable.

1027 Received a cheque for $16 from the collection agency for the recovery of Mr. Brady's previous account balance of $16, which was written off last month.

1028 Mr. L. Bobyk, whose outstanding account balance of $70 was written off last month as uncollectable, appeared in person to pay $70 cash.

1029 Mrs. M. Rivard appeared and requested the return of her overpayment of account of last Friday. The transaction of October 1 showed that a cheque for $37 was received, resulting in a credit balance of $13. Issued a cheque for $13.

1030 Received a debit memo and an enclosed NSF cheque from the bank. The bank charged back the NSF cheque of Mr. T. Moore for $35, which was originally deposited on September 29.

Key Check Figure Balance on Oct. 4 = $35

17-6 Use the journal sheet solved for Problem 17-5. Show the proof of posting the accounts receivable transactions for October 4. Show this proof in the appropriate section of the journal sheet. Be sure to follow the procedure recom-

Key Check Figure $540 = Column C Total

mended in the Mardan system. *Note:* Save the journal sheet for use in the next problem.

Key Check Figure $4 988 = Present Accts. Rec. Balance

17-7 Use the journal sheet solved for Problem 17-6. Assume that the balance forward of Accounts Receivable, carried forward from last day's journal sheet, was $4 785. Show a proper calculation for Accounts Receivable Control on October 4. Use the formula given in the text for the Mardan one-write system.

Key Check Figure Total = $865

17-8 Use the journal sheet solved for Problem 17-7 to do the daily cash summary from the following information: the float at the beginning of the day, $25; cash received during the day agrees with the total cash receipts shown on the bank deposit slip; there are no cash shortages or cash overages. This dental practice supports the cash control measure of depositing all daily cash receipts intact.

Key Check Figure Difference = $10

17-9 Assume that the transactions for October 31 have been recorded and posted correctly, and that the total charges and payments for that day have also been posted to the appropriate line on the yellow monthly summary sheet. Assume also that the following information has been verified: total of column A on the summary sheet, $10 705; total of column B on the summary sheet, $9 470; total balances of accounts receivable as at the beginning of the month, $4 785; total outstanding balances on patient ledger cards as listed on an adding machine tape, $6 010.

Prepare the trial balance of accounts receivable as at October 31.

Key Check Figure Approximately 100

17-10 Suppose that an aged analysis for the accounts receivable reported for Problem 17-9 consisted of an average amount overdue of $60.

a How many billings would be required to collect the total amount of accounts receivable as at October 31?

b Do you feel that this dental practice has adequate control of its accounts receivable? Explain your answer.

Case Study 17

Mary X is employed as a receptionist/clerk in the dental office of Brown and Johnson. Among her duties, Mary is required to bill patients and to record accounts receivable transactions on a one-write system.

On one particular morning, a new patient, John Blinkhorn, was given a checkup and cleaning. After the dental service, Mary X received the services-rendered portion of the stub with the following information: (1) opposite *Examination* $8.00, (2) opposite *X-Ray* 2 totalling $14; (3) opposite *Cleaning* $22, (4) Dr. Johnson's initials at the bottom. Mary then approached the new patient as follows:

"Your total bill comes to $46. Will that be cash or charge?"

Mr. Blinkhorn replied: "I'm sorry, but all I have is $10. Can I pay you at the end of the month?"

Mary smiled and answered: "Yes, that's fine. I'll write out the receipt for a complete charge." With that, Mary entered a receipt number, the date, description code, and $46 in the *Charge* column. She then removed the main receipt portion and handed it to the patient, saying: "Here is your bill. Please send a cheque by the end of this month. Goodbye for now."

a Did the clerk record the dollar results of the transaction correctly? Explain why or why not.

b In the same situation, how would you have handled the delicate matter of billing the patient? Give reasons for your views.

CHAPTER 18

COMPUTER APPLICATIONS

In the last chapter, you learned how many small firms used the one-write system to process accounting applications such as accounts receivable, accounts payable, and the payroll.

As a firm's volume of transactions grows, however, even the one-write system becomes inefficient. Consider, for example, a clerk's trying to process a weekly payroll made up of several thousands of employees on a one-write board. Or picture that clerk's having to process five hundred or more invoices or fee bills every day on the one-write board. Of course, the most efficient method today is to use a computer to process any accounting application where a large volume of transactions occurs.

In this chapter, you will be introduced to computers as they relate to the processing of common accounting applications. In offering these concepts, care has been taken to keep discussion of the technical aspects of computers to a minimum.

• Topic 1 (the only Topic in this chapter) deals with simple computer concepts as they relate to accounting.

TOPIC 1 COMPUTER CONCEPTS IN ACCOUNTING

Accounting Data versus Accounting Information

Think of a computer as an electronic box receiving accounting data, processing that data by turning currents on and off, and producing useful accounting information. There is a clear distinction between accounting data and accounting information. A computer receives accounting data and *processes* it to produce accounting information. Follow the simple example of the processing of part of a payroll application on page 635, top.

Analysis: Accounting data can take the form of numbers, letters, or special symbols. In the example, there are two pieces of accounting data: hours worked and the hourly rate. Since data must be entered into the computer, all data are called input data

Input data: a general term used to describe any or all facts, numbers, letters, and symbols to be entered into the computer.

Once data are put into the computer, they are processed. In the example, the processing is the computation of multiplying two numbers.

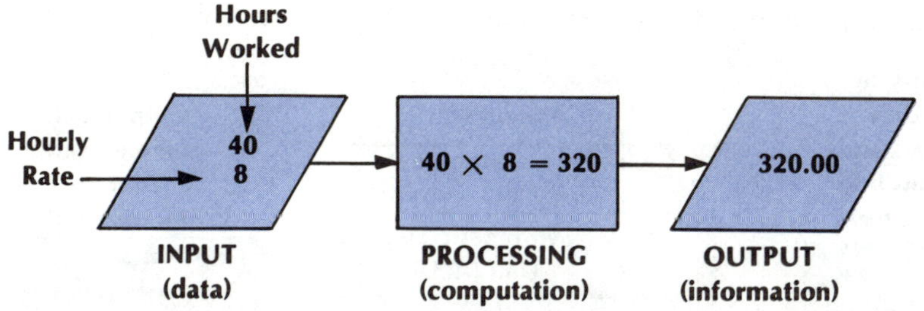

The result is output. Here, the output produces useful information in the form of the gross wages of the employee.

Output: processed data (information) transferred from a computer to any device outside of the computer.

Of course, this information can also be input data for a second stage of processing. For example, to obtain the employee's net pay, you would show:

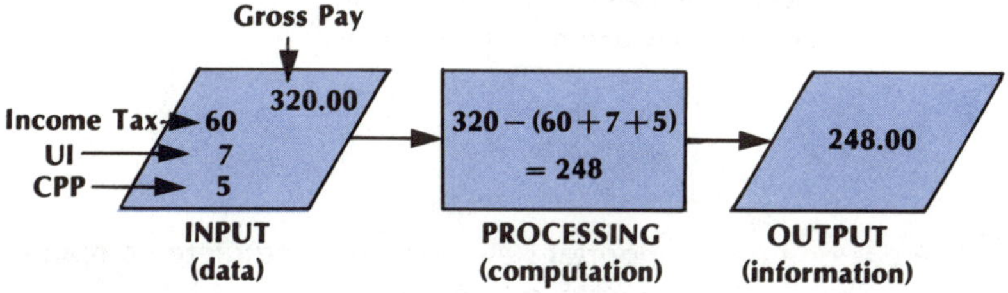

Analysis: Here, input data consist of the employee's gross wages and deductions for the Canada Pension Plan, unemployment insurance, and income tax. As the illustration shows, the computer processes the data by subtracting the total payroll deductions from the gross pay. The result is output information called the employee's net pay.

Without accounting data, there can be no accounting information. Accounting information is the output (the end result) of a processing operation for a specific accounting application.

Elements of a Computer System

To receive accounting data, process that data, and produce accounting information, our electronic box will need a series of interconnecting parts. This electronic box and connecting parts form a computer system. The system may be broken down into three distinct parts:

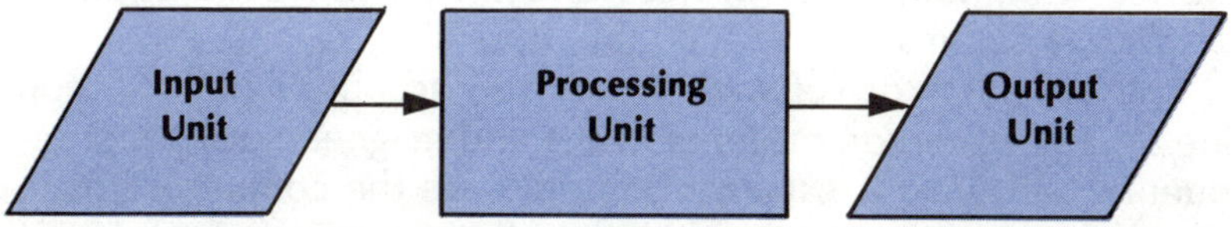

In turn, each of these three units may be broken down as follows:

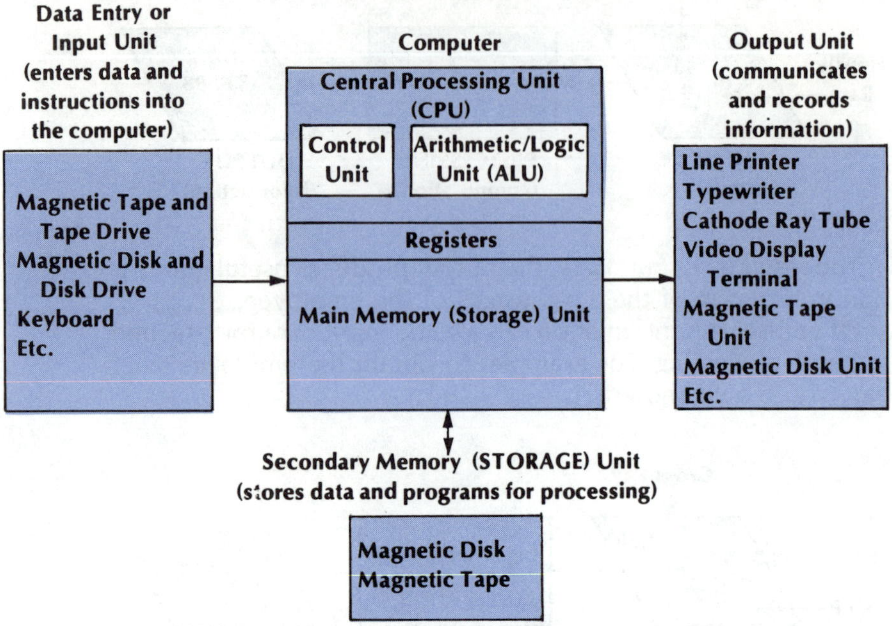

Software: a set of computer programs, procedures, and associated documentation concerned with a computer system.

There is one other important element in a complete computer system. That is the software or stored programs which tell the computer what to do. Let's look at each part of the complete computer system in more detail.

Data Entry or Input Unit

Input to a computer consists of the data related to a particular accounting application. For example, input to a payroll application requires employees' names, SIN, hours worked, rate of pay, and payroll deductions. In addition, the input consists of the set of instructions — software — that tell the computer what to do with the data.

To get accounting data and the program into the main memory of the computer, some form of input medium and input device are required.

Data may be recorded on a variety of media such as punched cards, punched paper tape, magnetic tape, or magnetic disk. The input unit (device) then "reads" the data on the media and enters the data into the computer's main memory unit. A magnetic disk reader (usually called "drive") is typical of this kind of input device. Common input devices and their corresponding input media are summarized in the table opposite.

The programs or software to run the accounting application are usually stored on magnetic tapes and magnetic disks. Consequently, software is usually "booted" into the computer's main memory unit through tape drives or disk drives respectively.

Magnetic Disk File Unit Courtesy of IBM

Magnetic Disk Pack Courtesy of IBM

Magnetic Tape Unit Courtesy of IBM

Input Medium	*Corresponding Input Device*
Punched card	Card reader
Punched paper tape	Paper tape reader
Magnetic tape	Tape Drive
Magnetic disk	Disk Drive
Source documents with magnetic marks, bars, or symbols	Scanning devices such as mark-sense readers, magnetic ink character recognition reader, and optical character readers

It is useful to remember that input devices transfer data (and programs) to the computer's main memory unit. But before data can be used by the computer, they must be converted to the computer's number code. How this is actually done is a technical matter beyond the scope of this text. Think of the input device as having the ability to convert all data into a series of electronic impulses which can be understood by the computer. Thus, all data entering the computer's memory will be in a number language the computer understands before actual processing begins.

There are other devices that allow data to be entered into the computer. A common one is the keyboard: you can "type in" data (letters, numbers, and symbols). The keyboard converts these data into the number code.

One other group of input devices, called terminals, is worth mentioning. Briefly, a terminal is an input device that can send data to a computer over communication lines. It can also receive data from a computer. Almost any input device — typewriter,

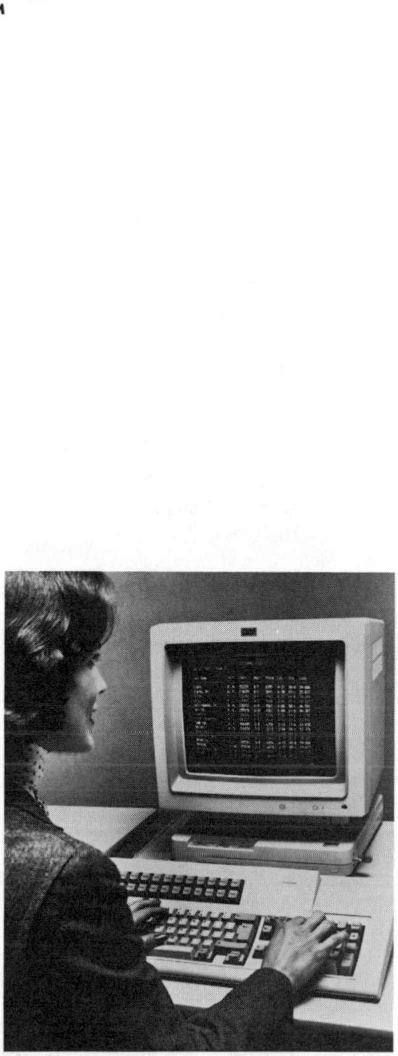

Display Station Courtesy of IBM

paper tape reader, etc. — can now be hooked up to a telecommunications system and become a remote input device to the computer. Even the human voice can be used as an input medium with this method.

Point-of-sale (POS) terminals: computer terminals used in retail stores as electronic cash registers.

Common terminals are keyboard display terminals and point-of-sale terminals. These usually have a printer so that "hard copy" is available. Point-of-sale (POS) terminals are cash registers which can transmit data to the computer. They can also be equipped with scanning devices to capture the price, item number, and description of each item checked out of a supermarket. The customer automatically gets a description of the product purchased on the bill, and the store gets a record which can be used in the inventory application.

The Computer

As you saw in the illustration on page 636, the computer or "electronic box" is subdivided into three main parts: the main memory or storage unit, a number of registers, and the central processing unit (CPU). You can also see that the CPU is subdivided into the control unit and the arithmetic/logic unit. Let's briefly explain these parts.

Main memory: the primary storage area in the computer for instructions and data.

Main Memory (Storage) Unit All accounting data and programs (instructions) go first to the computer's main memory unit. Computer storage must be large enough to hold the accounting data and instructions to process specific accounting applications. We will discuss the main memory unit in more detail later.

Register: a device capable of storing a specified amount of data, such as one computer word; often contained within the CPU.

Registers A number of registers provide a mechanism for transferring data and instructions between the CPU and the main memory. On most modern computers, a register is physically part of the CPU; on others, registers are located between the main memory and the CPU. Regardless of their location, think of registers as simply the path connecting the main memory unit and the CPU.

Central processing unit (CPU): the unit of a computer system that includes the circuits which control the interpretation and execution of instructions.

The Central Processing Unit The central processing unit (CPU) is regarded as the heart of the computer — where all the action occurs. It is responsible for interpreting and executing (carrying out or processing) instructions. Our earlier illustration shows the CPU as being divided into the control unit and the arithmetic/logic unit.

Control unit: a sub-unit of the CPU which controls and directs the operations of the entire computer system.

The main job of the control unit is to direct the operations in accordance with the instructions in the program. Think of the control unit as having the circuitry to analyze — one at a time — each instruction in the program. It also directs the other parts of the computer to prepare to execute the specified operation. For example, if the instruction calls for an ADD operation, the control unit will set the circuits to carry it out.

Arithmetic/logic unit (ALU): the unit of a computer system that contains the circuits that perform arithmetic and logical operations.

The arithmetic/logic unit (ALU) is involved in the execution of arithmetic or logic instructions such as an ADD or COMPARE operation. Data are brought from the main memory into the ALU and the required operations are then performed. Prior to output, all results must be returned to main memory. From there they can be sent to the output device. As the margin illustration shows, during processing data are constantly being moved back and forth between the arithmetic/logic unit and main memory.

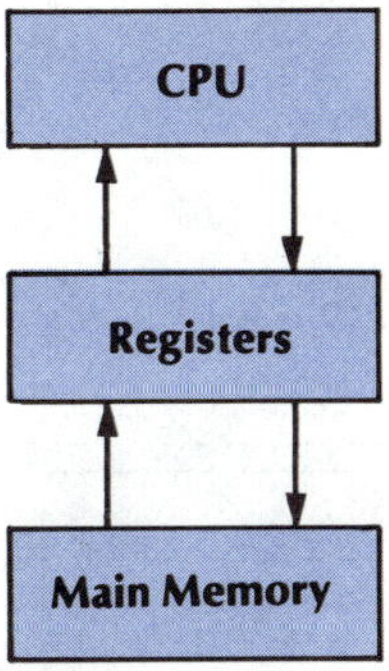

It is worth noting that some people understand the term CPU to mean the entire computer; in other words, in our illustration, the CPU plus the registers and main memory. However, the most widely accepted definition limits the function of the CPU to the interpretation and execution of instructions, which is the meaning used here.

The Output Unit

When the computer finishes processing accounting data according to the instructions provided by the program, it is ready to produce its results. Of course, these become accounting output or information.

Although there are a number of output devices, in accounting practice the *printer* is by far the most common and most important. If the computer has been programmed with a set of instructions to move the processed data through an output device such as a high-speed printer, that information can be transferred onto accounting documents in the form of a continuous roll. Such output can include invoices, customer statements, payroll cheques, payroll registers, journals, ledgers, financial statements, and special-purpose reports of all kinds.

IBM 4248 High-Speed Line Printer Model 1

Courtesy of IBM

Although the printer is by far the most common output device, it is by no means the only one. Common output devices and their corresponding output media are summarized in the chart below and on the next page.

Output Device	*Output Medium*
Printer (at least seven varieties are available)	Paper forms and documents of all forms
Video screen (CRT [cathode ray tube] or video display terminals)	Display on a TV-like screen
Audio response unit	Voice (recorded or synthesized)
Graphic plotters	Paper documents showing business graphics (charts and various kinds of graphs)
Magnetic disk unit	Storage on magnetic disk

Magnetic tape unit	Storage on magnetic tape
Microfilm unit	Storage on microfilm
Punched card unit	Storage on punched cards (becoming obsolete)
Paper tape unit	Storage on paper tape

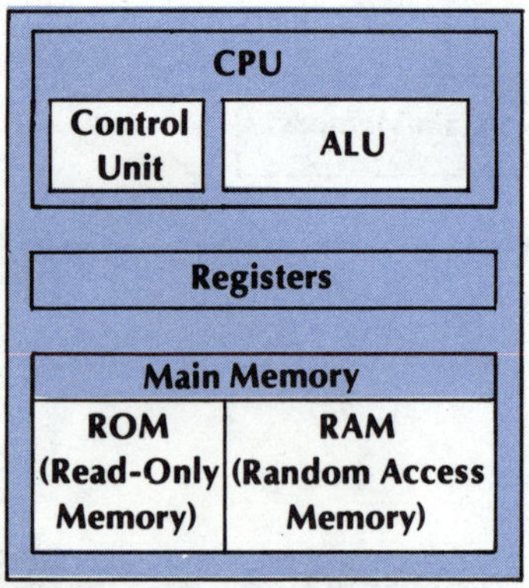

A Closer Look at Computer Memory

You learned earlier that the CPU is tied to the computer's main memory unit. All data and instructions must be placed in main memory before they can be processed in the CPU. All processed information returns to main memory before being reported through some output device.

There are two kinds of memory within the computer: *read only memory* or ROM and *random access memory* or RAM. In addition, all modern computer systems have secondary memory or auxiliary units. Because the size of memory is important in processing accounting applications, it is useful to learn a few things about memory and the size of storage capacity.

ROM: read-only memory, which cannot be erased and rewritten. This memory is used for permanent storage within the computer.

Read-Only Memory ROM usually contains the programs built into the computer by the manufacturer. For example, the programming language BASIC (Beginner's All-Purpose Symbolic Instruction Code), an easy-to-learn high-level computer language, widely used in small business and personal computers, may be part of the computer's ROM.

ROM is sometimes used to control the activities of programmers working for a large firm. Suppose, for example, a program has been written to control access to a 24-h bank teller terminal. A skilled but dishonest programmer might be tempted to change the program so that it instructs the machine to give out all the cash he or she wants. Clearly, this is a risk that the bank cannot afford to take. The answer is to store the program in read-only memory. That way, programmers cannot change the content of the memory locations containing the control access program.

Many people think of a computer as having a brain, because ROM becomes the "thinking" part of the computer. Why? Once the program is stored in ROM, you cannot ordinarily change it, add to it, or subtract from it. And even when the computer is shut off, programs in ROM always remain.

Operating system: collection of computer programs for carrying out such jobs as input/ouput control, memory allocation, and program read-in.

In some machines, ROM provides the computer with just enough intelligence to do a few simple tasks such as loading a program with a disk, tape, or cartridge. This program becomes part of the computer's operating system. In others, ROM contains enough intelligence to operate the computer and to "understand" a programming language like BASIC. That way you can write your own programs.

To sum up, ROM contains control programs, operating systems programs, and other programs which are put into memory permanently. As the name suggests, ROM can only be "read."

Random Access Memory RAM is far more important to the user. It's the amount of RAM that normally defines the computer's maximum capacity to receive data and the accounting applications program. You can put data into it, change it, and eliminate it. For that reason, RAM is often called user or usable memory.

RAM: random access memory, which is that part of main memory that can be changed by writing over previous contents. Used for temporary storage of data and programs during processing.

RAM is "random" because it provides access to any storage location point in memory immediately. The computer can go directly to any location, either "reading" its contents, or "writing" (storing) new information there. In other words, the computer can rapidly access pieces of information at random — there is no need for it to search in sequence all through memory looking for something. With RAM, however, it is important to know that whatever is entered into memory is lost if electric power is interrupted. RAM, therefore, is temporary memory.

RAM is usually made up of many rows of tiny electric switches called cells. Think of each memory cell as containing only a tiny "bit" of information. Some people like to think of these cells as electronic mailboxes because each cell has its own address. These "mailboxes" can hold data or program instructions for immediate use by the CPU.

Cells: locations in memory.

Address: a label, name, or number identifying the location where information is stored.

Like a light switch, the cell can be switched on or off. To picture this idea, let's use a 1 for every memory cell in the on position and a 0 for a memory cell that is in the off position. Look carefully at this illustration:

ONE MEMORY CELL

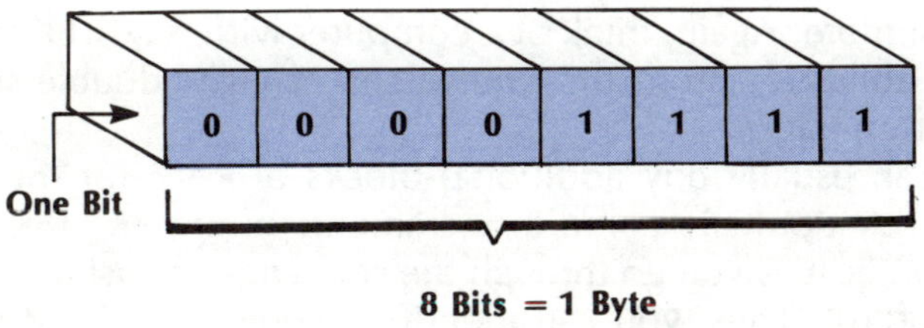

Analysis: These points should be read along with the illustration above:

- The word bit is short for *binary digit.* To explain *binary,* think of the computer using a numbering code with only two digits. Instead of using ten digits (from 0 to 9), as we do, computers use number codes with the digits 0 and 1 only.
- A grouping of eight bits is called a byte. The byte is the basic block of information stored within the computer.

Bit: abbreviation for "binary digit." The smallest unit of computer data, represented by 1 (on) or 0 (off).

Byte: a consecutive sequence of bits, generally eight bits long. One byte translates into one character.

Character: the actual or coded representation of a digit, letter, or special symbol.

• Each byte represents a character of information. For example, a byte can hold one letter of the alphabet (say *A* or *a*); an arithmetic or written symbol (say the "-" or ";"); or two digits (say 15).

K: an abbreviation for "kilobyte," a unit for measuring computer memory. One K is equivalent to 1 024 (2 to the 10th power) bytes or characters.

Memory Size You can measure computer memory in thousands of bytes called kilobytes. One byte is what it takes to store a single character in memory. So a kilobyte (1K) could contain a document of about 1 000 characters. The symbol for *kilobyte* is K.

Notice we said "about" 1 000 characters. To be more precise, however, the computer industry uses the metric *K* to represent 1 024 storage positions. Why? Because computers use binary digits. Remember the two digits 0 and 1. For 1K, think of the two digits raised to the power of 10; that is, 2 multiplied by itself nine times as follows:

2	× 2	× 2	× 2	× 2	× 2	× 2	× 2	× 2	× 2
	=4	=8	=16	=32	=64	=128	=256	=512	=1 024

Think of one kilobyte or 1 024 bytes as about half of a double-spaced typewritten page. How many kilobytes would be needed to store about 32 double-spaced typewritten pages? Your answer should be 64K.

Although a memory size of 64K is really 65 536 storage positions (64 × 1 024), in practice such exactness is often disregarded to simplify description of a computer's RAM. In small business computers, RAM usually contains from 16K bytes (1 024 × 16 = 16 384 bytes) to 128K bytes (1 024 × 128 = 131 072 bytes) or more. Again, think of a computer with, say, 16K as having the ability to store the equivalent of eight double-spaced typewritten pages.

You can usually buy additional blocks of RAM for the computer. They normally come in increments of 4K, 8K, 16K bytes and so on (just as you go through the sequence of raising 2 to the power of 10). Thus, you can identify a computer's RAM as 4K, 8K, 16K, 32K, 128K, 256K, etc.

It is important to know that the capacity of RAM is limited even if it is expandable. Thus, the usual size of RAM may be advertised as 16K and expandable to 64K. This would mean that RAM would be limited to 16K + 64K or 80K.

In general, the larger the RAM size, the larger the program and data which can be held in main memory. This point becomes clear when you consider a common accounting application such as setting up a separate accounts receivable file.

Suppose you have 500 customer accounts and you want each to show the following information: customer's name, a special account number (say 6 to 8 digits long), and address and telephone number. Say your count of characters (all the numbers, letters, and special symbols) for one customer account totalled 300. If you wanted a file of 500 customers, you would need 500 × 300 characters each, or 150 000 characters of information in your customer account file. Now, say the program to process the accounts receivable application requires 64K of RAM. How much RAM would you need to process the entire file? 64K? No. You would need 64K plus 150K, or 214K. Since RAM normally comes in increments of the digital number 2 raised to the power of 10 (4, 8, 16, 32, 64, etc.), your computer will need 256K bytes of usable memory to process this accounts receivable application.

It is worth noting that once one million characters of RAM are required, the term megabyte is used, abbreviated M. Some of the very large computer systems would even need more than a million bytes of memory cells; hence, the following table of memory size and *K* terminology is commonly used:

M: abbreviation for "megabyte," consisting of approximately one million bytes (actually 2 to the 20th power or 1 048 576 bytes).

					Kilobytes (thousands)		*Megabytes (millions)*
2^{10}	=	1 024	bytes	=	1K		
2^{11}	=	2 048	bytes	=	2K		
2^{12}	=	4 096	bytes	=	4K		
2^{13}	=	8 192	bytes	=	8K		
2^{14}	=	16 384	bytes	=	16K		
2^{15}	=	32 768	bytes	=	32K		
2^{16}	=	65 536	bytes	=	64K		
2^{17}	=	131 072	bytes	=	128K		
2^{18}	=	262 144	bytes	=	256K	=	1/4M
2^{19}	=	524 288	bytes	=	512K	=	1/2M
2^{20}	=	1 048 576	bytes	=	1 024K	=	1M

Bytes in the billions are called gigabytes.
Bytes in the trillions are called terabytes.

Word Size Earlier, you learned that accounting data and related program instructions are transferred by electronic circuitry from main memory to a series of registers and then to the CPU for processing. It is important to learn that this transfer occurs in a basic grouping of binary digits called the word.

Word: a set of bits making up the smallest unit of information to be processed by the CPU.

In simple terms, the word length of a computer is the number of bits (binary digits) that are processed by the computer in a single step. The longer the word length of a computer, the more data it is able to handle in a single step. Earlier, we illustrated a "word" length consisting of 8 bits. That same "word" could be shown in 16 bits as follows:

0	0	0	0	0	0	0	0	0	0	0	0	1	1	1	1

16-Bit Computer "Word"

This seems like a waste of bits, but the majority of computers use fixed word lengths to process data. An 8-bit machine can handle 8 bits of information at a time; 16-bit processors work with information in 16-bit chunks.

Typical word lengths for computer systems today are 8, 16, 32, and 64 bits.

Why are these numbers so important? Imagine a city requiring a great deal of traffic to cross over a river. Which would be faster, and 8-lane or a 16-lane bridge? Obviously, we can move traffic over 16 lanes much faster.

Computers transfer bits to registers and the CPU in bits. The greater the word length, the more bits the computer can transfer, and the more bits the CPU can process in one chunk. A 32-bit computer will have 32-bit registers and will be designed to process 32-bit numbers. A 16-bit computer will have 16-bit registers and will be designed to process 16-bit numbers. The more digits the computer has to work with, the greater the precision of calculation. Contrast, for example, your working with a pocket calculator with only 8 digits. A computer will tend to be more accurate because it can process larger "words."

To sum up, 8-bit machines can transfer and process only 8 bits of information at one time; 16-bit machines are faster because they can process 16 bits of information at once; and 32-bit machines are much faster because they can process 32 bits of information at once.

Secondary (auxiliary) storage: storage in addition to the main memory of a computer.

Secondary Storage Unit Even with the largest computer, it is impractical to store all of the accounting files and accounting programs used by the firm. Here are four reasons why secondary (auxiliary) storage is needed in all computer systems.

- A very costly "mainframe" with millions of RAM would be required to store the large files of data and program instructions to process common applications for accounts receivable, accounts payable, inventory, payroll, and the General Ledger. It is more practical to store data and instructions in secondary storage units until they are required for processing.
- Many of the accounting programs are used infrequently. For example, the payroll application would not be required until the end of the payroll period. Similarly, the General Ledger application would not be required until the end of each month.
- Some of the accounting programs are used only at year-end. For example, special payroll programs are used in February

of each year to print the required T4 slips and government year-end reports. It is not necessary to store these programs in main memory when they are not needed.

- And, finally, only one type of file is usually needed at a given time. For example, if the computer is printing pay cheques, the data on the accounts receivable file is not required.

For the above reasons, the files and programs used to process common accounting applications are not stored within the computer itself. They are placed on external storage media such as magnetic tape or magnetic disk.

Disk and tape storage capacity is also measured in kilobytes and megabytes. In general, secondary storage units hold more bytes of information than RAM. For example, small disks generally store 250K to 5M bytes, while larger disks can store 5M and up.

Magnetic Disk Pack Courtesy of IBM

It is important to know that data and programs stored in secondary memory units must be brought into the computer's main memory unit for processing. When the processing of a given accounting application is completed, the result is "written" on the proper output device. The next data record and instructions can then be brought from secondary (sometimes called auxiliary) storage into main storage. Secondary storage, then, is used to hold both accounting data and accounting programs until required by the CPU.

How a Computer Works: A Summary

You are now familiar with the major parts common to all computers (input, CPU, output, and memory). All of these parts have to be put together to explain how a computer works.

First, you enter the data (names, payroll amounts, payroll deductions — whatever you desire to process) into the computer's RAM. The data can be entered through an input device such as a keyboard, or it can be loaded from a secondary storage medium such as magnetic tape or magnetic disk.

You also have to load the sequence of instructions (the program), usually stored on magnetic tape or magnetic disk, into RAM. In the language of computing, loading a program disk is called booting the disk.

Booting: loading a program via a disk drive into computer memory.

Then, the CPU reads the first instruction from memory, interprets it, and performs the required operation (add, subtract, compare, etc.). The result is stored in memory.

The next instruction in sequence is automatically read and processed, and then the next one, and so on until the final instruction is executed.

Certain instructions "tell" the computer to move data in and out of the computer to and from the input/output devices.

Completed information may be instructed to be printed or stored on secondary storage devices.

In simple terms, that is how all computers work.

Mainframe, Mini, and Micro Computer Systems

Mainframe computer: a large-scale computer with millions of bytes of memory.

The use of computers for accounting may be traced back to the early 1950s. During that decade, only the large-scale or mainframe computer was manufactured to process accounting data. Needless to say, only very large businesses could afford to buy or rent a mainframe system.

During this "first generation," the mainframe computer system was housed in a separate central data processing department. Thus, a centralized data processing system was formed. Separate accounting departments such as payroll, accounts receivable, accounts payable, and general accounting would supply the data. Central data processing would then complete the processing for those separate departments.

Under centralized data processing, it is important to understand that accounting departments originated and controlled all accounting data. Central data processing was created to process that accounting data. Hence, all accounting departments were regarded as functional units. They were responsible for the creation of data and the checking of that data before it was processed. On the other hand, central data processing was regarded as the service centre which provided the method of processing other departments' data. This division of responsibility is still used today with firms which have mainframe computer systems.

Today, large-scale computers contain modern electronic circuits and cost in the millions of dollars. Their capacity is several megabytes of internal memory. With large main memories and at least 64-bit processors, these computers are capable of handing many related programs and large amounts of data at the same time.

One of the chief characteristics of modern mainframe computers is their ability to act as the host or central computer for terminals located in different departments. This central system allows communication with the user in an interactive, dynamic way with fast response.

Minicomputer: a medium-sized computer, larger and usually more powerful than a microcomputer, but smaller and less powerful than a mainframe.

As new electronic technology developed in the 1960s, a smaller-scale computer known as the minicomputer became available for the middle-range business enterprise. One of the outstanding features of the development of these minicomputer systems is the availability of accounting software packages. In general, accounting applications for payroll, accounts receivable, accounts payable, etc. are programmed for the user, thus eliminating the need to hire computer managers, systems analysts, computer programmers, and computer operators.

In addition, the majority of these minicomputer systems

feature a keyboard/display direct entry unit. After a short training period, any reasonably skilled clerk with a knowledge of typewriting and the ten-key adding machine can enter accounting data by following the instructions according to the "prompting" messages shown on the screen, and then visually checking the data before it goes to the CPU. A high-speed printer generally completes the three basic elements of a minicomputer system.

Courtesy of Mardan Business Systems Limited

Although it is often difficult to classify computers, generally today's minicomputer systems cost in the tens of thousands of dollars. They have storage capacities of at least 256K bytes of internal memory and usually run on 32-bit processors.

The most recent development in computing is the introduction of the microprocessor. In general, advances in electronics in the early 1970s have put the basic functions of a CPU onto a large-scale integrated chip the size of approximately one square centimetre. This "computer on a chip" is the key element in the new generation of microprocessors now taking over the computer market.

Microprocessor: an integrated circuit component that contains the logic of a complete CPU.

Chip: a device not much larger than a pinhead, containing an entire integrated electronic circuit.

Descriptively, the microprocessor may contain the elements of storage, process, and control on a single chip. See the sketch below. When input/output devices and secondary storage units are added, we have a microcomputer system.

Microprocessors are physically small, programmed ready for use, fast, and inexpensive. While the costs of the mainframe and mini are measured in hundreds of thousands and thousands of dollars respectively, the microcomputer for business use is in the five- to ten-thousand-dollar range. The most common microcomputer system consists of a microprocessor with an 8-bit or 16-bit processor and RAM sizes ranging from 64K to 128K, a keyboard/CRT display monitor, a line printer, and one or two disk drives to load data and instructions stored on disks.

Microcomputer: a small, self-contained digital computer whose mainframe is based on a microprocessor.

1. Read-Only Memory
2. Random Access Memory
3. Control Decode
4. Arithmetic/Logic Unit
5. Clock
6. Input/Output Decode

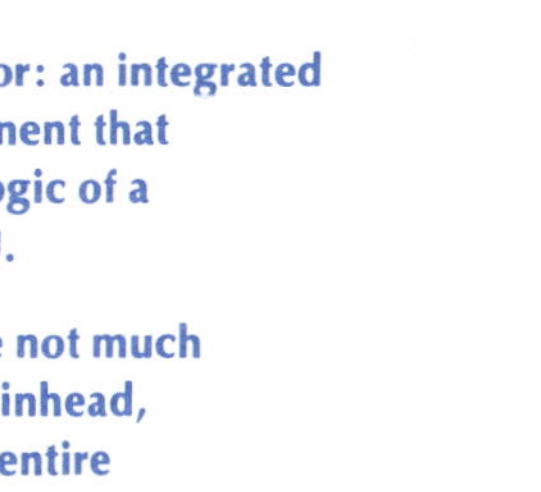

MICROPROCESSOR ON A CHIP

Some computer manufacturers feel that by the late 1980s there will be nothing left but microcomputers — no minis and no mainframes. Recent developments in technology point to increases in main memories and word sizes on microprocessors. At the time of writing, microcomputers are starting to be produced with 32-bit processors and 256K to 512K bytes of RAM. According to these firms, even the smallest office will be processing its accounting applications on inexpensive microcomputers.

With the recent technological advances in data entry through keyboard/display terminals, together with advances in mini and microcomputers, many firms have now turned to the concept of distributed data processing. In simple terms, distributed data processing refers to the idea of transferring the data entry function from the central computer department to the source, that is, to the end-user of the data. Two forms of distributed processing have developed.

Distributed data processing: data processing wherein data entry is performed by the end-user instead of a central computer department.

One form of distributed data processing is more common in the large business where an attempt is made to build a system out of the various terminals, minis, and microcomputers that are located in the end-user's department. All of these minis and microcomputers may be connected to each other or to a large central computer located elsewhere. Under this system, a central computer department would function; however, personnel from this central department would service the user department by supplying the programs. On the other hand, the end-user would now be able to enter accounting data and receive accounting information without delay. Because the jobs are entered away from the central computer centre, data processors have called this system remote job entry (RJE).

Remote job entry (RJE): a system wherein data entry is done by the end-user, usually through a terminal far removed from the CPU.

A second form of distributed processing may be found in small and medium-sized businesses. In general, the mini or microcomputers are unconnected and are operated by users without any centralized management of data processing. Under this form of distributed processing, most of the users do not have data processing skills; nor do they wish to spend time in programming equipment. Consequently, manufacturers now supply the software packages (standard) programs along with their systems. With a software package programmed for a particular accounting application, an accounting clerk simply enters the data via a keyboard/display unit and the small computer system then performs all the necessary calculations and produces the required printouts. Under distributed data processing, therefore, data entry becomes no longer time-consuming and error-prone. Furthermore, distributed processing is under the supervision and control of the user, all without the usual expense of computer managers, systems analysts, and programmers.

A Closer Look at Microcomputers

As stated earlier, many people believe that microcomputers will replace all mainframe and minicomputer systems in the near future. Here are some prevailing arguments favouring the wide use of microcomputers.

Advances in Technology Science has reached the point where it is possible to place all of the electronics for one or more of the computer's main parts on a single LSI (large-scale integration) chip no bigger than the nail on your little finger. One chip might hold the CPU, another the memory units, and a third the circuits needed to attach input and output devices. Linked, these components form the main frame of the microcomputer.

Lower Cost It is possible today to purchase, for less than $2 000, a complete computer system more powerful than the UNIVAC I (a first-generation computer developed in the early 1950s). UNIVAC I sold for over one million dollars.

Increased Word Size New 32-bit microprocessor chips are being developed for microcomputers. These have as much processing power as some models of large-scale computers.

Acceptance in Manufacturing Microprocessors and microcomputers are being used in factory robots which are programmed to produce a wide variety of consumer goods.

Acceptance in Mainframe and Mini Computers Microprocessors are being "embedded" into mini and mainframe computers to increase their speed and power.

Replacement for Typewriters Microcomputers with programs for word processing are replacing manual and electric typewriters in modern offices and in the home.

Acceptance in Education Microcomputers are providing education for children of all ages. Your school has probably equipped one or more classrooms with microcomputers.

You may even have one for home use. Let's take a closer look at microcomputers.

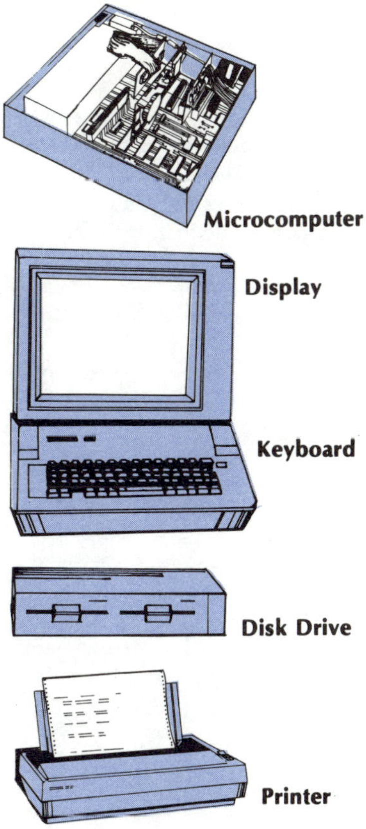

Microcomputer Hardware

The simplest kind of microcomputer system for small-business and educational use has four main parts as shown in the margin.

In practice, manufacturers may package these parts in one or more combinations. For example, the microcomputer may come as a separate rectangular box or it may be housed as part of the keyboard/display unit. Similarly, the keyboard may be separated from the display monitor or the two may be combined as one unit. And the disk drive(s) may come as a separate unit or may be combined with the keyboard/display unit. All manufacturers package the printer separately.

Typical of a microcomputer system for small-business and educational use is the Apple IIe as illustrated below. Can you identify the main parts?

Courtesy of
Apple Canada Inc.

Observe that the display monitor rests on top of the microcomputer box. The keyboard and two disk drives are built into the electronic box, while the printer is a separate unit. Let's examine each of the four parts in greater detail.

Motherboard: a chassis or cabinet designed so that several electronic circuit boards (cards) can be connected to it.

Inside the Microcomputer Once you lift the cabinet cover of the microcomputer, you will find a motherboard holding the CPU, main memory unit, and one or more input/output interfaces. This concept may be shown as follows:

MICROCOMPUTER

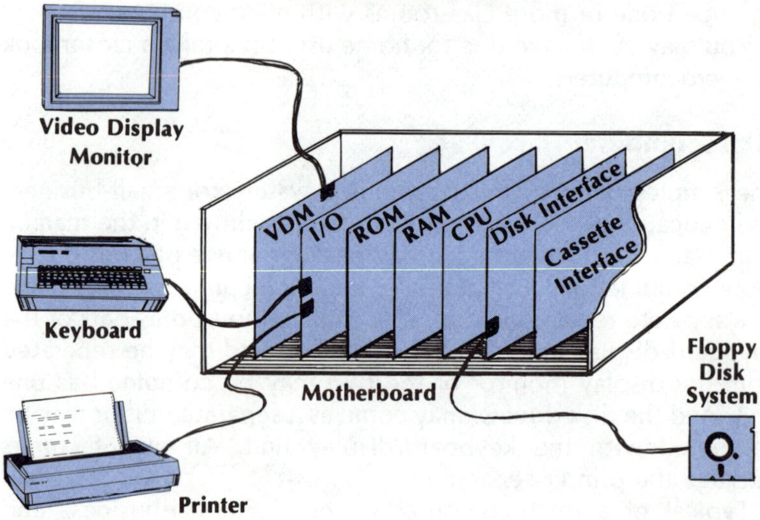

Analysis: The above shows the idea of a single "motherboard" holding several cards in slots. These cards would hold the electronic circuitry (the large-scale integrated chips, often called wafers) for the CPU, ROM and RAM memories, and input/output interfaces (connections) to the video display monitor, keyboard, printer, and disk system. One or more extra slots may be provided by the manufacturer to allow for expanded memories and to connect other input/output devices. The illustrations at the top of the next page show what the inside of the Apple IIe would look like if you took its cover off.

Further Analysis: These points are made in support of examining the inside of the majority of manufactured microcomputers.

- The heart of any microcomputer is the microprocessor which is a separate cental processing unit (CPU) on a chip. Registers are normally part of the CPU microprocessor chip.
- Most microcomputers use an 8-bit word length in their processing operations. The Apple IIe features such an 8-bit microprocessor. However, a trend is emerging today towards microcomputers that use 16-bit word-length microprocessors as

Courtesy of
Apple Canada Inc.

Courtesy of
Apple Canada Inc.

well as 32-bit microprocessors. Of course, the greater the word length, the more costly the microcomputer.

Keyboard/Display Unit All microcomputers for small businesses usually have a keyboard/display unit. As the next photo illustrates, the keyboard looks and feels like the keyboard of an electric typewriter. On the other hand, the display unit is like a TV screen; it is usually called a computer monitor and serves to display both input data and output information.

Keyboard: the chief data entry device for most mini and microcomputers; consists of keys arranged in the same fashion as the keys of a typewriter.

Monitor: a device like a TV screen, usually with higher resolution than a colour TV; may be black and white or colour.

Courtesy of
Apple Canada Inc.

Courtesy of
Apple Canada Inc.

The Disk Drive As you recall, when there are too many data and programs to store in the limited internal computer memory, data and programs can be stored in auxiliary memory units. There are two basic types of auxiliary or external memory: magnetic tape and magnetic disk. Of the two, magnetic tape is slower and less convenient because records are read off the tape in sequence. On the other hand, the magnetic disk is preferred for microcomputers because you have direct access similar to a

Disk: a storage device, shaped somewhat like a phonograph record, designed to hold computer data and programs.

Courtesy of Apple Canada Inc.

Floppy disk: an inexpensive form of disk storage in the form of a flexible plastic magnetic disk; usually stored in a cardboard envelope.

Bootstrap: a short sequence of instructions to get the operating system to load a program into computer memory.

Courtesy of Apple Canada Inc.

Hard disk: a disk in the form of a rigid platter; generally more expensive, but faster, more reliable, and with greater storage capacity than a floppy disk.

long-playing record album. On a long-playing record, you can play, say, the fifth song on the first side by simply picking up the tone arm and placing it at the beginning of the desired song. A magnetic disk is equipped with a movable read/write head that works in a similar fashion. You simply place a command to the disk unit instructing it to position the read/write mechanism over the track containing the desired record.

Two types of disks are used in practice. One is called the floppy disk or diskette (so called because it is made of a flexible plastic). The other is called the hard disk.

Most floppy disks come in one of two sizes, 8-inch or 5¼-inch.[1] The size refers to the disk's diameter. Some manufacturers now are producing a 3-inch diskette.

A floppy disk may contain from 50 000 to 750 000 bytes of information. Thus, they become important for the mass storage of data and programs when they are not required in the computer's main memory unit.

All floppy disks (diskettes) require disk drives. These are the hardware devices into which the diskette is inserted. A small, special program called the bootstrap is placed in ROM. The bootstrap program gives the instructions to the disk drive to "boot" what's on the disk into the RAM of the computer.

Although it is sometimes possible to store part of a file on a program disk, replace the program disk with a fresh, blank disk, and store the rest of the file on the second disk, this practice is most inefficient. For that reason, many of the accounting applications work better with separate program disks and separate storage disks working with a dual-disk drive system. Using a dual-disk drive, you would usually insert the program disk in one drive and a blank disk for file storage in another. Dual-disk drives are also more convenient than single-disk drives for copying programs and making backup files of important data.

Floppy disks are removable. They may be placed in their disk drives when being used for "reading" and "writing," then removed and stored away in a safe place until needed again.

All floppy disks are relatively limited in their storage capacity — usually 90K to 360K depending on the computer. Thus, when more mass storage capacity is required, a hard disk is preferable.

Hard disks come in both 5¼- and 8-inch sizes. It is important to learn that the majority of hard disks are mounted permanently into their drives. Therefore, there are no separate disk drives for hard disks.

Hard disks offer much more storage capacity than floppies. You usually measure memory capacity on hard disks in the

---

1. At the time of writing, disk sizes are reported in inches only. The computer industry has yet to use SI units. 8 inches = approximately 20 cm; 5¼ inches = approximately 13 cm; 3 inches = approximately 9 cm.

megabyte category; for example, 5-, 10-, or 20-megabyte disks are quite common.

Hard disks also last much longer than floppies. Of course, hard disks will be more costly.

Many accounting systems use both hard disks and floppies. In this case, floppies can be used for the initial program loading and for backup files. Thus, hard disks can then be used for the heavy daily operations.

It is important to realize that the program on disk (or tape) made for one computer generally will *not* run on another. And, in some cases, a program written for one disk of one brand of computer will *not* run on another brand of the same computer manufacturer. The reason for this incompatibility is that the disk format — the pattern in which the information is physically placed on the disk — is not the same.

Nearly every make of computer handles disk information layout in its own unique way. However, computer manufacturers are coming to recognize that compatibility among their different models is essential. Consequently, you will find that programs which run on a lower-priced model can usually be loaded onto a higher-priced model of the same computer manufacturer, as long as they contain the same microprocessor chip and the same disk operating system. For example, programs on the Apple II plus can run on the more expensive Apple IIe, because they contain the same microprocessor chip. Similarly, programs on the lower-priced Apple Macintosh can run on the more expensive Apple Lisa because they contain the same microprocessor chip.

Printer: an output device connected to the CPU which produces hard copy in the form of printed pages and forms.

The Printer Although a printer is considered a "peripheral" (an extra piece of equipment), almost all accounting applications require this valuable output device. You cannot print payroll

Courtesy of Apple Canada Inc.

Accounting Software

Before presenting an overview of programs to run common accounting applications, it is important to present a few general ideas on computer software. In particular, you should be able to:

- define software in general
- classify software into two main groups
- explain briefly the difference between system software and applications software
- distinguish among packaged software, custom software, service-bureau software, and do-it-yourself software

Software is the term for the instructions given to the computer. These instructions permit the computer to operate correctly. Another way to look at the general meaning of software is to think of all types of programs which direct and control computer hardware to carry out the processing of accounting applications. Software, therefore, must be thought of as a collection of programs and not just one program.

Software: a collection of programs either internal to the system as a set of instructions or external on a mass storage device.

In practice, software is usually divided into two groups: system software and applications software. Each is subdivided into smaller programs.

System software: that part of computer programs dealing with jobs such as loading programs, copying, providing error messages, and operating the various parts of a computer system.

System software (Firmware) has to do with the overall operation of the computer; hence, it is usually called the operating system's program. You can think of the operating system software as the traffic cop directing all traffic from input devices into the computer and to output devices.

All operating system software, whether it is internal or external, contains smaller programs. For example, one set of instructions may handle security. In some computer systems, the use of passwords becomes critical. These security identity codes allow only authorized operators to use certain programs or to gain access to valuable files such as payroll.

Passwords: short security system programs to prevent unwanted access to the computer.

Some operating system software deals with instructions to load data and programs stored on magnetic tape or magnetic disk into the computer's main memory. These "utility" programs dealing with the disk and disk drive make up the disk operating system, or DOS for short. Since the majority of accounting applications are supported by a disk system, let's examine DOS in more detail.

Disk operating system (DOS): that part of the system program that tells the computer's CPU how to transfer information to and from a disk.

One valuable small program under DOS is the bootstrap program. As you recall, this program helps you to "boot" the contents of a disk into computer memory. Other smaller programs in DOS help you to keep a "library" of programs and data files so you can locate them on the disk and bring them into the computer. Another, smaller DOS program allows you to make copies of data files and some program files. With DOS, then, you can store data and programs in files, copy a file, print a file, and list the contents of a file.

cannot even see the larger computer in operation. In fact, accountants must wait until the central computing centre's listings are delivered before they can find out what happened when the accounting application was processed.

- In medium- and small-sized businesses, using mini and microcomputer systems, accounting software is usually available as either packaged software, customer software, service bureau software, or do-it-yourself software. We will discuss each in turn.

Packaged software: programs created by computer manufacturers and software firms designed to carry out practical uses of the computer.

(a) Packaged software is bought off the shelf and is simply installed on the company's computer by the computer dealer or computer manufacturer. If the business can buy what it needs from the computer dealer, the cost may be as little as a few hundred dollars for each accounting application. Sometimes, however, packaged software needs some modifications. For example, a payroll program made in the United States would have to be changed for Canadian deductions such as UI, CPP, and income tax. These modifications could be very costly; consequently, Canadian-designed software should be a strong consideration.

Custom software: programs written to meet the needs of specialized applications such as accounts receivable for a dental firm.

(b) If no appropriate packaged software can be found, then custom software may be the answer. This software is designed to meet the special needs of businesses. For example, a software firm may be hired to program the accounts receivable application for a dental office. Of course, custom software might end up costing ten times the price of the firm's hardware. Since there is a shortage of good qualified specialists, custom packages often take as long as two years.

Service bureau software: programs written by a company that processes customer's inputs to produce customer-required outputs.

(c) Service bureau software is a third method of obtaining possible application programs. These service bureaus have specialist programmers who design software systems for the bureau's computers. Some of their developed software may fit the needs of a particular firm.

(d) Finally, there is the *do-it-yourself software*. You write the programs using a computer language like BASIC. However, the business may end up spending hundreds of thousands of dollars in programming labour. For this reason, small businesses normally buy packaged programs and middle-sized businesses turn to custom-made software packages.

- Regardless of how application programs are obtained, experienced systems specialists offer this warning: Beware of programs that do not interact. For example, programs to process common accounting applications such as accounts receivable, accounts payable, and payroll affect the General Ledger. Thus, a General Ledger program should be able to work with those other accounting programs. For this reason, experts believe in acquiring accounting software which contains the same formats so all programs can be processed with the same operating system.

- The typical accounting application for mini and microcomputer systems is *menu-driven.* This means that an

Menu: a video display of tasks the computer can be ordered to perform. The task is chosen usually by entering an appropriate command.

accounting clerk sits at the keyboard/display unit to process applications. The clerk is guided by a breakdown of the application on the screen — the menu. A series of commands instructs the clerk how to enter the data through the keyboard display. The entire application is done in the accounting department where the clerk and accountant are able to follow the processing on the display unit.

Menu-driven Application: A Simple Example

To see how a menu-driven software package works in accounting, assume you are using a microcomputer with a disk operating system. Also assume that you have loaded the program disk correctly. Many of the current operating systems will allow you to load a disk by simply inserting it into the disk drive and putting on the power switch. Some systems, however, require your entering a command at the keyboard to load the disk into the computer's RAM.

Once the disk is loaded, assume the following menu appears on the screen:

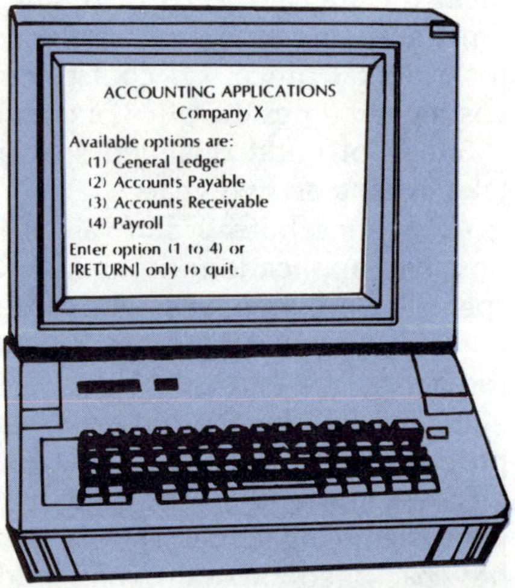

Step 1: Load the disk into RAM; the general menu appears on the screen.

Analysis: Since you want to work with the payroll application, you simply pick out the Payroll file, which is 4 on the program disk. Simply enter the number 4 on the keyboard and press the [RETURN] key. The computer's disk operating system searches the disk and finds the payroll file. Remember, a program disk can store more information than RAM; therefore, the disk operating system simply picks out the fourth file, as shown in the margin.

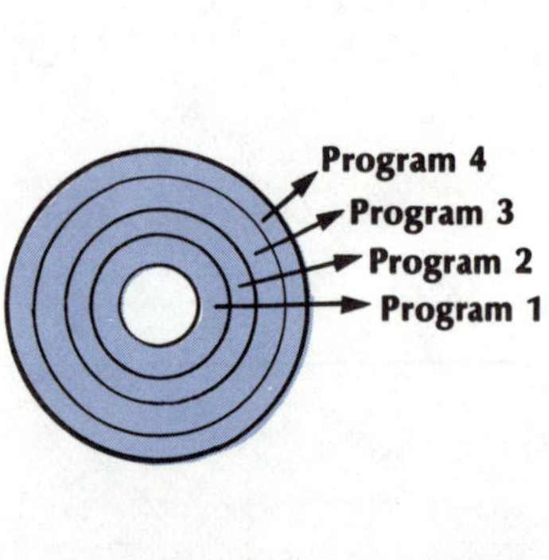

Once the Payroll file has been requested, the computer display may show a sub-menu strictly to process the firm's payroll as follows:

cannot even see the larger computer in operation. In fact, accountants must wait until the central computing centre's listings are delivered before they can find out what happened when the accounting application was processed.

• In medium- and small-sized businesses, using mini and microcomputer systems, accounting software is usually available as either packaged software, customer software, service bureau software, or do-it-yourself software. We will discuss each in turn.

Packaged software: programs created by computer manufacturers and software firms designed to carry out practical uses of the computer.

(a) Packaged software is bought off the shelf and is simply installed on the company's computer by the computer dealer or computer manufacturer. If the business can buy what it needs from the computer dealer, the cost may be as little as a few hundred dollars for each accounting application. Sometimes, however, packaged software needs some modifications. For example, a payroll program made in the United States would have to be changed for Canadian deductions such as UI, CPP, and income tax. These modifications could be very costly; consequently, Canadian-designed software should be a strong consideration.

Custom software: programs written to meet the needs of specialized applications such as accounts receivable for a dental firm.

(b) If no appropriate packaged software can be found, then custom software may be the answer. This software is designed to meet the special needs of businesses. For example, a software firm may be hired to program the accounts receivable application for a dental office. Of course, custom software might end up costing ten times the price of the firm's hardware. Since there is a shortage of good qualified specialists, custom packages often take as long as two years.

Service bureau software: programs written by a company that processes customer's inputs to produce customer-required outputs.

(c) Service bureau software is a third method of obtaining possible application programs. These service bureaus have specialist programmers who design software systems for the bureau's computers. Some of their developed software may fit the needs of a particular firm.

(d) Finally, there is the *do-it-yourself software*. You write the programs using a computer language like BASIC. However, the business may end up spending hundreds of thousands of dollars in programming labour. For this reason, small businesses normally buy packaged programs and middle-sized businesses turn to custom-made software packages.

• Regardless of how application programs are obtained, experienced systems specialists offer this warning: Beware of programs that do not interact. For example, programs to process common accounting applications such as accounts receivable, accounts payable, and payroll affect the General Ledger. Thus, a General Ledger program should be able to work with those other accounting programs. For this reason, experts believe in acquiring accounting software which contains the same formats so all programs can be processed with the same operating system.

• The typical accounting application for mini and microcomputer systems is *menu-driven*. This means that an

Menu: a video display of tasks the computer can be ordered to perform. The task is chosen usually by entering an appropriate command.

accounting clerk sits at the keyboard/display unit to process applications. The clerk is guided by a breakdown of the application on the screen — the menu. A series of commands instructs the clerk how to enter the data through the keyboard display. The entire application is done in the accounting department where the clerk and accountant are able to follow the processing on the display unit.

Menu-driven Application: A Simple Example

To see how a menu-driven software package works in accounting, assume you are using a microcomputer with a disk operating system. Also assume that you have loaded the program disk correctly. Many of the current operating systems will allow you to load a disk by simply inserting it into the disk drive and putting on the power switch. Some systems, however, require your entering a command at the keyboard to load the disk into the computer's RAM.

Once the disk is loaded, assume the following menu appears on the screen:

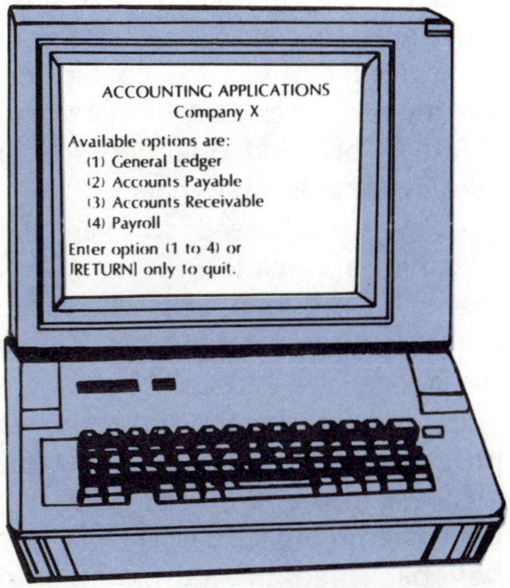

Step 1: Load the disk into RAM; the general menu appears on the screen.

Analysis: Since you want to work with the payroll application, you simply pick out the Payroll file, which is 4 on the program disk. Simply enter the number 4 on the keyboard and press the [RETURN] key. The computer's disk operating system searches the disk and finds the payroll file. Remember, a program disk can store more information than RAM; therefore, the disk operating system simply picks out the fourth file, as shown in the margin.

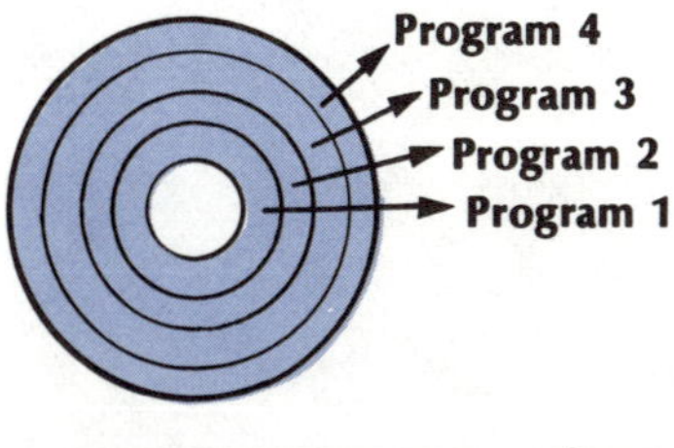

Once the Payroll file has been requested, the computer display may show a sub-menu strictly to process the firm's payroll as follows:

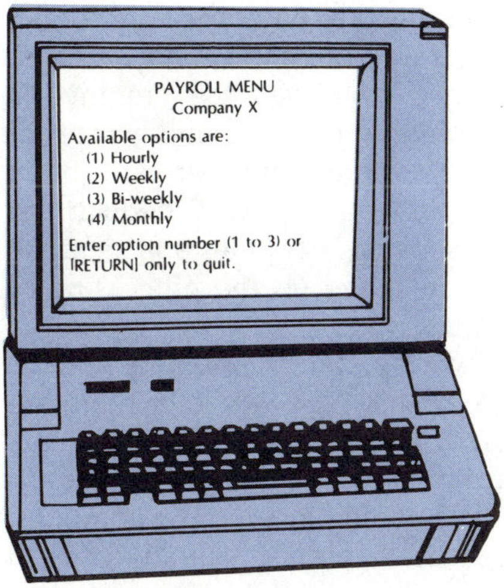

Step 2: Payroll menu appears on the screen, asking you to select the payroll category.

Analysis: In the above menu, you are asked to select either "Hourly Payroll," "Weekly Payroll," "Bi-weekly Payroll," or "Monthly Payroll." Of course, the menu could have been enlarged to take care of other plans such as a commission payroll. Assume in this case that you want the hourly payroll. You simply enter 1 on the keyboard and press the [RETURN] key.

Selecting the hourly payroll plan causes the computer to go into its third step, called the data entry phase. To help the clerk with data entry, the program may show a screen display as follows:

Step 3: Enter the payroll data for each hourly-rated employee from approved clock (time) cards.

Analysis: From the illustration, you can see how easy it is to enter data. It is like filling out a blank form for the hourly payroll using clock (time) cards approved by a payroll officer. Of course, these are the main items needed to process the gross pay of each employee.

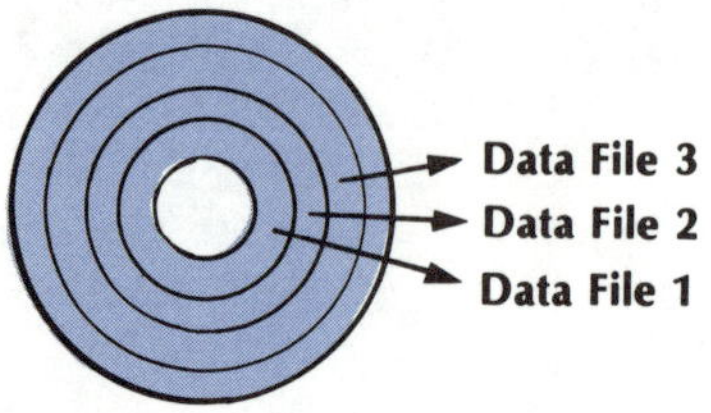

In some systems, you would not need to enter the data for the employee's rates of pay. Why not? By using the employee's SIN, the computer can be programmed to obtain the employee's hourly rate from a separate disk file that contains hourly rates of all employees. And, from other files, the computer can obtain data for CPP, UI, income taxes, and other payroll deductions. Remember a point made earlier. Separate data files and separate program files are normally used to speed up the processing of common accounting applications.

Go back to the illustration showing step 3, data entry. Note that the form displayed on the monitor asks whether there are more employees to be processed. You would answer the question by entering an appropriate command on the keyboard. In this case, entering the letter *Y* (yes) would instruct the computer to show another blank form to process. Entering *N* (no) would tell the computer to return to the payroll menu so you could follow the next step.

What would be the remaining steps to complete the payroll application? Of course, these would include instructions to print a complete hourly payroll register, print the individual employee's earnings record, and print each employee's pay cheque and earnings statement. Naturally, the payroll menu would show option numbers to process these and any other required steps.

Once the hourly payroll is processed, you would return to the payroll menu to process any other payroll plan. From this simple example, you should realize how easy it would be to follow any menu-driven program to process any accounting application.

Here are some good questions to ask yourself:

- *Under what menu would you process the accounting entries for the hourly payroll and the employer's payroll taxes?*

Of course, your answer would be the General Ledger menu because these journal entries affect General Ledger accounts.

- *Under what menu would you process the pay cheques and the various payroll remittances?*

Naturally, your answer would be the accounts payable menu, because payroll remittances would appear in the cash payments (disbursements) journal.

Packaged Accounting Software: A Closer Look

Hundreds of firms have emerged to offer packaged accounting software for leading makes of microcomputers. One firm, Software Dimensions, Inc. offers an easy-to-use, interactive accounting package available for small business. The entire package, called Accounting Plus Super/e, can be processed on leading microcomputers like the Apple IIe system.

The package includes five interactive modules that together perform all accounting applications needed by small businesses. These interrelated modules include the General Ledger, accounts payable, accounts receivable, inventory control, and payroll. You can purchase the entire package or separate modules to meet the specific needs of a small business. For example, a firm may wish to acquire the software for the General Ledger, accounts receivable, and accounts payable as shown below.

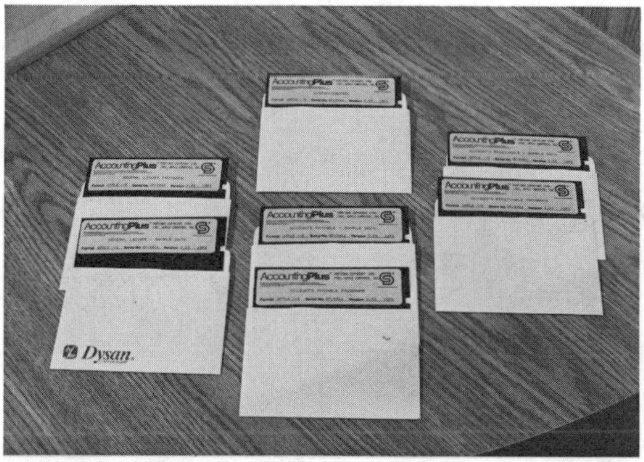

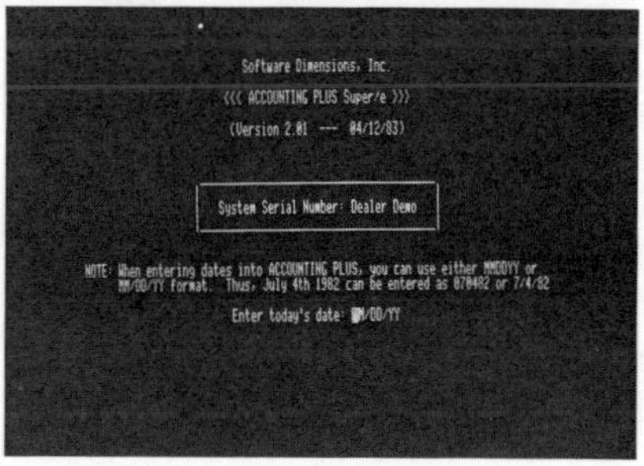

Analysis: As the illustrations show, applications software consists of program disks and data disks stored on floppies together with supporting instruction manuals. The Accounting Plus Super/e is designed for easy operation because it uses a user-friendly package that is totally menu-driven. You are guided by helpful prompts every step of the way. Let's look at the menus of the three modules.

General Ledger After loading the program disk, the monitor would display the Accounting Plus Super/e trademark as shown in the margin. You are then shown a display asking you to enter today's date. Once the date is entered correctly, the main menu appears on the screen as follows:

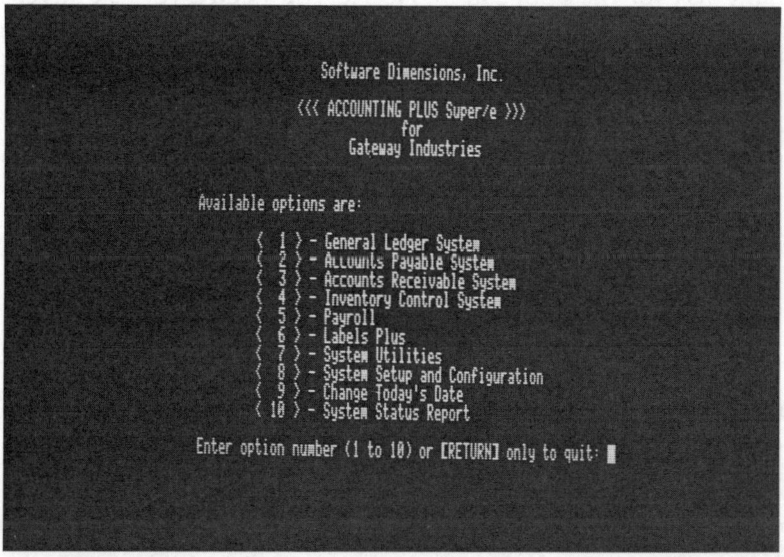

Analysis: The main menu shows the available accounting applications and other options. Notice the prompting message at the bottom: "Enter option number (1 to 1Ø) or [RETURN] only to quit." (Many displays use Ø for zero.)

Since you want the General Ledger application, you would enter the number 1 (not the letter "ell") on the keyboard and press the [RETURN] key. The monitor would display the following request:

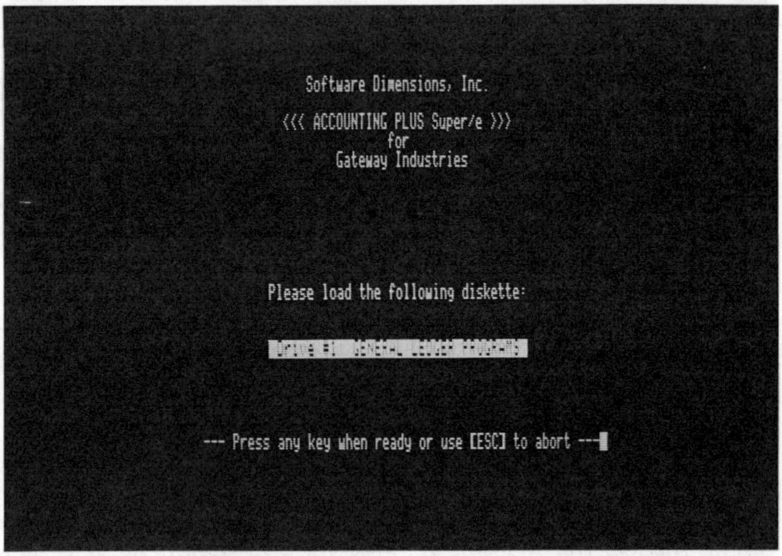

Analysis: The display asks you to load the GL program disk into Drive No. 1. Drive No. 2, then, would be used to load the data disk for the application. Notice you need two disk drives: one to load the GL program diskette, and one for the GL data diskette. If you had a single disk drive, you would have to keep interchanging program and data disks. This is time-consuming and often requires modification of the software dealing with the operating system.

Once the disks are loaded into RAM, you would press any key to get to the next step, which would display the General Ledger Reports Menu, illustrated next.

Analysis: Observe that the General Ledger Reports Menu shows a breakdown of the separate tasks making up the GL application. Of course, you could not print the financial statements without going through the various steps of the accounting cycle. Consequently, you would have to update the General Ledger accounts before the trial balance report and financial statements are printed. In other words, you do have to know a little accounting in order to use the various menus correctly.

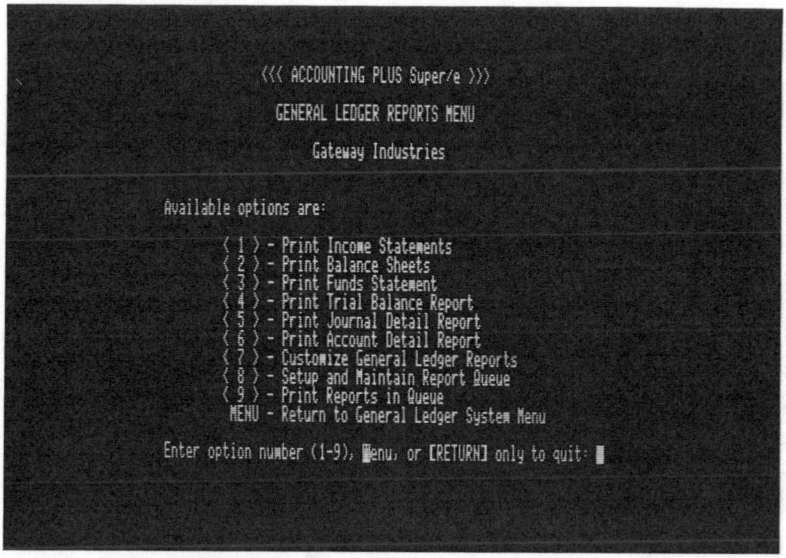

As the display directs, you would then enter *Menu* and [*RETURN*] to show the General Ledger Systems Menu as follows:

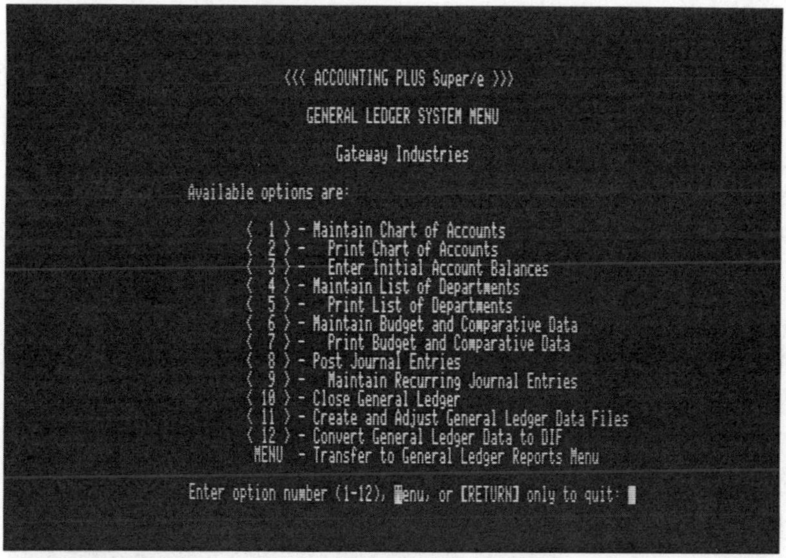

Analysis: The General Ledger Systems Menu shows the options to update the General Ledger. For example, option 2 instructs the computer to print the Chart of Accounts, which may be printed as in the next photo.

Analysis: With a printed Chart of Accounts, you could then update any account balance or enter a new account and balance. Once all the journal entries have been posted, you could get

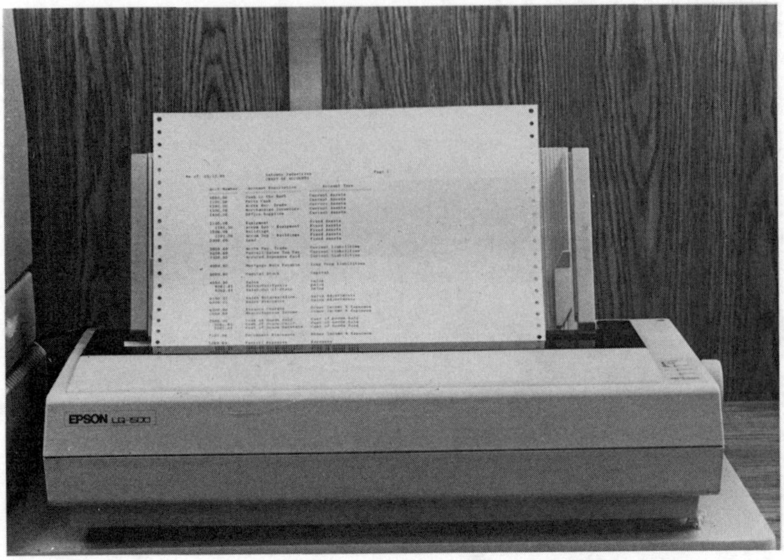

back to the General Ledger Reports Menu by entering *Menu* and [*RETURN*]. From that menu, you could enter option 4 to print the trial balance. This provides you with an opportunity to examine and analyze accounts in detail and make any necessary adjustment before generating financial statements. As you can see, other options allow you to complete the accounting cycle for the General Ledger.

Accounts Receivable Module You should have little difficulty in analyzing the menu-driven application for accounts receivable.

After loading the program and data disks, you would be guided by the main menu to process the sub-menus for accounts receivable. Note that the main accounting menu always appears first so you can select the desired module. You can then instruct the computer to display either the Accounts Receivable System Menu or the Accounts Receivable Reports Menu as shown below.

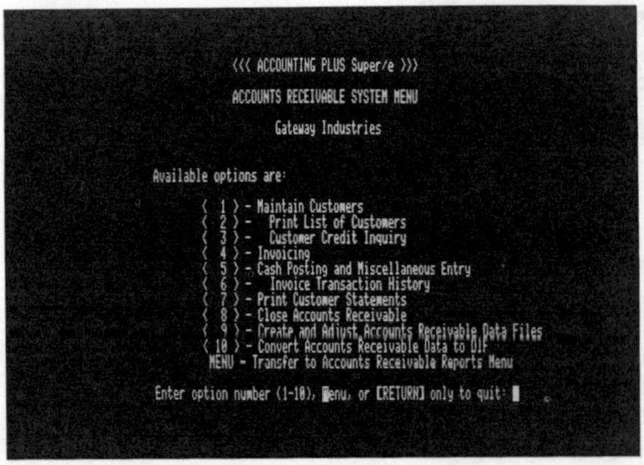

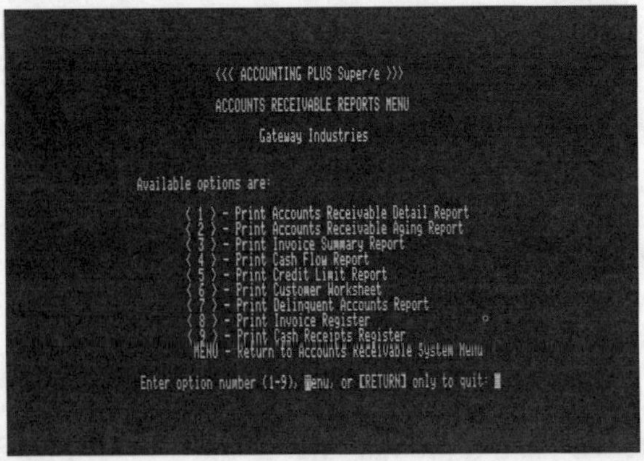

Analysis: Normally, you would work first with the System Menu to set up individual customer accounts. The program can handle up to 500 customers on floppy disk or 5 800 on hard disk. The menu is designed so as to cover all aspects of accounts receivable, from invoicing to the printing of customer statements. Notice that the System Menu is interrelated with the Reports Menu. From the Reports Menu you can call for the computer to print the essential reports related to accounts receivable.

It is important to realize that the accounts receivable module is programmed so that totals are automatically posted to the General Ledger system. This is one of the strong advantages of packaged accounting software.

Accounts Payable Module This module works the same way as the one for Accounts Receivable. Of course, you have to know what makes up the accounting for accounts payable before you can understand the options on the System Menu and the Reports Menu, as illustrated below.

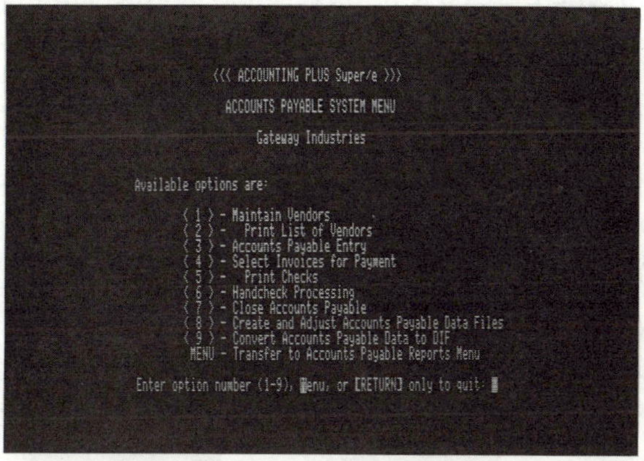

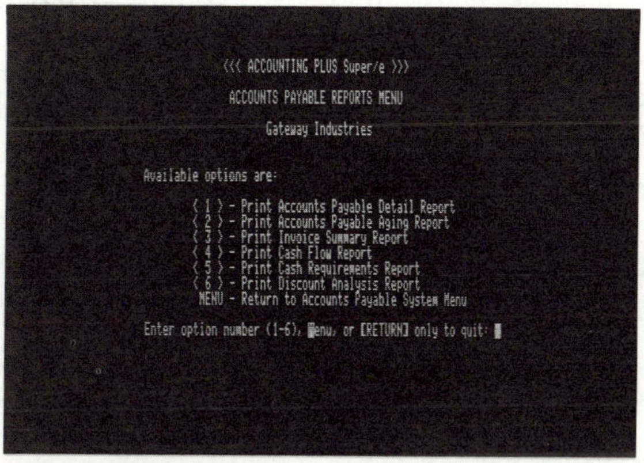

Analysis: This module supports up to 500 individual accounts payable on floppies, or 6 400 on a hard disk. As the System Menu shows, the options cover most of the tasks related to accounts payable. The related Reports Menu permits printing of the essential reports related to accounts payable. The program also allows for posting the totals automatically to the General Ledger system.

An earlier point is worth repeating. While packaged accounting software may work well for many small businesses, some modifications in the program are inevitable. For example, the accounts receivable module may do well for a small manufacturing or merchandising firm, but it would be inadequate for, say, a large dental practice. For this reason, some firms look to custom packages to meet their accounting software needs.

A Closer Look at Custom Accounting Software

One group of professional practices requiring a tailor-made computerized accounting system are the large medical and dental offices. A Canadian firm, Mardan Business Systems Limited, offers these practices custom accounting software to process especially their accounts receivable function. Mardan is ideally suited to design such software since they also provide one-write systems for smaller offices. With a good background and experience in manual systems, Mardan is able to convert a well-organized manual one-write system into a highly efficient large-scale computer system. Let's look briefly at their accounts receivable system.

Hardware Flourishing medical and dental practices would serve approximately 2 000 or more families in a specified residential area. To serve that size of practice would require a minicomputer system consisting of a large minicomputer, a hard disk drive with 20 megabytes of storage capacity, a terminal/keyboard display unit, and a printer. Some practices also keep a floppy disk system for their backup operations.

In many cases, the actual minicomputer and hard disk drive are kept in a back room where space is not a problem and where the noise generated won't disturb either the staff or patients. Locating the mainframe and disk drive there is also a security measure. The fragile equipment is not likely to get bumped and only authorized personnel may be given access to the hardware.

The terminal and printer may then be located at the reception desk where a front-office person may run the various aspects of the tailor-made accounting software. A typical terminal/display unit, suitable for large practices, is illustrated below.

Custom Software Mardan offers tailor-made packages for both medical and dental practices. The package for dental

Courtesy of Mardan Business Systems Limited

practices is called the Dental Office Management System. It covers the accounts receivable and General Ledger modules. Limited space does not permit our covering all aspects of this system. Let's examine how part of the accounts receivable application works.

Each morning before receiving the first patient, a trained office clerk turns on the terminal/display unit. The clerk does not need to know programming; all he or she needs is to be able to type and to know something about how a professional dental practice operates. Since Mardan bases its package on its one-write system, a knowledge of one-write accounting to process accounts receivable also helps.

After the terminal/display unit has been turned on, the display shows the main menu of the software package for accounts receivable as follows:

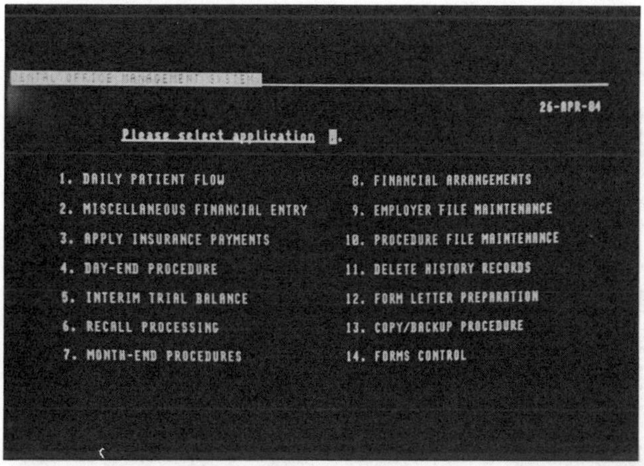

This is Mardan's main menu. The heading: "Dental Office Management System."

Analysis: The main menu works just like any other. Here, the options cover all aspects of the accounts receivable application for a dental office. Notice the built-in request *Please select application.* Like all well-written software, the clerk is guided by prompting messages to process any specific task.

In most of the daily operations, the assistant-clerk would be using option 1, *Daily Patient Flow.* The number "1" is entered via the keyboard and the [RETURN] key is pressed. Of course, this menu on the daily patient flow would be divided to allow for tasks such as setting up a new patient file, recording charges, and recording payments received. Of course, the assistant-clerk is always guided by sub-menus such as the partial ones that follow on the next two pages.

Observe that the sub-menu helping the clerk to set up a new patient file is like an actual information form. The clerk is guided by headings to complete the form right on the screen. Once the form is completed correctly, the data can be stored in RAM for

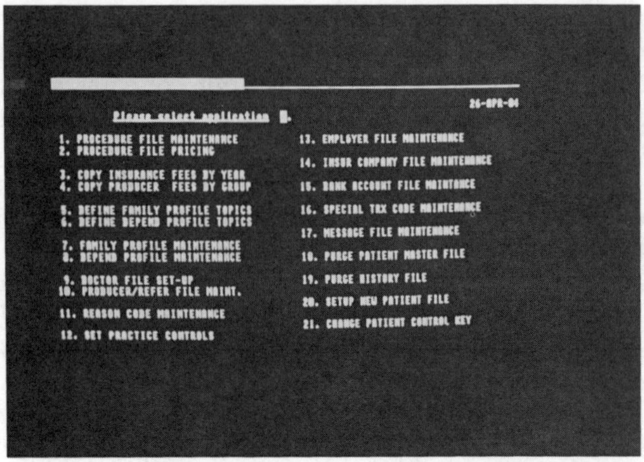

This sub-menu would be used to set up a new patient file. The heading: "Daily Patient Flow."

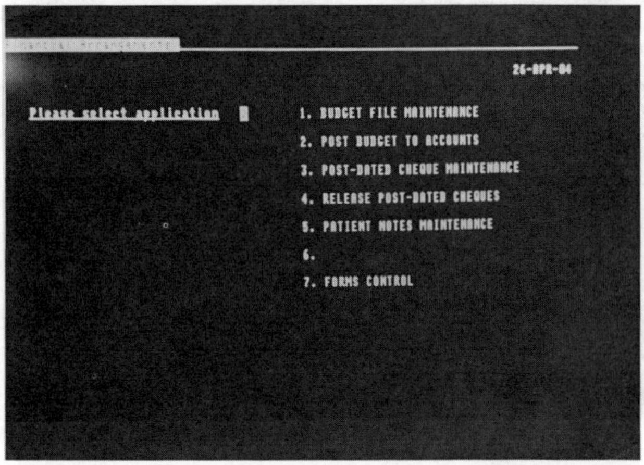

This sub-menu deals with the financial arrangements contracted for each patient. The heading: "Financial Arrangements."

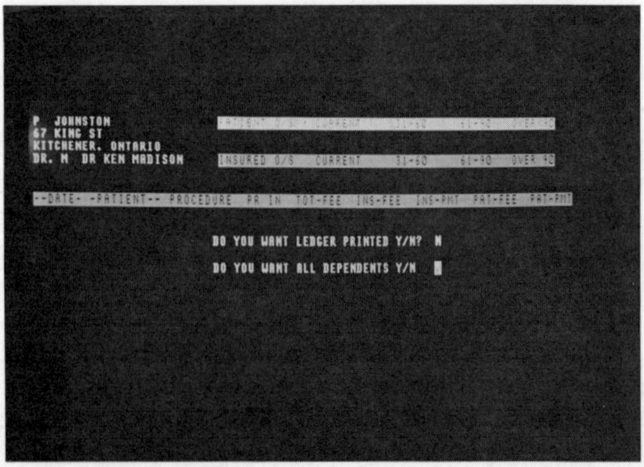

This display prompts the clerk in the printing of customer statements. First line: "Patient O/S, Current, 31 – 60, 61 – 90, Over 90."

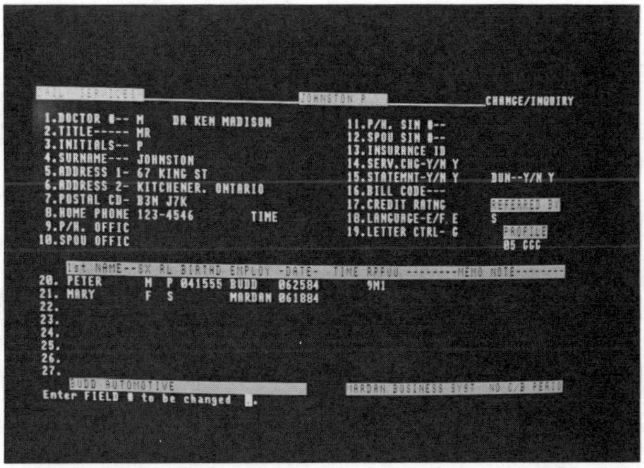

This sub-menu of Daily Services helps the clerk to set up a new patient file. The heading: "Daily Services."

further processing. Typical of processing daily accounts receivable are charges and payments as illustrated on the displays below.

This terminal shows the updating of a patient's account.

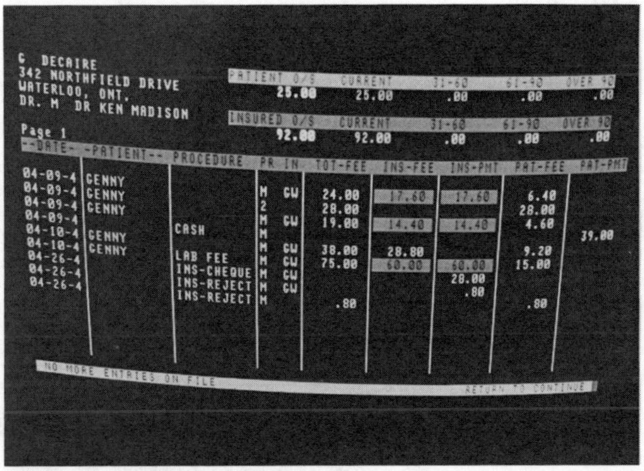

This close-up of the display shows an accounts receivable account in the accounts receivable file.

In summary, Mardan's custom software generates the patient bill/receipt, insurance claims, the day sheet (similar to the one-write system), the day sheet by doctor (since several would share the same practice), bank deposit sheet, voucher control sheet, aged trial balances, patient statements, delinquent account listing, and a listing of recalls. In addition, the main menu provides for personalized form letters and file reports. A separate General Ledger module is available to generate monthly income statements and balance sheets. Typical of the printouts resulting from the software are those illustrated on the next page.

YOUR PRACTICE NAME HERE

PAGE 003

DAYSHEET FOR 15-MAR-82

SERV DATE	VOUCH	IN	FAMILY NAME	PATIENT	DR	PR	PROCEDURE CODE	DESCRIPTION	TOOTH ##	SURFAC	STU I	CREDIT AMOUNT	I	CHARGES FEE	CHARGES LAB	CHARGES TOTAL	BALANCE OWING
03-15	0109	K	FRENCH	KYLE	S	S		PAYMENT P-CASH				30.00					
03-15	0109	K	FRENCH	KYLE	S	S		PAYMENT P-CHEQ				10.00					
												40.00		87.00		87.00 *	
03-15	0110	D	GREGORY	DON	J	J	12400	APPLY FLUORIDE G						11.00		11.00	64.00
03-15	0110	D	GREGORY	DON	J	J	21212	AMAL/2 SURF./PER	41	MO			Y	33.00		33.00	
03-15	0110	D	GREGORY	DON	J	J	13200	ORAL HYGIENE INS						11.00		11.00	
03-15	0110	D	GREGORY	DON	J	J	02142	POSTER. BITEWING						9.00		9.00	
03-15	0110	D	GREGORY	DON	J	J	01110	ORAL EXAM-PRIM D						23.00		23.00	
03-15	0110	D	GREGORY	DON	J	J		PAYMENT P-CASH				40.00					
03-15	0110	D	GREGORY	DON	J	J		PAYMENT P-CHEQ				10.00					
												50.00		87.00		87.00 *	
03-15	0111	J	JONES	JIM	S	S	21212	AMAL/2 SURF./PER	41	MO			Y	33.00		33.00	88.00
03-15	0111	J	JONES	JIM	S	S	13200	ORAL HYGIENE INS						11.00		11.00	
03-15	0111	J	JONES	JIM	S	S	12400	APPLY FLUORIDE G						11.00		11.00	
03-15	0111	J	JONES	JIM	S	S	02142	POSTER. BITEWING						9.00		9.00	
03-15	0111	J	JONES	JIM	S	S	01110	ORAL EXAM-PRIM D						23.00		23.00	
03-15	0111	J	JONES	JIM	S	S		PAYMENT P-CASH				10.00					
03-15	0111	J	JONES	JIM	S	S		PAYMENT P-CHEQ				50.00					
												60.00		87.00		87.00 *	
03-15		KL	JONES		S			RETURNED CHEQUE						100.00		100.00	110.00
03-15		KL	JONES		S			SERVICE CHARGE						10.00		10.00	
														110.00		110.00 *	
03-15		RR	JONES		J			DEBIT ADJUST.						50.00		50.00	50.00
03-15	0112	A	MARTZ	ANNIE	J	J	02142	POSTER. BITEWING						9.00		9.00	112.00
03-15	0112	A	MARTZ	ANNIE	J	J	13200	ORAL HYGIENE INS						11.00		11.00	
03-15	0112	A	MARTZ	ANNIE	J	J	21212	AMAL/2 SURF./PER	41	MO			Y	33.00		33.00	
03-15	0112	A	MARTZ	ANNIE	J	J	01110	ORAL EXAM-PRIM D						23.00		23.00	
03-15	0112	A	MARTZ	ANNIE	J	J	12400	APPLY FLUORIDE G						11.00		11.00	
03-15	0112	A	MARTZ	ANNIE	J	J		PAYMENT P-CASH				21.00					
03-15	0112	A	MARTZ	ANNIE	J	J		PAYMENT P-CHEQ				15.00					
												36.00		87.00		87.00 *	
03-15	0113	E	MOONEY	ELIZABETH	S	S	02142	POSTER. BITEWING						9.00		9.00	89.00
03-15	0113	E	MOONEY	ELIZABETH	S	S	13200	ORAL HYGIENE INS						11.00		11.00	
03-15	0113	E	MOONEY	ELIZABETH	S	S	01110	ORAL EXAM-PRIM D						23.00		23.00	
03-15	0113	E	MOONEY	ELIZABETH	S	S	21212	AMAL/2 SURF./PER	41	MO			Y	33.00		33.00	

Here is a typical daysheet filed for future reference.

DR GH SMITH
100 KING ST. S.
SUITE 234
TORONTO ONT.
M3D 4D4

STATEMENT
FOR PROFESSIONAL SERVICES RENDERED

MISS P BROWN
55 KING ST. W.,
KITCHENER, ONTARIO
N2J 4J5

STATEMENT DATE (MO. DAY YR.): MAR 31 82

PRESENT BALANCE: 92.00

PAYMENT ENCLOSED: $

PLEASE DETACH AND RETURN THIS PORTION WITH YOUR PAYMENT BROWN P

STATEMENT DATE	MO. DAY YR.		PHONE	BALANCE FORWARD	
	MAR 31 82	DR GH SMITH	885-2274		250.00

DATE MO. DAY YR.	PATIENT	DESCRIPTION	CHARGE	PAYMENT	BALANCE
03-15-82		RETURNED CHEQUE	50.00		300.00
03-15-82		CREDIT ADJUST.		10.00	290.00
03-15-82	PAT	PAYMENT CHEQUE		25.00	265.00
03-15-82	PAT	PAYMENT CASH		50.00	215.00
03-15-82	PAT	MINOR ASSESSMENT	13.50		228.50
03-15-82	BRENDA	PAYMENT CHEQUE		50.00	178.50
03-15-82	BRENDA	PAYMENT CASH		100.00	78.50
03-15-82	BRENDA	MINOR ASSESSMENT	13.50		92.00

Please note that your account is past due 90 days.
Collection proceedings commence in 10 days

PLEASE PAY 92.00

Here is a typical patient's statement of account.

After studying this section on custom software, you may have asked these questions:

- *Why is payroll not part of the main menu?* It is interesting to learn that the majority of large dental and medical practices cannot justify the costs of computerizing a payroll involving, say, 20 or 30 people. Consequently, it is normal to use the one-write system to do the firm's payroll application. The computer can be used to process the heavy volume of transactions dealing with accounts receivable.

- *How much would a minicomputer system such as this cost?* The answer is approximately $30 000 — around $25 000 for the hardware and $5 000 for the software (programs).
- *Could a microcomputer system do the same job?* At present, no. Microcomputers are so far designed to meet the needs of small businesses and personal-use applications. With technological advances in electronics, however, it may well be that the micros of the future will replace all minis.

A Brief Look at Another Accounting Program

So far, we've covered software packages related to traditional accounting applications only: accounts receivable, accounts payable, payroll, and the General Ledger. No chapter on computer applications in accounting would be complete without an introduction to the electronic spreadsheet.

The Electronic Spreadsheet Many accounting problems have been commonly solved with a calculator, a pencil, and a wide sheet of columnar accounting paper. Calculating sales projections, income taxes, financial ratios, cost estimates, accounts receivable, accounts payable, and payroll are typical examples of accounting problems solved on the accountant's traditional worksheet.

With the introduction and wide use of microcomputers in the mid-1970s, software companies have introduced a powerful worksheet called the electronic spreadsheet. This new applications software combines the convenience and familiarity of a pocket calculator with the powerful memory and electronic screen capabilities of the personal-use microcomputer.

Electronic spreadsheet: an applications program in which the computer's memory serves as a large worksheet.

Like a columnar worksheet pad, the electronic spreadsheet allows you to develop a systematic way of recording and analyzing accounting problems. Because the program has a variety of built-in functions, it acts as a powerful business calculator. While using the program, you can adjust formulas or values and then instantly recalculate the entire worksheet.

Applications suitable for the electronic spreadsheet appear unlimited so long as the computer's RAM is able to handle the program and data. Picture working with a worksheet the size of 63 columns by 254 rows. That size permits applications such as corporate planning, security analysis, mortgage-loan schedules, and the traditional accounting problems related to accounts receivable and accounts payable. In short, whatever involves repetitious analysis with pencil and calculator and structured layout on paper can be done more efficiently on the electronic spreadsheet.

One of the most powerful applications of the electronic worksheet is to get instant answer to *What if?* questions. "What if we priced Product X 10 percent higher and Product Y 8 percent lower?" "What if sales revenue increased by 5 percent for the next six months?" "What if inflation were increased by 1 percent per month over the next twelve months?" The traditional method of answering such questions took time by erasing figures and re-calculating new ones. With an electronic spreadsheet, the same questions can easily be solved in seconds. You simply store a formula within RAM and let the computer do all the changes.

The first successful electronic worksheet for microcomputers was created by an American software firm called Software Arts, Inc. That firm introduced VisiCalc in the mid-1970s. Since that time, copyrights of VisiCalc have been awarded to other leading software companies. Today, you can find VisiCalc available on leading makes of microcomputers. (At the time of writing, VisiCalç has been replaced by an improved version called FlashCalc.)[2]

Since VisiCalc was originated, other software companies have developed their own versions of the electronic spreadsheet. These include SuperCalc, Lotus 1,2,3, Symphony, Perfect Planner, Multiplan, and LisaCalc. VisiCalc, however, is still considered the "granddaddy" because it's available on the majority of microcomputers in use today.

Most spreadsheet programs cost between $100 and $600. The more expensive require at least 128K of RAM memory because they have some database and graphic capabilities. A typical package includes a reference manual and one or more floppy disks to store the program.

It is important to realize that VisiCalc (and other similar spreadsheets) is only one type of software. The spreadsheet cannot replace every application in accounting. You will still need separate software applications for the General Ledger, accounts receivable, accounts payable, payroll, and other specialized applications. The spreadsheet should be considered as the accountant's electronic worksheet in helping to solve problems requiring decisions.

Space does not permit our presenting an in-depth view of the electronic spreadsheet. Instead, we offer the following introductory view of VisiCalc:

- To operate the software, you need a microcomputer system consisting of the keyboard/display unit, a CPU with at least 32K of RAM (most small businesses recommend at least 64K), one or two disk drives for floppy diskettes, a special integrated circuit (a chip for VisiCalc), a set of blank diskettes, and the VisiCalc program diskette. The printer is optional but most useful to give you hard copies as needed.

---

2. FlashCalc is a trademark of VisiCorp, Inc., a California-based software firm.

• VisiCalc is available with a screen showing 40 characters across or an 80-character screen. The wider screen is recommended because it offers greater flexibility.

• A typical VisiCalc spreadsheet, after loading the program disk and entering data for an income statement, appears as follows:

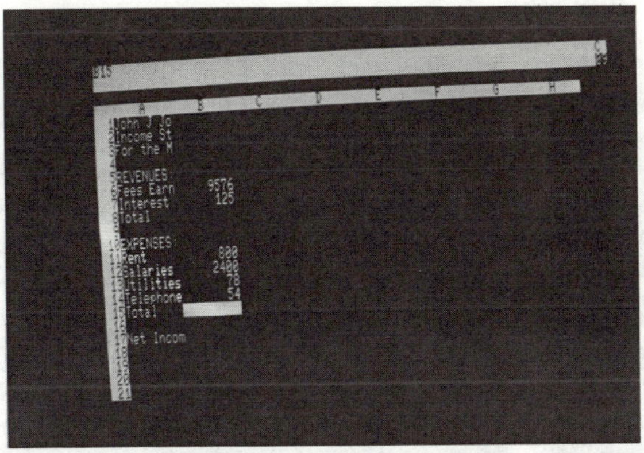

Analysis: These points are related to the above illustration:

• Down the side, the spreadsheet shows rows numbered from 1 to 21. Across the top, you can see eight columns headed A, B, C, D, E, F, G, and H respectively. Each column permits you to enter nine characters; thus, each column is normally nine characters wide. This is the usual view of the worksheet with an 80-character screen. Remember, however, that RAM contains the rest of the spreadsheet. When you move the sheet up or across the screen (an action called scrolling), you can obtain the maximum dimension: 254 rows down the side, and 63 columns across the top.

• VisiCalc has many built-in functions. For example, column width may be narrowed to 3 characters or widened up to 77 characters per column on an 80-character screen. Here's what the last illustration on the income statement would look like if the column width were increased to 33 characters per column:

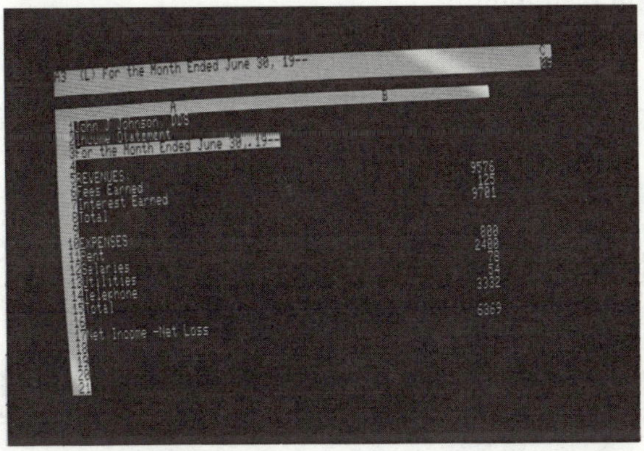

Analysis: By increasing the width, you can see all data entered earlier into RAM.

• As stated earlier, one of the most powerful uses of any spreadsheet is to answer *What if?* questions. VisiCalc allows you to change any previous data. The power of VisiCalc takes over to give you in seconds the new information, as illustrated in the next two photos.

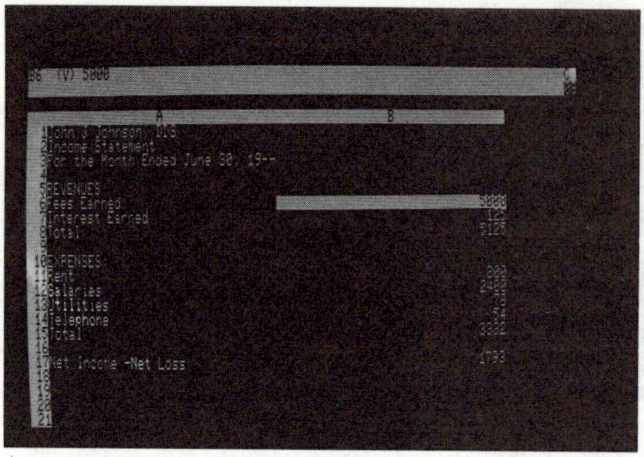

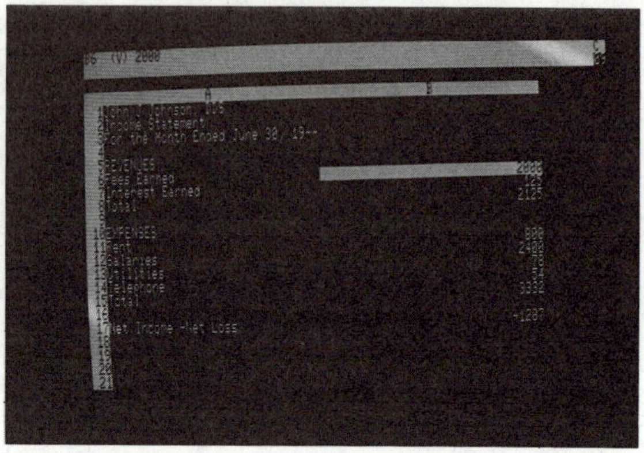

Analysis: Note that sales revenue has been changed twice. In the left photo, sales was changed from $9 576 to $5 000. In the right photo, sales was again changed from$5 000 to $2 000. VisiCalc calculated all of the resulting changes to report a new net income figure in the left photo and a net loss figure in the right photo.

In conclusion, spreadsheets are excellent planning tools which can eliminate hours of work on traditional accounting problems. With spreadsheet software, you won't have to explain your requirements to a programmer. Most spreadsheets come with a manual and "user-friendly" guides to help you solve problems on the electronic screen. Of course, you will need to know a few things, such as how to operate your microcomputer, how to load and change disks, and how to make printouts. Above all, you will still have to know something about accounting and how to solve accounting problems.

TOPIC 1 PROBLEMS

18-1 Perform the following exercises:

a Use the preparation of a sales invoice to explain the difference between accounting data and accounting information.

b Use the same example in **a** to explain how the accounting output produced becomes accounting data for a second stage of processing accounts receivable.

18-2 The five major components of a computer system are (1) the input unit, (2) the output unit, (3) the memory unit, (4) the arithmetic/logic unit, and (5) the control unit.

Briefly explain the *role* of each of these components. *Hint:* Do not merely describe each part. Explain the function (purpose) that each unit serves in a computer system.

18-3 Assume that a small business has a microcomputer system with 128K of RAM and a floppy disk system to process its common accounting applications.

a Why are two disk drives recommended in this system?

b Assume that your computer has enough RAM to store the program and data. Would you still recommend one or two disk drives? Explain your answer.

c Suppose the business could afford a hard disk rather than floppies. Give three advantages of a hard disk over floppies.

18-4 Suppose you plan to do your mailing list of customers on a computer system capable of printing mailing labels. Suppose further that you have shopped around and the software you plan to buy for this application requires 12K of memory for the program plus 16K of memory for temporary storage. And suppose the operating system requires 12K.

How much total memory would you need to support your mailing list application? Explain your answer.

18-5 Assume a small business has the capital to acquire a microcomputer system with either a 16-bit word-length microprocessor or a 32-bit word-length microprocessor.

a What is the difference between a bit and a byte in computer terminology?

b Would you recommend the purchase of the 16-bit or 32-bit microprocessor in the above case? Explain your answer.

18-6 Assume you plan to buy a microcomputer system for the General Ledger, accounts receivable, accounts payable, and the electronic spreadsheet.

a Briefly explain the difference between the General Ledger, and the electronic spreadsheet.

b Would you buy your system without the computer monitor and simply save costs by plugging in your home TV set? Explain your answer.

18-7 Answer the following questions:

a What is a canned program (also known as a software package or packaged program)?

b Name *three* advantages and *two* disadvantages of using a canned program.

18-8 Answer the following questions:

a Distinguish between mainframe, mini, and microcomputers.

b Distinguish between centralized and distributed data processing.

c Under centralized data processing, why is accounting recognized as a functional responsibility rather than a method?

18-9 You have been hired to help plan the menu-driven accounting software for a small business using a microcomputer system. You learn that the main accounting menu consists of these options: (1) General Ledger, (2) Accounts Receivable, (3) Accounts Payable, (4) Payroll. Assume the payroll consists of bi-weekly salaried employees only. Remittances are made by cheque.

a What options would you show on the main sub-menu for the General Ledger? Number these options beginning with 1.

b What options would you show on the main sub-menu for Accounts Receivable? Number these options beginning with 1.

c What options would you show on the main sub-menu for Accounts Payable? Number the options beginning with 1.

d What options would you show on the main sub-menu for Payroll? Number the options beginning with 1.

Hint: Think of your previous study of each of these applications under the manual system.

18-10 A business friend has recently acquired an off-the-shelf accounts receivable package. You have been asked to check out the package against some of the firm's present accounts receivable data. You test the package and find the following:

(i) The program will accept Smith, but not smith.

(ii) The program only accepts names up to 16 letters long, but you discover a customer with an 18-letter name.

(iii) The program "blew up" (got lost) because you exceeded its limit of 500 customers. You find there are 520 customers in the accounts receivable ledger.

(iv) The program flashes an error message when a particular customer's balance goes negative (that is, a credit balance).

a There is a technical name given to these software errors. What is it?

b What should your friend have done before buying the package?

c What should be done to solve the problems?

18-11 Assume you have graduated from dental school with a D.D.S. and plan to purchase an established dental practice from a doctor who is about to retire. The practice is located in a small community.

You are able to borrow $150 000 from the bank, but you have no extra money. Suppose you pay $100 000 for the old practice and an additional $35 000 for new dental equipment.

You learn that the established practice has 500 active patients with one hired front-office person and one dental assistant.

You learn also that the accounting system consists of making out source documents and placing copies in marked envelopes. No journals or ledgers are kept to process accounts receivable, accounts payable, and the payroll for two persons.

You investigate the possibilities of investing in an accounting system to handle the three applications. You learn that Mardan Business Systems Limited will supply manual one-write systems to process accounts receivable for approximately $300 per year, accounts payable for $200 per year, and the payroll for $150 per year.

Before purchasing the one-write systems, you read an ad in the local paper offering a real "buy" on a microcomputer system. The ad offers a package deal for keyboard/display, CPU with 32K of RAM, expandable to 64K, a single floppy disk drive, and a dot-matrix printer for a total cost of $3 000. The package includes BASIC and a disk operating system stored on a floppy. A 90-day warranty is quoted.

Would you invest in the one-write systems or purchase the microcomputer system? Give reasons for your answer.

Case Study 18

After completing separate courses in computer studies and accounting, one student was overheard making the following comments and future predictions:

(1) "With the wide use of microcomputers, I predict the computer will eliminate all manual accounting in the next five years."

(2) "Costs of microcomputer systems are decreasing all the time. All small businesses will be able to computerize their accounting applications. Consequently, I predict the computer will eliminate all bookkeepers and accounting clerks in the next five years."

(3) "I am convinced that the Japanese and the Americans will develop a computer in the 1990s that will be able to think just like any human. Consequently, I predict the computer of the 1990s will eliminate the need for professional accountants before the turn of the century."

What are your views on *each* prediction made? Give reasons to support your view.

INDEX

Note: The symbol *def.* precedes pages containing a definition in the margin or text; *illus.* precedes pages containing an illustration.

9

7

200

14.000 x 2
100

1360
122
2720
136
1632

1168
12
2336
1168
14.016
2
28

280 | 12
24 | 23
40

1500

11600

2500 | 12
24 | 20

146.000
8 4
1168
132
1300
26 2%
40 3%
1366